Planning in the Public Domain

John Friedmann

Planning
in the Public Domain

From Knowledge to Action

Princeton University Press

PRINCETON · NEW JERSEY

To Harvey S. Perloff

IN MEMORIAM

Contents

vii

Illustrations

Acknowledgments

This book was over five years in the making, and my debts can never be adequately expressed to all those who, directly or indirectly, have had a hand in shaping its arguments and presentation. In particular, I wish to express my gratitude to Peter Marris, Carl Boggs, Goetz Wolff, and Stephanie Pincetl, whose comments on various parts of the manuscript helped me greatly in revising early drafts. Marco Cenzatti spent over a year discussing with me the ideas in Parts One and Two. He also wrote Appendix C and devoted weeks to the preparation of the Index. To him I am deeply grateful. Special recognition must also go to Richard Foglesong and Manuel Castells, who read the entire manuscript as it was nearing completion, and from whose many detailed comments I benefited greatly.

Above all, I should like to thank the students and faculty of the Urban Planning Program at U C L A who created the ambiance in which the ideas contained in this book could flourish. Generations of students struggled with me through introductory courses in planning theory, and surely, without their probing and frequently contentious questions, this book would never have been written. My colleagues Edward Soja, Allan Heskin, and Dolores Hayden gave me an education in different facets of radical thinking: historical materialism, social anarchism, and socialist feminism. They may not recognize their contributions to this book and, indeed, may not like what I have written, but I am grateful to them all the same. They were my teachers.

Three decades ago, I had other teachers to whom I am indebted beyond measure. Let their names be inscribed in these pages: Rexford G. Tugwell, Edward C. Banfield, and, above all, Harvey S. Perloff, whose untimely death in 1983 deprived us all of mentor, dean, and lifelong inspiration. It is to him that this book is dedicated. Harvey's intrepid optimism would have led him to different conclusions than mine, but it was his belief in the importance of theory in planning that sustained my enterprise throughout all these years.

Some of the chapters went through a great deal of editorial revision at the hands of Eugene Tanke, to whom I am gratefully indebted for producing a more readable manuscript. Although his work was professionally impeccable, we eventually parted ways. But if he should read the chapters in which he had a hand, he will surely recognize his contributions.

The preparation of the manuscript was a selfless labor of love. Ets Otomo started out on the early versions of some of the chapters, and Erika Roos magically assembled the extensive bibliography into its present format. But the bulk of the work of readying the manuscript was Marsha Brown's, who summoned up an incredible reservoir of patience in plowing through the repeated revisions. Last, but not least, it was Janet Stern who saw the manuscript through press. Her impeccable sense of style preserved me from numerous errors, oversights, and inconsistencies.

Los Angeles, California
November 21, 1986

Planning in the Public Domain

Introduction

The eighteenth century bequeathed to us a dual legacy of reason and democracy. Reason meant trust in the capacity of the mind to grasp the orderly processes of nature and society, and to render them intelligible to us. Democracy meant trust in the capacity of ordinary people for self-governance. It presupposed a capacity for reasoning in all of us.[1]

For one brief moment in the flow of history, these two powerful beliefs came together in the luminous figure of Thomas Jefferson (1743–1826). Jefferson's most earnest wish was "to see the republican element of popular control pushed to the maximum of its practical exercise" (Garraty and Gay 1983, 793). As he wrote a friend in 1816, what he envisioned was a self-governing republic whose basic units would be rural neighborhoods, or wards (letter to Joseph C. Cabell, in Abbott 1947). Only questions that could not be resolved at this lowest level of governance would filter upward, to be resolved at successively higher levels. The presumption was that there would be relatively little that people could not adequately handle by themselves in their own communities.

Jefferson's image of an "elementary republic of the wards" has affinities with the proud Swiss traditions of local self-governance and with Proudhon's anarchist principles of federation (Proudhon 1979; orig. 1863). All three of these models (of which only the Swiss remains operational) try to forestall an excessive concentration of power in the hands of a remote and abstract state. But Jefferson was the last of a great line. An agrarian fundamentalist, he was unable to imagine the urban-industrial America of the future. For him, the "chosen people of God" were yeoman farmers, self-reliant, upright people "who labor in the earth" (Garraty and Gay 1983, 793).

More prophetic of things to come was Alexander Hamilton, a lawyer and banker. As secretary of the Treasury under George Washington (1790), Hamilton was successful in getting Congress to

1. For a classical introduction to the intellectual history of the Enlightenment, see Cassirer (1951) and Gay (1969).

3

charter the First Bank of the United States. A mercantilist by conviction, he was untiring in his advocacy of public measures to support the growth of private manufacturing. Hamilton believed in the state. His faith in democracy was considerably more limited. "Take mankind in general," he wrote. "They are vicious—their passions may be operated upon" (Garraty and Gay 1983, 793). To constrain the fickle passions of the people, Hamilton proposed a senate chosen for life, "a permanent body that will check the imprudence of democracy" (Wood 1972, 554). Matters of state required cool and steadfast minds and the charismatic leadership of the well-educated and well-bred. Ordinary people might confabulate about the goals and values of the polity, but the serious business of devising policies for the Republic must be left to experts. Government, wrote Hamilton, is a "complicated science, and requires abilities and knowledge, of a variety of other subjects, to understand it" (ibid., 508).

In this all-too-brief summation of the two major currents of political thought in the early decades of the Republic, we encounter a theme that would take two centuries to unfold. This theme is the frequently made distinction, so peculiar to the modern period, between values and fact. Values are conceived to be relatively stable preferences drawn from human nature, social tradition, and self-interest, whereas facts are things in themselves, bits of truth that only scientific reason can discover. It was Hamilton's conviction that politicians, as the people's representatives, should concern themselves primarily with general goals of policy ("values"), leaving the choice of the appropriate means ("facts") to specially trained experts.

These specialists, expert in mediating knowledge and action, I shall call planners, although that specific designation did not appear until the 1920s, when it was usually modified to mean a particular kind of planning expertise, such as physical or economic planning. In their most general signification, however, planners-as-experts have always argued that the selection of means is primarily a technical question, to be decided on grounds of efficiency (the "least-cost" principle). It is not surprising, therefore, that engineers were among the first practitioners of the new vocation.[2]

By the end of the eighteenth century, the idea of reason had begun to pass through a subtle transformation. Moral reason was left with the role of gaining general insight into human affairs, but in the hierarchy of authority, reason in its scientific and technical form ranked first: it was reason of a higher order. The conviction that

2. On the origins of engineering as a modern profession and its relationship to planning, see Hayek (1955) and Noble (1977).

public affairs should be informed by planning was grounded in the popular belief that science, which formed the foundation of planning, was essentially concerned with the investigation of "facts" and the discovery of "laws." Simplistic as it now seems to us, this understanding helped to shore up the authority of planners. According to Saint-Simon, one of the prophets of the new age, society would henceforth be ruled not be men but by scientific principles (Wolin 1960, 361). Ordinary minds, untrained in the subtleties of the scientific method, were no match for the rationality of those who knew how to make judgments about efficiency in relating means to ends. Parliaments could talk, but the real business of the state would be conducted by men of public spirit and far-reaching vision who had received the proper education. Tied to entrepreneurial talent and finance capital, the myriad applications of science would ensure the steady forward march of social progress.[3]

As a self-conscious application of scientific technique, however, social planning did not begin until the twentieth century, when it emerged from the matrix of industrial management. During World War I, the czars of the German and American war economies, Walther Rathenau and Herbert Hoover, applied planning principles to the task of mobilizing national production. For both men, as planners, the political process was of little consequence. This matter was especially clear in the case of Herbert Hoover, who has been called "the engineering method personified." First as head of the War Industries Board, later as Secretary of Commerce, and finally as President of the United States, he labored tirelessly to concert all powers within his reach to "meet the growing needs of corporate industry" (Noble 1977, 286). To his way of thinking, the implicit equation was simple: whatever was good for industry was also good for the country. Conflict between the public and the private interest was inconceivable. And if industry was run by private capital and gov-

---

3. At the root of the idea of social progress was a major contradiction. If progress meant a steady increase in the general happiness of the people, the economic system, which was one of progress's principal levers, called for the competitive and unrestrained pursuit of self-interest. The economic calculus, which eventually would encompass virtually all aspects of social life, rendered traditional methods of communal self-control antithetical and, given the goal of economic rationality, even irrational. They were replaced by the pitiless laws of the market and the police powers of the state. The natural passions of human beings had thus to be controlled through planning by the state, all the more so in view of the blatant injustices that the economy engendered, and that might inflame the passionate anger of those who were its victims. Social control theory (F. A. Ross 1901) expressed the fear of the bourgeoisie that its game might be discovered, engendering massive civil disobedience and revolt.

ernment was run by engineers, where was there a need for politicians?

With the onset of the Great Depression in 1929, the objectives of public intervention changed. Under Franklin Delano Roosevelt's New Deal, the state moved to control industrialists, not only to ensure a measure of social justice, but also to put people back to work and thus to save capitalism from itself. But even in these efforts planning remained the ideal. Although more rationalized than before and newly equipped with "theory," it asserted the public interest over private greed and profiteering.

One of the most ardent advocates of planning during the New Deal was Rexford Guy Tugwell. In what was to be the first of a long string of public appointments, ending with the governorship of Puerto Rico, Tugwell was called to Washington in 1933 to serve as a member of Roosevelt's "brain trust." His imagination fired by Frederick Winslow Taylor's ideas of scientific management, Tugwell was appalled by the enormous waste he saw in America's industrial system. Like Hamilton, he was profoundly suspicious of politics, but his reasons were significantly different. His strong sense of the public purpose was outraged by the willingness of politicians to cater to business interests. If planning "in the public interest" was to prevail, it would have to be safeguarded from the self-serving meddling of politicians (Tugwell 1975c). Planning would become a "scientific endeavor," he announced. In their collective wisdom, planners would produce a comprehensive plan and budget. The future would be laid out as a rational design.

Not everyone, of course, welcomed this prospect. By the 1940s, the early faith in science, particularly the social sciences, had been seriously undermined by skeptical inquiries. No one now claimed to understand how society "really" worked, or to understand it well enough to propose plans for the whole of it. An Austrian school of critics, led by Friedrich von Hayek and Karl Popper (in exile in Britain during the war), proposed that the scientific reason of social planners such as Tugwell or Karl Mannheim be replaced, either with the "invisible hand" of an unfettered market economy (Hayek) or with the piecemeal reformism that Austrians call *Schlamperei*, or "muddling through." Popper, a social democrat, was emphatic about the ascendancy of politics over the market (Popper 1974). But Hayek, in a more abstract vision, considered politics dispensable altogether. Reflecting a Hobbesian pessimism about human nature, he thought reason could not be trusted much beyond the "night watchman" role assigned to it in the liberal conception of the state (Hayek 1944). Left to its own devices, the market would allocate resources efficiently, maximizing economic growth. Little more was needed for a happy and contented life.

Beginning in the 1940s and despite Austrian skepticism, social planning experienced a remarkable period of efflorescence. Once again, as it had during World War I, global conflict required the mobilization and management of the war economy by the state. In the United States, planning methods were applied to production, price control, and rationing; to manpower training and allocation; to logistical problems; to the location of war-related industries and the construction of workers' housing nearby; and to special undertakings such as the Manhattan Project, which produced the first atomic bomb.

When the return to a peacetime economy posed equally challenging tasks, the state was again the decisive agent. Industries had to be reconverted to peacetime use. In Europe and Japan, entire cities demolished by bombing had to be rebuilt. The state's new role as a major provider of social services had to be planned. Keynesian economics was applied to ensure full employment and stable growth. And in rapidly decolonizing countries, development planning became a popular instrument for accelerating economic growth and rationalizing the use of foreign assistance.

The 1950s and 1960s were periods of vigorous theorizing about planning. Some thinkers perceived the rise of a "new professional class"—a technical intelligentsia—and speculated about its relationship to the older social classes of capitalists and workers (Walker 1979). The main emphasis, however, was on ensuring the rationality of decisions (H. Simon 1976, Dahl Lindblom 1957; Lindblom 1959). Planners wanted to be absolutely certain that their counsel was reliable. They saw planning as a form of scientific management which differed from traditional management because it brought special skills to the rational analysis and solution of social problems. Unlike administrators who dealt with the tasks of everyday management, planners were primarily concerned with making nonroutine decisions.

In this role, planners were sustained by a widely held belief that science and the new technologies of decision-making, such as game theory and cybernetics, could help provide what they promised: rational counsel for charting courses of action into the future. As members of the state apparatus, planners were inclined to see the managerial state as a guardian of the public interest and an instrument for social progress. So long as everyone played his part well, the system was fail-safe; the state would plan, the economy would produce, and working people would concentrate on their private agendas: raising families, enriching themselves, and consuming whatever came tumbling out from the cornucopia.

But the dream of endless progress did not last. Within two decades after World War II, the United States was bogged down in the quagmire of Vietnam. Poverty was rediscovered: there were as many poor people, proportionately, as there had been a generation earlier. In absolute numbers, there were many more. Black power became restless, and the inner cities burned. National leaders were assassinated. Militant students read Marx and Marcuse and organized themselves for political struggle. It was an intense period of heightened political awareness and popular protest. A contemporary historian interpreted what he saw in this way: "What Western civilization is witnessing . . . is the last phase of the great emanicipation promoted in the eighteenth century, and that last phase resembles the first, when all enlightened men agreed that authority and the State were always and a priori wrong" (Garraty and Gay 1983, 1150). The state responded to this frontal challenge in the accustomed way: with the mailed fist of repression and the velvet glove of social planning. Many experimental programs were started in the 1960s to combat poverty and to respond to the escalating demands of inner city residents. During these years, planners listened more attentively to the voice of the people, and "maximum feasible participation" was given an official blessing.

So far as the theory of planning is concerned, the culminating work of this period was Amitai Etzioni's *The Active Society* (1968). Etzioni proposed a model of societal guidance in which the people make demands, the state responds by providing answers, the people (now pacified) accept the state's authority, and the state builds a consensual basis for its policies. In making the state the principal player in his scenario, Etzioni was no exception among planning theorists. From Auguste Comte to Rexford Tugwell, planners had always sought support from ruling elites. They saw themselves as doing what the dean of Berkeley's Graduate School of Public Policy referred to as "speaking truth to power" (Wildavsky 1979). In the days of royalty, such speech had been the privilege of trusted chamberlains—and the court jester. Now it was the planners' turn.

But in the literature on the relation of knowledge to action, there was still another tradition that specifically addressed the needs of those who lacked substantial power. Because its chief proponents, drawing on certain strategic aspects of three political movements—utopianism, social anarchism, and historical materialism—saw power in collective action, I shall call this tradition *social mobilization*.

These movements arose in response to the dark underside, the injustices and exploitation, of industrial capitalism. Addressing the victims of that system, writers in this tradition began inevitably with a far-reaching, radical critique of present conditions. Unlike social guidance theorists who codified the world of power holders, these writers sought a radical transformation of society. In time, two major approaches to social transformation evolved. Utopians and some anarchists looked to self-reliant communities that could make a living in the nooks and crannies of the capitalist order, where the state did not intrude. A second group, composed chiefly of historical materialists, looked to a revolutionary practice aimed at transforming the structure of the existing power system, either through a direct assault on its strongholds or through a series of radical reforms. Rather than retreat from society into an ideal communitarian world, they would hold their ground and struggle within the existing system for a new order. Their political strength was based on social movements, particularly of labor.

As we approach the end of this century, the social mobilization tradition is becoming ever more relevant to planning. For there are signs that the system of industrial capitalism is so deeply mired in crisis that it may never fully recover. Here are some of the symptoms.

1. The weakening of the nation-state, as capital continues to leave its national "incubator" to become a truly global force.

2. The growing impoverishment of peasant societies in Latin America, Asia, Africa, and the Middle East, which together hold roughly two thirds of the world's population.

3. The growing awareness that our physical environment has only a finite capacity to accommodate growth in population and production.

4. The increasing redundancy of labor throughout the world, a result of several interactive trends, including the general slowing of economic growth and the spread of new labor-saving technologies (electronic computers, industrial robots, lasers).

5. The staggering volume of international indebtedness, especially in semi-industrialized countries such as Mexico, Brazil, Argentina, and Chile, which is placing extraordinary strains on the international monetary and credit system and forcing countries to choose among the equally unpalatable options of bank-

ruptcy, export-led strategies of growth, increased domination by transnational capital, and rampant inflation.

6. An increasingly intense rivalry between the United States and the Soviet Union for control of strategic areas, which in both countries has led to the formation of a military-industrial complex that controls a vast arsenal of nuclear weaponry.

Because it is invariably integrated into the state apparatus, planning for societal guidance is incapable of coping with the crisis of industrial capitalism. More often than not, the solutions it attempts to implement only make matters worse. If metropolitan countries impose tariffs to protect their national markets against Brazilian steel, for example, they exacerbate problems of economic recovery in a peripheral country that is increasingly dependent on exports. If a peripheral state takes Draconian measures to reduce hyper-inflation, these measures may stifle new investments, shrink internal markets, and encourage capital flight. Because it is so tightly linked to the system-in-crisis, the state itself has become part of the problem.

As a result, citizens around the world have begun to search for an "alternative" development that is less tied to the dynamics of industrial capitalism. Emancipatory movements have emerged to push for a more positive vision of the future than the present system-in-dominance holds out to us: a world working to eliminate the threat of a nuclear winter and in serious pursuit of a balanced natural environment, gender equality, the abolition of racism, and the eradication of grinding poverty. Though diversely inspired, these social movements appear to coalesce around two central strategies: collective self-reliance in development and the recovery of political community.

Thus there is renewed urgency in the question posed by the philosophers of the Enlightenment: Are reason and democracy compatible? Can ordinary people be trusted to use their heads in the conduct of their own affairs, or is superior wisdom needed? Can people free themselves from tutelage by state and corporate power and become autonomous again as active citizens in households, local communities, and regions? Industrial capitalism has answered these questions in the negative. It has placed its trust in men of wealth and power, the formally educated, and the experts. This position is still vigorously defended by Hamiltonian centralists, who remain profoundly suspicious of the "masses" (Crozier et al. 1975; Huntington 1981). In this book, I shall defend the contrary view: technical reason, when separated from democratic self-governance, is bound to have destructive consequences. The scientific mind, applied to prac-

tical affairs, cannot be trusted to itself; it lacks the "requisite variety" (Ashby 1956).[4] By serving corporate capital, it is caught up in the vortex of unlimited economic expansion. By serving the state, it works for the economy of destruction. Only by serving people directly, when the people are organized to act collectively on their own behalf, will it contribute toward the project of an alternative development.

The story I wish to tell is divided into three parts and an epilogue. Part One introduces the reader to the basic vocabulary of planning. It is described as a forward-looking activity that selects from the past those elements that are useful in analyzing existing conditions from a vantage point of the future—the changes that are thought to be desirable and how they might be brought about. Focusing on the problem of how knowledge might be linked to action, planning shares in the traditions of both academic scholarship and political practice. Yet it is fully at home in neither.

Notwithstanding its importance, the planner's role in history is not a determining one. Thought follows practice, and planners have to take their cues from practice, responding to actors' need for information, interpretation, problem definition, projection, evaluation, and strategic programming. Because of this "organic" relationship to the requirements of political practice, planning must also deal with purposes, motivations, contingencies, and risks. Unlike other disciplines, it seeks, in Tugwell's words, the utility of the future in the present.

In Part Two, the reader is introduced to four major traditions of planning thought. Convenient categories for organizing the many intellectual contributions to the problem of linking knowledge to action, they include social reform, policy analysis, social learning, and social mobilization. The first and last of these are the oldest; from their beginnings in the early nineteenth century, they established a dialectical tension in social practice that continues to this day. The dominant tradition of social reform deals with planning as a form of societal guidance; its radical counter is the tradition of social mobi-

4. Ashby's "law of requisite variety" states that "R's capacity as a regulator cannot exceed R's capacity as a channel of communication" (Ashby 1956, ch. 11). When the statement is applied to the solution of social problems, being short of requisite variety means nothing more than that scientific knowledge is *too simple* to cope with the actual complexity of the situation. Compared with the "real world," all scientific knowledge, no matter how elaborate its equations, must appear simplistic. Although to be simple is the strength of scientific methods, to leave the "real world" to scientific "simpletons" is a dangerous business.

lization, which deals with planning in a context of social transformation.

The *social reform* tradition of planning originated in France with Saint-Simonian engineers and, particularly, with Auguste Comte, whose "science of society," he thought, would guide the world on the certain path to social progress. From these early beginnings in the wake of the French Revolution, the tradition can be traced through the works of some of the great macrosociologists and political economists of this century, including Max Weber, Karl Mannheim, Rexford G. Tugwell, and more recently, Charles Lindblom, Amitai Etzioni, and Harvey S. Perloff. Their writings searched for the proper place of planning in society, explored devices for institutionalizing planning, developed models of social rationality, and studied the variety of social controls available to the state for obtaining compliance with plans.

In sharp contrast, the counter-tradition of *social mobilization* arises from the interactions of utopian, anarchist, and Marxist thought. Its origins are found in the early social criticism of what was then the new order of industrial capitalism. Its object was emancipation. Where social reformers addressed primarily the authorities of the state, and occasionally "enlightened" business elites, radical planners in the mobilization tradition spoke directly to working people, women, and oppressed races.

The other two traditions in the theory and practice of planning are more recent. *Policy analysis* is essentially a post–World War II phenomenon that grew out of the fields of management science, public administration, the neo-classical revival in economics, and the new information sciences called cybernetics. Its practitioners thought that correct solutions could be derived from the scientific analysis of data. This approach was often referred to as systems analysis. Although various schools can be distinguished, all of them lead back to Herbert Simon's work on decision theory. Another influence was the Rand Corporation in Santa Monica, California, whose principal client in its early days was the U.S. Air Force. Initial promises, however, were not fulfilled, and today policy analysts have grown considerably more cautious in their claims. Under the influence of Aaron Wildavsky and Giandomenico Majone, some of them have begun to shift toward a social learning model of planning.

The *social learning* tradition is in some ways different from all the others. Less unified as a "tradition" it tends to be narrowly conceived of as a theory of knowledge, or epistemology. Its progenitor was the American philosopher John Dewey. A powerful advocate of "learning by doing," Dewey conceived of social policy as a quasi-scientific experiment, and of democracy as a form of scientific politics. Dewey's precepts influenced two very different streams of planning practice. On the conservative side, his concepts were adapted by theorists of organization development (an offshoot of the scientific management movement), who applied them primarily to problems of corporate control. Leading figures in this group include such well-known social psychologists as Kurt Lewin, Chris Argyris, Donald Schön, and Warren Bennis. A second, revolutionary stream emerged in China with Mao Tse-tung. Here, Dewey's influence was perhaps more indirect. In any event, through Mao's famous essay "On Practice," the social learning perspective was introduced to the larger tradition of social mobilization, in which a favorable disposition already existed in the form of an older Marxist doctrine concerning the unity of theory and practice.

All four traditions are shown in Part Two to suffer from internal contradictions, some of them serious. But the real problems, it turns out, are historical-political. This aspect is discussed more systematically in Part Three, which addresses the future of planning.

In Chapter 7, several reasons are advanced to account for the present crisis in planning: (1) the theories about how we obtain valid knowledge about society are being radically revamped, (2) the sheer pace of historical events seems to outpace our abilities to harness the forces of change to a social purpose, and (3) the kind of problems we face and their magnitude render historically derived knowledge of little use in attempting to solve them. Cognizant of these dilemmas, planners have sought to escape along different routes: high technology, deregulation, and propaganda and repression are the most common. None of them are likely to work in the longer term. There remains yet a fourth route, however, which is to *re-center political power in civil society*. The concluding chapters are about this alternative.

The central argument in Chapter 8 concerns the public domain. The question is whether we are jointly responsible for the condition of our lives, having in common certain interests and concerns, or whether, in the final analysis, each individual, each corporate entity, and each social aggregate must go its own way in a Darwinian struggle without pity. Arguments pro and con are rehearsed. Although the debate continues, democratic theory has always asserted the sovereign right of the people to determine their own forms of governance. But as a form of governance, democracy implies the acceptance of an encompassing view of the whole that is more than the sum of its parts and more than a residual after private interests are somehow subtracted. The very concept of citizen presumes the prior existence of a sovereign political community more authoritative than the state.

Political communities have four characteristics that define their essence: their power extends over a given territorial base, they enjoy historical continuity, they are composed of citizen-members, and they are part of an ensemble of communities among which citizenship is shared.

If the present crisis is to be overcome at the root and not merely in its apparent manifestations, then the sense of an active political community must be recovered. It is through a renewal of politics, initially at the local scale of citizen encounters and moving out from there, that a new state and a new economics can be fashioned. Four arenas are discussed in Chapter 9. They include the household economy (which is also the smallest political community), the regional nexus of work place and home, the peasant periphery of the Third World; and the global community, which is the largest set of interdependencies for which we are collectively responsible.

The argument is both visionary and theoretical. It ends by affirming oppositional movements that will lead to a genuine political life with widespread citizen involvement, a measure of territorial autonomy in production and politics, the collective self-production of life, and the discovery of one's individuality in the context of specific social relations.

The final chapter takes up the question of how radical planners can help in mediating theory and practice in the current period of social transformation. The epistemological grounding for these mediations is found in the paradigm of social learning whose organizational counterpart is the small action group, which is loosely linked to similar groups elsewhere through informal networks and political coalitions. Radical planners are committed to an alternative world-historical project that points to greater self-reliance and a more active political life. As part of this undertaking, they perform critical roles in their facilitation and promotion of efforts that will lead to the self-empowerment of households, local communities, and regions; encourage thinking without frontiers; help to devise practical visions of the future; assist in building political coalitions to advance the aims of the counterforce; inform the strategic choices of activists; and encourage the practice of dialogue and mutual learning.

So conceived, radical planning cannot be subsumed under familiar categories such as "participation" or "decentralization." As an oppositional form of planning, it aims at ever-widening circles of liberated space on the terrains of state and corporate economy.

In sum, this book is an attempt to outline a history of planning thought and, at the same time, to suggest where the emphasis in future planning practice ought to lie. For this reason, it concludes by outlining a theory and practice of radical planning. Because radical planning encounters the powers of the state and corporation on all sides, the theory is self-limiting. It points to a dialectical process in which both traditional planning modes and radical planning modes interact to produce the kind of society we are able, collectively, to achieve.

In the next chapter, the major terms of the discussion are introduced, and some questions in planning theory are posed.

Part One / Concepts

1   The Terrain of
Planning Theory

When we say that someone has acted rationally, we usually imply approval. But what, precisely, do we mean by a "rational" action? For some, an action is rational when it adheres to a formal criterion, such as economic efficiency. If I can get more of something for the same cost, I am said to be acting rationally. For others, conforming to socially expected behavior is rational. Thus, if I quit my job for one that pays better, people will nod with understanding: I have acted rationally. Or if, as an industrialist, I shut down my factory in Cleveland, because I can increase my company's profits by moving operations to Arizona or Brazil, that action, too, will be widely hailed as rational. Although the shutdown may have put thousands out of work, my first responsibility is to myself and to my stockholders.

Market Rationality and Social Rationality

In the market as well as in society, rationality identifies a relation between means and ends in which the ends are generally taken to be the self-regarding interests of an isolated individual or firm. The linked interests of all those workers in Cleveland were not expected to enter into my profitability calculus. And yet, strictly speaking, I cannot entirely ignore them either, because as a value that enjoys social approval, rationality needs to be justified in terms that are broader than mere self-interest. I need to demonstrate that my actions will tend to benefit the collectivity as well as me. As Charlie Wilson once tried to argue, "What's good for General Motors is good for the nation."

This, as everyone knows, was also Adam Smith's basic position. Following Mandeville, he argued the doctrine of the natural harmony of interests. In his famous poem *The Fable of the Bees* (1714), Bernard Mandeville had said that human pride and the desire for luxuries would lead to general prosperity (Dumont 1977, ch. 5). Or as Smith expressed it, "private vices yield public benefits." This "logic" still informs the work of contemporary economists. Social

19

welfare is enhanced, they say, so long as an action makes at least one person better off than before and no one's situation is made worse. The underlying assumption is that the gain of some is not necessarily inconsistent with the gain of all, which therefore implies that the interests of capital and labor can be unified. This principle of practical philosophy, called the "Pareto optimum" after the Italian sociologist who first stated it, is the most widely accepted criterion for analyzing the costs and benefits of actions in the public domain (Mishan 1981b).

The unrestrained pursuit of self-interest by individuals and corporations came to be known as *market rationality*. Because its social outcomes were not planned with any conscious effort, market rationality could be presented as a quasi-natural phenomenon, something beyond human intentions. Yet it was obvious from the beginning that social welfare was not being unambiguously promoted by transactions in the marketplace. Even the weak conditions of a Pareto optimum were rarely, if ever, achieved. As the "blind" forces of the market increased the prosperity of some, they also stepped up the exploitation of labor, drove peasants from their land, dehumanized work, caused mass unemployment, produced urban squalor, hurled small businesses into bankruptcy, exacerbated inequalities of wealth and power, and ravaged the earth. In the face of these realities, a different kind of rationality was needed to balance the calculus of private gain.

Market rationality was grounded in a metaphysics of "possessive individualism" (Macpherson 1962). According to this doctrine, the individual is assumed to be logically prior to society, and the satisfaction of material needs is said to be the principal reason people live in social groups. The contrasting doctrine of *social rationality*, which came into prominence during the nineteenth century, made the opposite assumption: social formations were said to be logically prior to the individual, whose separate identity as a person derived from membership in a specific group. Reason, therefore, ought to be exercised in the name of the group, so that its collective interests might be properly formulated and pursued through appropriate actions. Since collective interests, in this view, always took precedence over the interests of individuals, the Pareto optimum ceased to be valid as a criterion for social welfare. In political terms, this implied that market operations would have to be curtailed or replaced; in either case, some form of central planning would be needed (Lindblom 1977).[1]

1. The problem with the doctrine of social rationality can be phrased as a question:

In the twentieth century, and particularly after the Depression, a third position was gradually adopted throughout the capitalist world. Though its rhetoric was deliberately vague, the practices it advocated were plain enough. Market rationality would be allowed free rein, but only within legal constraints designed to protect the collective interest. To mitigate the negative consequences of market rationality for people and their communities, then, the state would intervene in markets with the instruments of planning in progressive income redistribution, basic social service programs, unemployment and old age insurance, laws to protect natural resources and human habitats, and so on.

While corporate planning continued to hold firmly to the original model of market rationality, public planners championed a modified form of social rationality that was explicitly concerned with social outcomes (Mishan 1976). Public planning was thus brought into head-on conflict with private interests. The respective criteria for determining what was rational were diametrically opposed. But business was powerful, and planners rarely accomplished more than private interests were prepared to accept. When civic passions were inflamed by some particular practice—such as the dumping of toxic wastes, to take a recent example—planners might move against the interests of property and business. But such moments were relatively rare, and once passions had cooled, earlier gains might be reversed. It is probably correct to say that in most cases public sector programs are successfully launched only when they are broadly compatible with the interests of corporate capital.

The Uses of Planning

The practice of planning, in the modern sense, began in the early decades of this century. But to trace its ideological roots, we must go back to the early nineteenth century, to the work of Henri de Saint-Simon and Auguste Comte, in which the vision of a science working in the service of humanity first took shape. A full century of material and perceptual changes had to pass before planning emerged as a distinctive practice, with its emphasis on technical reason and social rationality. The first and most important among these changes was the gradual breakdown of the "organic" order of feudal society and

---

Who is to speak in the name of the collective interest, where that interest is understood as an undifferentiated whole? In practice, and where social rationality has prevailed over market rationality (as in the centrally planned economies of socialist countries), it is a Leninist vanguard party that presumes to speak in the name of the people, or the proletariat.

the emergence of the economy as a system of interrelated markets (Polanyi 1957). As economic pursuits came to be governed chiefly by the principle of private gain and were spurred on by competition, nearly all social relations outside the household came to depend upon money. Second, a science of society, together with its several distinctive disciplines, had to grow to maturity and gain a measure of social acceptance before the new planning could be based on it. Third, the industrial revolution had to mature before the bureaucratic state would take an active role in promoting the new economic forces, maintaining the necessary internal and external balances, and coping with the enormous social problems that industrialization had engendered.

Before the nineteenth century, a very different sort of planning had prevailed. Because it tended to impose a rational, Euclidean order upon the organic forms of nature, I shall call it *orthogonal* design (Houghton-Evans 1980). For architects and engineers, who were its chief practitioners, the straight lines and right angles of orthogonal design were classic instances of an artificial, rational ordering of space. The proto-cities of the ancient world—for example, the ceremonial centers of the Chou Dynasty; Teotihuacan in the central plateau of Mexico; and Angkor Wat, the magnificent temple city of the Khmer empire—are classical instances of orthogonal design (Wheatley 1971). Pierre Charles L'Enfant's imposing design for the federal capital at Washington, D.C. (1791), is a more recent example. In its purest form, orthogonal design can be found in the conceptions of utopian space expressed in Campanella's seventeenth-century City of the Sun, with its symmetrical-hierarchical patterns (Campanella 1981), and in the twentieth-century city of Brasília, designed by Lucio Costa and Oscar Niemeyer in the shape of an airplane with sweptback wings. It was master builders like these who had planned the great cities of antiquity; devised the complex irrigation systems of the early "hydraulic" civilizations of Egypt, Mesopotamia, the Indus Valley, and China; and laid out the roads that sent the Roman legions marching from the imperial hub to the furthest reaches of the empire (Childe 1956; Wittfogel 1959; Mumford 1961).[2]

2. According to Houghton-Evans (1980), the great virtue of "orthogonal" design is its *intelligibility*. Design, he avers, calls for "an orderly approach" in which separate functions are connected in space so that their logic becomes visible, creating a coherent system of spatial relations. In this view, orthogonal design appears to be the very opposite of Ian McHarg's *Design with Nature* (1969). It is not by obeying Nature that we shall master her, says Houghton-Evans; instead, we must impose upon Nature's

Orthogonal design had many historical and local variants, but its salient features can be readily described.[3]

1. It was primarily concerned with the physical arrangement of activities in two-dimensional or three-dimensional space.

2. It was intended for a static, hierarchical world that was construed as part of a cosmic order whose ultimate meaning could only be grasped through mystical revelation.

3. It had to conform to divine reason as interpreted by priests, shamans, theologians, geomancers, astrologers, and sometimes royalty. Because divine reason could only be "revealed," it became authoritative knowledge. Orthogonal designers were not obliged to justify their work in rational discourse. It was sufficient that designs came from an acknowledged master, and that the relevant spiritual authorities declared them in accord with divine purpose. Two kinds of knowledge were thus required for validation: pragmatic knowledge based on experience and knowledge of the "will of Heaven."[4]

4. Pragmatic knowledge of orthogonal design was typically passed from master to apprentice in actual work situations. Professional secrets were closely guarded, and design theory was a set of learned, pragmatic rules of procedure.

With the period we call the Enlightenment (ca. 1650–1850), Western European culture began to make a drastic break with the past, and by the mid–nineteenth century planning began to acquire features that had virtually nothing in common with the orthogonal design tradition. Although architects continued to work along traditional lines, most modern planning has been of an entirely different order.

---

subtle complexities (which presumably are not "intelligible" to men) an orthogonal order that is in accord with "human" reason. Presented in this way, orthogonal design becomes an example of patriarchal domination.

3. A lively description of the process of orthogonal planning is found in Arthur F. Wright's account of the planning and construction of the new capital city of the Sui Dynasty in sixth-century China, which by the eighth century was to become "the glittering cosmopolis of eastern Asia and by far the world's greatest city" (Wright 1978, 83ff.).

4. An outstanding example of authoritative design in this sense is the plan of the Benedictine monastery of St. Gall, Switzerland. Drawn up by monks in the ninth century, it was to serve as the paradigmatic design for Benedictine monasteries throughout Christendom. The plan of St. Gall was conceived as an ideal order, a proto-city, consistent with divine purpose (see the splendid book by Price 1983).

1. As a form of technical reason, modern planning is applied to the full range of problems that arise in the public domain.[5]

2. Planning takes place in and is adapted to a rapidly changing and increasingly turbulent world. Many aspects of this world will remain opaque to human understanding and can be only partially controlled.

3. In contemporary planning practice, knowledge derived from scientific and technical research has been added to the pragmatic knowledge of experience. Expressed in arch, conceptual language and in the form of quantitative models, scientific knowledge comes to us only in fragments, from different disciplines and focused experiments. Despite the lack of a unified "scientific" world view, these fragments, even when they are in conflict, tend to be stated as universally valid hypotheses.

4. Modern planning practice must conform to human (as opposed to divine) reason. Sharpened by science and logic, specific statements about the world must be validated in rational, open discourse, in which the burden of proof is generally on those making the initial statement. Unlike orthogonal design, modern planning has to justify itself politically, in open forum. As a result, the support for specific planning proposals generally takes the form of a fragile consensus that is constantly beset by rival theories and proposals. Far from being authoritative, modern plans are historically contingent and rest on democratic processes of decision-making.

One of the first demonstrations of the new planning practice was the allocation of raw materials to the German war machine during World War I. The technical genius responsible for applying the "scientific method" to central resource allocation was Walther Rathenau, who had apprenticed as president of Germany's largest public utility, the Allgemeine Elektrizitätswerk. An early exponent of scientific management and the world's first technocrat, Rathenau was

---

5. The discovery of a public domain may be seen as the crowning achievement of the Enlightenment. As a social movement, the Enlightenment had, for the first time, projected the masses of ordinary people into the stream of historical events, legitimated a democratic politics, and given birth to the "fourth estate" of the press—which helped to establish, for a rapidly urbanizing society, a shared sense of the "public." Problems that rose to public consciousness were thus, by definition, of general concern. This development helps account for the multiplication of planning activities in the post-Enlightenment period.

assassinated by political and racist enemies in 1922 (Berglar 1970).[6] But the idea of scientific planning had already taken root elsewhere. In the United States, Herbert Hoover, an engineer, had used methods almost identical to Rathenau's in mobilizing America's war economy. And over the next two decades, planning ideas proliferated, especially at the urban and regional levels (Scott 1969; Sussman 1976; Krueckeberg 1983). The first professional degree program in city planning was started at Harvard University in 1923 (Sarbib n.d.).

The full range of contemporary planning practice is illustrated in Chart 1. Although this is only a rough classification, some conclusions can nevertheless be drawn.

1. In market societies, the central coordination of all planning activities is patently impossible.

2. The same planning activity may cut across several levels of territorial organization—national, state, and local.

3. Physical planning or design is now only a small area of planning, and even in that sphere the orthogonal tradition has been largely replaced by scientifically based modes of analysis that involve modeling, projections, and spatial synthesis.

4. Modern planning practice is a social and political process in which many actors, representing many different interests, participate in a refined division of labor. Among these actors, the more important ones are lawyers, agronomists, economists, water engineers, city planners, social workers, statisticians, systems analysts, professional soldiers, civilian defense analysts, political scientists, social psychologists, public administrators, geographers, foresters, architects, environmentalists, community organizers, and demographers.

---

6. Rathenau stands in the direct line of succession to Auguste Comte. At the university, he had studied mathematics, physics, and chemistry, yet he was also at home in philosophy, the social sciences, and the new science of management. Starting his career as a chemical engineer, he soon switched to banking and eventually held a series of high-ranking posts in the wartime and postwar German governments. He was clearly the epitome of Comte's Ruler, the sort of man to whom the fate of the world should be entrusted. He wrote prolifically on economic and political subjects, and today we would call him a futurist. His book *The New Economy* (1919) urged (1) the unification and standardization of the whole of German industry and commerce into one great Trust, where it would work under a state charter and be armed with extensive powers; and (2) an intensification of the application of science and mechanization to production. For a summary in English, see Rathenau (1921).

Chart 1   **Planning in Market Societies**

National Security Planning

Economic Planning (national, state, local)
   investment for economic growth
   full employment (anti-cyclical)
   monetary policy (anti-inflation, pro-growth)
   trade policy (tariffs, etc.)
   incomes (redistribution)
   employment (education, job training)
   strategic resources (energy)
   science policy (research and development)
   sectoral policies (agriculture, transportation, etc.)

Social Planning (national, state, local)
   "safety net" for the victims of market rationality (unemployment insur-
      ance, workmen's compensation, retraining)
   social welfare services and transfer payments
   meeting individual and collective needs (health, education, housing, old
      age, day care)

Environmental Planning (national, state, local)
   residuals management and anti-pollution
   public lands management
   water resources
   resources conservation
   wilderness preservation
   protection of rare species
   protection of fragile and unique environments
   energy (alternative energy)

City Planning
   land use (zoning, public facility location)
   local transport (highways, rapid transit, airports, ports)
   urban redevelopment
   urban design
   conservation of the built environment
   community development (neighborhood planning)

Regional Development Planning
   natural resources development (irrigation, hydro-energy, integrated
      river basin development)
   regional economic development (inter-regional inequalities, special
      problem areas, urban-rural "imbalance")

Chart 1   **Planning in Market Societies** (*cont.*)

---

migration and settlement policy
location of industry (growth centers)
regional transportation
comprehensive rural development

We can gain further insight into modern planning practice by viewing the many heterogeneous activities listed in Chart 1 as a much smaller number of *uses* to which planning is put in the "management of change" within territorially organized societies. These uses are shown in Chart 2. It will be readily apparent that all ten uses correspond to some notion of *social* rationality and not one to a theory of *market* rationality. The state, which is the principal though not the only collective actor in the public domain, is forced to couch its deliberations in terms of a collective purpose, or what is also called the general or public interest. Although this interest may be nothing more than a fleeting political consensus, the state must maintain at least the appearance of serving it. If it does not, its very legitimacy may be in doubt.

In practice, concern with a collective good may lead the state to support profit-making activities in the private sector, activities that correspond primarily to market rationality. Because in capitalist societies most people gain their livelihood principally through private business, the proper functioning of the private sector is essential. State planning is therefore generally supportive of business, and it usually includes general economic guidance, the provision of public services (which account for a large part of the costs of reproducing the labor force), major infrastructural investments, business subsidies, and the protection of property rights (items 1 through 5 in Chart 2). Activity in each of these policy areas engenders political struggle. For example, the kind of general economic guidance that is offered will depend a great deal on which theory is invoked— Keynesianism or supply-side economics in domestic affairs and neomercantilism or free trade policy in the international arena, for instance. The relative importance of various social needs may also be in dispute, and the recipients of public subsidies will usually try to hold on to them even after the objective need for them has disappeared. Specific property owners may take exception to the application of, say, a zoning law, or to the projected distribution of costs and benefits of government, intervention. But even after all allowances for conflict have been made, it is still possible to maintain that

---

Chart 2   **The Uses of Planning**

---

1. Guiding overall economic stability and growth in national societies (monetary policy, full employment planning, international trade policy, etc.).

2. Providing public services to meet the general needs of the population (national defense, public housing, education, health, etc.).

3. Investing in areas that are of little interest to private capital because of low rates of return, diffused benefits, and the large size of the investment required (basic physical infrastructure, such as highways, mass transit, major hydroelectric facilities, land acquisition in urban redevelopment, etc.).

4. Subsidizing corporate interests and farmers to encourage specific actions (sectoral growth, redevelopment, infant industries, acreage reductions, relocation of industry, employment of handicapped, etc.).

5. Protecting property owners and local business interests against the ravages of unrestrained market rationality (land use planning, zoning, anti-pollution planning, etc.).

6. Redistributing income to achieve a more equitable and just social order.

7. Applying comprehensive and coordinate planning approaches to area development (multipurpose river basin development, comprehensive rural development, etc.).

8. Restraining market rationality in the name of social interests (coastal planning, job protection, wilderness preservation, etc.).

9. Transferring income to the victims of market rationality (unemployment and workmen's compensation, etc.).

10. Ameliorating other dysfunctional consequences of market rationality (social and spatial inequalities, business cycle planning, resource conservation, etc.; see also 1, 4, and 6 above).

---

planning for these uses, although generally supportive of the interests of capital (and therefore rational in market terms), is nonetheless applied in name and in substance to the furtherance of a general territorial or social interest.

State planning, of course, also includes policies and programs that correspond primarily to social rationality, and these may bring the state into conflict with interests that adhere to the market principle of conduct. The major planning uses that are resolved primarily with reference to socially rational criteria are income redistribution, coordinated planning for regional and rural development, restraints on market rationality, income transfers to victims of the market, and efforts to ameliorate the effects of market rationality (items 6 through 10 in Chart 2). The point of greatest potential conflict with market forces is the use described in item 8, which concerns policies that restrain the normal operation of markets. Historically, it is precisely here that the major public-private battles have been waged. And from these battles we have learned that *only large-scale political mobilization can hope to constrain the single-valued logic of the market.*

Five main conclusions can be drawn from this analysis of the role of planning in market societies. First, even in a country like the United States, with its fervent dedication to the principle of market rationality, many planning activities are undertaken at all the pertinent territorial levels. Second, these planning activities correspond to criteria of social rationality, which in turn derive from a conception of society that assigns primacy to territorially bounded collectivities. Third, although some varieties of socially rational planning aim at helping private business plan its own actions successfully, other varieties place severe restraints on market forces, and some of them even substitute political decision-making (aided by planning) for the operation of the market. Fourth, because planning in the public domain is politically inspired, it creates conflict. And fifth, in a head-on collision with private capital, state action based on planning is likely to be successful only when it is supported by large-scale political mobilization.

These conclusions, which are fundamental to an understanding of planning in capitalist societies, can be stated even more pointedly. Planning in the public domain occurs only in territorially organized societies in which both market rationality and social rationality contend for dominance. Production and livelihood depend largely on market rationality, but unrestrained profit making destroys the bonds of human reciprocity that lie at the foundation of all social life (Price 1978). For this reason, the state, which expresses the political community and is therefore accountable to it, is obliged to play a dual role: it must encourage and support the interests of capital, but it must also prevent those interests from eroding the foundation of a common life. When it opposes capital, the state typically can act with no more resolution than its political support allows. In the final analysis, its legitimacy depends on the political mobilization of the people acting in defense of their collective interests. As an instrument of societal guidance, actual planning practice inevitably reflects this complex, conflict-ridden role.

Planning and the Political Order

How does planning in the public domain fit into the system of political order? What tasks are assigned to planning in the whole ensemble of "guidance" activities to which technical reason is applied? And how is planning articulated with other elements of the social system? We can begin to find answers to these questions by referring to Figure 1, a model of planning in the public domain. Though necessarily static and abstract, this model introduces the major concepts that will be used throughout this book, shows relations between them, and locates planning activities within the spectrum of bureaucratic-political actions of the modern state.[7]

It will be useful to proceed by "reading" the model from top down. Each horizontal bar in the figure represents a definite conceptual space. Two overlapping lines, therefore, signify the coexistence in conceptual space of the activities or functions that they sym-

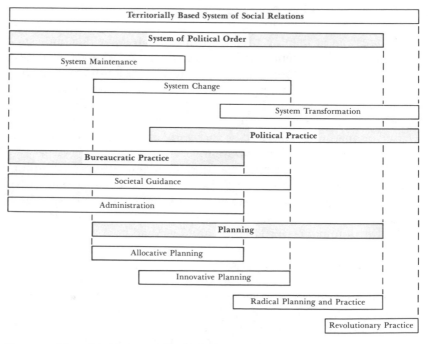

Figure 1. Planning in the public domain: basic concepts.

7. Many of the concepts discussed here were first introduced in my book *Retracking America* (1973). Since then I have made some changes in definition and have considered some new concepts that seem relevant to a discussion of planning theory. The present version is intended to supersede the earlier one in all respects.

bolize, but only to the extent of the overlap. For instance, the bar labeled planning hovers over allocative planning, innovative planning, and radical planning and practice, which are the three basic forms planning can take. The first two (allocative and innovative) overlap, as do the second two (innovative and radical), but allocative and radical planning barely come together: they are the extremes that are mediated through innovative planning. At the same time, radical planning and practice shades off into revolutionary practice, which in turn extends beyond the conceptual space of planning and therefore also beyond the system of political order.

This model tells us nothing about specific institutions, or about the relative importance of different forms of planning, or about the character of the political order, or about the nature of the political process. It is a purely conceptual model that is intended to clarify meanings and to show relations between major concepts in the theory of planning. After we have "read" through it, I shall point out certain of its properties.

The Territorially Based System of Social Relations

The most comprehensive concept of the model refers to social systems that are geographically bounded. Examples include the nation-state (the United States, Canada, France); states or provinces that are part of a federal system (California, Quebec, Rhône); and cities (San Francisco, Montreal, Lyon). Above the nation-state, territorial systems are encountered as multi-nation regions (the European Economic Community) and the global community (the United Nations); below the level of the city, we can identify the proto-territorial systems of neighborhood, borough, and village. We should bear in mind that territorial systems are arranged in the form of a nested hierarchy, so that people simultaneously belong to different orders of territorial relation.

Very large systems (the world, multinational regions, a large country) are heterogeneous with respect to culture, religion, political system, ethnic composition, and regional economic interest. But whatever the scale, territorial systems tend to look back on a common history and forward to a common destiny. Although individuals may escape this destiny by migration, most members of a territorial community have no choice but to remain where they are. This is obviously true for all of us with respect to the world as a whole; to some extent, it is also true at very local levels of territorial integration. Because of this social circumscription, territorial communities generally seek some measure of political control over their destiny; they are real or potential systems of political order (Carneiro 1970).

Members of territorially based communities tend to develop strong feelings of attachment, and these feelings are divided among the different communities to which people belong; some consider themselves citizens of the world, others are ardent nationalists, and still others identify primarily with local values. There are also competing loyalties to other agencies of social integration—family, social class, religion, and linguistic grouping—as well as more tenuous functional associations. Among these potential claimants on people's loyalties, family and state tend to have particular salience.

System of Political Order

Territorially organized social systems are typically organized as political systems. They have, or aspire to have, the basic institutions of self-governance: legislative, executive, and judiciary branches of government; political parties; an organized system of legitimate coercion (military or paramilitary forces, police, courts, jails); a constitution or charter that establishes the legal framework of the political order; and a political culture, which is a set of sanctioned practices for conducting the political affairs of the community. The bar labeled system of political order does not extend for the full length of the territorial system. The leftover space is taken up by revolutionary practice (at the bottom right of Figure 1), which is the practice of social forces that reject the legitimacy of the established political order and organize in violent opposition to it. Examples are terrorist actions in Northern Ireland, Israel, Lebanon, Peru, and the Basque Country in Spain and guerrilla movements in El Salvador and the Philippines.

Maintenance, Change, and Transformation of the System

The next three bars of Figure 1 suggest the basic dynamics of territorial systems: maintenance, change, and transformation. System-maintaining practices, articulated by the state, are chiefly bureaucratic in nature, whereas system-transforming practices involve a mobilized political community acting autonomously vis-à-vis the state. Mediating these extremes are system-changing practices through which radical proposals become integrated with the structure of the guidance system of society. The process through which this occurs is riddled with conflict and compromise. For this reason, special importance attaches to innovative planning which, from a certain perspective, may be regarded as the terrain for the resolution of these conflicts. Processes of system transformation are shown to overlap with both revolutionary practice and radical planning. To the extent that they overlap with radical planning, they must be regarded as a legitimate part of an established political order that tolerates system-transforming activities. Such transformations generally take the form of structural or radical reforms that are engendered through a political process of radical planning and practice from below. It is entirely possible, of course, that the state will attempt to repress system-transforming actions. Whenever this happens, the political system in effect shuts itself off from further transformation from within and openly expresses the will to power and the material interests of its ruling class.

Societal Guidance
This concept covers activities comprising primarily system maintenance and change. Though mediated by the state, processes of societal guidance are also promoted by central institutions from other domains, especially from the corporate economy. Which specific subset of guidance institutions is activated in a particular case will depend on the nature of the issues that emerge as politically salient. The meaning of societal guidance will be discussed in more detail later. For now, it will be sufficient to note that it usually means a top-down management of public affairs, which includes administration and planning as well as political practices that remain within the constraints of the political culture. Specifically, it excludes both revolutionary practices and the more politicized forms of radical planning.

Administration and Planning
These two bars should be looked at simultaneously. Administration refers to the management of program routines and is therefore concerned chiefly with activities of system maintenance and with those elements of system change that are on the verge of being institutionalized. Planning, by contrast, is concerned mainly with informing processes of system change, which forms its boundary on the left. From there, it extends the entire length of the bar representing political order, because planning presupposes and established politics and the institutions that make it possible. It is also shown to coincide with radical, though not with revolutionary, practice. As a counterpart to societal guidance "from the top," planning "from below" merges with the system-transforming practices of political radicalism.

Allocative, Innovative, and Radical Planning
Next, our model shows the three principal forms that planning can take. Allocative planning is concerned with the central disposition

of scarce resources (financial, land, labor) among competing claimants or uses. Innovative planning is concerned with institutional changes in the system of societal guidance. Radical planning is distinctive in drawing on organized citizen power to promote projects pointing toward social transformation. Examples of allocative planning include program budgeting, land use planning, economic development planning, and various forms of sectoral planning. Innovative planning practices have given rise to such new institutions (in the United States) as the Appalachian Regional Commission in the 1950s, the Office of Economic Opportunity in the 1960s, the Environmental Protection Agency in the 1970s, and various financial programs, such as federal revenue sharing. Examples of radical planning efforts are found in conjunction with action-oriented citizen movements, where they mediate between theory and practice in such matters as alternative economic development, producer cooperatives, feminist projects, and alternative energy programs. As with other categories, the three main forms of planning are shown to overlap with each other. Allocative planning may involve some innovative planning, as when a new program is getting funded, and innovative planning may be a response to radical planning and practice. On the other hand, allocative and radical planning barely come together. Almost the only point of overlap occurs when radical planners succeed in getting central authorities to fund radical projects, as occurred as a result of the special circumstances surrounding the Johnson administration's War on Poverty in the 1960s.

Revolutionary Practice
Overlapping with radical planning and practice, some parts of revolutionary practice may infiltrate and work within the still existing system of political order (Marris 1983). Ultimately, however, revolutionary practice seeks the dissolution and breakdown of that order. In its pure form, revolutionary practice remains outside the public domain.

In reviewing this model as a whole, we should note certain important features.

1. The practice of planning in the public domain has both political and technical aspects.

2. Technical aspects are especially pronounced in bureaucratic practice; political aspects predominate in political practice.

Both, however, are present to some extent in both forms of practice.

3. Bureaucratic practice is articulated through the institutional structures of the state; political practice has its origin in the politically active community. Although effective territorial governance requires both forms, bureaucratic and political practices are often in conflict. The need to resolve conflicts between them must be seen as a limiting condition; their normal state of relation is one of tension.[8]

4. For this reason, the state will attempt to bypass or suppress political practice whenever it can. But because political practice is the major source of structural innovation, suppressing or neutralizing the political community makes it more difficult for the state to find ways of coping successfully with changes external to the system itself. Repression feeds upon itself and becomes increasingly costly. Political critiques of planning policies are silenced. With the political community quiescent, the state becomes vulnerable to revolutionary practice.

Planning as a Theoretical Object

As planning theorists, we need to work with a general concept of planning. Without it, what shall we think and talk about? For everyday use, a pragmatic definition—such as planning is what planners do—may suffice; we can comfortably do planning without having a definition in the pocket. But theory cannot dispense with concepts, and for planning theory, the central concept is obviously planning itself. We need to know what *phenomena* should be investigated,

8. David Apter and Nagayo Sawa, in a brilliant dissection of the prolonged people's struggle against the Narita International Airport near Tokyo, offer trenchant commentary on the relation between citizen protest and state action in a democracy.

> Each successful democratic system is a living example of how extra-institutional protest can be transformed into institutional reform. Protest, even in its extra-institutional form, is a commonplace of democratic politics . . . By making accountability a function of direct opposition, the two become inseparable, a relationship converting democracy from a form of government in which political participation is passive, a form of complicity in power, into something dynamic, an expression of mutual responsiveness. (Apter and Sawa 1984, 276)

But what if the state cannot respond, because the state itself is the problem? Then, say Apter and Sawa,

> what will need reviewing in detail are all the old matters once regarded as settled: jurisdictions, political accountability, alternatives of opposition, institutional politics. (Ibid. 228)

They seem to be saying that we have already reached that point.

what *questions* should be asked, and what *philosophical perspectives* should inform our inquiry. The field of planning study needs bounding, and only a conceptual definition can provide that (Wildavsky 1973). Two main criteria should guide our search for a suitable concept: it should be general enough to cover all the specific areas of planning application identified earlier in this chapter and it should open up interesting questions for theoretical study.

In each of the substantive areas of planning, such as national defense, social planning, economic development, and urban design, planners draw on special theories that inform their work. Thus regional planners lean heavily on theories of location and population migration; urban designers work with theories of city form; and public health planners study epidemiology, or how diseases are transmitted in geographical space. At this level of analysis, planners are viewed in the context of specific tasks, and one necessarily dwells on the differences between them, which include not only differences in their objective planning concerns but also differences in their academic and professional training.

In the present inquiry, my focus is a different one. I shall assume that all specific planning applications face certain common methodological problems, such as making forecasts, obtaining appropriate forms of citizen participation, and constructing models useful in exploring alternative action-strategies. But I shall also assume that all planning must confront the *meta-theoretical problem of how to make technical knowledge in planning effective in informing public actions.* The major object of planning theory, I shall argue, is to solve this meta-theoretical problem. If it is not solved, planners will end up talking only to themselves and eventually will become irrelevant.

For many years, planning was defined as the art of making social decisions rationally (Robinson 1972; Faludi 1973). Rationality was defined as a kind of recipe for making decisions (identify objectives, consider all the relevant or most important alternatives, trace the major consequences of each course of action, and so on). It came to be labeled "synoptic" planning, and as a recipe it was difficult to apply. Charles Lindblom proposed, as an alternative decision model, a strategy of "muddling through" (Lindblom 1959, 1979). The theoretical content of both conceptions was quickly exhausted, however. Some authors, such as Etzioni (1968), proposed improvements in the recipe for rational planning. The "muddlers," on the other hand, scored few theoretical points. Their proposals for incremental decision-making, "mutual partisan adjustment," and "satisficing" were fancy arguments to extend the market model of the economy to the public domain (Simon 1976; Lindblom 1965). The implementation of their model would leave things precisely as they were. This was planning theory in its most apologetic form.

The rational-choice model of planning has stagnated for nearly two decades. Since the early major contributions of Simon, Banfield (Meyerson and Banfield 1955), Lindblom, and Etzioni, little that is new had been added.[9] Despite extensive and even virulent criticism (Caiden and Wildavsky 1974; Wildavsky 1979), the model continues to be in vogue, chiefly, one suspects, because nothing better has come along. The time would therefore seem to be ripe for a new conceptual approach.

An Operational Definition of Planning
When planners apply technical reason to the specific problem areas identified earlier, we find them engaged in some or all of the following activities.

1. Defining the problem to be addressed in ways that will make it amenable to action or policy intervention.

2. Modeling and analyzing the situation for the purpose of intervention with specific policy instruments, institutional innovations, or methods of social mobilization.

3. Designing one or more potential solutions in the form of policies, substantive plans of action, institutional innovations, and so on. These solutions are typically expressed in terms of:
    a. Futurity—specification of goals and objectives, as well as forecasts, probability judgments, action sequences, and so on.
    b. Space—location, spatial organization, physical design.
    c. Resource requirements—cost estimates and other claims on scarce resources such as foreign exchange, skilled labor, and so on.
    d. Implementation procedures.
    e. Procedures for feedback and evaluation.

4. Carrying out a detailed evaluation of the proposed alternative solutions in terms of their technical feasibility, cost effec-

9. A possible exception might be the work in welfare economics by Edward T. Mishan (1976, 1981a, 1981b). Mishan's theories hover uneasily on the margins of contemporary planning practice. They have been taken most seriously by environmental planners; planning theorists have taken little note of them.

tiveness, probable effects on different population groups, political acceptability, and so on.

Where these activities are found, we can safely assert that planning exists. In this pragmatic definition, planning appears as a mode of decision-making-in-advance, as an activity that precedes both decisions and action. But useful as it is in identifying what lies at the core of technical planning expertise, the definition is inadequate for theoretical inquiry. A more formal concept must be articulated.[10]

Formal Concepts of Planning
The broadest definition of planning as a form of technical reason is this one:[11]

I. Planning attempts to link scientific and technical knowledge to actions in the public domain.

In this definition, planning is not wholly concerned with either knowing or acting, but rather serves as a link: its specific task is to make scientific and technical knowledge useful to specific actors in the public domain. But we need a more precise definition if we are to connect our conceptual definition of planning to our model of a territorially based system of social relations (Figure 1). To meet this need, two further definitions suggest themselves:

II. Planning attempts to link scientific and technical knowledge to processes of societal guidance.

III. Planning attempts to link scientific and technical knowledge to processes of social transformation.

The operative terms in these definitions are *societal guidance* and *social transformation*. Whereas the former is articulated through the state, and is concerned chiefly with systematic change, the latter focuses on the political practices of system transformation. Planners engaged in these two practices are necessarily in conflict. It is a conflict between the interests of a bureaucratic state and the interests of

10. The pragmatic definition of planning is nevertheless useful in pinpointing problems in planning methodology, such as how to build policy models, how to make forecasts more reliable, what criteria to use in selecting the location of public facilities, how to design urban space, what method of shadow pricing to adopt in resource analysis, and how to make social evaluations more meaningful. The education and training of planners is concerned mainly with these and related questions applied to particular problem areas.

11. In the following, we shall not consider private sector (strategic) planning for corporate decision-making.

the political community. The bulk of public planning, of course, is related to societal guidance and includes both allocative and innovative forms. The pressure for system-wide transformation is intensified when, in the course of a system-wide crisis, the legitimate authority of the state declines, and the state itself is so weakened that it can no longer successfully repress the radical practices of the political community.[12]

Each of the three definitions of planning has roots in a different intellectual tradition.

DEFINITION I. The concept of action is central here, in the sense that action is viewed as being prior to any need for scientific and technical knowledge. Actors request the services of planners; they are in charge. The concept is taken from political philosophy (Arendt 1858), in which action signifies both a departure from routine behavior (a new path or an innovative practice) and the initiation of a chain of consequences that, except for the action, would not have occurred.[13]

DEFINITION II. Societal guidance is a concept drawn from macro-sociology (Etzioni 1968). It implies a central involvement of the state and incorporates both allocative and innovative forms of planning. Related theories include neo-classical and institutional economics, public administration, and organization development.

DEFINITION III. The language of social transformation is drawn primarily from both anarchist and Marxist literature, and from what is best described as a separate utopian tradition. Related concepts of political community and sociopolitical movements are taken, respectively, from political theory and political sociology.

A comprehensive exploration of the terrain of planning theory must cull from all the relevant disciplines those elements that are central to an understanding of planning in the public domain. The theory of planning is an eclectic field, bounded by political philosophy; epistemology; macro-sociology; neo-classical and institutional

12. In addition to outright repression, the state has several options for dealing with radical practice. It can co-opt radical politics by buying off its leadership, or give token recognition to radical movements, or make a strategic retreat. Any of these strategies may effectively neutralize the picture of a radical politics (see Apter and Sawa 1984 for examples).

13. Definition I represents a conscious turning away from decision-models of planning. Although in practice actions are inclusive of decisions, action is the more comprehensive term. Actors strive to make a difference in the world. They must mobilize power. They must concert the actions of others. All this is not part of planning but rather part of the situation to which planning is directed.

economics; public administration; organization development; political sociology; and anarchist, Marxist, and utopian literature. It is from the rich mine of these varied intellectual traditions that we must develop the answers to our questions about planning.[14]

Some Questions in Planning Theory

The conceptual definitions of planning raise questions that are central to any inquiry into planning theory. By way of illustration, and without attempting a systematic overview and ordering of questions, I should like to formulate some of them as they arise out of Definition I. This definition contains three key terms: knowledge, action, and the public domain.[15] In the remainder of this chapter, we shall discuss questions pertaining to knowledge and action. The question of the public domain and other questions concerning the state and the radical practice of political communities will be discussed at appropriate points throughout the book.

Our intention here is to raise questions, not to answer them. It is to show how a conceptual definition of planning as the relating of knowledge to action can be useful for theory, which is to say, for a more precise understanding of the possibilities and limits of planning in the public domain.

The Question of Knowledge

This question concerns what we can and cannot know about. Are there different forms of knowledge, and are some forms inherently superior to others? How does knowledge come to be validated? How is it different from what is *not* knowledge? And to what extent and in what ways can scientific and technical knowledge about the world be made available and useful to actors in the public domain?

Planners claim that their advanced degrees in relevant disciplines and professional fields give them privileged access to scientific knowledge and technical know-how. They also claim that this knowledge is generally superior to knowledge gained in other ways (from practical experience, for example). In this respect, they speak as the true heirs of the Enlightenment, the age in which central au-

14. Disciplines and modes of inquiry *excluded* from this list are psychology (particularly individual psychology), cultural anthropology, geography, history, political science, micro-sociology, and the humanities, including design theory.

15. A fourth concept is *linkage*. The basic question here is *how* knowledge is to be linked to action. It is an instrumental question to which an answer can be forthcoming only when we have satisfactorily responded to the prior questions about both knowledge and action, the two phenomena that are to be linked.

thorities in the secular world began to base their decisions on science and its technical correlates rather than on divine inspiration. In the Enlightenment tradition, two crucial assumptions are made. The first is that the world is objectively knowable through the instruments of positive science. The truth of the world, as it emerges from a myriad of scientific inquiries, is validated by becoming the basis for the mastery of the world. Learning the secrets of nature, we learn to fly, to harness the sun's energy, and to transmit voice signals over vast distances through space. We can do these things because scientific statements are statements about the world "as it really is." The second assumption is that there is an unbroken line of evolution between the physical or natural world and the human or sociocultural world. Seen in this perspective, the science of human behavior is a continuation of natural science "by other means," and its present lackluster performance in application is proof only of its relative immaturity. One or two generations (or centuries) hence, the argument goes, we will know a great deal more about the social world and how it works, so much more that we will be able to manipulate it at will, in much the same way that we now turn the natural world to our use.

The social validation of knowledge through mastery of the world puts the stress on *manipulative* knowledge. But knowledge can also serve another purpose, which is the construction of satisfying images of the world. Such knowledge, which is pursued primarily for the world view that it opens up, may be called *appreciative* knowledge. Although science (astronomy, for example) used to be primarily appreciative, it has become almost entirely a form of manipulative knowledge. Contemplation and the creation of symbolic forms continue to be pursued as ways of knowing about the world, but because they are not immediately useful, they are not validated socially and are treated as merely private concerns or entertainment.[16]

16. These brief allusions to the philosophy of science are based on eclectic readings. One of the best histories of science as a form of manipulative knowledge for mastering the natural world is Gillespie (1960). For the assumption of objective knowledge, I have relied chiefly on Popper (1975), and for the further assumption of continuity between the natural and social worlds, and of the respective domains of science, I have relied on the writings of evolutionists such as Steward (1955), Montagu (1956), von Bertalanffy (1960, 1962), Dunn (1971), Monod (1971), Wilson (1975, 1978), and Bateson (1979), in addition to the influential work of Popper. On appreciative knowledge, see especially Langer (1953) and, for a physicist's point of view, Schroedinger (1956a, 1956b). The contemporary tendency to return to an appreciative science is especially evident in such hybrid works as de Chardin (1959), Capra (1975, 1982), Hofstadter (1979), and Lindholm (1981).

The following questions about knowledge will be put from the perspective of planning and its linkage-to-action requirements. They are questions for which there are no easy answers; indeed, they may have no definitive answers at all. It is precisely this quality, however, that makes them intriguing.

1. All knowledge gained by applying the methods of science is knowledge about past events. But planners need some knowledge of future events, and so they engage in making forecasts, projections, and predictions. What assumptions must be made, particularly during periods of rapid structural change, in order to claim that knowledge of events in the past is relevant to "knowing" the future? Do these assumptions yield *reliable* knowledge about the future? And are the uncertainties inherent in statements about the future anything more than subjective feelings of risk, even when these feelings are "pooled," as in the Delphi method?[17] Are planners likely to assess risks in the same way actors do?

2. The hypotheses, theories, and models through which all scientific and technical knowledge is expressed are radical simplifications of the world: they are stated in universal terms, and their validity depends on the assumption that the world external to the model will remain unchanged. But in planning for the real world, "all other" conditions cannot be held constant. Rational actions must be based on holistic analyses of specific historical situations. Does knowledge, then, lose its "objective" character when the assumptions under which it is claimed to be true are "relaxed," so that more and more variables can interact with the endogenous variables of the model in ways that cannot be calculated with precision? In other words, does the scientist-planner who is forced to engage in holistic analysis produce knowledge that is superior to the hopes and expectations of ordinary people who are concerned with solving their own problems?

3. All scientific and technical knowledge is either theoretical or methodological. Theoretical knowlege is knowledge that is still being talked about; theories argue and are argued against (even when they are the "best" available theories at the moment). By what criterion, then, do planners choose among con-

17. The Delphi method, developed at Rand, is used to pool "expert" opinions about the future in a process of iteration which tends to move from diversity in the spectrum of replies to a convergence on a relatively stable forecast.

tending theories? Is the "safe" bet always the best? And is choosing one theory instead of another a political act? Methodological knowledge can be acquired only by great expenditures of money and time (the process of validation itself requires years), and these are resources that are not usually available to planners. On the other hand, "quick and dirty" solutions do not yield scientifically validated knowledge. On what grounds, then, do planners claim superiority for the kinds of knowledge they make available within existing constraints? Is it true that scientific-technical knowledge, whether validated or not, is always better than knowledge based on other methods of inquiry?

4. What are the proper claims of that knowledge that is based on the experience of acting in the world and that in its articulate, particularistic, and embodied form is sometimes called personal or experiential knowledge (Polanyi 1962)? On what grounds can scientific and technical knowledge, with its presumptive universal validity, claim to be superior to personal knowledge, especially when the application of each kind of knowledge yields a different result?

5. All empirical knowledge—scientific and technical as well as personal—is validated, before an action is taken on it, by talking about the evidence. The construction of knowledge must therefore be regarded as an intensely social process, with its own interpersonal and group dynamics. Because human beings pursue ends, have desires, and want their views to be accepted by others, communication processes are structured both politically and theoretically. The knowledge that we have about the world is in part a reflection of our passions. When we say that we "know about the world," we are talking of stories in which, by relating facts, experiences, beliefs, and visions in a narrative, we attempt to make sense of the world. We construct the world out of these stories in a process that is at once individual and social. This does not mean that knowledge is like fiction, a pure invention. Scientifically grounded statements about the world—to the extent that they are accepted as valid (and their validity is always historically contingent—can have very real effects on the world. They have the function of affirming or negating, of making useful, and of changing the existing order of relations. If may be argued that all knowledge is inherently tied to some form of practice, and that it qualifies as knowledge only insofar as it produces consequences in the real world.

This interpretation challenges the claims to objectivity made for science and minimizes the differences between scientific-technical and personal knowledge. It portrays the creation of all knowledge as a social process that remains unfinished and open to the future. Given this construction, on what grounds shall planners argue that their view of the world ought to prevail? Can we assume that their knowledge is always more reliable than personal knowledge? Do the conditions of knowing require at least a dialogue between planner and actor? If they do, how shall such a dialogue be structured? And by whom?

6. Personal or shared beliefs about the world—the ideologies of actors—are an important obstacle to gaining objective knowledge. Powerful beliefs influence the kinds of knowledge we obtain when we investigate the world or act within it. If all knowledge is permeated by ideology, how can planners claim privileged access to objective knowledge? And when the personal knowledge of actors clashes with the scientific and technical knowledge of planners, is there any reason to think that one or the other is inherently better and should therefore be followed?

7. What is the utility of ignorance for actors?

The Question of Action

If we identify actions rather than decisions as the principal focus of planning practice, then being effective in the world becomes the decisive criterion. Planning that changes nothing of substance is scarcely worth talking about. As a concept, action has usually been used to mean goal-oriented action, a use that places the accent on its presumptive rationality (Parsons 1949). Here, we use it in a different sense. Following Arendt (1958), we shall say that action means to set something new into the world. Goal achievement is not an essential part of it. For example, actions may be undertaken to discover new objectives or to explore the meaning of a particular constellation of values. The only fixed requirement for an action is that it can be attributed to an actor who can be held accountable for at least its proximate consequences. Following are action-related questions.

1. Who are the actors in the public domain to whom knowledge is being provided? Are they individuals, organizations, collectives? What is the institutional setting in which actors in the public domain are working? What are the dynamics of their

relations with each other? What material interests divide them, and what values are at stake in the actions they contemplate? Can planners remain indifferent to these and other characteristics of the action field, or should they have to relate their own work in some manner to the internal dynamics of the field? If they should, what implications follow?

2. To be effective, actors must have sufficient power to concert the actions of others and to overcome the resistance of vested interests. Is planning, therefore, always addressed to those who are powerful enough to launch a successful action? And if it is, can we say that planning is primarily an instrument of domination in the hands of actors who have the capacity to prevail in promoting their own interests? Alternatively, if planning is addressed to the weak, how shall plans be carried out? Are social mobilization, confrontation, and protest the only ways by which the weak can create a political space for themselves? Should planners help the powerless acquire power? If so, by what means? And how would this effort by planners affect their claim to objective knowledge?

3. All action represents a departure from the routine; it initiates a course of change. This implies that actors must overcome resistance, the counteractions of those whose life situation they would rearrange. Action is thus a dynamic process that requires to adopt strategies for change. But is the devising of strategies part of the process of applying scientific and technical knowledge to action? Or is the knowledge that goes into the fashioning of strategies derived primarily from experience, and therefore *personal* knowledge? And if this is the case, is not personal knowledge also the most valuable form of knowledge-in-action?

4. In the long term, the outcomes of a chain of action and counteraction are unpredictable. What does this tell use about the supposed ability of planners to "know" the future through forecasting models? Assuming that these models are not totally useless, what legitimate uses can be made of them?

5. Action requires value commitments strong enough to enable the actor to persist with the action long enough to overcome resistance. The culture of actors, therefore, is very different from that of planners. Planners share a passion for dispassionate reason, which is the hallmark of scientific work, and they champion its requirements for a skeptical mind, for attentive

listening, for the rejection of rhetoric, and so forth. What problems arise from this apparent incompatibility of cultures? And if planners should become more like actors in their passionate commitment to the action itself, what would happen to their claims about objective knowledge, and to their special status as "experts"?

It could be argued that actors look to planners for contributions precisely because planners are "remote" from the action itself. Planners, for example, might be expected to correctly define the situation actors face, to suggest realistic expectations of the future, to indicate major options and risks, to weigh the costs and benefits of an action, to provide feedback on the effects of potential actions as well as changes in the external situation, to assess the strengths and weaknesses of opponents, to estimate the resources that are needed and can be mobilized, and to predict the likely occurrence of critical events. It is not clear, however, that actors really want such advice. Their passionate commitments may lead them to insist on an equally committed analysis. Are actors who are passionately engaged likely to listen with an open mind to counsel that is inconsistent with their own perceptions and beliefs? What systematic biases do these circumstances introduce into planning analysis and the communication of its results to actors?

6. Do planners have any responsibility for the knowledge and values they press upon actors? To what extent should planners lobby for acceptance for their theories, proposals, and projects? Are planners co-actors or merely hired consultants?

7. The apparent lack of concern among planners about the values of actors would seem to contribute to the overall irrationality of technocratic planning. On the other hand, to the extent that planners do show concern with long-run, structural consequences, is the reasoning they use still predominantly technical, or does it merge with what we might call political reason? And if the latter, what kind of knowledge becomes most relevant then? Is it knowledge based on science or knowledge based on action and accumulating experience? And whose experience would be more relevant, that of planners or of actors? Knowledge based on action is a form of learning. Is it not the responsibility of planners, then, to help structure settings that will allow both actors and planners to increase learning from

experience, and to use what has been learned as a basis for further planning and action

Conclusion

The idea of planning is elusive and frequently misunderstood. "Make me a plan," someone will say, expecting to be provided with a document that rationally lays out a course of action in relation to specified goals. But there are many forms of planning and many specific applications, and underlying these specifics there are some general characteristics of planning that define a generic problematic. This chapter has tried to lay out the arguments for such a view.

With reference, then, to planning in the public sphere, and in contrast to corporate planning in the private interest, we found the following characteristics.

1. Planning is concerned with making decisions and informing actions in ways that are socially rational.

2. Scientific and technical planning as practiced today contrasts sharply with earlier "orthogonal" planning. Concerned chiefly with physical design, orthogonal planning was intended for a static, hierarchical order, was practiced in conformity with a divine or cosmic reason, was based on authoritative (secret) knowledge, and was learned in accordance with traditional practices of apprenticeship.

3. Planning in a market society, such as the United States, is found in virtually all areas of state intervention.

4. Where planning is used, it is meant to serve a public or general purpose, such as ensuring the stability and growth of the economy; undertaking selected public investments and, in the absence of private sector interest, inducing desired actions on part of the private sector through various forms of subsidy; restraining private sector actions to safeguard the well-being of the population at large; redistributing income on grounds of equity; protecting individuals and businesses against the uncertainties of the market; and so forth.

5. Three major forms of planning may be identified—allocative, innovative, and radical—roughly corresponding to the three possible states of political systems: maintenance, evolutionary change, and structural transformation.

6. Planning can be defined in many ways, but in a theoretical perspective, only a few definitions are of possible interest.

Three linked definitions of planning in the public domain were advanced. At the most basic level, planning was said to be an attempt to relate scientific and technical knowledge to actions in the public domain. Two broad types of action were identified, concerned, respectively with societal guidance and social transformation. To illustrate the significance of these definitions, the chapter concluded with a series of questions in the theory of planning.

With this discussion as background, we can now proceed to look at the major traditions of planning thought as they have evolved in the course of the last two hundred years.

Part Two / Traditions

Two Centuries
of Planning Theory:
An Overview

Introduction

The idea that scientifically based knowledge about society could actually be applied to society's improvement first arose during the eighteenth century. It was given great momentum by Jeremy Bentham, the iconoclastic theorist and prison reformer whose most significant work appeared in 1789 in the midst of a period of revolutionary turmoil. Until then, ethics had been a moralistic "science," concerned chiefly with rules of proper conduct and with right intentions. But Bentham, convinced that any worthy idea had to be practical, focused with mathematical rigor on the consequences of action which he made the basis for ethical judgment, and therefore also for evaluation and choice. This shift of focus to a consideration of consequences had revolutionary implications, and despite its simplicities and naive assumptions, Bentham's pain-and-pleasure calculus was a major invention.

Bentham's influence on European thought was immense, but different national traditions selected different messages from it. In England, John Stuart Mill refined Bentham's elementary notions and passed them on, under the label of utilitarianism, to the "neo-classical" economists who came to dominate the field toward the end of the nineteenth century. In France, Bentham's ideas were picked up by Saint-Simon, whose radar-like mind was attuned to even the slightest tremors of modernity. But the Saint-Simonian transformation, carried forward by Comte, took a very different path than the one charted by Mill. Although he was an early admirer of Comte's "positive philosophy," Mill came to reject the lockstep authoritarianism of Comte's later work. Henceforth, the two traditions of the modern temper—a British liberalism rooted in concern for the individual and his liberties and a French socialism that assigned a decisive role to the state—would go their separate ways.

Important as Bentham's contributions were to the budding methodologies of planning, it is Saint-Simon who should rightfully be regarded as the father of scientific planning. This enigmatic figure has been appropriated by several social sciences as the progenitor of a long line of presumptive heirs, including sociology (Gouldner 1958), political science (Vidal 1959), public administration (Ionescu 1976; Krygier 1979), and even "socialism" (albeit not the Marxist variety), which until well into the 1880s referred primarily to state intervention in the economy (Durkheim 1958, Bernstein 1955). Planning, of course, draws on all these disciplines and philosophical traditions. But if their common ancestor is Saint-Simon, why not then claim him for planning as well? In the myth of creation, order arises from chaos. And from the inspired, disorderly writings of Saint-Simon came the main themes that would eventually be taken up by more systematic planning theorists in our time.

What Saint-Simon referred to as his social physiology suggested an image of the body social whose physicians would be scientists and engineers who placed their work in humanity's service. Familiar with society's "organic" laws, they would consciously set out its future course "according to a comprehensive plan." It was their ability to predict future outcomes of present actions that would enable society to control its destiny. It was a brave conception! As a practical matter, the scientist-physicians of society would offer their knowledge to those most capable of steering humanity's progress toward the new industrial order: the engineers, entrepreneurs, and banker-financiers who would build it; the artists, writers, and musicians who would serve as its ideologues; and the political leaders who would wield their baton over the whole ensemble.

At the time Saint-Simon developed his theories, the ultimate victory of industrialism was by no means assured. His theories were seized by the nascent bourgeoisie as an ideological weapon in their struggle for domination. As a class, they would derive great benefit from a philosophy in which scientific planning was to be the midwife of humanity's liberation from the darkness of its feudal past.

An interesting parallel can be observed in the economic development doctrines that became popular during the 1950s and 1960s, when the industrialization of the newly independent nation-states of Asia and Africa and the accelerated growth of the older Latin American countries fired peoples' imaginations. Prosperity would soon be universal, they thought; poverty would be banished forever; happiness was about to become the common human lot. All this would be achieved through (scientific) planning. It was a fantasy that would soon lead to a soberer view of things, but for a while, it was invested with idealism and hope (Wolfe 1981). It was the same hope and idealism that had inspired Saint-Simonian engineers a century before.

The soberer view in the first industrial age came less than a generation after Saint-Simon's death in 1825, with the publication of Proudhon's *Philosophy of Poverty* (1846) and, two years later, coincident with the Paris uprising, *The Communist Manifesto*. Here, for the first time, were "radical" views of planning enshrined in the doctrines of anarchism and historical materialism. (Meanwhile, the "conservative" vision was marching forward under the banner of Comte's Religion of Humanity.) What made radical planning different was its political message: it was addressed not to the ruling class, as both Saint-Simon and Comte had addressed theirs, but to the carrier of revolutionary struggle, the urban proletariat. Proudhon's ringing exclamation "Property is Theft!" scarcely endeared him to the princes of capital; neither did Marx and Engels' "Workers of the World, Unite!" All three wished for a change in the relations of power, Proudhon by denying the legitimacy of any coercive form of power whatsoever, Marx and Engels by demanding structural reforms, such as the ten-point program of the *Manifesto*. Both saw the answer to the planning powers of an oppressive bourgeois state in a broadly based social mobilization of working people.

Conservative and radical traditions of planning thought were thus established early on. The actual realization of scientific planning as a technique for guiding social progress would take another century. Inaugurated with production planning during the war years, 1914–1918, it came into regular use with the installation of the Soviet planning system in the 1920s. Although other forms of planning, such as urban design, piecemeal social reforms, and administrative city planning, can be found from the middle of the nineteenth century onward, they did not as yet embody a scientific practice. It is only the concept and ideology of a scientifically based planning that will concern us here. Long shadows of this conception, such as the faith in a meritocracy of scientific and technical elites (Tugwell 1975a, b), in an objective social knowledge (Popper 1975), in the possibilities of a directed process of societal change (Etzioni 1968), and in the ultimate harmony of social relations finetuned to an ever-widening social consensus, reach down to this day (Habermas 1979).

The path of this germinal idea was obviously not going to be a straight line. For one thing, different tasks required different solutions, and these were taken up by new disciplines as the need for them arose. Also, there were contending conceptions of the state and, indeed, of actors other than the state. In time, then, there emerged a great variety of planning traditions. Some would lean toward the technical side of the equation—decision-making and the design of alternatives—others more to the political and institutional side. The remainder of this chapter is devoted to a perspective of the evolutionary history of scientifically based planning.

The Intellectual Traditions

The period covered by Figure 2 is roughly two hundred years. As we move down from the late eighteenth century to the present, the time scale on the left of the diagram expands to accommodate the large number of contemporary authors: since 1945, there has been a virtual explosion in planning literature.

Intellectual traditions and authors are placed along a continuum of social values, from conservative ideology on the left-hand side of the figure to utopianism and anarchism on the right. To simplify exposition, we can divide this continuum into three parts. On the extreme left of the diagram are shown those authors who look to the confirmation and reproduction of existing relations of power in society. Expressing predominantly technical concerns, they proclaim a carefully nurtured stance of political neutrality. In reality, they address their work to those who are in power and see their primary mission as serving the state.

Systems Analysis derives from a cluster of theories that may be grouped loosely under the heading *Systems Engineering* (cybernetics, game theory, information theory, computer science, robotics, and so on). Scientists in this tradition work chiefly with large-scale quantitative models. In specific planning applications, they may use optimizing techniques such as operations research; alternatively, they may construct long-range forecasting models. Most futures research leans heavily on systems-analytic languages.

More closely allied to Public Administration than to Systems Analysis, *Policy Science* subjects specific issues in public policy to socioeconomic analysis. Stock-in-trade concepts include the analysis of costs and benefits, zero budgeting, cost effectiveness, and program evaluation. Overall, there is a preference for problems that are well-bounded and for goal statements that are unambiguous. Note, too, that policy science is heir to a long intellectual tradition. Such logic as it has derives largely from neo-classical economics with its several offshoots of welfare economics and social choice theory.

An amalgam with the institutional approach of public administration, however, is its very own.

Public Administration, finally, has been more generally concerned with the functions of central planning, the conditions for its success, and the relation of planning to politics. In recent decades, a special area of concern has been the implementation of public policies and programs. A central contribution to planning theory from the traditions of public administration was made by Herbert Simon, whose early work, *Administrative Behavior* (1976; orig. 1945), approached the bureaucratic process from a behavioral perspective that stressed conditions limiting rationality in large organizations.

On the opposite side of the spectrum (the extreme right of Figure 2) are authors who look to the transformation or transcendence of existing relations of power within civil society. Here, it is no longer the state that is addressed but the people, particularly those of working-class origins, who, it is believed, are fundamentally opposed to the bureaucratic state and, more generally, to every form of alienated power. The mode of discourse adopted by the authors is frankly political.

Most extreme in their rejection of power are the *Utopians* and *Anarchists*, who deny all claims of higher authority in their search for a world of non-hierarchical relations. Parallel to this tradition is *Historical Materialism* and, more recently, *Neo-Marxism*. Writers in this vein tend to espouse the revolutionary transformation of the prevailing "mode of production." In contrast to utopians, they accept the state as a necessity. Class relations constitute a central analytical preoccupation of historical materialists. It is through relentless class conflict, they argue, that existing relations of power will eventually be "smashed" and replaced with a socialist state that will reflect the organized power and material interests of the working class as a whole.

Midway between utopian anarchism and historical materialism we have located a secondary tradition, especially important for planning theory, which is known as the Frankfurt School of Critical Sociology (Jay 1973). Its principal concern is a radical critique, grounded in Hegelian and Marxist categories, of the multifaceted cultural manifestations of capitalism, including the deification of technical reason itself.

Moving toward the central portions of Figure 2, we enter the grey area of overlap between the conservative pole of "ideology," where present relations of power remain largely unquestioned, and the radical pole of "utopia," with its transcendent vision. Here we en-

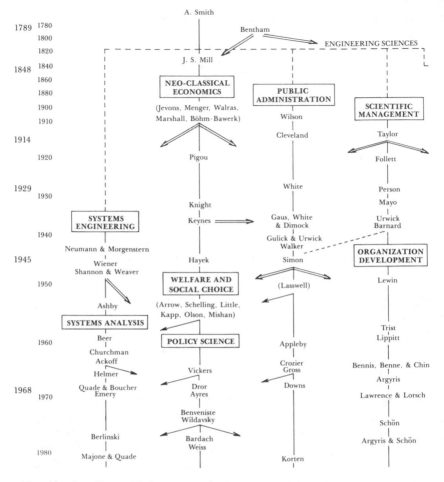

Figure 2. Intellectual influences on American planning theory.

counter the reformist traditions of planning and their immediate antecedents. Close to public administration, which may be partly regarded as its offshoot, is the tradition of *Scientific Management*, which had its start with the seminal work of Frederick Winslow Taylor (1919; orig. 1911). His doctrine enjoyed remarkable success. And despite its clear subservience to business interests, it had a compelling attraction even for radical thinkers, such as Veblen and Lenin, who conceived of society as a large workshop and of planning as a form of social engineering. For all of them, conservatives and radicals alike, the watchword was efficiency, and in an age of industri-

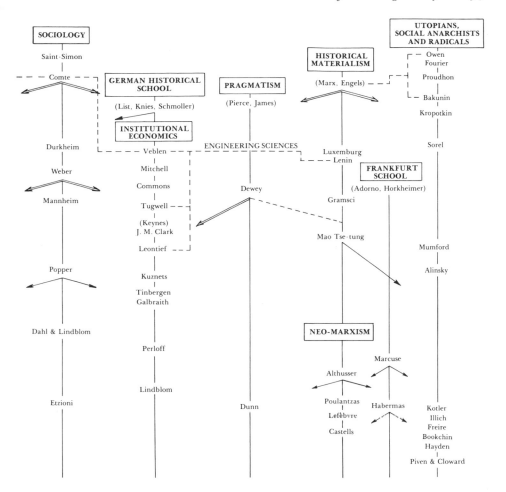

alism its invocation would magically unlock the gateway to the future.

After 1945, scientific management spawned the new field of *Organization Development*. Its principal client was the large, private corporation to which it tendered a message steeped in humanistic rhetoric. With works by Eric Trist, Chris Argyris, Donald Schön, Charles Hampden-Turner, and others, the field produced a literature that moved gradually away from profit as the sole criterion of management, bringing psychological values of self-development to the foreground.

Along more conventional liberal lines is *Institutional Economics*. An

American branch of the nineteenth-century *German Historical School*, but by no means rigorously defined, it emphasizes the study of existing economic and social institutions over abstract theorizing in the style of neo-classical economics. Institutionalists prefer to examine the failings of specific institutional arrangements in relation to social purpose and to identify reforms. They have contributed major ideas for planning full employment, economic growth, regional resources development, New Towns policies, public housing schemes, and social welfare. The institutionalization of a planning function was one of their major concerns.

Institutionalists tend to regard the state as a relatively benign and rational actor, responsive to political pressure. In this sense, they stand very much in the tradition of Comte, who thought that social scientists should offer their knowledge to the rulers of nations. Like the father of positive philosophy himself, they believe in the powers of technical reason to determine what is correct, to persuade the ignorant and doubtful, and to forge the consensus needed for action. Suspicious of a freewheeling democratic politics, they place their faith in a technocracy of the meritorious.

Located between the traditions of institutionalism and historical materialism, we find the philosophical school of *Pragmatism*. For present purposes, this is an important tradition primarily because of John Dewey's exceptional influence on the intellectual history of planning. His influence is especially notable in the case of the institutional economists, many of whom came to accept Dewey's championship of a "scientific politics" in which learning from social experiments was regarded as fundamental to the development of a healthy democracy. A more recent exponent of a Dewey-like pragmatic philosophy is Edgar Dunn.

For want of a better term, the center line of Figure 2 is labeled *Sociology*. Here we meet with the great synthesizers of social knowledge. Without exception, sociologists have argued the case of technical reason in human affairs: Emile Durkheim and Max Weber, the first stressing the importance of consensual values in social organization and the "organic solidarity" of the division of labor, the latter emphasizing the dominant role of bureaucratic structures in an industrial society devoted to the worship of functional order; Karl Mannheim, the most distinguished continental sociologist of his time, a critic of mass society and an advocate of "rational planning" as a way of overcoming the evils of unreason that had overtaken Europe; Karl Popper, an Austrian emigré scholar living in England, whose polemical masterpiece, *The Open Society and Its Enemies* (1974; orig. 1945), advocated piecemeal social engineering;

Robert Dahl and Charles Lindblom, two social scientists from Yale University, whose joint endeavor, *Politics, Economics, and Welfare* (1957), was the first major American theoretical statement on planning; and Amitai Etzioni, an Israeli sociologist residing in the United States, whose *The Active Society* (1968) may be read as a worthy successor to Mannheim's *Man and Society in an Age of Reconstruction*, written during another period of general crisis a generation earlier (1949b; orig. 1940).

A dashed line labeled *Engineering Sciences* runs across the top of Figure 2, connecting Saint-Simon and Comte in the center with Scientific Management, Public Administration, Systems Engineering, and Institutional Economics. (An influence on Lenin is also shown.) A case can be made for the idea that the methods of engineering informs major sectors of the planning theory tradition. At his celebrated Paris dinners during which his basic ideas took shape, Saint-Simon played host to some of the leading professors of the new École Polytechnique (established in 1794), and later he surrounded himself, by preference, with young *polytechniciens* who were both his audience and inspiration. Among them was Comte, who for disciplinary reasons had been excluded from the École only months before he was to graduate.

The École Polytechnique may be seen as the prototypical institution of the new industrial age and the source of its managerial ideology. Engineers applied the knowledge of the natural sciences to the construction of bridges, tunnels, and canals. By the same logic, why should not a new breed of "social engineers" apply their knowledge to the task of reconstructing society? In his brilliant essay on the École tradition, Friedrich von Hayek tells us how the new institution, born in revolutionary times, shaped the character and outlook of its pupils.

> The very type of the engineer with his characteristic outlook, ambitions, and limitation was here created. That synthetic spirit which would not recognize sense in anything that had not been deliberately constructed, that love of organization that springs from the twin sources of military and engineering practices, the aesthetic predilection for everything that had been consciously constructed over anything that had "just grown," was a strong element which was added to—and in the course of time even began to replace—the revolutionary ardor of the young polytechnicians. . . . It was in this atmosphere that Saint-Simon conceived some of the earliest and most fantastic plans for the reorganization of society, and . . . it was at

the École Polytechnique where, during the first twenty years of its existence, Auguste Comte, Prosper Enfantin, Victor Considérant and some hundreds of later Saint-Simonians and Fourierists received their training, followed by a succession of social reformers throughout the century down to Georges Sorel. (Hayek 1955, 113)

The engineer's sense of certainty (and his ignorance of history) informed some of the most prominent of later planning theorists, among them Thorstein Veblen, Rexford Tugwell, and Herbert Simon, all of whom were enthralled by the idea of "designing society." Even Simon, who was certainly aware of the difficulties inherent in the project, could not resist discussing social planning as the task of "designing the evolving artifact," as though society were merely a somewhat complex machine (Simon 1982). It is precisely when we turn from designing genuine artifacts to society that the design model breaks down. Simon seems to be conscious of the contradiction.

Making complex designs that are implemented over a long period of time and continually modified in the course of implementation has much in common with painting in oil. In oil painting, every new spot of pigment laid on the canvas creates some kind of pattern that provides a continuing source of ideas to the painter. The painting process is a process of cyclical interaction between painter and canvas in which current goals lead to new applications of paint, while the gradually changing pattern suggests new goals. (H. Simon 1982, 187)

An oil painting is not a machine, and designers do not paint in oils. What is more, and to confuse the metaphor, society is not a canvas to be painted by an inspired artist. Engineers can build bridges and automata; it is an illusion to think that they can "build" society. There was a moment in time when aeronautic and space engineers though that, having reached the moon, they could now turn their energies to solving the problem of growing violence in cities, along with other urban "crises." But the two types of problems—how to conquer space and how to eliminate urban violence—were of an essentially different nature, and the engineers' discovery that urban violence would not yield to engineering solutions was not long in coming (Rittel and Webber 1973).

This "quick read" across the horizontal axis of Figure 2 needs to be complemented now with a more detailed discussion of the time dimension in the evolution of planning thought. Certain key dates are set in larger type in the left-hand margin.

Our story begins in 1789 with the publication of Bentham's *Introduction to the Principles of Morals and Legislation*. Written only a few years after the American Revolution and coincident with the storming of the Bastille, Bentham's treatise marks the transition from the genteel voices of the Enlightenment—Locke, Hume, Montesquieu, Diderot, Voltaire, Condorcet—to the era of capitalist accumulation—dynamic, brash, materialistic, and incurably optimistic. Bentham transformed the language of natural reason he had inherited into the precise instrument of technical reason. His work symbolizes the great divide.

The next major break occurs in 1848 when popular revolts swept with lightning speed throughout the continent of Europe. Within little more than a year, however, the revolutionary forces had spent themselves. Bourgeois hegemony was firmly reestablished, and a long period of national unification was initiated. Except for individual precursors, nearly all the major planning traditions date from 1848. Paradoxically, the development of scientific planning parallels the rise of the liberal state.

The Great War of 1914–1918 cast a deep shadow over bourgeois illusions of unlimited progress. Subterranean, disjunctive forces were being discovered by philosophers such as Bergson and Heidegger, psychologists such as Freud and Jung, composers such as Schönberg and Weber, and novelists such as Kafka and Joyce (Hughes 1977). The dark clouds of unreason were beginning to draw together. Fascism was on the rise. But the war had shown the possibilities of centrally directed planning, and within a decade the Soviet Union had inaugurated its first Five-Year Plan.

Then came the Crash in 1929. Intensive social reforms were undertaken everywhere, especially in the United States. The new Keynesian economics legitimated an interventionist role for the state with an appeal to science. Key figures in the evolution of planning theory made their debut at this time. A few, like Rexford Tugwell, were planners in both deed and word. Karl Mannheim managed to escape the Nazi juggernaut to England. Antonio Gramsci languished in a fascist jail, and Keynes and Mumford lived in comfort and security, the first in Cambridge and the second in a small town in upstate New York. Always prolific, their writings were at various times exhortatory, technical, cautionary, philosophical, and political. To some of these theorists planning meant reform; to others, it meant revolution and transcendence.

With World War II (1939–1945), the Depression ended abruptly.

It is said that fifty million people lost their lives during the war. Even so, when the end of the war came, recovery was rapid and spectacular. Cities were rebuilt; the welfare state was installed; economic growth accelerated to an unprecedented pace; new nations proliferated; nuclear energy was harnessed to both peaceful and military uses; astronauts took moon walks and brought back rock samples from outer space; communication satellites televised images around the globe, projecting "history" into the living room; a communist China emerged as a world power; national wars of liberation were fought on nearly all the continents . . . the list seems endless. With history speeding up and becoming global in scope, the searth for meaning amid chaotic change intensified.

Major new planning traditions now appeared on the scene, including systems analysis, policy science, and organization development. There were, in addition, outstanding individual contributions, most notably by Herbert Simon, Robert Dahl and Charles Lindblom, and the Dutch economist Jan Tinbergen. Scientific planning had finally arrived. Against the turmoil of global events, it proclaimed the triumph of technical reason.

Our last historical "hinge" is 1968, the year when yet another wave of revolutionary fever swept across the world, from Beijing to Berkeley, from Paris to Mexico City. For the first time, a revolutionary social movement had acquired global reach, sending shivers through all the corridors of power. In the end, of course, the movement was defeated, just as it had been in 1848, but in at least one respect it had succeeded. It had revealed the total bankruptcy of the established order. While it is true that finance and industrial capital had succeeded in organizing global markets, the number of the world's poor was rising year after year; in the rich countries, consumerism had become more of a burden than a pleasure; the human soul was in the grip of unknown terrors; devastating wars were fought to bitter conclusion in Southeast Asia and Central America; economic restructuring had made many millions of able-bodied workers redundant; the state itself was sinking ever more deeply into debt, even as economic growth was slowing to a crawl. The welfare system, which had been so elaborately devised, lay shipwrecked on the shoals of fiscal crisis. The easy optimism of the immediate post-war decades was crumbling fast.

The indisputable prophet of the period was Herbert Marcuse, whose *One-Dimensional Man* (1964) was read by students who desperately sought a rational explanation for their distemper. The enemy, said Marcuse, was technical reason. It poisoned our consciousness, it threatened the survival of the human race. But beyond magisterial rejection of contemporary life, Marcuse offered no answers. It was left for more positive thinkers to search for new responses. Some saw the future in a new style of planning based on dialogue; others drew the outlines of social utopias beyond the coercive apparatus of state and corporation; neo-Marxists extolled the logic of the class struggle in social transformation.

But the heady, swirling pace of events continued. To many, it seemed to have skidded out of control. No one knew what the future would bring; the Saint-Simonian dream was dashed. On the political left, the shift was to communal action, on the right, to the libertarian philosophy of Milton Friedman. Both were movements away from the state.

Under these conditions, the paradigm of scientific planning, which had held sway for over a century and a half, was suddenly besieged by doubts. Familiar voices argued for "national planning," but the actual thrust of events pointed away from traditional solutions. Though it still possessed the power to make war and sow universal destruction, the nation-state (at least in the West) was losing credibility at home. President Reagan was ready to dismantle it. Others tried to fill the vacuum of political power through communitarian approaches. As we near the turning of another century, the meaning of scientific planning is in doubt.

On the Origins of Planning Thought

Claude Henri de Rouvroy (1760–1825), the Comte de Saint-Simon, was the quintessential modern man. He sensed that forces had been set in motion that would utterly transform the world into which he had been born. And in celebrating the dawn of the age of industry, he became the most brilliant publicist of his time. Had he lived in the mid–twentieth century, he might have been a manager-aristocrat, perhaps an Antonio Peccei, whose book *The Chasm Ahead* announced a grand plan for the unification of the world and led, as the first step, to the founding of the Club of Rome (Peccei 1969). Or he might have been an enthusiastic trilateralist, devoted to the cause of making the world safe for capital (Sklar 1980). He was, in short, a man in love with the future and astute at detecting the hidden currents of his time. He was also hopelessly and passionately romantic.

While still in his teens, Saint-Simon enlisted to fight "for the cause of industrial freedom" (as he would later describe it) in a faraway

America (Ionescu 1976, 101). On his return to France, where another revolution had broken out, he speculated in requisitioned
Church properties, winning a fortune that he was soon to lose. During the Jacobin terror of Robespierre, he was imprisoned and
nearly fell victim to the guillotine. Once released, he conducted one
of the most splendid intellectual salons in Paris. His stormy love affairs ended in marriage and almost instantaneous divorce. On the
shores of Lake Geneva, he unsuccessfully wooed the most brilliant
woman author of his time, Germain de Staël. By now reduced to
penury, he was taken in and cared for by his former servant. A
stream of essays, pamphlets, speeches, and letters on the reorganization of society attracted young disciples who revered him as their
guru and helped support his work. Toward the end of his life, as
self-made prophets are inclined to do, he laid the basis for a short-
lived religion, New Christianity. Surrounded by his acolytes, he
died, philosophical to the end, giving instructions and counsel. "Remember," he is supposed to have whispered in his dying breath,
"that to achieve great things we must feel passionately" (Markham
1952, xvii).

To get a feeling for this style, and a better idea of why he can be
called the father of that slightly disreputable enterprise known as
planning, let us listen to him speak. Following is an extract from his
"Sixth Letter," which appeared in the second and last issue of his pe-
riodical *The Organizer*.

> Once we have done the three things I have spoken of, we find
> ourselves in a position to proceed to the establishment of the
> new political system, for the new composition of the lower
> chamber would have made it possible to establish the social or-
> ganization required by the present state of civilization and the
> lower chamber is invested with supreme political power be-
> cause it votes the taxes.
>
> I will describe the course which the chamber of deputies . . .
> should take. In order to explain more clearly and rapidly, I
> shall let the chamber itself speak:
>
> There shall be a first chamber which will be called the Cham-
> ber of *Invention*.
>
> This chamber will have three hundred members; it will be di-
> vided into three sections, which can meet separately, but
> whose work will only be official when they have debated in
> common.

Each section can call the assembly of the three sections together.

The first section will be composed of two hundred civil engineers; the second of fifty poets and other literary creators, and the third of twenty-five painters, sculptors, or architects and ten musicians.

This chamber will concern itself with the following:

It will present, at the end of its first year of existence, a plan of public works to be undertaken for the enrichment of France and the improvement of the lot of its inhabitants, to cover every aspect of usefulness and amenity; it will thereafter give its advice annually on what should be added to the initial plan and on the improvements which can be made to it.

Irrigation, the clearing of land, opening up new roads, digging out canals will be regarded as the most important parts of this plan; the roads and canals should not be seen solely as means to facilitate transport; their construction should be conceived in such a way as to make them as pleasant as possible for travellers. (. . . The whole of France should become a superb park in the English style . . .)

This chamber will undertake another task, which will be to prepare a plan of public holidays.

These holidays will be of two kinds; those of *expectation* and those of *commemoration*.

They will be celebrated successively in the capital (and also) in the capitals of the departments and districts, so that able orators, of whom there are never very many, can spread the benefits of their eloquence.

In the feasts of *expectation*, the orators will explain to the people the plans for the public works which parliament has in hand, and they will encourage the citizens to work eagerly by making them aware of how greatly their lot will be improved when they have put these plans into execution.

In the feasts consecrated to *commemoration*, the orators will try to convince the people of how much better is their position than that of their ancestors . . .

A second chamber will be formed which will take the name of Chamber of *Examination*.

This chamber will be composed of three hundred members; one hundred of them will be physicians engaged in the science of living organisms, one hundred physicians engaged in the study of animals, and one hundred mathematicians.

This chamber will be entrusted with three kinds of work. . . . It will draw up a plan of general public education . . .

The Chamber of Commons will be reconstituted when the first two have been formed; it will then take the name of Chamber of *Implementation*. This chamber will see that, in its new composition, each branch of industry is represented and that it has a number of deputies proportionate to its importance.

The members of the Chamber of Implementation will not receive any salary because they ought all to be rich, as they will be drawn from among the main leaders of industry.

The Chamber of Implementation will be in charge of carrying out all the resolutions; it alone will be entrusted with setting the scale of taxation and of collecting the taxes.

The three chambers together will make up the new parliament which will be invested with sovereign power, both constitutional and legislative . . . (In Ionescu 1976, 147–149)

We may smile indulgently at this vision, but we should remember that Saint-Simon was describing what he considered to be "the organization required by the present state of civilization." He was writing in the year 1820, when the European continent still stood at the threshold of the age of industrial capitalism.[1]

There are four major provisions in his scheme for a new polity. First there would be a parliament composed of a meritocracy of scientists, engineers, industrialists, artists, and intellectuals—people whose interests and intellect would naturally combine to bring about the inevitable reforms. It was to be a government of "the best and the brightest." Second, the parliament's main task would be to prepare not only an annual plan for public works but also a corresponding budget and appropriate levels of taxation. (This idea of preparing parallel material and financial plans, we may recall, is a

1. Saint-Simon's predilection to redesign the basic political institutions of his country reminds one of the no less ardent labors of yet another planner-aristocrat, Rexford G. Tugwell, who spent half a lifetime redrafting the U.S. constitution. His objective, like that of his predecessor, was to bring the political system of his country in line with the supposed requirements of his age. (See Tugwell 1970, 1974.)

forerunner of PPBS, the planning-programming-budgeting system used by Robert McNamara during his reign as U.S. Secretary of Defense from 1961 to 1968.) Third, there would be an ingenious series of holidays whose purpose would be to gain wider popular support for the plan, and incidentally for the government that proposed it. Fourth, a key role in this scheme would be reserved for wealthy industrialists who would serve the state without pay (but would clearly enrich themselves by their "service," as the text implies.[2] Their job would be to implement the plan, and, most important, to levy and collect the necessary taxes.

Saint-Simon's claim to be the father of scientific planning does not rest exclusively on the new pages of the "Sixth Letter," however. His championship of a meritocracy must be seen in the context of his total vision for society, a vision to which he devoted the last twenty-five years of his life. A nobleman déclassé, Saint-Simon was certainly no democrat. The common folk, he thought, should be kept at a distance from government. What he wanted was *not a government of men, but the administration of things* (Krygier 1979, 39)—a slogan that would be repeated by Marx and a long line of socialist theoreticians. Furthermore, it was clear to him that the "administration of things" should be entrusted to the real movers of the new society, the industrialists, who would be aided by a court of scientific advisors with the requisite talents for calculation and design. In Saint-Simon's world, planning and administration would be based squarely on a science of observation and measurement, a new "social physics" that would discover the basic laws of historical movement. This, he thought, would eventually remove planning from the passion of politics. In fact, if politics were left with no other task than to ratify scientific proposals that emerged from the planning laboratories of the state, it might even become unnecessary altogether.

Sooner than most, Saint-Simon understood that the industrial system which was about to conquer the world required continually expanding markets. He thus became an ardent pamphleteer for a United States of Europe. A federal parliament, he thought, composed of industrialists, savants, and artists—resembling today's Eurocrats—would be able to plan and carry out public projects on a continental scale. Had he lived a little longer, he would have witnessed the unification of the world, not through politics but

2. This provision evokes memories of the "dollar-a-year-men" who happily flocked to Washington during World War II to serve their government.

through the grandiose schemes of transportation, such as the Suez and Panama Canals, conceived by his disciples. For them, E. J. Hobsbawm writes, "the world was a single unit, bound together with rails of iron and steel engines, because the horizons of business were like their dreams world-wide. For such men, human destiny, history and profit were one and the same thing" (Hobsbawm 1979, 58). In his continent-spanning enthusiasm, Saint-Simon foresaw a sustained growth in production that would break up, once and for all, the tight little worlds of agrarian feudalism. The heroes of his drama were men who performed honest work. His planning criteria were those of engineering: functional fit and efficiency.

Like all prophetic utopians of the early nineteenth century, Saint-Simon wanted to believe in the possibility of a consensual society. "What he genuinely thought was that he was proposing a neutral, value-free system, one might even say . . . a systems analysis, based on scientific conceptualization and empirical research, and through which he could predict what kind of institutions and processes the emerging industrial society would require" (Ionescu 1976, 7). The value question was swallowed up by what was supposed to be obvious and therefore reasonable to all who were properly informed. As another writer said in reference to Durkheim, although the judgment would equally pertain to Saint-Simon, "knowledge about the *spontaneous* development of values could . . . be used to further the *planned* development of a morality suitable to modern times" (Gouldner 1958, xxi). The idea was simply to catch up with what was already in place—or surely coming. A spontaneous reality would be studied as though it were a natural event, and knowledge so obtained would be applied, as by an engineer to the construction of a new and better world. This was the kernel of Saint-Simon's thought. It would subsequently emerge as the philosophy of positivism, exerting a profound and lasting influence on later theorists.

Disenchanted toward the end of his life, seeing neither the blessings of a universal prosperity nor social harmony, Saint-Simon developed a new religion—an ideology for the industrial age—that would do for the masses what science had done for the elites: it would give them faith in the powers of science and an ethics of service. To high and low alike he preached this constant refrain: Love and help one another.

New Christianity is called upon to achieve the triumph of the principles of universal morality in the struggle which is going on with the forces aiming at the individual instead of public interests. This rejuvenated religion is called upon to organize all peoples in a state of perpetual peace . . . mobilizing them against any government so anti-Christian as to sacrifice national interests to the private interest of the rulers. It is called upon to link together the scientists, artists, and industrialists, and to make them the managing directors of the human race . . .

Finally, New Christianity is called upon to pronounce anathema upon theology and to condemn as unholy any doctrine trying to teach men that there is any other way of obtaining eternal life, except that of working with all their might for the improvement of the conditions of life of their fellow men. (From "New Christianity, 1825, in Markham 1952, 105)

With its intermingling of a universal faith, harmonious class relations, the public interest, elitism, and a commitment "to do good competently," the language here is remarkably similar to that of many liberals in the reform tradition of American planning.

In 1818, Saint-Simon took on Auguste Comte, then a mere twenty years old, as his secretary and "intellectual son." Although by all accounts it was a stormy association and ended after six years in mutual recrimination, Comte made Saint-Simon's enterprise his own and carried it forward with vigor. Compared to the romantic Saint-Simon, Comte was a plodder who craved system and order. He seemed to have conceived most of his important ideas under Saint-Simon's tutelage, but what he lacked in originality he more than made up for in grand systematization.

Comte's obsession became an encyclopedic classification of the sciences, which he hoped would demonstrate the essential unity of human thought and of the world it reflected. At the very apex of his archetypal pyramid he placed a *social physics* (later sociology) modeled on Newton's *Principia Mathematica* (1687). His orderly mind made some of his master's wilder notions more acceptable. At the same time, he disseminated a naive and wholly unfounded view of the role of the social sciences within the scientific undertaking generally, and thereby did untold damage to the cause of planning.[3]

3. The Comtean dream of a unified science persists nevertheless! It inspired both Otto Neurath's *International Encyclopedia of Unified Science*, published at the University of Chicago, and Ludwig von Bertalanffy's "General System Theory." On the former, see Johnston (1972, ch. 12); on the latter, see von Bertalanffy (1962).

An engineer by training, and thus familiar with the mathematical and physical sciences of his time, Comte came to think of history as being governed by objective laws. "True history," he wrote in 1822, is "conceived in the scientific spirit" and at "the discovery of those laws that regulate the social development of the human race" (Lenzer 1975, 66). Borrowing quietly from Condorcet, he summarized history in the Law of the Three Stages, the steady progression of human thought from theology to abstract metaphysics to a culminating stage of positive philosophy, or science. J. B. Bury explains: "Each of our principal conceptions, every branch of knowledge, passes successively through these three stages . . . and the proof . . . that any branch of knowledge has reached the third stage is the recognition of invariable natural laws" (Bury 1932, 292). According to Comte, the Law of the Three Stages tells the whole story of human development.

Comte was firmly convinced that human freedom lay in submission to "natural, scientifically established laws," just as free-falling bodies submit, as it were, to the law gravity. Like most of his ideas, this one is both deceptively simple and wrong. It is also dangerous. Since the laws that "govern" history would be announced by the very scientists who had "discovered" them, it would be to the word of the scientists that people would be asked to submit "in freedom." To ensure this submission—and here a note of realism creeps into his work—Comte felt called upon, like his master, to engage in that most thoroughly French of pastimes, inventing a civic religion; in this case it was the Religion of Humanity, whose priesthood of savants would insist upon the detailed regulation of public and even private lives by rules "that are inflexible because they always admit of verification" (Lenzer 1975, 4).

Of special interest to us here is Comte's understanding of planning. At a time when he was still closely identified with Saint-Simon, he wrote in his *Plan of Scientific Works Necessary for the Reorganization of Society* (1822):

> The formation of any plan for social organization necessarily embraces two series of works as distinct in their objects as in the intellectual efforts they demand. One, theoretical or spiritual, aims at developing the leading conception of the plan— that is to say, the new principle destined to coordinate social relations—and at forming the system of general ideas, fitted to guide society. The other, practical or temporal, decides upon the distribution of authority and the combination of adminis-

trative institutions best adapted to the spirit of the system already determined by the intellectual labors. (In Lenzer 1975, 19)[4]

Two things are noteworthy about this extract. First, and most important, there is a rigid functional division of labor between theoretician-planners on the one hand and practical administrators on the other, or in military language a division between staff and line. Second, politics is reduced to an inconsequential role: it fails to appear as an autonomous, norm-giving force. For Comte, science can generate knowledge not only about what is, but also about what ought to be. As a vocation, it is beyond the reach of the masses; it is a hieratic discourse among initiates bathed in the shadowless light of Olympian skies.[5] Thus he writes:

There can be no doubt that man's study of nature must furnish the only basis of his actions upon nature; for it is only by knowing the laws of phenomena and thus being able to foresee them, that we can, in active life, set them to modify one another to our advantage. . . . The relation of science to art may be summed up in a brief expression: from science comes prevision; from prevision comes action. (In Lenzer 1975, 88)

In Comte's understanding, it is the business of science to establish facts and immutable laws. For planners is left the task of guiding the course of social progress in accordance with these laws. Contrary to the modern Popperian view that scientists establish their hypotheses by falsification,[6] Comte held that science progresses by a process of verifying its hypotheses. Given his conception of scientific work as the steady accumulation of verities, it is not surprising that he thought humanity's highest stage would be reached when sociolo-

4. Saint-Simon published this essay under his own name in 1824. It was over this issue of priority in authorship, which has never been satisfactorily resolved, that the two men broke off their longstanding association.

5. Marx had a very different conception from Comte's, and it is perhaps here that we must look for the radical break between bourgeois social science and historical materialism. For Marx, thinking and doing, theory and praxis, are part of the same operation. Interpenetrating each other's domains, they coexist, so to speak, on the same plane. Theory and praxis either work together or they do not work at all.

6. For Popper's philosophy of science, see his recent compendium *Objective Knowledge* (1975). Though his logic is faultless, his rule-making for scientists has been seriously challenged by another Viennese philosopher, Paul Feyerabend (1975), on historical grounds. Popper's influence on planning has been positively assessed by Andreas Faludi (1983), a planning theorist and also Viennese, and critically assessed by Marios Camhis (1979).

gists would begin to take over God's work on earth. It was, he fancied, a future not far off.[7]

John Stuart Mill, being more concerned with actual liberties than with a fictitious order, eventually came to repudiate Comte's teaching in the strongest possible terms. Having been attracted to his early work, he wrote in 1859:

> Some of those modern reformers who have placed themselves in strongest opposition to the religions of the past, have been no way behind either churches or sects in their assertion of the right of spiritual domination: M. Comte, in particular, whose social system, as unfolded in his *Système de Politique Positive*, aims at establishing (though by moral more than by legal appliances) a despotism of society over the individual, surpassing anything contemplated in the political ideal of the most rigid disciplinarian among the ancient philosphers. (Mill 1974, 139)

The view that emerges from this backward glance at the origins of planning thought is a familiar one, best described in the current language of management science. It is also, in retrospect, an extremely conservative view; confirming existing relations of power, it is addressed to the rulers of society. And by claiming the dispensations of science, it ignores political community. So long as the established powers could claim a measure of success—chiefly in providing continous economic growth whose fruits might be shared, albeit unequally, with the masses of working people—the central assumptions behind this view of planning would remain unchallenged. But we have now moved into an era when, as Jürgen Habermas de-

7. The difference between verificationism and falsification in science is resolved in logic. "All cows are black" can be verified only by actually observing the total universe of cows, whereas observing a single brown cow would be sufficient to "falsify" the assertion. According to Karl Popper, the vigorous search for the negative evidence defines the substance of scientific procedure. But it is otherwise in planning. Here something new must be set into the world, even if the new is nothing more exciting than a new regulation. Every innovation is a wager with the future, based, one may assume, on the best information and knowledge available at the time. Planners spend most of their time thinking up new solutions of this sort. They would not survive for long if all they did was to collect evidence to show why a proposed solution would *not* work. Society is not a laboratory, and history does not repeat itself. Each posit is a new throw of the dice. Some learning can go on within a given situation, but what works in China will not necessarily work in Zaire.

Whether one holds with Comte or with Popper, therefore, the business of planning is a very different thing from science. Its object is not the perfection of knowledge but the perfection of the world. The two objectives are clearly related, but the paths to them are very different.

scribes it, there is a general crisis of legitimation: the system is no longer delivering on its promises of material sufficiency, social equality, and democratic rights. This is nowhere more evident than in the decolonized countries of the world. Though they are integrated into the capitalist world system, most of them are unable to meet even the minimal needs of their growing populations. There are exceptions, to be sure: certain indicators of "progress," such as longevity of life and average years of schooling, are pointing upward. But overall, the system is failing them.

At the same time, our understanding of science, and particularly social science, has become more sophisticated and subtle. We are no longer prepared to accept statements about "immutable laws of human progress." The physical and engineering sciences, having made possible the technological marvels of the modern world, are still highly regarded. But when it comes to the social sciences, the matter is quite different. The problem is not primarily one of method but of history: the constant flow of interlocked events has accelerated to a point where our understanding of the world actually seems to be decreasing. Even economics, that most precise of the social sciences, is unable to keep up with the rapidly changing character of the global economy; and the efforts in other contemporary social sciences often seem to be little more than a fancy form of journalism. This crisis in the social sciences may explain the recent popularity of "futurology" (for example, Toffler 1970, 1980). Strictly speaking, futurology is a bogus science—at best a form of disciplined guessing about the future, at worst sheer fantasy. But given our seeming inability to understand the world by studying its past, the flight into the future is comprehensible. As we shall see in the next section, however, planning in the style of Saint-Simon and Comte, though increasingly irrelevant to our day and age, is still very much alive.

Four Traditions of Planning Thought

Figure 3 places certain key figures in the history of planning thought within four major traditions. To be grouped into a common "tradition," authors had to meet three requirements: (1) they had to be thoroughly familiar with one or more of the "languages," such as economics or mathematics, in which their scientific work is carried out; (2) they had to have some commonalities in philosophical outlook; and (3) they had to address a small number of central questions that defined for them the major matters in dispute. All four traditions revolve around one core concern: how

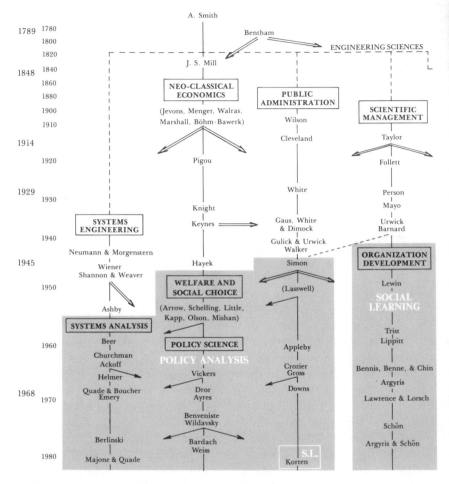

Figure 3. Major traditions of planning theory.

knowledge should properly be linked to action. They extend across the entire ideological spectrum, from support for the state and affirmation of its authority to the abolition of every form of authority, including that of the state. The two older traditions, social reform and social mobilization, reach back to the first half of the nineteenth century. The other two, policy analysis and social learning, originated in the period between the Great Depression and World War II.

If we arrange these traditions according to the formal definitions of planning offered in Chapter 1, the result is a fourfold political classification (Figure 4).

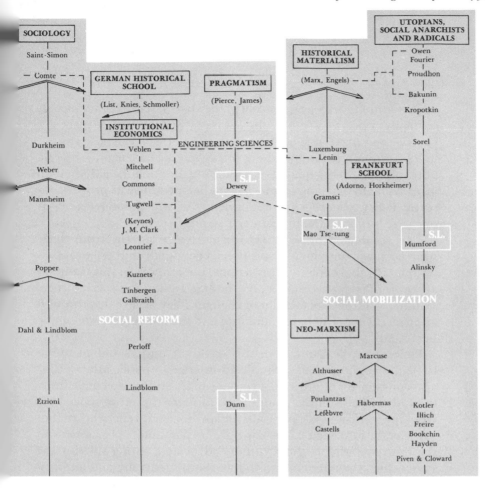

This classification indicates certain tendencies. As we saw from Figure 1, societal guidance and social transformation are overlapping categories (as are conservative and radical in Figure 4). Their overlap suggests that a healthy social system cannot remain the prisoner of only one mode of linking knowledge to action; it will need to draw on all four traditions for its planning practice. Fundamental differences remain, of course, and during certain periods and for certain purposes, one or two forms of planning discourse will tend to dominate. As we shall see in Part Three, the traditions of social learning and social mobilization seem to be especially pertinent today. Before we discuss these traditions at length in Chapters 3 through 6, it will be useful to describe very briefly the focus, vocabulary, philosophical position, and central preoccupations of each one.

Social Reform

This tradition focuses on the role of the state in societal guidance. It is chiefly concerned with finding ways to institutionalize planning practice and make action by the state more effective. Those writing in this tradition regard planning as a "scientific endeavor," and one of their main preoccupations is with using the scientific paradigm to inform and to limit politics to what are deemed to be its proper concerns. Policy Science—Karl Mannheim's *wissenschaftliche Politik*—is one of its products (Mannheim 1949a, orig. 1929).

The vocabulary of social reform derives primarily from three sources: macrosociology, institutional economics, and political philosophy. In their political convictions, the authors in this tradition affirm representative democracy, human rights, and social justice. Within limits they are tolerant of change. They believe that through appropriate reforms both capitalism and the bourgeois state can be perfected.

Philosophically, authors in this tradition understand planning to be the application of scientific knowledge to public affairs; they also consider it a professional responsibility and an executive function. Many fields in the planning terrain are therefore fenced off from the intrusions of politicians and ordinary citizens, who are not sufficiently informed to be engaged in planning. As planners in the reform tradition, these authors advocate a strong role for the state, which they understand to have both mediating and authoritative functions. Since the publication of Keynes's *General Theory* in 1936, they have argued for three areas of scientifically based and legitimate state intervention: the promotion of economic growth,

Political Ideology

KNOWLEDGE TO ACTION	Conservative	Radical
In societal guidance	Policy Analysis	Social Reform
In social transformation	Social Learning	Social Mobilization

Figure 4. The politics of planning theory: a tentative classification.

the maintenance of full employment, and the redistribution of income.

The central questions addressed by planners in this tradition tend to be of a broad philosophical nature.

1. What is the proper relation of planning to politics?

2. What is the nature of the public interest, and should planners have the power (and the obligation) to articulate and promote their version of it?

3. In the context of planning, what should be the role of the state vis-à-vis the market economy? To what extent would "social rationality" be served through market interventions by the state? Under what conditions would such interventions be considered legitimate?

4. If planning is a scientific endeavor, what is the correct meaning of science? Is it Karl Popper's view that scientific knowledge is the residue of hypotheses that has successfully resisted all efforts at "falsification" through contradictory evidence? Is it Thomas S. Kuhn's celebrated theory of science as the dynamic interplay of "normal paradigms" and "scientific revolutions" (Kuhn 1970)? Or is it John Dewey's pragmatic epistemology, in which knowledge exists only in the act of knowing and the validity of any statement is derived from its usefulness in application? Which of these views is appropriate for planning, and what would be the implications of adopting it?

5. There is great debate within the social reform tradition over the institutionalization of planning. Should planning be used comprehensively as an instrument of central guidance, coordination, and control by the state? Should it be divided among a large number of relatively autonomous actors working on more narrowly defined problems, who can therefore adapt their calculations more precisely to a constantly changing environment for decision-making? Or does the "correct" organization for planning lie somewhere in between synoptic central planning and a decentralized planning that involves "mutual partisan adjustments" among actors?

Besides debating these philosophical questions, social reform theorists, and particularly the economists among them, have fashioned the tools needed by a state that is increasingly determined to manage the economy "in the public interest." These instruments, so important to mainstream planning, include business cycle analysis

(Mitchell), social accounting (Kuznets), input-output analysis (Leontief), economic policy models (Tinbergen), urban and regional economics (Perloff), and development economics (Hirschman). Major specialized fields of study have evolved out of these pioneering efforts, and several of the inventors of planning tools have been honored with the Nobel Prize in economics.

Policy Analysis

This tradition was strongly influenced by the early work of Herbert Simon, whose revolutionary study, *Administrative Behavior*, published in 1945, focused on the behavior of large organizations, and particularly on how they might improve their ability to make rational decisions. Simon had absorbed several intellectual traditions into his own thinking, among them Weberian sociology and neoclassical economics, and his approach stressed synoptic analysis and decision-making as the means of identifying the best possible courses of action. What was "best," of course, would inevitably be limited by the normal constraints on rationality, which include the resources, information, and time that are available for making decisions. Simon's was a model of "bounded" rationality.

The ideal-typical decision model applied by authors in the policy analysis tradition has seven identifiable "stages."

1. Formulation of *goals and objectives*.

2. Identification and design of *major alternatives* for reaching the goals identified within the given decision-making situation.

3. Prediction of major sets of *consequences* that would be expected to follow upon adoption of each alternative.

4. *Evaluation* of consequences in relation to desired objectives and other important values.

5. *Decision* based on information provided in the preceding steps.

6. *Implementation* of this decision through appropriate institutions.

7. *Feedback* of actual program results and their *assessment* in light of the new decision situation.

For the most part, policy analysis has concentrated on stages 2, 3, and 4. In recent years, some excitement has also been generated about the implementation problems of policies and programs (stage 6), leading to a modification of the original decision model: implementation concerns are now incorporated as early as stage 2, the design of alternative courses of action. The vocabulary of policy analysis tends to be as specialized as its overall technical orientation. Most analysts are versed in neo-classical economics, statistics, and mathematics. Beyond this, they tend to cluster into specialized sub-disciplines, such as systems analysis (with its emphasis on mathematical modeling), policy science (with its combined emphasis on neo-classical economics and political science), operations research (which tends to focus on problems having determinate outcomes), and "futures research," which is still a rather eclectic field. In addition, much of the language in policy analysis derives from work with specific analytical techniques, such as gaming, simulation, evaluation research, linear and nonlinear programming, and the like.

Policy analysis has, strictly speaking, no distinctive philosophical position. On larger issues of society and justice, its practitioners are typically conventional in their thinking. They tend to regard themselves as technicians, or more flatteringly as "technocrats," serving the existing centers of power—large private corporations and the state. On closer inspection, some of their views are remarkably similar to those of Saint-Simon and Comte. They believe that by using appropriate scientific theories and mathematical techniques, they can, at least in principle, identify and precisely calculate "best solutions." They are social engineers. If challenged on epistemological grounds, policy analysts are likely to reply that it is better to arrive at decisions through an imperfect (but perfectible) science than through a process of unmediated politics that is subject to personal whim, fickle passion, and special interest. The reliance of policy analysts on the tools of neo-classical economics implies that the value premises of that discipline are built into their work; chief among these values are individualism, the supremacy of the market in the allocation of resources, and the inherent conservatism of the equilibrium paradigm. Because market outcomes are regarded as "rational" for the actors involved, deviations from them are normally thought to require special justification and are admitted only reluctantly.

The central questions informing this tradition, in keeping with its basic ethos, are essentially technical.

1. What are the relative advantages of comprehensive and incremental policy analysis? Comprehensive models provide an extensive overview of a given terrain but are subject to huge, if

indeterminate, error. Incremental analysis is modest in its demands for information, concentrates on the consequences of limited change, and can be modeled to yield determinate solutions. Which model is to be preferred, and under what conditions?

2. Different models yield different types of solution. Some are structured to allow for the maximization of "payoff" variables such as profits, employment, or travel time. Others are essentially "optimizing" models that yield "best combinations" of results over a variety of objective variables. Still others yield only second-best solutions (in Simon's neologism, they are merely "satisficed"). The choice of a model for evaluating consequences and recommending technically correct solutions to political decision-makers matters a great deal in policy analysis. And how should decision-makers be informed? Should they be given, for example, the one "best" solution? Should they be given the results of various "simulations" together with the assumptions that were used to obtain them? Or should they be asked to take part in "gaming situations," in which they simulate the group dynamics of strategic choices, much as the Army General Staff might simulate war games or conduct field maneuvers?

3. How might market prices be modified to express social criteria of valuation? Should cost-benefit studies, for example, use current market rates of interest or some "shadow" price of money that reflects social preferences? If so, and in the absence of political guidance, how might shadow prices be calculated? Or, in the case of goods for which there is no ready form of market valuation, what conventions of "social accounting" might permit them to be included in the overall policy calculus? Should women's household work, for instance, be assigned a shadow price, and if so, what should it be?

4. Policy analysts make forecasts about economic variables, expected changes in reproduction behavior, environmental impacts, technological innovations, changes in settlement patterns and land use, and many other trends. What are the best methods for medium and long-range forecasting?

5. Most policy analyses contain huge areas of uncertainty about the future and even greater areas of ignorance ("What are the chances of a nuclear holocaust within the next twenty years?"). How should these great unknowns be treated, and

what advice should be given to those responsible for decisions? Are there ways of controlling for uncertainty, and what mathematical values should be assigned to express different degrees of subjective uncertainty? Should alternative courses of action be designed to be compatible with the known areas of ignorance ("planning without facts"), especially when the consequences of a *wrong* decision might be politically, environmentally, or in some other way disastrous?

Social Learning

This tradition focuses on overcoming the contradictions between theory and practice, or knowing and acting. Its theory derives from two streams. The first is the pragmatism of John Dewey and more specifically his scientific epistemology, which put so much stress on "learning by doing." A second stream evolved within Marxism and has its origins in Marx's "Theses on Feuerbach" (1978; orig. 1844), which ends with the famous declaration, "The philosophers have only *interpreted* the world, in various ways; the point, however, is to *change* it." From this immortal sentence derives the basic Marxist proposition concerning the essential unity of revolutionary theory and practice, which found its fullest expression in Mao Tse-tung's 1937 essay "On Practice" (1968; orig. 1937).[8]

Social learning may be regarded as a major departure from the planning paradigms of Saint-Simon and Comte. Whereas these early founders of the planning tradition had treated scientifically based knowledge as a set of "building blocks" for the reconstruction of society, theorists in the social learning tradition have claimed that knowledge is derived from experience and validated in practice, and therefore it is integrally a part of action. Knowledge, in this view, emerges from an ongoing dialectical process in which the main emphasis is on new practical undertakings: existing understanding (theory) is enriched with lessons drawn from experience, and the "new" understanding is then applied in the continuing process of action and change. Whereas Comte and his fellow

8. The connection between Mao's theory of knowledge and Dewey's pragmatism has not gone unnoticed. As John Bryan Starr points out in his unexcelled study of Mao's political philosophy (1979), Dewey "exerted considerable influence on the Chinese intellectuals with whom Mao had contact during the May Fourth period. Like Dewey, Mao sees ideas growing out of practical experience and, in turn, shaping that experience. For both, the world is regarded as a series of problems, which are the occasion for both theory and action. Indeed, the resemblance was clear to Mao, since he on more than one occasion described himself as a pragmatist. . . . In Mao's view, however, pragmatism is not enough" (70–71).

positivists believed that the social world corresponded to immutable "social laws," social learning theorists have asserted that social behavior can be changed, and that the scientifically correct way to effect change is through social experimentation, careful observation of the results, and a willingness to admit to error and to learn from it.

Not surprisingly, the central questions of the social learning tradition are primarily instrumental.

1. How can the normal processes of social learning, which are found in all cases of successful and extended action, be used to spread social learning techniques to all forms of social undertaking?

2. Since human beings are reluctant to alter their habitual ways and are prone to believe that their own opinion or ideology is the only correct one, and since there is an evident connection between ideology and power, how can change be accomplished? How might people be motivated to participate in a form of social learning that depends on openness, dialogue, a willingness to risk social experiments, and a preparedness to let these experiments affect their own development as persons?

3. How might formal and informal ways of knowing be linked to each other in a process of change-oriented action that involves mutual learning between those who possess theoretical knowledge and those whose knowledge is primarily practical, concrete, and inarticulate?

4. The social learning paradigm involves, among other things, frequent face-to-face transactions that require a relation of dialogue between the participating parties (Friedmann 1981, 1979). But under conditions in which specific tasks must be performed, dialogic relations are difficult to bring about and maintain. What techniques might facilitate relations of trust and dialogue, especially between "planners" and "client-actors"?

5. What is the relationship of the social learning paradigm—with its emphasis on dialogic, non-hierarchical relations and its commitments to experimentation, tolerance for differences, and radical openness in communication—to democratic political theory? And what is its relationship to the growth and development of the autonomous, self-actualizing personality?

Social Mobilization

This planning tradition departs from all the others by asserting the primacy of *direct collective action "from below."* It stands in particularly stark contrast to the traditions of social reform and policy analysis, which address the role of the state and look toward a "scientific politics." In the social mobilization tradition, planning appears as a form of politics, conducted without the mediations of "science." Nevertheless, scientific analysis, particularly in the form of social learning, plays an important role in the transformative processes sought by social mobilization.

The vocabulary of social mobilization comes in part from the long tradition of mutually antagonistic social movements on the left: Marxists on one hand and utopians and anarchists on the other. Only Marxism ever developed a full-fledged ideology, but the mutual attractions and repulsions of various factions and groupings on the left provide much of the rhetoric in which even today's struggles are expressed—rhetoric that also stems from the collective memory of two centuries of struggles and communitarian effort. It is a history of oppression and triumphant revolutionary movements, from the Paris Commune to the Spanish Civil War, with its own pantheon of heroes and heroines, its own moments of glory in defeat. The language of social mobilization draws on this history as much as it does on the more abstract discourse of its philosophers, theoreticians, and gurus.

Philosophically, this tradition embraces utopian communitarianism, anarchist terrorism, Marxist class struggle, and the neo-Marxist advocacy of emancipatory social movements. These divisions are chiefly historical, however, and reflect disagreements over strategy and tactics more than basic differences in ideology. One might reasonably claim, for example, that various proponents of social mobilization are of one mind in their condemnation of the pervasive oppression and alienation of human being under the institutions of capitalism and the bourgeois state. Social mobilization is an ideology of the dispossessed, whose strength derives from social solidarity, from the seriousness of their political analysis, and from their unflinching determination to change the status quo.

Two kinds of politics may be involved in social mobilization. For utopians and anarchists, there is a *politics of disengagement* carried on by "alternative communities" that demonstrate to others new ways of living. For Marxists and neo-Marxists, there is a *confrontational politics* that emphasizes political struggle as necessary to transform existing relations of power and create a new order that is not based on the exploitation of labor and the alienation of man from what is distinctively human.

Among the central questions faced by adherents to this tradition are these.

1. What is the proper role of "vanguards," community organizers, and the leaders of movements for social mobilization? If emancipation is the ideological goal, does it not require leadership elites to abide by thoroughly democratic procedures, including the full participation of everyone in collective decisions, a tolerance for open dissent, and non-manipulative method of organizing group action?

2. How can the disinherited and those who have never had effective power suddenly gain confidence in their ability to "change the world"? How can the poor empower themselves to gain their freedom from oppression?

3. How can the commitment to a new life in community (utopians and anarchists) or a new life in struggle (Marxist and neo-Marxists) be maintained when only an occasional and partial victory occurs in the seemingly interminable struggle against the enemy?

4. What should be the basic components of a strategy? What role should be given to violence, to the choice of arena, and to the timing and duration of actions ("long march" or Armageddon), and what kinds of specific actions should be undertaken (strikes, demonstrations, street theater, terrorism, noncooperation with the state formation of political alliances, establishment of alternative communities)?

5. What should be the characteristics of the "good society," the social ideal to be realized in practice, now or in the future? What relative importance should be given to such goals as a non-hierarchical and inclusive social order, the practice of self-reliance, voluntary cooperation, dialogic processes, and a radical leveling of the social hierarchy?

New chapters in the history of planning thought are still being written. Specific modalities and styles of planning may become obsolete, but the link between knowledge and action will remain a lively concern, both ideologically and in practice. We cannot wish *not* to know, and we cannot escape the need to act. As social conditions and human understanding change, the actual and theoretical links between knowledge and action will surely undergo changes as well. If we wish to ensure the continued vitality of planning in the public domain, we will do well to examine, carefully and in a critical spirit, the traditions we now have. This is the task of the next four chapters.

3   Planning as Social Reform

Social reform may be called the central tradition in planning theory. In this chapter, I propose to follow the evolution of this tradition and to identify its major themes, models, and personalities.

There are five sections. After a brief account of the beginnings of "thought at the level of planning" in the United States—an account which highlights the distinctive contribution of Thorstein Veblen—I sketch the theories that dominated discussions during the early 1930s when, for a few critical years, the question of planning formed part of the national agenda. The section closes with an account of a comprehensive planning paradigm introduced in 1934 by Harlow S. Person, a consulting economist and president of the Taylor Society, the high citadel of scientific management.

Section two addresses the complex and controversial subject of rationality. Modern planning is said to be scientific or "rational," and so it is essential to undertake a serious inquiry into the various meanings of rationality in public life. The concept will be traced in the writings of Max Weber, Karl Mannheim, and others, and its significance for different planning traditions will be shown.

Sections three and four turn to a discussion of major debates in the reform tradition: the relation of planning to politics and the closely related question of calculation and control. Section three focuses on the patrician figure of Rexford Guy Tugwell, whose passionate advocacy of what he called the "collective mind" continues to find a sympathetic echo among leading planning theorists. Charles E. Lindblom, a political economist at Yale, dominates the following section with his no less sustained and closely reasoned arguments for a radically decentralized system of decision-making, which he calls "disjointed incrementalism" or "partisan mutual adjustment." Occupying opposing ideological positions, Tugwell and Lindblom frame the central debates about planning in its institutional form. Both claimed to have discovered the exclusive route for achieving greater rationality in the direction of public affairs. The

87

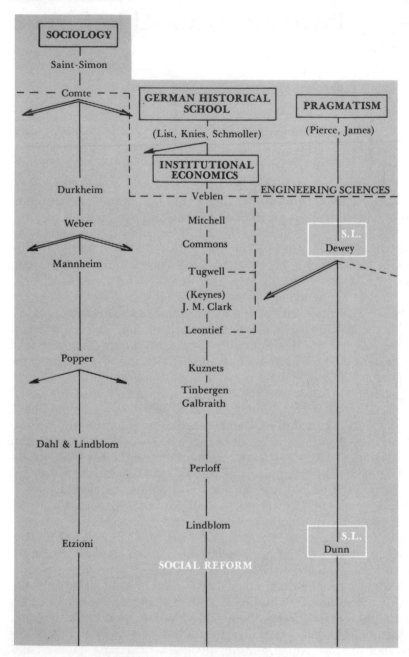

Figure 5. The social reform tradition of planning.

chapter concludes with a few general observations on the reform tradition in planning theory.

Control from the Top: An Early Planning Paradigm

Major wars appear to form the great divides in history. Whatever the reason—the trauma of death and destruction, the catharsis of a collective effort whose object is to defeat a common enemy, or the need to take one's bearing anew at the war's end—it seems that great conflicts often give rise to new ways of perceiving, new questions, and new voices.

World War I was no exception. As Lewis Lorwin has observed, the idea and practice of planning had its origin in the managed war economy. American planning can be seen, he wrote, as

> the logical culmination of two basic movements which already before 1914 began to cut the foundations from laissez-faire, namely *scientific management* and *public regulation*. The former slowly evolved techniques which may now be utilized for the coordination of inter-plant and inter-industry relations. From the latter comes the economic doctrine that industry is invested with a public interest. (Lorwin 1932, 572; italics added)

The war had speeded up a change in public opinion that made it seem less outrageous than before that government should regulate business for a public purpose. Although the devising of social controls is not identical with planning, a growing number of influential people came to believe that without some form of intervention by the state, the "spontaneous" discipline of the market would merely exacerbate the evils of inefficiency, waste, and injustice. The once comfortable belief in universal progress had been wiped out by a century of unfettered capitalist expansion and the horrors of the first global war in history.

The powers of the government might, of course, be used for a variety of ends. When Herbert Hoover became the new secretary of commerce in 1921 (he was to remain in this position until his presidency in 1929), he was by no means alone in thinking that scientific rationalization and social engineering could achieve "a synthesis of the older industrialism and the new without sacrificing individual effort, grassroots involvement, and private enterprise" (Hawley 1974, 117). As a result of such a synthesis, he argued, the "American System" would become preeminent in the world. It would raise living standards, humanize industrial relations, and integrate conflicting social elements into a harmonious community of interests. The key to this development would be the cooperative institutions of civil society: trade associations, professional societies, and similar organizations among farmers and workers. Unlike government bureaus, these associations would be "flexible, responsive, and productive, built on service and efficiency rather than coercion and politics" (ibid. 118). Over the past thirty years, the new industrialism had developed "the moral awakening, the commitment to science and productivity, and the mutuality of interests that would convert the associational structures around which the new system was taking shape into instruments of social progress" (ibid.). It was the duty of the state, Hoover believed, to manage, speed up, and guide this evolution toward what he variously called the Cooperative Committee Conference System or Progressive Democracy, but the role of the state was to be that of midwife only. Once the Conference System had taken hold, the state would fade away, leaving civil society to manage for itself.

For an engineer, it was a surprisingly utopian vision. To implement it, Hoover turned what had been a sleepy secretariat where, his predecessor had told him, he would need to work only two hours a day "putting the fish to bed at night and turning on the lights around the coast" into a beehive of activity (Murray 1981, 21). For its time, it performed in much the same way as the French Planning Commissariat was to perform forty years later during another postwar period of recovery and reconstruction (Cohen 1969).

> Essentially, [Hoover] believed, he had created [a] governmental tool that . . . functioned as an economic "general staff," business "correspondence school," and national coordinator, all rolled into one, yet preserved the essentials of American individualism by avoiding bureaucratic dictation and legal coercion, implementing its plans through nearly 400 cooperating committees and scores of private associations, and relying upon appeals to science, community, and morality to bridge the gap between the public interest and private ones. . . . Like the war to end all wars, it was the bureaucratic empire to end future bureaucratic empires; and in theory at least it was supposed to wither away once a new order was built. (Hawley 1974, 138–139)

In retrospect, Hoover appears to have been a true Saint-Simonian, one of the prophet's admired "industrialists," a man of the new order. Like his predecessors who had built railroads and canals, spanning the continents, he was an enthusiastic supporter of vast engineering schemes, among them the St. Lawrence Seaway and the Hoover Dam on the Colorado River.[1]

While Hoover worked furiously to harness business to his vision of an associative state, others bitterly attacked the American System as it had actually evolved. The most influential of these critics was Thorstein Veblen, a professor of economics, who at various times had taught at the University of Chicago, Stanford University, the University of Missouri, and the New School for Social Research. Like Hoover, Veblen praised the virtues of an engineering frame of mind, but he diverged radically from his younger contemporary in his ideas about the good society. The Great Depression seemed to vindicate Veblen's deep-seated pessimism about the American Way of Business; it sent the more buoyant Hoover into political oblivion.

Beginning in 1919, Veblen had published a series of polemical essays in *The Dial* which were subsequently collected in book form (Veblen 1983). In these essays, he struck out, as was his custom, at what he called the Vested Interests, by which he meant the absentee financial owners of American corporations.[2] Veblen saw these interests as fostering "a regime of continued and increasing shame and confusion, hardship and dissension, unemployment and privation, waste and insecurity of person and property" (ibid. 128). The answer to this abomination, he contended, was to pass control of the country's industry from the financiers to the "technicians," who would speak, so he thought, not for extraneous commercial interests but for the industrial system as a "going concern." Being in close touch with the production process, technicians should form themselves into a *directorate* whose general purpose would be the "care of the community's material welfare" (ibid. 134). Its task would be

> the due allocation of resources and a consequently full and reasonably proportioned employment of the available equipment and man power; . . . the avoidance of waste and duplication of work; and . . . an equitable and sufficient supply of goods and services to the consumer. (Ibid. 142)

Here, then, was a call for national planning that would promote efficiency and welfare, even as it overcame the "anarchy" of the market. It semed self-evident to Veblen that by removing the con-

1. For a thorough reassessment of Herbert Hoover's role as secretary of commerce, see Hawley (1981).

2. The change of corporate ownership, signaled here by Veblen, from producer-entrepreneurs to financial capital was massively documented by Berle and Means in their classic study, *The Modern Corporation and Private Property* (1932). For a recent excellent survey of this same terrain, see Herman 1981.

trol of production from the "price system," which he said reflected
merely "commercial valuation," and basing it on "tangible performance," it would be possible to lay out a rational plan for industrial
expansion. Such ideas would later be worked into the material-bal-
ances approach of Soviet planners and Leontief's input-output
analysis.

> The technology—the state of the industrial arts—which takes
> effect in this mechanical industry is in an eminent sense a joint
> stock of knowledge and experience held in common by the
> civilized peoples. It requires the use of trained and instructed
> workmen—born, bred, trained, and instructed at the cost of
> the people at large. So also it requires, with a continually more
> exacting insistence, a corps of highly trained and specially
> gifted experts, of divers and various kinds. These, too, are
> born, bred, and trained at the cost of the community at large,
> and they draw their requisite special knowledge from the
> community's joint stock of accumulated experience. These ex-
> pert men, technologists, and engineers, or whatever name
> may best suit them, make up the indispensable General Staff
> of the industrial system; and without their immediate and un-
> remitting guidance and correction the industrial system will
> not work. (Ibid. 82)

Through technical planning, Veblen believed, the productive powers of the industrial system might be increased by as much as 300 to
1200 percent (ibid. 83)!
   Veblen was not alone in this call for the rule of technical reason.
His contemporary, James Harvey Robinson, a distinguished social
historian and founder of the New School for Social Research, was
yet another believer in the efficacy of scientific planning.

> [M]an is now in a position . . . to have some really clear and ac-
> curate notion of the world in which he dwells and of the living
> creatures which surround him and with which he must come
> to terms. It would seem obvious that this fresh knowledge
> should enable him to direct his affairs more intelligently than
> his ancestors were able to do in their ignorance. (J. H. Robin-
> son 1921, 157)

As in Veblen's case, this bright view of the future veiled an underlying pessimism. The dangers "lurk on every hand," he said (ibid.
Preface). Unless knowledge keeps pace with historical change, the
system will veer out of control. Only scientific planning, which he
called intelligence, can save the world from itself. Ten years later,

during the Depression, his book, like Veblen's, was reissued in a new edition and helped to fuel the outgoing debates on planning.

The decade from 1929 to 1939 witnessed an explosion of planning literature. Perhaps the prophets of doom had been right after all. Perhaps, as Lorwin suggested, the time for planning had finally arrived. Perhaps the Soviet Union, with its experiments in national planning, was gaining ground on the United States, and perhaps it was true after all, as some were arguing, that the country needed to be managed "scientifically" in a spirit of open-minded social experimentation. Much of the writing during this period was exhortatory. Some was cautiously optimistic. Outright critical views were few. Nearly everyone agreed that the country needed planning on an unprecedented scale.[3]

To chart the new course, Franklin Roosevelt, immediately on taking office, set up the National Planning Board. It consisted of three members: chairman was Frederick A. Delano, Roosevelt's uncle and a businessman who had been closely associated with metropolitan planning in Chicago and New York; the two other members were Wesley C. Mitchell, a well-known economist who had founded, in 1920, the National Bureau of Economic Research, had helped to develop the *Survey of Current Business* under Hoover's reign in the Department of Commerce, and since 1929 had chaired the President's Committee on Social Trends, and Charles E. Merriam, a professor of political science at the University of Chicago. In their *Final Report* (National Planning Board 1934), they recalled the halcyon days of planning under Herbert Hoover, that "strong individualist" under whose leadership there was "perhaps the most striking development of collectivism in governmental trends in relation to business" (ibid. 71). Planning, according to the board, involved three general functions: *coordination, projection,* and *scientific analysis.* But not everything required national planning, and much planning could be effectively decentralized to state and local governments.

In language not unlike that of Mannheim, who was expressing similar thoughts in Europe, the board pointed out that "wise planning is based on control of certain strategic points in a working system. . . . It involves the continuing reorganization of this system of control points as the function and situation shifts from time to time" (ibid. 31). It then went on to recommend the establishment of a permanent intelligence and planning function for the United States.[4]

3. For a good cross section of writing on planning in the mid-1930's, see the compendium *Planned Society: Yesterday, Today, and Tomorrow* (MacKenzie 1937). Lewis Mumford wrote the preface to this impressive volume of nearly one thousand pages.

4. Successors to the National Planning Boad included the National Resources

The *Final Report* was a political document produced by advocates of planning within the federal government. Its phrasing had to be cautiously circumspect. No such constraints quelled the enthusiastic Stuart Chase, the most brilliant publicist of his time, when, only weeks after Roosevelt had been nominated as the standard-bearer of the Democratic party, he published *A New Deal*, which had every earmark of being the marching orders for the left wing of the party (Chase 1932).

Chase introduced his book with a pithy quotation from Veblen's *The Engineers and the Price System.* Without the slightest hesitation, it declared that the country would be better off if it were turned over to the continued administration of technological experts and production engineers. In this brief quotation, sixteen lines in all, can be found all of Veblen's major preoccupations: progressive advance, industrial system, coordination from the top, expertise, professionalism. Within a decade after Veblen wrote his essay, these terms had entered the language of social reform. They would continue to be the major organizing ideas for American planning theory until the 1950s.

In a series of short exclamatory essays unclouded by doubts, Chase set out the major reform program of the New Deal. There was to be "segmental" planning in America, with professionals in charge, and they would all be engaged in doing more or less the same things: measuring, calculating, establishing rules, evaluating results, projecting futures, making budgets, and drawing up physical plans. In addition, however, there was need for a *central directive*, without which there would be only chaos. There was, proclaimed Chase, a desperate need for *control from the top.*

> The drive for collectivism leads toward control from the top. . . . All planks are related parts of one central project—to build a sturdy bridge from production to distribution. . . . At bottom the conception of economic planning is science supervising people's housekeeping. Not its morals, not its play, not its loves or its living. Science is to be only a good cook, making sure we have enough to eat. (Chase 1932, 213–214)

And according to Chase's logic, this coordination of parts "is not a financial problem nor a political problem but an engineering problem" (ibid. 215).

Chase's planning model had more than a surface resemblance to

Board (1934–1935), the National Resources Committee (1935–1939), and the National Resources Planning Board (1939–1943).

the work of Harlow S. Person, a towering figure in the scientific management movement. Person, an economist among engineers, had acquired his expertise as a consultant for corporate management. Now, he was saying, the time had come to apply the techniques of business to the business of government (Noble 1977).

Person had been appointed to the Mississippi Valley Committee, which was to investigate and report on the "principles, policies, conditions, and problems of the use and control of water in the Mississippi Drainage Area." Its Report, issued on October 1, 1934, featured a chapter on planning which had been drafted by Person himself. In only a few pages it succeeded in outlining a complete paradigm of central, coordinative planning (Mississippi Valley Committee 1934, 221–228). Because I have reproduced the full text in Appendix A, I will confine my observations to Person's summary chart which, in graphic form, manages to convey the principal provisions of his paradigm (Figure 6).

Planning, said Person, is channeled through an "institutional mind" that is more powerful than the sum of any of its parts. Through perception, memory, and reasoning, the institutional mind *undertakes scientific analysis, designs a comprehensive plan of action, and coordinates the subsequent actions.* For this complex task, it brings together many specialists, shown at the top of Figure 6 "in the round." Once the institutional mind has produced a blueprint, a *decision* is made at the top, and the appropriate *commands* are given through which the plan is to be *carried out.* In a sequence of programmed stages, the several elements of the plan are *fitted together* until the *final objective* is reached, and the blueprint becomes a reality on the ground.

The hierarchical structure of this planning process is plainly evident. Not only is the flow of information shown to be in only one direction—from the top down—but each level of planning is composed of a three-tiered hierarchy: director, clerical worker, and manual laborer, all working harmoniously together under the general guidance of the plan. The result, shown at the bottom of Figure 6, looks much like the orthogonal planning that, five thousand years ago, produced the pyramids in the valley of the Nile!

Person's model is not merely an historical curiosity. Its influence was pervasive. On the positive side, it was echoed by Rexford G. Tugwell, Roosevelt "brain truster" and America's leading planning theorist (Tugwell 1932, 1940, 1975a, b, c); by Nobel Prize winner Jan Tinbergen (1964); and by Harvey S. Perloff, dean of UCLA's Graduate School of Architecture and Urban Planning and a Fellow of the American Academy (1980). On the negative side, it became

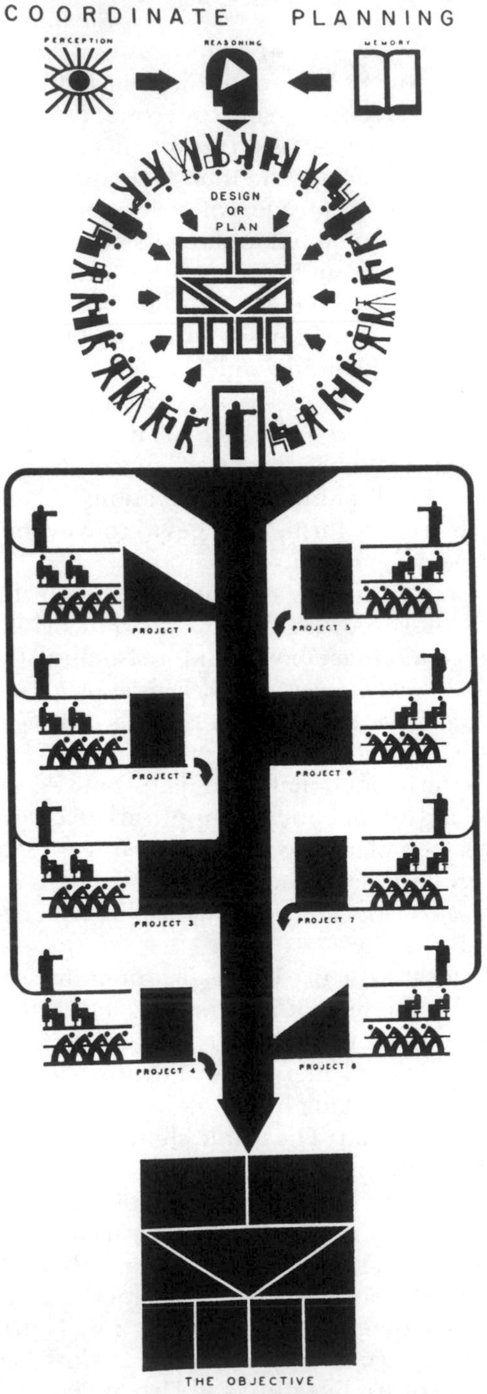

Figure 6. An early planning paradigm: co-ordinate planning. (From Mississippi Valley Committee, 1934)

the bête noire of the major critics of "synoptic" planning, from Karl
Popper (1945) to Aaron Wildavsky (1979).

As a planning paradigm of considerable staying power, its leading
idea was simple enough: the "institutional mind"—Person's quaint
term for the Central Planning Board—has the ability to lay out the
future in advance with something approaching scientific rigor. It
knows how problems must be defined to be amenable to solution,
and it can also determine which solutions are likely to be the most
cost-effective. Operating on the basis of a strong social consensus,
the institutional mind can rely on the willing cooperation of all participants in the planning process and on the acquiescence of a more
or less silent, demobilized lay public. With nothing more than a simple command or set of instructions, the blueprint will begin to materialize in stone and mortar. It was an altogether beguiling vision
and a manager's dream.

The Theme of Rationality

If there is one theme that runs through all the discussions and debates on planning, it is that of rationality. Whether you argue in favor of planning or against it, sooner or later you end up with the
question of whether and to what extent planning is or can be "rational." Is it possible, critics ask, to be rational in public affairs? What
does rationality mean? How can decisions and actions be made
more rational? In attempting to be rational, do we make things better or worse? Because of their belief in the possibilities of rational
action, planners lean heavily on the scientific nature of their calling.
This belief accounts for their ambivalence toward politics as an alternative to calculation.

Whereas the use of a term such as *technical reason* is close to ordinary speech, *rationality* is a formal concept that must be carefully defined. And so we begin our investigation with the writings of Max
Weber, who was the first to state the theme in all of its complexity.
Although Weber's sociological writings are chiefly interpretive—
unlike Mannheim, he was not primarily interested in planning—his
methodological focus was on rational action (Parsons 1964). It was
his preoccupation with the conditions for rational action that led
Weber to exert a lasting influence on theory in planning.

Weber distinguished between rationality—a cognitive function—
and rationalization, which referred to social processes through
which modern institutions are progressively brought into conformity with the principles of rational thought. In relation to action,
Weber further distinguished between two forms of rationality. For-

mally rational actions correspond to a particular logic of decisions: they must be instrumentally efficient. Substantial or material rationality refers to particular social arrangements and their suitability with respect to the declared purposes of the society. Formal and material rationality, said Weber, are dialectically linked to each other: they exist in a state of continuous tension.[5]

The U.S. military procurement program may serve as an example. The program, is, of course, based on rigorous technical thinking. It makes use of the latest analytical techniques, including linear and nonlinear programming, simulation analysis, cost-effectiveness studies, forecasting techniques, and so forth. In short, it is a result of the highest degree of formal rationality attainable. Yet, when it is measured against the broad requirements of national security, military procurement is in many of its aspects found to be *materially irrational*, producing less defense for more money. The conflict is neatly summarized by Fallows:

> My argument so far is that the realities of economic constraint, of an unpredictable future, and of the special nature of combat should shape our plans for war. The next step is to contrast those factors with the prevailing ethic of modern American defense. That is the "managerial" view of the military, which assumes that organizing for conflict is similar to organizing for other activities and that the most important choices about defense can be justified by the same tools of rational, often economic analysis that might be used in adjusting the federal budget or developing a new style of car. That mentality leads to tactics based on oversimplified, abstract models; to an emphasis on machinery rather than on men and strategies; and to a tendency to neglect the human element that, through history, has often determined the outcome of conflict. (Fallows 1981, 18)[6]

5. Why Weber thought that the contradictory relation between formal and material rationality was a structural one is particularly revealing of his understanding of social dynamics. Human beings strive for formal rationality in their actions, but the more they try, the more they run headlong into trouble: society is not a logical structure designed by engineers but rather consists of both logical and illogical elements and relations. To forget this, and to emphasize only the logical elements, as planners are inclined to do, leads to the aforementioned contradictory results.

6. Fallows quotes defense analyst William D. White's remark that "waging war is no different in principle from any other resource transformation process, and should be just as eligible for the improvements in efficiency that have accrued elsewhere from technological substitution." Commenting on this attitude, Fallows writes, "The

Fallows describes as the "managerial" approach what Weber would no doubt call an instance of formally rational action. It involves the analytical isolation of the part from the whole, the objective analysis of each separate part, and the eventual reassembly of the several parts into new wholes as either scientific theories or plans of action.

Weber was extremely careful to set forth the conditions for objective analysis. He argued passionately for an intellectual asceticism in which factual statements would be held rigidly apart from statements of value. He contended that a social science had to adhere to the same formal standards as the physical sciences, specifically to the principle by which personal inclinations and preferences were to be brutally excised from analysis.[7] Value judgments, he asserted, had a nonscientific origin. They were a result of culture, tradition, social position, and personal preference, and they had no place in scientific discourse.[8]

This methodological commitment—which, despite persistent criticism, continues to dominate the practice of the social sciences today—led not only to the demarcation of two tangential spheres of discourse, science and politics, but also to the formulation of the rational decision model of Herbert Simon and others in the 1940s and 1950s. When the intention is to reach a given objective, declares Weber in a manner reminiscent of Bentham, scientists can legitimately identify both the intended and unintended consequences that might be expected from the proposed action. But only the decision-maker (significantly, Weber calls him the actor, or *der Handelnde*) can assess the real costs of his projected undertaking and draw the appropriate conclusions. The decison to act or not to act, as well as the manner of action, is a subjective political choice, and

---

natural legacy of viewing war as a 'resource transformation process' is an over reliance on technology and an underemphasis on the intangibles of leadership and esprit" (Fallows 1981, 34).

7. This idea, that the existing should be separated from the desired, was not original with Weber. Weber refers to a 1914 essay by Schumpeter, who, in turn, attributes the separation of "is" from "ought" to Thomas Malthus's Introduction to *Principles of Economy* (1820) (see Weber 1956, 532).

8. In light of Weber's conviction that formal and material rationality are dialectically related, it is curious that he should hold so fiercely to a position that he knew would lead to false conclusions in practice. The reasons for this are undoubtedly complex. There was first, his interest in contemplative understanding rather than political practice. Since he was only concerned with thought processes, the distortions introduced by a value-free scientific methodology did not particularly disturb him. Second, personal factors were most likely involved, such as his own psychic instability which made him fearful to face human questions with all their emotional force. For details of Weber's life, see Bendix (1962).

the scientist, as scientist, has to remain silent (Weber 1956, 188, 273).[9]

The principle of rationality, then, is closely related to the notion of objectivity in scientific work. For Weber, science was a means for mastering the irrational, and the irrational, to which he felt himself irresistibly drawn, could be contained within its own sphere only through the most severe of personal struggles. He was determined to grasp the irrational forces of life, among them politics and religion, with only the instruments of reason; the passions had to be controlled.[10]

It is interesting to note how, in their less observed moments, aggressive rationalists often express a quite irrational fear of what they are evidently unable to control. We encounter this fear in Comte, Veblen, and Robinson; we shall come upon it again in Karl Mannheim. Not all planning theorists, by any means, were afraid of values, instincts, and the inchoate forces unleashed by what Mannheim would call the fundamental democratization of life. To cite only one instance: in common with many utopians and anarchists, Lewis Mumford affirmed the "irrational" as a life-enhancing and constructive force. He, at least, saw no essential contradictions with rationality. The real danger, he averred, *lies rather in the severance of rationality from its irrational roots.* For Mumford, only a value-committed, critical scholarship could be called good scholarship. If utopian thinking should ever become identified with central power, tacitly accepting the dominant values in the name of "objectivity," it would cease to be utopian.

The increasing rationalization of the world was Weber's other obsession. He affirmed its relentless progress even as he lamented its results in the progressive demystification—the *Entzauberung*—of the world. Here, he introduced one of his most enduring concepts, the ideal-typical construct of bureaucracy as the rationalizing, and *rationalized*, contemporary institution par excellence. According to Weber, bureaucracy was functionally specialized; it was concerned with abstract rules of universal application; its decisions were based

9. This separation of fact from value, and the correlation of this logical distinction with the distinction between science and politics, underlies modern welfare economics. Economists such as T. W. Schultz argued that their expertise allowed them to prescribe the course for economic growth, but now how the resulting product might be distributed. They regarded the latter as an eminently political question in which economists, as scientists, had not particular expertise. See Schultz (1949).

10. The frontispiece gracing Hirschman's *The Passions and the Interests* (1977) is an emblem dating from 1617 whose inscription reads, "Repress the Passions!" It shows a hand emerging from a cloud. Above a tranquil landscape, in a pair of iron tongs, the hand firmly grasps a heart and holds it rigidly in the sky. It is a chilling image.

on the deliberate calculation of means to given ends; and its purpose was to coordinate and control the actions of subordinate subjects so that the objectives of the state might be attained (Weber 1964, Pt. 3). Though he made no explicit reference to planning, planning was necessarily a part of this construct. It, too, was functionally specialized, instrumentally rational, concerned with universal norms and criteria for decision-making and evaluation, and dedicated to the controlled implementation of its programs.

Just where the dividing line between calculation and control should be drawn remained somewhat hazy. Later theorists argued for their joint consideration in practice; others for their functional separation. Either planning was part of the bureaucracy or it stood "above" it. Regardless of how this dilemma might be resolved, planning would appear as an element in the bureaucratization of life. And as Weber described it, bureaucracy was "the most rational means for exercising control over human beings" (Jacoby 1973, 149).

The last of Weber's concepts to which I wish to draw attention is his distinction between an *ethics of responsibility* and an *ethics of ultimate ends*. In the first, an actor shoulders responsibilities generated by himself; in the second, he stands firm on ultimate principles: like Martin Luther, he declares, "Here I stand; I can do no other."

In actual practice, responsibility and ultimate concerns are usually intertwined. The question has to do with the relative importance of each term. It is scarcely surprising, then, when we learn that, with increasing rationalization and the improved capacity of the social sciences to predict the probable outcomes of action, the balance in decision-making has gradually shifted away from "ultimate concerns" to "responsibility for the results." What Weber could not know, or did not want to know, is that a politics of ultimate concerns would eventually reassert itself, as we observe today, for example, in the worldwide upsurge of the ecology movement. He might have argued that this resurgence is nothing more than an eruption of the irrational into the sphere of planning. But another way of looking at it is to say that any innovation in policy or, more generally, any public action, requires an intense commitment to values. Without it, opposition cannot be overcome, counteractions cannot be deflected, the movement cannot be sustained.

The rationalization of the world—Bentham's dream and Weber's nightmare—has its own limits and contradictions. The tension between an existential commitment to values and responsibility for the consequences of one's actions must be maintained. When it is not, the actual results for the system will be disastrous: either the sacrifice of happiness for principle or the total mummification of society.

Karl Mannheim was not, as Weber was, a Protestant by nurture; as a Jew, he cherished the utopian, reality-transcending moment more than the rationalized order of the present. He was also less interested than Weber in merely "understanding" society; like Marx, he wished to change it. His sociology was oriented to change and, more particularly, to planned forms of change guided by a technical intelligentsia.

Planning, said Mannheim, is the rational mastery of the irrational (Mannheim 1949b, 265ff.). But "the irrational" he had in mind was not the demonic forces with which Weber struggled but more general sociological categories: the institutions of a free, unregulated market; mass behavior under conditions of fundamental democratization; and a pseudo-democratic politics in which the most powerful, most ruthless, least scrupulous elements would bully their way to the top.

In a manner akin to Weber's, Mannheim distinguished between two forms of rationality: *functional* and *substantial*.

> Whether a series of actions is functionally rational or not is determined by two criteria: (a) functional organization with reference to a definite goal; and (b) a consequent calculability when viewed from the standpoint of an observer . . . seeking to adjust himself to it. (Ibid. 53)

And by substantial rationality he meant

> an act of thought which reveals intelligent insight into the inter-relations of events in a given situation. . . . Everything else which is either false or not an act of thought at all (as for example, drives, impulses, wishes, and feelings, both conscious and unconscious) will be called "substantially irrational." (Ibid.)

In addition to these basic categories, Mannheim introduced the idea of *self-rationalization*, which he understood to be the individual's "systematic control over his own impulses" (ibid. 55). This term was an important addition to the vocabulary, especially when the concept was extended to an organization or collectivity in which the implied reflection, self-observation, and taking account of one's own situation "assumed the functions of self-reorganization" (ibid. 57).

> [I]t becomes apparent that a society which must carry out more complicated processes based upon thinking and acting

with a purpose in view, will, in certain situations, necessarily tend to produce the reflective type of person. From this point of view it is clearly fallacious to regard reflectiveness—as many romantic thinkers do—as being under all circumstances a life-extinguishing force. On the contrary, in most cases, reflectiveness preserves life by helping us to adjust ourselves to new situations so complex that in them the naive and unreflective man would be utterly at a loss. (Ibid. 57)

Here we encounter a theme that was echoed also in American writings of the period. Person's talk of an "institutional mind" and Tugwell's construct of a "collective mind" were not unlike Mannheim's call for self-rationalization *at the level of society*. In a profound aside, probably written after his arrival in London at the start of World War II, he recounts a conversation with friends.

Someone said: "We have progressed so far as to be able to plan society and even to plan man himself. Who plans those who are to do the planning?"

To which Mannheim replies:

"The longer I reflect on this question, the more it haunts me. . . . We can indeed direct and control the rational and irrational forces in certain spheres, but after a certain point they are beyond our reach and dominate us. (Ibid.)

Mannheim's reputation as a sociologist had been established with *Ideology and Utopia* in 1929 (Mannheim 1949a). This early work had helped to lay the foundations of the sociology of knowledge, one of the important branches of the still emerging field of sociology. Its practical conclusion was that all thinking about social questions, reflecting a person's social position and experience, is ultimately "perspectivist" and partial. A purely objective knowledge does not exist. As he addressed the question of planning, Mannheim's problem was how a comprehensive and unbiased view of the whole might nevertheless be achieved. For if planning were ever to provide reliable guideposts to the future, a more or less "objective" understanding was clearly a basic requirement.

Mannheim ventured several answers to this perplexing question. One was that thinking at the level of planning was *situationally concrete* and therefore bounded, historically specific, and of necessity contextual. A second answer was that, within a given situation, planners would focus on the emergent and mediating forces that articulate the changing social field. He called these forces the *principia media* of the situation. Third, planners would think pragmatically about the means for controlling social change by searching out the *strategic heights* or key positions in the social field. And fourth, planners would be schooled in the art of *interdependent thinking*, including interdisciplinary work.

> Interdependent thinking is most useful when it works out as fully as possible all the relevant factors—their relevance being determined by the problem to be solved. . . . It is into concrete *situations* that one integrates the otherwise disconnected elements of knowledge. (Mannheim 1949b, 230, 236)

Objectivity in planning was thus perceived as a question of *praxis* rather than of abstract knowing. In concrete situations, the pure objectivity of thought might well be impossible; to this extent, the sociology of knowledge was vindicated. But purity might not be a relevant requirement for planners. What planners needed was controlled, strategic knowledge that could be verified by its consequences.

Here Mannheim comes close to a pragmatic position. Knowledge for practice was situationally specific, focused, strategic, and interdependent. It was in these characteristics that its objectivity would be found. This conclusion was surprisingly close to the views propounded by the U.S. National Planning Board in its *Final Report* (1934).

This emphasis on praxis was a courageous step for a European academic writing in the 1930s. Shortly before his death, Weber had valiantly tried to protect "science" from an involvement with practice in order to preserve its fragile objectivity; Mannheim, no less a sociologist than Weber, enthusiastically embraced practice. And as a practitioner, he refused to be limited to an instrumental application of rationality in which means were to be fitted to ends that themselves remained unexamined. Instead, he argued that rational actions had to conform to rationality in both its forms, substantial as well as functional. The purpose of planned action would thus emerge from a process of systematic study in which "intelligent insight" would be gained into the interdependencies of existing situations.

These several ideas, drifting like a nimbus around the Matterhorn of rationality, eventually worked their way into the major planning traditions, albeit on a selective basis. They led to the theory of rational decision-making in policy analysis; they had very different methodological implications in the work of the social learning theorists; and they even surfaced on the left wing of planning where social mobilization was proposed as a "rational" response to the material irrationalities of the capitalist system. At the same time, planning's master theme provided the background to the two major topics of debate within the social reform tradition: first, the relation of planning to politics and second, the question of calculation and control.

Planning and Politics

From the beginning, planning was regarded as an alternative to politics. Already implicit in Bentham's calculus of costs and benefits, this understanding became increasingly clear with Saint-Simon's managerialism that inspired later theorists to describe administration as a "science." Even Mannheim, though less of a positivist than most planning theorists, was moved to ask whether politics might not become a scientific endeavor. It was reasonable to infer from this question that, if politics could indeed be successfully turned into a science, it would cease to be politics in the common understanding of the word.

For many rationalists, politics was merely a residue of the past. In the modern era, its place would be taken by a "calculus of consent." Though for a while it might still serve the limited functions of formulating objectives and legislating plans into law, politics would eventually be rendered obsolete by science and become a more or less empty ritual. Planning was seen as one of the major rationalizing forces in social life. And planners were often tempted to regard the political process as a major obstacle to the materialization of reason in the world.

More than anyone, Weber had helped to bring about the rift between politics and planning. Though not original with him, the separation of the objective study of what "actually exists" from one's beliefs of what "ought to exist" has become strongly identified with him. His Lutheran ethics of responsibility was based on the presumed capacity of scientists, however circumscribed that capacity might be, to project the hypothetical consequences of actions into the future, and to do what Bentham had advocated more than a century earlier: objectively to measure the pains and pleasures that would be inflicted upon people by public choice among alternative actions.

As a sociologist oriented to planning, Mannheim was less troubled than Weber about preserving objectivity. As the dark shadow side of reason, he saw a ghost of politics in almost Jungian terms. But in America, there were other perspectives. Mannheim's contemporary, a somewhat aloof professor of economics from New York who, in other times, might well have been a Roman senator, dramatically declared planning to be a *superpolitical* activity. For Rexford G. Tugwell, it was to be a Fourth Power of Government (Tugwell 1940, 1975c).

Tugwell's career is worth describing in some detail. More than any other theorist of planning, he had a distinguished public career that carried him to the very heights of public power. When Roosevelt was elected to the White House in 1932, Tugwell was already a successful and much published economist at Columbia University. Roosevelt took a liking to the debonair and controversial professor with his arrogant manner, and he appointed him to be the new assistant secretary of agriculture. (He was later to be promoted to under secretary.) With the Department of Agriculture as his base, Tugwell helped devise the new emergency legislation that was known as the Agricultural Adjustment Act of 1933 and which, by limiting production, succeeded in raising crop prices, thus saving millions of independent farmers from almost certain ruin. Within his department, Tugwell was also responsible for the Resettlement Administration, which was concerned with the relocation of poor and landless farmers on public lands (Banfield 1951).

Despite these substantial commitments to farming as a way of life, Tugwell was quite convinced that the future of the country did not lie with small-scale or even cooperative farming. Sympathetic to the efforts of the Regional Planning Association of America to build New Towns after the British model, he set up a suburban division of his short-lived Resettlement Administration which would initiate a government-sponsored program of New Town construction. Perhaps these Towns would set a new spatial pattern for metropolitan expansion (W. H. Wilson 1983).

Like Tugwell's other initiatives, it met with implacable opposition from the U.S. Supreme Court, which declared government involvement in the program unconstitutional. But Tugwell remained unyielding. A prolific and style-conscious writer, he took his ideas to the public in an awsome series of essays, intending to convey a sense of drama. He entitled the series *The Battle for Democracy* (1935).

By the mid-1930s, Tugwell had become for corporate business and its media a symbol of everything that was hateful to them in the New Deal. His left-wing views were beginning to be seen by the president as a liability, and late in 1936 Tugwell resigned his position.

Only two years later, however, he resurfaced as the first permanent chairman of the New York City Planning Commission. New

York's mayor, Fiorello La Guardia, was not only a progressive and dynamic leader but also a consummate politician, getting elected to an unprecedented three terms in office. The real powerhouse in New York City, however, was Park Commissioner Robert Moses, whose style for getting things done—building highways, tunnels, bridges, and parks—was, to say the least, improvisational and completely uncongenial to Tugwell's "master planning" ideas (Caro 1975; W. H. Wilson 1983).

Moses and Tugwell sparred bitterly over what were, in essence, different conceptions of government and the public interest. Moses was a doer, and to get things done in New York, one had to be a "power broker." Moses excelled in this role. And even as the patrician Tugwell projected New York's future in the austere offices of the City Planning Commission, the aggressive park commissioner was out tunneling, bridging, paving, landscaping, and transforming the very image of New York City according to his own likes and dislikes, without even the slightest bow to the professor from Morningside Heights and his "collective mind." Needless to say, the two men had little use for each other.

Tugwell's situation in New York was becoming precarious; then, at the urging of Harold Ickes, Roosevelt appointed him in 1941 to be governor of Puerto Rico. At last, Tugwell was to be master in his own domain. It was wartime now, and Puerto Rico played a key security role in the Caribbean. Moreover, as governor, he had substantial executive powers. But even more significant than these circumstantial events, Tugwell found in Puerto Rico a certain receptivity to and understanding of his conception of planning and reform. Perhaps a "Fourth Power" did not frighten Puerto Rican politicians who, at that time, had not yet managed to gain full control of even the first three! As it turned out, Tugwell's original idea of setting up a planning board independent of executive authority faltered also in Puerto Rico. But this is another story (Goodsell 1965, ch. 6).

Working hand in hand with Muñoz Marín, the Popular Democratic party official who, before the end of the decade, was to serve as the island's first elected governor, Tugwell created the planning machinery that years later would become renowned as Operation Bootstrap, Puerto Rico's accelerated effort, under its own government, to turn the backward and largely rural island economy into an industrial commonwealth.

After five fruitful years in San Juan, a period that was full of struggle and accomplishment, Tugwell returned to the mainland in 1946. Robert Maynard Hutchins, the iconoclastic chancellor of the

University of Chicago, had invited him to head up and organize an interdisciplinary Program for Education and Research in Planning in the Division of the Social Sciences. After two years as its chairman, Tugwell resigned in favor of Harvey S. Perloff, a brilliant young economist whose path-breaking research on Puerto Rico's economic development (Perloff 1950) had come to Tugwell's attention. After another eight years spent in writing and teaching, Tugwell retired from the university in 1957.

But his creative life was far from over. Hutchins, who had left the university at about the same time, had moved to California where, with the help of the Ford Foundation, he founded, in Santa Barbara, the Center for the Study of Democratic Institutions. In 1966, he invited Tugwell to join him there as one of a small group of Senior Fellows. The Center turned out to be a somewhat cerebral hillside retreat for scholars, reminiscent of Plato's Academy overlooking the Aegean. Here Tugwell spent his remaining years in research and writing. Among his many projects was the redrafting of the American Constitution, a document which, he believed, had in large measure become obsolete. It was an undertaking that brought him few admirers (Tugwell 1970, 1974).

Tugwell's ideas on planning are the most complete statement of a coherent planning philosophy America has produced. For this alone, Tugwell's name will be long remembered. On the event of his move to Washington in 1932, he would write:

> War in industry is just as ruinous as war among nations; and equally strenuous measures are taken to prevent it. The difficulty in the one case is precisely the difficulty in the other; so long as nations and industries are organized for conflict, wars will follow, and no elaboration of machinery for compromise will be altogether successful. There are vast, well-meaning endeavors being made in both fields which must necessarily be wasted. The disasters of recent years have caused us to ask again how the ancient paradox of business—conflicts to produce order—can be resolved; the interests of the liberals among us in the institutions of the new Russia of the Soviets, spreading gradually among puzzled business men, has created wide popular interest in "planning" as a possible refuge from persistent insecurity; by many people it is now regarded as a kind of economic Geneva where all sorts of compromises may be had and where peace and prosperity may be assured. It is my belief that practically all of this represents an unconsidered adherence to a slogan, or perhaps a withdrawal from

the hard lessons of the depression years, and that it remains unrelated to a vast background of revision and reorganization among our institutions which would condition its functioning. Most of those who say so easily that this is our way out do not, I am convinced, understand that fundamental changes of attitude, new disciplines, revised legal structures, unaccustomed limitations on activity, are all necessary if we are to plan. This amounts, in fact, to the abandonment, finally, of laissez faire. It amounts, practically, to the abolition of "business." This is what planning calls for. (Tugwell 1932, 75–76)

It was enough to make a businessman wince. Tugwell had thrown down the gauntlet and was not about to retreat. Seven years later, back in New York City, he broadened his conception.

Planning is not direction when it is at the service of special interests in society; it becomes direction only when it can affect economic divisiveness; becoming a unifying, cohesive, constructive, and truly general force. (Tugwell 1975c, 157)

Surfacing here are some of Tugwell's most basic convictions. In anticipation of Etzioni's "societal guidance," he calls planning a *directive* force that would be used in the interest of the people as a whole, that is, in the "general" interest. Like Veblen (and, for that matter, like Comte), he had a horror of divisiveness, conflict, and competition. Planning would achieve a clear vision of the future, above the din of petty politics, by becoming institutionalized as a fourth branch of government, with its own autonomous sphere. Armed with substantial authority, planners would be charged with devising the general plan or blueprint for the development of the whole, be it the national economy, the physical form of a city, or some other set of interlocking social processes requiring societal guidance from the top. In many respects, the model was not unlike Person's paradigm of planning.

In his next major essay on planning, Tugwell restated his ideas in more accessible language. He described planning as a

conjunctural institution which, through gradual and experimental change, may come to dominate social drift. . . . The arrival of agreed standards and procedures, of close measurement, of specification, furnish the opportunity for excluding, in wider and wider areas, both business and political appeals, and for admitting technical standards in administration as well as a more sophisticated sense of time than is now in use. Our total economic organization shows its contemporary instability because of our avoidance of large and exact projection of probabilities with a spacing out of time in program form. We cannot expect conformity to a design which does not exist, nor to a sequential program which is not laid out. And we do not expect it. The question here is whether, given such a design and such a program, conformity might be reached without "politics." (Tugwell 1940, 97–98)

For Tugwell, politics signified "personal competition for place." In this sense, he said, it was a disreputable activity, competitive, short-range, and unsavory in its practice of wheeling and dealing. Moreover, it was frequently aimed at the consolidation of privilege. What was needed was a countervailing power of experts who would bring to government "technical freedom, the protection of proficiency, the insuring of competence" (ibid. 101). Experts would lay out everyone's future in advance. Only in this way could the general interest be served. In discussing technical expertise, Tugwell waxes almost lyrical.

The ability to permit the future to govern social conduct is an old art but new science. . . . The master plan and the capital budget are useful for expressing what has been called here a drift toward competence but which might equally well be described as the displacement of demagogic romancing by future reality or what, at least, can, on the basis of available evidence, be judged to be future reality. . . . The function of the future changes. . . . It is no longer possible for individuals, much less societies or governments, to exist naively and spontaneously, though it is very human to desire that type of irresponsible living. It is this impulse toward the uncomplicated and undisciplined past which gives demagoguery its best opportunities. When the future is laid out in clear and objective—even if tentative—terms, the result is equally unacceptable to politician and business man. Both live by uncertainty. Neither can survive exactitude. Yet it is in this clear understanding that the public interest has its best chance to prevail. (Ibid. 112–113)

Tugwell's most mature statement on planning comes in a paper he read in 1948 to the Michigan Academy of Sciences (Tugwell 1975b). It is a remarkable essay in which he tackles the question of planning from the standpoint of sociobiology. Society is now likened to an organic body, whose specialized parts are controlled by a collective mind.

[T]he rationale of planning rests on the recognition that well-outlined, distinct, and autonomous colonies of men exist and that they move in coherent ways toward defined objectives, constantly searching for redefinitions of direction and for better means of movement. (Ibid. 215)

To establish an appropriate direction for the evolving social organism, a specialized planning agency is set up. Tugwell describes what it does.

[I]t surveys, for understanding, the whole organism of which it is a part, . . . it appraises most carefully the operation of the parts as they affect the functioning whole, . . . it undertakes a meticulous study of the resources and the developing direction of the organism, . . . and it produces the Development Plan which it will propose for public examination . . .

The Plan must represent not only expert analysis and synthesis but something like a community judgment that the synthesis is acceptable. It must be a device which, when put into effect, will not involve such substantial dissent as will hamper its operations by nonconformance. It is the responsibility of the collective mind . . . to represent the conscience, the good intention, the disinterested moral judgment, of the social organism as well as its detached and objective designation of the emerging Gestalt. (Ibid. 219–220)

In this essay, Tugwell reveals yet another facet of his transpolitical thinking. Planning, he says, requires public agreement. To be effective, it must have the cooperation of the whole community, which is portrayed here as a multicellular organism, something like a colony of ants or a Portuguese man-of-war.[11] But such cooperation, it seemed to Tugwell, would surely be forthcoming so long as the experts did their jobs well. There might be public hearings and the like, but the most important thing was for the experts to think and feel *for* the organism and to decide what is right. Patients are not inclined to challenge the skilled diagnoses of their physicians. Why, then, should society challenge the professionals who compose its collective mind?

The organic metaphor, which had become so dear to Tugwell, alienated many even among his admirers. Still, "possessive individualism" was not an acceptable alternative. Collectivist though they

11. Among the biologists cited by Tugwell in support of his organic metaphor were C. Warder Allee (1932), J. W. Bews (1935), and A. E. Emerson (1946). See also the allusive sequel by Allee (1958).

were, and thus seriously at odds with the American ethos, Tugwell's
ideas were gradually absorbed by others and found their way into
the literature as a persistent tradition of "planning in the public interest."[12]

On the practical side, the planning machinery for Puerto Rico, in
whose design he had played a leading part, was the first instance of
a development planning agency in what eventually would be known
as the Third World. When John F. Kennedy helped to create the
Alliance for Progress to promote economic growth with justice in
Latin America, many of the national planning agencies established
at that time looked to Puerto Rico as a model (Perloff 1969). Both in
theory and practice, Tugwell's influence on the world of planning
has been strong and pervasive.

Among those who worked within the Tugwellian paradigm was
Harvey S. Perloff, who had succeeded Tugwell as chairman of the
Chicago School of Planning. In his last book, *Planning the Post-Industrial City* (1980), Perloff presents, in more technical language, a
vision of planning very similar to Tugwell's. He writes:

> At the core of urban planning is the concept of a set of ac-
> counts that help to guide the functioning of an urban commu-
> nity into the future towards certain goals by means of precon-
> ceived strategies. (Perloff 1980, 91)

Here we have Tugwell's "directive power" in new language. The use
of the term *urban community* is of particular interest. Although Perloff avoids Tugwell's organicism, he uses "community" to suggest a
basic harmony of interests. Conflict, the lifeblood of a democratic
politics, is notable by its absence from Perloff's formulation. Planning the future, he seems to be saying, is a job chiefly for experts; it
calls for "an understanding of the requirements and possibilities for
systemic changes in the socio-economic-political forces and human
behavior" (ibid. 114). If we are to reach a broad understanding such
as this one, we require technical skills that will:

1. Analyze developments over the past generation.

2. Speculate on the implications for the municipality of possible developments over the next generation.

12. I was Tugwell's student at the University of Chicago and fully conversant with
his ideas at the time. Although I found it difficult to accept what seemed to me to be
Tugwell's corporatist views of the state, many of his themes, in particular the question of the public interest and the uses of the future in the present, had a lasting influence on my thinking.

3. Design (with members of the community) a small number of alternative futures and forecast the impacts of each.

4. Create an operational framework for implementation (ibid. 287).

The complexity of the elements that must be brought together into a single, time-dependent vision of the city is awesome indeed. Like Tugwell, Perloff sees planning as a "conjunctural" activity whose purpose is to produce a virtual cascade of plans, expertly drawn up, with the agreement of the community. They include:

1. An asset account plan.
2. A land use/natural resources account and plan.
3. A manpower account and plan.
4. An investment plan.
5. A fiscal plan (ibid. 294).

Perloff sees planning as performing an important *hinge function* that will relate the development activities of government to those of the private sector. With this in view, "planners must seek to involve all the major institutions as well as the citizenry in the various phases of planning and development processes" (ibid. 253).

We discover here a major clue to Perloff's understanding of the relation between planning and politics. Essentially, Perloff calls for a participatory process *outside* the normal channels of politics. The critical task of goal setting is described as a "community activity" that should be conducted on a periodic basis, perhaps every ten years (ibid. 238). People from the "poorer neighborhoods" must be involved. It might be difficult, at first, but the effort must be made if the goals are to be "meaningful" (ibid. 232). Nothing in this or any other passage in Perloff's book suggests the rough and tumble of city politics. Instead, he advocates use of "the newer methods of dialogue, including TV, class room projects, computer gaming, and similar methods" (ibid. 231).

Goal variety for different neighborhoods is to be encouraged. But "few cities have yet elaborated goals which reflect the true diversity of city life and city residents" (ibid. 231). How conflicting claims on global resources should be adjusted he does not say. Presumably, planners would find some acceptable compromise, reached in the course of public hearings and lengthy negotiations. Like Saint-Simon, Perloff stresses, over and over again, the need for cooperation and dialogue. In this search for consensus, planning techniques might play a significant role.

> [U]se can be made of the Delphi tool in the formulation of goals. The very purpose of a Delphi exercise is the establishment of an expert view of a given subject. Thus, the use of questionnaires asking about the preferred goals of a variety of expert groups can be a valuable supplement to the typical neighborhood-oriented goals effort. This would help ensure that certain considerations in goal setting, such as changing technology and changes in population structure, were brought to bear in the goals efforts. (Ibid. 232)

For Tugwell, politics had seemed to carry "a connotation of slight unscrupulousness" (Tugwell 1940, 98), whereas public planning was simply a "normal extension and development" of contemporary business practice (Tugwell 1932, 76). Such planning was obviously ill-suited for an environment in which politics was the very air which people breathed. In Perloff's understanding, half a century later, technical planning needed to get people involved; if it was to work at all, and maintain an appearance of being "democratic," it would have to be based on an evolving social consensus. Either the question addressed by planners had to be defined as a strictly technical matter, such as the design of an airplane engine or the alignment of curves on a freeway, or else some practical means had to be found for demobilizing public opinion. The new politics of goal setting was to be part of the engineering of consent. Based on "dialogue," rational argument, and negotiation among the interested parties, it would be decentralized, civilized, and emphatically suburban.[13]

During the later 1960s, Amitai Etzioni had written in a somewhat similar vein. He called his construct "interwoven planning" and presented it as part of a more comprehensive theory of "societal guidance." Because of this difference in contexts, it will be rewarding to examine Etzioni's concept in more detail.

Etzioni was a microsociologist, like Mannheim, and Israeli-born. The vision that inspired him was of an "active society" pursuing its chosen destiny. This chiliastic vision led him to define major components of what he called the active orientation: a self-conscious actor or actors, one or more societal goals to which a commitment had

13. A cartoon facing the title page of Perloff's *Planning the Post-Industrial City* shows a group of white, middle-class American suburbanites at what appears to be a planning meeting; the caption reads, "I may be a tad early, but my instinct is the future is coming back" (Perloff 1980).

been made, and access to power sufficient to attain these goals. To be activated, says Etzioni, "is to be aware, committed, and potent" (Etzioni 1968, 5).

But immediately the question must be raised, active for what? Etzioni's answer is that of an empirical sociologist. Societal objectives, he suggests, are reached through a process of authentic *consensus formation* among the relevant actors. But does not this stress on consensus conceal, as Marxists insist, that conflict is at the base of organized society? Not at all, replies Etzioni. Although societal consensus often reflects the will of some members of the society more than others, *societies often evolve a shared pattern with conflict occurring with and around it.* Conflict, in Etzioni's view, presupposes a system of political order, a political community. The nature of that order, and who controls it, was not his concern.

The process of consensus-formation was crucially important for Etzioni.[14] It is, he says, a process that is partly "guided" from above by the controlling "overlayer" of society and partly voluntaristic. *Societal guidance* itself he defined as a combination of downward control and upward consensus-formation. In its overlayer, society requires technical elites and guidance institutions that are "responsive" to the needs of the non-elite population below them.[15] A simplified model of this process might look something like the diagram in Figure 7.

14. In 1937, Karl Mannheim had written about a similar concept.

He who plans freedom, that is, assigns self-determination free spaces in the regulated structure, must plan, to be sure, also the conformity needed for the life of the society. . . . In the immediate future we shall have to devote much energy to substituting a new conformity for the traditional one, which is in process of dissolution. In this effort, we shall rediscover values that we had forgotten in the age of unlimited competition: identification with the other members of society, collective responsibility, and the obligation following from it to possess in common with the others a basis of attitudes and ways of behavior. (Mannheim 193, 364)

Mannheim would plan for social solidarity where Tugwell assumed it under his overarching metaphor of a social organism. Planned solidarity was a problem for education. Etzioni's consensus-formation process was presented as a form of social mobilization. From a certain distance, all these concepts seem to be saying the same thing; on closer inspection, however, they turn out to have very different meanings and implications.

15. Etzioni's language is somewhat opaque on this point. In his formal definition, however, he does not mince words. Elites, he says, are *control units* that specialize in the *cybernetic functions* of knowledge-processing and decision-making and in the *application of power* (Etzioni 1968, 668).

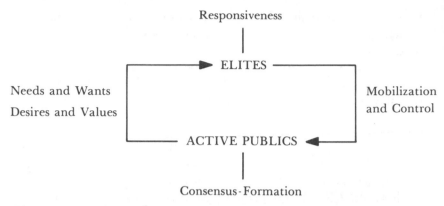

Figure 7. A simple model of societal guidance (after Etzioni).

This "functional-genetic" view of society (the characterization is Etzioni's) is only a hair's breadth removed from Tugwell's bio-social organicism. Collectivities, says Etzioni, "have properties of their own and . . . consciousness is one of them (ibid. 228). Being such a collectivity, the active society has, therefore, the "potential capacity to *act in unison* by drawing on a set of normative bonds" which binds its members to each other in a social collectivity (ibid. 667; italics added). The bonds are said to constitute "quasi-organic relationships" among its members. Societal guidance, it turns out, is simply an updated version, in the jargon of sociology, of Tugwell's more metaphysical "directive in history."[16]

The role of interwoven planning can now be understood more clearly. Referring to "post-modern" societies, Etzioni declares that they "experiment with new organizations and techniques of contextuating control so as to link control more closely to consensus-formation" (ibid. 486). He therefore rejects the master planning approach as being antiquated and unworkable. In its place, he proposes to put a planning that is "interwoven" with the more general processes of societal guidance. This interweaving is a matter of degree, as planners assume frankly political roles (they are, of course, members of the "internal social elite"). Some may "attempt to learn about the perspectives of the decision-makers and take these perspectives into account in their planning." Others will wish to "explore the perspectives of those who are likely to be affected by the plan." Yet a third group of planners will seek a "much higher" level of articulation with societal guidance institutions, such as the

16. Etzioni's collectivist model of society is derived from Durkheim and Marx, though he is at pains to distinguish his own formulation from those of his illustrious ancestors.

planners who work for the European Economic Community, the French Planning Commissariat, or the British National Economic Development Council, all of which, Etzioni insists, are "post-modern" agencies of control (ibid. 486–487).

Interwoven planning, then, is an elite function, part and parcel of the twin processes of consensus-formation and societal guidance. To be effective, planners must tack close to the winds of power. Indeed, they may be tempted to manipulate power themselves. Tugwell would have understood. Like the former colonial governor of Puerto Rico, Etzioni is disdainful of legislative politics which, in his view, is becoming every day less relevant to the needs of the society (ibid. 488–489).

Such understandings did not go unchallenged. Whatever differences divided them, the critics of technocratic planning all attempted to rehabilitate a democratic politics and show that political interaction, far from having been rendered obsolete by planning, continues to play a major role in "societal guidance."

Critics split mainly into two groups: those who held that social reforms from the top were desirable and those who were skeptical of any form of government intervention. A possible third group is more difficult to define. Its aim was less to criticize than to describe and account for actual planning processes. Nevertheless, the work of this group yielded conclusions that are pertinent to our discussion.

The Critic as Social Reformer
Karl Popper's two-volume study, *The Open Society and Its Enemies* (1974), has often been seen as a bitter attack on planning in all its forms. In fact, however, Popper's critique is leveled only at "utopian engineering" which, in the present context, would mean the writings not only of the early scientific managers, such as Harlow Person, but also the more sophisticated statements of Tugwell and Perloff. Popper writes:

> What I criticize under the name of Utopian engineering recommends the reconstruction of society as a whole, i.e., very sweeping changes whose practical consequences are hard to calculate, owing to our limited experiences. It claims to plan rationally for the whole of society, although we do not possess anything like the factual knowledge which would be necessary to make good such an ambitious claim. We cannot possess such knowledge since we have insufficient practical experience in this kind of planning, and knowledge of facts must be

based upon experience. At present, the sociological knowledge necessary for large-scale engineering is simply non-exist-
ent. (Popper 1974, I, 161–162)

Here, Popper appears to be saying that even though the knowledge
we now have may be inadequate for what he calls utopian planning,
it is conceivable that we may have the necessary knowledge at some
future date. More than a matter of knowledge, however, is involved.
It is a question of principle whether to gear planning to the perfection of society or to piecemeal social engineering that is seeking to
remove specific hurts.

> The politician who adopts this method may or may not have a
> blueprint of society before his mind, he may or may not hope
> that mankind will one day realize an ideal state, and achieve
> happiness and perfection on earth. But he will be aware that
> perfection, if at all attainable, is far distant, and that every
> generation of men, and therefore also the living, have a claim;
> perhaps not so much a claim to be made happy, but a claim
> not to be made unhappy, where it can be avoided. They have a
> claim to be given all possible help, if they suffer. The piece-
> meal engineer will, accordingly, adopt the method of search-
> ing for, and fighting for, its greatest ultimate good. (Ibid. 158)

The spokesperson here is a politician-planner. As far as Popper is
concerned, politics and planning go hand in hand. Though he appears here as an incrementalist, his concern would seem to be with
large-scale reform: he calls it a "rational political programme for the
protection of the economically weak." The real question is not about
change itself but about who should be in charge. Popper is anxious
that the levers of central power should remain with politicians, and
that they not be seized by the technicians of planning with their naive and dangerous notions about the perfection of the world. Pragmatic politics should remain firmly at the helm. It is not, one should
think, a totally unreasonable proposition.

> Our analysis considers political power as fundamental. Politi-
> cal power . . . can control economic power. This means an im-
> mense extension of the field of political activities. We can ask
> what we wish to achieve and how to achieve it. We can, for in-
> stance, develop a rational political programme for the protec-
> tion of the economically weak. . . . And when we are able by
> the law to guarantee a livelihood to everybody willing to work
> . . . then the protection of the freedom of the citizen from eco-
> nomic fear and economic intimidation will approach com-

pleteness. From this point of view, political power is the key to economic protection. Political power and its control is everything. Economic power must not be permitted to dominate political power; if necessary, it must be fought and brought under control by political power. (Popper 1974, II, 126)

What is striking about this powerful statement is that its message is not, after all, very different from that of the "utopians." The latter praised technical planning as the most suitable instrument for achieving economic growth with social justice; Popper looks to the primacy of politics. Unfortunately, he neglects to investigate either the social basis of politics or the theory of the liberal state. To this extent, his critique of planning remains only a partial one.

Another prominent critic, Albert O. Hirschman, was, like Popper, concerned with the rehabilitation of politics. In the book that brought him to the attention of a wide public, *The Strategy of Economic Development* (1958), he argued, in opposition to the prevailing views of development economists, that "balanced," comprehensive planning might not be the most effective way of ensuring accelerated economic growth. Via market and political processes, imbalances in growth and development had a way of being self-correcting. The process might be most costly in terms of resource utilization, "but the imbalances at the same time *call forth* more resources and investment than would otherwise be available" (Hirschman and Lindblom 1962, 212).

In a subsequent essay (1963), Hirschman developed a series of models of "reform mongering" that pointed up such political dimensions of reform as "log rolling" and "shifting alliances." He was, of course, fully aware of the intellectual appeal of "simultaneous solutions," in which all problems are "grasped" by a central intelligence and are transformed into appropriate programs of directed change. Yet, he continued to advocate a Machiavellian strategy of political gamesmanship ("shifting alliances") as a means for reforming society.

In a third paper (1967a), Hirschman presented an ingenious argument for man's imperfect knowledge of the future—in fact, for a vision of the future *without* planning, in direct contradiction to Perloff's cascade of central planning devices.

Creativity always comes as a surprise to us; therefore, we can never count on it and we dare not believe in it until it has happened. In other words, we would not consciously engage upon tasks whose success clearly requires that creativity be forthcoming. Hence, the only way in which we can bring our crea-

tive resources fully into play is by misjudging the nature of the
task, by presenting it to ourselves as more routine, simple, undemanding of genuine creativity than it will turn out to be.
(Hirschman 1967, 13)

Ironically, he called this argument the Principle of the Hiding
Hand. Planners want as much as possible to reduce uncertainty
about the future. (For Tugwell, the reduction of uncertainty was
one of the major reasons for planning.) They see their task as outlining, in advance of the action itself, what will need to be done and
prescribing for each of the actions involved the specific tasks to be
accomplished. According to Hirschman's thesis, this kind of planning would lead to less social innovation rather than more, and
therefore also to less overall economic and social change. Formally
rational behavior, he seemed to be saying, does not necessarily improve the material rationality of actions. It is a conclusion we have
met before.

The Critic as Skeptic

Among the severest critics of technocratic planning are two political
scientists, Edward C. Banfield and Aaron Wildavsky. Both look with
a dispassionate eye on political behavior: "Here is what it is," they
seem to be saying. "Don't try to change it; endure. Maybe the world
is not perfect, but we have little faith in human nature. When people
meddle—and planners with their theories of 'world improvement'
are incorrigible meddlers—things will only get worse."

A senior professor of politics at Harvard, Banfield had been an
early collaborator of Tugwell's at the University of Chicago (Tugwell and Banfield 1951). His doctoral dissertation (Banfield 1951)
was an empirical study of one of Tugwell's institutional inventions,
the Resettlement Administration, and how it had failed. Skeptical
about the claims of rationalists, he turned to the study of urban politics. In his key work on the subject, written jointly with his former
student, James Q. Wilson, also a Harvard professor, he pleaded for
a political view of planning, which he believed was incompatible
with blueprinting the city's future.

Planners are . . . becoming increasingly aware that the decentralization of authority and power that is so characteristic of
American local government is radically incompatible with the
ideal of master planning; . . . the political system continues to
work mainly by bargaining and compromise, not by "implementing the general interest," and the main decision in a master plan must (as Mowitz and Wright said those in Detroit did)

"reveal the power distribution in the community at that particular time." (Banfield and Wilson 1963, 203)

Here, Banfield still allowed for the possibility of piecemeal engineering in Popper's sense. Only five years later, however, he contended that government was totally incapable of solving the urban
problem. In fact, he added with a flourish, the intervention of government would tend to make things worse (Banfield 1968). It was an
extremely conservative, if not misanthropic, view of the world.

> Faith in the perfectibility of man and confidence that good in-
> tentions together with strenuous exertions will hasten his
> progress onward and upward lead to bold programs that
> promise to do what no one knows how to do and what perhaps
> cannot be done, and therefore end in frustration, loss of mu-
> tual respect and trust, anger, and even coercion. (Banfield
> 1974, 280–281)

By this time, the intellectual gulf between Tugwell and Perloff and
their former colleague at the University of Chicago had become un-
bridgeable.

Although Aaron Wildavsky writes in a style very different from
Banfield's, in the end he too lashes out at the reform tradition. Planning is wasteful, he asserts. Its brave attempts at coordinating everything end up helter-skelter. The many interlocking plans in practice
lack consistency, and planners' claims to contribute to a rationally
ordered society are self-deluding. The political system, says Wildavsky, works better than planning; direct interaction is preferable to
cogitation.

> The injunction to plan (Think!) is empty. The key terms asso-
> ciated with it are proverbs or platitudes. Pursue goals! Con-
> sider alternatives! Obtain knowledge! Exercise power! Obtain
> consent! Or be flexible but do not alter your course. These im-
> peratives have a noncontroversial ring to them, in part be-
> cause they contain no operational guidance. (Wildavsky 1979,
> 134–135)

Just what Wildavsky intended to put in place of planning is not
clear. Interest group politics is certainly part of the answer. Another
is the free, unfettered market. But there is more here than is immediately apparent. Wildavsky, after all, was founding dean of
Berkeley's Graduate School of Public Policy. Even as he was lam-
basting planning, he was advocating "policy analysis." Here is how
he thought this new expertise might function in the real world.

Policy analysis . . . is about change in patterns of social interaction. How does change happen? By joining planning to politics, social interaction gives analysis a historical outlook made up of the past pattern of agreements, including agreements to disagree until next time. From the organized actors, the constituent elements of this interaction, analysis gets its abiding interest in incentives to alter their behavior. And planning helps analysis bring intelligence to interaction, by rationalizing movement to a different pattern that may lead to improved future outcomes. (Ibid. 139)

Wildavsky's language here is uncharacteristically opaque. Is policy analysis a form of planning, only by another name? Is it simply "intelligence" made available to political actors who might do with it as they please, because intelligence is supposedly "neutral" with respect to values? Is it a sly scheme to manipulate behavior through a hidden motivational structure? It is difficult to tell. In his more recent work, Wildavsky appears to have taken a further turn to the right, with a populist tract on the reduction of taxes and the limitations of government (Wildavsky 1980).

The Critic as Empiricist
Of the many empirical studies of planning practice, I have selected two for their special relevance to our argument. In their classic study of the community action program of the sixties, Peter Marris and Martin Rein (1982; orig. 1967) emphasize a point that the advocates of rational planning seem to have lost from view. It is that any social reform is best regarded as an *innovative action* which, because it must overcome opposition, is not only inherently biased (it must at least favor the reform) but also political. Although they do not refer explicitly to "innovative planning," Marris and Rein's intention is clear: social reform requires a style of political practice that is light-years removed from the theoretical models of comprehensiveness. (Hirschman's plea for the "hiding hand" comes to mind in this connection.) Conflict is the very medium of social reform. They write:

[N]o movement of reform in American society can hope to supplant the conflicts of interest from which policy evolves. It can only act as advocate, not as judge. If it is to be persuasive, it must be single-minded about the interest it represents, and so willing to surrender claim to universal authority. Once this is recognized, community action can be seen as the starting point of a variety of innovations, each of which, if it is to influence the progress of reform, must be disentangled from the constraint of its rivals. Perhaps the most far-reaching was the development of a new political structure. (Marris and Rein 1982, 230)

There is much else in this book that is worth pondering, and those interested in innovative planning are referred particularly to its closing chapters.

The second empirical study I wish to discuss is a short history I wrote of CORDIPLAN (Friedmann 1965), Venezuela's national planning agency—an agency that might have been devised by Tugwell himself. One of the aspects that puzzled me most when I studied CORDIPLAN's operations in 1963 was, on the one hand, the growing discrepancy between planned targets and the actual performance of the economy and, on the other, the growing political prestige enjoyed by the agency. How was it possible, I asked, that a failure to perform on the level of master planning (here it was called the National Development Plan) should lead to increasing public respect for CORDIPLAN? The answer came as a surprise. Perhaps the job of planning was not, primarily, to lay out the future in advance but to serve the presidency as a political instrument in what Etzioni would call the process of consensus-formation.

In this light, economic modeling appeared to be largely a symbolic activity that, by showing planning to be a highly technical skill, would legitimate the role of planners in the political process (interwoven planning). My attention was therefore drawn to what I called the latent functions of national planning in Venezuela (ibid. 50ff.).

1. Strengthening the presidency vis-à-vis other political actors in the guidance system.

2. Improving the political process through better information.

3. Creating a "new mentality" oriented to national development.

4. Reducing social conflict through negotiations with capital and labor on the basis of the plan that represents the government's position.

5. Mobilizing foreign aid and other external resources.

As it happened, Venezuela's planning scored well on these criteria, at least through the mid-1960s. Planning had helped to restructure the country's internal political process, a conclusion very much like that of Marris and Rein (see above). It was itself a part of that process. Even at the highest executive level, planning and politics were closely intertwined. The much desired separation of fact and value, science and politics, had turned out to be a chimera.

Calculation and Control

With the question of calculation and control, we approach the very heart of technical planning. Planning implies the ability of actors to gain some understanding of the emergent future, to correctly analyze perceived problems from a standpoint of either ameliorative change or goal achievement, to identify practicable means of action in the present, and to predict and assess the probable consequences of their actions, both for themselves and for others. We shall call this faculty for comprehensive analysis the capacity for *calculation*.

Control refers to the ability of actors to carry out their intentions. In the more technical sense, it means implementation. And because implementation often requires the coordination of others' activities, control, implementation, and coordination will here be taken to mean much the same thing.

Calculation

Virtually all writers in the social reform tradition address the question of calculation,[17] but only a few approach it concretely in terms of specific analytical techniques. The philosophers of planning—Mannheim, Tugwell, Mumford—all stress the need for comprehensiveness in planning analysis, though they use different words to describe it. Mannheim speaks of *interdependent thinking* grounded in specific situations, Tugwell uses the metaphor of a *collective mind* capable of overcoming the partial and fragmented knowledge of disciplinary specializations, and Mumford declaims eloquently the need for *simultaneous thinking*. He wrote:

> We have still to develop . . . the art of simultaneous thinking: the ability to deal with a multitude of related phenomena at the same time, and of composing, *in a single picture*, both the qualitative and quantitative attributes of these phenomena. Specialists, as such, cannot plan: for planning involves the job of coordinating specialisms, focussing them in common fields of knowledge and canalizing them in appropriate channels of common action. (Mumford, in MacKenzie 1937, vii)

In practice, simultaneous thinking would be accomplished in two ways: through the interdisciplinary training of planners (see, for example, Perloff 1957) and through effective teamwork on the job.

Of course, the requirements for a planning synthesis occasionally were set excessively high. In his last book, Harvey Perloff called for

17. The more technical and epistemological aspects of calculation in relation to planning will be taken up in Chapter 4.

the integration of nearly everything: economic, political, social, physical, and environmental analysis; multilevel territorial analysis; "sectoral" or functional analysis; and planning over different time horizons (Perloff 1980). In the absence of cross-disciplinary, multi-sectoral, and multilevel models operational in time and space, something like a game plan for four-dimensional chess, Perloff's ambitious program for coordinative planning remains an ideal capable of only fragmentary implementation.

A number of outstanding institutional economists avoided the philosophical debate over the possibility of comprehensiveness in planning, devoting themselves instead to the practical elaboration of *comprehensive information systems*. The most important of these included national economic accounts (Kuznets 1937); input-output analysis (Leontief 1937, 1966); and economic policy models (Tinbergen 1952). Although embracing less than the totality of the components for comprehensive planning as required by Perloff, these models were made operational and provided the intellectual foundations not only for national economic planning but, in an adapted form, for regional and urban-metropolitan analysis as well (see, for example, Isard 1960).

An early and particularly important contribution to calculation was made by Wesley C. Mitchell, founder of one of the country's premier scientific institutions, the National Bureau of Economic Research, in 1920. Mitchell had served on President Hoover's Committee on Social Trends and Roosevelt's National Planning Board. In a speech at Harvard in 1936, he called for a national organization to undertake the "deliberate and systematic study of social problems." More realistic and modest in his ambitions than either Person or Tugwell, Mitchell understood that national planning would be "vastly more difficult than to design an efficient bridge across the Golden Gate" (Mitchell 1937, 131). His proposal was to establish, on a continuing basis and at the national level, a small board that would be responsible for seeing that the appropriate studies were made and, on the basis of their findings, devising the appropriate policies. With the establishment a decade later of the President's Council for Economic Advisors, Mitchell's proposal finally became reality.[18]

18. Mitchell was ever careful not to claim too much for social science in policy analysis. After one year's service with national planning, he wrote in 1935:

How much a National Planning Board with advisory powers might improve upon our efforts to solve social problems by taking thought no one can tell in advance. What I have said about the difficulties that beset the social sciences warns us that success is not a foregone conclusion. To supply deficiencies in knowledge the board would doubtless have to undertake much research

The power of the new quantitative models that were widely adopted in the years following World War II should be noted. They helped to focus the national effort, giving emphasis to economic growth and full employment. Because they modeled economic relationships, they raised economists to a position of preeminence in policy analysis. Even the thinking of non-economists was molded by these models, whose logical structure was impeccable and whose results, to a lay person at least, seemed amazingly precise and accurate.

Goals came to be expressed in terms of "growth of GNP." Sectoral planning was guided by the classification of national social accounts. Short-term forecasting took the form of Tinbergen's system of simultaneous equations, which distinguished neatly between policy and outcome variables and were easily dovetailed into the Kuznets-Leontief models of economic structures. While the philosophers talked, it was the new information systems that helped to form the kind of planning that was being done.

In light of this development, one wonders at the skepticism expressed by some of the critics of comprehensive planning, such as Friedrich Hayek, who declared that central calculation was impossible. Although it was one thing to see the limitations of current information systems, it was quite another to argue, as Banfield and Wilson would do, that planners should therefore "think small." Big or small are ideological categories that have little to do with the actual possibilities of central calculation—possibilities that were, in fact, expanding rapidly during this period, as the demand for information grew.

One of the more dramatic failures of calculation was the social indicators movement that flourished between 1965–1975 (see, for example, Gross 1966, Duncan 1969). After the initial eagerness to develop social indicators to complement economic accounts, the movement collapsed before its promise had been fulfilled. It seems reasonable to conjecture that the implications of social policies planning were felt to be more threatening to the established powers than was the use of fiscal-monetary instruments to manage the economy. No one objected to "philosophers" so long as they did not threaten to actually fashion the tools of comprehensive planning. When they

---

through its own staff or through other agencies. But after doing its best to lay a scientific foundation for its plans, the board would often have to advise proceeding in an experimental fashion on the basis of probabilities. It would be doing pioneer work; for it would be trying to better the social organization of one of the most advanced countries in the world—to do things that have not yet been done. (Mitchell 1937, 101–102)

moved from advocacy to technics, support for their work quickly evaporated.

Control
We recall Harlow Person's top-down paradigm of planning presented in the first section of this chapter. Here the principal control device was hierarchy: a simple command from the top would suffice to set the implementing machinery in motion. Were it not for its prevalence—particularly in socialist systems—this model would scarcely be worth considering further (Lindblom 1977; Bahro 1979; Ellman 1979). A relatively costly method of implementation, the appeal of hierarchy rests on its conceptual simplicity. Everyone understands a command to which negative sanctions are attached: if you don't do as you're told, you're fired.

A more sophisticated command model was developed by B. F. Skinner, who invented a system with *positive* sanctions whereby compliant behavior was rewarded. This seemed to render meaningless the bothersome question of freedom which would so frequently surface in discussions of command systems. Experiments had shown that Skinner's people (and pigeons) did what they were supposed to do—and enjoyed doing it—*by internalizing the implicit commands that they were carrying out* (Skinner 1971). Of course, hierarchy was not eliminated; all that Skinner did was to provide the ruling elites with an instrument of benign coercion.

Theoreticians like Tugwell and Perloff had largely ignored the question of controls. Once the plans were made official, they would be carried out, they thought, through the normal workings of the state bureaucracy. Plans, of course, would have to be acceptable to people, and for this purpose they proposed public hearings and other means of getting people "involved." But planners would retain control over the entire process.

Aside from this concession, they hoped that the relevant publics would remain passive and compliant. It was Tugwell's opinion that planners should always devise their plans with a view to what he called the general interest of the collectivity (Tugwell 1975a). His disdain for politics did not allow for fundamental conflicts of interest. The general interest would be secured through the collective mind.

Mannheim had already perceived a problem in this connection. In his two major books on planning (1949b, 1951), he devoted considerable space to the question of control. It was his sociologist's good sense that led him to advocate *strategic* planning (not everything had to be "planned"), the selection of *key positions* for government intervention, and the employment of *indirect controls* that would operate on a person's subjective field of expectations, fears, and hopes. Mannheim, like Skinner, preferred positive rewards to oppressive sanctions.

Dahl and Lindblom (1957) were rather more ambitious in their classification. They identified four *control processes:*[19]

price system (control of and by leaders)

hierarchy (control by leaders)

polyarchy (rule of the many, or control of leaders)

bargaining (control among leaders)

together with four *control techniques:*

spontaneous field control

manipulated field control

command

reciprocity

This way of looking at controls proved to be useful. For the first time, the market was identified as a possible instrument for planning, as were polyarchal politics and bargaining. The authors suggested the possibility of using the market specifically for implementing planning. Their classification also opened the way to a *negotiated* planning (sometimes referred to as "indicative") which, at the time, was being successfully applied by the French Planning Commissariat under Pierre Massé and, with the creation of CORDIPLAN, would soon be introduced to Venezuela under Hector Hurtado. Planners might even design "polyarchal" systems as an instrument of control. It was a heady prospect.[20]

19. Dahl and Lindblom conclude their treatise with a brief mention of a fifth control process, which they refer to as "small group processes" (Dahl and Lindblom 1957, 519–521). Clearly intrigued by its prospects, they write, "For those in search of adventure and Revolution within the framework of the Renaissance-liberal-socialist core of values, perhaps no route offers such exciting possibilities" (ibid. 521). In practice, small group processes were extensively used as a means for control in Maoist China (Whyte 1974). In a very different context, they were also advocated by Friedmann (1979b), for whom task-oriented, dialogic groups constitute the very essence of a "good society."

20. Despite its reputation for failure, the community action program during the 1960s was essentially a political design to produce a new range of policy outcomes by giving voice to a segment of the population that until then had remained invisible: the urban poor (Marris and Rein 1982).

Lindblom's Interactionist Model

After his brilliant collaboration with Robert Dahl, Lindblom pursued the question of calculation and control in a way that was rather upsetting to the proponents of central, comprehensive planning. His work was nothing less than a sustained attack on their position. In a famous essay (1959) and in two subsequent books (Braybrooke and Lindblom 1963, Lindblom 1965), he developed a two-phase model for calculation and control and called the phases "disjointed incrementalism" and "partisan mutual adjustment."

In his work with Robert Dahl, Lindblom had presented incrementalism as one of four "comprehensive processes for rational calculation," the others being science, calculated risks, and utopianism. Science received rather low marks as a helping hand in decision analysis, and the remaining two processes could hardly be considered instances of "rational calculation" at all. This left incrementalism. It was to the exploration of this approach that Lindblom turned in his provocatively entitled essay "The Science of Muddling Through" (1959). Over the next several years, he continued to work intensively on the subject.

Because of excessive information requirements, said Lindblom, central, comprehensive planning, which he called "synoptic," did not work at all. The only reasonable alternative was to divide large decisions into smaller ones and distribute them among a large number of actors who would make their decisions independent of each other. In Lindblom's model, each actor would pursue his own interests on the basis of information received about the actions of all the other actors in the situation. With each actor pressing for his own advantage, all relevant points of view (and the supporting information) would eventually be brought out for their joint consideration. Under given circumstances, the outcome of such a process would also tend to be the most rational that was practically attainable.

An attractive feature of this model was that it appeared to substitute social interaction for purely mental processes in systemic calculation. For David Braybrooke, Lindblom's co-author in 1963 and a utilitarian philosopher, it was a happy discovery that, it seemed to him, managed to solve with one brilliant stroke the many perplexing problems of Bentham's felicity calculus. Logical conundrums in utilitarianism, such as the question of the correct weighting of preferences or the impossibility of intersubjective comparisons, vanished in view of a solution that bore all the marks of genius: policy decisions might be made like decisions in a perfect market! So long as no single actor could assert appreciable influence over policy outcomes, the result would indeed lead to the "greatest happiness of the greatest number."

"The Science of Muddling Through" was reprinted over forty times. Both the periodic reappearance of the essay and the controversial nature of his model eventually prompted Lindblom to reassess his argument (1979). So far as calculation was concerned, he thought the model had withstood the test of time. His current doubts focused rather on the suitability of an incremental *politics*, which had once seemed to be merely a logical corollary of incrementalism in analysis. Lindblom begins his reassessment with a restatement of his basic position: "[N]either revolution, nor drastic policy change, nor even carefully planned big steps are ordinarily possible" (Lindblom 1979, 517). The "enemy" is *big* and *drastic* change. Lindblom proposes to array changes along a continuum from big to small, but doubts about the usefulness of this artifice surface immediately when he refers to the introduction of the Federal Reserve System as "still incremental," with the abolition of money cited as a counter-instance of a drastic, structural change (ibid.). With examples like these, the problem is defined out of existence: in some perspectives, virtually any change can be shown to be "incremental."

Lindblom proceeds to define three modes of incremental analysis arranged in a nested hierarchy as shown in Figure 8.

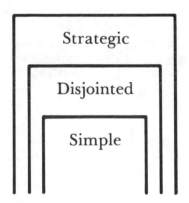

Figure 8. Incremental policy analysis as a nested hierarchy (after Lindblom).

He offers specific arguments why an incremental mode of analysis should be pursued as an alternative to "synoptic" decision analysis.

I will not rehearse the arguments here, except to say that his incrementalism is presented as a remedial form of planning—a planning without overarching goals—not unlike Popper's "piecemeal engineering." From a more practical standpoint, the implications of Lindblom's model carry the following three prescriptions.

1. Decentralize decision analysis to many small actors, none of whom controls a very big slice of the total action.

2. Give each actor substantial autonomy over decisions.

3. Improve the network of communication between all actors in the system.

Having reasserted his faith in the incremental method of analysis, Lindblom turns to the more vexing question of an incremental politics. Referring to the market-oriented state systems of North America and Western Europe, his conclusions are worth quoting at length.

> Having assigned many or more of the great organizing and coordinating tasks of society to business enterprises, then subjecting the managers of these enterprises to market inducements rather than commands . . . the only way to get the assigned jobs done is to give businessmen whatever inducements will in fact motivate them to perform. That renders these political systems incapable of following many lines of policy that, however attractive they might look for, say, energy conservation or environmental protection, threaten to undercut business inducements to perform.

> [T]he problem is not incrementalism but a structure of veto powers that makes even incremental moves difficult and insufficiently frequent. . . . If we could imagine an incremental politics without the veto powers that now abound in it, I suggest we would find incremental policies a suitable instrument for more effectively grappling with our problems.

> Another source of timidity in American politics is ideological conservatism having its course in the many indoctrinations that grow out of the structure of private enterprise. It is difficult for many political leaders, and for ordinary citizens as well, to open their minds to the possibility that the American Constitution, with its many curbs on the popular will. . . . is not an adequate set of rules for coping with our current great problems. It is no less difficult for them to let their mind freely explore—and reconsider the traditional justifications of—the

extraordinary autonomy of the business corporation and its capacities to obstruct government problem solving. (Ibid. 520–521)

Lindblom's advocacy of constitutional reform to constrain the powers of the large private corporation remind one of Tugwell's life-long efforts in the same direction. It is also noteworthy that Lindblom argues for the necessity of "broad-ranging, highly speculative, and sometimes utopian thinking about directions and possible futures" as a counterpart to incremental analysis (ibid. 522). This is not unlike Etzioni's advocacy of a critical intelligence in societal guidance outside the existing system of power or, as he slyly suggested, in "bohemia" (Etzioni 1968, ch. 8).

Lindblom concludes his ruminative essay by suggesting that "the possibilities of intelligent and democratically responsive policy making" are still insufficiently explored, and by declaring his belief that the future lies with "improved combinations of incremental analysis, incremental politics, and partisan mutual adjustment" (Lindblom 1979, 524).

In *Politics and Markets* (1977), Lindblom undertook a masterful analysis of policy making in societies under the alternative regimes of central planning and markets. In this his last major work, he proposed "social interaction" as an alternative to planning analysis in pluralist or polyarchal societies. Analysis, he argued, cannot find the correct solutions. How, then, are institutions and policies to be designed? The answer, according to Lindblom, is "by social processes of interaction that substitute for conclusive analysis" (Lindblom 1977, 253). Suppose, he says, a large society wants to decide how to allocate its resources. In centrally planned systems, an elite would study the question in an attempt to find correct decisions. In polyarchies like the United States, it would establish an interaction process that would make a diagnostic study unnecessary: "the market system is the obvious example" (ibid.). But there are social interactions other than the market—negotiations and political horse-trading, for instance. And, on balance, these methods of interactionist planning are superior to central calculation. Lindblom is careful not to claim too much for his model. "It is not assumed that interactions produce perfect solutions to problems, only that they will often be superior to the solutions attempted by the intellect. Either can be a disaster" (ibid. 255). To this pessimism of the intellect, he opposes a stoic acceptance of politics as he finds it.[21]

21. Lindblom's dilemma is a real one. On the one hand, he had so committed himself in public to a philosophy of incrementalism (and a Weberian ethics of responsi-

In concluding this section, I should like to draw attention to four major assumptions that would seem to underlie Lindblom's interactionist model of planning. They are necessary assumptions, for only to the extent that they are satisfied can the normative claims of the model be justified.

1. Lindblom's society is not, as it was for Tugwell or Etzioni, a collectivity having certain "organic" properties, but rather an assembly of individuals in which legally constituted persons are expected to pursue their self-interest aggressively.

2. The policy context is always "normal times." Lindblom does not deal with situations of crisis in which there might be a great public clamor for "structural" change.

3. Access to power, including information, is evenly distributed among all of the actors in the decision system, so that not one of them carries significantly more weight than any other. No group is permanently disenfranchised.

4. Society is not deeply divided over issues of class, ethnicity, or any other matter. Moreover, actors tend to be kindly disposed toward each other, they do not attempt to exert undue influence to gain their objectives, and they are ever ready to abide by the bargains that are struck.

Except for the last, there are also the assumptions required by classical price theory. Since none of them correspond to any known reality, however, Lindblom's advocacy of incrementalism and partisan mutual adjustment would seem to be ill-advised as a general model.

Lindblom appeared to be aware of this dilemma when he turned

---

bility), that anything "central," including, of course, synoptic planning, seems "impossible" and, if not impossible, immoral: it would only make things worse! In this, he agreed completely with Banfield and Wildavsky. Yet, on the other hand, it now turns out that decentralized decision modes, which involve an incremental *politics*, are also unlikely to work, because of (1) the fickle nature of populist democracy—"[t]he erosion of class indoctrination and the ability of opponents to veto any public measure they did not like"—a position that echoes the "ungovernability of democracy" thesis of the Trilateral Commission (Crozier et al. 1975) and (2) the exceptional power allowed corporate enterprise under the American Constitution ("The large private corporation fits oddly into democratic theory and vision. Indeed, it does not fit") (Lindblom 1977, 356). This last statement earned him a nasty editorial by the Mobil Corporation on the Op-Ed page of the *New York Times* (February 9, 1978), but the fact is that Lindblom is impaled on the horns of a dilemma. With Tugwell, he would agree that the power of corporations must be checked. But with Banfield and Wildavsky, he is led to argue that any form of "central decision-making" is bad, because synoptic decisions are either "impossible" or "immoral."

to examine the actual workings of American society. As early as the mid-1970s, it was clear to him that we were not living in "normal" times, that large private corporations had effective veto power over decisions in the public domain, and that there were defined social classes whose interests are often diverging. The polyarchal system, then, is at best lumpy. And historical reality is very different from the ideal-type of mutual partisan adjustment. Still, when it comes to resolving this conflict, Lindblom retreats to his model even while talking vaguely about constitutional reform. Human ability to do comprehensive planning analysis is so deeply flawed that we are condemned to grope forever in the dark. The answers we derive from analysis are illusions.[22] Better, then, to rely on short-term "interactions" among the principals involved in given situations—a pluralist politics—than to make grandiose plans whose consequences we cannot hope to control. The outcomes of such a politics might not be the best we would hope for; they are simply all we can get. Alternative planning systems, based on synoptic analysis such as the Soviet Union's, where citizen-subjects are forced to live with planners' error-prone analysis, do even worse.

Conclusion

From Bentham to Lindblom, from Saint-Simon to Etzioni and Perloff, social reform is the grand tradition of planning theory. Over the past fifty years, it produced not only the first models of institutionalized planning in the United States (Person, Tugwell), but also scores of notable monographs as well as three great synoptic treatises; Mannheim's *Man and Society in an Age of Reconstruction*, Dahl and Lindblom's *Politics, Economics, and Welfare*, and Etzioni's *The Active Society*. In addition, it encouraged the invention of the major quantitative models for calculation in central planning, including social accounting, input-output analysis, economic policy models, and models for urban and regional analysis.

Major philosophical systems inform the tradition. From the eighteenth century, it inherited Bentham's utilitarianism; from the nineteenth century, Comtean positivism; and from the twentieth century, Dewey's pragmatism and Popper's critical rationalism. Each of

22. In a little book on the uses of the social sciences in problem solving, Lindblom and Cohen report on a conversation with a critic. "Do you want to suggest," asks the critic, "that professional social inquiry fails to do as well as it might, or do you want also to suggest that it often positively obstructs social problem solving?" To which Lindblom and his co-author curtly reply, "We want to suggest both" (Lindblom and Cohen 1979, 86).

these thinkers added a distinctive feature to the tradition. From Bentham, the social reformers learned to look at the consequences of potential action and to measure their costs and benefits; from Comte, they acquired a deep respect for the empirical study of society; from Dewey, they borrowed the image of social experimentation; and from Popper, they learned about the difference between piecemeal and utopian engineering.

Finally, we must again be reminded of the towering figure of Max Weber, who traced the lineaments of a rationalized society and believed that in the practice of each, science and politics could and should be held apart. Only in this way could the practitioners each do that for which they were best suited: scientists to produce knowledge and politicians to produce policy decisions. All social reformers were interested in reforms, particularly in "grand" reforms of the "guidance system" of society. Economists developed information systems of considerable power, while the more philosophically inclined dreamed of central planning institutions, the "directive in history," and a "collective mind." In modified form, many of these institutional innovations were actually put in place.

As Banfield noted, reformers tend to believe in the perfectibility of the world. This was as true for early planning theorists as for later contributors. Dewey, for example, credits Bentham with "radical" social change, which he calls a "capacity for bold and comprehensive social intervention combined with detailed study of particulars and with courage in action" (Dewey 1963a, 15). And Saint-Simon, like his English contemporary, was a world improver of the most ambitious sort. In our own century, Mannheim searched for a "third way" between market anarchy and totalitarian dictatorship, and a full generation later, Etzioni dreamed of an "active society" pursuing common projects that define its destiny. In the early 1950s, Dahl and Lindblom laid out seven basic ends of action; freedom, rationality, democracy, subjective equality, security, progress, and appropriate inclusion. In one form or another, these values have instructed all of the contributors to the reform tradition. Among them were centralists, such as Tugwell and Perloff, who thought that it was necessary to strengthen the state by establishing within the executive branch (or independently) an institutionalized intelligence that would lay out the future for the collectivity as a whole. Others stressed more decentralized, problem-avoiding strategies. But virtually all reformers believed in the need for some form of institutional change. And when an opportunity presented itself, as it did for Tugwell in the 1930s and early 1940s and for the planners of the community action program in the 1960s, they behaved very much like innovative planners, marshaling resources and acting in committed, politically conscious ways to produce a significant change in the system of societal guidance.

There has been a tendency to write off these efforts as failures. I do not believe this to be an accurate, fair judgment. It is true that hopes and expectations often outpaced actual accomplishments. Had they not done so, the accomplishments might well have been less. Some forms of planning were successfully institutionalized at central levels in the United States (in the Office of Management and Budget, for example); the Puerto Rican planning system continues to function to this day as a regular part of the Commonwealth Government; Wesley Mitchell lived to witness a Council of Economic Advisors installed in the president's office; and thanks in large measure to the efforts of Harvey Perloff, the regional approach to planning has become a worldwide practice. None of these planning institutions have delivered, perhaps, all that their originators dreamed they might. Perhaps they have not made the world more perfect. But to say this is not to write them off as failures.

Social reformers, it is true, typically addressed themselves to the rulers of society. Reforms came from the top, they thought. Some were convinced that only "comprehensive" planning had merit; others permitted only "piecemeal social engineering." Most of them stayed shy of politics, which they tended to equate with all that was "irrational" in society. Like Weber, they were torn between an asceticism of the mind and a passionate commitment to orderly change. On the whole, they believed that a "general interest" could be formulated through the instrumentalities and procedures of planning, that most people of good will would subscribe to such an interest, and that it was therefore safe to suppose that the consensus necessary for democratic planning might actually be obtained. Some, like Mannheim and Etzioni, thought that such a consensus would itself have to be planned: they regarded the process of consensus-formation as a central and continuing elite activity, Mannheim through reforming education and altering personality structures, Etzioni through more frankly political activity.

It was different for Tugwell. Long experience in public life and many disappointments had taught him that consensus-formation, although possible, might not be probable, and that more structural changes were needed. He spent the final years of his long life on a project of constitutional reform. It was for him what a civil religion had been for Saint-Simon and Comte, the desperate end-of-life project of one who had set out to leave the world more perfect than he had found it in his youth.

4   Planning as Policy Analysis

What Is Policy Analysis?

The years 1968–1972 witnessed the emergence of policy analysis as a fledgling field of professional practice. As it greeted the world, it had something of the brashness of youth, but like any adolescent who steps out into the world, its swagger disguised an underlying insecurity and doubts about its own identity.

By the end of the sixties, it had been in gestation, so to speak, for most of a generation. Over a period of three decades, analytical techniques and methods had been developed, and there had been abundant opportunity, both during and after the war, to try out its skills at "problem solving," especially in the military services. Then came that turbulent decade of victory and defeat, with John F. Kennedy's assassination, the War on Poverty, the rise of black power, the assassinations of Martin Luther King and Robert Kennedy, and Vietnam—a decade that culminated, in 1969, in the dramatic landing of the first human beings on the moon. Despite the widespread conviction that America was passing through an unprecedented cultural revolution, or perhaps precisely because of this consciousness, Etzioni's *The Active Society* (1968) seemed to sum up what we wanted most to believe as a people: that perhaps it was possible, after all, to accomplish great things as a nation, that societal guidance was not merely a utopian dream. Policy analysis promised to become the gyroscope that would help to keep us on a steady course. It was, proclaimed Herbert Simon, a new "science of design" (H. Simon 1982; orig. 1969).

But, as an astute critic observed, it was also a business.

> Taught in universities, bought by private business and government agencies, and sold by a growing cadre of experts, systems analysis is a commodity commanding high prices and ready acceptance at home and abroad. (Hoos 1972, 1–2)

137

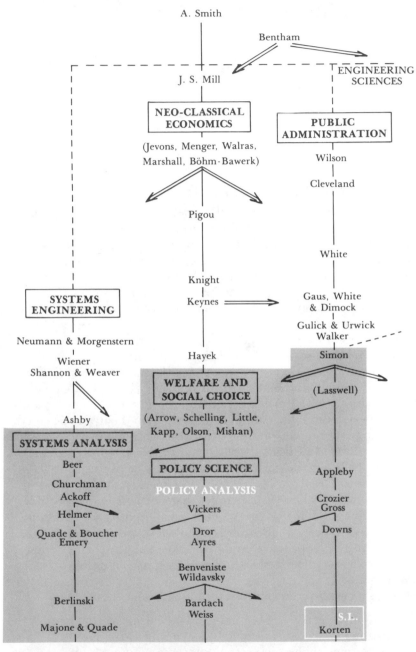

Figure 9. The policy analysis tradition of planning.

The basic model is shown in Figure 10, below.

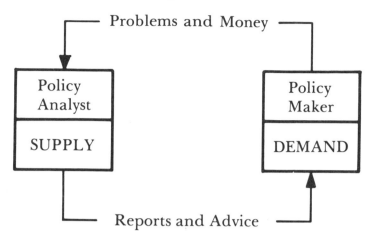

Figure 10. An economic model of policy analysis.

With proper packaging, suppliers might actually succeed in creating a demand for what they had to sell.[1]

As a field, policy analysis resulted from the confluence of three streams of intellectual discourse: *systems engineering* with its strong bias for quantitative modeling (Quade 1966; Quade and Boucher 1968); *management science* with its leanings toward a general-systems-theory approach that emphasized the cybernetics of "open" systems (Churchman et al. 1957; Ackhoff 1962; Beer 1966; Emery 1969; Ackoff and Emery 1972); and the *political and administrative sciences* with their behavioral orientation, focus on political institutions, and greater acknowledgment than either of the other two traditions of the role of nonrational behavior in human affairs (Bauer and Gergen 1968; Dror 1968, 1971; Lasswell 1971). What made the convergence of these three traditions possible was a shared belief that, first, the objective methods of science could and, indeed, should be used to make policy decisions more rational and second, that more rational decisions would materially improve the problem-solving abilities of organizations.[2] In addition, proponents of all three

1. For well-documented studies of policy research conducted for the U.S. Government, see Horowitz and Katz (1975) and Guttman and Willner (1976).

2. The Comtean ideal of a nomothetic social science continues to inform the social scientific establishment, especially in the United States, despite its epistemological impossibility. For example, the ethos of the National Science Foundation (NSF) has been described by one of the foundation's high functionaries as "modeling the social

"streams" of policy analysis worked with a concept of system that involved, at its most elementary level, inputs, outputs, an environment, and complex "feedback loops." The vocabulary of systems tended to drive out the more discursive language of the social sciences. Society was being assimilated to the image of a machine.[3]

Addressing a spellbound audience at Massachusetts Institute of Technology in 1968, Herbert Simon stated convincingly that the new meta-discipline of design would replace older humanistic traditions.

> The proper study of mankind has been said to be man. But I have argued that man—or at least the intellectual component of man—may be relatively simple, that most of the complexity of his behavior may be drawn from man's environment, from man's search for good designs. If I have made my case, then we can conclude that, in large part, the proper study of mankind is the science of design not only as the professional component of a technical education but as a discipline for every educated person. (H. Simon 1982, 159; orig. 1969)

Some of the subjects that Simon thought should supplement, if not replace, history, art, literature, and speculative philosophy included statistical decision theory, linear and dynamic programming, imperative and declarative logics of design, heuristic search procedures, the theory of hierarchical systems and design organization, and problems of representation. Simon envisioned the dawn of a new age in which artificial intelligence, linked to human minds in synergistic fashion, would triumph.

Once it had broken free of its chrysalis, policy analysis quickly developed all the characteristics of a maturing field of professional expertise. Within fourteen years, sixteen journals were started; several graduate programs were established at major universities; areas of professional sub-specialization were identified; and there

science after the natural sciences" (Aborn 1984, 34). (On the epistemological errors of this equation, see Ulrich 1983, ch. 1.)

3. Murray Aborn concludes his historical essay on the social indicators project at the NSF with these words: "[T]he most important single factor in the success of any future revival of the social indicators movement will not be what the social sciences have to offer, but rather *the extent to which society has shaped itself around the concepts underlying the employment of social indicators as well as the mechanisms of their production*" (Aborn 1984, 41; italics added). In short, says Aborn, society must be fitted to the technology of its domination by planners and the social interests they serve. For it is altogether idealistic to suppose, as Judith de Neufville does in her social indicators book (1975), that indicators can serve some neutral purpose in policy discussion.

was both a growing self-consciousness about the use of analytical methods and a tough-minded critique from within the profession that contributed, in the late 1970s, to the emergence of a second generation of policy models. These marks of a growing professionalization are documented in Appendix B.

During its halcyon days—a scarce two decades ago—policy analysis was inclined to declare itself bravely "a new science, a new ethos." I have already cited Simon's vision of a "science of design." Policy analysis was clearly to belong to this new science, and it found the world sadly corrupted. In order to be showered with its blessings, declared the prophets, the world would first have to reform itself! Some of the pronouncements of the period sound every bit a parody of Luigi Pirandello's famous play *A Science in Search of a Client*.

> If, however, evaluative research is to make its full contribution, substantial changes must be made in society's overall approach to social programming. Legislators and other public officials reflecting widespread public concern must raise significantly their demands for the effectiveness and efficiency of programs. In addition, they must learn to focus more on program goals so that they can assume a more experimental attitude toward specific programming strategies. . . . Such fundamental changes in attitude would lead to greatly expanded interest in evaluative research. (Caro 1971, 28)

One of the originators of operations research (and pamphleteer *extraordinaire*), Sir Stafford Beer, announced "Complexity is the very stuff of today's world," as though it were a big discovery. And to *manage* complexity—this was his favorite expression—a new science was required that would offer the means to:

1. Measure and manipulate complexity through mathematics.

2. Design complex systems through general systems theory.

3. Devise viable organizations through cybernetics.

4. Work effectively with people through behavioral science.

5. Apply all this to practical affairs through operational research (Beer 1975, 380–381).

Beer thought that society was "frivolling" away its opportunities. "Society," he reflected gloomily, "proceeds instead by *consensus*, that lowest common denominator of alternative democracies" (ibid.). And like his predecessor, Saint-Simon, he piously concluded:

Change cannot occur within the framework of the existing ethic: mankind needs to formulate a new ethic relevant to the problems that face the species today. The basis of this ethic is a true and not spurious compassion for the real and not imagined plight of mankind—two thirds being undernourished and three thirds being under threat of extinction. The key to applying this ethic is:

* recognition that technology makes mankind as a whole unimaginably wealthy
* recognition that this wealth is largely consumed by massive waste
* a willingness to reorganize society to eliminate waste thereby to finance the eudemony of man
* facing up to and conquering any entailed threat to personal freedom. (Ibid. 389)

Like most manifestos of the period, Beer's message was addressed to other analysts, and it exhorted them to learn the new skills of their craft.

It is true that leaders of the policy analysis movement insisted, time and again, that techniques were not enough, that simple techniques were frequently more effective than sophisticated ones, that questions of problem and goal definition were vastly more important than optimization procedures, and that professional judgment was absolutely essential in all phases of analysis (Quade and Boucher 1968). But analysts were left to discover for themselves how to acquire this wisdom.[4]

Given the significance attached to professional judgment, it is surprising how little attention was paid in the early years of the profession to the subject matter of specific analysis. After all, the analyst's effectiveness as an advisor was said to depend, in large measure, on his or her knowledge of the historical and institutional context for decision. To obtain such knowledge, an extended period of exposure to reality was essential, and this suggested a sectoral

---

4. As Horowitz and Katz pointed out, professional judgment may not be very much in demand.

Policy makers prefer the use of quantitative aspects of social science in the formation of decisions. The presumed exact and orderly nature of the quantitative approach has inherent appeal to the policy makers in their attempts to order and audit political options and the implications of their choices. The rising value of the social sciences to basic types of decisions requires its growing use at a time of internal turmoil over the essential nature and tasks of the social sciences. (Horowitz and Katz 1975, 46)

breakdown of analysts according to major specializations (for example, transport, land use management, national defense, public health, food and agriculture, energy, housing, and education). Although many of these planning specializations are embodied in identifiable communities of professional analysts, universal problem-solving abilities were proclaimed as the most distinctive feature of an analyst. Wrote the first dean of Berkeley's Graduate School of Public Policy:

> *Emphasize analysis, not subject matter.* Keep moving from one substantive area to another—from health, to welfare, to transportation, to energy, to whatever. . . . Analysis is a stance, not a technique: no one set of operations can be taught as the essence of analysis. But there is a way of looking at things in terms of opportunity costs, or what must be given up to do whatever one wishes, or problem solving and a "can-do" view of the world. . . . There is a model, a structure of resources and objectives, with a criterion for choosing among alternatives. Confidence grows. (Wildavsky 1979, 414)

If policy analysts have a language in common, it is, as mentioned earlier, the language of systems, with its reference to boundaries, environment, equifinality, steady state, recursiveness, feedback, and black box. This language has changed the very ways we think about the world, and before we pass on to a brief account of the history of the field, it may be useful to sum up in what specific ways it has done so.[5]

1. Systems theory has changed our views about causality. We no longer think in terms of linear relations of the form $A \longrightarrow B$, but instead we take into account the possibility of feedback: $A \quad B$. Causality, we now know, is complex and circular. This knowledge relieves us of Weber's burden of responsibility, since actions are seldom efficient, setting in motion a complex web of actions and reactions whose ultimate outcome is unforeseeable.

2. Systems theory has introduced us to the notion that every "open" system is surrounded by an "environment" with which it is in constant interchange, gathering or dissipating energies or achieving a "steady state." Systems must consequently adapt

5. The following is culled from eclectic reading in systems theory. See, for example, von Bertalanffy (1968), Emery (1969), Ackoff and Emery (1972), Lilienfeld (1978), and Churchman (1979a, b).

to their environment by introjecting parts of it (enlarging system boundaries), controlling other parts (which requires energy), or conforming to external conditions in ways that will maintain a condition of steady state within.

3. Systems theory is based on the implicit assumption that all systemic relations are fundamentally harmonious, so long as the system itself remains in a state of equilibrium with its environment. Fundamental conflict is not a systems concept. This assumption allows us to think of systems as inherently benign and manageable.

4. All systems, it is said, conform to the principle of hierarchy, which is perceived as the "deep structure" of the world. This assumption makes it easy to accept the notion of "controlling overlayers" and sociopolitical elites (Etzioni). Hierarchies are derived from natural laws (the conservation of energy, the capacity of information channels, distance-decay relationships) and are therefore unavoidable.

5. Systems theory tends to be reductionist. As Lilienfeld has noted, "All things are systems by virtue of ignoring the specific, the concrete, the substantive" (Lilienfeld 1978, 192). This accounts for the reluctance of policy analysts to declare their substantive, sectoral interests. The search for a General System Theory, with its alluring prospect, has so far failed to yield significant meta-theories capable of integrating all knowledge. Still, from time to time, world-shattering conclusions are announced which, because they are unverifiable, substitute for the more empirically grounded knowledge of separate disciplines or specific interdisciplinary work.[6]

A Brief History

The emergence of three mainstreams of policy analysis from their parent disciplines—systems engineering, management science, and the political and administrative sciences—was the outcome of several decades of increasing interaction between academia and the main poles of power in American society, business and government. On one hand, there was substantial new theoretical work in a number of sciences that, in skilled hands, could be transmuted into "operational" analysis; on the other, there was a growing demand for such analysis, accelerated by a succession of events unprecedented

6. For a withering critique of General System Theory and its related modeling efforts, see Berlinski (1976).

in their scale and severity: a world economic depression, a global war of shattering ferocity, and a period of rapid recovery paralleled by the dissolution of empires, national wars of liberation, and the emergence of a score of newly sovereign nations in Asia, Africa, and the Middle East. But this demand for policy analysis, a heretofore nonexisting commodity, had to be generated first before it could translate into contracts, money, and fame. The growth of policy analysis was a supply-led expansion that raised to positions of influence what many believed were members of a new professional-managerial class (P. Walker 1979; Gouldner 1979).[7]

Social scientists were no more averse to climbing to the top than ordinary folk. The indomitable Auguste Comte had spent a lifetime currying the favors of the powerful; his dearest wish was to be summoned as an advisor to the rulers of the world. Max Weber had been a member of the Verein für Sozialpolitik, which was dedicated to the use of scientific surveys as an instrument of social reform. Karl Mannheim thought that a free-floating intelligentsia, disconnected from social class, was uniquely fitted for the tasks of social reconstruction; and Rexford Tugwell had actually been successful in his quest for power, becoming first a major force in the councils of government in Washington, D.C., and subsequently governor of Puerto Rico.

On the eve of World War II, the distinguished American sociologist, Robert Stoughton Lynd, wrote a small book bearing the urgent title *Knowledge for What?* (1939). Addressed to his fellow academicians, it held out to them an exciting vision of how their work, directed at what he believed to be the proper questions, might contribute to major structural reforms in the political economy of the country. In a series of what he called outrageous hypotheses, he suggested that social scientists engage in probing, among other things:

> the need for a large and pervasive extension of planning and controls to many areas now left to casual individual initiative
>
> . . .

---

7. The emergence of such a "class" had been announced by James Burnham's notorious *The Managerial Revolution* (1941), which has set many a sociologist in search of a new constellation of power in America. But as Goldhammer (1978) astutely observed, there is all the difference in the world between being powerful and being an advisor to the powerful. And policy planners had no choice but to become advisors or the teachers of advisors. By themselves, they had no power at all, not even a realistic prospect of power.

> the need to extend democracy markedly as an efficient reality in government, industry, and other areas of living . . .
>
> the proposition that private capitalism does not now operate to assure the amount of general welfare to which the present stage . . . entitles us. (Lynd 1939, 209–220)

Social-scientific knowledge, he admonished his peers, should be placed in the interest of "functionally more useful kinds of order" (ibid. 126). It must become a weapon in the struggle against Veblen's "vested interests," helping to restore a sense of hope to a culture in the midst of crisis.

It is ironic to observe the contrast between Lynd's idealistic radicalism and the technical roles that academicians would actually assume as analysts of public policy. Among the scientists working for the Rand Corporation and MITRE in the 1950s, there was very little talk of structural reform: their client was the U.S. Air Force. Even when a number of consulting firms, Rand among them, began to shift into civilian work, this was still true; reform was not their business. Policy analysts had an image of themselves as experts working to improve the decision-making of the powerful. If they succeeded in this, it would reinforce their power. Under the guise of scientific objectivity, they played a profoundly conservative role.[8]

During World War II, many social scientists drifted into Washington, D.C., where they worked on problems of psychological warfare, military selection and training, military intelligence, propaganda, production planning, rationing and price control, and strategic services. They joined another group of scientists, mathematicians, and engineers who, albeit geographically more dispersed, were working for the government on new weaponry such as radar and rockets and the atomic bomb. This opportunity to work against deadlines and with few restrictions on expenditure no doubt enabled them to speed up processes of innovation that might otherwise have taken decades to accomplish. Their wartime effort issued in new theories that would soon find practical application—through the electronic computer and communication satellites, for example—in civilian life as well.

8. This is made abundantly clear by the massive involvement of policy analysis with the military services. But, as Horowitz and Katz point out, the matter is not quite so simple, and social science may also, on occasion, promote social change. "Social science," they write, "not only encourages change (when a prior consensus dissolves) but may also protect order (when a prior consensus is present). Thus, social science cannot be seen as simply a 'change agent' or as an 'establishment tool' " (Horowitz and Katz 1975, 50).

After the war, Sputnik and the arms race ensured that, at least for a while, there would be plenty of jobs for systems analysts and engineers. The matter was different for social scientists. Having moved in the ambit of power during the war, many were reluctant, when peace broke out, to return to their poorly paid jobs in the academy. In the wake of Stouffer's impressive two-volume treatise on *The American Soldier* (1949), they rallied themselves to produce a rather odd collection of essays, bravely entitled *The Policy Sciences: Recent Developments in Scope and Methods* (Lerner and Lasswell 1951).[9] The authors could hardly have guessed that it would take another twenty years before their collective work would mature to the point at which they might actually lay claim to the terrain of policy analysis (Lasswell 1971).

Setting the tone for the volume, Charles Easton Rothwell of the Hoover Institute and Library at Stanford University began by invoking the terrible reality of the atomic bomb.

> General Omar Bradley recently described our age as one of "nuclear giants and ethical infants." He found much to be apprehensive about in a civilization whose fumbling efforts to resolve the problems of human relations are in such tragic contrast with its mastery over the inanimate. Each new atomic explosion symbolized more ominously the disaster that can overtake mankind unless we learn to meet the problems of harmonious living as skillfully and surely as we have conquered those of organized violence. (Lerner and Lasswell 1951, vii)

The answer to this awesome discrepancy between the "mastery over the inanimate" and "fumbling efforts to resolve the problems of human relations" was to be planning, he said.

> Planning suggests a systematic attempt to shape the future. When such planning becomes a prelude to action, it is policy making. (Ibid. ix)

Part I of the symposium concerned the scope and focus of the policy sciences, with contributions from Ernest Hilgard and Daniel Lerner on the person, Edward Shils on the primary group, Mar-

9. Name changes are sometimes meant to work like magic, creating a reality that is not there. In the early decades of the nineteenth century, when the status of the natural sciences was at high tide, a social *science* was newly born, though it was but the old scholarship tradition in new clothes. When social scientists wanted to be hired as advisors by government, they called themselves *policy scientists*. And when they looked at possibilities of planned intervention, they added psychology to the lot and called it *behavioral* science.

garet Mead on national character, Clyde Kluckhohn on culture, and Lasswell himself on world organization. Even this abbreviated listing makes it apparent that, at the time, the so-called policy sciences were still closely identified with the humanist tradition in sociology, cultural anthropology, and social psychology. How these theories were to be mapped into practice was, in 1951, still far from clear.

Part II was concerned with research procedures. Here, the shift from the language of philosophical discourse of the first 120 pages to the language of technical analysis is striking. Hans Reichenbach reviewed probability methods in the social sciences, Kenneth Arrow wrote on mathematical modeling, Paul Lazarsfeld discussed qualitative measurements, Alex Bavelas looked at "communication patterns in task-oriented groups," and Herbert Hyman of the National Opinion Research Center took a critical look at interviewing as a scientific procedure.

A third part, entitled Policy Integration, was devoted to a series of disconnected essays on such diverse topics as the psychology of economic behavior, sample surveys, psychological warfare, the natural sciences in policy formation, and research policy. It was not at all what the section title promised in somewhat programmatic fashion. Indeed, without a specific problem in view, it is difficult to see how the intergration of policy could have been anything but a rhetorical phrase.

In retrospect, one can see how, only a few years after World War II, the social and behavioral sciences were still searching for a legitimate role for themselves. Distinguished scientists all, the authors were talking chiefly to themselves rather than to potential clients. They were unsure of what they had to offer. Unlike Lynd, they had no radical program in view.

The Lerner-Lasswell symposium was followed within the next twelve years or so by a series of theoretical and methodological innovations that would give the newfangled "policy sciences" a tough core of common ideas. Only a brief listing of these innovations is possible here (see Chart 3). Notably absent are the speculations concerning national character, culture, and world organization that had been prominent at an earlier time. The world of the social sciences was being taken over by the engineers. Cybernetics, statistical decision theory, and organization theory were the new code words.[10]

10. In British usage, which attempts to suppress the use of nouns as adjectives, American operations research becomes operational research. But the two are identical in meaning.

Chart 3   **Major Innovations in Policy Analysis:**
Theory and Method, 1944–1966

---

1. *Systems Engineering, Applied Mathematics, and Statistics*
   Game theory (von Neumann and Morgenstern 1953 [orig. 1944]; Luce
   and Raiffa 1957)
   Cybernetics (Wiener 1950, 1959 [orig. 1948])
   Information theory (Shannon and Weaver 1949)
   Statistical decision theory (Savage 1954)
   Operations research (Churchman et al. 1957; Ackoff 1962; Beer 1966)
   Linear programming (Dantzig 1963)

2. *Economics and Political and Administrative Sciences*
   Welfare economics (Reder 1947; Myint 1948; Baumol 1952; Little 1957)
   Choice theory (Arrow 1963 [orig. 1951]; Olson 1965; Barry and Hardin
   1982)
   Econometrics (Cowles Commission monographs; Tinbergen 1951,
   1964; Theil 1964)
   Organization theory (H. Simon 1976 [orig. 1945]; H. Simon 1957;
   March and Simon 1958; Cyert and March 1963)

In 1951, Harold Lasswell may have been a harbinger of good tidings, but the key personality in the development of policy analysis was indubitably Herbert Simon. His book *Administrative Behavior*, originally published in 1945, was like a time fuse that, a full quarter century later, would set off an explosion in the tremendous excitement about policy analysis. It also contributed to a major reworking of the intellectual foundations of public administration (H. Simon et al. 1950).[11] Simon's early work, in municipal administration (Ridley and Simon 1943), had shown him to be a careful observer of bureaucratic practices, even as it revealed his interest in the formal problem of allocative efficiency. How was a public administrator to know whether his or her decisions were correct?[12] Throughout Simon's life, the question remained one of his central concerns.

11. Woodrow Wilson's essay "The Study of Administration" (1887) is regarded as the starting point of public administration as a professional field. It quickly absorbed the lessons and concepts of scientific management (Taylor 1919; Follett 1920, 1924) and moved on to develop its own language and concerns. Like scientific management, the study of public administration was Comtean in its inspiration, an influence that ultimately traces back to Saint-Simon. The early public administration, roughly to the end of World War II, leaned heavily on the formulation of "normative" principles of good administration (Waldo 1948). A behaviorally oriented public administration begins with Simon (1976; orig. 1945) and with the textbook to which Simon himself was a major contributor (H. Simon et al. 1950).

12. This question echoes the existential cry of R. D. Laing: "I want to live correctly.

In a major departure from Weber's ideal-typical mode of description, Simon focused on actually existing bureaucracies, carefully describing, and then modeling, observed behavior. The result of this inductive process was a large number of specific hypotheses which, in keeping with the prevailing spirit of positivism, were presented as having potentially universal validity. Two major commitments guided Simon's exploration of organization theory. The first was an assumption that organizations are hierarchical in structure. The second was his concern with central (policy) decisions and how they might be made more rational.[13] Hierarchy, decision-making, and control went hand in hand. As a student of administration, Simon was interested in top management, and management values inform all of his work. Given his behavioral perspective, however, it is curious how little attention he paid to the shadow side of management, the dynamics of power. The word *power* does not even appear in the index of *Administrative Behavior*. Though pervasive in all organizations, power struggles were incapable of being reconciled with Simon's model of "administrative man" (H. Simon 1957). Power was consequently excised from his studies. This omission was not without consequences, since the counterattack of conventional social science on the scientific model of policy analysis came precisely from those who, like Aaron Wildavsky, were primarily students of the politics of power.

On the other hand, the decision-making approach was analytically very strong. Among other things, it allowed Simon to link the study of administration to neo-classical economics, the information sciences, and systems engineering, a route that eventually led him to a long involvement with studies in the psychology of decision-making and the logic of artificial intelligence.

To live correctly cannot be wrong. There must be a correct way to live. That way must conform to the nature of life, and to what is the case." Should bureaucrats be so very different from psychiatrists?

13. One is never quite sure with Simon whether he is merely describing existing conditions or prescribing ideal behavior. This is an inherent difficulty also in neo-classical economics, from which Simon draws heavily. There was a time in Simon's career when he was concerned with the question of how to make better decisions. "The rationality of decisions," he wrote, "that is, their appropriateness for the accomplishment of specified goals—becomes the central concern of administrative theory" (H. Simon, 1976, 240). In his introduction to the third edition of *Administrative Behavior*, however, he proposes the "boundary between the rational and the non-rational aspects of human behavior" as a new central concern (ibid. xxviii). Lest this remain obscure, he clarifies: "Administrative theory is peculiarly the theory of intended and bounded rationality—of the behavior of human beings who *satisfice* because they have not the wits to *maximize*" (ibid.).

A significant contribution to the problem of decision-making was Simon's notion that administrative rationality was "bounded." Decision makers, said Simon, could never be completely rational in the sense of having *total* knowledge of a situation and the alternatives available to them. In practice, there were always limitations of time, resources, and intelligence. In practice, a person's knowledge of consequences was at best fragmentary and the alternatives examined always few. Under the circumstances, one had to make decisions the best one could. One had to select the course of action that would somehow manage to satisfy major organizational values. The pragmatic decision problem was rarely how to optimize one's values; to "satisfice" them was all that one could reasonably expect. One simply chose that course of action that appeared to be "good enough." And how did one know that it was good enough? Well, said Simon, "the first test, and perhaps not the least important, is the test of common sense" (H. Simon 1976, xxx).

As a decision rule, it was as comfortable and ultimately as meaningless to live with satisficing as it was to follow Lindblom's "muddling through": neither criterion helped very much when one wanted to do things a mite better. They seemed to be advising, in the language of the social sciences, what everyone was doing anyway, that is, to somehow manage to get by.

More important than the elusive criterion of satisficing was Simon's focus on the making of decisions. In the first place, decision-making elevated *cognition* over *action*.[14] Simon paid scant attention to the problem of implementation. So long as decisions were made rationally (and planners were to have a major role in this), it was assumed that the rest would take care of itself. Action, counteraction, and strategy were not part of Simon's vocabulary. His framework also made it difficult to consider informal organizations, such as small groups; non-hierarchical forms of decision-making (participatory processes, networks); non–goal-oriented behavior (social learning);[15] the politics of implementation; and other conflictive processes. Simon also assumed, and presumably this, too, stemmed

14. Strictly speaking, Simon's focus was on *pre*–decision-making, since decisions that commit moral, physical, or economic resources to certain tasks are evidently also a kind of action. The logic of action, however, can be shown to be very different from the logic of decision. One is driven to conclude that decisions are located at precisely the point where logics of thinking and of action intersect.

15. In his more recent work (1982), Simon appears to be backing away from his earlier insistence on goal-directed behavior. In a fascinating essay on "Social Planning: Designing the Evolving Artifact," he suggests a process of designing *without* final goals. With this concept, he moves very close to the position of the social learning theorists to be discussed in the next chapter.

from his blindness to the possibilities of an action model of organizational behavior, that rationality is always to be preferred, that *to be rational is good*.

Now it is easy to demonstrate that this last assumption, actually a particle of faith, is factually incorrect. Hirschman (1967), for instance, argued that it was precisely our *ignorance* of consequences that made us dare to undertake new ventures, and Moore and Tumin (1964) added other reasons: ignorance as a preserver of privileged position, as a reinforcement of traditional values, as a preserver of fair competition, and as a preserver of stereotypes. Ignorance, concluded Moore and Tumin, "is an active and often positive element in operating structures and relations" (Moore and Tumin 1964, 527). But rationality requires the replacement of ignorance with knowledge. It follows that, in given circumstances, greater rationality (in the sense of having fuller knowledge) may well run counter to the best interests of a decision maker.

Nevertheless, Simon's decision model became the centerpiece of a reconstructed theory of organizations. Overall, it was a static theory, emphasizing structure over developmental change.[16] Eventually, it would be supplemented by Charles Lindblom's more dynamic, interactive model of partisan mutual adjustment (1959, 1965), which was discussed at length in the preceding chapter.

Even as Lindblom was developing his theories, the Rand Corporation in Santa Monica, California, was attempting to package a so-called systems approach to policy questions. Established in 1948, Rand—the name stood for Research and Development—was a nonprofit think tank for the U.S. Air Force. In the course of its work, it brought together a remarkably talented group of men. Many Rand analysts were drawn from academic life, and virtually all of the world's leading analysts worked, at one time or another, as Rand consultants or else, like Yehezkel Dror, spent time there as a research fellow.

The major promotional literature was put together by two Rand scientists: Edward S. Quade, who wrote *Analysis for Military Decisions* in 1966, and W. I. Boucher, who, in collaboration with Quade, wrote *Systems Analysis and Policy Planning* in 1968. Based on lecture courses at Rand in 1959 and 1965, respectively, both books were primarily intended for *users* of systems analysis (at the time, most of the users were with the military services), and they were designed to answer questions such as, What is systems analysis? Why is it neces-

16. The process theory of organizations came to be known as *organization development* and will be discussed in the next chapter.

sary? When and where is it appropriate? How does one approach and carry out systems analysis? What methods can be used? How can a good analysis be recognized? What can one expect from a systems analysis? How has analysis changed over the years? Why? What changes can be expected in the future (Quade and Boucher 1968, vi)?

In an early memorandum, Quade had defined systems analysis as an "approach to complex problems of choice under uncertainty" (Quade 1963, 1). But he candidly admitted that the approach was "by no means fully developed, nor were its successes and failures . . . completely understood" (Quade 1966, v).

According to Quade, systems analysis involved four discrete steps (see Figure 11).[17] They were presented as an iterative process in which the "complexity of the 'full' problem frequently far outruns analytic competence" (Quade 1963, 10), and analysis "must be tempered with and used alongside experience, judgment, and intuition" (ibid. 28).[18]

A recurrent theme in Quade's writings is the importance of "considered judgment." This is true for all steps in the process, as in modeling, for instance.

> For most phenomena, there are many possible representations; the appropriate model depends as much *on the question being asked* as on the phenomenon about which it is asked. There are . . . no universal models. (Ibid. 17)

17. A fifth step, or verification, was added for the sake of logical completion. Since real-world experiments can rarely be carried out, however, verification is usually impossible. Because of this, the learning curve of systems analysis tend to be rather low: ideal proposals succeed each other over time, but there is little advance. (See, however, the proposals to use social experimentation as a method in policy and program evaluation: Campbell 1971 and Riecken and Boruch 1974.)

18. According to Quade,

> there is no clear line of demarcation between operations research and what we are calling systems analysis. Until recently, operations research has tended to emphasize mathematical models and optimization techniques. . . . The systems analyst, on the other hand, is likely to be forced to deal with the problems in which the difficulty lies in deciding what ought to be done, not simply in how to do it. In such a situation, far more attention must be devoted to establishing objectives, criteria, and alternatives. The total analysis is thus a more complex and less neat and tidy procedure which is seldom suitable for a quantitative optimization over the whole problem. (Quade 1963, 2)

At the time, the most advanced text in operations research was probably Ackoff (1962). But the distinction that Quade was trying to draw in 1963 has become blurred.

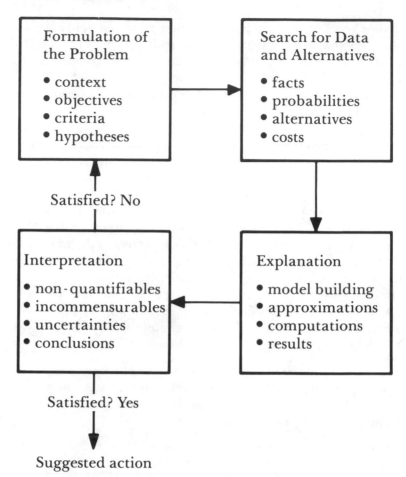

Figure 11. Activities in policy analysis. (From Quade 1963, 11. Reproduced with permission of the Rand Corporation)

Models, in fact, are ad hoc theories, and their elaboration is a skill resembling the practice of an art or craft.

> Considered judgment differs from intuitive judgment in that the logic behind the opinion is made explicit. Both are based on an individual's experience and background, but when the reasoning is explicit, an observer can form his own opinion from the information presented. Judgment permeates systems analysis. . . . The ideal is to keep all judgments in plain view. (Ibid. 14)

The matter of judgment was difficult to discuss. The books sponsored by Rand preferred to deal with topics such as linear programming, the theory of games, applied dynamic programming, mathematical optimization techniques, and the theory of branching processes. It was for its quantitative approach and other esoteric "social technologies" that Rand had achieved fame. After all, there might be many people who would claim to know about a problem and have a "judgment" about it. But mathematicians were few.

The field of management science showed less restraint than Rand in its approach to policy analysis. Its point of departure was General Systems Theory (GST) which, for about a decade, had held a number of very capabale scholars in thrall, among them Kenneth Boulding (an economist) and Anatole Rapoport (a mathematical biologist), with whom the originator of GST, the Austrian biologist Ludwig von Bertalanffy, had founded the Society for General Systems Research in 1954. The society's functions were to:

> (1) investigate the isomorphy of concepts, laws, and models in various fields, and to help in useful transfers from one field to another; (2) encourage the development of adequate theoretical models in the fields which lack them; (3) minimize the duplication of theoretical effort in different fields; (4) promote the unity of science through improving communication among specialists. (von Bertalanffy 1968, 15)

Von Bertalanffy described systems as a "complex of interacting elements" (ibid. 55). They were presumed to exist in reality (as opposed to being merely mental constructs) and were arranged in a hierarchy of scale, from single cell to the cosmos. Von Bertalanffy drew a crucial distinction between *closed* and *open* systems and, as a biologist, he was primarily interested in the latter. He argued that all open systems were subject to the same set of structural laws regardless of the empirical relations being modeled.[19] In a rigorous development, he hypothesized, "general systems theory would be of an axiomatic nature" (ibid.). General systems theorists made much of the fact that systems could pass through a series of developmental phases: they could become more highly organized (negative entropy), achieve a condition of "steady state" with their environment, or fall apart (positive entropy). They might also evolve toward the same objective from different initial conditions and by different

---

19. Von Bertalanffy writes: "*If open systems . . . attain a steady state, this has a value equifinal or independent of initial conditions.* A general proof is difficult because of the lack of general criteria for the existence of steady states; but it can be given for special cases" (von Bertalanffy 1968, 132).

routes (equifinality), and they were continuously engaged in an exchange of energy with their environment.[20]

Von Bertalanffy's ideas were quickly absorbed into Anglo-American management science, the result of a rare and fruitful collaboration, lasting over many years, by Churchman (1957, 1979a [orig. 1968]); Churchman and Verhulst (1960); Emery and Trist (1960, 1965); Emery (1969); and Ackoff and Emery (1972). The reasons for GST's appeal to management scientists are somewhat obscure. Emery's selection of readings suggests a preference for systems language as a metaphor. Management scientists like to think of business organizations as *open systems* that draw *energy* from their *environment* to develop new *structures*. They found it useful to describe human organizations as *adaptive* to conditions in their environment, and to think of technical processes as being linked into *socio-technical systems*.

The systems-theory approach was heavily attacked on both technical and philosophical grounds (Berlinski 1976; Lilienfeld 1978; the "reply" by Churchman 1979b). But by then, it was already firmly entrenched. The theory appeared to satisfy management's yearning for unity of purpose and cybernetic guidance, and, with some notable exceptions (Ulrich 1983), it was strongly supportive of central control and planning from above.

The sixties had seen the rapid development of the several strands of policy analysis. As the decade came to a close, it appeared that a critical mass was being formed. The resulting fireworks of policy analysis have already been described.

Policy Analysts and the Decision Process: A Behavioral Critique

Judged by the continued growth of policy analysis, the quest for a willing client was spectacularly successful. The executive branch of the government proved to be more than accommodating: policy analysis became big business. In 1976, the Center for the Study of Responsive Law published its carefully documented report on "pri-

20. It appears that the yearning for a *unified* science is a Viennese specialty. Both Otto van Neurath (founder of the Encyclopedia of Unified Knowledge) and von Bertalanffy were Viennese, and both had achieved their basic insights prior to coming to the United States and Canada, respectively. But in an offsetting fashion that, in its own way, is no less Viennese, Austrian economists—among them Carl Menger, Böhm-Bawerk, Friedrich von Hayek, and Karl Popper—were also among the leading advocates of incrementalism in economic analysis and, by implication, in life itself. For details, see Johnston (1972).

vate managment consultants, 'experts,' and think tanks." In his introduction, Ralph Nader explained:

> Social Security and veterans' benefits aside, the predominant activity of government is letting contracts, grants, and subsidies to corporations for the purpose of performing governmental missions. Although the regulatory functions of government provoke the most publicized outcries, the contracting activites, in sheer dollars and personnel, are vastly greater—more than 100 times greater in revenue terms alone. The growth of Federal government expenditures in the last twenty years (from $70 billion to $365 billion) has not resulted from an increase in the number of employees, which has remained relatively stable. Instead, it has resulted from a growth of government by contract and grant—a staggering $110 billion in 1973. The subcontracting work—concerned with policy formation, organizational models, and even the recruitment of Federal executives—to private corporations whose stock in trade is alleged to be expertise accounts for the bulk of these huge expenditures. (Guttman and Willner 1976, x–xi)

In view of the government's extraordinary degree of reliance on private contractors and consultants, it is surprising that, until quite recently at least, very few analysts regarded their relationship to clients as being in any way problematic. Analysis was treated like any other commodity. There were both service providers and consumers who presumably derived some satisfaction from the product. If they did not, why would they continue to spend huge sums of money to obtain it? It was a comfortable logic. Analysts might occasionally wonder by what formal criterion one might judge the quality of policy decisions, as in the claim that the purpose of analysis is "to improve decisions." But such wondering has not been very productive. The best one could respond was that policy decisions were "good" to the extent that they were based on *rational and scientifically sanctioned procedures*. But analysts were experienced enough to know that, however tempting it might be to use them, inputs are an illegitimate measure of performance.

The reason for this failure to look beyond the market model of analysis can be traced to Simon's original formulation of the decision-making paradigm. Analysts posited a "rational" decision maker (Simon's "administrative man") who was personified even though "he" might be an entire government bureaucracy such as the U.S. Air Force or the Pentagon. This mythical creature, it was asserted, invariably sought to make decisions rationally or, as they say in the business, to get the "biggest bang for the buck," though in practice it was, in Simon's terms, sufficient to "get by."[21]

In the common language of policy analysis, decisions were equated with actions, and the basic model of rational decision or action contained the following well-known terms:[22] *goals and objectives, alternatives, consequences, choice.* As Graham Allison put it, "rationality refers to consistent, value-maximizing choices within specific constraints" (Allison 1971, 30). It follows that rationally acting persons could be fully "explained" by their explicitly formulated goals.

> The rigorous model of rational action maintains that rational choice consists of value-maximizing adaptation within the context of a *given* pay-off function, *fixed* alternatives, and consequences that are *known* (in one of the senses corresponding to certainty, risk, and uncertainty). (Ibid. 31)

Set out in this form, these were heroic assumptions, even when they were toned down with reference to a concept of "bounded" rationality. Policy analysts were fully aware of this dilemma. The brave new world of PPBS (Planning-Programming-Budgeting System) was failing or had failed (Novack 1965; Wildavsky 1975). Social indicators and, even more, social accounts were buried even before they were properly implemented (Bauer 1966; Gross 1969; Duncan 1969; Juster and Land 1981).[23] And critics such as Ida Hoos (1972) were raising fundamental questions about the ability of policy analysis to come to grips with America's pressing social problems. Could the practitioners of policy analysis actually deliver on their promise

21. The technical words for "getting by" varied according to the model. Simon proposed "satisficing," but statistical decision theorists derived their language from the theory of games and spoke of "minimax" strategies, the principle of "minimum regret," and other such concepts that differed significantly from maximization or optimization rules.

22. The logical equivalence of decisions and action could be maintained only under the assumption that the execution of decisions was a frictionless and automatic process in which the actors in the play would each carry out to perfection the parts assigned to them in the script. In this model, it was essential that the central authority—the analyst *cum* decision maker—write a script that would not constrain its own actions. For a given play, there could be only one actor having a genuine free choice. It had to be assumed further that there were no other plays in process at the time, and that the stage for the play was a closed system. (See also note 14.)

23. Aborn (1984) points out that even though work on social indicators is no longer funded as a separate rubric at the NSF, large-scale data gathering continues to be funded at substantial levels. The latter has, so to speak, assimilated the former. As a result, quantitative social science—the anti-theoretical approach preferred by policy makers who seek out the advice of policy analysts—has become stronger than ever.

to "improve decisions"? At least one experienced hand in the business thought that they could not.

> The consensus seems to be that most research studies bounce off the policy process without making much of a dent on the course of events. Support for this notion surfaces in many quarters, among social scientists, executive branch officials, and members of Congress. (Weiss 1977, 68)[24]

The critical self-examination of which Carol Weiss's paper is an example took essentially two forms. One group of critics focused on the analyst's role in the decision process; the work of this group will be reviewed in the remainder of this section. Another group looked more deeply into the logic of policy analysis. It provided epistemological critiques and its work will be reviewed in the next section.

In a major study of two fateful weeks in October 1962, known to history as the Cuban missile crisis, Graham Allison contrasted a model of pure rationality with two alternatives. The first alternative, which he called the "organizational process" model, dealt with the *patterned response* of formal bureaucracies.

> For some purposes, governmental behavior can be usefully summarized as action chosen by a unitary, rational decision-maker: centrally controlled, completely informed, and value maximizing. But this simplification must not be allowed to conceal the fact that a government consists of a conglomerate of semi-feudal, loosely allied organizations, each with a substantial life of its own. Governmental leaders do sit formally and, to some extent, in fact, on top of this conglomerate. But

---

24. Weiss here falls into a rhetorical trap that should not pass unnoticed. She assumes that "research studies" should make at least some "dent on the course of events." But by what reasoning? As we saw earlier, the problem of what constitutes an improved decision could not really be solved by arguing that an improvement would be observed if only the "decision maker" would accept the policy analyst's recommendations. One was, therefore, driven back to the even weaker position that it would be sufficient for an "improvement" to be noted if policy research were used as an "input" in the decision process, regardless of outcome. It is therefore easy to see why Weiss should have hoped otherwise, placing emphasis on results. But the matter is troublesome. On the one hand, along with her peers, she must have held to the theoretical position that decisions and actions are virtually identical (see note 22). In a more pragmatic mood, had she been asked, she would have said that decisions are one thing and implementing actions quite another. Still, within the framework of policy analysis, she had no choice: unless a new paradigm were to be substituted for Simon's classical decision model, the logical equivalence of decisions and actions had to be maintained. It is therefore a major disappointment and source of unending frustration to analysts that their work never seems to make any "dent" in the real world.

governments perceive problems through organizational sen-
sors. Governments define alternatives and estimate consequences as their component organizations process information; governments act as these organizations enact routines.
Governmental behavior can therefore be understood . . . less
as deliberate choices and more as *outputs* of large organizations
functioning according to standard patterns of behavior. (Allison 1971, 67)

The second alternative to rationality, or the model of "government politics," was constructed with the dynamics of bureaucratic
rivalry in mind. Like its predecessor, governmental politics

sees no unitary actor but many actors as players—players who
focus not on a single strategic issue but on many diverse in-
tranational problems as well; players who act in terms of no
consistent set of strategic objectives but rather according to
various concepts of national, organizational, and personal
goals; players who make government decisions not by single,
rational choice but by the pulling and hauling that is politics.
(Ibid. 144)

Allison suggested that policy decisions generally result from a convergence of bureaucratic routines with political struggles, struggles
that are frequently linked with the wider politics of the outside
world. One should by no means conclude from this that policy decisions arrived at in this way are in some mysterious sense "irrational." Organizations as well as individuals might well differ over
objectives that would lead to very different results. And since there
is not likely to be any criterion that is acceptable to all the actors for
deciding among objectives or for assigning relative weights to them,
and since there are almost always important side values to consider
along with the main stakes in the game, a process composed of both
normal bureaucratic routines and politics is not an unreasonable
proposition. As Lindblom might say, it substitutes interaction strategies for theoretical solutions.

The outcomes of complex bureaucratic games, actually of a whole
ecology of games played simultaneously, are indeterminate. The attainment of an overriding objective—of some strategic meta-
game—may well be, for most actors, a merely secondary consideration.

With this admission, however, the rational model falls apart.
Without a clear objective function, policy analysis loses its blind assurance of functional rationality. It becomes an open-ended and in-

determinate process. We already saw the rationality criterion wobble when we discussed Simon's ambiguous concept of "satisficing." Analysts nevertheless persisted in their belief that, in the final analysis, all rational behavior *must be* goal-directed. But what if people should act otherwise? Suppose the problem for an actor is not how to "achieve goals" but how to devise appropriate strategies in an ecology of games in which the stakes are survival and power? In that case, an action model may be more appropriate than a formal model of decision-making (Wildavsky 1978; orig. 1963).

Organizational decision-making, which is a commitment of moral and material resources by those who command them, is a complex, time-dependent process. Inherently conflictive, it involves bargaining among all the players, who themselves control only bits of the requisite power for their projects. And for some players, the excitement of the game may be sufficient reason to engage in it.

The more one looks at organizational behavior, the more explicit decision-making seems to fade into the background. Documents pass up and down corridors; there are always meetings; telephone calls are made to allay suspicions, confirm impressions, and obtain consent; and in the end, when signatures get put on documents, the climax is already past, the decision has merged into the normal stream of organizational responses. Decisions, then, are ususaly minute and continuous; they constitute an evolving process that has its own dynamic form.

If this account is correct, policy analysts should be asked to have more modest aspirations than the heroic role in which Simon's "science of design" had cast them. Even the scaled-down rhetoric of the Rand Graduate Institute, "to apply and adapt academic theories . . . in order to solve real-world policy problems," might have to be revised (Rand Graduate Institute 1982, 2). Organizational actors unquestionably need technical advice, and information can become an important political weapon. There are alternatives to be explored and options to be thought through systematically. There are reports to be written, presentations to be made, budgets to be defended. The results of past actions must be recorded and evaluated. From time to time, in the councils of government, the voice of skepticism must be raised to keep from blundering. Channels of communication to the "world of knowledge" must be maintained so that practise might not depart too greatly from the existing "state of the art" in fields important to the mission of the agency. Consultants must be selected, and their work must be monitored. There is, then, no shortage of things legitimately to be done, and bureaucracies frequently have responded by setting up their own internal units for this purpose.

In addition to the in-house base for policy analysis in the bureaucracy, the profession has also established bases in the private economy (consulting firms) and the academy. At each of these bases, analysts tend to have very different ambitions and views of the world.[25] *Bureaucratic* analysts will want to gain voice and influence within their own organizations. They must please their superiors even as they hold their respect for independent judgment. Some of them may eventually want to leapfrog into the academy or, as the case may be, return to it, and so they will want to nurture their continued credibility as scholars. But above all else, to survive in the bureaucracy, they must learn to be pragmatic, know how to work within impossible deadlines, and possess a sixth sense for the politics in the agency's environment.

The key to understanding *private* analysts is money. Consulting firms must survive in a highly competitive world. They must be able to sell themselves to potential clients, to attractively package their wares, to work within fixed budgets, and to maintain a good public reputation. They must also learn to work contentedly with their client's basic assumptions: too many challenges of this framework will almost certainly lead to nonrenewal or, worse, cancellation of contract.

Academic analysts, finally, tend to be "loners" whose success as analysts is to a large extent based on their personal standing within the academy, where careers depend primarily on the quality of one's scholarship. Unlike their confreres in the bureaucracy and private business, they cannot afford to take pragmatic shortcuts in their work, which is carefully scrutinized in the specialized journals of the academy. This process of peer review, which can be pitiless, may bring them academic honors and an independent standing as consultants. But this gain is purchased at the price of ignorance. Their absorption into scholarly work often leaves them little time to become familiar with the shifting sands of the policy terrain. As a result, their specific advice will often have a somewhat abstract air about it. Moreover, academics typically work without fixed deadlines, and they are rarely available to the bureaucracy at the precise times they are needed.

And yet, these three groups of analysts, differing in their con-

25. Relations among these three worlds of policy analysis are analyzed in Friedmann and Abonyi (1976). The academy and some private research tanks also undertake contract research. This aspect of their work is not reviewed here, even though its contribution to the practice of policy analysis may be extremely important.

cerns, perspectives, and behavior, also stand on common ground: they are purveyors of advice to the powerful. And this, it turns out, is a challenging task in itself that requires skills not normally taught even in graduate schools of public policy. Although the art of advice is an ancient one, relatively few studies have been devoted to it (Jöhr and Singer 1955; Meltsner 1976; Goldhammer 1978; Szanton 1981; House 1982). One of the best of these is Guy Benveniste's *The Politics of Expertise* (1977). A seasoned analyst of educational policy and a professor at Berkeley, Benveniste stresses the importance of the expert's knowledge of the policy terrain.

> The would-be experts cannot expect to draft policies without knowing a considerable amount about the policy environment. They must be able to recognize the arguments of practitioners, to realize their strengths and weaknesses, and to temper their own narrow field of expertise with the kinds of generalized folklore and knowledge that prevail in the environment. In most social situations, the folklore and conventional wisdom have been acquired over time by trial and error. The would-be experts trained in an analytical discipline can question aspects of this conventional wisdom. But they should not be so foolish as to assume that it is all rubbish. Parts are dysfunctional and should be changed, but parts are needed. (Benveniste 1977, 93)

Few advisors are able to live up to these high requirements, and the majority of those who do will be found inside bureaucracy. In any event, good experts are rare, and policy makers are frequently cynical about the advice they get (Horowitz and Katz 1975, 151–155).

One of the really serious problems in policy analysis is the lack of attention given to the question of policy or program implementation. The starting point for academic interest in implementation is an ingeniously wrought case study of anti-poverty programs in the city of Oakland, California (Pressman and Wildavsky 1979). At the time of its first publication in 1973, the authors of this pithy little volume had been able to locate only one detailed case study of implementation (Derthick 1972). They seemed rather astounded at this failure of policy analysts and other social scientists seriously to address the question of how ideas get translated into practice.[26]

During the past decade, however, spurred on by Pressman and

26. Strictly speaking, their search was not complete. Other early studies of the politics of implementation include Banfield (1951), Meyerson and Banfield (1955), and Hirschman (1967b).

Wildavsky's example, there has been a strong revival of interest in the question, with a number of outstanding studies on the politics of implementation (for example, Bardach 1977; Grindle 1980). Of particular interest, in the present context, is a chapter contributed to the second edition of Pressman and Wildavsky (1979) by Majone and Wildavsky. Its authors argue for an evolutionary interpretation of implementation. Policy implementation, they say, is not like building a physical structure such as a bridge—a process that has a clear beginning and an end. Rather, it is a continuously evolving set of problems that arise at different levels of decision-making.

> Policy ideas in the abstract . . . are subject to an infinite variety of contingencies, and they contain worlds of possible practical applications. . . . They have no resting point, no final realization; they are endlessly evolving. How then, and why, then, separate analytically what life refuses to tear apart? . . .
>
> Implementation is evolution. Since it takes place in a world we never made, we are usually right in the middle of the process, with events having occurred before and (we hope) continuing afterward. At each point we must cope with new circumstances that allow us to actualize different potentials in whatever policy ideas we are implementing. When we act to implement a policy, we change it. . . . In this way, the policy theory is transformed to produce different results. As we learn from experience what is feasible or preferable, we correct errors. To the degree that these corrections make a difference at all, they change our policy ideas as well as the policy outcomes, because the idea is embodied in the action. (Majone and Wildavsky 1979, 190–191)

As far as policy analysis is concerned, the evolutionary perspective on implementation has two major implications. First, it tells us that policy analysts never start with a clean slate. There is always a history of prior actions and their consequences, and every problem, if it is to be correctly understood, must be related to a sociopolitical context. Second, implementation is not simply whatever happens once a policy has been decided, but a pervasive concern that helps to shape the very contents of that policy. This argument for a close and continuing consideration of implementing measures in policy and program formulation cannot be emphasized enough. Unless implementation problems are taken into account in the design of policies, expert advice will be stillborn.

Epistemological Critiques

In the following pages, I propose to examine some facets of logic internal to the traditions of policy analysis. Ever since Herbert Simon, these traditions have been sharply focused on decision-making understood as an event in time preceding action. Decisions first, then action: that was the basic model. The object was to make decisions on public policy more rational by undertaking certain kinds of studies that involved forecasting, mathematical modeling, dynamic programming, policy and program evaluation, impact analysis, cross-impact analysis, gaming and simulation, and similar well-known techniques. Despite repeated disclaimers by leading practitioners that policy analysis could be reduced to a bundle of methods, the field became increasingly identified with concepts and methods derived from systems engineering and economics (Allen 1978; Carley 1980).

This section is devoted to a critical look at these concepts and methods.[27] In the first part, I shall consider the question of whether they are the right tools for the job. This will be followed by a review of some questions inherent in the logic of social forecasting. Finally, I will examine the general crisis into which policy analysis was plunged when it became apparent that its central paradigm of rational decison-making was no longer tenable.

"Benign" or "Wicked" Problems?

Is there anything about social problems that is different from, say, a problem in civil engineering, such as designing an airport? And if there is, what are the differences, and what implications do they have for policy analysis?

In an early paper, two professors in Berkeley's School of Environmental Design thought they had discovered what was unique about the sort of problems that policy analysts were being asked to think about: the problems, said Rittel and Webber, were "wicked."

> The problems that scientists and engineers have usually focused upon are mostly "tame" or "benign" ones. As an example, consider a problem of mathematics, such as solving an equation; or the task of an organic chemist in analyzing the

27. The most thorough epistemological critique of systems-scientific approaches is by Werner Ulrich (1983) The remarks that follow are not based on his work, however, which is a full-blown philosophical treatise along neo-Kantian lines. Unfortunately, Ulrich's argument does not lend itself to brief summation, and the more superficial epistemological critique that follows will have to stand in for the more solid analysis this former student of C. West Churchman accomplishes.

structure of some unknown compound; or that of the chess-
player attempting to accomplish checkmate in five moves. For
each the mission is clear. It is clear, in turn, whether or not the
problems have been solved.

Wicked problems, in contrast; have neither of these clarify-
ing traits; and they include nearly all public policy issues—
whether the question concerns the location of a freeway, the
adjustment of a tax rate, the modification of school curricula,
or the confrontation of crime. (Rittel and Webber 1973, 160)

"Wicked," problems, they explain, are those that are " 'malignant'
(in contrast to 'benign') or 'vicious' (like a circle) or 'tricky' (like a
leprechaun) or 'aggressive' (like a lion, in contrast to the docility of
a lamb)." And it is "morally objectionable," they conclude, "for the
planner to treat a wicked problem as though it were a tame one, or
to tame a wicked problem prematurely, or to refuse to recognize the
inherent wickedness of social problems" (ibid. 160–161).

Their paper presents convincing arguments in support of this position and raises serious questions about the suitability of rational
techniques which, in the view of their advocates, are designed to
"solve" problems quickly and clearly. Some characteristics of
"wicked" problems are:

1. There is no definitive formulation of a wicked problem . . .

2. Wicked problems have no stopping rule . . .

3. There is no immediate and no ultimate test of a solution to
a wicked problem . . .

4. Wicked problems do not have an enumerable (or an ex-
haustively describable) set of potential solutions, nor is there a
well-known set of permissible operations that may be incorporated into the plan . . .

5. Every wicked problem can be considered to be a symptom
of another problem . . .

6. The existence of a discrepancy representing a wicked problem can be explained in numerous ways. The choice of explanation determines the nature of the problem resolution. (Ibid.
161–166)

Rittel and Webber's essay reads like a modern-day version of
Hans Christian Anderson's fairy tale "The Emperor's New
Clothes." It devastates the rational decision model—insofar as the
class of wicked problems is concerned—by demonstrating that the
model is inappropriately applied: it is based on a faulty epistemol-

ogy. As Majone and Wildavsky would do six years later, the authors argued for an evolutionaray perspective. In this view, social problems are never solved; they are merely displaced by other problems.

Take, for instance, a relatively "simple" problem of perennial concern to the American public: the low average performance of high school students on standard achievement tests. That is how the "problem" may be handed to an analyst, but it is not the "real" problem with which the analyst must come to grips. The "real" problem is one that can be "attacked" with the hope of improving average test scores across the nation. What is it, then? Is it that teachers are not paid enough, so that the best talent is not attracted into the profession? Is it a personal story of poverty and broken homes? Is it a temporary problem of cultural adjustment on the part of immigrant children in central cities? Is it that the more affluent middle class has started to pull out its children from public schools to give them a private education?

One could continue to ask questions in this vein. Politically, however, it is impossible to postpone a decision when public concern is at high tide. Voters are impatient, and politicians cannot wait for the research community to provide answers which, in any event, are always inconclusive. So they do what they can. With such support as they can get from already existing studies, politicians will pick an answer out of thin air: teachers' salaries, for instance. For a while, more resources are shifted to education, and for good measure school boards are admonished to pay more attention to the basic disciplines.

Although this flurry of activity in no way "solves" the problem of low test scores, both politicians and the public will breathe a little easier, for they have done their best. In time, another problem comes along to absorb their attention—an energy crisis, perhaps, or rising interest rates, or acid rain.

Some might wish to argue that it is grossly unfair to present the educational conundrum in this way. They might even say that, *given time*, the techniques of policy analysis are powerful enough to provide a definitive solution to the problem of scholastic under-performance. Perhaps, but the whole point of the exercise is that *there is never time to do all the research that might be needed*. Over many decades, an extraordinary amount of money has been spent to understand how learning takes place. We know a great deal, but the experts do not agree. They do not agree, in part, because their starting positions and basic philosophies of education differ. Education, then, is one of those "wicked" and "malignant" problems for which there is never a solution. For policy makers and their analysts, there is only a continuing development of policy—an evolution—and at any given moment, one does what one can with whatever wisdom is at hand.

The Veil of Time

One of the most perplexing questions in policy analysis is how to deal with the future. Forecasters from Bentham, Saint-Simon, and Comte to modern ones such as Olaf Helmer (1966), Henri Theil (1966), Kahn and Wiener (1967), and Robert Ayres (1969) have claimed that scientific methodologies exist by which we can push aside the "veil of time" and forecast future events as the consequences of past trends and present actions. Forecasts are typically conditional statements of the sort "If a, then $b, c, \ldots, n$." The desire to know what does not yet exist but may happen at some future time is a very powerful human desire. But the naive belief that science can peer beyond the rim of the present is a misunderstanding that stems from the classical view of experimental science as a methodology that advances by making predictions (hypotheses) and then testing them.[28] The procedures of classical science require that:

1. The experiments that are conducted are those for which the conditions surrounding the experiments can be controlled.

2. The events predicted are recurrent and part of an orderly sequence.

3. The research methodologies adopted have no significant influence over the outcome of the experiment.

4. The research itself aims at falsifying the hypothesis, rather than adducing supportive evidence that will more firmly establish the prediction.

5. The predictions are either part of a causal sequence or else are randomized outcomes, not of the events themselves, but of the statistical distribution of a class of events.

The contrast with policy analysis—Simon's "science of design"— could not be more dramatic. In policy analysis:

1. Analysts rarely control the conditions for their "experiments." They operate in real time with total situations in which external conditions cannot be held at bay, and in which the in-

28. For a very different understanding of the scientific enterprise, see the works by Kuhn (1970), Lakatos (1971), and Feyerabend (1975).

ternal environment of the policy experiment is inevitably subject to dynamics of human relations and institutional change.[29]

2. Every situation encountered by analysts is essentially unique in terms of the total constellation of interactive forces. The past, therefore, has only limited relevance for the future, and beyond very short-range projections, analysts are always "groping in the dark."

3. Social events are frequently dominated by a "tipping point" phenomenon in which an equilibrium situation is suddenly disturbed when a key variable reaches a magnitude sufficient to upset the existing balance of relationships. Almost always, the results of such "tipping" come as a surprise.

4. Social research frequently influences outcomes, even decisively, as when forecasts of higher interest rates contribute to the rise of interest rates, or the prediction of racial outbursts heightens the probability of racial outbursts. The phenomenon is well-known under the heading "self-fulfilling prophesies." There are other situations, too, in which research may lead to unintended changes in behavior.

5. Increasingly popular statistical forecasting models tend to have very large, indeterminate errors (Morgenstern 1963; Lee 1973; Meadows et al. 1982).

Most social forecasts are exercises in logic in which events are projected on the basis of a long series of assumptions. Since the assumptions are established a priori but are usually determining, the logic of forecasting turns out to be circular: given the assumptions, forecasts represent the working out of the inevitable conclusions. The assumptions themselves, on the other hand, are subject only to expert judgment, and they are not controlled (Miles and Irvine 1979).

Despite the invention of various ingenious methods for spying through the veil of time, the outlook for social and economic forecasting is fairly bleak.[30] Claims that anything like a full range of consequences of an action can be predicted in advance of the action itself cannot be sustained. All the same, the art and science of forecasting is unlikely to disappear: our desire to know what is written in the "book of time" is more powerful than any logic. And it is

29. Within the last decade, however, the idea of policy experiments has gained some ground, as, for example, in the workability of educational vouchers. See Riecken and Boruch (1974).

30. The current state of confusion in the modeling community is well illustrated in a recent volume sponsored by the International Institute of Applied Systems Analysis (IIASA) (Meadows et al. 1982).

not an altogether futile exercise. Properly conceived, forecasting can play a significant role in policy analysis, even when it falls short of our ardent wish to know the path ahead. For example:

○ Certain dimensions of a projection can be tested, such as the resistance of forecasting models to changes in the values of parametric variable.

○ For many purposes of policy formation, projected orders of magnitude may be all that is needed.

○ Because short-term forecasting models operate with a great margin of certainty, emphasis on this dimension of planning may gain in popularity.

○ Especially when they are kept simple and transparent, forecasting models may be used as learning devices for analysts.

○ Forecasting models may improve the availability and quality of the data necessary for their construction.

○ Forecasting models may be used to send up warning signals of coming crises.

Pitfalls or New Paradigm?
By the mid-1970s, it was evident that policy analysis was in serious trouble. Partly in response to this, the International Institute of Applied Systems Analysis (IIASA) in Laxenburg, Austria, sponsored a major conference in 1977 on *Pitfalls of Analysis* (Majone and Quade 1980). The occasion brought together an illustrious array of analysts from major universities, private business, and nonprofit research groups. The proceedings, a small, well-edited volume, is the best currently available state-of-the-art report. It makes for distressful reading.[31]

Pitfalls are traps into which even experienced analysts may fall. And if they *may* fall, cynics might venture, fall they will! There are pitfalls strewn about in areas almost too numerous to mention: in formulation and modeling, data analysis, the analysis of costs, optimization methods, communication, implementation analysis, evaluation, and even the language of policy analysis. With this in mind, it is scarcely surprising that the conference ended with repeated calls not only for extreme caution in analytical work but, more significantly, for everyday human qualities such as judgment, intui-

31. *Pitfalls* is not without precedent. From the beginning, policy analysis was very conscious of its weaknesses. See earlier work by Koopman (1956), Kahn and Mann (1957), Hitch and McKean (1960), Morgenstern (1963), and Quade (1968).

tion, sensibility, and the art of effective communication. Kathleen Archibald is puzzled by it all.

> Majone does here refer to interpretive tools—to "imagination, judgment, and analogical and associative thinking." And the Hitch quotation Quade turns to does refer to "inventive and ingenious analysis." But where in the literature, and where in the training of analysts, is attention given to methods of improving imagination, judgment, analogical and associative thinking, inventiveness and ingenuity? What proportion of books and articles and classes are devoted to such topics, compared to the space and time devoted to improving rigor and technical skills? It is a minute fraction of the total verbiage on policy analysis. (Archibald 1980, 192)

The solution she seeks has some of the strangeness of Richard Hofstadter's *Goedel, Escher, Bach* (1979).

> Through the looking-glass is no idle metaphor; what better way to imply self-referentiality than going through a mirror? Self-referentiality is a characteristic of both culture and consciousness. It can be demonstrated that this self-referentiality generates a basic indeterminacy that in turn gives rise to (a) the presence of uncertainty and those serious pitfalls associated with it in analysis; (b) the possibility of novelty, of creative solutions; and (c) the indissolubility of language creation and problem-solving and thus the need to use old words in new ways. (Ibid. 194)

It is by no means clear, however, whether "going through a mirror" will help to rescue policy analysis in its existing form, *so long as its central paradigm of rational decision-making continues to weigh on analysts' thinking.* There are some indications that a paradigm shift is underway, as in Majone and Wildavsky's evolutionary perspective on policy implementation (1979) and their frank advocacy of a political and interactive approach to policies planning. It is to a consideration of this groping for alternative models in policy analysis that we now turn.[32]

32. Does policy analysis, indeed, does any professional field, need a central paradigm, or should one be content with the buzzing confusion in which all paradigms are equally valid, and it is all a matter of taste and preference? In other words, are paradigms important in professional work? Is it not true that the test of a good professional is pragmatic; in the final analysis, is it not the satisfaction of clients that really matters?

But the question cannot be disposed of so easily. Professions learn from practice,

Enlightenment or Engineering: The Second Generation Models

By 1977, the year of the IIASA conference on pitfalls, it had become clear that the entire rationale for policy analysis would have to be rethought. The great expectations of the 1950s and 1960s had not been fulfilled. The internal critique had revealed major inconsistencies of both a logical and empirical nature. This was particularly true for that branch of policy analysis that traced its origins to systems engineering, but, to a certain extent, it also involved the claims of analysts who followed the lead of Dror and Lasswell and leaned more heavily on the political and administrative sciences.

Convinced of the need for a dramatic turnaround, some of the leaders of the field cast about for new roles and intellectual paradigms. The most persuasive of these proposals came from Carol Weiss (1977, 1982). Basing her advocacy on earlier studies, she argued that

> to a large (but unknown) degree, research actually affects policy less through problem-solving or social engineering than through what Morris Janowitz has called "enlightenment." The studies by Nathan Caplan at Michigan and Karin Knorr at Vienna, as well as our research at Columbia, suggest that the major effect of research on policy may be the gradual sedimentation of insights, theories, concepts, and ways of looking at the world. (Weiss 1977, 77)[33]

What was particularly important to Weiss was that the critical function of scholarship should not be impaired. She contrasted "conventional wisdom" with the new model of "enlightenment," with its faint echoes of Voltaire and Condorcet.

> This is the conventional wisdom: the social researcher whose work is to enter the policy sphere should reach consensus with some important segment of policy actors on the basic value-

---

but they also learn from graduate study in particular disciplines, and academic work centrally depends on traditions of discourse for its quality. Traditions of discourse require the rigors of a paradigm that constrains, for the period during which the paradigm is accepted as valid, the questions being asked, the answers that are sought, and the assumptions that are allowed as legitimate for purposes of inquiry. If these are suddenly relaxed and "anything goes," the result will not be an advance of knowledge but a babbling Tower of Babel and the collapse of knowledge. That is why paradigms resist replacement, and why in every kind of inquiry there is always a leading paradigm: no scientific discipline or profession can be without one (Kuhn 1970; Churchman 1971).

33. The reference is to Janowitz (1970).

orientation of his work. For maximum research utility, the researcher should accept the fundamental goals, priorities, and political constraints of the key decision-making group. He should be sensitive to feasibilities and stay within the narrow range of low-cost, low-change policy alternatives.

The enlightenment model of research use does not make such assumptions. It does not consider value consensus a prerequisite for useful research. It sees a role for research as social criticism. It finds a place for research based on variant theoretical premises. It implies that research need not necessarily be geared to the operating feasibilities of today, but that research provides the intellectual background of concepts, operations, and empirical generalizations that inform policy. As new concepts and data emerge, their gradual, cumulative effect can be to change the conventions policymakers abide by and to reorder the goals and priorities of the practical policy world. (Ibid. 80)

Weiss was blowing the bugle of retreat to the academy. Henceforth, from their base in the universities, policy analysts would be able to broadcast their insights, criticisms, and good counsel to a generalized audience of policy makers and other influentials. Through a process of sifting, ideas in good currency would eventually emerge to become the basis of whatever orthodoxies ruled the world of policy. At the same time, other academics, operating from different value premises, would attempt to displace the reigning ideas by models of their own, through criticism, argument, and persuasion. It was an idea increasingly attractive to policy analysts who had burned out in the front lines of their profession and welcomed a more sheltered existence (Bulmer 1982).[34]

Another prominent academic who had been deeply involved in policy analysis, Richard Nelson of Yale University, echoed Weiss's theme in a brilliant essay on institutional economics. Provocatively

---

34. An important side aspect of Weiss's "enlightenment" model of policy research is that analysts would be able to drop their pose of scientific neutrality and actually become advocates for their ideas. This is an aspect not sufficiently stressed in critiques of the scientist bias in policy analysis, where mainstream thinking still holds that "the facts will speak for themselves." If the object is *knowledge*, the refutation of hypotheses becomes a basis for advance. But in action-oriented analysis, the aim is to bring something new into the world; *it is to generate new practice*. Even in the nether world of science, advocacy is very much part of the game of getting ideas accepted, but in the world of political practice, advocacy is all there is: policy ideas are never defeated, the way certain hypotheses in science may be rejected. They are merely replaced by other ideas.

entitled *The Moon and the Ghetto* (1977), the essay was originally delivered as the Fels Lecture on Public Policy Analysis at the University of Pennsylvania in 1974. Much of the volume is taken up with a
methodological critique of the systems analysis tradition applied to
civilian problems in ways already familiar from the earlier work of
Ida Hoos (1972). What makes the essay unique, however, is its advocacy of a major new role for policy analysts: devising organizational innovations, or what Nelson called "new regimes of governance."

Neo-classical economics, which exerted a powerful influence on
policy analysis, saw its core problem as the efficient allocation of resources. Nelson now argued the perfectly reasonable proposition
that a major reallocation of resources to new activities would require
a rethinking of the organizational structure through which the new
programs would have to be administered. As they face new circumstances and a new institutional environment, older organizational
arrangements became outdated. Thus, there is a need to continuously monitor the system of economic organization generally—and
the organization of sectoral activities more specifically—for its continuing "fit" with the environment. Economic organization, according to Nelson, is an adaptive, evolutionary system.

The third major reassessment came from Giandomenico Majone
and Aaron Wildavsky in their joint chapter included in the second
edition of Pressman and Wildavsky (1979). The evolutionary perspective with regard to economic organization, which was so attractive to Nelson, is here applied to the question of implementation.
Beginning with the premise that policy analysis must become more
closely linked to action (and must therefore move away from the decision model with its cognitive bias against an interaction model),
Majone and Wildavsky propose to view the implementation of programs as a continuing, evolutionary process involving social learning, adaptation, and occasional redirection. Policy analysis would
somehow have to fit into this ongoing process of societal guidance,
contributing to the dialectic of its practice.

> Reducing, bounding, limiting contingencies is the analytical
> function. Discovering the constraints under which policy ideas
> may be expected to operate—applying negative knowledge, if
> you will—is the main task of analysis. Fixed prescriptions—
> "knowing that"—give way to "knowing how"—adopting the
> right rule at the right moment when events unfold, in order to
> bring out one potential result over many others. Knowing how
> is a craft, not a science. (Majone and Wildavsky 1979, 190)

"Knowing how is a craft, not a science." That sentence sets the new direction.

The importance of judgment in policy analysis had been recognized since at least the mid-sixties. But by relating it back to the implementation process, Majone and Wildavsky raise it to a new position of eminence. It is clear that even though they are not prepared to abandon the front lines of policy analysis, they are writing off the engineering model—"fixed prescriptions"—for a model that comes very close to social learning (discussed in Chapter 5).

Finally, it is worth mentioning again the essay by Majone (1980) in which he endeavors to assimilate policy analysis to the new developments in the philosophy of science. (This essay is strongly reminiscent of Camhis's earlier work on planning theory [1979].) Majone is fascinated by Lakatos (1971) and the later Popper (1975), both of whom "concentrate on the growth of theories rather than their refutation" (Majone 1980, 185). Popper, in particular, was now asserting a view of science that lifted it above the ordinary concerns of everyday life. Science takes place, he asserted, in a world of its own, a world of "objective structures that are produced by human minds but which, once produced, exist independently of them as theories, artistic creations and styles, norms, institutions, problem situations, critical arguments" (ibid.). Popper called it World 3 and distinguished it from World 1, the world of physical objects and physical states, and World 2, the world of mental states, beliefs, and personal preferences. Though linked to the other two, World 3 exists autonomously with little reference to the everyday worlds of human concerns.[35]

Following Popper, Majone now argued for a similarly autonomous policy space "consisting of (actual and potential) policy problems, policy arguments, norms, constraints, tentative solutions and their institutional embodiments" (ibid.).[36] The focus of policy analysis would consequently be on what, following the lead of Lakatos, he calls "action programs." It would shift from individuals and groups as *actors* to "objective features like policy content, evolving doctrines and problem situations, changing constraints, and interaction among different policies" (ibid.). The object would be to keep the process of policy development moving along; it would *not* be to predict or to falsify or, indeed, to optimize; and it would certainly not be to generate new practices. Policy development was sui ge-

35. For a critique of Popper's three worlds from the perspective of an epistemology of social learning, see Friedmann (1978).

36. Majone proposes to treat this policy space as a subset of Popper's World 3.

neris, but exactly what he meant by it, Majone had some difficulty in explaining. One criterion, he thought, might be the disposing of issues.[37]

Whatever one might think of an *autonomous* policy space as an appropriate metaphor, this much is clear: like the authors cited earlier, Majone was calling for a retreat into the cloisters of the academy or of research institutions like his own (IIASA). Only in the relative projection from day-to-day crises of real policy making would an autonomous policy science be able to flourish.

Carol Weiss's argument seemed to carry the day. If policy is an evolutionary process in which decisions are merely markers along the way, all intellectual perspectives might be helpful. No single approach could be given a priori preference. And if the context of policy analysis was indeed a form of generalized decision-making, then one need not pay too close attention to the operational requirements of policy (though implementation questions ought not to be ignored). And if the object of the analysis was action programs rather than decisions, and if the process of analysis itself was dialectical, then indeed there was new scope for policy analysis.[38] The retreat to the academy would be a liberating experience. And one might reasonably hope that the results of academic work would somehow filter into the policy making process.

The process of "filtering" itself was not closely examined, however. It might be well, therefore, before we agree that the enlightenment model points the way to the future to consider the institutional setting for policy analysis.

As we saw earlier policy analysis had developed on three distinct institutional bases. The first was bureaucracy. Here, policy analysis was seen as an internal function of governance (Meltsner 1976; House 1982). The second was private corporations (either for profit or not-for-profit) such as Rand, IIASA, the Brookings Institution, SRI, Resources for the Future, Inc., and the Institute for Defense Analysis. These corporations worked as consultants to government and tended to regard policy analysis as a commodity. (Nonprofit in-

37. "Disposing of policy issues" as a criterion of policy develoment is not as empty a concept as it might first appear. It fits into the evolutionary view of policy, in which problems are never solved but merely succeed each other in historical sequence. "Disposing of a problem" was also John Dewey's suggested criterion for the truth value of a statement.

38. Wildavsky had argued that the process of policy analysis is best thought of as involving contradictory pairs, such as descriptive/prescriptive and objective/argumentative (Wildavsky 1979, 14–15).

stitutions, however, might also undertake long-range policy research.) The third was the academy, where analysis was carried out in the form of policy-relevant research that was funded either by private and public foundations or by the university itself, or was conducted simply as a matter of individual initiative, without significant financial support.

Independent of each other, these three bases for policy analysis are nevertheless linked in various ways, and as a set they constitute a scholarly community of policy analysts (or planners). There are many such communities, and they are typically organized around particular policy sectors. Thus, we find communities of environmentalists, urban designers, regional scientists, labor analysts, transport planners, housing specialists, public health planners, defense analysts, and agronomists. They tend to be interdisciplinary and problem-focused. Other communities are organized around methodological approaches, such as operations research, futures studies, and econometrics. Each community is composed of members from all three bases for policy analysis. Typically, it is distinguished by having an organizational format (association, society, network, "invisible college") and by publishing its own journals, newsletter, and other communications that maintain the flow of information and ideas among its members, who in turn identify themselves with certain "classics" in their field that provide them with a focus and direction in establishing the major research paradigm.

Within such a community, migration from one base to another is quite frequent, and the best analysts typically spend time on all three bases: bureaucratic, corporate (commercial and/or not-for-profit), and academic. This experience, as well as periodic meetings and conference and the journal publications, helps to knit the field together and give its practitioners an informal, tacit understanding and a common language. It is through these scholarly communities that policy research "filters" from the academy into the more operationally oriented bases of bureaucratic and corporate policy analysis. But the role of these communities goes substantially beyond communication. It can be further characterized by the following major contributions they make, as communities, to the policy making process.

1. Scholarly communities create a stable research environment for policy analysis that is characterized by recognized leaders, elder statesmen (and women), basic research questions, a set of

generally accepted hypotheses, common research methods, and a sense of the community's own origins and history.

2. Scholarly communities help to ensure the quality of policy advice by exercising critical and screening functions through their journal publications, book reviews, contact networks, and other means. The communities set their own standards of excellence, and these are enforced through both formal and informal processes.

3. Scholarly communities provide a setting for acting out the inevitable tensions between theory and practice by encouraging encounters between academic and practical policy analysts and planners. These tensions lead invariably to conflicts over journal policies, professional education, and the agenda for annual conferences in which all members of a community are brought together. Even as these tensions are fought out, however, there is a growing understanding within that community of the several positions and perspectives, because its members not only move frequently from base to base but also maintian friendships and professional contacts *across* bases.

4. Scholarly communities allow for the gradual modification of their central research paradigm as they adapt to changing circumstances in the policy environment and to sustained and increasingly persuasive critiques from outside the dominant tradition. Occasionally, one research paradigm may be substitued for another within the same community, though what is more often the case, a new community will be formed with its own intellectual heroes and contact network.

It appears then, as we move toward the twenty-first century, that we are finally leaving behind us the Comtean vision of an engineered society. There remain the command system of the state and the enormous power of the corporations and financial empires that operate increasingly on a global scale. Technical reason is still enshrined in these systems, even if policy analysis as a "science" has shifted its emphasis from optimization to a looser model in which organizational design plays as large a role as the efficient allocation of resources.

Conclusions

Policy advisers have existed since time immemorial. We moderns have technified and institutionalized the advisory function, and we have clothed it in a mantle of science, but the function remains the same. An activity that has survived thousands of years must meet a need in the structures of governance. And although modern policy analysis, with its array of sophisticated models and computers, is of very recent origin, there is no question that, in one form or another, it will survive indefinitely into the future. Its fortunes may wax and wane, and its characteristic mode of operation may undergo some change, but it was surely no accident that it was the Rand Corporation that sponsored Herbert Goldhammer's *The Adviser* (1978), a history of policy advice through the ages, from Delphic oracles to councils of state, from ancient Chinese emperors to Winston Churchill. The Rand people saw themselves as standing in the long line of an old and honorable profession.

Still, the recent shift in emphasis from on-line analysis to "enlightenment" and from decision theory to implementation and interactive models is a significant one. Once decision theory has been displaced as the principal focus of policy analysis, the way is open for many different approaches, some of which may well depart from the hallowed traditions of the field.

A major alternative to decision is "action," and actions imply the existence of actors who act. When the latter are substituted for decision makers as the focus for planning, one is no longer bound to consider the ruling overlayers of society, as Etzioni would have it, as the only or even the principal actor in given situations. In the public domain, there are always multiple actors, such as political parties, social movements, trade unions, and farmers' granges, whose roots are deep in civil society (Ulrich 1983).

This new focus on action leads us to different models of planning and, indeed, to new traditions. These models have two things in common: (1) they are not specifically addressed to the ruling elites, and (2) they focus on actions rather than on decisions. Because of these inherent biases, the planning traditions we shall now discuss—social learning and social mobilization—are more oriented to social change and system transformation than to the maintenance of existing power structures. With them, we move into a new terrain of planning.

5 Planning as Social Learning

Writings in the tradition of social learning have common intellectual roots and many branches. For some, social learning serves chiefly as a metaphor to denote a certain style of linking knowledge to action; for others, it is a social technology, much like policy analysis. Yet, it stands in the sharpest possible contrast to the latter.

Policy analysis is focused on decisions; it is a form of anticipatory decision-making, a cognitive process that uses technical reason to explore and evaluate possible courses of action. The client for this exercise is a "rational decision maker" who is implicitly regarded also as the executor of policy who will follow up his or her choice with the appropriate implementing actions. A structural model of policy analysis would look like the diagram in Figure 12.

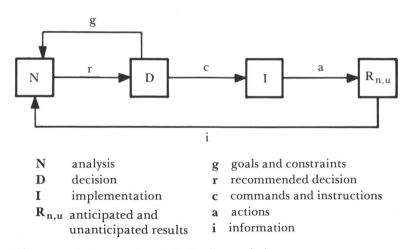

N	analysis	**g**	goals and constraints
D	decision	**r**	recommended decision
I	implementation	**c**	commands and instructions
R$_{n,u}$	anticipated and	**a**	actions
	unanticipated results	**i**	information

Figure 12. A structural model of policy analysis.

Social learning, on the other hand, begins and ends with action, that is, with purposeful activity. It is a complex, time-dependent process that involves, in addition to the *action* itself (which breaks

181

into the stream of ongoing events to change reality), *political strategy and tactics* (which tell us how to overcome resistance), *theories of reality* (which tell us what the world is like), and the *values* that inspire and direct the action. Taken together, these four elements constitute a form of *social practice*. It is the essential wisdom of the social learning tradition that practice and learning are construed as correlative processes, so that one process necessarily implies the other. In this scheme, decisions appear as a fleeting moment in the course of an ongoing practice. They are embedded in a learning process that flows from the attempt to change reality through practice (Figure 13).

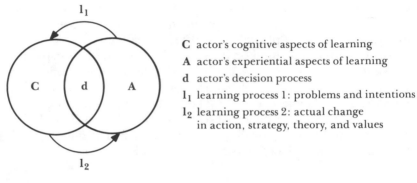

C actor's cognitive aspects of learning

A actor's experiential aspects of learning

d actor's decision process

l_1 learning process 1: problems and intentions

l_2 learning process 2: actual change
   in action, strategy, theory, and values

Figure 13. A simple model of social practice and learning.

As a conscious mode of practice, social learning derives from the philosophical pragmatism of John Dewey. Indeed, until the end of World War II, all the principal statements of social learning were philosophical, including essays by Lewis Mumford and, surprisingly, given his vastly different cultural and political setting, Mao Tse-tung. With the establishment of the National Training Laboratory in Group Dynamics at Bethel, Maine, in 1947, social learning was transformed into a "soft" technology. The new field of professional study and practice that evolved from this experience came to be known as organization development. Initially a technology in the service of corporate management, its concepts have been extended into the public domain, where social learning is closely linked to transformative practices originating in civil society, "from below."[1]

The remainder of this chapter is divided into three main parts. The first is an attempt to characterize the social learning approach by its principal features. There follows a survey of the historical de-

1. This statement needs to be qualified to the extent that a social learning model was successfully applied on a large scale during the Chinese revolution.

velopment of the approach in both its philosophical and technical aspects. The chapter closes with a critical assessment of the tradition and a brief look at some of its most recent developments.

The Social Learning Approach

The purpose of this section is to give the reader a synoptic overview of social learning as an approach to planning. It is a risky business. Among those who use the metaphor of social learning, there is little agreement on the meanings of even basic categories, such as action and learning. Nevertheless, I shall proceed, but with this warning: this is not an altogether innocent undertaking. In choosing among possible meanings of social learning, I choose an ideology as well.

What Is Action?

The principal focus of the social learning approach is on action—that is, on purposeful activity undertaken by an actor, individual or collective—within the actor's environment. Often, as for example in Marx, the concept of action is used in the sense of practical activity (Novack 1975, ch. 9). Since we are concerned here only with planning in the public domain, it will be useful to distinguish between activity as either *working* or *historical* practice. A peasant farmer pushing his plow through the field is engaged in one form of practical activity; it is his working practice. The same farmer joining with others from his village to form a dairy cooperative, village improvement association, or support group for guerilla fighters is engaged in public, historical practice. Because it is repetitive, working practice is often codified; historical practice, on the other hand, is always unprecedented and unique.

When we say that someone is engaged in an action, we generally mean that the action was taken autonomously, that the person (or organization) had a genuine, that is, noncoerced margin of choice. We tend to regard the actor as the center of his or her action. Because action must overcome resistance—though generally true, this holds with particular force for historical practice—it calls for a strategy and tactics that will guide the actor through the action itself. As resistance is successfully overcome, the actor acquires useful information that may lead to cumulative learning. Each new cycle of action, however, leads to a new start.

Who Is the Actor?

Actions imply an actor who acts. In the social learning approach, actors appear variously as individual persons, small groups, and what the organization development literature refers to as "human organ-

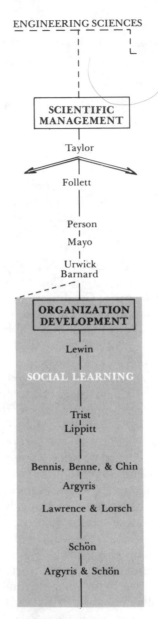

Figure 14. The social learning tradition of planning (selective).

izations" and "communities." To these categories may be added urban social movements. But the principal focus of the social learning
approach is the *task-oriented action group*, a dynamic, interactive totality involving fewer than a dozen participants, the smallest group
being the dyad of two persons. Collective actors, such as organizations, communities, and social movements, may be disassembled
into component action groups. These groups appear as relatively
impermanent structures within the larger whole that they compose
(Friedmann 1979b).

Who Learns?
In the social learning tradition, actor and learner are assumed to be
one and the same. It is the action group that learns from its own
practice. Whether organization, community, or movement also
learns will depend on the nature of intergroup relations and the
formal structure of authority. In organization development, it is
usually assumed that the relevant actors are the top management of
business firms; during the Maoist period in China, the relevant actors were said to be the peasant masses under the tutelage of political cadres. Yet despite rhetorical references to the "masses," small
groups played an extremely important role in China's revolution-
ary-historical practice (Whyte 1974).

What Are the Principal Modes of Learning?
First, learning manifests itself as a change in practical activity. Directly woven into social practice, it is rarely systematized or articulated in the formal language of scientific discourse. Social learning
is typically a form of tacit and informal learning (Polanyi 1966).

   In the second place, social learning may involve so-called change
agents who encourage, guide, and assist an actor in the process of
changing reality. They are generally professionals or paraprofes-
sionals (trainers, facilitators, process consultants, organizers; in
China, cadres and members of the Communist party) who bring
certain kinds of formal knowledge to the ongoing social practice of
their "client group." To be effective, change agents must develop a
transactive relationship with their client conducive to *mutual learning*
(Schein 1960: Friedmann 1973).

   Finally, one may speak of either *single-* or *double-loop learning* (Argyris and Schön 1974, 1978; Argyris 1982). The former involves a
simple change in the tactics or strategy of the action to solve a given
problem; the latter requires an adjustment of the norms governing
the action process and, specifically, a change in the actor's theory of
reality, values, and beliefs. It requires a major cognitive restructur-

ing that will have far-reaching practical consequences for self-image, human relations, formal authority, and the ultimate distribution of the costs and benefits of action.

Does Social Learning Require Theory?

All learning requires theory, where theory is understood as a set of categories that will guide practice and help to process information generated in the course of the action itself.

In what I have called historical practice, two kinds of theory are involved: a theory of reality and a theory of practice. The first can be further divided into (1) a theory of history, that is, how an actor is inclined to view the world (for example as a zero-sum game from the perspective of class struggle, as a natural order, or as inherently progressive), and (2) a theory of the situation, that is, an actor's understanding of the specific situation in which he or she is engaged. The theory of practice relates to an actor's conduct in specific roles. It consists of codes derived from theories of normal practice—for example, bureaucratic, political, commercial, professional, and revolutionary practice. Theories of practice are sets of expectations about appropriate behavior.

In social learning, knowledge of reality and of practice exert a mutual influence on each other. Theory, however, is based not only on an actor's evolving experience, but on prior learning as well, reflecting the actor's class position, work experience, and formal education. Prior learning is far from being a chaotic jumble of beliefs, ideas, and memories. Supported by one's peer or reference groups, theories about the world acquire a definite structure and are difficult to change. Such change has been compared to a process of re-education that involves not only cognitive but also affective-behavioral reconstruction.

These somewhat tentative generalizations concerning the conceptual scheme of social learning may now be drawn together into a more synthetic statement.

1. Actions in the public domain usually involve many collaborators acting through small, task-oriented groups which, in their internal relationships, display psychosocial dynamics that are not reducible to the characteristics of individual participants. Continuously forming and reforming, action groups are temporary social systems.

2. Embodied in group relationships, social learning is a cumulative process that lasts for the duration of a given action cycle. When a cycle terminates and the group dissolves or undergoes

a major change in composition, what has been learned is dissipated and lost. Action groups are a form of collective memory.

3. Action groups are oganized around specific tasks. In addition to the objective requirements of the tasks, group behavior is influenced by the way the personal needs of its members for love, esteem, and self-expression are being addressed within both the group and the larger environment of which it forms a part.

4. Social learning in small groups takes place primarily through face-to-face relations, or dialogue. But dialogue requires interpersonal skills, such as the art of listening, the ability to trust others and make oneself vulnerable to them, a willingness to suspend rank and material power, and a responsiveness to others' needs. These and related skills of dialogue can be acquired, at least in rudimentary form, through appropriate training.

5. In social learning, objectives tend to emerge in the course of an ongoing action. To bring about a significant redirection of objectives, however, may involve a long and painful process of "double-loop" learning.

Antecedents and Development

I now propose to outline the evolution of the social learning tradition, beginning with John Dewey's instrumentalism, or the pragmatic theory of knowledge. Dewey's influence will then be traced in the writings of three very different individuals, Mao Tse-tung, Lewis Mumford, and Edgar S. Dunn, Jr. I will then follow the tradition after World War II, when Dewey's philosophical treatment of social learning was transformed into a "soft" technology for changing social reality. The work of behavioral scientists, inspired by Kurt Lewin and institutionally connected with schools of business administration (Harvard, MIT, Michigan), social learning led to development of a new field of professional expertise know as organization development. A brief assessment of this approach in terms of its usefulness in planning, closes this section.

Dewey's Pragmatism

Pragmatism derives from the Greek word *pragmata*, meaning an act, or the state's business. It is the theory of getting things done. There is general agreement that the approach to planning that we have called social learning is rooted in this peculiarly American philosophy, which, in addition to Dewey's writings, is chiefly the work of his predecessors Charles Peirce and William James (James 1974). My purpose, however, is neither to search out the origins and derivations of Dewey's pragmatism, nor to undertake an exhaustive critical study of his monumental work. Rather, it is to look at those aspects of his philosophy—its epistemology, its political theory—that are immediately relevant to the development of social learning as a model for planning.

During the period between the great wars, John Dewey, who lived for nearly a century, from 1859 to 1952, ruled as dean of American philosophers. He was the first among his peers to be read widely in both Europe and China, and his approach, "learning by doing," virtually became a household expression. Dewey was also the last American philosopher to believe seriously in the reality of historical progress that would carry society upward and onward on the shoulders of what his Chinese admirers called Mr. Science and Mr. Democracy.

> The Golden Age lies ahead of us not behind us. Everywhere new possibilities beckon and arouse courage and effort. The great French thinkers of the later eighteenth century borrowed this idea from Bacon and developed it into the doctrine of the indefinite perfectibility of mankind on earth. Man is capable, if he will but exercise the required courage, intelligence and effort, of shaping his own fate. (Dewey 1950, 59: orig. 1920)

This ardent declaration, albeit 120 years too late, came from a true believer in the Enlightenment. Dewey's world was like a continent whose frontiers had not yet closed in upon themselves.[2] Its vast and unexplored expanses stretched out before a human race that was eager to explore it, to settle it, and to make the land fertile and productive. The only true end of human effort, declared Dewey, was growth itself. It would lead, he thought, to an as yet unimagined improvement in the conditions of life and to the moral perfection of the race.

> Government, business, art, religion, all social institutions have a meaning, a purpose. That purpose is to set free and to develop the capacities of human individuals without respect to race, sex, class or economic status. And this is all one with saying that the test of their value is the extent to which they edu-

2. Dewey was thirty-four years old when Frederick Jackson Turner proclaimed his famous frontier theory of American history and in the same breath declared the "era of the frontier" at an end.

cate every individual into the full stature of his possibility. Democracy has many meanings, but if it has a moral meaning, it is found in resolving that the supreme test of all political institutions and industrial arrangements shall be the contribution they make to the all-around growth of every member of society. (Ibid. 147)

Empirical science was the medium through which social progress would be achieved. Dewey's imagination was captivated by its unique method of knowing, which was self-corrective in operation and enabled scientists to learn from both their failures and successes.

> The heart of the method is the discovery of the identity of inquiry with discovery. Within the specialized, the relatively technical, activities of natural science, this office of discovery, of uncovering the new and leaving behind the old, is taken for granted. (Ibid. 22)

Uncovering the new, leaving behind the old—with this phrase, Dewey gave pointed expression to the mythology that underlay the American "experiment." To untold millions, America appeared as the Promised Land. Immigrants streamed to her shores from abroad, the fabled land shimmering before their eyes. One's personal history, they found, counted for very little here, the present was forever in transition, and the future beckoned seductively on the horizon. All you had to do was to let go of your past and set to work.

Dewey's epistemology was meant to reflect and serve this vision of America. All valid knowledge, declared Dewey, comes from experience, by which he meant the interaction between human subjects and their material environment. "In its primary integrity," he said, "experience recognizes no division between act and material, subject and object, but contains them both in an unanalyzed totality" (Dewey 1958, 8; orig. 1929). It was an active mode of being in the world. Through experience, we come not only to understand the world but also to transform it. As in a spiral movement, from practice to plan and again back to practice, it is the way we learn.

> The plans which are formed, the principles which man projects as guides of reconstructive action, are not dogmas. They are hypotheses to be worked out in practice, and to be rejected, corrected, and expanded as they fail or succeed in giving our present experience the guidance it requires. (Dewey 1950, 89, orig. 1920)

Each "plan" is an experiment, and history unfolds as a succession of experiments in a progressive movement. With each cycle of hypothesis and testing, we consolidate what we know, and we eliminate error. But in historical practice, how shall we know what constitutes truth and what error? Dewey strove mightily to bypass these troublesome terms. Although he did away with truth and error, the question of whether an assertion was valid remained. His first, tentative answer was simple enough: hypotheses are to be rejected, corrected, and expanded as they fail or succeed in giving present experience the guidance that it needs (ibid. 128–130).

In the end, this answer would prove unsatisfactory. To a maker of violins, it may be fairly evident when his "hypothesis" of how to build a master instrument has been successful: experienced musicians will tell him so. But in the domain of historical practice, where problems are nortoriously "slippery" and even "wicked," success and failure are not as readily determined. The question of what is valid knowledge requires deeper exploration.

By 1929, Dewey thought he had advanced over his earlier formulation. Truth, he had always insisted, is adverbial. "That which guides truly is true." And since there is no final truth, its pursuit as such is folly. Every statement is tentative, provisional. *Knowledge is validated*—this was his basic insight—*only when it helps an actor to dispose or settle a problem* (Dewey 1980, 229; orig. 1929). And a problem is settled when "conclusions emerge in which objects once uncertain and confused are rendered clear and stable" (ibid. 230).

It seemed like a reasonable solution. On closer inspection, however, this answer, too, proved troublesome. Could it be that each actor had knowledge that was valid only for himself? Was it not distinctive of all articulated knowledge that it was shared with others?

With his treatise on logic (1938), published when he was already in his eighties, Dewey proposed a category that would replace the classical criteria. He called it "warranted assertability." Reliable statements about the world must have a guarantor. And how shall we know, in the specific case, that they in fact have such a warrant? We know it, he explained, not from their proven correspondence with an objective reality, or from their resilience to repeated efforts at "falsification," but from the "opinions of mankind" for which, he admonished, we must have a "decent respect." Valid knowledge, he concluded, rests on a *consensus theory of truth* (Novack 1975, 178).

Dewey fails to show us how individual hypotheses are to be combined into larger theoretical constructs. Apparently, every hypothesis is to be treated as a new throw of the dice. Although in *Experience and Education* (1963a) he wrote with great insistence about the *con-*

tinuity of human experience and its significance for knowing, this was a rather belated admission, and its consequences for epistemology were not explored. Taking into account the immense body of his writings, it is not at all certain that Dewey had anything more elaborate in mind than one provisional hypothesis after another. He did not regard the production of knowledge as a social enterprise, as was subsequently suggested both by Kuhn (1970) and by Feyerabend (1975). In Dewey's process theory of knowledge, the true pragmatist must be prepared to let go of a hypothesis the moment he finds that it no longer gives him the guidance he thinks he needs. As an actor in the public domain, he must continuously explore the new and leave the old behind. *The past has no claims on the present.* Commitments, stakes, interests, fear of loss, attachments are so many irrational impulses that must be overcome by a properly scientific approach.

Dewey was extremely elusive about the actors whose experience in the public domain would form the basis of their knowledge. In many situations there was little doubt. In the classroom, for example, the active learner was the student, and in the laboratory it was the scientist. But who "produced" the history of humankind?

For Dewey's answer, we must turn to his theory of politics (Dewey 1946; orig. 1927). What we find here is surprising. The members of a polity, said Dewey, cluster around issues of common concern; in this way, they constitute different publics. At any one moment, there will be as many publics as there are common issues. At first inchoate, these publics acquire coherence as government officials organize them and act in behalf of their interests (ibid. 28). Public officials, Dewey asserted, are the caretakers or "guardians" of the public interest or, to be more precise, of the special interests under their tutelage. It is the business of the publics to *discuss* what is of interest to them and, in the form of wishes and complaints, to pass the word on up to the officials of the state. But the state takes counsel only with itself. This potentially orderly and stable process is difficult to carry out, however, because as new issues arise, the state is in continuous flux, shuffling and reshuffling agencies and publics.

> [T]he problem of discovering the state is not a problem of theoretical inquirers engaged solely in surveying institutions
> which already exist. It is a practical problem of human beings
> in association with each other. . . . The formation of states
> must be an experimental process. (Ibid. 32–33)

A semblance of order amidst chaos is maintained by an elite corps of experts, the technocrats of the modern state. Most public concerns are technical matters, said Dewey. They involve the same kinds of problems as the design and construction of an efficient machine. Such problems

> are to be settled by an inquiry into facts; and as the inquiry can be carried out only by those especially equipped for it, so the results of inquiry can be utilized only by trained technicians. What has counting heads, decision by majority and the whole apparatus of traditional government to do with such things? (Ibid. 124–125)

Even as he wrote these lines, in apparent approval of decisions by experts (in this, echoing Thorstein Veblen's call for a "soviet of engineers"), Dewey worried about the decline of politics. "What, after all," he cried, "is the public under present conditions? What are the reasons for its eclipse?" (ibid. 125). Unable to resolve the contradiction between the need for technical experts and the recovery of politics, he sought refuge in a utopia of the Great Community, which would be sustained, he argued, by an intimate dialogue on public questions.

> Signs and symbols, language, are the means of communication by which a fraternally shared experience is ushered in and sustained. But the winged words of conversation in immediate intercourse have a vital import lacking in the fixed and frozen words of written speech. Systematic and continuous inquiry into all the conditions which affect association and their dissemination in print is a precondition of the creation of a true public. But it and its results are but tools after all. Their final actuality is accomplished in face-to-face relationships by means of direct give and take. Logic in its fulfillment recurs to the primitive sense of the word: dialogue. Ideas which are not communicated, shared, and reborn in expression are but soliloquy, and soliloquy is but broken and imperfect thought. It, like the acquisition of material wealth, marks a diversion of the wealth created by associated endeavor and exchange to private ends. It is more genteel and it is called more noble. But there is no difference in kind. (Ibid. 218)

It is a noble vision, but how should we find the path to take us there? Dewey thought that to reach the Great Community one had to start at home. The journey had to begin in the community of neighbors.

A man who has not been seen in the daily relations of life may inspire admiration, emulation, servile subjection, fanatical partisanship, hero worship; but not love and understanding, save as they radiate from the attachments of a near-by union. *Democracy must begin at home, and its home is the neighborly community.* (Ibid. 213; italics added)

As a political theme, this was as durable a one as could be found in America (McWilliams 1973). And Dewey gave it its maximum expression: "The local is the ultimate universal," he wrote, "and as near an absolute as exists" (Dewey 1946, 215; orig. 1927).

With this remarkable apotheosis of the local community, Dewey closed his inquiry into the nature of politics. Transcending class divisions, public action is to be restricted to a dialogue among friends, neighbors, and kinfolk. Unfortunately, he never "disposed" of the question of how a republic might survive its growing legions of experts who, immune to political pressure, would govern locals from above.

Dewey's Influence
During his lifetime, Dewey's influence was wide and pervasive, especially in the United States. His optimistic faith in the future, his "plain talk" (so different from the obscurantism of contemporary European philosophers), his generous reading of democracy with its double affirmation of equality and science, and his ardent belief in the possibilities of human self-realization through experiential learning—all these made Dewey a leading spokesman for his age. It was natural that he should also become a strong advocate of planning. Indeed, in the period between the wars, Dewey was the great oracle of scientific planning. In *Liberalism and Social Action*, he wrote:

Organized social planning, put into effect for the creation of an order in which industry and finance are socially directed in behalf of institutions that provide the material basis for the cultural liberation and growth of individuals, is now the sole method of social action by which liberalism can realize its professed aims. Such planning demands in turn a new conception and logic of freed intelligence as a social force. (Dewey 1963b, 54–55; orig. 1935)

It was not difficult to be a faithful disciple. Dewey's message was of the simplest sort: only ideas that work matter; the scientific method points the way to human progress; one learns by changing reality.

Ideas like these might surface in many different settings. Three individuals who were strongly influenced by Dewey's ideas on social learning were Mao Tse-tung, Lewis Mumford, and Edgar S. Dunn, Jr.

Mao Tse-tung. The case of Mao Tse-tung is surely the strangest of the three. There is no reason to believe that Mao ever read any of Dewey's writings or, for that matter, heard him lecture in person. Yet, there is strong circumstantial evidence that Mao's essay "On Practice" (1968a; orig. 1937), one of the most important statements in the social learning tradition, was directly influenced by Dewey.[3]

In 1919, invited by one of his former students at Columbia University, Dewey still robust at sixty-three, arrived in China, where he was persuaded to remain for two years of intensive lecturing and writing. It was during this period that he put the finishing touches on his *Reconstruction in Philosophy* (1950; orig. 1920).

> Neither Mao nor his various biographers indicate that he attended any of Dewey's lectures or that he had any direct contact with the American philosopher. Mao speaks of his own shift from liberalism to Marxism as having occurred in the spring and summer of 1920. Prior to that time and during the first year of Dewey's stay in China there were several occasions on which it would have been possible for Mao to have attended one of Dewey's lectures. The importance of establishing this kind of direct contact between Mao and Dewey is mitigated, however, by the fact that the journals and newspapers of the period which we know that Mao followed closely were filled with discussions of Dewey's ideas. Thus it would have been impossible for Mao to have avoided extensive (if secondhand) contact with these ideas. (Starr 1983, 4–5)

Mao's essay was composed in 1937, fully eighteen years after Dewey first set foot in China. According to Mao's official editors, the essay was occasioned by his desire "to expose the subjectivist errors of dogmatism and empiricism in the Party, and especially the error of dogmatism, from the standpoint of the Marxist theory of knowledge" (Mao Tse-tung 1968a, 1–2). Its significance for the future of his country was Mao's insistence, even at this early date and in the rhetoric of a philosophical discourse, on a Chinese road to socialism. China's historical circumstances were very different from those of

---

3. For this and other observations on the relation between Dewey and Mao, I am deeply indebted to John Bryan Starr of Yale University, who was kind enough to let me see a draft of his forthcoming essay on the subject (1983).

the Soviet Union—the self-proclaimed mother country of international socialism at the time—and if Chinese revolutionaries were going to be successful, they would have to examine their own reality, *they would have to learn from their own practice*.

The essay makes no mention of Dewey. All the same, at a first reading, the parallels are striking.

> Marxists hold that man's social practice alone is the criterion of the truth of his knowledge of the external world. What actually happens is that man's knowledge is verified only when he achieves the anticipated results in the process of social practice (material production, class struggle, or scientific experiment). If a man wants to succeed in his work, that is, to achieve the anticipated results, he must bring his ideas into correspondence with the laws of the objective external world; if they do not correspond, he will fail in his practice. After he fails, he draws his lessons, corrects his ideas to make them correspond to the laws of the external world, and can thus turn failure into success; this is what is meant by "failure is the mother of success" and "a fall into the pit, a gain in your wit." The dialectical-materialist theory of knowledge places practice in the primary position. (Ibid., 3)

In this quotation, which provides the key to Mao's essay, social practice is variously defined as the practice of material production, class struggle, and scientific experiment. This is a sharper, more hard-edged focus than Dewey's category of experience, which he described as an interactive totality between humans and their environment.

A second point of difference with Dewey's pragmatism is Mao's insistence that practice must be brought into "correspondence with the laws of the objective external world." Mao adopts the realist position according to which the world has an objective existence. It is the task of theory correctly to interpret this reality and to bring social practice into conformity with it. This supposition allows Mao to use freely the terms "error" and "truth," which Dewey was straining to avoid. According to George Novack (1975), Dewey replied evasively when challenged on the question of the realist position. Although he offered different answers at different times, his formulations were consistently non-dialectical. His basic category of experience remained an "unanalyzed totality." It failed, says Novack, who is both a Marxist and a realist, to transcend the "real dualism" between subject and object (Novack 1975, 170).

Leaving these differences aside, Dewey and Mao fundamentally agreed that the source of all valid knowledge is the practice of changing reality. Mao's language on this point is vivid and concrete.

> If you want knowledge, you must take part in the practice of changing reality. If you want to know the taste of a pear, you must change the pear by eating it yourself. If you want to know the structure and properties of the atom, you must make physical and chemical experiments to change the state of the atom. If you want to know the theory and methods of revolution, you must take part in revolution. All genuine knowledge originates in direct experience. (Mao Tse-tung 1968a, 8)

Perceptual knowledge is the start, but social practice must be guided by appropriate theory, which in turn must be revised according to the lessons of experience.[4] The process of mutual adjustment between theory and practice is never ending. According to Mao, who, like Trotsky, espoused a theory of permanent revolution, even the revolutionary theory of Marxism is subject to this law. There is no omega of history; change and transformation are pervasive and eternal.

> As man's practice which changes objective reality in accordance with given ideas, theories, plans or programmes, advances further and further, his knowledge of objective reality likewise becomes deeper and deeper. The movement of change in the world of objective reality is never-ending and so is man's cognition of truth through practice. Marxism-Leninism has in no way exhausted truth but ceaselessly opens up roads to the knowledge of truth in the course of practice. Our conclusion is the concrete, historical unity of the subjective and the objective, of theory and practice, of knowing and doing, and we are opposed to all erroneous ideologies, whether "Left" or "Right" which depart from concrete history. (Ibid. 19)

4. When Mao spoke of theory, he had in mind of course, the Marxist-Leninist theory of revolutionary practice. The counterpart in Dewey was a scientific hypothesis. But Dewey used the option of a hypothesis inconsistently. Sometimes, he seemed to refer to a whole chapter of history, as in "America: an experiment in democracy." At other times, he referred simply to a "working hypothesis." His pragmatic convictions made it difficult for Dewey to put forward a global hypothesis of historical practice. He was a reformer and pluralist at heart who believed in the essential correctness of democratic procedures, specifically in their American form, as the medium that would reconcile the contradictions of historical practice.

In typical fashion, Mao interpreted this process of interaction and adjustment as a dialectical cycle between whatever is immediately given and conceptual knowledge.

> Practice, knowledge, again practice, and again knowledge.
> This form repeats itself in endless cycles, and with each cycle,
> the content of practice and knowledge rises to a higher level.
> Such is the whole of the dialectical-materialist theory of
> knowledge, and such is the dialectical-materialist theory of
> knowing and doing. (Ibid. 20)

The problem of what constitutes *valid* knowledge remains, however. When is guiding theory in error and in need of change, and when is failure to attain anticipated results merely a result of unexpected events whose causes are not structural but accidental?

In his short essay "Where Do Correct Ideas Come From?" (1968b; orig. 1963), Mao elaborates on his conviction that knowledge is valid only when it brings the results expected by an actor. This is true, he says, of "man's struggle with nature." But in social struggle, failure may be either historical, and therefore structural, or accidental.

> [T]he forces representing the advanced class sometimes suffer
> defeat not because their ideas are incorrect but because, in the
> balance of forces engaged in struggle, thcy are not as power-
> ful for the time being as the forces of reaction; they are there-
> fore temporarily defeated, but they are bound to triumph
> sooner or later. (Ibid. 135)

But who is to decide the question in the title of the essay, and on what authority? Two possibilities present themselves: either unlimited communication—a full public discussion of the event in question—all opinions being heard, and a vote taken, with a majority deciding, or the ex cathedra pronouncement of a Hobbesian Sovereign. On the whole, Mao inclined toward the latter position, Dewey toward the former (Starr 1983, 10).

We may therefore conclude that the epistemology of social learning, at least in its application to historical practice, is grounded in political theory about the nature of the state. For Dewey, the political framework for social learning was in the Anglo-American tradition of liberal democracy: pluralist, open-ended, egalitarian, and respectful of civil rights. For Mao, it was the theory of democratic centralism (Starr 1979, 148–156 passim).

Lewis Mumford. The second social learning theorist significantly influenced by Dewey's thinking was Lewis Mumford. The influence
was indirect, because Mumford's intellectual roots were not in pragmatism, and he was given even less than Dewey to abstract theorizing. His passion was the city in its historical concreteness (we may
recall here Dewey's lack of interest in historical thinking). His first
great book was a masterful synthesis of the city's cultural history
(1938).

In two short chapters on the unity of city and countryside in regional planning, about fifteen pages in all, Mumford outlines a vision of planning that to this day remains unsurpassed. In the preceding decade, Mumford had thought hard about regional
planning (Sussman 1976). Now he distilled his thinking to propose
a view of planning as a self-educative process of social transformation projected onto an entire region. From the hands of experts into
which nearly everyone had placed their trust, Mumford would de-
volve planning, as a form of regional praxis, to the people themselves.

According to Mumford, the practice of regional planning has
four distinctive phases: (1) an initial series of surveys to obtain a
multilayered image of the region in its historical dimension; (2) an
outline of regional needs and activities expressed in terms of social
ideals and critically formulated purposes;[5] (3) an imaginative reconstruction and projection of the region's future; and (4) most important, the "intelligent absorption" of the plan by the regional population and its translation into action through the appropriate
political and economic agencies (Mumford 1938, 375–380).

The entire effort was conceived by Mumford as an educative
process.

> Regional plans are instruments of communal education; and
> without that education, they can look forward only to partial
> achievement. Failing intelligent participation and understand-
> ing, at every stage in the process, from the smallest unit up,
> regional plans must remain inert. Hence the need for positive
> organs of assimilation. Regional plans must provide in their
> very constitution the means of future adjustments. The plan
> that does not leave the way open to change is scarcely less dis-
> orderly than the aimless empiricism that rejects the plan. Re-
> newal: flexibility: adjustment: these are essential attributes of
> all organic plans. (Ibid. 380–381)

5. Mumford had written, "Not merely does planning . . . require a visualization of
resources and activities and processes, by means of the regional survey: it demands a
critical formulation—and revision—or current values" (Mumford 1938, 377).

Hence, there follows the unusual image of "intelligent absorption": the plan, properly understood, is to form the context of day-to-day choices, decisions, and inventions. It will percolate outward into the fine web of social relations in local communities to animate the appropriate actions.

Social learning had to be pushed down to the neighborhood and village. In this respect, Mumford was at one with Dewey. But where Dewey trusted in experts, Mumford thought that people could do a lot for themselves. In his heart, he was a Jeffersonian democrat.[6]

> The real alternative to the empty political patterns of the nineteenth century lies, not in totalitarianism, but in just the opposite of this: the restoration of the human scale in government, the multiplication of the units of autonomous service, the widening of the cooperative processes of government, the general reduction of the area of arbitrary compulsion, the restoration of the processes of persuasion and rational agreement. Political life, instead of being the monopoly of remote specialists, must become as constant a process in daily living as the housewife's visit to the grocer or the butcher, and more frequent than the man's visit to the barber. (Ibid. 382)

It is the concrete, everyday experiences of people in their local and regional surroundings that form the basis of all reliable knowledge for guiding their actions in the present.

We glimpse here a vision of a learning society in which people are politically active and informed and can engage each other in a rational discourse over the kind of regional life they would want for themselves. Mumford thought that to realize this vision people would need to undergo a special educational experience. Beginning with children, both boys and girls, as they became active in various kinds of regional activity, it would culminate in their participation in regional surveys, which is where planning starts.

> Beginning with the crawling of an infant in his home, the systematic contact with the environment should broaden out until it includes the furthest horizon of mountain top and sea: in a bout of sailing, fishing, hunting, quarrying or mining every child should have a firsthand acquaintance with the primitive substratum of economic life: the geography and geology of the textbook should be annotations to these experiences, not substitutes . . .
>   The next step toward a rational political life . . . is the hitch-

6. See Jefferson's letter to Joseph C. Cabell on "The Elementary Republics of the Wards," written in 1816. (Reprinted in Friedmann 1981, 219–222.)

ing of these concrete experiences to local surveys, more systematically undertaken. The soil survey, the climatic survey,
the geological survey, the industrial survey, the historical survey, on the basis of the immediate local environment, are the
next important instruments of education: this is a process of
grasping in detail and as a whole what has hitherto been taken
in through passive observation in city and countryside. (Ibid.
384)

Mumford concludes his essay with a veritable manifesto of social
learning.

We must create in every region people who will be accustomed, from school onward, to humanist attitudes, cooperative methods, rational controls. These people will know in detail where they live: they will be united by a common feeling
for their landscape, their literature and language, their local
ways, and out of their own self-respect they will have a sympathetic understanding with other regions and different local
peculiarities. They will be actively interested in the form and
culture of their locality, which means their community and
their own personalities. Such people will contribute to our
land planning, our industry planning, and our community
planning the authority of their own understanding, and the
pressure of their own desires. Without them, planning is a
barren externalism. (Ibid. 386)

Like Mao, Mumford was concerned with pushing social learning
down to localities in a praxis of regional reconstruction. It was to be
an effort directed at transforming the relations of countryside and
city "from below." But unlike Mao—and this made Mumford a utopian rather than a revolutionary—he had no program for overturning the existing structures of power which, in Mumford's case, were
the institutions of monopoly capitalism that, even as he was writing
about a revived political life, were undermining his dream. His life
ended in bitterness and disillusion.[7]

Edgar S. Dunn, Jr. The third major social learning theorist writing
under Dewey's sway is Edgar S. Dunn, Jr., an economist with a
Washington think tank and a former deputy assistant secretary for
Economic affairs of the U.S. Department of Commerce. His book
Economic and Social Development (1971) carries the provocative sub-

7. For a wider perspective on Mumford's thought in American regionalism, see
Friedmann and Weaver (1979, especially ch. 2).

title *A Process of Social Learning*. Its basic orientation is directly derived from Dewey's writings, and its overall approach is evolutionary and progressive.

Dunn's central concept is what he calls *evolutionary experimentation*,
and in accord with many noted biologists such as George Gaylord
Simpson and Theodosius Dobzhanski, he sees history as the natural
successor to biological evolution—an evolution "by other means," so
to speak. The general trend of historical movement is in a steadily
upward direction. But where evolution in the natural sphere is
guided by the interaction of necessity and chance in selective muta-
tion, social evolution is purposeful and a result of planning. Dunn's
"moral imperative" derives from this general understanding: "we
must improve the efficiency of evolutionary experimentation and
its directed character" (Dunn 1971, 157).

At this juncture, Dunn pauses momentarily to ask how history
might be given a stronger sense of collective purpose in the event of
there being a disagreement about the nature of the improvement to
be made. It is the question that continues to haunt the pragmatist
philosopher of social learning: how can we tell that the knowledge
we apply is valid? Difficult enough to decide for a single actor, the
problem is compounded when the action to be taken affects an entire political community. Dunn's stiff and Olympian reply is that
conflicts over goals—that is over the correct course of action to be
taken—"can only be resolved by goal modification or by subordinating the goals in conflict to a higher order goal that embraces
both" (ibid. 158–159). All told, it is a counsel of despair.

The fact of the matter is that, like Dewey and Mumford before
him, but unlike Mao, Dunn cannot conceive of a situation in which
there might be a fundamental disagreement over what he calls "the
direction of history." History follows a course of progressive evolution, and who could be opposed to that? All that is necessary, Dunn
suggests, is for people "to iron out their differences" and reach
agreement on what needs to be done. He refuses to see this as anything other than a rational process of discussion and debate.

Like Dewey, too, Dunn is tantalizingly vague about who should be
the actor in his system of evolutionary experimentation. For Mao,
the historical actor was the peasant masses of China under the collective leadership and guidance of the Communist party; for Mumford, it was the inhabitants of a region acting through their own institutions. But the former Washington bureaucrat conjures up "the
social system experimenter," the *dues ex machina* of pragmatism, who
magically creates order out of choas.

> The basic point of departure is the fact that the social system
> experimenter is not exogenous to the system. He exists as an
> endogenous component of the system he is attempting to un-
> derstand and transform. He is immersed in the act of social
> system self-analysis and self-transformation. He is the agent of
> social learning—a purposive, self-actuating, but not fully de-
> terministic process. . . . He is engaged . . . in formulating and
> testing developmental hypotheses. (Ibid. 241)

Alas, we never discover the nature of this potent male. We encounter him as a faceless Administrator of Social Change who will ensure
that the process of social transformation is "conscious, orderly, and
controlled" (ibid. 244). Political mobilization plays no evident part in
this process. And while the people talk (dialogue is eulogized by
Dunn and Dewey both), the real action is decided at the top.

Organization Development (OD)

The behaviorist approach to planning the human side of enterprise
is an intellectual hybrid. Its origins are in the older management science of Frederick Winslow Taylor and Harlow S. Person. It is from
this tradition that OD draws its major clients—the top management
of corporations—as well as its principal assignment—enhancing the
long-term profitability of enterprise.[8] But its wellspring of inspiration is psychology.

When OD researchers began to evolve a professional identity and
to look at workers as something other than abstract symbols on an
organization chart, the earlier emphasis of leading theorists on "efficiency" and "time and motion studies" began to give way to the humanistic psychologies of Carl Rogers and Abraham Maslow, which
stressed self-actualizing personalities and hierarchies of human
needs. These psychologies subtly undermined the prevailing totalitarian ethos of corporate management, which continued to regard
workers as prefabricated components in a carefully designed machine.

With the introduction of humanistic psychology, OD acquired a
quasi-spiritual dimension. Although OD practitioners continued to
regard themselves as exponents of empirical science and clinical
practice, their approach to the structuring of the human work experience became increasingly normative. Some of the public pronouncements of its doyens, such as Warren Bennis and Chris Ar-

8. See, for example, Likert (1967), in which end-result variables of the preferred
"system organization" are higher sales volume, lower sales costs, higher quality of
business sold, and higher earnings by salesmen.

gyris, carried an almost messianic message. Their humanistic vision for America promised to transform the industrial capitalism of the past into a fluid "post-industrial" society from which coercive power, exploitation, and oppression were absent (see, for example, McCluskey 1976). The tendency was to portray these traits as atavistic residues from an earlier era. Coercive power, said the doyens, was no longer necessary. The organization of the future would be decentralized, spontaneous, and non-hierarchical.

The Hawthorne Experiment and Its Lessons. Our interest in OD derives from its explicit social learning approach, which it perfected as a clinical method for intervention in organizational change. The Hawthorne story, where it all began, takes us back to the mid-1920s, when the scientific management movement was at its height and Harlow S. Person was evolving ideas on management planning that would soon make their way into the national debate on planning America's future.

In collaboration with the National Research Council and the Western Electric Company, the Harvard Graduate School of Business initiated in 1927, at Western's Hawthorne plant in Chicago, a series of experiments that would make history. Work at Hawthorne continued until 1932. It was the first time that the socio-behavioral sciences were put to the test as a technology; by all accounts, the results were a resounding success (Mayo 1933; Roethlisberger and Dickson 1939).

The original studies had to do with the relation between conditions of work and the incidence among workers of fatigue and monotony. The second phase of these studies involved six workers who were segregated from a regular operating department of the plant for special study and observation.

> The operation selected was that of assembling telephone relays. This consisted in putting together a coil, armature, contact springs, and insulators in a fixture and securing the parts in position by means of four machine screws; each assembly takes about one minute, when the work is going well. The operation is ranked as repetitive; it is performed by women.
> (Mayo 1933, 55)

The problem to be solved was which changes in working conditions would lead to a sustained increase in output per worker. To their great surprise, researchers discovered that changes in the women's physical environment made virtually no difference in the level of their performance. Changes in *social* working conditions, on the other hand, not only led to higher output but appeared to increase worker satisfaction as well. Harvard scientists made the "epochal" discovery that workers are human beings who respond favorably when they are treated with consideration and respect. They concluded that an industrial organization was essentially a social system whose patterned regularities could be measured and whose behavior could be altered through appropriate interventions by management.[9]

The Hawthorne studies demonstrated that women, even as disciplined factory workers, retained a *core of free choice* over their work, that despite their machine-like, repetitive tasks, they were not robots, and that a hidden reservoir of motivation could be tapped by management so long as the workers were treated as feeling and thinking beings with other needs beyond the need to earn a living. Elton Mayo quotes M. L. Putnam of the Western Electric Company about the lessons management drew from the Hawthorne experiments.

> The records of the test room showed a continual improvement in the performance of the operators regardless of the experimental changes made during the study. It was also noticed . . . that there was a marked improvement in their attitude toward their work and working environment. This simultaneous improvement in attitude and effectiveness indicated that there might be a definite relationship between them. In other words, we could more logically attribute the increase in efficiency to a betterment of morale than to any of the . . . alterations made in the course of the experiment. We concluded that the same relationship might exist throughout the plant and that the best way to improve morale . . . was through improved supervision. (Ibid. 74)

9. The flavor of these experiments comes across in this description by Elton Mayo, who inspired the work at Hawthorne.

Undoubtedly there had been a remarkable change of mental attitude in the group. Reference is to the group of women involved in the experiment. This showed in their recurrent conferences with high executive authorities. At first shy and uneasy, silent and perhaps somewhat suspicious of the company's intention, later their attitude is marked by confidence and candor. Before every change in program, the group is consulted. Their comments are listened to and discussed; sometimes their objections are allowed to negative a suggestion. The group unquestioningly develops a sense of participation in the critical determinations and becomes something of a social unit. This developing social unity is illustrated by the entertainment of each other in their respective homes, especially operatives one, two, three, and four. (Mayo 1933, 69)

The approach of the behavioral scientists who undertook these studies was, of course, highly manipulative. They had penetrated into the secret of human motivation and had used this knowledge to alter workers' behavior in ways that were ultimately beneficial to management. In their own science, the consequences were far-reaching, and what had started as an obscure micro-experiment in a small corner of the giant Hawthorne Works would blossom out into a social movement.

Group Dynamics, Personality, and Human Growth. The Hawthorne experiments gave rise to a new field of research: the study of small groups and the dynamics of their interactions. The relay assembly room at Hawthorne had consisted of a group of six workers; once one began to look around, groups of approximately this size might be found almost everywhere. When managers talked about their "span of control," they meant a small group of four to six others (Urwick 1956, 59–60). Military organization was based on the ten-men squad as the smallest operating group, and World War II had taught the importance of the "buddy system" for the survival of soldiers in combat. There were study groups in universities and groups of active citizens meeting in each others' homes to map out strategies of political struggle. And there was, of course, everybody's group, the ubiquitous nuclear family. In the foreshortened perspective of the evolving machine of OD, small groups were seen as ideal social settings for changing behavior.

The major catalyst for the study of small groups was a refugee scholar from Berlin, Kurt Lewin. A social psychologist, Lewin had developed what he called a field-analytical method for describing social interactions (1951). After coming to the United States in 1932, he dedicated a major part of his professional life to the study of face-to-face relations in small groups. In 1944, he founded the Research Center for Group Dynamics at MIT, which opened up a whole new range of inquiries with immediate implications for behavioral restructuring.[10]

Lewin's basic teaching was that groups are *interactive wholes* that cannot be further broken down into their individual elements without having their existence as an organic unity destroyed. The smallest possible group is the dyad. This and all larger groups, argued Lewin, are constituted as a relationship (or set of relationships). *When this relationship is severed, the group, which had its own dynamics until then, will disappear without leaving a trace.*

10. Upon Lewin's death in 1947, the center moved to the University of Michigan, where it continued to flourish under the direction of Dorwin Cartwright.

Groups, said Lewin, form the basis for our development as persons because they are "the ground on which a person stands." Even though the strength of an individual's attachment to specific groups may change, and members will "read" each others' relationship to the group as a whole and to each other quite differently, groups have an exceptionally high potency for all of us. From childhood on, we are accustomed to using group relations to further our own ends. Because we are ubiquitously members of groups, a change in personal circumstances is often a direct result of a change in the situation of the groups of which we are a part. Finally, the group is for all of us part of the life space in which we move about, and to reach or maintain a certain status or position within a group is one of our vital goals (Lewin 1948, 85–86; orig. 1940).

To study group behavior scientifically, theorists had to devise an appropriate methodology. Again, the Hawthorne experiment provided the key: *the way to study groups was to try to change their behavior.* Group dynamic research was thus a form of "action research" in which theory would be linked to the practice of changing reality. It was precisely at this point that the study of group dynamics, which would soon change into OD, was linked directly to Dewey's social learning approach (Lewin 1951, ch. 7; orig. 1943–1944).[11]

The major difference between group dynamics and the social learning paradigm as it had evolved up to this point was that changing behavior groups was thought to require an outside "agent" who, ever since the halcyon days of the Hawthorne experiments, was inevitably also a researcher. Properly speaking, the actor was not the group itself but the outside "change agent" who, while engaged in the modification of group behavior, was also studying the very process of this change.

It was only a matter of time, however, before a different conception would prevail. Now it was thought that successful behavioral change on the part of groups—Lewin called it the process of re-education—required that members experience themselves as *acting subjects* and that the group itself, as it collectively acted upon its own environment, become the relevant subject for learning. Henceforward, change agents were called by softer, less threatening names, such as facilitator and trainer.[12]

To give reality to this new conception, which came to be embodied in the laboratory method, a training workshop was conducted in New Britain, Connecticut, in 1946.

11. In his preface to *Resolving Social Conflicts* (Lewin 1948), Gordon W. Allport notes the striking kinship between Dewey's work and Lewin's.

12. For Lewin's theory of "re-education," see the perceptive, critical essay by Kenneth D. Benne in Bennis et al. (1976, ch. 8.1).

The four major leaders at Connecticut, Kurt Lewin, Kenneth D. Benne, Leland P. Bradford, and Ronald Lippitt, each brought different knowledge and experiences which made the events at Connecticut feasible and possible. Kurt Lewin brought high competence in research concepts and methodologies, original theories of group dynamics and of the processes of social change, and an active interest in action research as a tool for social improvement. Kenneth Benne brought knowledge of philosophy, particularly educational philosophy, as well as experiences in the use of workshop and discussion methods of learning and in intercultural education. Leland Bradford contributed knowledge and experience from the growing field of adult education as well as a background in educational psychology and knowledge of workshop methods and discussion experiments in adult education. Ronald Lippitt brought knowledge of social psychology, particularly of group behavior, through his work with Lewin, skills in research technologies, and a background in educational theory through his work with Piaget. (Benne et al. 1975, 3–4)[13]

Out of this initial experience came the National Training Laboratory in Group Dynamics, which, in the summer of 1947, moved into Gould Academy in Bethel, Maine. The training offered stressed the unity of theory and practice, an experimental approach, face-to-face relations among the members of a T-group (training group), and the participation of a professional "trainer." It sought to develop growth in the self-awareness and improvement in the interpersonal skills of the participants. Greater competence in managing group relations, it was thought, would be the principal lever for changing the organizations to which the participants eventually returned. The direction of the intended change was greater adaptiveness to changing conditions in organizational environments and, on

13. This brief account of the originators of the laboratory method calls attention to several cross-influences. Reference to Benne's background in educational philosophy is a specific reference to John Dewey, whose educational theories at that time were dominant. Lippitt's involvement with Piaget is of interest in light of Piaget's later work on "genetic epistemology," which had much in common with Dewey's instrumentalism. According to Piaget (1970), a child is capable of learning before it begins to verbalize: learning proceeds from manipulating one's environment. It is evolutionary, rising from primitive institutions through a variety of novel constructs to complex understandings of reality. "To my way of thinking," wrote Piaget, "knowing an object does not mean copying it. It means constructing systems of transformation that can be carried out on or with this object systems of transformations that correspond, more or less adequately, to reality. They are more or less isomorpic transformations of reality" (Piaget 1970, 15).

the part of business firms, increased long-term growth in productivity.

From the initial experience at Bethel, the idea of group training spread rapidly, as various universities across the country set up training laboratories of their own. By the mid-1950s, the name of the original organization was shortened to National Training Laboratories (NTL), and participants were drawn in greater numbers from nonbusiness organizations such as community groups and educational institutions. In 1967, an NTL Institute for Applied Behavioral Science was formed, with program divisions on community affairs, education, international programs, organization development, Black affairs, administration, and (subsequently) voluntarism. After several reorganizations, the four major "centers" that made up the Institute in 1975 were the Center for the Development of Individual Potential, the Center for Macro-System Change, the Center for Professional Development, and the Center for System Development. Each year, one hundred laboratory programs were conducted with organizations and institutions around the world (Benne et al. 1975, 3–9).

In time, the laboratory method became more normatively oriented and "therapeutic." It became a therapy applied to otherwise healthy people whose "potential" as loving and creative human beings was "locked up." The laboratory method would help them to become more truly human. The explicit values for this approach were drawn from the writings of Carl Rogers, Abraham Maslow, and other leaders in the newly fashionable school of "humanistic" psychology.[14]

A Basic Rogerian assumption is that

> individuals have within themselves vast resources for self-understanding and for altering their self-concepts, basic attitudes, and self-directed behavior; these resources can be tapped if a definable climate of facilitative psychological attitudes can be provided. (Rogers 1980, 115)

Following on this assumption, the step to a "psychology of being" is a relatively easy one: it leads to the discovery of a possible new selfhood in the context of supportive, change-oriented, non-judgmental groups. Small, unstructured groups such as these, theorized the Rogerians, would encourage mutual trust and the practice of "dialogue." They would help to "release" human potential. Reading the

14. Both Rogers and Maslow have published voluminously. For Rogers, a useful starting point is his latest book, *A Way of Being* (1980), which also contains a complete bibliography of his work. Maslow is best represented by *Toward a Psychology of Being* (1968).

qualities of a fully developed person according to Carl Rogers' image of "The Person of Tomorrow," we catch a glimpse of what many of the people at the NTL were trying to achieve:

1. Openness.
2. Desire for authenticity.
3. Skepticism regarding science and technology.
4. Wish for intimacy.
5. Process persons ("the certainty of life is change").
6. Caring attitude (gentle, subtle, non-moralistic, non-judgmental").
7. Closeness to and caring for elemental nature.
8. Antipathy for any highly structured, inflexible, bureaucratic institution.
9. Trust in one's own experiences and a profound distrust of external authority.
10. Unimportance of material things.
11. Yearning for the spritual ("their heroes are spiritual persons—Mahatma Gandhi, Martin Luther King, Teilhard de Chardin. Sometimes, in altered states of consciousness, they experience the unity and harmony of the universe"). (Ibid. 351ff.)

It is the wish list of every person who sees himself or herself sucked up into the mega-structures of the state and global corporation.

From Group Dynamics to OD. The next major step in the evolution of OD was the linking of small group research with change in formal organizations. The Harvard Business School and MIT's Sloan School of Management were already involved. Research centers were established at the University of Michigan, the University of Chicago, UCLA, and elswhere. Corporate management could be sold on the idea: Hawthorne had demonstrated the effectiveness of action research; worker productivity could be markedly improved by changes in the social environment; and beyond this immediate payoff, OD would guide corporations toward long-term adaptability, growth, and innovation. The earliest text of the new professional field, dedicated to "Kurt Lewin and our colleagues at the National Training Laboratories," was seductively entitled *The Dynamics of Planned Change* (Lippitt et al. 1958). Within three years, it was followed by a textbook of selected readings (Bennis, Benne, and Chin 1961) that soon became the standard reference in the field. Each of its three successive editions was quite different from the preceding one and afforded readers a good overview, at regular intervals, of this rapidly evolving field.

The new social technology spun off a language of its own by which its practitioners might know each other at first meeting. It included code words such as planned change, change agent, client system, T-group, internal and external environment, temporary system, socio-technical system, helping relation. A procedure for planned change, involving the following five distinctive phases, was codified.

1. Development of a need for change ("unfreezing").
2. Establishment of a change relationship.
3. Working toward change ("moving").
4. Generalization and stablization of change ("freezing").
5. Achieving a terminal relationship. (Lippitt et al. 1958, 130)

The text was meant to instruct future practitioners. By including phase 1 in the list, the authors seemingly wished to ensure that, when the time came to look for a job, OD consultants would be prepared to develop a market for their skills.

Four potential target systems were identified: personality, small group, organization, and community.[15] The basic theoretical assumptions of OD were spelled out clearly by Robert Chin and Kenneth D. Benne (1976). Its central tradition, they said, was normative–re-educational, in contrast with rational-empirical and power-coercive models of social change.[16]

> Patterns of action and practice are supported by sociocultural norms and by commitments on the part of individuals to these norms. Sociocultural norms are supported by the attitude and value systems of individuals—normative outlooks which undergird their commitments. Change in a pattern of practice or action, according to this view, will occur only as the persons involved are brought to change their normative orientations to old patterns and develop commitments to new ones. And changes in normative orientations involve changes in attitudes, values, skills, and significant relationships, not just changes in knowledge, information, or intellectual rationales for action and practice. (Chin and Benne 1976, 23)

15. Organization development placed primary emphasis on the middle pair of target systems, while the popular human potential movement focused on personality change. Despite promising beginnings (see, for example, chapters 6 and 7 in Bennis et al. 1976), the application of OD methodologies to entire communities remained more promise than actual delivery.

16. The first of these roughly corresponds to what we have called the tradition of policy analysis and the second to social mobilization.

What is immediately apparent from this message is the intensely idealistic character of the proposed change strategy. It brings to mind the following passage from the Confucian classic, *The Book of Rites*.

The ancients who wished clearly to exemplify illustrious virtue throughout the world would first set up good government in their states. Wishing to govern well their states, they would first regulate their families. Wishing to regulate their families, they would first cultivate their persons. Wishing to cultivate their persons, they would first rectify their minds. Wishing to rectify their minds, they would first seek sincerity in their thoughts. Wishing for sincerity in their thoughts, they would first extend their knowledge. The extension of knowledge lay in the investigation of things. (de Bary et al. 1960, 115; orig. ca. 200 B.C.)

"The Great Learning" as Confucians call it, is, without doubt, a wise moral teaching. But will it set the empire aright? One may question the nested logic of the passage. Chin and Benne's principles or organizational development are questionable in the same way. They violate the basic rule of pragmatist epistemology that *learning comes exclusively from the attempt to change reality*. In the laboratory settings of the NTL, participants may undergo psychic bombardment through an intensive group experience, but *there is no objective practice beyond the narcissistic practice of the group itself*. And surely, as participants nurture each others' psyches, they must be dimly aware that back at work, in the real world of office and factory, they are involved in intricate and often brutal games of power. To act the part of a Rogerian Person of Tomorrow, as though these games did not exist, scarcely recommends itself as a recipe for human survival.

The mapping of the re-educational theories of group dynamics and the normative theories of personal growth onto the larger canvas of OD called for a deeper understanding of organizations as such.[17] And this call led to contributions of a somewhat different sort than the literature we have discussed up to now.

Organization theory cuts across many different traditions of social scientific research. We might call it an "intermediate" social theory, located between the microanalysis of small group behavior and the macrotheorizing of the likes of Marx, Mannheim, and Etzioni,

17. Revealing the inherent bias of the new technology, OD literature frequently refers to organizations as "human systems." Many OD theorists, in fact, are prepared to reduce organizations to patterns of social interaction that are ultimately traceable to individuals.

who investigate the structure and dynamics of the whole society. We have already noted the contributions to our knowledge of organizations by such scholars as Max Weber, James March and Herbert Simon, Anthony Downs, and Michel Crozier. Rensis Likert (1967) was the first from within the traditions of OD to write about organizations. Like his professional colleagues at the NTL, Likert was a behaviorist with a mission. His business was to change organizations, and to this end he developed four normative models of management system, arranged in an ascending hierarchy of desirability: System 1—exploitative-authoritarian; System 2—benevolent authoritarian; System 3—consultative; and System 4—participatory. Experimental evidence, claimed Likert, showed that participatory System 4 management is the most likely to be effective in doing what business is supposed to do: buy, sell, make a profit. The critical point for an OD theorist, however, was that existing management systems could actually be changed and brought into conformity with the characteristics of System 4.

> The causal variables have two essential characteristics: (1) they can be modified or altered by members of the organization; i.e., they are neither fixed nor controlled by external circumstances; (2) they are independent variables; i.e., when they are changed, they cause other variables to change, but they are not, as a rule, directly influenced by other variables. (Likert 1967, 75, 77)

Not unexpectedly, the major "causal variables" identified by Likert were what he called the principle of supportive relationships; group decision-making in a multiple, overlapping group structure; and high performance goals.

Likert's main theoretical contribution was his proposed format for System 4, which softened the traditional organization chart of administration theory by introducing the notion of a "multiple, overlapping group structure." This, asserted Likert, is a fundamental requirement that must be met in adapative learning systems.

Likert came from the University of Michigan branch of OD. At the time his book was published, two professors from Harvard's Graduate School of Business Administration, Paul R. Lawrence and Jay W. Lorsch, produced one of the most important organization-theoretical studies in the entire OD literature (1967). They succinctly restated their main theses two years later in a work that was part of a series of short OD texts (1969).

The authors start with a subtle and highly original conception of an organization, which they say, is "the coordination of different activities of individual contributors to carry out planned transactions with the environment" (Lawrence and Lorsch 1969, 3). This definition encompasses the traditional division of labor and establishes coordination and guidance as the essential attributes of an organization. The uniqueness of this conception, however, is its explicit recognition that an organization operates in an *environment* that it cannot completely control and to which, therefore, it must learn to adapt even as it must carry out transactions with it in order to survive and grow. But organizations carry out many different functions and tasks; their work is *differentiated* into subsystems, each of which deals with a different "region" of the organizational environment overall.[18] According to the authors, the long-term effectivenss of organizations will depend on the degree to which their internal structure reflects the differentiated external environment and the ability of the organization *as a whole* to integrate its several parts into a common strategy of action.

Environments, said Lawrence and Lorsch, can be characterized by the two intersecting continua of certainty/uncertainty and stability/change (Figure 15).

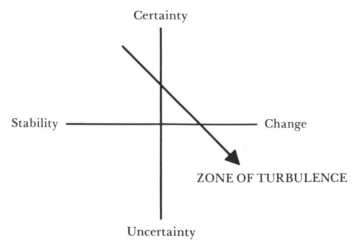

Figure 15. Organizational environments and the drift to turbulence.

18. The notion of an organizational environment did not originate with Lawrence and Lorsch. The usual reference is to von Bertalanffy's various writings on "living" systems. Within the OD literature, the following two antecedents are particularly significant: Burns and Stalker (1961) and Emery and Trist (1965). The practical definition of an environment is an empirical question. For instance, in the corporate environment of a business firm, there will be an environment for sales (the firm's customers and competitors), for research (pertinent science and technology), for personnel (labor and professional markets), and so forth.

According to a well-known essay by Emery and Trist (1965), contemporary organizations are moving from the relatively slow-changing environments of the past into a "zone of turbulence." This movement is indicated in Figure 15 by the diagonal arrow pointing toward the southeastern quadrant of the diagram, where a turbulent environment exists, and where forecasting becomes exceedingly troublesome, requiring not only a high-density information environment with very short feedback loops, but the utmost in response capacity, adaptability, and strategic reserves.

When these conditions are translated back into the language of OD, they suggest a refocusing of organizational structures on *temporary, overlapping groups*, that are *oriented to specific tasks* and whose working style is *interpersonal and transactive* ("relations of dialogue"). From the standpoint of the whole organization, each of these groups constitutes a *learning environment*, which, within the framework of broad organizational objectives and the requirement of accountability, enjoys considerable *autonomy of action*. Under conditions of turbulence, it is through a group structure of this sort that organizations can maximize not only their learning and response ability but their overall effectiveness as well.

A similar theme is addressed by Donald Schön's more journalistic treatment of organizational adaptiveness to turbulence in *Beyond the Stable State* (1971). Schön proposes the useful concept of a "network structure" to "knit together the still autonomous elements of the functional system in networks which permit concerted action" (Schön 1971, 183). These networks reach beyond organizational boundaries—they become "boundary-spanning"—and extend into parts of the organizational environment proper. For example, an agricultural extension service includes within its operating network a group of "demonstration" farmers, or a university medical school employs physicians on its part-time staff who have a lively outside practice. When this occurs, the very notions of fixed boundaries, internal and external environments, and central management controls tend to evaporate. A new organizational format takes shape, one that is characterized by *temporality* and *fluidity* and requires continual redesign and adjustment (ibid. 184). The older center-periphery, or top-down model or organization gives way to a new form of decentralized administration which depends more on multidirectional communication flows than on formal authority structures.

Curiously, at this point, seemingly light-years removed from Dewey's *Reconstruction in Philosophy*, we return full circle to an acceptance of change as the primary datum of human experience, to an emphasis on the tentative, experimental approach to changing reality and on intensive learning processes in small-group, face-to-face settings.

With its strong normative impulse, OD research had broken through the traditional concerns of organizational analysis and developed a startlingly different model. As it appeared to OD theorists, the problem was how to get organizations to change ongoing practices and move in the direction of a differentiated management structure. Or, as Argyris and Schön (1974, 1978) argued, it was to shift organizations from an existing capacity for "single-loop" learning to a new and more sophisticated capacity for "double-loop" learning. The former is defined as straightforward problem solving. But double-loop learning involves forms of "organizational inquiry which resolve incompatible organizational norms by setting new priorities and weightings of norms, or by resturcturing the norms themselves together with associated strategies and assumptions" (Argyris and Schön 1978, 24). Double-loop learning, they said, "involves a major reorganization that will allow an organization to adjust itself to new circumstances in its environment." It is presented as a form of inquiry into the persisting mismatch between an organization and its environment, an inquiry that is expected to lead to a serious reexamination of an actor's theory of reality, values, and beliefs, and to their eventual reformulation, resulting in new strategies of action.

The theory of double-loop learning echoes an early Lewinian insight that true learning involves a restructuring of one's relations to the world, a process of re-education or, still more powerfully, cultural change. The problem is that any restructuring is painful, and organizations, like people, are reluctant to inflict such pain on themselves, unless not doing so is likely to cause even greater pain. Even then, mechanisms are at work that will tend to discount the pain of the present while magnifying in the mind the pain of future changes. We tend to think that our present troubles will not last, that things will soon get better, that pain has compensating benefits.

Argyris and Schön adopt the characteristic OD model that purports to show how an organization that displays certain positive characteristics (it is cooperative and inquiry-oriented, creates a trustful environment, reduces "dysfunctional" norms and "games of deception") will be better equipped to engage in double-loop learning than organizations that do not. But the means for putting this model into effect are, it would seem, the same old methods of OD, involving laboratory training and other small-group learning experiences designed to teach participants the esoteric skills of "learning to learn" (Argyris 1982, ch. 19).

The main problem with this approach is that it abstracts from power relationships. The ideology of OD is focused on small-group and intergroup relations, and it expects these to change concomitantly with changes in individual personality behavior. Power, which is central to a correct understanding of how organizations are actually put together, is "bracketed." More often, it is treated as if it were counterproductive. Because of this, much of OD literature and practice remains a futile endeavor.

This is not to say that its ideas are useless. Small groups are important, and the discovery of non-hierarchical forms of organization (as in Likert and Lawrence and Lorsch) is a major advance. So is the idea of "process consulting" (Schein 1969), which has much in common with "transactive" planning, with its emphasis on informal, person-centered relations within organizations. What makes OD an incomplete approach is its steadfast refusal to face up to the realities of power and confrontational struggle, which form the basis of the next chapter.

One reason that power can be made to disappear in OD theorizing is that OD's therapeutic program is primarily addressed to management elites, that is, to the very people who wield effective power in organizations. It is easy for these elites to take power for granted (one is tempted to say "they tend to overlook it") and to talk of more edifying matters with which they are less familiar.

The situation is very different for those who remain outside the executive chambers—the white- and blue-collar workers and the masses of ordinary people, whether they have jobs or not, for whom the real deprivation of power is an everday experience, and who understand very well who sits on top and why. The theory of OD is not addressed to them, as, indeed, it is not addressed to problems more generally in the public domain. It remains primarily a science for board rooms.

Critique and Prospect

In comparison with policy analysis, the tradition of social learning represents a major step forward. With it, we move from anticipatory decision-making to action and social practice. The social learning approach works with a process concept of knowledge: its central assumption is that all effective learning comes from the experience of changing reality. As a form of knowing, it is intrinsically related to human activity, focusing attention on dynamic social processes (as opposed to pure cognition), examining problems from the perspective of an actor actually engaged in practice, highlighting the mediating role of small groups, using the concept of a social environment as a major category in the analysis of learning situations, and emphasizing the crucial importance of dialogue for social practice.

But there are major problems with the social learning approach that need to be addressed. Although some of them have already been mentioned, it is time to pull the strands together and lay the groundwork for a more systematic critique.

Philosophical Foundations
There are two problems here: the rationalistic bias of the social learning approach and the validation of knowledge. Both John Dewey and Edgar S. Dunn, Jr., posit a learning process that functions not unlike a *perpetuum mobile* machine: once it is set in motion it never stops, because its motion generates no friction. Since in the actual world friction always requires an equivalent amount of energy to surmount it, the *perpetuum mobile* remains an alchemist's dream. The philosophers of social learning have constructed a learning model that is based on an idealized model of how science works: error is recognized and ways are quickly mended. The "friction problem" reappears the moment an active subject is restored to this sentence. Actors (as opposed to scientific abstractions) are not, as a rule, eager to acknowledge error; they have far too much at stake, money and reputation being the more obvious interests. Nor is it always clear when an error, so to speak, has been committed, or what the nature of the error is.

There is a more profound reason still why people persist in doing what they do despite the difficulties they encounter. People (and organizations) may actually come to treasure certain practices and ideas, not for their instrumental qualities but for being what they are. The Catholic Church is an institution that has been very slow to change its ways and probably, for that very reason, has survived two thousand years. For many hundreds of millions of faithful, the Church, precisely because it is so slow to change, provides a sheltering haven for the soul. Indeed, an attachment to familiar relationships and patterns of behavior is a fundamental characteristic of all human behavior, and to part with the familiar is inevitably painful, experienced as a loss, and mourned (Marris 1975).

One might go further and say that in order to undertake an action, which is to overcome resistance in the environment, it is absolutely essential to believe in what one is about to do. And the more extended the prospective action (and the more deeply rooted the potential resistance to it), the more of a commitment is entailed. Actions, from this perspective, are not "experiments" conducted by bloodless scientists who are "neutral" about their outcome (Watson 1969). They are commitments that will be abandoned only when their unworkability is clearly demonstrated, when the calamity of failure is already imminent. Even then, as a last desperate gesture, actors may be tempted to ask whether the impending disaster might not be otherwise explained, and instead of seeking fault with their own practice, search for scapegoats in the environment instead.

And thus we may conclude that contrary to the rationalism of the philosophers, interests act as a powerful conserver of human energy. If we do not learn easily, it is not that we are "irrationally" attached to the past, but that the basis for our reasoning is broader than pure, frictionless knowing. Even in the face of mounting problems, we will tend to fight for what we have as well as for our beliefs.

The second philosophical issue in social learning is what I have called the "validation problem." Dewey deals with it in two ways: first, he argues that knowledge is valid if it *disposes* of a problem; second, it is valid when people *agree* that they can trust it and rely on it for guidance. There are problems with both of these criteria.

If we follow Rittel and Webber (1973), social problems (and this is the category of problem that concerns us here) are "wicked" in the sense that they elude solution. What happens, as a rule, is that the symptoms addressed are those whose treatment will lower the temperature of the patient, so to speak, and divert people's attention, even as another problem surfaces which has an even greater claim on the public's attention. So far as historical practice is concerned, "disposal" turns out to be no criterion at all. A problem goes away not because it has been solved, but because another problem has displaced it.

The second criterion, which asserts the consensual basis of knowledge, arises from the obvious need to treat knowledge as a social product. People who find no one to agree with them are often labeled "deranged" and placed in mental institutions. To avoid the madhouse, I must find at least one person who will validate what I believe to be the case. Usually, the requirement for sharing is more stringent. In science, for example, knowledge is validated by the relevant community of scholars through a dynamic social process that is far from the popular image of science as a form of dispassionate reason.

Even with this proviso, it is true that scientific communities, more than the human community at large, employ modes of discourse that not only are formalized but whose rules of validation are strictly enforced. Among scientists, there is a high level of tolerance for open discourse, a general bias that favors empirical evidence and logical reasoning, and an alert, critical skepticism regarding all assertions. In their own way, then, scientific communities do show how far a process of "undistorted communication" is possible (Habermas 1979). When we leave this minority community to plunge into the wider society, the situation changes dramatically. In political discourse, for example, there are no rules at all. Passionate rhetoric to the point of deception is far more common in politics than is dispassionate reason: the channels of communication are denied to those who have little or no power; and the consequences that flow from the resolution of a particular debate are frequently immediate and direct, affecting vital interests and commitments.

But the consensual-basis-of-knowledge criterion must assume, if it is to be taken seriously at all, that access to the media of communication is roughly equal, that the intelligence required for understanding a given issue is equally distributed among the population, and that there is no attempt at conscious deception (including the suppression of negative evidence). In practice, these are difficult if not impossible conditions to fulfill. Even in principle, they require a full-blown political theory of democratic governance to make them plausible (Barber 1984).

It now becomes apparent that the democratic ethos pervading all of Dewey's writings and forming the basis of his theory of knowledge is by no means an objective, uncontested fact. A theory of the state underlies it, and there are many theories of reasonable appeal in the literature. Earlier in this chapter, for example, I suggested that Mao Tse-tung's "democratic centralism" is a plausible formulation for the specific historical circumstances of China's revolutionary era. That being so, and given that there is no objective basis for saying that one form of state system is naturally superior to another, the unadorned consensus criterion of truth must be rejected out of hand.

Epistemological rules have political consequences, and the question of the validation of knowledge requires a *political criterion* for its resolution. This question has not been previously debated in the literature.

Social Technology (OD)

There are four main criticisms that can be leveled at OD, the only serious attempt until now to translate the theory of social learning into a set of professional practices. Since these criticisms have already been mentioned, it will be sufficient to recall them briefly at this point.

First, and most important, OD refuses both to face up to differences in people's access to the bases of social power and to take seriously the basic relations of dominance and dependence that exist in every social system. Unequal access to power, which includes surplus time above the needs for reproduction, knowledge, organization, means of production, information, social networks, financial resources, and adequate physical space, must be addressed as a central concern in every process of change. Unless strong countervailing measures are devised, the tendency will be for existing power relations to be reproduced or, worse, for inequalities to be increased. Only in small, face-to-face groups can power relations be partially suspended.

Second, lacking a macro-social theory, whether of a Weberian or Marxist cast, OD is at present unable to apply its technology in the public domain.

Third, as an ideology and professional practice, the teachings of OD are addressed primarily to management. Despite its claims to be deeply concerned with humanistic values, OD hands tools to management that will be used to management's advantage. The ultimate effects on workers, or, for that matter, on society at large, remain uncertain. Through its blindness to differences in access to the bases of power, OD helps to consolidate the structures of domination in society.

Fourth, the claims of OD theorists that their practice has a "scientific" and "experimental" basis are only partially correct; OD is also a highly normative field, and a major school within the profession has embraced the values of Carl Rogers's "self-actualizing" Person of Tomorrow, along with Rogers's nondirective, therapeutic approach to small-group interaction. Although specific models of organizational behavior are constantly being proposed as intrinsically desirable, their full consequences, even for management clients, have not been explored. The public claims of OD tend to exceed its actual ability to perform.

In light of these comments, what are the prospects for the social learning approach to planning? A major new development is a shift in the application of the paradigm to the public domain. The steps are still tentative, but they are moving in a hopeful direction.

Some years ago, in *The Good Society* (1979b), I developed a group-based model of what I called radical practice, which is a practice, articulated through the network structures of social movements, that aims at the realization of emancipatory values with regard to such social problems as the role of women, the worlds of work and education, and forms of governance. The "good society" is portrayed as a small, task-oriented action group (a "temporary system") governed by relations of dialogue within but engaged in political struggle with the dominant powers of the larger society that impede the realization of its political objectives. The model conforms to the actual practices used in the major political struggles of recent decades (labor, ethnic group, gender, environmental, anti-nuclear) and is decidedly non-utopian.[19] Nevertheless, it, too, fails to confront the question of power, and its message remains incomplete.

A second example of the move to apply the social learning model to the public domain currently is being seen in relation to problems of rural development in the Third World. David Korten (1980; Korten and Alfonso 1981; Korten and Klaus 1984) has introduced a social learning approach to development administration, a subfield of public administration. He calls it a "people-centered" development that involves building local, territorially based regional economies in a spirit of self-reliance; mutual help in the provision of social services; community-level management of natural resources; and reorienting bureaucratic practices facilitate social learning in local organizations and communities.[20]

Third, a splendid example of an application of Lewis Mumford's vision of regional planning as a social learning process is the beautiful publication put out by the staff of RAIN (Portland, Oregon) called *Knowing Home: Studies for a Possible Portland* (1981).[21] Like it,

19. The pragmatic message of the book has generally gone unnoticed; critics have been more impressed by its poetic imagery and the unusual manner in which quotations from other authors are introduced into the text. Nevertheless, the book is intended as a serious contribution to the theory of planning and should be read as such.

20. For a parallel approach, see Friedmann (1982). For a Chilean case study, see Chonchol de Ferreira (1982).

21. The introduction to this little volume illuminates the process of regional self-education.

This book began more than a year ago as a brief paragraph describing a possible pamphlet on "community self-reliance in Portland. . . ." We soon realized we were on to something bigger and more exciting than we had anticipated. Plans for a pamphlet became plans for a book, and the book became much more than simply a guide to community self-reliance projects in Portland. In hundreds of scribbled research notes, in endless discussions among ourselves, and in fascinating conversations with dozens of Portland people who generously shared their special insights and knowledge, we explored a whole range of challenging questions relating to community values, economics, and ecology. . . . In seeking answers . . . we have come to a much fuller understanding of who we are and where we are in this special place called Portland. . . . A vision has emerged in our minds and on these pages of

there is a growing number of publications exploring other places in America. In Europe, where regionalism takes somewhat different forms, there is a notable upswelling of interest in small-area, self-reliant development that will inevitably rely on social learning.[22]

Finally, there is a vast and rapidly expanding literature on citizen participation in which this approach is viewed not simply as yet another form by which people are co-opted into the existing structures of domination, but rather as an autonomous political practice.[23] Although social learning has not been specifically addressed in this literature, it is clearly implicit in both the structure of the movement and its objectives.

These recent efforts, it may be hoped, will overcome some of the difficulties and contradictions of the earlier social learning literature. We see them being directed at concrete questions in the public domain, where the answers that are proposed take the form of community self-help and local self-reliance. Both forms require intensive processes of social learning.

Although such answers are attractive, they assume no fundamental change in the existing relations of power. At best, they are answers for small groups out of step with their society; they are quasi-utopian. If self-help efforts are to work on a larger scale, whether in the industrialized countries of the West or in the Third World, they must bring about fundamental changes in the relations of power within the larger society—changes that can only be achieved through social mobilization and conflict.

We therefore turn to examine the fourth tradition in planning. It is the only tradition that specifically addresses the powerless and disinherited. It tells them that in order to emancipate themselves from domination, they must first acquire countervailing power through numbers and organization. Ordinary people who have no social

---

how Portland and other communities around the country can meet the special challenges of the coming decades, and become more democratic, more beautiful, and more self-reliant places in which to live. (RAIN 1981, 5–6)

22. See, for example, the papers presented at the International Conference on Selective Self-Reliance and Development from Below in Industrialized Countries, sponsored by the Swiss National Research Program on "Regional Problems" and UNESCO, at Sigriswil, Switzerland, September 7–9, 1983.

23. See the various publications of the Center for Responsive Governance (1100 17th St., NW, Washington, D.C., 20036) and its bimonthly journal, *Community Action*. A Third World approach to participation is being studied, under the direction of Matthias Stiefel, by the United Nations Research Institute for Social Development, Geneva. Its major publication medium, *Dialogue About Participation*, can be obtained from Selina Cohen, UNRISD Popular Participation Programme, Queen Elizabeth House, 21 St. Giles St., Oxford, X1 3LA, England.

power of their own can expect to bring about the changes they desire only when they act collectively. Because they challenge the existing structures of dominance and dependence, such changes tend to be called radical, and planning that shares these aims is a form of radical planning.

6   Planning as Social Mobilization

Oppositional Movements

In the traditions already discussed (Chapters 3 to 5), planning is treated as a form of societal guidance; it is concerned with the management of change "from above." Beginning with Saint-Simon, writers in these traditions took existing relations of power as given; invariably, they addressed the rulers of society. Even when they argued for a more equitable distribution of opportunities, they did so within the constraints of mainstream politics. Social reformers invested the new planning technology with powers to design and implement reforms through action by the state and corporate management, while policy analysts tended to withdraw from the question of purpose and objectives altogether.

The case of social learning is more ambiguous. An epistemology, originally with no formal application, social learning came to be accepted as the leading paradigm for a professional movement, Organization Development, which looked to corporate management as its principal client. However, the successful application of the social learning paradigm to China's revolution suggests the possibility of a very different connection. I shall argue that social learning is not only compatible with radical planning but essential to its practice as well.

The planning tradition of social mobilization (SM), which encompasses the three great oppositional movements of utopianism, social anarchism, and historical materialism, developed as the great counter-movement to social reform. Emerging simultaneously in France and England around 1820, and thus contemporaneously with Saint-Simon and Comte, it responded to the social upheaval, human pain, and brutalization that accompanied the industrial revolution. Its perspective was that of the victims, the underclass of society; its starting point was a critique of industrialism; and its purpose was the political practice of human liberation.

Like the social reform tradition, the roots of social mobilization reach deep into the eighteenth century. It was from the Enlight-

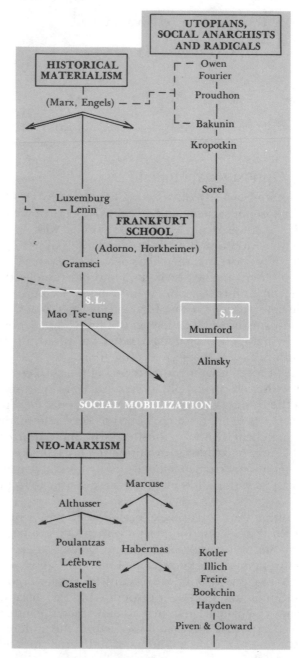

Figure 16. The social mobilization tradition of planning.

enment philosophers that SM theorists learned to look at social institutions as historical constructs capable of being changed by human effort, that they took the discovery—or was it the invention?—of the human individual and of society as separable and distinctive entities, that they learned to assert the natural right to revolution against the oppressors of humanity, that they appropriated the idea of social progress, and that they received their faith in the saving grace of science and the powers of human reasoning.

In the following pages, I shall endeavor to outline the great traditions that comprise SM.[1] But before proceeding, it will be useful to identify and comment briefly upon the several features that they have in common.

From the very beginning, it was customary to treat utopian movements, social anarchy, and historical materialism as incompatible alternatives to one another. The stress was put on the differences between them and on their conflicting approaches to their common project of human liberation. We need only recall Engels' dismissal of early socialism as "utopian"—as best a mere forerunner of "scientific" socialism—and the continuing polemics between anarchists and Marxists (Engels 1975; Thomas 1980). Yet the very fact that the polemics continue down to our own times are plain proof of the intertwined nature of these oppositional movements.

Each of the separate traditions contributed important elements to SM as a whole. From utopianism we learned the possibilities of a secular life lived in small communities apart from the state, the possibility of a money-free economy based on the exchange of labor time, the influence of the social and physical environment on the formation of human character, the importance for human development of a balance between industrial and agricultural pursuits, the importance of giving free rein to the passionate nature of human beings as the first break with the Benthamite tradition of rational calculation, and the role of play in education and learning. From social anarchism we learned, in addition, the possibility of a world based on reciprocal exchange; the use of a federative principle in joining into larger mosaics units of associated labor, self-managing communes, and regional communities based on landscape and cultural traditions; the profound suspicion of all hierarchical relations, and especially the state, as a repressive force; the virtues of spontaneity as opposed to an administered life; the principles of mu-

1. For this purpose, I will treat the "critical theory" of the Frankfurt School as a branch of historical materialism, though its actual ideological location is exactly between this movement and the radical movements of the non-Marxist Left.

tualism and cooperation as an alternative to competition in social organization; and the use of mass action in defiance of the state and corporate authority. And finally, from historical materialism, we learned to understand the class nature of social life, to view historical change as a political process originating in class struggle, to recognize the importance of class consciousness in the revolutionary practice of the masses, to analyze the present from a scientific and critical perspective, and to acknowledge the key role of theory in sustaining political practice that aims at structural social change.

Proponents of all three oppositional movements were chiefly motivated by their moral outrage over the conditions of early industrial capitalism. They were guided in their quest for a better society by their belief in the possibilities of social emancipation; they were concerned with changing the course of history through varieties of collective action; and they asserted their firm belief in the necessity of scientific and technical knowledge for radical action: it was through the application of scientific thought that the tasks of revolution and social reconstruction would be accomplished.[2]

Central to SM was the idea of social emancipation. In all preceding history, it had been argued that true emancipation could be attained only through spiritual discipline. The world was pictured as a "vale of tears," its hierarchies had been ordained by God Himself. With the Enlightenment philosophers, however, the inevitability of hierarchy was questioned.

It was Rousseau who propounded the idea of the "natural" human being in touch with both his inner and his outer nature. Actually existing human beings, he argued, were crippled in the development of their capacities by artificial social arrangements. It was therefore just and proper that these circumstances should be changed. Passionately devoted to individual self-realization, we would join together in collective action and break the fetters that restrain us. So liberated, we would set about the task of building a new society in which we might develop freely, happily subservient to the

---

2. It was precisely on this last point that the Frankfurt School dissented, launching its counterattack against the harvest of the Enlightenment—a harvest of serpents as they saw it. Their argument opposed those Marxists and others who saw in science and technology the instruments for liberation from necessity. Scientific rationalism had created a new system of domination that so regimented and controlled human life that it turned human beings into Calibans, craving their submission and continuing enslavement to the machine. Critical theorists feared that even the will to liberation might be squashed by the new system of total domination and ideological hegemony (Horkheimer and Adorno 1982; Adorno 1978; Marcuse 1964).

collective will of all, which also was the will of each and every one of us (Manuel and Manuel 1979, ch. 17).

Rousseau's ultimate vision was paradoxical. As Manuel and Manuel have pointed out,

> The greatest evil for Rousseau is dependence upon others, yet final liberation can be achieved only through the instrumentality of the general will, which has absorbed into itself all individual wills, *and has eradicated every vestige of independence*.
> (Manuel and Manuel 1979, 437; italics added)

It is precisely this impossible dream, this "myth" as Georges Sorel might have said, that has sustained the emancipatory movement to which we still adhere. As vision and as myth, it has informed utopianism, social anarchy, and historical materialism in equal measure.

The Utopian Movement
The utopian impulse takes us back into the misty origins of human thought. It concerns the perfectibility of life on earth. Modern utopias, however, have their beginnings with two remarkable men: Robert Owen (1771–1858), a Scot, and his French contemporary, Charles Fourier (1772–1837). It was their visionary imagination that gave rise to the building of "intentional communities," which followed blueprints for perfection. The communitarian movement they inspired flourished especially in America—a country which, it might be argued, was part utopian phantasy itself—in the three decades between 1830 and 1860. In another upsurge of utopian sentiment, during the 1960s, it enjoyed a brief revival (Kanter 1972; Rexroth 1974).

Utopianism is not like other intellectual traditions, in which author is linked to author across the generations, each one building on what has gone before. Rather, each instance of utopian thinking stands by itself, without acknowledged antecedents. Utopias are inventions. Their inventors might borrow elements from one another (though usually without acknowledgment) and use ideas in common currency. But as Arthur Bestor (1950) has observed, each utopia is a "patent office model" of a designed community with everything in place. History implodes into a single, ecstatic moment that is meant to last forever.

Utopians are chiefly concerned with a moral ordering of human lives. As Rosabeth Kanter has put it,

> The ideas informing the communal life style—perfectibility, order, brotherhood, merging of mind and body, experimen-

tation, and the community's uniqueness—all represent its *intentional* quality, with harmony as their principal theme: harmony with nature, harmony among people, and harmony between spirit and the flesh. (Kanter 1972, 54)

Another focal element in the utopian movement is its ardent embrace of voluntarism. For utopians, the creation of the good society is not a political act but rests squarely on the force of ideas, moral persuasion, and human determination. The analysis of historical change or questions of political strategy are of scant interest to them. Impatient with contingency and process, they are convinced perfection can be realized now. It is all a matter of commitment.

Towering above all others in the utopian movement is Robert Owen. A contemporary of Bentham, he shared his belief that individual happiness is gained through the pursuit of an enlightened self-interest (Harrison 1969, 84). For Owen, the progressive mill owner and capitalist, this notion came to be associated with the idea of an organic community in which the interests of capital and of labor would be harmoniously combined. By keeping workers happy and content, productivity would be increased, he thought, and this, in turn, would increase profits. Thus, workers and capitalists alike would benefit.

Owen wrote with the fervor of an evangelist preaching the Second Coming. But unlike the religious millenarians who were his contemporaries and whose ecstatic language he borrowed in his later years (Harrison 1969, 101ff.), he and his followers held high the flame of social progress. New Harmony was an embodiment of their vision.

The experiment at New Harmony lasted exactly two years (1825–1827). At its peak, the community had a membership of one thousand, but its promise was always more than it was able to deliver (Fogarty 1972, ch. 8). A clear exposition of Owen's ideas for a better world can be found in his famous "Report to the County of Lanark" (Owen 1972, 425–498). Here, his justification for "utopian" reforms was still expressed in the matter-of-fact language that capitalists like himself would have no difficulty understanding. Science, he declared, would lay the foundations of a common prosperity (ibid. 247–248).

First, it must be admitted that scientific or artificial aid to man increases his productive powers, his natural wants remaining the same . . .
Second, that the direct effect of every addition to scientific or mechanical and chemical power is to increase wealth; and it

is found accordingly that the immediate cause of the present want of employment for the working classes is an excess of production of all kinds of wealth . . .

Third, that, could markets be found, an incalculable addition might yet be made to the wealth of society . . .

Fourth, that the deficiency of employment for the working classes cannot proceed from a want of wealth or capital . . . but from some defect in the model of distributing this extraordinary addition of new capital throughout society . . .

A behaviorist at heart, Owen was a firm believer in the idea that changing people's environment would result in changes in their behavior. Thus happiness could be induced through acts of deliberate intervention—by philanthropists such as himself—in people's external surroundings. His plan for social reconstruction reads like a page from Skinner's *Walden Two*.

The reflecting part of mankind have admitted, in theory, that the characters of men are formed chiefly by the circumstances in which they are placed; yet the science of the influence of circumstances, which is the most important of all the sciences, remains unknown for the great practical business of life . . .

Through this science, new mental powers will be created which will place all those circumstances that determine the misery or happiness of men under the immediate control and direction of the present population of the world, and will entirely supersede all necessity for *the present truly irrational system of individual rewards and punishments* . . .

The science of the influence of circumstances over human nature . . . will prove how much more easily men can be trained by other means to become, without exception, active, kind, and intelligent—devoid of those unpleasant and irrational feelings which for ages have tormented the human race.

This science may be truly called one whereby ignorance, poverty, crime, and misery may be prevented; and will indeed open a new era to the human race; one in which real happiness will commence, and perpetually go on increasing through every succeeding generation. (Ibid. 270–272)

Not unexpectedly, this extensive and universal rearrangement of society would be carried out in "peace and quietness, with the good will and hearty concurrence of all parties, and of every people" (ibid. 271).

In fairness to Owen, his plan was not devoid of merit.

- It was based on communal villages of between 800 and 1,200 members who would pursue agriculture as their primary activity, though there would also be some manufacturing for local use.

- Children's education was to be a central feature of the plan, and Owen proposed that children be reared separately from their families, though parents might have access to them in the course of the day.

- Food, dress, and lodging would be rationally designed in accordance with common-sense principles of health. Cooking as well as eating would be done communally.

- Communes would be either self-governing or managed on "scientific" principles by administrators who were appointed.

- Experimental learning would be allowed for. The communitarian design merely established principles; the specific situation as well as actual experiences would lead to the gradual perfection of communal life.

- The goods produced by the community would be equitably distributed among all members: each person would have a right to his or her "fair shares."

The successful implementation of his ideas, Owen claimed, would help to overcome the major contradictions which, until his time, had plagued humanity: the division between mental and manual labor, the division between public and private interest, and national rivalries (ibid. 274).

The desire for a merging of the public and private realms was not unique to Owen. We find it again and again in the writings of communitarian socialists and anarchists. It is a wish that should be carefully examined—not for whether it is possible: we may assume that it is—but for its desirability on social, political, and philosophical grounds. In practice, the hoped-for identity would seem to imply the invasion of the private by the public sphere, and its complete subordination to the latter.

The picture of a nonpolitical life informs not only Owen's communitarian idea; it is found with social anarchists as well. In the idealized constructs of these dreamers, the community functions very much like a "black hole" in astrophysics whose gravity potential is so great that it swallows up all rays of generated light. The antipolitical stance of both utopian movements and social anarchy is their point of greatest vulnerability. And so it is that Owen's utopia can flip-flop easily into the most rigid form of domination.

Owen does talk about the governance of his communities. If they are formed by the middle and working classes, he writes, they should be governed by themselves, guided by principles "that will *prevent* divisions, opposition of interests, jealousies, or any of the common and vulgar passions which a contention of power is certain to generate. Their affairs should be conducted by a committee" (ibid. 287). In the more likely case that they are founded by "land-owners and capitalists, public companies, parishes, or counties," they should be administered in accordance with the rules and regulations laid down by their founders (ibid.).

In common with many utopians, Robert Owen was both a rationalist and a moralist. The true and the good were coterminous for him. Harmonious relations, not contradictions, were the rule in life. The pursuit of power and the desire for domination were not part of his prophetic vision.

The second major inventor of utopias was Charles Fourier. Unsung in his own country, and considered mad by most, Fourier had a substantial influence in the United States. In English translation, his more extravagant notions could be filtered out, while the rest could be adapted to the American ethos. That remainder found a huge response.

What sort of man was he? Manuel and Manuel present us with a vivid portrait.

> Fourier the bachelor lived alone in a garret and ate table d'hote in the poorer Lyons restaurants, disliked children and spiders, loved flowers and cats, had a mania for measuring things with a yardstick cane, had a sweet tooth, could not digest bread, adored spectacles and parades, loathed the philosophers and their Revolution as much as he did rigid Catholicism. From all accounts he was a queer duck. Men called him mad, but no evidence has been adduced to sustain this clinical diagnosis; his autopsy revealed no signs of brain damage. (Manuel and Manuel 1979, 641)

Fourier's writings were a mixture of the fantastic, the pedantic, the lucid, and the poetic. In an age devoted to the worship of scientific reason, he praised the splendid passions of humanity. There were twelve passions in his system: the classical five senses, leading to a life of luxury; four affective passions, pointing the way to a libidinal life; and three "distributive" passions which he called the cabalist, composite, and *papillone* (the fluttering butterfly), suggesting a distribution of work in harmony with human nature. A thirteenth passion, finally, resulted from the *union* of the other twelve.

> . . . the inclination of the individual to reconcile his own happiness with all surrounding him, and of all humankind, today so odious. It is an unbounded philanthropy, a universal goodwill, which can only be developed when the entire human race shall be rich, free, and just. (Fourier 1976, 61; orig. 1808)

Fourier's basic teaching was that the passions must be allowed free rein. Human beings were born unto pleasure, and a society freed from repression was in accord with the will of heaven.

> Voluptuousness is the sole arm which God can employ to master us and lead us to carry out his designs; he rules the universe *by Attraction and not by Force*; therefore, the enjoyments of his creatures are the most important object of the calculations of God. (Ibid.)

This way of putting things was light-years from Jeremy Bentham's crabbed moral calculus. After reading Fourier, one wonders whether Bentham truly understood the passionate life at all. Fourier—forerunner of Alex Comfort and Fritz Perls—proclaimed the realm of sensuous pleasures. Pain would be abolished in this realm. It was a popular idea.

Fourier proposed that every pleasure, including every "innocent mania," should be indulged in "provided that its devotees can gather together the nucleus . . . of at least nine persons, and arranged in a regular group." In typical fashion, he continued:

> No matter how comical a fancy may be, it is breveted a useful and respectable passion, if it can offer this feature of corporative union. It has a right to a standard in its reunions, a right to outward insignia for its members, and a place in the ceremonials of a certain degree, province, or region, if it may not figure in those of the Phalanx. Thus God knows how to attain the goal of unity by the double road—
> *Of the infinitely small as well as the infinitely great;*
> *Of the infinitely ridiculous as well as the infinitely charming.*
> (Ibid. 161–162; orig. 1822)

Life, said Fourier, was to be experienced passionately. A century before Freud, he posited the connection between the repression of the libido and human misery. His catalogue of miseries was an impressive one: extortion . . . the art of devouring the future . . . commercial plundering and knavery . . . the decline of agriculture . . . the overthrow of intermediary bodies which imposed limits on central power . . . alienation . . . barbarous usages, vendettas, guerillas . . . war . . . the immorality of politics (ibid. 94–95).

Against incipient social chaos, Fourier offered the Phalanx or Phalanstery, an ideal community which has been described as a kind of hotel-pension for upward of 1,800 people. Its economic base was to be agriculture, but there were also workshops that would produce for its inhabitants.

Although life in the Phalanstery was to be ruled by the clock, the clock ticked differently for rich and poor. Everyone rose at 3:30 in the morning. But during the course of their work all day in the stables and fields, the poor ate only three times and then retired at 10, while the rich indulged themselves in five meals, went hunting and fishing, read newspapers, discussed horticulture, went to church, visited the library, engaged in exotic gardening and fish hatching, and closed the day with entertainments in the arts: the theater, dances, receptions (ibid. 167–168). Fourier's idea was that if everyone did as he pleased, and did not stay too long with any one activity—here the passion of *papillone* did its work—everything would be accomplished, yet no compulsion was needed.

> The chief source of light-heartedness among Harmonians is frequent change of sessions. Life is a perpetual torment to our workmen, who are obliged to spend twelve, and frequently fifteen, consecutive hours in some tedious labour. Even ministers are not exempt; we find some of them complain of having passed an entire day in the stupefying task of affixing signatures to thousands of official vouchers. Such wearisome duties are unknown in the associative order; the Harmonians, who devote an hour, an hour and a half, or at most two hours, to the different sessions, and who, in these short sessions, are sustained by cabalistic impulses and by friendly union with associates, cannot fail to bring and to find cheerfulness everywhere. (Ibid. 166; orig. 1829)

This vision created much excitement in America, where a virtually empty continent beckoned settlers to experiment with short-circuiting history. Within a few years, dozens of Phalansteries would be established. Kenneth Rexroth gives a vignette of a group of colonists setting out to build one in the 1840s.

> [C]rowds of a hundred or more colonists trouped off with flags flying and music playing to the wilderness, or to abandoned farms for which they had paid high prices. The first

day began with a picnic, and ended with dancing, drinking, and the fulfillment of Fourier's *parcours*, the concurrence of all sensual pleasures in perfect bliss. Within a few days, provisions began to run short, necessary skills were found to be in even shorter supply, and tempers were shorter yet. Soon competition for what little was available seemed worse than in the world they had left, and they began to quarrel and accuse each other of stealing. Some colonies lasted only a few weeks, and left the leading members seriously indebted. (Rexroth 1974, 253–254)

The picture has, to use a favorite Fourier expression, charm. And yet, in Fourier's febrile imagination, it is often difficult to pick out the sense from the nonsense, the serious from the fantastic and the droll.

Fourier's utopia displays the same curious contradiction that we found with Robert Owen: the juxtaposition of an emancipated society with the complete regimentation of life. It is the totalitarianism of any closed society designed to work as a harmonious whole. Christian-inspired utopias, in their desire to regain Paradise, are especially prone to this conception. Static and ahistorical, communitarianism offers a prescriptive model that is ultimately dangerous: in the name of total emancipation from conflict and pain, it destroys our autonomy as individuals. Without a politics, we are reduced to a society of drones!

Social Anarchism
The major clue to understanding social anarchism is its passionate denunciation of all forms of authority, especially the state's. It might thus be called a political movement to abolish politics. In this as well as in other respects, social anarchism resembles the utopian movement, but the differences are clear.[3]

Two branches may be usefully distinguished. (We shall leave aside here the extreme individualist forms of anarchism whose most famous representative is Max Stirner.) The first branch advocates peaceful means of cooperation as the road to an anarchist social order; its chief representatives are Proudhon and Kropotkin. The second branch champions the route of physical violence in the destruction of all authority relations. Its spokesmen are Bakunin and Sorel.

Pierre Joseph Proudhon (1809–1865) is generally acknowledged to be the "direct ancestor" of social anarchism as a movement. Born

3. The best, most readable history of anarchist thought is by George Woodcock (1962), a Canadian historian.

in Besançon, a little town in the region known as the Franche-Comté at the foot of the Jura Mountains, Proudhon was a master in the art of printing.[4] Largely self-taught, and proud of his regional origins, he was deeply distrustful of the cosmopolitan city—Paris in his case—with its network of global contacts and its immense concentration of economic and political power. In rejecting the metropolis, he was much like other utopians and anarchists who preferred intimate social groupings to larger and more complex constructs.

Proudhon was a prolific writer. His words reached out and touched his countrymen, influencing their thoughts and beliefs, if not their actions, until well into this century. Abroad, his influence was even stronger. The Yugoslav experiment with socialist self-management is deeply indebted to his work.

Proudhon urged a path of peaceful, structural reform which, in the midst of the ongoing capitalist system, would create an alternative order based on self-governing working communities. His central ideas were well summarized in the following extract from a letter written in the year prior to his death.

> By the word anarchy I wanted to indicate the extreme limit of political progress. Anarchy is . . . a form of government or constitution in which public and private consciousness, formed through the development of science and law, is alone sufficient to maintain order and guarantee all liberties. In it, as a consequence, the institutions of the police, preventive and repressive methods of officialdom, taxation, etc. are reduced to a minimum. In it, more especially, the forms of monarchy and centralization disappear, to be replaced by federal institutions and a pattern of life based on the commune. When politics and homelife have become one and the same thing, when economic problems have been solved in such a way that individual and collective interests are identical, then—all constraint having disappeared—it is evident that society will be in a state of total liberty or anarchy. Society's laws will operate by themselves through universal spontaneity, and they will not have to be ordered or controlled. (Letter to Mr. X***, August 20, 1864, in Horvat et al. 1975, I, 84)

4. Proudhon called himself an anarchist, at other times a "mutualist." In her pamphlet on the mass strike (1971; orig. 1906), Rosa Luxemburg ignores Proudhon's contributions to the theory of social anarchy and singles out Bakunin as the "founder" of the anarchist movement. Bakunin was, indeed, more in the center of the working-class movement than Proudhon had ever been. Still, practical politics aside, it is Proudhon who can rightfully be called the intellectual parent of social anarchism, though even he had forebears, notably William Godwin (1756–1836).

Let us take up these ideas in turn. What is the Proudhonian understanding of the good society?

1. Proudhon advocates a *minimalist state*; in the course of time, this state would evolve into anarchy, which he calls the state of total liberty and is conceived of as a social order regulated by the principle of fair exchange.

2. Proudhon revives the *communal tradition*, which in Europe goes back to the eleventh and twelfth centuries. It is the tradition of municipal self-governance and establishes a corporate order in which the authority of the commune extends to all affairs, private as well as public. Worker-owned companies and banks are woven into the fabric of public life.[5]

3. Communes are joined to one another through a *principle of federation* in which lower-order units retain more powers than they relinquish, and dissociation is always possible. The natural unit above the commune is the province or region, which is governed autonomously through its constituent communes. As are all social relations, the federal system is ruled by commutative justice.

4. According to Proudhon, anarchy is the "extreme limit of political progress." The text does not tell us how this progress is to be achieved, but we know from other evidence that it will be chiefly through economic action that liberty must be attained. Workers associate in self-governing companies. As these spread and federate among themselves, self-managing political institutions will spring up of their own accord.

5. Complete anarchy is a social order that is *spontaneously generated and maintained* by enlightened individuals and the self-governing institutions they themselves create. Their consciousness, according to Proudhon, will be formed by two specific practices: science—which is the systematic investigation of things—and the law of commutative justice or fair exchange, which he called mutualism.

6. In his ideal vision, there takes place a final convergence of the public and the private, the collective and the individual. When this happens, says Proudhon, "society's laws will operate by themselves through universal spontaneity."

7. Proudhon's system presupposes a classless society; it also requires the complete autonomy of each person as he enters into

5. For a review of the communal tradition, see Friedmann (1982), where the relevant literature is cited.

associate relations with his fellows. (Proudhon was a traditionalist concerning female roles and pictured women exclusively in the domestic sphere.)

8. Proudhon's society charts an austere course in which there is a sufficiency of material necessities. Although money is in circulation, there is little trade beyond the immediate region which, in most respects, remains a self-sufficient entity.

The second major figure of social anarchism is Michael Bakunin (1814–1876), a Russian aristocrat turned revolutionary. This untidy mountain of a man contributed little to the basic doctrine of social anarchism (he borrowed freely from both Marx and Proudhon). But he was singular in the expression he gave to his revulsion in the face of all authority relations. Contemporary terrorists take inspiration from his inflammatory rhetoric.

Bakunin was possessed by a passionate belief in the cleansing powers of destruction. Like his predecessor Fourier, he believed in the priority of passion over reason. Freedom for him was the absence of all external restraint. Hence, the state, which was the principal restrainer of liberty, had to be utterly destroyed. There could be no revolution, thundered Bakunin, "without a sweeping and passionate destruction, since by means of such destruction, new worlds are born and come into existence" (Pyziur 1968, 65). Revolution means the total destruction of everything. It wells up from the underclasses of society and explodes every obstacle in its path to total liberty.[6]

A non-revolutionary, liberal politics was, in his view, not only futile but contrary to the working class's best interests. The working class, argued Bakunin, should engage in acts of mass defiance and not in endless parliamentary debates in which the proletariat is inevitably the loser. It was primarily over this issue—the nature of working-class struggle—that Marx and Bakunin divided in their competing claims to the leadership of the First International (P. Thomas 1980, ch. 5). It was a struggle that Bakunin lost.

Georges Sorel (1847–1922), though less flamboyant, was Bakunin's worthy successor in his advocacy of violence as a redemptive agency. In contrast to the "terrible Russian," he was a scholarly and

6. It is difficult to read the many passages in Bakunin's writings that echo this theme without thinking of contemporary examples—the Baader-Meinhoff gang in Germany, Italy's Red Brigades, and Pol Pot's teenage destroyers of Cambodia. There is something immensely seductive, even erotic, in the act of total violence, at least for the male of the species. In his personal life, Bakunin was a cautious man, innocent of all physical acts of violence. His advocacy of pan-destruction sprang from the theater of his tragic imagination.

dour man, little inclined to political action. His lifelong quest was for the hero—a collective actor aflame with historical passion. When he discovered this hero in Marx's proletariat, he worshipfully addressed his writings to this bearer of a tragic destiny. Through its revolutionary syndicates, the proletariat becomes engaged in the struggle for its ultimate liberation. But the end of this struggle is foredoomed by humanity's incapacity to realize the historical projects in which it is engaged.

The self-liberation of the proletariat must be carried out on its own ground; it must be an economic action, indifferent to bourgeois tactics. Only a violent break with the normal order of established relations can accomplish its purpose. The specific instrument Sorel had in mind was the general strike.

> The social revolution is an extension of that war in which each great strike is an episode; this is the reason why Syndicalists speak of that revolution in the language of strikes; for them, Socialism is reduced to the conception, the expectation of, and the preparation for the general strike, which like Napoleon's battle, is to completely annihilate a condemned regime. (Sorel 1950, 274; orig. 1906)[7]

For Sorel, the general strike was to be a kind of Twilight of the Gods, when the very foundations of the social order would begin to crumble. Yet beyond this apocalyptic image, he had only the vaguest of ideas for the "day after" the general collapse. His model for a future society was the self-governing communes of Switzerland. More important, he thought that the general strike would shape working-class consciousness even if it failed. For the failure would merely reaffirm the rightness and indeed the necessity of the struggle, which would become its own reason for being.

---

7. The mention of Syndicalists refers to the anarcho-syndicalists whose American counterpart was the International Workers of the World (iww or "Wobblies," as they were popularly known). The iww grew out of the reaction of Marxists, socialists, anarchists, and progressive trade unionists to the conservative policies of the American Federation of Labor. The strong commitment of the afl and its head, Samuel Gompers, to the capitalist system and to craft unionism in particular led to the despair of many radicals of ever turning the afl into a revolutionary organization. Consequently, on June 27, 1905, the iww was formed.

Based on syndicalism, the iww sought to organize all workers, regardless of race, skill, or sex, into "one big union." Through this one industrial union, a unified working class could wage class war through strikes and sabotage. Ultimately, the iww sought to induce the collapse of capitalism through a general strike in which the vast majority of workers would seize power (Foner 1965; I am indebted to Dewey Bandy for this account).

People who have devoted their lives to a cause which they identify with the regeneration of the world could not hesitate to make use of any weapon which might serve to develop to a greater degree the spirit of the class war. (Sorel, in Kolakowski 1978, 164)

The final object of the war was to abolish the state. Like Bakunin, Sorel was intoxicated with the prospect of apocalypse.

Sorel's sense of the tragic led him to identify the role of "myth" in sustaining the Sisyphean struggles of the human race. Action was not, in his view, a carefully calibrated series of incremental actions toward attainable goals. That smacked of bourgeois reasoning. Genuine action—the action of heroes—occurred as an eruption of irrational forces which needed a nourishing ideology to carry them forward. "Myth is needed to overcome the world of scientific fact," wrote I. L. Horowitz. "Ideology, the conscious representation of class interests, is the basis of social practice" (Horowitz 1961, 133).

Sorel himself was more specific.

[E]xperience shows that the *framing of the future, in some indeterminate time,* may, when it is done in a certain way, be very effective, and have very few inconveniences; this happens when the anticipations of the future take the form of those myths which enclose with them all the strongest inclinations of a people, of a party, or of a class, inclinations which recur to the mind with the insistence of instincts in all the circumstances of life; and which give an aspect of complete reality to the hopes of immediate action by which, more easily than by any other method, men can reform their desires, passions, and mental activity. (Sorel, in Horowitz 1961, 132–133)

In the face of disaster, it is the myth alone which allows us to endure heroic actions.

Sorel's influence on world events was only marginal. Anarcho-syndicalists referred to him; Mussolini praised him as his *maestro.* But Sorel retired to the countryside, where he would dream of an "untamed warrior class fighting for survival rather than wealth and comfort, valiant but not cruel, proud in spite of their poverty, devoted to their tribal customs and their freedom, ready to fight to the death against foreign rule" (Kolakowski 1978, II, 169). In the end, one sees his kinship more to Don Quixote de la Mancha, the knight of the dolorous mien, than to Bakunin's angel of destruction.

Peter Kropotkin (1842–1921) is the fourth and last of the great nineteenth-century anarchists. With him, we reenter a zone of peaceful transformation. Like his countryman, Bakunin, Kropotkin was an aristocrat of ancient lineage. His father was a landowner and holder of more than one thousand serfs. At the age of fifteen, Peter Kropotkin joined the Imperial Corps of Pages in St. Petersburg, where he remained until his twentieth birthday. The next ten years were spent in the military and the civil service. For much of this time, he served on geographical missions in eastern Siberia.

Kropotkin retained an immense respect for the scientific method. His ethics of mutual aid—and Kropotkin was if nothing else an ethicist—had to be framed in the rhetoric of science. Did not the social Darwinists base their vicious doctrines on scientific grounds? As with other leading intellectuals of his age, Kropotkin believed in the grace of the scientific method. In keeping with his convictions, Kropotkin's language is restrained and notably free from the passionate outbursts that characterized Bakunin's writing.

> Anarchism, the no-government system of socialism, has a double origin. It is an outgrowth of the two great movements of thought in the economic and the political fields which characterize the nineteenth century, and especially its second part. In common with all socialists, the anarchists hold that the private ownership of land, capital, and machinery has had its time; that it is condemned to disappear; and that all requisites for production must, and will, become the common property of society, and be managed in common by the producers of wealth. And in common with the most advanced representatives of political radicalism, they maintain that the political ideal of the political organization of society is a condition of things where the functions of government are reduced to a minimum, and the individual recovers his full liberty of initiative and action for satisfying, by means of free groups and federations—freely constituted—all the infinitely varied needs of the human being. (From "Anarchist Communism: Its Basis and Principles," in Baldwin 1970, 46; orig. 1887)

We can easily detect here a strong family resemblance to Proudhon's "mutualism." Like his predecessor, Kropotkin speaks of the minimalist state, the recovery of individual liberty in free association with others, the principle of federation as the preferred mode of joining into voluntary associations with each other. Social classes are abolished, and from this follows the abolition of the state as an instrument of oppression. "The no-capitalist system," writes Kropotkin with his usual directness, "implies the no-government system" (ibid. 52).

Kropotkin advocates a form of communism in which land, labor, and capital are the "common property of society," to be "managed in common by the producers of wealth." On this question, he is more explicit than Proudhon. The latter had spoken of self-management and, in his youth, exclaimed that property is theft. But on the question of the ownership of the means of production, particularly of land, he had remained remarkably ambiguous.[8]

The no-government system of anarchy, Kropotkin believed, would emerge spontaneously from the cooperative activity of working people. It required struggle, but not the violent, revolutionary struggle of a Bakunin or Sorel. Kropotkin's gradualism is dramatically underscored in the following excerpt from his historical encounter with Lenin.

The year is 1918, and the place is Moscow. The revolution is in full swing. Life is hard. Through a mutual acquaintance, a meeting is arranged between the anarchist sage (Kropotkin is seventy-six) and the fiery leader of the Bolsheviks. What ensues is a dialogue of the deaf.

> Vladimir Ilich (Lenin) got up from his chair, having said all this clearly and distinctly, with animation. Peter Alekseevich (Kropotkin) leaned back in his chair and, with an attentiveness which changed to listlessness, listened to the fiery words of Vladimir Ilich. After that, he ceased speaking about cooperatives.
>
> "Of course you are right," he said. "Without a struggle, nothing can be accomplished in any country, without the most desperate struggle . . ."
>
> "But only a massive one," exclaimed Vladimir Ilich. "We don't need the struggle and violent acts of separate persons. It is high time that the anarchists understood this and stopped scattering their revolutionary energy on utterly useless affairs. Only in the masses, only through the masses and with the masses, from underground work to massive red terror if it is

8. According to George Woodcock, Proudhon did not literally mean that property is theft. The very concept of theft implies a legal claim over the thing expropriated. Proudhon's "boldness of expression was a form of shocking emphasis, and whatever he wished to be understood by property was, as he later explained, 'the sum of its abuses.' He was denouncing the property of the man who uses it to exploit the labor of others without any effort of his own. For 'possession,' the right of a man to effective control over his dwelling and the land and the tools he needs to work and live, Proudhon had only approval; in fact, he regarded it as a keystone of liberty, and his main criticism of the communists was that they wished to destroy it" (Woodcock 1962, 113–114).

called for, to civil war, to war on all fronts, to a war of all against all—this is the only kind of struggle that can be crowned with success. All other ways—including those of the anarchists—have been surrendered to history, to the archives, and they are of no use to anyone, ill-suited for everyone; no one is attracted to them and they only demoralize those who for some reason are seduced by this old, worn-out road . . ."

Vladimir Ilich suddenly stopped, smiled kindly and said: "Forgive me. It seems that I've gotten carried away and am tiring you. But that's the way it is with us Bolsheviks. This is our problem, our cognac, and it is so close to us that we cannot speak about it calmly."

"No, no," answered Kropotkin. "It is extremely gratifying for me to hear all that you say. If you and all your comrades think in this way, if they are not intoxicated with power and feel themselves secure from enslavement by state authority, then they will do a lot. Then the revolution is truly in reliable hands."

"We will try," Lenin answered good-naturedly, "and *we will see* (he used his favorite phrase) that none of us become conceited and thinks too much of himself. This is a terrible sickness, but we have an excellent cure: we will send those comrades back to work, to the masses." (Kropotkin 1970, 330–331)

It was a rather pathetic moment, this wintery day in the suburbs of Moscow. For Lenin, it was self-evident that the Communist party and the state would have to lead the masses into socialism. It was a simple question of power. Kropotkin thought less highly of the state, which he believed to be inherently corrupt. There was no way that these two men—the one riding the crest of revolutionary victory, the other a venerated but powerless philosopher—could ever meet on the same ground. Lenin's historical materialism was incompatible with Kropotkin's humanist doctrine.

Historical Materialism
The third major movement in the tradition of SM is the monumental work of the founders of "scientific" socialism as a revolutionary movement.[9] Its major components are shown in the diagram in Figure 17.

9. For the classical distinction between "utopian" and "scientific" socialism, see Engels (1975). Historical materialism is treated here as the theoretical base of scientific socialism, which, because it is a revolutionary movement, must extend its meaning to theory as well as practice.

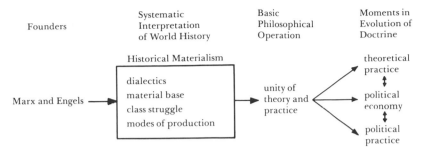

Figure 17. Intellectual foundations of socialism as a revolutionary movement.

Several aspects of this diagram require comment. Historical materialism is portrayed as an approach to the understanding of world history that is characterized by a series of methodological commitments.[10]

1. A *dialectical* mode of analysis grounded in the belief that the world can be correctly apprehended as a dynamic "unity of opposites." Dialectics is the philosophical predisposition to see historical development as an expression of contradictory social forces that stand in opposition to one another. According to Marx who, in turn, relied on Hegel but turned him "upside down," it is the clash between a "thesis" and "antithesis," as two opposing material forces, that leads to their sublation in an historical "synthesis," which preserves whatever is positive and useful in the first two terms while resolving the tension between them into a new set of opposites through an operation called "the negation of the negation," which carries history progressively forward.

2. A mode of analysis that starts with the *material base* in the forces and relations of production and looks on the realm of culture, ideas, and institutions as interdependent with this base and not as an autonomous social force in its own right.

3. A mode of analysis that interprets the movement of history from a perspective of *class struggle*, in which each of the two major social classes is seen as having mutually antagonistic interests, depending on its specific relation to the means of production. Under a system of fully developed capitalism, the

10. For the best discussion of Marx's methodological commitments that continue to inform historical materialist scholarship, see Ollman (1980). The following miniaturized account follows Ollman only in part.

hegemonic class (the bourgeoisie) is locked in battle with the dominated class of the dispossessed (the proletariat). Within themselves, however, these massive social classes are not homogeneous—there are class fractions—and in agrarian societies, one has to reckon, in addition, with the peasantry as yet another class and, indeed, as the most numerous.[11]

Though the origins of capital are national, and the development of the capitalist system is geographically uneven, capital moves inexorably to the organization of a world economy (Wallerstein 1974). Thus, historical materialism carries the implicit notion that social classes, and particularly the proletariat, are not essentially defined by territorial loyalties. Both accumulation and the class struggle are articulated through a system of "world cities" that organize the capitalist system in its spatial dimension (Soja 1980; Friedmann and Wolff 1982).

4. An analysis that focuses on *modes of production* as a historical construct and major theoretical framework. Each mode of production is defined by a unique set of economic, political, and ideological characteristics, though in historical analysis economic relations are always taken as the point of departure. The relations of production define the form in which the extraction of surplus value takes place. Under capitalism, the dominant class owns and controls the means of production and lays claim to the possession of the entire product at the point of production. The dominated class, or proletariat, is left with no other possession than its own labor power and receives a level of wages that is barely sufficient for its social reproduction. In the global periphery, with its vast "reserve army" of labor, the remuneration of both urban and agricultural workers is often *below* even the official minimum, a fact that is reflected in the high incidence of infant mortality and the short average life span of the working masses in these societies.

These four modes of analysis are interdependent and mutually reinforcing. What renders them unique and distinguishes them from any other scientific undertaking is their basis in a passionate commitment to a revolutionary practice. Historical materialism cannot be discussed apart from scientific socialism in its Marxist-Leninist versions without seriously distorting its meaning. It is not simply another form of social science but a *science of social revolution* which is aligned on the side of the revolutionary class. Therefore,

11. For an account of China's rural class system in 1926, see Mao Tse-tung (1965).

the questions of practice—Does the proletariat have sufficient consciousness of itself as a revolutionary class and its historical mission? What is the role of the militant cadres in the leadership of proletarian masses? What is the most advisable strategy for the struggles ahead? With what other social groups should revolutionary alliances be made?—are central to an understanding of historical materialism as social theory.[12]

Here it is necessary to draw a distinction that, when it fails to be made, can lead to wrong conclusions. As Gertrud Himmelfarb points out, the paradigm of class struggle is conceived in world-historical terms; it is enacted at the macro-level of historical happening.[13] But as *revolutionary practice*, class struggle necessarily takes place in territorially delimited settings, where the issues of struggle are always specific, and where loyalties other than class, such as gender, race, or religion, are often more compelling than people's self-image as "workers." At the level of world history, local events may well reduce to the simplicities of a life and death struggle between a universal class of proletarians and an equally universal class of bourgeois bankers and their minions. But in the small worlds of everyday

12. These questions do not dominate what Perry Anderson has called the "western Marxism" of the past fifty years (Anderson 1976). Contributors to its debates were principally militants who were deprived of meaningful political activity, such as Gramsci, whose major work was written in a fascist prison cell, or university professors and philosophers, such as Horkheimer, Habermas, Sartre, Colletti, Poulanatzas, and others, including Louis Althusser, who convinced themselves that their political practice could be justified in terms of their *theoretical* work alone. These men (there were few women among them until the appearance of socialist feminists in the late 1960s) had little reason to worry about the class consciousness of the proletariat; they were chiefly concerned with systematizing and expanding Marxist categories.

13. Gertrud Himmelfarb has pointed out the significance of Marx and Engels' use of the concept *working class* to refer to population groups that non-Marxists prefer to call the "urban poor." Citing Steven Marcus's commentary on Frederick Engels' *The Condition of the Working Class in England* (1845), she notes with interest how the poor are "taken to connote an attitude of passivity or acquiescence, and "working class" or "proletariat" an attitude of rebelliousness" (Himmelfarb 1983, 495). She observes that Engels' proletariat was "something more than an historical abstraction . . . a 'world-historical' class furthering the 'world-historical' movement of communism." It was, in fact, a "specifically English production, located in real towns and villages, living in real cottages and cellars, working at real jobs, participating in real events, suffering real hardships, and indulging in real vices" (ibid.).

This dual aspect of the proletariat—as world-historical class and as living human beings caught up in real situations—typifies the dialectics of theory and practice in scientific socialism. For it is real social classes that must be mobilized to make the revolution happen. And to this end, we need a theoretically as well as practically adequate account of the principal collective actors. The considerable dilemma this poses for historians is discussed at length in McLennan (1981).

life, this is not how events appear. At this level, revolutionary practice may not be the issue at all.[14]

Marxists see the evolution of capitalism as a necessary step in world-historical development. Capitalism had resolved the contradictions of European feudalism, releasing prodigious and completely unprecedented forces of production which have led not only to an enormous accumulation of private wealth in a few hands and a few favored regions, but to the creation of the proletariat as a universal class from whose labor this wealth was being extorted. In creating this class, which was necessary for its own historical achievements, capitalism laid the basis for its eventual self-destruction. This passage into oblivion—as inevitable as the demise of feudalism, both being merely historical, not ontological, modes of production—may well be drawn out over many decades and even centuries. But when it happens—and, according to some the process is already underway—it will come as a consequence of both the mounting contradictions internal to capitalism itself and the tenacious struggles of the working class and its immediate allies.

The image of a necessary historical process and the contingent actions of the proletariat not only gives historical materialism its distinctive flavor as a science—one thinks in this connection of the analogous construct of biological evolution which is likewise a product of necessity and chance—but also locates social struggle in specific contexts. This raises questions that are of fundamental importance to the success of the revolutionary project. We return to the question of practice.

Historical materialism has only recently been forced to take cognizance of social revolutionary forces other than class (Barrett 1980; Omi and Winant 1983). I shall address this question in the concluding section of this chapter. But even its classical position on the central role of class analysis in revolutionary struggle leaves open criti-

14. At the level of everyday practice, indeed, it is questionable whether the Marxist paradigm of revolutionary struggle has contemporary relevance in Western industrialized countries, especially the United States. For this reason, as well as for other reasons which he makes clear, Manuel Castells has recently made public his disenchantment with the Marxism of Althusser and Poulantzas, who had once been his teachers. He now favors a less rigidly articulated radical socialism based on a belief in the progressive political actions of urban social movements in their struggles for a better life. These movements are no longer necessarily of a classist nature but rally around questions of what he calls collective consumption (Castells 1983). Castells may be criticized for his lack of interest in class formation at the point of production, but his formulation at least has the merit of dealing with actually existing struggles in the world rather than with world-historical abstractions. For a brilliant critique of Castells's earlier work, see Evers (1981).

cal questions that have engaged Marxist theoreticians from early on. Their resolution has had profound historical consequences on international working-class solidarity and the structuring of post-revolutionary societies.

Historical materialism draws a fundamental distinction between social class in its passive and active states. A class "in itself" is an objective category of analysis, a sleeping giant who needs to be awakened. A class "for itself" is that giant roused from sleep, fully conscious of himself as a collective actor struggling for his own liberation. The proletariat's consciousness of itself as a revolutionary class is said to be a result of social learning from concrete experiences in strikes, political repression, civil war, and other instances of struggle. The process of gaining consciousness, however, also requires guidance, it is argued, and this guidance must be provided by those whom both Bakunin and Lenin call professional revolutionaries, whose dedication to the coming revolution is total. Their specific task is to establish the connection between the politically diffuse economic struggles of the working class and their ultimate political objective, which is the seizure of state power (Lenin 1975, 96–156). A fully mobilized proletariat in the vanguard of the popular forces, and intervening in the historical process when the capitalist system as a whole, beset by multiple crises, is creating the conditions propitious for the final phases of the revolutionary struggle, is capable, in a given country, at a given time, to "smash" the bourgeois state and so transform it in the process of wielding revolutionary power that it will serve the working class, the peasantry, and other oppressed groups, substituting a social mode of production for the tottering institutions of capitalism. The socialist mode of production, however, is said to characterize merely a transitional period that will guide the world into the era of full communism and so to the recovery of our full humanity.

This is not the place to undertake a theoretical critique of this interpretation. What can be done is to point to its actual results. Revolutionary socialism has failed not only in the heartland of industrial capitalism where Marx had predicted that it would occur, but also in its broad emancipatory objectives. For in post-revolutionary societies, the working class has not only been subjected to the tyranny of a bureaucratic-managerial class but has also been deprived of political space. Indeed, so thorough is its subjugation to the state that any meaningful distinction between public and private has been virtually erased: in post-revolutionary societies, almost all private concerns are under public scrutiny and guidance (Hegedus et al. 1976; Bahro 1979; Ellman 1979; Rossanda et al. 1979).

The struggle continues nevertheless, as theory is continuously adjusted to practice and the latter to the evolving world-historical realities. For the unity of theory and practice, which is the basic philosophical operation of historical materialism, forces Marxists perpetually to reinterpret world events in the light of an overarching ethos of emancipation and the perennial source of energy that nourishes the daily struggles in which they are engaged.

Major characteristics of utopianism, social anarchism, and historical materialism are contrasted in Chart 4. This chart must serve in place of a more detailed account of how each movement connects with others in the rich history of revolt and revolution that is the counterpoint to the ideology-in-dominance. Readers are encouraged to deepen their understanding of the several movements that constitute this tradition by going directly to the authors who are identified with them.

So far, we have said little about the relevance of this history for planning and, more specifically, for the kind of planning I call radical (Chapter 1). It was scarcely a decade ago that some planners began to admit to being, in some sense, radical, but their numbers are steadily growing, though the movement is not yet very large. What I shall therefore have to say in the following pages does not rest on a broad consensus. No agreed-upon doctrine has emerged. Nevertheless, in a variety of ways, its leading members tend to conform to the model of radical planning that I propose to sketch.

Radical planners draw selectively from the entire body of the relevant literature and experience. In making this claim for an intellectual tradition of "radical planning," I am aware that I depart from the customary ways of looking at the oppositional movements that compose it. In the past, each movement has jealously defended its own turf. Moreover, both anarchism and historical materialism are linked to revolutionary movements that have nothing in common with "planning" as it is normally understood. For revolutionaries, "planning" is simply another form of bourgeois domination that must be resisted (see Appendix C). If we should therefore wish to consider the classical opposition movements as a tradition within the theory of planning, a reconceptualization is required. This is made possible when planning is defined as an activity in which knowledge is joined to action *in the course of social transformation*.

Because we are interested in public domain planning, I shall argue that social mobilization must be included in any discussion of planning theory. For "the people," that is, civil society and, more particularly, the popular classes whose only possibility of gaining ac-

---

Chart 4   **Utopianism (U), Social Anarchism (SA), and Historical Materialism (HM): A Synoptic View**

Final Goals (The Good Society)

U: Detailed description of particular forms of the Good Society. The typical utopian community is small and engaged in agricultural as well as industrial production. The community would look after the basic material needs of its membership and, in so doing, limit contact with the outside world. Owenite communities make education a central preoccupation; Fourierists stress the principle of passionate attraction. In both types of community, public and private spheres would merge. In both, the design of the physical space for a communitarian life is of the utmost importance. Propagation of the good society is by example.

SA: Abolition of the State as an instrument of class coercion. Autonomous units of "associated labor" are linked into larger ensembles by following the Proudhonian principle of federation, which reserves the right of "exit" for each federated member. The goal is to achieve a non-acquisitive society in a regional setting, practicing self-reliance. Small, decentralized units of production, organized on mutualist or cooperative principles, serve chiefly local and regional markets. Because workers learn to engage in every type of work, the distinction between headwork and handwork disappears. Social control is from within the community and occurs spontaneously through the practice of fair exchange.

HM: A classless, cosmopolitan society based on abundant cooperative wealth and furthering the all-round development of the individual: "from each according to his ability, to each according to his need." Contradictions characteristic of earlier modes of production, such as the social division of labor, especially the distinction between headwork and manual labor, and the spatial division of labor between city and countryside, are overcome.

Intermediate Objectives

U: Establishing "intentional" communities embodying specific forms of the Good Society.

SA: Two versions must be distinguished: Bakunin's revolutionary strategy of direct action and the peaceful means for reaching anarchist objectives promoted by Proudhon and Kropotkin. For Bakunin, the immediate task was the physical destruction of the state in all of

Chart 4   **Utopianism (U), Social Anarchism (SA), and Historical Materialism (HM): A Synoptic View** (*cont.*)

its forms—economic, political, religious, educational. The physical infrastructure of the capitalist state would have to be totally demolished by violent means. From its still smoldering ashes would rise the new forms of anarchist society.

According to Proudhon, the objective at hand was the formation, on the margins of the still existing state, of an alternative society, based on what came eventually to be called "autonomous units of associated labor" in workshops and factories by the free consent of individual workers ("social contract"). Proudhon referred to his system as "mutualism" and imagined a form of credit and labor exchange that would maintain a rough equality of power among the small units of anarchist society by impeding private accumulation. These units, thought Proudhon, would eventually federate into larger ensembles, even as they retained the unrestricted right to "exit" from the federation. The territorial base of anarchist society would be the small locality, or "commune." In the formation both of larger production units and of communes, the principle of delegation and accountability to the base must be strictly observed.

HM: Popular forces, led by the proletariat and its "vanguard" political organizations, "capture" the state and establish a transitional "dictatorship" over the remnants of bourgeois society. The means of production are socialized and the surplus extracted from production is managed in the interest of the working class by the state. (In recent years, European communist parties have abjured the idea of a "dictatorship" in favor of continuing struggles through the parliamentary system. Under this version, however, the prospect of a social revolution recedes into the hazy future.)

Strategy:
Organization

U: Formation of "intentional" communities by like-minded individuals who adhere freely to the principles of the Good Society embodied in the communal order.

SA: For Bakunin, it was necessary that "in the midst of the people's anarchy, which is the very life and entire energy of the revolution, the unity of revolutionary thought and action find an organ. This organ must be the secret and universal association." But for Proudhonists and indeed for most social anarchists, no organization, se-

Chart 4	**Utopianism (U), Social Anarchism (SA), and Historical Materialism (HM): A Synoptic View** (*cont.*)

cret or otherwise, was needed, because participatory, non-hierarchical groups of workers would merge to carry out the revolution and establish units of associated labor by their free consent as the basic form of anarchist society. A branch of anarchism, the anarcho-syndicalists, did work through trade union organizations or syndicates that had a more formal structure, but syndicates were typically small, and their leadership was decentralized.

HM: Formal organizations, such as political parties and labor unions, are essential to the successful waging of class war. Political parties may play a "vanguard" role by assuming leadership of the revolutionary movement, setting its political direction and deciding on questions of strategy. (An alternative movement within the traditions of HM has stressed the formation of workers' councils, or soviets, in factories, but these attempts have not been successful in practice and play no significant role in contemporary revolutionary organization.) The principle of internal organization governing the vanguard political party is "democratic centralism," which means free discussion at the base and binding collective decisions at the top.

In the decades since World War II, mass political parties adhering to principles of HM have appeared in Italy, France, Spain, and Portugal. Increasingly, however, these parties assume bourgeois characteristics and abandon their revolutionary objectives for a peaceful transition to socialism.

Strategy:
  Nature of the Struggle

U: Withdrawal from society; establishment of "intentional" communities. Means and ends of action are viewed as largely identical: the chosen means must be ethically consistent with the ends.

SA: According to Bakunin, the structures of state domination must be smashed to create the conditions for the reconstruction of society along anarchist lines. "Smashing" is a physical act that involves the apocalyptic violence of a mass-based and spontaneous revolutionary movement. Alternatively, there is symbolic terrorism, or "propaganda by the deed." Institutional politics must be avoided at all costs. In its place, anarchists propose economic actions, such as the general strike, which at the turn of the twentieth century became a strategic weapon for the anarcho-syndicalists. The creation of au-

Chart 4	**Utopianism (U), Social Anarchism (SA), and Historical Materialism (HM): A Synoptic View** (*cont.*)

tonomous units of associated labor is in accord with emancipated human nature and is consequently a spontaneous process requiring neither foresight nor coercion.

HM: Revolutionary struggle, using both political (institutional and legitimate) and extra-political (violent) means. The culminating revolutionary act is the seizure of state power. In general, it is argued that the ends justify the means, which stand in a purely instrumental relationship to the immediate objectives of the revolutionary struggle.

Strategy:
  Timing

U: The future is now.

SA: Immanence of the Good Society, although the possibility of progress through social learning is admitted.

HM: Exploitation of the internal contradictions of capitalist society. The struggle for control of the state must be waged pragmatically in relation to the actual historical "conjecture." Critical to the success of the revolutionary movement is the creation of a "revolutionary situation." Once the proletariat has seized the powers of the state successfully, there ensues a long period of "transition" (called socialism) in the direction of a "higher phase of communist society" when the state as an instrument of class domination will "wither away." (This ultimate vision is in many respects similar to the end-state of social anarchism.)

The Enemy

U: The enemy is a morally corrupt and bankrupt society. But the enemy is ignored, as the "intentional" community turns inward upon itself.

SA: The enemy is the bourgeoisie, which, together with the institutions through which bourgeois domination is secured, has expropriated the means of production and reduced workers to wage slaves. Although all relations of domination are rejected as morally pernicious, the ultimate evil is the state. Only authority relations that emerge spontaneously from within the moral order of a free community are genuine.

Chart 4	Utopianism (U), Social Anarchism (SA), and Historical Materialism (HM): A Synoptic View *(cont.)*

HM: The class enemy is the bourgeoisie, which, by controlling the means of production, has established itself as the ruling class in capitalist society and is the ultimate source of exploitation, oppression, and alienation of the working class.

The Human Individual

U: Different conceptions, according to different versions of the Good Society. In one famous version (Fourier, Reich, Marcuse), human beings are portrayed as, above all, sensual, passionate beings.

SA: Human beings have a natural tendency to be loving, generous, and cooperative; they are innately social beings. This nature is distorted, and human beings are reduced to moral cripples, because they are subject to the repressive institutions of organized violence, principally the state. Freely chosen productive work is essential to the realization of one's full humanity.

HM: Under capitalism, essential aspects of individual humanity are "alienated" by the powers of capital, state, and religion, in whose hands they assume the form of a repressive authority. Under socialism, these powers will once again be internalized by individuals, releasing immense creative potential for self-development. Human beings are regarded as "open" to the future; they are perfectible without limit. This self-transformation, which is a gradual process, takes place in the course of engaging in the political practice of changing reality, and it will be furthered by the non-repressive institutions of the new society as they emerge from struggle. As with SA, freely chosen productive work is regarded as essential to the realization of one's full humanity.

cess to power is through social mobilization, are not merely the silent objects and sufferers of elite planning by the state. According to democratic theory and their own view of the world, they have a fundamental right to co-determine their own destiny. And that implies not only political struggle and collective self-empowerment; it also frequently involves some sort of planning "from below." Sometimes (though rarely) the struggle may be revolutionary in the sense of seeking the overthrow of the entire system of existing power relations. But what is institutionally defined, then, as the public domain, will be consciously subverted, albeit in the name of a higher morality. Here, planning has little to contribute because, as I use the term, planning presupposes an existing system of consensual order without which a public domain does not exist.

Radical planners, perforce, walk the thin line that divides licit from subversive action. For some of them, the utopian tradition may be sufficient inspiration (Kropotkin 1975 [orig. 1888–1890]; Buber 1949; Goodman 1960; Illich 1973; Hayden, 1984). Interested in right ways of living together, they would persuade us by the moral force of their arguments. How to implement their (utopian) solutions is of only secondary importance to them. For others, the question of revolutionary practice is posed in hard, existential terms.[15] There is yet a third form of radical practice and planning, however, that is neither utopian (though it may be informed by utopian visions) nor revolutionary, but is interested in transformative action. It is to this kind of planning that I now turn.

Granting its essentially eclectic nature, social mobilization or radical planning nevertheless has certain characteristics, including at least the following, that set it apart from other traditions.

1. SM serves emancipatory values. Specifically, it addresses the concerns of working people who themselves exert no significant influence on societal guidance and consequently bear the brunt of dehumanizing oppression and exploitation. Their social movements, whether based on gender, class, ethnicity, religion, or some other common bond, seek above all liberation from their degrading position in society.[16]

2. SM views history as a contradictory process in which the route to social progress remains open. SM rejects the harmony model of society, which is the stock in trade of the social reform

15. See Piven and Cloward (1979), Katznelson (1981), and Castells (1983) for a discussion of urban social movements and their potential as agents of revolutionary transformation. In Western Europe, the current political debate concerns the strategies of so-calleld Euro-communism, which is the parliamentary road to revolutionary power. See Boggs and Plotke (1980).

16. The concept of working class is too narrow and sectarian to serve as the exclusive basis for SM planning. In agrarian societies, for example, "the people" include the small peasantry, landless workers, the under- and unemployed urban masses, as well as workers who enjoy steady employment. In the United States, the cohesive bonds of ethnicity and gender are frequently stronger than those of class, and urban social movements tend to cut across class boundaries, uniting people in common action on the strength of their primary identification. I do not wish to exclude class as a relevant organizing concept for radical practice, but I regard its exclusive designation for this purpose as quite simply wrong. See Katznelson (1981) for an extended treatment of this argument.

tradition, in favor of a model based on conflict within the dominant society, its institutions, and its agents.[17]

3. SM involves a radical political practice by actors collectively committed to bringing about specific forms of structural change within society. In the course of producing these changes, individuals taking part in the collective action reform themselves as persons as they seek to become truly social beings who experience in their own lives the tensions and contradictions between the individual self with its many needs and the equally powerful claims of the collectivity of which they are a part and in whose needs they share.

4. SM is informed by a paradigm of social learning that expresses the dialectical unity of theory and practice. In SM, knowledge is regarded more as a flow than as a stock of resources. Groups engaged in political struggle learn from the practice of changing reality. To be effective, this learning must be integrated with a theory of social transformation. Without theory, radical practice cannot achieve its broad objectives of emancipation. It must be something other than moral fervor combined with spontaneous reflex. Embedded within a strategy of action, radical practice must be saturated with theory.

In the next section, I propose to examine some aspects of critical consciousness and ideology within the tradition of SM. This will be followed by a discussion of alternative strategies for radical practice. Finally, I will return to the basic question of whether and to what extent SM may be regarded as a major tradition within planning (as I have claimed), and I will identify some of the possible roles for "planners" within this tradition.

Critical Consciousness

Whatever its variant, the starting point of planning in the tradition of SM is a thoroughgoing social critique. Listening to this critique, we hear the voices of those without substantial power, whose suffering

17. There is, within the tradition of SM itself, a tendency to toy with a model of society that envisions the harmonious integration of all elements into a single, noncontradictory whole. This tendency is especially strong in utopianism, though traces can also be identified within anarchism and even within historical materialism (Marx's "utopian" vision of full communism). In its political doctrine, however, historical materialism insists on a dialectical view of historical process. It is this instance of the dialectical nature of the struggle in the here and now that I wish to appropriate for the tradition of SM as a whole.

is a double burden of oppression and a dim awareness of this oppression. Social criticism is thus the inevitable prelude to radical practice.

Even as Saint-Simon was singing hosannas to the new industrial age, Robert Owen and Charles Fourier, the first utopians of the new century, were lashing out against the moral corruption and inhumanity of what they called the manufacturing system.

This scathing indictment comes from Robert Owen's pen.

> It has been and still is a received opinion among theorists in political economy, that man can better provide for himself, and more advantageously for the public, when left to his own individual exertions, opposed to and in competition with his fellows, than when aided by any social arrangement which shall unite his interests individually and generally with society
> . . .
>
> Yet when they shall know themselves, and discover the wonderful effects which combination and union can produce, they will acknowledge that the present arrangement of society is the most antisocial, impolitic, and irrational that can be devised; that under its influence all the superior and valuable qualities of human nature are repressed from infancy, and that the most unnatural means are used to bring out the most injurious propensities; in short, that the utmost pains are taken to make that which by nature is the most delightful compound for producing excellence and happiness, absurd, imbecile, and wretched.
>
> Such is the conduct now pursued by those who are called the best and wisest of the present generation. (Owen 1972, 269)

Or consider these words from Charles Fourier, who quotes from a Dublin newspaper of 1825.

> "There is an epidemic prevailing here among the people: the sick that are taken to the hospital recover as soon as they have been given food." Their sickness, then, is HUNGER: one need not be a sorcerer to divine that, since they are cured as soon as they have something to eat. Have no fear that this epidemic will attack the great: you will not see either the Lord-Lieutenant nor the Archbishop of Dublin fall ill from hunger, but rather from indigestion.
>
> And in places where the civilized masses do not die of *pressing* hunger, they die of *slow* hunger through privations, of

speculative hunger which constrains them to nourish themselves with unwholesome food, of *imminent* hunger through
overwork, through engaging in pernicious pursuits, enduring
excessive fatigue, which gives birth to fevers, to infirmities.
(Fourier 1976, 84–85)

In these passages one senses the depth of the authors' moral outrage. But in contrast to earlier centuries, their invective has secular
roots: it is the right to personal excellence and happiness that is
being violated. In common with many of their contemporaries,
Owen and Fourier were convinced that life could be something
other than a story of privation and repression, that the evils of the
manufacturing system could be abolished, that it was within human
capacity to change the world and bring it into accord with a vision of
life as it might be and *ought* to be.

The major motivating force in the writings of these critics and
dreamers, the ethics of their social criticism, was the idea of emancipation, by which they had in mind the removal of those "artificial"
social barriers that block the full development of human potential.
Here was how Jean-Jacques Rousseau visualized the individual self
in its full splendor.

The ideal moi [self] has harmoniously educated manual and
mental powers; it cannot conceive of *luxuria*; it is autonomous,
entire, whole. It lives fully and totally within the bounds of
time and space that happen to be its environment. Identity,
the consciousness of self, grows like a plant. Once it is fashioned, man can preserve that self whatever the vicissitudes of
fortune. (Manuel and Manuel 1979, 442)

The "ideal moi," then, was a generous and loving self. It was, in
addition, a spontaneous self, simple and pure in its intentions. Properly nurtured through education and in communion with nature,
human beings would grow into beautiful persons. There are no intimations here, however subtle, of the killer instinct, the death
drive, Thanatos, which Freud claimed was eternally engaged in
struggle with the creative life-enhancing urge of Eros (Freud 1962,
69).

In Rousseau's view, human beings were perfectible. This belief
was closely related to his understanding of our social nature, of what
he called the *moi comun*. True individuality, he argued, could be developed only in the context of a well-ordered polity to which we
would gladly subordinate our separate wills, because we would take
an active part in fashioning its laws. Based on a concept of our social

nature, Rousseau's individualism required a political community in which citizens would be both sovereigns and subjects (Colletti 1976).[18]

Rousseau's belief in human perfectibility was made possible by a naturalistic conception of the human individual. The anticlericalism of the eighteenth century had succeeded in pushing the Christian sense of guilt into the background. Thus released from the burden of original sin, the "natural" human being could develop his given faculties. All that was needed was a benign environment that would nurture rather than oppress.[19]

Such an environment, unfortunately, was not to be. Industrial capitalism enforced new forms of servitude. Marx's thesis of the progressive immiseration of the proletariat was no hyperbole. It was under the sign of massive immiseration that the radical counter-traditions were born. Their historical project was the abolition of capitalism and its replacement with patterns of social relations that would accomplish what the American and French revolutions had merely promised: the recovery of our essential humanity in free association with others.[20]

If the emancipatory ethos was pervasive among writers in the SM tradition, the specific sources of their criticism were diverse. At its most elementary level, social criticism was simply an expression of

18. Colletti cites a telling passage from Rousseau's *Emile.*

> The man of nature is everything to himself; he is the numerical entity, the absolute whole. . . . Civil man is only a fraction of the whole, his value lying in his relation to the whole, which is the social body. Good social institutions are those which best strip man of his nature, taking away his absolute existence to give him a relative one, and transferring his *self* into a common unity; so that each individual no longer believes himself to be one, but a part of a unit, and is no longer aware except in the whole. (Colletti 1976, 173)

Colletti's comment on this passage is revealing. "To create a society is to create a common interest, an association or real socialization of interests. . . . This is the basic originality of Rousseau's 'contract.' "

19. For Robert Owen, a benign environment included grade schools that were open to light and air, in which dancing, singing, and gymnastics were part of the daily curriculum and in which play and the playground were treated as an educative agency. "So original were these educational views," writes John F. C. Harrison, "that Owen had difficulty in finding teachers whom he could trust to carry them out" (Harrison 1969, 160).

20. Given a belief in human perfectibility—of the divine spark in every human being, as an earlier generation might have put it—there were no natural limits to emancipation. It had to be a *total* liberation. It would eventually take Freudian psychoanalysis to strike down the devils in our soul and, still later, Jürgen Habermas's "ideal speech situation" with its demand that even the slightest urging to gain power over others be forever banished from the public domain (Habermas 1979).

outrage at man's inhumanity to man, a spontaneous and visceral re-action to evident evil. Time and again we encounter this moral fury, from Owen and Fourier to William Morris, John Ruskin, and the impassioned rage of Lewis Mumford.

A second major source of social criticism is an image of humanity constructed by reason. The beginnings of such an image emerged already with Rousseau and the utopians with their belief in the nat-ural self, the *moi comun*, the passionate nature of the human soul, and the molding influences of the environment on character. But unquestionably the most ambitious effort to devise such an image was that of Karl Marx. As a young man, Marx developed a philo-sophical conception of humanity that would serve as a foundation for all his later work. It allowed him to proceed to a critical analysis of actual forms of alienation, and from this knowledge to recover an integral vision of the human being who would emerge, he thought, in the communist society of the future.[21]

For Marx, the human individual is, in essence, (1) a natural and sentient being; (2) a moral being who stands in free, autonomous re-lation to others like himself; (3) a being who has needs which, above the level of survival and biological reproduction, and in accord with human experience, become progressively higher and more com-plex; and (4) an active, malleable being, capable of changing the reality that surrounds him even as he changes and transforms him-self.

Free, conscious, practical activity, or *labor*, is the highest expres-sion of humanity. According to Marx, it is through labor that we sustain our livelihood, make our history, and create those needs that must be satisfied to raise our capacities as human beings to ever higher levels of perfection.[22]

21. Basic sources for a discussion of Marx's philosophical anthropology include Avineri (1970), Schaff (1970), Heller (1976), and Ollman (1980).

22. Marx's concept of labor is equivalent to free, conscious, self-generated activity. He means it to be coterminous with life itself. For a very different reading, see Arendt (1958). Arendt not only distinguishes labor from work on the basis of what is being produced (labor produces livelihood while work produces our physical envi-ronment), but she also identifies political action as yet a third category, which is placed, as a capstone, over the remaining elements of human practice.

Under capitalism, however, labor is reduced to a quantitative expression. It is equivalent to abstract labor power which the worker, in competition with others, sells on a "free" market to potential buyers. By so limiting the concept of labor, all unre-munerated work such as women's traditional work in the home is diminished and de-meaned. The language of capitalism forces on us a sphere of consumption and lei-sure that is seen as essentially restorative or hedonistic, and so is robbed of its wider significance.

Before the exchange economy enforced on us a very different regime, most of what humanity produced was meant for self-consumption, and products were simply an extension of ourselves into the material world: they were embodiments of our labor.[23] Let us look at an example. The Indian peasant woman grinds maize in a mortar, she mixes the dough, slaps the tortillas into their traditional shape, and cooks them over a fire she herself has made; in a very real sense, the tortillas are hers and hers alone: she makes a gift of them to those whose lives are nourished by her work. Most kinds of production, however, and also hers, require the cooperation of others. Maize for the tortillas must be sown and harvested, wood must be collected and slowly burned into charcoal, water must be drawn from a well or nearby stream, salt made by other workers must be obtained in exchange. And so it comes about that our individuality can fully develop only in a context of social groups in which all are mindful of each other.

From this image of the emancipated individual, Marx proceeds to a first critique of capitalism. Alienation occurs, he says, when the owners of capital appropriate the product of our labor and sell whatever we produce as commodities in a market. Thus torn from natural relation to self and community, the things we produce are objectified; they are turned into a fetish. The pecuniary gains from their sale are recycled to produce still more, resulting in the ever greater accumulation of capital and the more rigid control of labor

---

23. Even before the appearance of an exchange economy, there was, of course, expropriation by Church and feudal lord, as well as the primitive exchange that occurs in all societies. The idea that the product of one's labor is the producer's own was first articulated by John Locke, who used it as a foundation for his theory of property:

> Though the earth and all inferior creatures be common to all men, yet every man has a *property* in his own *person*. This nobody has any right to but himself. The *labor* of his body and the *work* of his hands, we may say are properly his. Whatsoever, then, he removes out of the state that nature has provided and left it in, he hath mixed his labour with it, and joined it to something that is his own, and therefore makes it his property. It being by him removed from the common state nature placed it in, it has by this labour something ananexed to it that excludes the common right of other men. For this labour being the unquestionable property of the labourer, no man but he can have a right to what that is once joined to, at least where there is enough, and as good left in common for others. (Locke 1948, 17–18; orig. 1690)

Marx's theory of exploitation, which is fundamental to his understanding of accumulation processes in capitalism and the source of much of its moral fervor, is based on the Lockean notion that the product of labor belongs to the laborer by right. Exploitation exists when capitalists expropriate that product. The specific rate of exploitation is the difference between the costs of social reproduction of labor and the value of the commodities produced by labor.

at the work place, through management, and at the place of residence, through propaganda. Alienation cripples our humanity; it destroys our natural sociality; it makes us dependent on powerful others; and, in the end, it reduces us to the pitiable condition of "one-dimensional man."[24]

As the cash nexus of the market drives self-interest between worker and worker, it breaks the spontaneous bonds of human cooperation. The social division of labor creates a further and unnatural distinction between hand and head labor, with the latter in dominance, and as tasks become ever more narrowly defined and specialized, workers lose their sense of the labor process as a whole and become progressively de-skilled (Braverman 1974).

A parallel process occurs in the political sphere. Virtual political power is appropriated from the political community by the state, which is the instrument of bourgeois rule, and the consequent bureaucratization of life renders human beings powerless vis-à-vis state agencies and the nameless officials who staff them. Although the fiction of democratic accountability is maintained, real power is concentrated in the coercive institutions of the state.

For Marx, it was in the nature of a "categorical imperative" to overthrow all conditions "in which man is a degraded, enslaved, neglected, and contemptible being" (Schaff 1970, 114). The point of revolution is the recovery of our true humanity through an emancipatory practice that, in due course, will institute the social conditions for a fully human existence. What might be the contours of such a world? All we have is a few pointers. Property would revert into the hands of "associated labor" or units of free, cooperative ac-

---

24. In the words of Herbert Marcuse:

> I have just suggested that the concept of alienation seems to become questionable when the individuals identify themselves with the existence that is imposed upon them and have in it their own development and satisfaction. This identification is not illusion but reality. However, the reality constitutes a more progressive stage of alienation. The latter has become entirely objective; the subject which is alienated is swallowed up by its alienated existence. There is only one dimension, and it is everywhere and in all forms. The achievements of progress defy ideological indictment as well as justification; before their tribunal, the "false consciousness" of their rationality becomes the true consciousness. (Marcuse 1964, 11)

Marcuse's concept of the "more progressive stage of alienation" is but an intensified echo of Antonio Gramsci's concept of ideological hegemony and his call for a counter-hegemony of the working class, that is, an independent cultural creativity of that class. It has not been observed before, but Gramsci's hopeful advocacy of a counter-hegemony is probably as utopian as was one of Fourier's phalanxes a century before (see Gramsci 1971).

tivity. Production would be chiefly for use, without a great deal of exchange beyond the local market. And because money would no longer be needed except, perhaps, as a unit of accounting, wage labor would also be abolished. With the consequent disappearance of social classes, the class struggle would vanish from memory, and as an instrument of class domination, the state would atrophy and be replaced, in work place and community, by a form of self-management in the hands of the workers themselves.

Linked to a comprehensive philosophical conception, systematic social criticism, and a utopian vision, the Marxian image of humanity is a powerful, compelling one. Despite the many efforts to erect critical philosophies based on alternative images of being human— Darwin's or Freud's, for example—none has succeeded to the extent of Marx's ingenious derivation of a concept of alienation in providing the ideological basis for a radical practice.

A third major source of social criticism is the scientific analysis of capitalism as a system of political economy. Some aspects of this analysis were discussed earlier and need not be repeated here. The power of its critique may be sensed from the following sketch.

In a daring flight of the imagination, Marx and Engels undertook to analyze capitalism as a dynamic, universal, and historical system, or *mode of production*, which was subject to its own "laws of motion." One of these laws was the inherent necessity of capitalists to engage in the constant innovation of both product and production processes. Innovation speeds up the pace of historical change, which an exultant Schumpeter called the "whirlstorm of creative destruction." As it renews itself from period to period, capital leaves no memory of itself: its glassy office towers reflect an ever-present NOW. Capital destroys the past, destroys whatever it needs to feed its insatiable appetite for profits and power—people, landscapes, resources, attachments to community and place, autonomy of production—destroys quite possibly more than it creates along with values that can never be replaced. To protect themselves from the memory of these horrors, people develop historical amnesia. And lacking history, they are more easily controlled.[25]

Marx pointed to capitalism's innate drive to expand over the

25. We may recall here a practice of the Chinese revolution that the Chinese called "talking bitterness." Older peasants would get up at a meeting of their fellow villagers, both young and old, to recall for them their sufferings at the hands of landlords, moneylenders, warlords, and brigands in the days before the revolution. It was oral history in a collective setting and one of the more effective means for social mobilization.

globe, organizing world markets for capital, commodities, and labor. He provided an explanation of the destructive "anarchy" of the market, with its ever-recurring, ever-deepening crisis of overproduction. And he predicted what he regarded as the inevitable polarization of social classes.

As struggles grew in severity, the state, which Marx understood to be an instrument of class domination, would set aside the rhetoric and institutions of liberal democracy as it intensified its repression of the working class. But in the end, this, too, would prove of no avail. Driven by internal contradictions and revolutionary struggles beyond a point of no return, capitalism would enter its final phase of mounting social crises and internal collapse.

A rather curious offshoot of historical materialism is *critical theory*. The term refers to the work of a group of scholars who, in 1923, founded the Institute for Social Research at the University of Frankfurt. Since then, critical theory has evolved into a vast investigation of all that classical Marxism had relegated to the twilight zone of the ideological superstructure of the dominant mode of production.

Forced to emigrate during the Nazi period, the Institute settled in New York and later in Los Angeles, but it failed to find a permanent home in the United States. Its two leading personalities during this period, Max Horkheimer and Theodor Adorno, returned to Germany after the war. However, many of their former associates and co-workers, among them Herbert Marcuse, Erich Fromm, Bruno Bettelheim, Franz Neumann, and Karl Wittfogel, decided to make their way independently in the New World (Jay 1973; Hughes 1975; Connerton 1980).

What distinguished the work of the Frankfurt school from historical materialism—though this was not immediately apparent—was its complete lack of interest in revolutionary practice. The working class had been co-opted into bourgeois society; revolutionary consciousness was dated. Despite the Frankfurt school's initial identification with Marxism and its concern with a critical reformulation of Marxist doctrine, its most powerful voices, among them Herbert Marcuse and Jürgen Habermas, moved beyond the framework of historical materialism to essentially utopian formulations.

Marcuse's work was, for the most part, a form of negative philosophizing. A phrase he borrowed from Alfred North Whitehead— the "Great Refusal"—may be allowed to stand for Marcuse's project as a whole. As he used it, the Great Refusal was a "protest against

unnecessary repression, the struggle for the ultimate form of freedom—'to live without anxiety' " (Marcuse 1964, 49–59).[26]

It was clearly an impossible demand. To make it plausible, Marcuse had to conjure up one of the archetypes of the utopian imagination, the Land of Cockayne, where even the slightest wish or desire is immediately gratified. For all of its evils, thought Marcuse, the
capitalist system had, in fact, brought humanity close to a cornucopia, where less and less work would be required to meet essential
human needs. Thus released from the "realm of necessity into the
realm of freedom," humanity would set about to create a ludic society of eroticized play in which language would turn to song and
life would be spent in the contemplation of beauty. "True civilization," he said, quoting Baudelaire, "lies in the reduction of the
traces of original sin" (ibid. 153).

It was a charming fable, and Marcuse recognized its kinship to
Fourier's phalanxes, where work had been changed into a form of
"passional attraction." His own demands for *total* freedom went beyond Fourier's, however, whom he criticized for the detailed blueprinting of his ideas (ibid. 218).

> The working communities of the *phalanstère* anticipate
> "strength through joy" rather than freedom, the beautifica-
> tion of mass culture rather than its abolition. Work as free
> play cannot be subject to administration; only alienated labor
> can be organized and administered by rational routine. It is
> beyond this sphere, but on this basis, that non-repressive sub-
> limation creates its own cultural order. (Ibid.)[27]

Jürgen Habermas, Marcuse's junior by a generation, eventually
took a similar course. His utopia, however, was infinitely more austere: it terminated in the search for and contemplation of truth
rather than beauty. Habermas began his project with a critique of
Marx, who, he thought, had failed to perceive the crucial importance of symbolic interaction as a domain co-equal and interdependent with the domain of instrumental action, or labor. Like

26. "To live without anxiety"—*ohne Angst leben*—is a phrase lifted from Theodor
Adorno's essay on Richard Wagner. *Angst*, however, is more than anxiety: it is an existential dread, and it is complete emancipation from this dread that Marcuse calls
the ultimate freedom. Another utopia? Return to the Garden of Eden?

27. "Strength through joy" is an allusion to a cultural movement organized by the
state in Hitler Germany. The final sentence in the quotation refers to Marcuse's recognition that the overcoming of necessity is only relative, and that a certain amount
of "repression" will always be necessary to meet the material requirements of a comfortable (!) life.

Marcuse, he sought to incorporate Freudian psychology, along with linguistics, into social analysis. But this research program led him into rarified regions of abstract thought, far removed from the pressing concerns of everyday life.

Habermas imagined an "ideal speech situation" in which the claims to the validity of what was being asserted would rest on a consensus concerning the intelligibility of the utterance, the truth of its propositional content, the sincerity of the speaker, and the appropriateness of the particuluar "speech act" to the situation. A breakdown in this consensus would require a more elaborate discursive justification, "the putting out of play of all motives except that of a willingness to come to an understanding; and . . . a willingness to suspend judgment as to the existence of certain states of affairs and as to the rightness of certain values" (Connerton 1980, 103).[28] An ideal speech situation exists, then, "only when for all participants there is an effective equality of chances to take part in the dialogue" (ibid.).

Communicative action is oriented toward reaching an understanding, ideally without attempting unduly to influence one's partners in rational dialogue. It is the ideal of a graduate university seminar, though for Habermas it describes the conditions of a perfect polity.

It was precisely this utopian urge and the density of his language that made Habermas into a cult hero among sociologists (Thompson and Held 1982). He allowed them to feel radical without actually being so. Though few bothered to read the fine print, felicitous phrases such as "legitimation crisis" were suggestive of a radical transformation of society but in typical Frankfurt fashion implied no political practice whatever.

At the end of *Legitimation Crisis* (1973), in a mini-chapter entitled "Partiality for Reason," Habermas equivocates between action and non-action, not unlike the philosopher Louis Althusser, whose counterpart to Habermas's communicative action he called "theoretical practice." Writes Habermas:

> One has already accepted his opponent's point of view if one resigns before the difficulties of enlightenment, and, with the goal of rational organization of society, withdraws into actionism. . . . Furthermore, the partiality for reason just as little jus-

28. The willingness to suspend judgment automatically removes discourse from action, and therefore from the moral contents of action. This alone renders the Habermasian utopia suspect. It is a utopia where nothing ever happens (except for good conversation!).

tifies the retreat to a Marxistically embellished orthodoxy . . .
Both paths are forbidden to a practice that binds itself to a rational will . . . that demands theoretical clarity about what we
do *not* know. (Habermas 1973, 142–143)

In Habermas's universe, critical thought is elevated above "ac-
tionism" (social reform) and "Marxistically embellished orthodoxy"
(revolution). In its search for consensual truth, the life of the mind
is portrayed as providing its own justification. Whether a meaningful social critique can be divorced from any social practice is a question Habermas fails to ask, though he answers it implicitly (see note
28). From the perspective of planning, the separation from political
practice is not permissible (Ulrich 1983). Critique unrelated to action is a respectable, bourgeois practice that is tolerated precisely because it is irrelevant.

In concluding this section on critical consciousness, I should like
to mention yet another strand of contemporary social criticism—the
feminist critique of male domination, or patriarchy. Going back at
least two centuries to the writings of Mary Wollstonecraft (1975;
orig. 1792), feminist theory offers by no means a unified critique.
There are radical, liberal, psychoanalytic and Marxist branches, as
well as sub-categories within each one of them, and they are not necessarily compatible with each other. In contrast to critical theory,
however, feminism is an emancipatory social movement, and feminist theory is the theory of this struggle. Each position within feminism has different implications for practice. And because the outcome matters, it is vigorously fought over and argued.[29]

A major focus of feminist theory is the household, traditionally
the center of a woman's world and the stronghold of patriarchal
practices (Zaretsky 1976; Foreman 1977).[30] The ambiguous relation
of the household to the capitalist economy; its crucial role in both
biological and social reproduction, including critical socialization
processes; women's specific repression and exploitation in its invisible and "private" worlds; and the reasons for the willing acquiescence of women to a situation considered by feminists to be intoler-
able accounts for the permanent interest of the household in
feminist studies.

29. Recent critical reviews of feminist theory, from very different perspectives, include Barrett (1980), Elshtain (1981), and Jagger (1983). For an instance of direct
application of feminist theory to practice, see Hayden (1984).

30. Use of the household concept rather than "family" is intended to underscore
the historicity of the bourgeois family (household), the institution with which we are
primarily concerned. It allows us to leave open the future development of households in new and unfamiliar directions.

Households are the central institution in civil society. And if the principal aim of a reconstructive practice is the recovery of political community as an autonomous domain through institutions of self-management, that community being the political expression of civil society, the reconstruction of the household in line with feminist conceptions is an essential step. I shall argue this position more fully in Part Three of this book.

The feminist case against the bourgeois household can be briefly stated.[31] Traditionally, women have been confined to the domestic sphere as men's "property," to be exclusively enjoyed by their husbands, who also appropriate the surplus product of their unwaged labor. Thus, women remain mute, invisible, and economically dependent.

From early on, young women are schooled in the arts of husbandry, which includes the bearing and nuturing of children; the domestic chores of cooking, cleaning, and sewing; and (where appropriate) the skills of gracious refinement to be displayed for the delectation of their husbands and their husbands' (male) friends. Because women's work is unremunerated, it fails to be socially acknowledged as important, and in a world that measures a man's worth by his income and position, it is held to be structurally inferior work. When women do venture forth to join the labor force, driven by economic necessity more often than by personal ambition, and yet not freed from the drudgery of housework, they command a price that is substantially below that of the skill-equivalent work of men. For this reason, women tend to see their earnings as merely supplementary to their husbands', and they suffer a loss of self-worth.

Women are not normally encouraged to get an education beyond the simple rudiments of knowledge unless, impelled by their class

31. I offer the following paragraphs with some trepidation. They are a caricature of some proto-feminist position that refers blithely to a bourgeois household as though a more precise class analysis were not important, as though national and ethnic differences counted for nothing, as though the household were forever frozen into a particular structure. Moreover, feminists come in different varieties, from radical-lesbian to liberal-hetero, and they do not by any means understand the household in the same way. Yet, even a caricature has value if it captures some essential features, though the importance of those features may be exaggerated. Women's role has been a subservient one, even in the modern era. Its subservience is of a specific kind, and in American society it is far less onerous than, say, in rural Turkey. Yet, for the most part, subservient it continues to be. With my attempt at a summary statement (the "caricature"), I hope to capture some of this subservience. For an assessment of the household by two radical-lesbian-socialist authors, see Helmhold and Hollibaugh (1983).

and station in life, they may need to become a "good and worthy companion" to their husband. Reduced to the nuclear group of husband, wife, and children, the bourgeois household becomes a claustrophobic, privatized world, dominated by men who move freely in the world of work and politics and seek, in the intimacies of their home, a "haven in a heartless world."

Feminist literature on the household economy attempts to account for these conditions, especially in relation to the workings of capitalism. It points to the historicity of the family household and its changing character over time. It explores alternative models of living together, devoting particular attention to the organization of household work and the gender division of labor. It examines in great detail the problem of child care with a view to allowing women full participation in public life, and it investigates alternative physical arrangements that would make a reconstructed household possible.

Feminists insist that their concerns extend to every human sphere, public and private, and that it is no longer acceptable to treat humanity as though it were distinguished by nothing but social class. The construction of gender must be introduced into all critical discussions; it is the basis for the oppression of women, and its reconstruction, beginning with the institution of the household, is the only road to women's liberation. By implication, it is the road to men's liberation as well.

Social criticism—this curious amalgam of moral passion, philosophical reflection, political economy, and prophecy—is the first and necessary step in the construction of an ideological framework for action. Such a framework is necessary to sustain and orient all political practice. A composite of several elements, it generally includes a description and explanation of reality from a critical perspective, a vision of the future, and an indication of what must be done. It was the extraordinary power of the Marxist critique, grounded in a concept of the human individual and in historical analysis, and pointing to the historical struggles between bourgeoisie and proletariat as the necessary path to the liberation of humanity from class domination, that made it prevail over competing ideologies, even as it was powerfully influenced by them, most recently by the feminist movement.

This is not to argue the case for either the completeness or correctness of the critique or the revolutionary doctrine to which it is linked. Ideology is an instrument of struggle and must be fashioned to meet the needs of the struggle. These needs come to a focus in the strategy for transforming basic structural relations in society. It is to a consideration of strategic alternatives in SM that we now turn.

The Question of Strategy

For radical practice, the question of strategy is both decisive and . . . divisive. All are agreed that the thrust for transformative, structural change must come "from below," that the struggle for liberation must be a form of self-liberation, that it is the people in their own communities who have to take hold of their lives, that society is their own handiwork and not that of the state. But beyond this very general agreement and a consensus on the ultimate ends of an emancipatory practice (a non-repressive, life-supporting community in which individual and collective needs are carefully balanced), there is a falling out over the strategy to be adopted—how the final goal might be achieved—and the closely related question of intermediate objectives. In part, the considerations here are ideological, in part they are of a practical nature.

The practical questions can be dealt with rather quickly. They turn on the immediacies of the situation in which the social struggle takes place. Strategy is not an abstract, universal set of categories, though it can also be that. Rather, it is a way of proceeding, in actual circumstances, with particular allies, against specific enemies, for particular objectives.

The more interesting considerations for our purpose are ideological. The political Left is fragmented precisely over disputes concerning the proper course of action. As it turns out, agreement on the decisive NO to every form of exploitation and oppression does not mean that there is consensus on the methods for struggle and for reconstruction.

Here are some of the issues on which radical movements typically divide.

1. Who should lead the movement: the people themselves, self-organized into revolutionary forces (for example, workers' councils), or a political elite of professional revolutionaries bound by disciplined commitments to a central authority?

2. What should be the social basis of people's organization for the struggle: class, ethnicity, gender, religion, or territory?

3. When there is conflict over the nature of the political struggle, which contradiction is primary and which is secondary? For instance, when gender and class struggles conflict, which

should take precedence and how is the question to be decided? Can two parallel struggles be waged at the same time?

4. Should long-term but uncertain gains be sacrificed for more immediate and certain benefits or should the ultimate revolutionary goal ("overturning capitalism") remain as the primary objective of organized working-class struggle?

5. What sort of alliances should be made and with whom? Are trans-class alliances, for example, a permissible expedient or should the struggle be confined to the committed militants of a single social class?

6. What role, if any, in the revolutionary struggle should be played by criminal elements, bandits, outlaws, unemployed workers, and "lumpenproletarians?"

7. Are violent means to be employed and, if the answer is yes, under what specific circumstances and in what form: as a last resort, as a basic tactic, only for defensive reasons? For what political objectives should violence be used?

8. Should the revolutionary movement be centrally organized and directed or should it retain a decentralized, informal structure?

The resolution of these and similar questions is what I mean by strategy.[32] They have been debated in the context of three political movements: Marxism-Leninism, Maoism, and social anarchism (both the Bakunin faction and the Proudhon-Kropotkin faction). In addition, debates over strategy have been influenced by the examples and the writings of charismatic leaders whose social movements do not readily fit into any preexisting mold, such as advocates of nonviolent struggle (Gandhi, Martin Luther King, Jr., the Society of Friends); populists such as Saul Alinsky; and professional revolutionaries such as Rosa Luxemburg, Leon Trotsky, and Antonio Gramsci.[33]

I do not propose to present a systematic account of the internal arguments and differences within the major ideological traditions

32. The language in which I have posed these questions is that of revolutionary socialism, but the issues would remain the same, even if a more moderate, less inflammatory rhetoric were used.

33. I am excluding from consideration the formation of utopian communities and similar experiments that involve only a handful of people who choose to turn away from society to create their own special worlds. Establishing intentional communities clearly involves questions of strategy, but they are of a very different sort than the strategy of sustained struggle for the transformation of the existing world, which is the topic here.

(the debates between Lenin, Trotsky, Pannekoek, and Gramsci, for example). This would surely be a worthwhile task, but it exceeds the scope of the present essay. Instead, I will attempt a synoptic account of a number of strategic issues in SM planning as they have become manifest over the last 150 years in the struggles for social transformation. The account will not be complete in the sense of capturing every ideological nuance, and the documentation will not be complete; however, they will be sufficient for present purposes.

Discussion will be organized around the following four topics: (1) spontaneity versus formal organization, (2) people versus elites in social mobilization, (3) organizing "for" or "against," and (4) forms of the struggle.

Spontaneity versus Formal Organization

One of the major controversies in the literature on SM concerns the origin and center of radical practice. The rhetoric has it that the "masses" can liberate themselves only through their own actions, that, in full consciousness of its mission, the working class erupts upon the stage of history to struggle with its common enemy, the bourgeoisie, for the control of its own destiny.

This classic, overblown image of the working class as demiurge leaves most basic questions of strategy unanswered, including these: who is to control the revolutionary movement, how much control should be wielded from outside, and to what purpose? At the beginning of this century, Rosa Luxemburg provided possible answers to these questions. Consciousness, she said, is gained in the course of the struggle itself. The revolution, which was imminent, would sweep like a whirlwind across the world. In a series of mass actions, workers would spontaneously lay down their tools and take up arms against the state and its agents (Luxemburg 1971). To be a worker, she believed, was to be predisposed to revolution, and her hope was for an "elemental outbreak" of working-class anger against the state and capital (Kolakowski 1978, 82). The mission of the revolutionary party was to cultivate the protean consciousness of the proletariat, to guide its passions toward specific politics ends, and to hasten the course of history through the conquest of power.

The very opposite of Luxemburg's "spontaneism" was Lenin's strategy of the "vanguard" party, a small, militant, and secret organization wholly dedicated to the revolutionary task. The Leninist party was to foment—not merely cultivate—a revolutionary consciousness among the masses and, when their enthusiasm was at a high pitch, and the situation ripe, to give out the parole for the final assault. Spontaneity, Lenin thought, would burn itself out; the revolution must be organized from above.

Luxemburg actively combated Lenin's strategy; she saw even the vanguard party as a potentially regressive agency that would restrain the revolutionary spirit of the masses.[34] And even though Mao Tse-tung subsequently succeeded in assimilating the two opposing strategies by embracing the doctrine of democratic centralism even as he held firm to his belief in the mass line (see below), he failed to resolve the inherent contradictions between them. Yet progressive change can be organized in other ways than through spontaneous self-mobilization or hierarchical organization. A complete list of organizational forms for social mobilization would include at least the five categories described below.

Spontaneous Uprisings. Spontaneous uprisings (for example, Watts in 1965, Paris in 1871 and 1968) may dramatize people's grievances in unforgettable ways, but their drive and dynamics are impossible to sustain. Much of the debate concerning "mass strikes," for example, turns on the question of whether political objectives can be achieved by this route. Piven and Cloward are very much to the point when they write that "insurgency is always short-lived" (Piven and Cloward 1979, xxi). Popular outbursts have chiefly a symbolic or cathartic value.

The bourgeois press often refers to such uprisings as "riots." The word suggests authority defied and reflects fear of uncontrolled violence. People are terrified by the destructive fury of crowds. And because they usually do not grasp the deeper issues involved, they are prepared to call for the quick restoration of "law and order." Subsequently appointed commissions of inquiry, such as the Kerner Commission in the wake of the Watts uprising, may yield information, insights, and suggestions as to how recurrences of similar events might be prevented, but positive corrective action is rarely taken.

Local Action Groups. Local action groups (informal organizations) may coalesce spontaneously around some public issue, such as a rent strike, but isolated within the local community they remain largely powerless and ineffective. They can, however, form the nu-

---

34. A contemporary counterpart to Luxemburg's spontaneism is found in Piven and Cloward's impressive work on social movements (1979). To describe the actions of social movements, they use such terms as strike, riot, disruption, protest, uprising, and mass defiance. Only spontaneous violence can leave a legacy of social progress. "Organizations," they write, "endure . . . by abandoning politics" (Piven and Cloward 1979, xxi).

cleus of a wider movement; like guerilla bands, they constitute the lowest-level links in a generalized struggle for a new society (for example, feminism, ecologism). The strength of local action groups lies partly in their having firsthand knowledge of the local situation, including its politics. Even more important is their reliance on personal interaction and commitment, the extensive use of face-to-face dialogue, the rational discussion of ideological questions in a supportive environment of comrades and friends, and flexibility in adjusting actions to local conditions (Friedmann 1979b).[35]

Networking. Local action groups may be brought together into larger movements. The least formal of these involves networking, a voluntary arrangement with easy conditions of entry and exit—the very essence of anarchist organization—which makes few demands on its membership beyond those of sharing information and making small financial contributions to maintain the network (mailing lists, newsletters, and so on). From time to time, local action groups may mobilize for larger, combined actions (a national protest, a people's referendum), but the real stage for struggle remains local. The collective energy required by networking is minimal, because the actions of the membership are not "coordinated" in the usual ways but rather tend to be convergent.

Coalitions. The next step up the organization ladder is the formation of coalitions for joint undertakings involving either local action groups or formal organizations (see below). Coalitions are possible when objectives are convergent or, as is more generally the case, when separate but parallel objectives can be effectively pursued through a joint effort.

Coalition-building requires leadership skills of a high order and the virtual full-time commitment of dedicated militants. As with formal organizations, coalitions tend to create a gap of perception and interest between the active leadership engaged in the high politics of the coalition and the "masses" with their everyday concerns. Another potentially divisive aspect of coalition-building is the struggle for power and for control of the coalition among its constituent groups, some of which are organizationally stronger than others, and which may have different ideological positions.[36] For all these

35. One of the best manuals for the mobilization of local action groups, reflecting a Quaker approach, is Coover et al. 1977.

36. Differences in ideology are especially pronounced in the popular front coalitions of European politics, in which communists and socialists of various stripes usually contend for hegemony within the movement—with inevitably disastrous results for the movement itself.

reasons, radical coalitions tend to be fragile, evanescent constructs that seldom last for more than the duration of a particular and short-lived action.

Formal Organizations. Finally, there are formal organizations that have the ability to link local action groups into city-wide, regional, national, and even international movements. Manuel Castells, a strong advocate of local citizen movements, nevertheless recognizes that they have severe limitations unless they coalesce into political parties. With post-Franco Spain as his background, he writes:

> The citizen movement in each neighborhood does not repre-
> sent the "people," because politics is not the sum of local and
> sectoral interests. Rather, it consists in the choosing of *global*
> *options* and *social organizations* that can only be elaborated and
> presented to the masses by political parties active at all levels
> of society, even when they fundamentally represent the inter-
> ests of only one social class and its political allies. (Castells
> 1977, 216; my translation)

Castells refers to parties of the Left, such as the Spanish Communists, which, he suggests, must mediate broader, class-transcending
interests than merely those of the proletariat and its "allies," which
constitute the political base of the Left.

Formal organizations seeking to articulate and carry out radical
policies include not only political associations but also labor unions.
Because they rely for their day-to-day management on professionals, controlling power rises to the top: Robert Michels (1915) called
it the "iron law of oligarchy." On the positive side, formal organizations may acquire legitimate standing in the community and carry
political weight. But these gains are purchased at a price. To the extent that organizations become part of the establishment, and as
Michels's "iron law" takes effect, they lose much of their radical lus-
ter. The extent to which formal organizations can be used to advance radical causes is therefore open to question. As Carl Boggs
(1982, ch. 5) has noted, radical practice and respectability do not, as
a rule, go hand in hand.

In conclusion, we might venture this observation: no single form
of organization is in itself sufficient to bring about radical change.
All forms have their place on the progressive agenda, sometimes
alone, at other times creating more complex patterns. One has to
choose which pattern to encourage, but the choice is not an either/
or; rather, it is between certain styles befitting given situations, in ac-

cord with actual possibilities, and in full cognizance of what each organizational form can uniquely accomplish.

People versus Elites in Social Mobilization

Mass-based struggles are often centered on some inclusive social identity, such as class, race, religion, or gender. Occasionally, too, the identity may be a territorial one, such as a neighborhood or region, though so-called territorial struggles often coincide with the struggles of a particular social group, as in black inner city neighborhoods, or the Francophone Province of Quebec. It is when groups sharing a social identity and occupying a definite territory feel themselves to be threatened or exploited that popular struggles are the most bitter and prolonged.[37]

Marx long ago distinguished between objective and subjective class identities. The working class was both an objective category, defined by social scientists on the basis of some criterion such as access to the means of production—it was, Marx said, a class "in itself"—and a subjective category, a collective actor conscious of its revolutionary mission—a class "for itself." The distinction has passed into everyday use. We know, for instance, that the U.S. Census has defined a category of Spanish-surnamed people (a class "in itself"), yet only a smaller number of Hispanics would declare themselves to be militants (a class "for itself"). We know, too, that the census counts the number of wage and salary workers in the country, and yet again, very few workers would declare themselves to be members of a revolutionary movement.

More generally, to be a working man or woman in the United States is not understood as a class identification at all. Social stratification tends to be perceived more by level of income than by a structural relation to the means of production.[38] To receive an income from wages and salaries is seen as a functional characteristic of the

37. There are also popular struggles that do not require a specific group or territorial identity. This appears to be the case with the peace movement, the consumer movement, and the ecology movement. Their basis is a common oppositional interest and, in the specific cases mentioned, it could be argued that the interest in question is predominantly middle-class and white. Since middle-class whites constitute the dominant majority, they tend to be blind to their own identity, finding it more convenient to express their opposition in universalistic rather than explicitly class or racial terms.

38. There is, however, a growing perception of a permanent "underclass" in America (mostly coincident with certain racial minorities), and during periods of labor militancy, something like a blue-collar, working-class identity, with its own culture, has in fact existed in this country. But this is a far cry from a working-class identity overall, including all wage and salary earners.

population without political significance. Largely for this reason, social class and especially working-class identity has not been, historically, a basis for radical movements in the United States.[39] A politics of liberation has been pursued far more effectively by racial minorities, especially blacks, Hispanics, and Native Americans.

Ira Katznelson explains this apparently anomalous situation—anomalous from a historical materialist point of view—with reference to the peculiar history of urban settlement in America.

> What is distinctive about the American experience is that the linguistic, cultural, and institutional meaning given to the differentiation of work and community, a characteristic of all industrial capitalist societies, has taken a sharply divided form, and that it has done so for a very long time. (Katznelson 1979, 19)

Already by the Civil War,

> the connections between conflicts at work and conflicts in residence communities were much more stark in the United States than elsewhere. . . . Away from work, ethnic and territorial identifications became dominant. . . . At work, workers were class-conscious, but with a difference, for their awareness narrowed down to labor concerns and to unions that established few ties to poliltical parties. (Ibid. 52)

Racial identification, initially imposed by the dominant majority, became, in the course of emancipatory struggles, transformed into a positive self-image of the group: ethnic minorities became politically active subjects, leading the way to what Omi and Winant (1983) call a "politics of difference." From a political perspective, race is conceived as a category that is continuously "in formation." Subjective group identification, or collective consciousness—the process of becoming a group "for itself"—is therefore not a precondition for a radical politics but its result. For this reason, liberation must always be a form of self-liberation.[40]

The concept (and reality) of self-liberation, however, does not

---

39. The puzzle of why the American working class has not become a class "for itself" has preoccupied a number of writers. (See, for example, Ollman 1972; Katznelson 1979; Omi and Winant 1983.)

40. The raising of consciousness is a critical process in the formation of radical social movements. It can happen in a variety of ways: spontaneously, through persecution by the hegemonic class or group; through struggle groups, study sessions, and literacy campaigns (Freire 1970); and through acts of terrorism, intimidation, and conformist social pressure.

dispense with the problem of leadership and, specifically, the relation of militant minorities to the movement as a whole. Lenin made the role of militant minorities famous with his theory of the "vanguard" party. After declaring that "the political struggle of Social Democracy is far more extensive and complex than the economic struggle of the workers against the employers and the government," he went on to argue in 1902 that this project required an organization of "revolutionaries" that must consist "first, foremost and mainly of people who make revolutionary activity their profession. . . . Such an organization must of necessity not be too extensive and as secret as possible" (Lenin 1975, 138; orig. 1902).

Lenin did not invent the idea of a conspiratorial minority. That honor belongs to his fellow Russian, the ex-aristocrat Michael Bakunin, who, despite his anarchist convictions, was seduced by the idea of manipulating the masses for what he took to be their own best interest (Pyziur 1968, 94–96). For if collective consciousness is learned only in political struggle, then it is altogether reasonable to assume that neither collective consciousness nor political militancy are ever equally distributed among the population. Moreover, struggle must be given a political orientation, and who but political elites should be prepared to give this direction? The Leninist solution of steering the course of revolution through dedicated cadres comes readily to mind. Yet it poses the serious ethical and, indeed, practical question of how elites and masses should stand in relation to each other.

It was Lenin once again who gave the classic formulation to an answer; he called it the principle of democratic centralism. Subsequently adopted by Mao Tse-tung, democratic centralism was made into a key political doctrine of the Chinese revolution. There would be free and open discussions among the membership "at the base," followed by a collective decision made by the leadership (the Central Committee of the Party) in full awareness of the people's views. The final phase would be the imposition of an "iron discipline" in the enforcement of that decision.

John Bryan Starr points out that democratic centralism is in many ways comparable to "Weber's notion of hierarchical structure of bureaucratic organization where information and compliance flow upward and directives backed by office-based authority constitute the downward flow through the hierarchy" (Starr 1979, 155). In Mao's hands, however, both Weberian bureaucracy and Leninist doctrine were fundamentally changed in meaning by his attempt to integrate them with his doctrine of the "mass-line." Mao defined this doctrine in a famous passage.

In all the practical work of our Party, all correct leadership is necessarily "from the masses, to the masses." This means: take the ideas of the masses (scattered and unsystematic ideas) and concentrate them (through study turn them into concentrated and systematic ideas), then go to the masses and propagate and explain these ideas until the masses embrace them as their own, hold fast to them and translate them into action, and trust the correctness of these ideas in such action. Then once again concentrate ideas from the masses and once again go to the masses so that the ideas are persevered in and carried through. And so on, over and over again, in an endless spiral, with the ideas becoming more correct, more vital and richer each time. (In Starr 1979, 148; orig. 1943)

Or, more succinctly, *"The people, and the people alone, are the motive force in the making of world history"* (Lin 1966, 118; orig. 1945; italics added).

In this statement, we recognize Mao's radicalized version of social learning. Yet only a few years earlier, he had written this forbidding warning.

We must affirm anew the discipline of the Party, namely:

(1) the individual is subordinate to the organization;
(2) the minority is subordinate to the majority;
(3) the lower level is subordinate to the higher level; and
(4) the entire membership is subordinate to the Central Committee.

Whoever violates these articles of discipline disrupts Party unity. (Lin 1966, 255; orig. 1938)

As these citations show, the marriage of the mass-line and democratic centralism was an uneasy one. Democratic centralism remained suspended between an almost Lincolnesque faith in the wisdom of the people and the pragmatic requirements of central control in political struggle. In practice, the application of these principles, apparently so contradictory, gave almost unlimited power to the central leadership and in particular to Mao, who could define the issues and terms of the debate, stop and start the debate at will, and eventually eliminate those critics who were becoming troublesome and inconvenient by their criticism of the party (or of Mao's leadership). Democratic centralism was a very limited democracy indeed.

In contrast to this Leninist-Maoist tradition, the questions of authority, hierarchy, and leadership and the related issues of formal organization and vanguardism are sheer anathema to anarchists. As a possible strategy, "Revolution from outside" is totally proscribed by them. The correct solution is reliance on the spontaneous action of small, localized groups and the formation of networks or, at the limit, loose, unruly coalitions. When anarchists allow themselves to think of formal organizations at all, it is primarily of self-managed cooperatives (Kropotkin) and federalist structures with plenty of power reserved at the base (Proudhon).[41]

Anarchist ideas on organization have been especially attractive to the movements of the New Left in the United States and Western Europe, with their profound opposition to both the state and mega-corporation, their deep suspicions of formal organizations and hierarchy, and their marked preference for self-reliance (Galtung et al. 1980). In a curious way, Mao's mass-line (though not his correlative doctrine of democratic centralism, a deliberate and questionable omission) intersects with American experience, which has its own populist roots. In the anti-poverty and civil rights campaigns of the early sixties, for example, we come upon not only the mass-line principle of "community control" but, linked with it, the ardent advocacy of nonviolence and civil disobedience by charismatic figures such as Martin Luther King, Jr., who understood that the unarmed people's most effective weapon, and its ultimate source of autonomy from both its own leadership and the state, is a commitment to what are essentially moral principles of action. In citizen movements based on these principles, the initiative always remains with the people acting within their own communities.

The real difficulties with the anarchist model of organization derive from the very sources of its strength: first, as Katznelson (1979) has observed, a community-based politics has been unable to tie into the work place: critical questions of industrial and economic state policy thus remain outside its scope;[42] second, the network and loose coalition practices that build up the oppositional movement from local neighborhood to nation are, at least for the present, po-

41. Bakunin's advocacy of a "secret society" of professional revolutionaries, which had so appealed to Lenin, must be regarded as an anomaly in the anarchist tradition. As a *revolutionary* anarchist, Bakunin was by no means typical of the movement as a whole, though his influence, especially in Italy and Spain, was strong.

42. See the fascinating debate in *democracy*, involving William Appleman Williams (1981), a comment by Robert Ross (1982), and a rejoinder by Williams in the same issue (1982), which hinges precisely on this question. Williams argues for a regional socialist politics; without choosing to offer an alternative of his own, Ross questions the relevance of such a politics in the face of global capital and the international state.

litically too weak and too disorganized to be effective in their struggle with the forces of the state and capital.[43] So far, the New Left has been unable to develop a coherent strategy of structural reform, and its legions remain encapsulated within the "city trenches" of local neighborhood and community. Their war, as Gramsci might have said, is a "war of position" (Gramsci 1971, 229–235).[44]

Organizing "For" or "Against": The Problem of Ideology
There is, in practice, a basic asymmetry between struggling *for* something and struggling *against* a perceived wrong. It is common knowledge, for instance, that it is easier to get people to agree on what is wrong—for instance, to rally communities and labor against plant closings in America today—than to decide on how to build a new and better world. There is no lack of visionary models, from "economic democracy" to "self-reliance." The difficulty is getting people to agree on which of the many futures that seem attractive and possible they should commit themselves. For such a commitment is considerably more than the relatively inconsequential task of choosing a "tomorrow" that will be only marginally different from today. It is a commitment to the structural transformation of society, to embarking upon a path of action whose ultimate consequences cannot be foreseen.[45] Because of this, it has been easier to organize protest movements, and to unite people in their struggle against some deep-seated wrong, than to mobilize them around a

43. What it would take to confront global capital and the state is called by Omi and Winant the strategy of "crossing many rivers" (1983, Pt. 2, 61ff.). Socialists should recognize, the authors say, that "in a majority of cases, minority-based political projects (1) have a progressive economic content . . . (2) have a lot to teach any oppositional grouping aspiring to majoritarian politics about cultural diversity and the variety of organizational approaches required to mobilize different groups against the dominant social order; and (3) can be supported in loosely unified blocs and alliances that do not require general agreement about the need for revolution, the national question, or the nature of the Soviet Union" (ibid. 62).

44. Gramsci distinguished between (class) wars of movement and of position. In the first, the object was to assault the state itself; in the second, civil society. Importantly, wars of position included an ideological struggle for cultural hegemony.

Gramsci thought that the "war of position" was the more appropriate strategy for Western bourgeois society, where civil society was at a high point of its own development, culturally creative, and resilient. On this basis, he criticized Rosa Luxemburg's pamphlet on the mass strike (1971) for its attempt to provide a theoretical justification of the war of movement in the West. A concise but very clear exposition of these difficult and sometimes contradictory concepts is found in McLellan (1979, 188–193).

45. Utopians, of course, experience no such problem: their moral commitment is to a radically different future *now*, which takes the concrete form of an alternative community.

reconstructive program for a "new society." In the ongoing struggles against an enemy, all that is needed is to hold out some general good, a symbol of emancipation.

> We hold these truths to be self-evident, that all men are created equal, that they are endowed by their Creator with certain inalienable Rights, that among these are Life, Liberty, and the pursuit of Happiness.

Beginning with Marx, socialists have been notably reluctant to spell out the ultimate goals of their struggle, and one is left with little more than a handful of stock phrases, such as "from each according to his ability, to each according to his need"; "the socialization of the means of production"; "the abolition of the state"; and similar slogans.[46] The argument has always been that the socialist society of the future will emerge out of immediate struggle, and that to describe it in advance of the action itself is to engage in an unproductive and utopian practice.

Anarchists have been more inclined to spell out a social vision beyond their basic demand for the "dissolution" of the state. But even Kropotkin, who was more explicit than most about the details of an anarchist society, thought he had to defend himself against the charge of being an "idealist."

> In the first place, in the ideal we can express our hopes, aspirations, and goals, regardless of practical limitations, regardless of the degree of realization which we may attain; for this degree of realization is determined purely by external causes.
>
> In the second place, the ideal can make clear how much we are infected with old prejudices and inclinations . . .

46. A very different view is propounded by Albert and Hahnel.

> Making a socialist revolution in the United States requires a clear vision of what the socialism we want will be like. How will it work, what will be its institutional and human relations, and how will its quality of life be superior to that we now endure?
>
> United States citizens are not going to rally to rhetoric nor to an amorphous set of promises, nor to a blurry vision . . .
>
> In order for people to care about socialism in this country, it will have to be evident that socialism means a new form of truly democratic society, a possible society which is so much more desirable than what we have now, that it is worth immense efforts to struggle in its behalf. (Albert and Hahnel 1978, 253)

Their "un-orthodox" Marxism has scarcely made a ripple in American politics. Is it because their vision is insufficiently attractive, or does the problem reside precisely in their attempt to elaborate the model of a socialist America?

In speaking about the definition of the ideal, we of course
have in mind the definition of only four or five prominent features of this ideal. Everything else must inevitably be the reali-
zations of these fundamental theories in life. (Kropotkin 1970,
47; orig. 1873)

On the practical side, there was always the fear that opening up
the question of a new society, or even the specifics of a structural reform, would divide the Left more than unite it.[47]

And yet, the issue of "for" or "against" must be confronted. If social movements are to sustain their action, they require an ideology
that provides its adherents not only with a satisfactory image of
present-day reality but tells them as well, and in appropriate language, what is needed to be done and why. Most programmatic
statements—doctrinal declarations, manifestos, and the like—contain both, a critique of the present system, along with the social
forces that sustain it, and a political or philosophical statement of
the kind of social order for whose eventual achievement the struggle must be waged.[48]

A curious exception to this generalization is Saul Alinsky, a self-
proclaimed radical community organizer from Chicago whose
influence on the American community movement has been considerable (Boyte 1980). Because he rejects a programmatic counter-
ideology as un-American, it will be worthwhile to examine his views
in some detail.

What ideology, if any, can an organizer have in a free society
[he asks], working for a free society? The prerequisite for an
ideology is possession of a basic truth. . . . A free man working
for an open society is in a serious dilemma. To begin with he
does not have a fixed truth, he has no final answers, no
dogma, no formula, no panacea. The consequence of this is
that he is ever on the hunt for the causes of man's plight and

47. The vision of a self-reliant society is given substance in Galtung et al. It is interesting to observe, however, that the authors are careful not to specify the details of
their model. As Galtung observes in his opening chapter:

One advantage with the term "self-reliance" is its open-endedness. The term
has a certain nucleus of content, but it is up to all of us to give it more precise
connotations (in fact, that would be the only self-reliant way of going about
defining the term "self-reliance"). The following is one *suggestion*, one effort to
fill it with content, even to build some kind of ideology around it; it is by no
means a set of prescriptions, a dogma. (Galtung et al. 1980, 19)

48. For a good example, see the Charter of the Malagasy Socialist Revolution,
which was introduced in August 1975 (in Galtung et al. 1980, ch. 16).

general propositions that help to make sense out of man's irrational world. He is constantly examining life, including his own, to get some idea of what it means. (Alinsky, 1969, xii–xiii; orig. 1946)

Alinsky then proceeds to state his own "basic truth."

> In the end, [the free-society organizer] has one all-consuming conviction, one belief, one article of faith—a belief in people, a complete commitment to the belief that if people have the power, the opportunity to act, in the long-run they will, most of the time, reach the right decisions. The alternative to this would be rule by the elite—either dictatorship or a political aristocracy of some form. I am not concerned if this faith in people is regarded as a prime truth and a contradiction to what I have already written, for life is a story of contradictions. (Ibid. xiv)

Alinsky seems to be only dimly aware of the substance of his own commitments. What he calls the "free society" is capitalist America, circa 1945. The "free world" had won the war against the Axis powers, and Franklin Roosevelt had proclaimed his Four Freedoms as the basis for a just world order. To advocate a free society was thus very much in keeping with the spirit of Alinsky's time.

To understand more fully what Alinsky had in mind, one must read further in his text. Toward the end of the book that established his reputation, Alinsky comes forward with his central thesis that "*in the world as it is, man moves primarily because of self-interest*" (ibid. 225; italics added). It is a bald restatement of the unmitigated cant of possessive individualism and its sustaining myth.

With this background, it is not difficult to guess of what Alinsky's "radicalism" fundamentally consists. It consists of nothing more, he says, than of helping the "poor of America" to get what they want. And what they want, he says, is *more*.

> Do you know what the poor of America or, I might add, the poor of the world want? They want a bigger and fatter piece of these decadent, degenerate, bankrupt, materialistic, bourgeois values and what goes with it. (Ibid. 229)

Rejecting any form of counter-ideology, Alinsky perforce accepts the reigning ideology. His radicalism concerns the means of action, not the end. It consists of going directly to the people to organize them on their own behalf: acting together, to be sure, but each one acting for himself alone. Thus, he combines his basic understanding of the world "as it is" with the grand populist declaration that "if the people have the power, the opportunity to act, in the long-run they will, most of the time, reach the right decisions." To set the world aright, all that is needed is to empower people.

There is here an implicit rejection of Gramscian doctrine that starts from a very different set of assumptions and specifically works within a historical materialist framework. A decade earlier, Gramsci had argued the need for a working-class "counter-hegemony" that would socialize the proletariat into a set of ideological and cultural categories different from that of the hegemonic class. The bourgeois state, he averred, would not be successfully "captured" until the proletariat had first developed its own comprehensive ideology to the point where it could speak for the whole of society and thus sustain its claim to be a "universal" class.

> To establish its own hegemony the working class must do more than struggle for its own narrow sectarian interests: it must be able to present itself as the guarantor of the interests of society as a whole. The establishment of a proletarian counter-hegemony was impossible without the active participation of the intellectuals of the working class. The Party was also an essential element here. (McLellan 1979, 187)

The issue could not be more clearly posed. Alinsky turned away from "ideology"—actually the expression of a "counter-ideology" in Gramsci's sense—because his own thought was being root-fed, invisibly, by the very bourgeois order that had brought on the working class poverty he wished to change. His radicalism was accommodationist. He wanted poor people to get a better deal but without transforming society. And the way to do this, he convinced himself, was to mobilize people where they lived, in their own backyards and not at the point of production. Gramsci's concept of counter-hegemony, on the other hand, requires a political party complete with elite leadership, militant vanguards, a central committee, and party discipline. His counter-ideology implies an oppressive social structure containing all the contradictions of "democratic centralism" that we have already noted.

It is for this reason, perhaps, that the American New Left has been so careful to "keep things loose" and to avoid major doctrinal commitments. New Left rhetoric tends to stress three "antis"—anti-bigness, anti-authority, anti-monopoly—and three "pros"—pro-people, pro-self-realization, pro-ecology. As an ideology, it may not be much, but it has the considerable merit of providing an uncontested basis for building coalitions and alliances that focus on immediate issues of political struggle (Shalom 1983).

Forms of the Struggle

Social mobilization inevitably involves some sort of "struggle" to make the world a very different place from what it is. The choice of conflict, which is often deliberate, has enormous practical implications. Here, we will briefly consider three sets of alternative conflict strategies and the theoretical positions from which they derive: the choice of means—nonviolent or violent, reform or revolution—and the strategy of political or extra-political struggle. Each set is best regarded as a facet of the same underlying predisposition: to see history as either a continuous flow of events which, because of cumulative changes, is nevertheless capable of producing a structural transformation in a given system of relations, or as a discontinuous process, with revolutionary ruptures marking the "turning points" of historical happening.

Historical materialists tend to believe in "turning points" and, more particularly, in a breakdown theory of capitalism. The crises and internal contradictions of capitalism, they predict, will build up to a revolutionary situation in which the proletariat, victorious at last, will rise to power. Such was the firm belief of Rosa Luxemburg, whom Lenin called the "eagle" of the revolution; it accounts as well for the extraordinary interest of Marxists in contemporary crisis theory; and it explains the allusiveness of a title such as Mandel's *Late Capitalism* (1975), with its intimations of an early collapse.

The millenarian character of so much Marxist thought has endowed both its rhetoric and strategizing with a peculiar sense of urgency and drama. In the 1920s, the Moscow-directed Comintern promoted policies that were firmly rooted in the belief that the collapse of European capitalism was imminent. These hopes were temporarily buried by the advent of fascism and nazism, by the military defeat of the popular front in Spain, and by the subsequent suffocation of the revolutionary workers' movement all over Europe, culminating in the Hitler-Stalin pact of August 1939. Today, the hopes have resurfaced. The restructuring of the global economy in the 1970s, the shaky nature of the international financial system, and the gradual advance of militarism, authoritarianism, and fascism across the continents have reawakened the millenarian faith that the historical transition to a revolutionary socialism cannot be far away.

The Choice of Means: Nonviolent or Violent. In many ways, the choice of means is both a critical and categorical question in strategic councils. Many strategists, among them the Proudhon-Kropotkin wing of social anarchism and charismatic figures such as Gandhi and Martin Luther King, Jr., explicitly disavow the use of violence as a legitimate means of struggle. They advocate instead an arsenal of nonviolent methods, including protest marches, sit-down strikes, acts of civil disobedience, symbolic protest actions, noncooperation with the state, boycotts, and work stoppages.[49] Being a kind of moral jiujitsu, nonviolent struggle can be extremely effective against the armed might of the state. But in order to achieve results, certain conditions must be met: a legal system that protects human rights and a civilian leadership with the moral authority to negotiate with the state. These conditions are not always fulfilled: the state may encourage right-wing terror, the mass following may not be prepared to accept the results of negotiation, or the leadership may be divided into factions contending among themselves for political ascendency within the movement.

To negotiate means to "give and take." It works well within a context of (expected) historical continuity, where each step along the road to social transformation is a small one but the whole builds up to social transformation. By unifying the Congress Party and rallying the Indian masses behind it, Ghandi hastened the coming of national independence. And Martin Luther King's forceful advocacy of nonviolence gave strength of resolution to the black power movement of the sixties. Neither leader, however, was able fully to realize his ideals in practice, and both, ironically, died a violent death.[50]

Struggles involving violence are of two kinds: terrorism and extended civil war.[51] Within the traditions of sm, the propensity for violence can be traced to Bakunin, whose advocacy of terrorist methods brought him into headlong conflict with Marx himself. Bakunin's anarchist imagination reveled in the possibilities of spontaneous violence, as he thundered against Marx's political road that would enmesh the working class in the spider nets of bourgeois institutions and the state.

But terrorist tactics can also be used in more disciplined fashion. Thus Carl Boggs tells us that Italian left-wing terrorists, whatever ideological differences there might be among them, share a single guiding objective:

49. A borderline case of nonviolence is violence against oneself as a symbol of protest, as in the case of a hunger strike or self-immolation.

50. Electoral politics as a major form of nonviolent struggle will be discussed in the section entitled "The Strategy of Political or Extra-Political Struggle."

51. The Rand Corporation claims that these modes of conflict are likely to be the dominant forms in the years to come. See Jenkins (1983).

to operate as a catalyst, through direct armed action, of an intensified class struggle that [will] lead to civil insurrection and, ultimately, to a revolutionary conquest of power . . . [and] to explode the contradictions of the "multinational corporate state" through exemplary struggles, opening the door to expansion of an anti-state popular insurgency. (Boggs 1982, 99)

Terrorist tactics, of course, are capable of being used by the Right as well as the by the Left; they may be targeted or sown at random; and the specific forms they take—bombings, kidnappings, lynchings, hijackings, assassinations—are as variable as death itself. Terrorism's psychological impact, however, is often far in excess of any real damage done. Magnified by the media and by the inevitable drama of violence, the fear of terrorism is out of all proportion to the actual suffering of material loss and death.[52] Terrorists are branded criminals, and their official repression, along with radical, non-terrorist groups for good measure, meets with widespread approval among the public, including even the "official" Left.[53]

It is only one small step from here to the appearance of counter-terror. Once a Latin American specialty, the practice has lately spread to other continents, and especially to the Middle East. The grizzly purpose of massive random killings by groups enjoying at least the tacit support of the state is to wipe out, once and for all, the vestiges of political opposition to the ruling elites and the economic interests they represent. Waves of terror and counter-terror can grow to such intensity that they may turn into a civil war without fronts, as has happened in Lebanon—a truly frightening propsect for any country.

Occasionally, a strategy of *combined* struggle is used in which violent and nonviolent methods are joined in concert. Often employed in struggles for territorial liberation, a combined strategy generally involves a legitimate organization willing to negotiate a political settlement with the reigning power, even as invisible terrorist groups keep up the pressure on the enemy. A good example of this is

52. This is not true, however, of the right-wing terror of Latin American death squads, whose combined victims already number in the hundreds of thousands.

53. Following the kidnapping and murder of former prime minister Aldo Moro in Italy, the Italian Communist Party (PCI) adopted a stern anti-terrorist stance, presumably to distance itself from terrorist groups such as the Red Brigades. Commanding about one third of the popular vote, the PCI is a mass party that necessarily reflects the conservative impulses of lower middle-class and working-class voters; on the whole, these are law-abiding citizens who vote the Communist ticket, not to bring about a proletarian revolution but to get a better economic deal. The Party intercedes for them with the state to which otherwise they have no access.

Northern Ireland, where Sinn Fein is the visible political arm of the nationalists and the terrorist group is the Irish Revolutionary Army. The close but not always harmonious coordination of the two is a well-known fact.

There are two major drawbacks of a combined strategy. First, the terrorist faction may be difficult to control politically, as it pursues ends of its own that may not agree with the political branch of the movement and indeed may run counter to its purposes. Second, terrorist action may erode the moral advantage that a more peaceful practice enjoys and may tarnish the revolutionary movement as a whole.

The second major form of violent revolutionary action, extended civil war, is distinguished from a situation of terror and counter-terror chiefly by the scale of its operations and by the clarity of its objectives: to gain political power, to seize the state apparatus, and to install a revolutionary government.[54]

War always represents an extraordinary commitment of resources on the part of both the revolutionary organization and the state. This commitment may lead both parties to the conflict to seek foreign allies capable of underwriting the struggle by supplying weapons, instructors, money, and even soldiery. But the so-called allies, usually powerful neighbors or the superpowers and their satraps, may exert so decisive an influence on events that they eventually assume control over the conflict itself. What was once a civil war becomes internationalized and trivialized as a mere incident in the global struggle for ideological hegemony.[55]

Reform or Revolution. Most struggles, even when they employ a revolutionary rhetoric, are for only limited gains. This is particularly evident in the case of urban social movements with their "revindicative" focus—what Castells (1983) likes to call their consumer trade unionism. It is also true for most popular struggles in the United States (Heskin 1983).

Historical materialists often denigrate such efforts as meliorist, asserting that they serve to perpetuate or "reproduce" the system of capitalist relations.[56] Instead, they advocate a strategy that aims at

54. Recent instances of successful civil wars occurred in Cuba and Nicaragua, but other wars continue to rage, for example, in El Salvador, the Philippines, Indonesia, and the Sudan.

55. Contemporary examples of countries whose civil wars became internationalized include Spain during the 1930s and, more recently, Kampuchea, Afghanistan, and El Salvador.

56. Social anarchists also reject reformism, but for very different reasons. They disdain any form of collaboration with statist power, however "cunning" the reasons.

an intensification of the contradictions internal to capitalism itself. As with Piven and Cloward (1982), their hopes may be pinned on the urban underclass and their "blind" demands for welfare benefits that will drive the system either into bankruptcy or hyper-inflation. Or they may look to Third World struggles, gnawing away at the overextended structures of the capitalist world system where it is the most exposed and vulnerable.

The criticisms of the historical materialists are probably not well founded. They overlook the historical record of the real social gains that have been made in both Europe and North America by struggle—the expansion of suffrage, the abolition of child labor, the forty-hour workweek, free education, anti-discriminatory legislation, social security, and so forth—and they are vague about the long-term revolutionary strategy. Arguments about "intensifying contradictions" make sense only in a millenarian epoch, but few would argue that a revolutionary situation actually exists, or that it is rapidly approaching.

Of particular relevance in this context is Antonio Gramsci's assessment of the revolutionary situation in Western Europe. I have already referred to his concepts of "counter-hegemony," "war of movement," and "war of position" (see note 44). Gramsci's was essentially a political argument (as against the dominant economism of Marxist theorists) in the great tradition of Italian political thinkers, particularly Machiavelli. Writing in the early 1930s, he did not think that a frontal assault on the state would succeed, and so he distanced himself from the Comintern and its preparatory strategies for the great event. History has largely confirmed the correctness of his judgment.[57] Instead of a "frontal assault," Gramsci counseled in favor of a "cultural" strategy which, supplemented by political action when appropriate, would create an alternative working-class culture embodied in specific institutions and practices capable of successfully challenging the cultural hegemony of the bourgeoisie, with its excessive individualism, political passivity, and consumerist passions.

Today, it is perhaps easier to see what Gramsci had in mind than when he wrote his *Prison Notebooks* in the 1930s. We have the example of the concrete practices of the Italian Communist Party (PCI) in its reformist city administration of Bologna and elsewhere, which have demonstrated the possibilities of "another" urban politics

57. The bureaucratic socialisms in Eastern Europe came in the wake of postwar political realignments and, in every case but Yugoslavia, were imposed upon an unwilling population by the Soviet Union.

based on democratic, participatory structures (Jaggi et al. 1977).[58]
And we have the countercultural practices of environmentalists,
feminists, and neighborhood activists, with their emphasis on
small-group work, self-reliance, substantial equality between men
and women, cooperative forms of production, and an ecological
ethic (Bookchin 1971; Perlman 1979; Morris 1982). Although these
new attitudes and practices may be compatible with the global structures of finance capital, they carve out enclaves from the larger system of power, where the hegemony of capital is reduced and perhaps eliminated altogether. Unlike anything we have inherited
from the past, these enclaves may "prefigure" the socialism of tomorrow.

It is equally true that these practices are not yet tied into a revolutionary strategy for the massive transformation of the system. For
such a strategy to appear, the "conjunctural" historical situation
must be propitious. Revolutions, as Rosa Luxemburg reminds us,
are not made as much as they are seized.[59]

The Strategy of Political or Extra-Political Struggle. The question of
whether to work within the system, and the terms on which one
might be prepared to work "within," is one of the perennial debates
in the sm tradition. Marx himself was basically a political person,
prepared, for tactical reasons, to walk the road of electoral politics,
if only for a time and when convenient, while Bakunin, who was
ready to destroy the state, was not: to collaborate with the arch-

58. Carl Boggs, in a private communication to me, wrote: "You tend to romanticize
the Bolognese experience, or rather you take at face value the treatment of Jaggi et
al., which is very uncritical of the pci's role there. From my own study of the situation,
there are a good many negative features which must be dealt with, including the institutionalized role of the pci and its organic relationship to the vested interests in the
community."

59. Whether capitalism as a global system can be "smashed" at all remains an open
question. Revolutions are political acts and necessarily take as their objective the capture of territorial power or the state. But as a global system, capitalism is unlikely to
be very much affected by a successful socialist revolution in some country, and it will
always strike back at the offender from its bastions in the United States, Western Europe, and South Africa. This reduces any national revolutionary "enclave" to the status of a local guerilla action against the capitalist world system, which is increasingly
drawing into its orbit the more consolidated, post-revolutionary regimes of the Soviet
Union, its European satellites, and apparently even China. This is not to argue that
capitalism has become immune to revolutionary struggles. But its powers to resist—
whether in Chile, Nicaragua, Angola, or Mozambique—are formidable, indeed.
Capitalism will no doubt eventually give way to another "mode of production," but
this transition may not happen in quite the way that Marx had imagined, it will not
happen in this next generation, and it may be driven not by the proletariat as the revolutionary class par excellence, but by quite another set of forces.

enemy was inconceivable to him. Instead, he believed in the revolutionary potential of spontaneous outbursts of popular fury, though the outbursts might be goaded, and even guided in their politics, by the secret conspiracy of which he dreamed.

The First International divided precisely over this issue, and in the next generation it contributed to the split within the German socialist movement between the so-called revisionists, under Edward Bernstein, who opted for the road of electoral politics and reform, and the radicals, under Liebknecht and Luxemburg, who marched off to revolution and a martyr's death.

Bernstein understood socialism as a series of structural reforms that could be achieved through parliamentary action. Capitalism, he thought, might last for a very long time. It was therefore reasonable to invest one's hopes and energies in the material improvement of working people's lives and the democratization of the political system. In a famous statement, written in 1898, he declared his position.

> It is my firm conviction that the present generation will already see realised a large part of socialism, if not in official form, at least in content. . . . There can be more socialism in a good factory law than in the nationalisation of a whole group of factories. I admit it openly: I have for what is commonly called "the final goal of socialism" extraordinarily little feeling and interest. This goal, whatever it may be, is nothing to me, the movement is everything. (In McLellan 1979, 31)

Rosa Luxemburg was animated by a very different spirit. For her, the imminent breakdown of capitalism was a foregone conclusion. It remained then to chart the course for the period of transition and to prepare for the event. The real energy for revolution would come, she thought, from the people themselves. Her language was passionate and her tone prophetic.

> [O]nly in the period of the revolution, when the social foundations and the walls of the class society are shaken and subjected to a constant process of disarrangement, any political class action of the proletariat can arouse from their passive condition in a few hours whole sections of the working class who have hitherto remained unaffected, and this is immediately and naturally expressed in a stormy economic struggle. The worker, suddenly arouse to activity by the electric shock of political action, immediately seizes the weapon lying nearest his hand for the fight against his condition of economic slav-

ery: the stormy gesture of the political struggle causes him to feel with unexpected intensity the weight and the pressure of his economic chains. (Luxemburg 1971, 50; orig. 1906)

Compared to this ardent, revolutionary spirit, this out-and-out idealism even, electoral politics was as nothing. In the movement of history it would scarcely amount to a ripple.

The "mass strike" became a heated topic of debate among the central leadership of the German Social Democrats. Karl Kautsky, the Marxist "pope," was critical of "comrade" Luxemburg's romantic bravado and counseled caution. For him, as well as for Bernstein, the mass strike was no more than a defensive weapon, an instrument of "last resort" (Kautsky 1914).

But the issue of electoral politics as a valid road to socialism did not vanish forever. It flared up again in the 1970s, disguised this time as Eurocommunism. In 1976, the French communist party officially renounced the classical Marxist dogma of the "dictatorship of the proletariat." Henceforward, if it should ever come to power, the party would conduct itself in accord with normal parliamentary procedure: it would stand for reelection! In the following year, Santiago Carillo, the leader of the Spanish communists, published his controversial *Euro-Communism and the State* (1977), which at length argued the case for a democratic road to socialism.

In an astute comment on the future of Eurocommunism, Carl Boggs questions whether it is "socialism" that will indeed lie at the end of this particular road.

After nearly fifty years of development, social democracy has established a broad and durable presence within the bourgeois state in many Western European countries, and it has carried out some far-reaching reforms. Nowhere, however, has it made much progress in democratizing the state or in breaking down the class structure. On the contrary, it has functioned to reinforce the social division of labor, to legitimate the relations of domination in those systems where it has achieved hegemony. The attempt to impart new "content" (socialism) to old "forms" (the bourgeois state) has proven illusory.

The outcome for Eurocommunism will probably be little different . . .

As we have seen, Eurocommunism lacks a schema for combatting both class and bureaucratic forms of domination; it seems clearly willing to accept a *modus vivendi* with (planned and regulated) capitalist enterprises and with permanent professional bureaucracies in national and local government.

Here the illusion of parliamentary democracy returns to
haunt the Eurocommunists: Democratization is attested within
the political infrastructure of bourgeois society. (Boggs 1982,
110, 111)

The American story is different, since a working-class politics has
scarcely ever existed here as a major force. Instead, progressive
movements have invested extraordinary hopes in the tripartite system of the state, with its division of powers among the legislative, executive, and judiciary branches, each independent and autonomous. Among the major radical critics of this "political road" are
Frances Fox Piven and Richard Cloward. But this formidable pair
of critics appears to advocate contradictory strategies. In 1977, they
took essentially Luxemburg's line of spontaneism (though carefully
avoiding her millenarian ardor).

[I]f the lower classes do not ordinarily have great disruptive
power, and if the use of even that kind of power is not
planned, it is the only power they do have. Their use of that
power, the weighing of gains and risks, is not calculated in
board rooms; it wells up out of the terrible travails that people
experience at times of rupture and stress. And at such times,
disruptions by the power may have reverberations that go beyond the institutions in which the disruption is acted out.
(Piven and Cloward 1979, 26–27; orig. 1977)

But six years later, they play a different tune: now their strategy
consists of massive registration drives to get the poor to vote its economic interest, that is, the reconstruction of the welfare state so un-
ceremoniously dismantled by Ronald Reagan (Cloward and Piven
1983). One can only infer from this contradictory approach to the
class struggle—spontaneous insurgency then, electoral politics
now—that their true strategy is one of radical cunning. Bourgeois
institutions are to be used for transformative ends whenever it is
convenient to use them. The electoral process can be used to defeat
capital on its own terrain. The 1984 election would be a skirmish,
just like the skirmishes and battles of the sixties, and the class
war will continue. But since there are always only skirmishes and
battles to be fought, the right tactics assume extreme importance.
And who should devise these tactics? It is not clear. Piven and Cloward are consistent in rejecting the formal organization of protest
movements.

How the issue of political versus extra-political struggle is finally
resolved will depend on two questions that have both theoretical

and practical aspects. The first we have already discussed: it is the immediate prospects of capitalism as a system and a conjuncture favorable to revolution. The second requires a brief comment. It concerns the relative autonomy of the state.[60]

For Marx, the state appeared in its somewhat simplistic role as an instrument of class domination. It was part of the ideological superstructure, an instrument of coercion, and it could be expected to act in the interests of the bourgeoisie to which it was subservient. This classical view prevailed until the early 1970s, when it was seriously challenged by O'Connor (1973), Offe (1974, 1975), and Poulantzas (1980; orig. 1978). These authors perceived the state in "structuralist" terms, not as an entity unto itself but as a system of relations and, more particularly (following Poulantzas's language), as a *condensation of class relations* and, therefore, as a *terrain* for struggle. This view made it possible to think of the state in dialectical rather than monolithic terms, and made it seem reasonable to engage in electoral politics *as a strategy*, so long as it was understood that the politics was part of the world revolutionary struggle—a mere episode in the long march to a socialist future.

In her important comparative study of major national revolutions (France, Russia, China), Theda Skocpol finds the structuralist theory of the state insufficient to account for reality. Her state is historically determined. States are actors in an international system, and they have an institutional materiality that cannot be dissolved into class relations.

> We can make sense of social-revolutionary transformations only if we take the state seriously as a macro-structure. The state properly conceived is no mere arena in which socioeconomic struggles are fought out. It is, rather, a set of administrative, policing, and military organizations headed, and more or less well coordinated by, an executive authority . . .
>
>   The perspective on the state advanced here might appropriately be labelled "organizational" and "realist." In contrast to most (especially recent) Marxist theories, this view refuses to treat states as if they were mere analytic aspects of abstractly conceived modes of production, or even political aspects of concrete class relations and struggles. Rather, it insists that states are actual organizations controlling (or attemping to control) territories and people. Thus the analyst of revolutions must explore not only class relations but also relations of states

60. The following discussion is based on Skocpol (1979, 19–32).

to one another and relations of states to dominant and subordinate classes. (Skocpol 1979, 29, 31)

Thus, Skocpol posits a degree of state autonomy that goes considerably beyond O'Connor, Offe, and Poulantzas and leaves room for the emergence of a "new class" of professionals and planners.

Both structuralist and realist theories of the state leave open the door for class-transcending political strategies. Yet extra-political mobilization, nonviolent as well as violent, must never be discounted, since it is the traditional way by which the people, occupying the space of civil society, can break into politics to assert, or reassert, their voice as the ultimate sovereign over their collective fate. To rely on the institutionalized processes of electoral politics exclusively would mean to abandon the revolutionary project forever. One might further argue that a political practice aimed at social transformation can be effective only when it is based on the extra-political actions of ordinary people gathered in their own communities.

Planning as Social Mobilization

What does planning have to do with the traditions of SM we have discussed? The question arises for two reasons.

1. For nearly two hundred years, planning has been tied to a reform tradition. It has always signified planning by the state and has involved central guidance and direction in support of capitalist development, including social and physical planning that would ameliorate, through social welfare programs, urban design, and land controls, the worst effects of unfettered economic growth.

2. SM is concerned with structural changes in the very society that the social reform tradition, with its paternalistic ethos, is trying to build up. Instead of beginning with goals and objectives, its starting point is social criticism. And it relies on action *from below*. It is the people themselves whose political practice is decisive. Their methods may be violent, sometimes subversive, and extra-political. How can this activity—barely tolerated by the state and often repressed—be called "planning"? It would appear to be a contradiction in terms.

These objections can be answered only in the context of the planning paradigm presented in Chapter 1. There we saw that planning, defined as the linkage between knowledge and action in the public domain, could be applied to two kinds of action concerned, respectively, with societal guidance and with social transformation. Both forms of planning are necessary if society is to perfect itself. We also saw that planning did not have to be centrally located and, indeed, that planning in the public domain could originate anywhere, including civil society. Planning was therefore not, *in principle*, exclusively a function of the state. And so, the basic objection that social mobilization has nothing to do with planning must be rejected; it misses the point that oppositional movements are essential to a healthy society, that our present predicament is not the end of history but merely another start, and that existing social movements point to the possibilities of a fuller humanity, centered in itself and free from external oppression.[61]

Nevertheless, there remains the question of the specific meaning that planning as sm—I shall call it radical planning—can have for us. Within sm, we saw three major sub-traditions. Let us briefly recall them.

1. Utopianism. Concerned with visionary social arrangements, utopians believe in the immanence of the Good Society concretely realized in "intentional communities."

2. Social anarchism. Rejecting both the state and capitalist relations of production as oppressive forces, social anarchists champion small-scale, decentralized, self-managing units of production, stressing their voluntary character, their mutualist cooperative nature, and the principle of confederation as the means of linking them into larger regional and national ensembles. Two very different paths to the goals of social anarchy contend with each other: the first is the spontaneous and peaceful emergence of anarchist forms within the "womb" of capitalist society; the second is Bakunin's path of pan-destruction, which seeks to eliminate all forces that may be hostile to the emergence of anarchist forms of social relation.

3. Historical materialism. A revolutionary critique of capitalist society, historical materialism understands society as rooted in a specific mode of production. As a mode of production, capitalism is subject to its own "laws of motion" that nevertheless are contradictory, leading to periodic crises, the eventual break-

---

61. The expression "external oppression" must be understood in the Marxian sense of powers of self-determination that rightfully belong to us, the birthright of every human collectivity (but not of every individual!), but that nevertheless have been alienated from us and now are turned against us, appearing as though they no longer belong to us and have come to weigh on us from the "outside."

down of the system, and its replacement by a new mode of production, in the event called socialist, which, in turn, points the way to the "post-historical" classless society of full communism. Historical materialist analysis is dialectical, emphasizing contradictory relations and, in the social sphere, class struggle between bourgeois rulers and proletarian workers. In the analysis of historically concrete situations, theory must be joined to revolutionary practice, but with regard to the latter, there are several contending schools: Edward Bernstein and Santiago Carillo's parliamentary route, Rosa Luxemburg's spontaneism, Lenin's vanguardism, the Gramscian "war of position" to create a counter-hegemonic force within civil society, and Mao Tsetung's theory of the mass line.

Historically, these three movements have informed planning within the social reform tradition even as they severely criticized it. Utopianism has been particularly influential in the field of city planning, where there exists a long tradition of ideal cities (Lynch 1981) and social utopias (Goodman and Goodman 1960; Illich 1973). Social anarchism has been important for both city and regional planning. Kropotkin's *Fields, Factories, and Workshops of Tomorrow* (1975; orig. 1888–1890), for example, was a direct precursor of the contemporary garden cities movement and of plans for metropolitan deconcentration, while the regionalism of Proudhon and Elisée Reclus is connected to contemporary territorial struggles for regional self-determination and a tradition within regional planning that looks upon regions as physico-cultural entities (Weaver 1984). Historical materialism, finally, has given us the actually existing practice of the planned economy with its unwieldy bureaucratic apparatus (Ellman 1979).

Thus, there is no question about the influence of SM on mainstream planning. In addition, both anarchists and Marxists have leveled severe critiques at "bourgeois forms of planning" (for a summary and comment, see Appendix C).[62] Chiefly ideological, they divide into two parts. On one hand, planners are seen as part of the repressive apparatus of the state, what Robert Goodman calls "soft cops." On the other hand, the prevailing bourgeois theories of planning are condemned for being ahistorical, abstract, and unrelated to social conflict and class struggle. But neither as mainstream planning nor as critique has SM given us a positive image of what a radi-

62. For the anarchist critique, see especially Goodman (1971); critiques from an explicit Marxist standpoint include Roweis and Scott (1977), Harvey (1978), and Preteceille (1982; orig. 1974).

cal, transformative planning might be like. There is, however, a beginning.

Like so much else, the discovery of SM as a tradition of radical planning followed in the wake of the turbulent sixties, with their massive protests, black and brown liberation struggles, and more quixotic movements, such as the Yippies, who ran a pig for president of the United States. Its earliest statement came from within the field of city planning in a polemical piece by Grabow and Heskin (1973), who coined the term "radical planning." Their essay "deconstructed" establishment planning as it existed at the time and proposed a new order of society evidently inspired by utopian and anarchist thought: the formation of small, spontaneous communities living a self-reliant life apart from corporate America.

The essay evoked much comment and controversy within the city planning profession, but its overall message was widely misunderstood. In 1973, planners were not yet ready to contemplate the possibility of a radical alternative to their own practice, particularly if that alternative would render most of what they knew irrelevant.

The Grabow-Heskin piece was preceded by an upsurge of so-called advocacy planning, which was a movement that "exploded" the myth of planning in the public interest and urged city planners to mediate the demands of the urban poor vis-à-vis state agencies (Heskin 1980). In retrospect, advocacy planning was not radical at all, though its flamboyant rhetoric initially suggested otherwise. As it turned out, the notion of advocacy fitted quite comfortably into the reality of a pluralist politics, with planners giving the poor a professional voice to defend their "interests" in an arena where other, better-endowed groups were already busy with advocates of their own contending for a share of the available resources. As advocates, planners assumed the role of "public defenders" of the urban poor, and like public defenders in the courts, their work typically was paid for by the state.

Neither Grabow-Heskin nor advocacy planners, however, succeeded in establishing a well-defined concept of radical planning as an alternative to social reform. The arguments for such a concept remain to be made. In the following pages I shall attempt this task, but I shall depart from the critical-historical approach of this and earlier chapters of Part Two. The task will be to extract from the rich tradition of SM the major elements for a theory of radical planning. I shall do so by attempting to answer five questions: (1) What is the project? (2) Who is the client? (3) What knowledge is relevant? (4) What do radical planners do? and (5) Can radical planners be professionals?

What Is the Project?

In its timeless, perennial dimension, the project is the emancipation of humanity from social oppression. It is a project undertaken in the face of all the forces of repression, chief among which are the bureaucratic state and the large corporation, and so it requires struggle. This struggle can be violent or nonviolent, political or nonpolitical, revolutionary or reformist. In every instance, however, it requires the overcoming of resistance.

Emancipatory struggle is always particularized and historical. It involves particular individuals and groups, in particular situations, facing particular problems. Thus, the general project becomes *this* project, the universal is joined to the specific, and radical practice proceeds experimentally, through a process of expanded social learning, until enough fragments of the new society exist so that they may be joined into a global network. A key principle in radical, transformative practice is that *no group can be completely free until freedom has been achieved for every group.* Thus, the struggle for emancipation leads to results that will always be partial and contradictory, until the final and possibly utopian goal of a free humanity is reached.

Some elements of a non-oppressive society and the tasks of radical practice for North America and Western Europe in the years ahead will be discussed in Chapter 9.

Who Is the Client?

If it is legitimate to use the word at all in this connection, the client is the mobilized community or group.[63] Because it is oppositional, radical practice (and the planning associated with it) cannot be organized and sponsored by the state. *The impulse for it must come from within the community itself.* Self-mobilization, however, involves gaining an awareness of the promise of emancipation and confidence in the possibilities for change. These processes may require the outside intervention of "organizers" and others who can teach both a new awareness and the necessary skills for a self-reliant practice. For the community must not only acquire a critical consciousness of its own conditions of oppression, but also learn to engage in direct

---

63. This statement is valid only for radical practice in the Western World. As I shall argue, in countries of the peasant periphery, the process of transformative change must be orchestrated by a revolutionary state. But such a state does not engage in "radical planning." As I am using the term here, radical planning always refers to an oppositional practice. And even a revolutionary state is a state and therefore claims a monopoly over the use of repressive force.

action, to negotiate, and to translate its passions into realizable, effective programs for structural change.

Yet even with the mobilized community as its focus, radical planning and practice are not wholly confined to it. At least as important as localized action is the building of linkages. There are three kinds: (1) functional, from place of residence to place of work, and from work place to work place; (2) horizontal, from community to community, region to region, into ever larger patterns of territorial cooperation; and (3) vertical, from community to region, region to nation, and nation to groups of nations and the world. These linkages require new institutions, and care in devising them, so that democratic control is maintained.

What Knowledge Is Relevant?
The social learning paradigm (discussed in Chapter 5) plays a major role in planning for social mobilization. We recall the model:

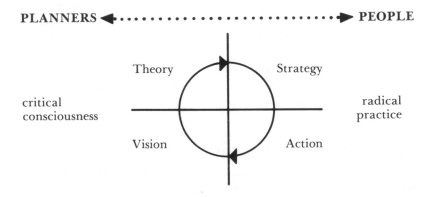

Step 1: From practice to consciousness

Step 2: From consciousness to practice

Figure 18. The social learning paradigm in radical practice.

The knowledge for radical practice, therefore, comes from practice itself; it is knowledge acquired by the mobilized group in the course of its own actions. Here we need to remember that the four phases of the social learning paradigm are primarily conceptual. In practice, they overlap, intertwine with, and penetrate each other. Thus, without vision, no radical practice; without radical practice, no theory; without theory, no strategy; without strategy, no action. More important, "planners" and "people" play interchangeable and interactive roles, so that it cannot always be determined who wears the hat of planner and who does not. (Later, I shall argue that planners do provide specialized skills and are consequently identifiable as separate individuals, even when they are not easily distinguishable in practice.) This intertwining of roles is possible because the mobilized community, which is the central focus for a transformative, radical practice, is inherently small, and the setting within which it works is not bureaucratized. A key to successful radical practice, therefore, is the avoidance of bureaucratic organization, and this implies an effort that, in its most fundamental form, must be conceived on a small scale.

What Do Radical Planners Do?

This is perhaps the critical question. If radical planners were, for example, in every respect like policy analysts, or even like process consultants in organization development, then what they do would have no intrinsic meaning; radical planning would not exist. But our conclusion is different. As we have extracted it from the sm tradition, radical planning is, like other forms of planning, concerned with the linkage of knowledge to action.[64] Yet there is more than one way this linkage can be effected: planning for societal guidance is very different from planning for structural change and social transformation. It is this last which is of interest here. And as we try to specify what radical planners do, the answers we have given to the preceding questions must be assumed. Instead of generalizing from empirical case studies, I have tried to construct a normative model of what a radical form of planning might look like. It outlines the dimensions of a possible practice. (The question of what radical planners do is taken up again in Chapter 9, where it will be linked to the emancipatory practices of households, communities, and social movements.)

  1. Radical planning begins with a critique of the present situation. This critique is not merely normative; it contains a strong analytical element which allows us to interpret, understand, and explain why things are as they are. Planners can help in the mobilization of radical practice by providing a *critical* account of the situation to be changed.

  64. Later, I will argue that this statement, in fact, is incorrect, and should be replaced with "the mediation of theory and practice in social transformation." Yet I retain the original formulation for its heuristic value. We are not yet ready for an "epistemological break" that would show radical planning to be something altogether different from planning for societal guidance.

2. Once we are aware that things are not as they might be, and that they are capable of being changed, the next question is, how? Planners can help communities and groups that are already mobilized to search for practical solutions to the problems perceived by them. To this search, they bring a strong analytical ability, a sense of what is likely to work and what is not, a knowledge of institutional constraints, a knowledge of what has worked or failed elsewhere, and an ability to assess and evaluate alternative solutions.

3. Devising an appropriate strategy, which is the next step in radical practice, requires timely, accurate, and richly textured information ("intelligence"); correct interpretations of this intelligence; a careful assessment of actual options; and the continuous monitoring of the action itself, its results, and the changing context of collective action. Planners can provide mobilized groups with the intelligence they need for devising a successful strategy of action.

4. Most solutions to deep-seated problems, even radical, transformative solutions, have technical aspects that must be considered: questions of design, of cost, of location, and so forth. Planners can help mobilized groups refine the technical aspects of transformative solutions.

5. The social learning model is iterative and recursive: it "feeds" on its own practice. But the learning is never direct; it must be passed through a theoretical and ideological filter where experience is sifted for what it has to teach us. It becomes available to us only in this "filtered" form. Planners can make conscious use of a social learning model by devising group process methods of "filtering" so that the group itself may learn from its own experience. These methods may involve open discussion, self-criticism, role playing, maintaining a collective memory, and other devices suitable for this purpose.

6. What has been learned from practice constitutes valuable knowledge, especially if the knowledge is also used to expand and revise theoretical and ideological components of transformative practice. Experiential knowledge is ephemeral, embodied in particular individuals who possess "know-how," but it tends not to be articulated and not to become more generally available. Yet for the project of emancipation, it is important that we learn collectively. This requires (a) that we abstract from our own experience, which may be called generalizing the solution, and (b) that we disseminate newly gained knowledge

in ways appropriate to the project: using video, film, and writing; sharing experiences by word of mouth; arranging for exchange visits with other mobilized groups who may be interested in the experience, and so forth. In this way, the fund of knowledge for radical practice is enriched.

7. Radical practice is oppositional. Sooner or later, it will run up against the state and its regulatory and repressive agencies. What happens then will be guided by the strategy that the mobilized group has adopted. In most cases, the encounter will be peaceful, and the group may even seek the active collaboration of the state, albeit under carefully controlled conditions. Radical planners can mediate these encounters with technocracy by adopting the latter's jargon and presenting group demands in ways that are likely to meet with the approval of the state. In doing this work of mediation, planners are never autonomous agents but have to act as representatives or delegates of the group for which they speak. This implies that planners must be ideologically committed to the transformative project of the group. They must see themselves as agents of collective struggle.

8. Group processes are difficult to manage, and the tendency to concentrate information, knowledge, and decision-making in a small leadership elite is very common, especially as decision time is always pressing and usually in short supply, so that only the most committed are prepared to make the necessary time available. Thus, in any group process, there is an oligarchical tendency. Radical planners have a responsibility to resist this tendency and to ensure the widest possible participation of all members of the group during the entire process involving the four phases of social learning: vision, theory, strategy, and action.

9. Action needs to be undergirded by structures of meaning or ideology, which is the point of both departure and return for radical practice. The meanings articulated by ideology do not remain constant but must continuously be tested in practice. Yet the process of devising an appropriate ideology, through a collective enterprise rather than through the work of any individual or group, requires special skills. Ideological statements must be persuasive not only to the membership of the mobilized group but to other groups as well. They must be at the same time coherent, intellectually sophisticated, morally persuasive, and simple in expression. Their function is to legiti-

mate emancipatory practice, to sustain this practice in adversity, and to disarm and de-legitimize the opposition. Planners who become integrally a part of mobilized groups—in Gramsci's language, organic intellectuals—may have the necessary skills to put together statements that will serve these several purposes.

10. For all the reasons enumerated above, radical planners must never be far removed from the action itself. The linkage of knowledge to action in social transformation must be accomplished through their own persons.

Can Radical Planners Be Professionals?

Despite the sharing of tasks in radical planning and practice and the process of mutual learning that must take place between planners and the mobilized group engaged in transforming reality, individuals identified as planners possess specialized skills. These skills are acquired through training and experience; they are professional skills. But the term professional also conjures up a gamut of institutional conditions (professional degrees, professional organizations, professional journals, professional codes of conduct) which belong to the state and may be irrelevant for an emancipatory practice. Planners are therefore needed for their manifest skills in radical planning, and not because they are certified professionals.

What are the skills required of radical planners? Among them are at least the following:

- Communicative skills
- Group process skills
- Familiarity with the social learning paradigm, its requirements, and its applications
- Familiarity with planning theory (history, problems, pitfalls)
- Analytical skills (particularly skill in analyzing complex and dynamic situations)
- Synthesizing skills in devising solutions
- Substantive knowledge (historical, theoretical, institutional)
- Experiential (tacit) knowledge in social transformation

But unless these skills are embedded in critical thinking and in a moral commitment to an ethics of emancipation, they are worse than useless for a radical practice. The Maoist slogan "red *and* expert" continues to be valid in its general meaning. Planners must be committed to the possibilities of a non-oppressive society. If they are not, they should not be radical planners but should go to work as policy analysts for the state.

Conclusions

When we compare it with the other traditions we have discussed, social mobilization has an immensely rich intellectual history. As the grand counter-tradition, it approaches the question of social order in the light of transformative theory and practice that hold considerable appeal for those who are without effective power in society. Intellectuals have been its principal proponents. It is they who have debated the grand themes of the tradition. But for better or worse, they have always done so in the name of those who are better at articulating their needs and hopes in the concrete settings of their daily struggles than at writing political tracts. And precisely because they stand in opposition, radical intellectuals have had to rethink society from the ground up, both to gain a foothold for a fundamental critique of existing social relations and to formulate a social vision capable of expressing emancipatory values.

Rethinking society has meant that one could not remain content with a metaphysics that merely underwrote existing relations of power. Radical knowledge might not reveal the ultimate truth of things; it would reach out instead to a historically contingent truth. And underlying this truth would be an image of "being human" based on social bonds rather than on the flawed assumption of the autonomous self-development of unattached, free-floating individuals. Finally, the theory would have to stay close to the experiences of everyday life. It would have to make sense to ordinary working folk.

Contrast this fascinating array of issues with those posed by social reform theorists who, like Machiavelli, would tell the princes of this world how they might stay in power. Even the best of social reformers thought of knowledge positivistically rather than as a process in which social actors intervened at all levels, since knowledge had to be internalized by them and brought into relation with their own practice. Within the social reform tradition, planners were consequently seen as performing technocratic functions in which people's views might be heard but not necessarily heeded. The reformer's main concern was with the institutions and techniques of societal guidance "from above."

The traditions of policy analysis and social learning are more one-dimensional yet. The central questions in both are epistemological. Ruling class values are accepted to an even greater extent than in the social reform tradition, though social learning models can be adapted also to radical planning. In policy analysis, the task is to lay out the choices before the decision makers and to spell out the probable consequences and uncertainities of each. Social learning has become a tool of bureaucratic management.

Because of the questions that it opens up for debate, the social mobilization tradition is intrinsically compelling. Yet it is also heavily flawed. Utopians have failed to bring the world closer to their ideals. Social anarchism has no living manifestations, and when it was seriously tried, it ended in pathetic failure (Mintz 1982). Historical materialism, finally, has scored greater successes in critiquing bourgeois society than in building a democratic socialism. Its legacy is the totalitarian, bureaucratic state.

But on the other hand, and to be fair, there have been hundreds of live utopian experiments, and though they were often little more than "butterfly passions" (Fourier), they did reach beyond brave words to the deeds of committed believers. The anarchist vision has been kept alive, along with its dream of cooperation, mutuality, and the self-production of livelihood. It has challenged the existence of hierarchy and has made that challenge stick. And historical materialism has served as the ideological foundation of some of the world's great revolutions, including those of Russia and China, and has left the world a very different place, though we might not agree that the character of these changes has always been politically benign.

With all that is manifestly wrong with social mobilization as a tradition in planning, it is nevertheless the only tradition that can stand up to the dominant order. It points to an economics, a politics, and a sociology that reject the seeming inevitability of uneven development, powerlessness, exploitation, and alienation that are the hallmarks of the capitalist world system.

Part Three / Emergents

7 Where Do We Stand?

Our historical survey of planning thought is now complete. Across a complex and difficult terrain, it has brought us, over a span of two centuries, to our present situation.

And now a secret must out. Talk to planners, and nine out of ten will describe their work as a "failure" or of "little use." They will say: "We no longer know what to do. Our solutions don't work. The problems are mounting." If they are right—and who would quarrel with them?—we are forced to conclude that mainstream planning is in crisis. Knowledge and action have come apart. The link is broken.

This crisis, of course, is not merely a tumor disfiguring an otherwise still healthy body. Wherever we turn today, the sense of crisis is pervasive. This is nowhere more evident than in the Third World. In country after country, Third World planners are unable to satisfy even the most basic needs of their population. On average, people eat less today than they did ten years ago; their real incomes are lower; there is less work; violence has increased. A small minority in each country continue to live well. But even this relative prosperity is tenuous, resting, as it does, on the repressive apparatus of the state. Material conditions are better in the First World of Western Europe, North America, Australasia, and Japan, but the fate of the First World is intertwined with that of the Third, even as the loss of direction is manifested in other ways—in the behavior of young people, for example, or in the paranoia of national leadership.

I do not wish to claim that the rupture between knowledge and action is responsible for the crisis of the world system as a whole. But there must be a connection. Action divorced from knowledge does not know where to turn next. It becomes blind action. And so, in this chapter, I will speak mainly of the crisis in planning, keeping in mind, however, that it is part of a larger set of circumstances that seems to be veering out of control.

In speaking of a crisis in planning, I have in mind mainstream planning by the state. It is fundamentally a crisis in the idea of societal guidance. Some would call it a crisis of the state. More precisely,

311

it is a crisis in the state's ability to satisfy the legitimate needs of the people.

There are at least three reasons for this crisis in planning. The first is a *crisis of knowing*. In knowledge about society, the certainties of positivism have suddenly become undone. Comte's disciples now speak in many tongues and have long given up on the discovery of universal "social laws." Even economics, that last stronghold of positivism, has fallen into disarray. Amid all the confusion, there is a search for alternatives. One increasingly popular alternative is *hermeneutics*, or the "science" of interpretation. In hermeneutics, what counts is not the putative social law, or the empirical regularity, but the meaning of an event in relation to the actors who are directly involved in it (Giddens 1982). The human subject is thus reintroduced into our theoretical discourses about society. As subjects, we choose to act. But the point of the action is not to be rational in the technical sense. What human subjects strive for is meaningful action.

As human subjectivity enters, knowledge becomes discursive and dialogical. Human subjects, grounded in their own implicit understandings of the world, "talk back" to students of society as well as to planners. Through this "talking back," knowledge becomes essentially transactive. It can no longer be addressed exclusively to other social scientists but must speak to actors who, for the most part, are found in the households, institutions, and social movements of civil society.

The result is that the process of knowledge-formation becomes increasingly fluid. What Habermas called "communicative acts" are at its core. Theorists who are obliged to speak plainly come face to face with ordinary citizens who have their own ideas. And in this confrontation, planning ceases to be a more or less humble "scientific endeavor" and assumes the characteristics of a craft.

The second reason for the crisis in planning is the *accelerated pace of historical events*. Mainstream planning requires a certain stability in its environment. How can there be forethought without it? How can plans be made, when exogenous events are forever upsetting the conditions that would make them possible, or even appropriate? Information must be filtered up to the center, where it is classified, analyzed, interpreted, and integrated into policies, plans, and programs. But all this is a time-consuming process. Budgets are on an annual cycle. Medium-term plans are projected for a period of five or six years. Longer-term strategic plans may look ahead a couple of decades. And while all this planning is going on, the world continues to change. Just now it seems to be changing more rapidly than at any other time in history—so fast, in fact, that when the plans and projects are ready for implementation, they are no longer appropriate (assuming that, at the time of their conception, they responded to a correct interpretation of the world). Central plans have become obsolete even before they are announced. And, contrary to the puff about them, computers are no help at all, since they can order information but are incapable of interpreting the data. Computers can give us neither theory nor meaning.

The third reason for the crisis in planning is the *unprecedented nature of the events we face*. There may indeed be structural "laws" that "explain" the behavior of historically contingent institutions, but these laws do not help us come to grips with problems that we have never before encountered: the massive environmental degradation from deforestation, salinization, and acid rain; the management of mega-cities with thirty or more million people; our ability to unleash the destructive fury of hydrogen bombs equal in energy to the sun; the environmental limits to a mode of production that thrives on the unlimited expansion of production. These are all first-time problems, and we have only recently become aware of them.

It is not, however, the sheer magnitude of these perils that is the central problem but the lack of any genuine knowledge about them. Given enough time, we might eventually get a handle on them. But planning cannot afford to wait. And so the experts throw up their hands in despair, even as they offer us another of their ad hoc theories in order to save face. The state is in retreat.

Four escape routes are open. The most popular is *salvation by technology*. According to a widespread belief, scientists and engineers will come to the rescue in the nick of time. The micro-chip, the laser beam, the artificial heart, genetic modification, breeding in vitro—these point the way to the promised land. As a last resort, we shall colonize space. The Strategic Defense Initiative has already captured people's imagination as the magic shield that will banish the specter of Armaggedon forever.

Escape route number two is *salvation by unfettered enterprise: the free market*. In this belief, the state is generally regarded as being part of the problem and, indeed, its principal part. Reduce the state's involvement in economic relations, advocates of this view assert, and all will be well. Growth will be recovered. Everyone who wants a job will find one. And the pleasant ascent up the candy mountain of consumption will resume. What those who would take this escape route fail to see is that it is precisely free, oligopolistic markets—split up among a shrinking number of global banks anad corporations—that is behind the many problems we confront: mounting indebtedness, hyper-inflation in the Third World, environmental devastation, jobless growth, and so on.

The third escape route, though common enough, is one that no one really wants to take: *propaganda and repression.* Through propaganda and related techniques of influencing consciousness, people are lulled into political inertia. Through police repression (including official terrorism), remaining dissidents can be wiped out. Although the route is unpopular, it can, for varying lengths of time, avoid the political consequences of dealing with the very real problems that confront a country, and that often get worse under the silence of repression. Without the feedback of an active polity, states are likely to go beserk.[1] And the worst rise to the top.

There remains yet a fourth route, which is the *re-centering of political power in civil society*, mobilizing from below the countervailing actions of citizens, and recovering the energies for a political community that will transform both the state and corporate economy from within. The next three chapters propose to outline this path and show how radical planners can help clear the way. It is in the recovery of political community and in the transformative vision that underlies it that the knot between knowledge and action that has come undone can be retied.

We shall proceed as follows. In Chapter 8, we take a deeper look at the present crisis and at some of the responses to it. As a project, the recovery of political community is already underway, and we can learn from the experience. Central to the chapter is a discussion of the public domain. Although there are strong arguments both for and against the concept of a public domain, the recovery of political community requires that we believe in the reality of common interests and, thus, in the possibility of the common good. Failing this, we clear the way for a retreat into privatism that will leave the political terrain undefended against an authoritarian and repressive state. There would be little sense in writing this book in a world where the public domain is thought to be an illusion, or worse, where it has fallen apart and more powerful neighbors have moved in to seize control, as in Lebanon and Northern Ireland.

Chapter 9 points to the recovery of political community as the central guiding vision of a project of social reconstruction. The actors who can appropriate this vision include neither the state and its

1. By this, I mean launching a war against one's own citizens or engaging in foreign adventures. The recent case of Argentina under the Generals comes to mind. Official terror took the lives of thirty thousand victims, and the Falklands imbroglio, while less devastating in human terms, cost the country dearly in many other ways, not the least of which was national pride.

related institutions nor the global corporation. We must turn to the intimate sphere of the household instead. But, in their role as places of private consumption, households have become enervated. What must be done, then, is to rethink the household as a sociopolitical entity for the self-production of life. It is in a reconstructed household economy, partially de-linked from the market and joined with other households into local and regional networks, that the first steps must be taken for the recovery of political community. In addition to the household economy, three arenas of action are discussed: the regional nexus of work and play, the peasant periphery (or Third World), and the global community. Thinking and acting must be done at all four levels *simultaneously* if the present world crisis is to be surmounted.

In Chapter 10, we return to the question of a radical planning grounded in the tradition of social mobilization. We are now ready to show radical planning as directly tied into the project of social reconstruction in each of the four arenas where planning is geared to transformative actions from below.[2] Radical planners must assume an ideological position; they cannot remain neutral. Standing in opposition to hegemonic power, they put their work in the service of emancipatory values and a strong political community.

Fundamental to radical planning is an epistemology beyond the still-entrenched positivism of social science. In social learning we have such an epistemology. It is an epistemology adaptable to the purposes of social transformations. A discursive mode of knowing, including dialogue, is central to it. The chapter goes on to discuss, from a normative perspective, what radical planners do. They focus, I will endeavor to show, on processes of collective self-empowerment and self-reliance; on being able to "think without frontiers"; on the recovery of meaning, purpose, and practical vision through radical practice; on social processes of networking and coalition-building; on strategic action; and on dialogue and mutual learning. The chapter concludes on a practical note, with a discussion of some of the dilemmas faced by radical planners, including economic survival.

The final chapter takes the form of an epilogue that sums up the entire journey we have taken.

2. The problem of planning in the peasant periphery is somewhat different. Here, a stronger role for the state is essential. The function of radical planning—which is necessarily an oppositional planning—is less clear in the Third World than in the First.

8   From Critique to
        Reconstruction

Mind at the End of Its Tether

Toward the end of his long and productive life, much of it devoted
to celebrating the achievements of modern science and engineering, H. G. Wells, the author of many science fiction novels, abandoned his faith in rationalism, years before the current generation
of planners. "Mind," he wrote in 1945, "has reached the end of its
tether" (Wells 1964). The world has become "a tale told by an idiot."
No longer could reason be taken as a reliable guide to Nature. The
past triumphs of science had been the consequence of a historical
rapprochement between reason and cosmos, a temporary, accidental conjuncture. Now the two were separating and traveling along
different trajectories. The cosmos had grown distant and inscruta-
ble, and the great achievement of the Enlightenment—the en-
thronement of reason—had revealed itself as an illusion.

   Wells was not alone in his disenchantment. At roughly the same
time, but coming from a very different background and by way of a
very different line of argument, Max Horkheimer and Theodor
Adorno, refugees from Hitler Germany, had become similarly dis-
illusioned. The reason of Enlightenment, they said, had issued in
the actual history of mass deception and genocide (Horkheimer and
Adorno 1982; orig. 1944). It had driven humankind to the edge of
the abyss. Henceforth, we were condemned to live under the sign of
the nuclear holocaust.[1]

   1. *Dialectic of Enlightenment* was written before Hiroshima. But its thought frame
was prescient. With the advent of the atomic bomb, nothing essential would change.
The bomb was already "prefigured" in the structure of the argument. Witness the
following note, entitled "Idle Horror."

   The observation of evil is a fascinating occupation. But this observation implies
   a measure of secret agreement. The bad social conscience of everyone who
   participates in an evil deed, and hatred for fulfillment in life, are so strong that
   under critical circumstances they turn against their own interests as a form of
   immanent revenge. One fatal example of this is provided by the French bourgeois who observed ironically the heroic ideal of the Fascists: they were de-

317

There is, however, another reading of this apparent failure of scientific and technical reason. Wells was an old-fashioned idealist, and though he had written a popular world history, he had always believed that what happened in history was, in the final analysis, a result of rational thought informing a collective will. And if thought could grasp the secrets of Nature through scientific reason, our human and imperfect world could eventually be made to coincide with the perceived harmony of the cosmos. The mass destructions of World War II, and especially the dramatic instance of the nuclear explosions over Hiroshima and Nagasaki, had shaken his faith in this potential outcome.

But what if thought were not, as he believed, autonomous? What if the constructions of the mind, including the models confected by scientific reason, were interwoven with history instead of rising divinely above it? We remember Rexford Tugwell. Like Wells, Tugwell believed that thought "at the level of planning" might become a directive force in history. It was, he believed, a force independent of history. But if Tugwell were wrong, and mind is actually a part of the historical process, both determined and determining, then the crisis of planning would have to be regarded as a specific instance of the historical crisis. And since the past two hundred years may be understood chiefly as the unfolding of industrial capitalism, the perceived crisis of planning would have to be interpreted in light of the crisis of this larger process. In this interpretation, the crisis of planning is not that abstract reason has failed to control the forces of historical change. Rather, the crisis foreshadows the end of the historical project that planning has so faithfully served.

If we pursue this line of argument—as I propose to do—and refuse to fall into the seductive arms of a cultural pessimism, we are obliged to look more closely into the crisis that confronts us. Only through a deeper understanding of this crisis can we decide what stand we ourselves should take.

In the view of those who hold power in the United States and, indeed, in most of the capitalist world, the crisis we are living through, in an acute form since the early 1970s, is said to be merely a cyclical event. Within the last generation, whole new technologies have come into use—micro-chips, robots, satellites—that are transforming the material conditions of our lives. Old industries are being dis-

---

lighted by the triumph of their fellows expressed in Hitler's rise to power, even if it threatened their own destruction; indeed, they took their own destruction as evidence of the justice of the order they represented. . . . In Fascism, they are presented with a synthesis of their desire to rule and self-hatred; idle horros is always accompanied by the words "I told you so." (Horkheimer and Adorno 1982, 230–231)

mantled, new industries, based on different technologies, are emerging. Accompanying these changes is a new spatial ordering of production. As older regions are retired, new metropolises blaze forth like meteors against the night sky of the Pacific Rim. A lengthy period of "retooling" and "capital restructuring" is underway. Once restructuring has been accomplished, a new long wave of growth can be expected to create a world of plenty. The marvelous age we are about to enter holds out the prospect of global prosperity far greater than the costs of this periodic bloodletting of "creative destruction," with its regrettable, if unavoidable, individual and social tragedies.[2]

Given this restricted cyclical view of the crisis—restricted, because it is limited to prices, foodstuffs, and raw materials—a wide spectrum of plans has been proposed to deal with the future. Pride of place must be given to the plans that are actually in execution, most notably in the United States and Britain. Their central idea appears to be the creation of a space for the free maneuver of private capital by "unleashing" what Raymond Williams (1983) calls the forces of strategic advantage. Accordingly, the welfare state will be dismantled, taxes will be reduced, the power of organized labor will be broken, competition from overseas will be encouraged, business will be deregulated.

Accompanying this neo-liberal policy, with its commitment to a philosophy of the minimalist state, are ideological efforts to reinstate old moral verities in an unlikely alliance with a frenzied and eroticized consumerism. More frightening still is a heated-up anticommunist rhetoric whose object is to pave the way for a massive recapitalization of the military-industrial complex. For the United States, the results of these policies, taken as a whole, have been a trillion dollar deficit; two-digit interest rates; a huge and growing trade deficit; the financial collapse of many small businesses, including thousands of small commercial farmers; the rise of super-conglomerates; rising unemployment; and the gnawing fear of a nuclear holocaust.

But, we are told, these are not the essentials. We should focus rather on the GNP, that ultimate gauge of a nation's health. If we hold the course steady, the promise is for a cornucopia to shower us with untold blessings. The expected scenario is painted for us in vivid colors by conservative economic historian W. W. Rostow.

2. The intellectually most ambitious effort to construct this scenario is by W. W. Rostow (1978), who speaks of the "price revolution of 1972–77 as the initial explosive stage of the fifth Kondratieff upswing confronted in a world economy which has experienced four marked, if irregular, cycles since 1790 in the relative scarcity or abundance of foodstuffs and raw materials" (Rostow 1978, 571).

By the year 2000, if we are wise and lucky, we will have
achieved the following:
—Gross birth rates in the developing world will have been
    brought down from their present explosive level . . . to 20
    or less.
—The level and productivity of agriculture, notably in the de-
    veloping regions, will have increased enough so that the ex-
    panded populations can be decently fed . . .
—The scientific and technical problems involved in creating a
    new energy source, based on renewable or essentially infi-
    nite sources, will have been solved.
—Air and water pollution will be under control.
—Expanded production . . . will provide, at reasonable costs,
    sufficient raw materials to permit industrialization to con-
    tinue . . .
—In order to accomplish the above results, patterns of invest-
    ment will have been restructured . . . and new technologies
    . . . will permit growth to proceed in the next century.
—High and steady rates of growth will have been reconciled
    with price stability.
—The developing nations . . . will have about doubled their
    present income per capita and acquired another quarter
    century's experience of modernization. . . . They will be
    much more capable of adjusting to changing circumstance
    and solving their problems in the century beyond. (Rostow
    1978, 580–581)

Against this neo-liberal revelation of paradise with its implicit policy
prescriptions, in which the public domain is all but dissolved into the
private economic concerns of large corporations, global financial institutions, the military establishment, and individual consumers, the
social reform tradition of planning has come up with its own solutions. As might be expected, the state is to play a more central role
in rescuing the domestic economy. Without it, the patient might die.
There are two concerns here, both of which stem from a vision in
which the public domain and its politics are still taken seriously. One
surmises a residual sense of social obligation.

   The first concern is with the social costs of capital restructuring
and with the traditional role of the capitalist state in assisting people
and regions that have been struck by the cyclone of "creative destruction," and thus in dealing with devastation caused by forces beyond their immediate control.

   The second concern has to do with the role of the state in the very process of restructuring. Some would decelerate this process by protecting older industrial sectors threatened with obsolesence or competition from low-wage labor areas abroad. Others, such as Lester Thurow (1981), argue for closer and continuing cooperation between major business interests and the government, with the latter helping to finance the innovative "high tech" industries that are emerging. A new form of public-private "partnership" would help to keep Japan at bay, a country in which the traditional tie-in of state and corporations is so close as to render the usual distinction between public and private domains irrelevant. This demand for an "industrial policy" is frequently coupled with proposals for joint economic planning by the new partnership, along the lines of indicative growth planning—a style of planning that was successfully introduced by France during the period of economic recovery following World War II (Cohen 1969).

In striking contrast to the social reform tradition's focus on institutional change and central planning, policy analysts have been unable to formulate a coherent position vis-à-vis the crisis. Again, this is not unexpected, given their pretensions to being value-free and concerned with only technical relations. As we saw in Chapter 4, some analysts have argued for a retreat to the academy to improve and sharpen the tools of their trade. Others have gone to work for transnational corporations where they now offer such new services as risk analysis for overseas investments. Still others, disenchanted with planning, have thrown their weight behind neo-liberal ideologies, proclaiming in loud voice that all planning in the public domain is vanity, and that the forces of the market are the lesser evil (Wildavsky 1980).

Finally, there are the exponents of the social learning tradition. Compared with the mainstream debates, theirs is only a small rivulet of a voice, so harmless and apparently insignificant that it tends to be tolerated with a certain wry amusement. Social learners speak of humanizing planning. With E. F. Schumacher (1973), they argue for a human scale of production, an appropriate technology. With David Korten, they speak of a "people-centered development" (Korten and Klaus 1984). With Johan Galtung, they would promote planning from below and self-reliance (Galtung et al. 1980).

Common to all the positions identified above is a solid confidence in the workability of the system of industrial capitalism. Though there might be some ultimate limits to growth, technology can be relied upon to push those limits further and further into the future. We are therefore obliged to submit to technology. The existence of mass poverty in the peasant periphery of the global economy is admitted. But, as Rostow said, if we are wise and lucky, progress will come, on "little cats' feet," eradicating famine as sustained economic growth resumes to spread its bounty into the far corners of the world.

There is, however, a more cataclysmic view of the present historical crisis. According to this view, mounting contradictions will throw the system into a tailspin of growing dissolution, even as they generate, based on altogether different principles of organization, collective movements for social reconstruction.

The basis of this view rests on four arguments which take, as their point of departure, the world economy as a whole, meaning the linked system of global markets and their spatial organization into core, semi-peripheral, and peripheral areas articulated through a global hierarchy of "world cities" (Friedmann and Wolff 1982; Friedmann 1986).[3] The four arguments can be briefly stated.

1. Industrial capitalism generates both costs and benefits. When these are calculated in socially relevant terms and on a global basis, it is highly probable that the costs of continued growth will exceed the benefits by a growing margin, creating an inherently unstable situation that cannot continue without limit.[4]

3. The emergence of a world economy is not without historical precedent. Wallerstein (1974) traces it to the beginning of the sixteenth century and characterizes its essential feature as a single (international) division of labor. Post–World War II developments, however, put an entirely different face on the situation. Transnational enterprise has become part of the language of everyday discourse (Froebel, Heinrichs, and Kreye 1980). According to one estimate, transnational corporations now market four fifths of world trade, exclusive of socialist countries (Cavanagh and Clairmonte 1982, 8). An accelerating trend of mergers has, within the last 20 years, created 200 industrial corporations, half of them American, whose combined sales in 1980 amounted to nearly 30 percent of world gross domestic product (GDP) (ibid. 11). Individually, their worldwide employees may number in the tens and even hundreds of thousands, and their sales may rival the GDP of all but the largest of national economies (Kidron and Segal 1981, map 35).

4. That there are costs and benefits accruing from economic growth, and that these values are calculated differently on social as opposed to private account, is completely obfuscated by the measurements currently in use. The onset of the world economic crisis in the 1970s led to a serious reexamination of the social accounts model by which the gross product of national economies was calculated (Nordhaus and Tobin 1972; Seers 1976; Hueting 1980). The main results of this reexamination are set forth below.

a. The social accounts framework includes a measure not only of final goods and services produced to satisfy individual and collective wants, but also of a great deal of intermediate production as well. From a welfare perspective, this in-

2. There is no inherent tendency toward equilibrium in the global market economy, as major oligopolistic actors seek short-term strategic advantage in a climate of mutual suspicion and growing social unrest. The weakened national economies of semi-peripheral and peripheral states react more violently to

---

volves double-counting on a heroic scale. The correct procedure would be to eliminate intermediate production sectors from the accounts. But this has not been done. Instead, we note how the steady, proportionate increase in intermediate production sustains an illusion of welfare-producing growth.

b. The social accounts framework makes no allowances for the environmental costs of production, or what Hueting calls compensation for and elimination of environmental losses (that is, the losses or displacements of specific environmental functions): "[W]hen production (and consumption) as a negative and unintentional by-product, destroys means of satisfying wants already in existence (the environmental functions), it is not logical to regard the expenditure incurred in compensating for and eliminating these as income" (Hueting 1980, 179). Hueting and others have provided evidence that environmental costs, like the intermediate costs of production, are substantial and growing. The principal difference between them is that environmental costs *are not counted at all*.

c. Another major uncounted cost of economic growth is psychological. Some of this (for instance, a certain proportion of expenditures on "human relations management," psychiatry, and psychological counseling) appears as an intermediate cost. Most of it, however, finds expression in the alienation, anxiety, boredom, sexual violence, fear, and loneliness that characterize so much of contemporary life. Though evidently related to the dominant mode of production and the labor processes specific to that mode, psychological costs do not enter into the accounts framework despite its implicit claim to measure "human satisfactions" (Marris 1975; Scitovsky 1976). With growing social polarization, economic restructuring, de-skilling, the removal of the "safety net," and a secular rise in the average rate of unemployment, the psychological stress on individuals is likely to increase. There may not be any ready way to substract these costs from the measure of the domestic product. Conceptually, however, the conclusion is clear. Our primary sense of well-being is not necessarily enhanced because the GDP goes up!

d. The social accounts framework incorporates nonmarket transactions in a wholly inadequate way, as in estimating the value of the self-production of food or assigning rents for self-built housing (Seers 1976). Not only are these estimates notoriously "flaky," but they also ignore huge areas of work and satisfactions without which social reproduction would be unthinkable (for example, the nurturing of preschool children). The volume of nonmarket activities is always very large, especially in the peasant periphery, where the social accounts framework is grossly misleading as a measure of collective well-being. But it is also misleading in advanced industrial societies, where a part of the ongoing struggle concerns the extent to which the economy should preempt traditional household functions (Pahl 1984).

e. The social accounts framework treats national economies as the appropriate unit of accounting. External economic relations are consequently treated as "inputs" to domestic production, while regional economic relations are not counted at all. But wealth and poverty have become interdependent on a world scale, and

the periodic ups and down of the global business cycle, and so contribute to a permanent crisis that gathers momentum, since the recovery periods are too short to permit even a lurching forward. As crisis mounts on crisis, political instabilities are added to market instabilities, with no general solution in sight.

3. In the past, the social costs of economic growth have typically been absorbed by households and the state. As these costs rise, there is a decline in the state's ability to alleviate hardship; to regulate private corporations in the public interest; and to repair the damage done to workers, resources, natural environments, and human communities rendered obsolescent by the surging drive of corporations for expansion and innovation. As a result, individual states will increasingly resort to measures that will protect them against the seemingly arbitrary actions of transnational capital. But such actions are counterproductive to the project of an ever-expanding world economy. As policy, protectionism is the very antithesis of a world economy, which must assume the unhindered movement of production factors, commodities, and information. Without such freedom (at least

---

the new political *regional* consciousness demands an appropriate accounting at that level also. The central state is no longer the exclusive locus for economic and social policy decisions. An adequate accounts framework would need to link the national economy with appropriate accounts at a multinational or world scale, as well as with sub-national, regional accounts.

These criticisms of the social accounts framework are not matters merely of opinion; neither are they of marginal importance. James Tobin, who was one of the chief critics, received the Nobel Prize in economics for his work, and Roefie Hueting's book is introduced by Nobel laureate Jan Tinbergen. The criticism goes to the root of the matter, it challenges the very logic of the framework. And the implications are serious. In Hueting's terse formulation, "the figures of national income, which are generally interpreted as economic or welfare growth, are giving wrong signals" (Hueting 1980, 177).

But if they are giving the wrong signals, *the entire logic of the liberal paradigm, which assigned centrality to economic growth, is thrown in doubt.* Gross national (or domestic) product can no longer serve as a guide to policy so long as the aim of policy is, as it must be, the well-being of citizens living in their own communities. In retrospect, it is indeed questionable whether an inclusive and theoretically adequate accounts framework can ever be constructed. The most that we can probably expect is a set of loosely related social indicators. Such indicators would not allow simple statements to be made about national "development." They would not allow for a single hierarchical ordering of national economies; neither would they tempt politicians to tout the short-term growth performance of a country as "miraculous." No single standard of performance could be unambiguously applied. Instead of economic experts pouring oil on troubled waters, the question of the "right" development would be opened up as a political question to differently constituted groups and interests: class, gender, ethnic, territorial, environmental.

for the strongest actors), the system as a whole cannot expand. And if it cannot expand, it must decline, for industrial capitalism requires continued growth for its very survival.

4. The impact of the global economy on semi-peripheral and peripheral countries is devastating. In the semi-periphery, inequalities both social and regional are mounting; the periphery as a whole is unable to feed its own population. Not surprisingly, such conditions, if they persist year after year, are politically destabilizing. Two contradictory, if related, outcomes have already become visible: increasing state repression of democratic opposition and growing revolutionary countermovements to seize power and initiate "another" development. These conflicts tend to attract involvement of the two superpowers, and to contribute to the general military buildup and paranoia. As more and more resources are sucked into these conflicts, the state's ability to attend also to civilian needs diminishes dramatically. Social callousness adds to the general instability. Some states collapse altogether (Lebanon). Others are mired in decade-long civil conflict of unprecedented violence and brutality (the Middle East, Central America). In some, racial and religious bigotry flares up (Northern Ireland, Sri Lanka, Punjab). In others, genocide threatens unwanted populations (Kampuchea, West Irian). An entire continent is ravaged by famine (Africa).

Faced with this apocalyptic prospect, technical reason is powerless. Neither the neo-liberal nor the proposed social reform solutions can stem the general dissolution—a dissolution that has already begun and that will soon be generally apparent—as the world system spins out of control. The only genuine "solution" that remains is for individuals to join in a collective struggle that seeks to plant, amid mounting violence and chaos, the germinal seeds of a new order.

Counterforce

It is difficult to write about the historical decline of a system of power as it is happening. It is even more difficult to imagine what might replace it. And yet we must try. For a counterforce is beginning to gather. Forged in resistance, it prefigures in its inventions the major alternatives to the dying order of things.

The grounding of the alternative is in a new mode of production. Centered in the household, though not confined to it, it produces life itself. The material base of life—food, water clothing, transport, and shelter—is part of this, though it is only a part, and indeed, most of it will still be produced by the traditional means of the factory system. The more important part and that which is completely under the control of the household and, more generally, of civil society whose nucleus is the household, is *nonmaterial* and relates to modes of interaction in which the significant and moral dimensions of our lives find expression.[5]

Like all work, the work of the household in the production of life is a cooperative endeavor. And if life is to be self-produced and not acquired secondhand in department stores, entertainment palaces, and other institutions of our hyper-commerical civilization, it will require access to the bases of social power—the information, knowledge, skills, organization, tools of production, and time and space that we need to produce our own lives. For this access we will have to struggle, and in this struggle begin to express the ultimate aim of the alternative movement, which is the reclaiming of territorial life for ourselves, constituted as a political community, autonomous and sovereign over the life spaces we claim as our own.

Although it is a lived reality, it is not yet a social movement in the fullest sense. Those who have joined the struggle recognize the special bonds of solidarity that unite them. At the present time, the strength of this incipient movement appears to be concentrated in the major cities of the core economies, where it constitutes a political counterforce that must be reckoned with.

The movement's goal is universal in its appeal: the collective self-production of life and the reclaiming of the political terrain from the state; in short, the recovery of a genuine political community. It

5. I have found that young, educated, urban Americans have difficulty accepting the household as the central institution of civil society. Many have succumbed to the ideology of individualism to such an extent that they see themselves as history-less atoms. I believe this understanding to be fundamentally wrong. They themselves have grown up in households, they have mothers and fathers and siblings and other relations, and for the most part, in fact, they retain strong ties to their immediate families. In their personal lives, perhaps until they are in their mid-thirties, they may experiment with different household settings for themselves, from living alone to joining an urban commune. But children have not yet been abolished, and the ties of blood are universally acknowledged. We do not make ourselves alone but in relation to other human beings, and particularly to those who are close to us. There are degrees of closeness, and to specify households as the central social configuration is not to insist that they be nuclear, private, and closed. On the contrary, the household unit that is emerging, and that must emerge if the political terrain is to be reclaimed by us, is one that allows for many different ties to significant others, even as it preserves an inner circle of intimacy for itself. In the new vision, the household becomes, with others, a co-producer of our individual and collective lives.

not only addresses the increasingly felt needs of ordinary people in the industrialized countries, but also speaks directly to the peasant masses of the world periphery (see Chapter 9). In strategic terms, this convergence of aims means that the alternative movement, though its origins are in the West, can declare itself in solidarity with social movements in the direction of collective self-reliance throughout the world.

Still, an important difference remains. In the peasant periphery, self-reliance is a matter of urgent priority in meeting people's immediate survival needs. To this end, peasant households must be mobilized, and the only agency capable of doing so is the national state. The same is not true of our own societies, which are more tightly organized, have better communication facilities, and a much stronger economic base. Here, the state is correctly seen not as a possible ally in social transformation, but as an obstacle to necessary change. In Western industrialized countries, therefore, the immediate aim is to enlarge the space of the household "mode of production" and, beginning from there, to branch out into other political communities: the locality, the region, and beyond, until the furthest limits of the globe are reached, which is the ultimate political community.

In the longer term, the state itself must be transformed. Its powers must be scaled down, redistributed among smaller political units, and rendered more directly accountable to the people. *The real struggle, then, is for a recovery of the political community on which our Western ideas of democratic governance are based.* Political community presupposes the recognition of a sphere of common concerns and the discourse about them: a public domain. Yet in many widely accepted social theories, the existence of this sphere and its correlative concepts of public interest and the common good has been explicitly denied. Because we cannot reclaim what does not exist, we must now turn to consider the relevant arguments of both its adversaries and its advocates.

The Case against the Public Domain

No one would seriously question that all of us live in a system of political order that reflects what Louis Althusser has called "structures in dominance." Throughout the Western world, the existing political order, that is, the ensemble of political institutions and practices of a territorially organized society, forms part of a civilization that essentially has been shaped by the bourgeoisie. If this is so, one might speak of a class domain and, with reference to it, the use of the term "public" would be vastly misleading. It is class interests that are primarily served by politics.

Three arguments explicitly deny the reality of a public domain. According to their philosophical origins, we may call them radical utilitarian, liberal, and Marxist. If the idea of a public domain nevertheless persists as an active term in the political life of a society, it is perhaps because certain historical residues point to a tradition beyond class interests. We take up the arguments for the public domain in the next section.

The Radical Utilitarian Argument

The radical utilitarianism of Jeremy Bentham was eventually absorbed into neo-classical economics and became its metaphysical ground (Schumpeter 1954, 87–88). Since neo-classical economics remains the dominant doctrine, especially in Anglo-Saxon countries, radical utilitarianism, conceived in the eighteenth century as a substitute for natural law, continues to be relevant today.

Jeremy Bentham declared the role of the state to be that of furthering the "greatest happiness."[6] "The business of government," he wrote, "is to promote the happiness of the society by punishing and rewarding" (Bentham 1948, 70). But the happiness he had in mind was that of the individuals who make up the society and not of the society as an entity in (and for) itself. Throughout his life, Bentham was chiefly concerned with legal reform, aware that there is scarcely an aspect of human happiness that is not, in some measure, affected or circumscribed by the law, which is a social institution. It would take Adam Smith's genial invisible hand to ensure the harmonious climax. Bentham's benevolent state, argued latter-day ideologues, was, after all, not needed. If each person strove exclusively to maximize his or her happiness through the market system of exchange, the resulting sum of individual happinesses would be the greatest attainable. Political life was, therefore, not of the essence.

In his major published work, *An Introduction to the Principles of Morals and Legislation* (1789), Bentham had written with doctrinal authority:

> The community is a fictitious *body*, composed of the individual persons who are considered as constituting as it were its *mem-*

6. The "greatest happiness" principle was also known, in earlier incarnations, as, first, the principle of "utility," and then as the principle of "the greatest happiness of the greatest number." The greatest happiness, declared Bentham, was the only right, proper, and universally desirable end of human action, and in particular that of "a functionary . . . exercising the powers of Government" (Bentham 1948, 1).

bers. The interest of the community then is, what?—the sum of the interests of the several members who compose it. (Bentham 1948, 3)

The "interests of the several members," of course, is to promote each his or her own happiness, which is the *net benefit* a person obtains from his efforts, once proper allowance has been made for the "mischief, pain, evil, or unhappiness to the party whose interest is considered" (Bentham 1948, 2).[7]

All this takes place within a state whose legitimacy is not yet at issue. The state exists; its palpable reality is its sole and sufficient justification. The problem, as Bentham saw it, was to align the state's actions with a hedonistic calculus. Since the object of the state was to effect the greatest happiness of its subjects—a value judgment for which, to his great regret, he was unable to find any objective basis—Bentham in effect proposed a giant computing facility for human happiness. This "machine" would calculate for each citizen the pains and pleasures of alternative state actions and, summing up over all citizens, recommend the course of action to the sovereign that promised to result in the largest overall gain of pleasure over pain.

Bentham proposed what was in essence a rudimentary form of scientific planning. The ringing phrases—so dear to the Enlightenment—of liberty, social contract, and natural right were as nothing to Bentham; contemptuously, he referred to them as "nonsense on stilts" (Monroe 1967, 285; Mill 1974, 87). Happiness would flow abundantly from central planning.

Bentham's uncritical view of the political domain is best summarized by a leading Bentham scholar. According to D. H. Monroe, Bentham held that "a man has political authority when other men habitually obey him. Laws are the commands of such men, when enforced by punishment or the threat of punishment" (Monroe 1967, 285). Bentham's "moral science" is thus placed at the disposal of the state. Because it has the capacity to impose sanctions, the state can force compliance with its laws.[8] But sanctions are painful. By causing pain, they govern human behavior, creating a habit of obedi-

7. For the changing historical meaning of "interest" in Western European languages, see Hirschman (1977, Pt. 1). Originally, interest referred only to rulers; later it came to be used in the sense of the material advantage of individuals and groups within nations. In a democratic society, its collective meaning, once concentrated in the absolute authority of the king as sovereign, became difficult to sustain: witness the vicissitudes attending Rousseau's concept of the General Will.

8. Bentham recognized, in addition to the authority of the state, the authority of religion and of popular morality. Both could impose sanctions of their own.

ence. Faced with this situation, human beings strive to maximize their pleasures in a field that has been structured for them by legal (and extralegal) constrains. In drawing up its laws, the state is to be guided by the expert advice of Bentham's moral calculators. Thus does the principle of greatest happiness become a neutral instrument in the employment of technical reason.[9]

This model recalls B. F. Skinner's utopian fantasy, *Walden Two* (1969). The radical utilitarian is there revealed as a behaviorist who has no need for a concept of the public domain. Words such as freedom are superfluous in the utilitarian vocabulary (Skinner 1971). People's happiness can be calculated with increasing precision by moral scientists, such as Skinner's Mr. Frazier, who is the maximum leader of the Walden Two community. The only significant distinction between Bentham's utilitarian calculus and Skinner's behaviorism is that the former is principally concerned with punishments, or negative sanctions, while the Harvard professor's fame rests chiefly on his theory of *positive* reinforcement as a means for social control. Punishments bring pain, but positive reinforcement increases a person's pleasure in doing the will of others. In the end, the question of who legitimizes the authority of the reinforcers is neither asked nor answered, perhaps because the term authority itself belongs to an outdated lexicon. Since in Skinner's utopia all punishments have been abolished, there is no longer any need for "authorities": they have become friends and genial companions. Science and happiness provide their own justifications.[10]

9. This outcome is paradoxical, because Bentham did not conceive of the state as a super-entity with purposes and a will of its own. For him, it was merely "a human contrivance to enable men to realize as many of their desires as possible" (Monroe 1967, 248). The sources of the paradox are three: (1) Bentham's uncritical acceptance of the state as sovereign, (2) his rejection of natural law doctrine, and (3) his belief in the scientific objectivity of the hedonistic calculus.

10. Skinner's *Walden Two* was one of the most popular books among the college generation of the 1950s, and it is still in print. It describes a utopian community of hierarchical design. A small group of self-selected managers and planners have the authority to initiate actions. They base their authority on their exclusive access to the results of experimental science and behavioral engineering. Below them, and properly engineered into conformist behavior, is the mass of the people. Although their happiness is proclaimed to be the greatest good of the community, their actual existence in the novel is a shadowy one. Invariably, they are found moving in small, usually animated groups, and they seem content enough. *But they do not act.* They conduct themselves instead in strict conformity with a program the engineering of which remains the responsibility of the planners alone. (There are also experimental scientists who are paid by the community to improve the behavioral basis of programs).

The people do not have a voice in their institutions of governance. They are said not even to want such a voice, conditioned as they are into passive acquiescence to the

The Liberal Argument

The extreme Benthamite position is that politics is superfluous, because the costs and benefits of programs can be calculated in advance by experts. But in modern democracies, politics is an incontrovertible fact. Like Bentham's state, it exists. And, if it exists, there must be a domain of the political, or a public domain. Political scientists have made this domain the object of their study. How, we might ask, do these experts conceive of politics and its sphere? In particular, we are interested in the views of political scientists in the liberal tradition, which is the post-Millian inheritor of utilitarian philosophy.[11]

Edward C. Banfield is a distinguished Harvard professor. His conception of politics is shared by many of his empirically minded colleagues. In an early work, he writes, "Politics is the activity (negotiation, argument, discussion, application of force, persuasion, etc.) by which an issue is agitated or settled" (Meyerson and Banfield 1955, 304). And an issue exists "when there is a conflict, real or apparent, between the ends of different actors (or within the end system of a single actor), *and not all of the conflicting ends can be realized*" (ibid.; italics added).[12]

Politics, in this view, is chiefly concerned with actors whose self-regarding ends are in conflict. Because they contest a limited good, all their ends cannot be realized simultaneously. Banfield describes a pluralist politics in which all contenders are grouped according to their particular interest. This interest may not always be engaged,

---

authority of science and behavioral engineering. They are happy. Why should they wish for things to be different? Their every whispered complaint is registered and "taken into account" by the authorities.

Science has replaced politics; it has even replaced God. The founder and guiding demon of Walden Two, Mr. Frazier, is the embodiment of abstract authority. At one point in the story, he imagines himself to be as Jesus on the cross, even as God Himself. Mr. Frazier clearly acts, but the members of his utopia do not. Having internalized their behavior, they are blissfully content.

11. John Stuart Mill (1806–1873) is considered to be the "father" of modern utilitarianism. In many ways, Mill humanized Bentham's hard-edged felicity calculus. To him we also owe the radical separation of fact from value, commonly ascribed to Max Weber, which is the basis for modern welfare economics. A man of expansive sentiments, Mill fiercely reigned in his moral passions. More than is true of most other writers, his thinking directly reflects his life experiences (Mill 1974b).

12. Banfield follows in the pluralist tradition of American political science, which received its original formulation by Arthur Bentley (1908) and its modern formulation by David B. Truman (1951). It was Truman who wrote, "In developing a group interpretation of politics, therefore, we do not need to account for a totally inclusive interest, because one does not exist" (Truman 1951, 51). Banfield has been cited in the text for his closer involvement with planning theory.

and the conflict is not always permanent. At given times, it comes to focus on specific issues, such as budget allocations, new legislation, and the election of public officials. Where a particular good is not contested, politics slumbers.

In this conception, the public domain appears as an arena for conflict. It is an abstract political space without specific attributes. Like the Colosseum in Imperial Rome, it sets the stage for spectacular gladiatorial battles. Since it has no independent role in this conflict, there is no "interest" that can be linked to it. Conflict is the name of the game; it is the relations of power among the actors playing in the political arena that determine the outcome.

It might be noted that politics in the pluralist conception is treated as the continuation of market relations by other means. Politics, not planning, substitutes for allocative choices which, for whatever reason, have been removed from the market. This close parallel between politics and markets has not gone unobserved, and some social scientists have proposed a market model of political behavior (Buchanan and Tullock 1962). In this model, politics tends to merge with a rational construct in which "utilities" are exchanged at the margin. Presumably, these utilities can be calculated *in advance* by expert forecasters. In a fantasy, one might arrive at the following conclusion. If the forecasting is reasonably accurate, why not dispense altogether with a politics that is unpredictable and expensive, and substitute for it an expert judgment of the balance of individual utilities at the margin? Losers would be compensated according to the criterion of the Pareto optimum; winners would get whatever they wanted. And so, we are back at the paradoxical position that we found in our analysis of the hedonistic calculus: a state unconstrained by politics and in the hands of those for whom technical reason is infinitely superior to the passions of political life.[13]

The Marxist Argument
Scholars in the Marxist tradition face a dilemma for which only political praxis is able to provide a solution. To the extent that they

13. The ideology of market rationality was originally proposed as a check on political passions. Buying and selling might be dull business, but it was peaceful (Hirschman 1977). Adam Smith, of course, never imagined that either markets or politics might be simulated, but that possibility has not only been noted, it has been acted upon. We now have short-term economic forecasting models of considerable power which are used in central planning, and we have extensive political forecasting at election times. It has even been suggested that these forecasts influence actual behavior. This has made of forecasting a "moral science" very much in the image of Bentham's felicity calculus.

critically analyze existing social (including political) relations, they must cast their discussion in terms of an implacable and fundamental opposition between class interests. The present reality, according to Marxists, is characterized by the struggle for domination between the two great eschatological classes of capital and labor—eschatological, because they are regarded as the last of social classes in the "pre-history" of humankind. The ultimate victory of labor in this titanic struggle is taken for granted, and with its victory begins the long and arduous transition to a classless society from which every trace of bourgeois memory has been erased.

This focus on the class struggle precludes acceptance, in any but pejorative terms, of political categories such as state, political community, or public domain, which are treated as essentially ideological constructs that suggest, when used by apologists for the existing order, a form of trans-class solidarity. It was not accidental that Marx and Engels argued so vehemently against any form of territorialism. Both capital and labor, they insisted, were universal social classes, and the struggle between them was a universal struggle. And just as the scope of capital was global, so labor, according to the authors of *The Communist Manifesto*, had been "stripped of every trace of national character. Law, morality, and religion are, to the proletarian, so many bourgeois prejudices, behind which lurk in ambush as many bourgeois interests" (Marx and Engels 1978, 482).

In other words, the only possible basis of a true solidarity is class, which is a solidarity based on a perception of common class interests. Bourgeois rhetoric, then, must be understood as the language of *any* social class that wishes to establish its hegemony.

> [E]very class which is struggling for mastery, even when its domination, as in the case of the proletariat, postulates the abolition of the old form of society in its entirety, and of domination itself, must first conquer for itself political power in order to present its interest in turn as the general interest, which in the first moment it is forced to do. (Marx 1978a, 161)

The dilemma for Marxist analysis arises in regard to the society of the future. The political element in bourgeois society is viewed as simply a conflict over power. It arises from the uneven distribution of power and the use of commanding positions within the state apparatus by one class to oppress and exploit the members of another. But the final goal of history is the abolition of all relations of power *and, therefore, of the political element as well.*

Marx solved this problem with a grand gesture of his utopian imagination. He envisioned the reabsorption of the state into a community of men and women in which exploitative relations were absent, in which the social division of labor had been abolished, and which in every aspect of its life was a self-governing community. Except for the fact that suffrage in this community of equals was universal—every adult member would be an active participant in every phase of communal life—this ideal picture of a cooperative commonwealth seems to have been inspired, at least in its political aspects, by the image of the classical city-state. Democracy would be direct, production chiefly for use. The needs of human beings for an encompassing and rich sociality would be amply met as life itself became political in the original Greek sense of *political* as a concern with the common good. "In the real community," wrote Marx, "the individuals obtain their freedom in and through their association" (Marx 1978a, 197). Only in the context of a cooperative commonwealth, which was to be the beginning of the "real" history of humanity, was it possible to speak of the *general* interest in ways that were more than pious phrase making (Avineri 1968, ch. 8).

Magnificent as this vision is, it leaves unanswered the urgent question of how this ideal might be reached and, indeed, whether it can be reached at all. Beginning in the 1960s, a group of Marxist philosophers attempted to deal with this question by appropriating Jean-Jacques Rousseau for Marxist analysis. In Rousseau's concept of the General Will they hoped to find a basis for inspiring a European Left whose confidence had been severely shaken by its knowledge of Stalin's murderous brutality and Soviet aggression (della Volpe 1978; Colletti 1976; Althusser 1972). It proved to be a difficult undertaking. In a more realistic vein, Nicos Poulantzas, a Greek political scientist working in Paris, attempted to open up the conceptual space for a politics of class struggle by developing a sophisticated *Marxist* theory of the state. The state, he wrote, "is a relationship of forces, or more precisely, the material condensation of such a relationship among classes and class frictions, such as this is expressed within the state in a necessarily specific form" (Poulantzas 1980, 128–129; orig. 1978). The state itself thus becomes a "contested terrain," reflecting in its actions the current balance of political forces. "Class contradictions are the very stuff of the State," wrote Poulantzas. "They are present in its material framework and pattern of organization, while the State's policy is the result of their functioning within the State" (ibid. 132). Therefore, and addressing himself to what he calls the popular masses, "we must grasp the state as a strategic field and process of intersecting power networks, which both articulate and exhibit mutual contradictions and displacements" (ibid. 136).

The Marxist model of the bourgeois state exhibits certain similarities to that of liberal political science. In both, attention is focused on conflicts over budgets, priorities, and material control over parts of the state apparatus. Where Poulantzas conjures up the imagery of the state as a battlefield, liberals such as Aaron Wildavsky (1978) describe the public domain as an arena for competing interest groups. Poulantzas uses the language of class struggle; ultimately, this puts his argument into a different tradition of discourse. The similarities between the two views are nonetheless striking.

On the other hand, Poulantzas carefully avoids any reference to a public domain. His central concern is the state. The public domain remains a bourgeois category. Unlike the state, it lacks a material base. For this reason, Poulantzas rejects the writings of della Volpe and Colletti, with their (to him) useless attempts to effect a marriage between social contract theory and Marxist class analysis. The idea of social contract, growing out of natural rights doctrine, is incompatible with the traditions of Marxist thought. Revolt against oppression is sufficient justification for the claims of people's power.

For Poulantzas, the great task is "to open up a global perspective on the withering away of the State" (Poulantzas 1980, 262). This involves "unfurling direct, rank-and-file democracy," particularly in the multiplication of self-management forms of organization, and the transformation of the state from within. Neither process requires recognition of a public domain.

The Case for the Public Domain

The case for the public domain must begin, as do all political questions, with a conception of what it means to be human. There are those, for example, who would argue the extreme individualist position that, as a human being, "we don't owe nothin' to nobody." We are self-made men and women, our own creators, *ex nihilo*. Competition and struggle shape our efforts. When we cooperate, it is for selfish reasons only, a form of antagonistic cooperation. It is always the others who constrain us by being there, by insisting, perhaps, on a different order of life than the one we would prefer. Libertarians come close to this *monadic* view of human life. It is also the anthropology of classical liberalism (Hobbes 1958; Locke 1948; Macpherson 1962).[14]

14. Monadic views may be benign or vicious. Where benign, they presume a natural harmony among human beings and their spontaneous cooperation in the absence of social and political constraints. This, in essence, is the anarchist position (Kropotkin 1902). But where the monadic model is vicious, as with Hobbes (1958), who imag-

As we saw in the preceding section, this view of human nature has no need for a concept of the public domain. Indeed, it is unable to come up with a general concept of the public, much less of the public good, as anything other than the addition of the several goods of individuals in a social aggregate. It follows that all external constraints on the power of individuals to realize themselves must be limited to the barest minimum. Any constraint, insofar as it infringes upon the natural right of each individual to his or her self-actualization, will be experienced as painful (Berlin 1969).[15]

Most of us, however, are conscious that we are born into the world as helpless creatures who could not survive for even a day without the nurturing help of others. We are born into families, communities, clans, and tribes that have a preexisting structure, normative coherence, and a history. The extraordinarily long period of our dependency on others, our slow progress into adulthood and personal autonomy, which is the universal human lot, is an exceptional period of learning (Portmann 1956). It is also an intensely social experience, involving numerous interpersonal exchanges, during which we learn the rules of accepted social conduct, including reciprocity, civility, and respect, along with other useful survival skills.

At the root of this learning process is the manipulation of the material world (sensory-motor activity) and language (symbolic interaction) (Piaget 1970). These are the two instruments with which we construct our world. It is a world we jointly make, and it is charged with meaning both for ourselves and for others. From this perspective, we appear as eminently social beings. We use symbolic language to communicate; therefore, we are human. In addition, work and politics are major sources of sociality.

Marx suggested that human beings distinguish themselves from animals "as soon as they begin to *produce* their means of subsistence" (Marx 1978a, 150). But this life activity, their *work*, is in a deep sense of cooperative undertaking. Marx referred to humans as a species-being (*Gattungswesen*) in whom society and the autonomous individual compose a "unity of opposites" that can only be grasped from a dialectical standpoint (Avineri 1968, ch. 3).

---

ined our natural disposition to be one of universal warfare, a "dread Sovereign" must be introduced to control the inherent viciousness of human beings toward each other and so avoid their mutual self-destruction. The "dread Sovereign," however, is introduced into the model in an ad hoc manner, since by the rules of the game he cannot also conform to the specifications for everyone else. He alone, of all humanity, is exempted from vicious, self-regarding behavior; he alone acts benevolently, in the general interest.

15. Monadic individualism is usually accompanied by a situational ethics: So long as you do not hurt anyone else, do as you wish.

After language and work, the third and final source of sociality is political, and it is defined by membership in a political community. In its origins, the concept of a political community is a specifically Western conception, but its appeal is nearly universal. In ancient Greek, the word "to live" was the same as "to take part in communal life" (Jaeger 1976, 113). At no time was the political community more closely identified with all that is distinctively human.

> The polis is the sum of all its citizens and of all the aspects of their lives. It gives each citizen much, but it can demand all in return. Relentless and powerful, it imposes its way of life on each individual, and marks him for its own. From it are derived all the norms which govern the life of its citizens. Conduct that injures it is bad, conduct that helps it is good. This is the paradoxical result of the passionate effort to obtain the rights and equal status of each individual. All these efforts have forged the new chains of Law, to hold together the centrifugal energies of mankind, and to coordinate them far more successfully than in the old social order. Law is the objective expression of the state, and now Law has become king, as the Greeks later said—an invisible ruler who does not only prevent the strong from transgressing and bring the wrongdoer to justice, but issues positive commands to all the spheres of life which had once been governed by individual will and preference. Even the most intimate acts of the private life and the moral conduct of its citizens are by law prescribed and limited and defined. Thus, through the struggle to obtain law, the development of the state brings into being new and more differentiated principles of public and private life. (Ibid. 108–109)

Citizenship in the polis was, of course, highly restricted. Just before the Peloponnesian War, an estimated 43,000 individuals in Athens held full citizen rights, out of a total population of 317,000 (13.6 percent). The three essential requirements for citizenship were gender (male); descent (proper birthright, accompanied by acceptance into the societal units of family, clan, brotherhood, and tribe); and property (ownership or use of land) (C. G. Thomas 1981, 47–48). Even so, the idea of a self-governing community emerged with the Greek city-states of the classical period (750–350 B.C.). Although Athenians stood in awe before the law, they knew very well who made it: it was they themselves, gathered in assembly. And so the polis was a politically as well as morally transparent community. Being of human design, materially as physical city and spiritually as city-state, it could be improved and perfected. Plato's *Republic*, the first ideal community, was a creation of the polis. It was a remarkable discovery.

We can sum up our discussion by observing that human life is experienced at three distinct and interactive levels; that of *individuality*—our "self" which seeks its differentiated expression and development; that of *dyadic* or *dialogic* communication in small groups, such as family, friends, and work mates; and that of *collective, political experience*, where the self is understood as part of an overarching whole that has the authority to assert certain claims which may override individual desire. Although at different times each of these levels may be regarded as primary, they all insist on being taken seriously, demanding an adequate space for their expression.

Let us look more closely now at the third, or political, level, which manifests itself through membership in a political community. The polis was one such community. But for Americans, the concept of political community has a more immediate origin in the eighteenth-century theory of the social contract, that is, in the general proposition that we have elected to live a life in common with each other, within a territory that we co-inhabit. The social contract declares that we are prepared to create and sustain institutions that will further our common welfare.

> In the name of God, Amen. We, whose names are underwritten . . . do by these Present, solemnly and mutually in the Presence of God and one another, covenant and combine ourselves together into a civil Body Politik, for our better Ordering and Preservation, and Furtherance of the ends aforesaid; And by Virtue hereof do enact, constitute, and frame, such just and equal Laws, Ordinances, Acts, Constitutions, and Offices, from time to time, as shall be thought most meet and convenient for the General Good of the Colony; unto which we promise all due Submission and Obediance . . . Anno Domini, 1620. (Mayflower Compact, in S. G. Brown 1941)

Social compacts are occasionally explicit, as with this solemn declaration of the Puritan settlers en route to establish the first colony in the New World. Essentially, they are acts of constitution making. But for those of us who come after and find a world already made, *the social compact is the continuing choice we make for ourselves as citizens*. It is the way we assert our sovereign rights, as a people, over a given territorial domain.

People's political sovereignty extends both outwards and inwards. Toward the outside, the political community defends itself against external powers that threaten to restrict or abolish its own powers. Toward the inside, it asserts itself over the remaining domains of public action: the *state*, from which it demands both responsiveness to people's wishes and accountability for its actions; the *corporate economy*, from which it demands service of the common ends of the community; and *civil society*, from which it demands conduct in conformity with the moral norms agreed to in assembly.

Finally, the idea of people's sovereignty implies their right to change the nature of their compact, including the system of political order if need be, and to change the rules of the economic order as well. In other words, the social compact implies the unrestricted right of the community to transform even its most basic institutions.[16]

In addition to their sovereignty in the making of collective decisions, political communities have four characteristics which together define their essence: (1) they have a territorial base, (2) they enjoy historical continuity, (3) they are composed of citizen members, and (4) they are part of an ensemble of communities among which citizenship is shared. Territorial limits define the reach of a people's sovereignty. They also define the natural resources and physical environment that must sustain the livelihood of the people. Historical continuity suggests a common past and a shared destiny for which the people are collectively responsible. Citizenship entails both rights and obligations, including the obligation to take an active part in the life of the political community through such actions as speaking in assembly, public demonstrations, voting, and (when necessary) acts of civil disobedience. Finally, shared citizenship implies that we are simultaneously members of different political communities, ranging in scale from the village and city neighborhood to the emerging world community.[17]

16. The Virginia Bill of Rights of 1776 contains this remarkable passage.

> The government is, or ought to be instituted for the common benefit, protection, and security of the people, nation, or community; of all the various modes and forms of government, that is best which is capable of producing the greatest degree of happiness and safety, and is most effectively secured against the danger of maladministration; and that when any government is found inadequate or contrary to these purposes, a majority of the community has an indubitable, unalienable and indefensible right to reform, alter or abolish it, in such manner as shall be judged most conducive to the public weal. (S. G. Brown 1941, 34)

17. I am aware of the ideal nature of this description of a political community. The description is in terms of *values* rather than actually existing institutions and historical practices. Within itself, the political community is, of course, divided: that is the

The following discussion presupposes the reality of a public domain—a sphere of common discourse and concerns, along with the
institutions and laws that regulate conduct within it. Without this
sphere, there would be no planning, not even radical planning.
There would be only a Hobbesian struggle for individual advantage. But my insistence on the need for a public domain as the
ground for political practice goes further by arguing for a revival of
political activism that will shift political initiative from the state, re-
centering it in civil society where it rightfully belongs. I call it the recovery of political community. It is the central project of a reconstructive philosophy.

Social Reconstruction as Project

The project of social reconstruction can now be stated with greater
precision. In the latter half of the eighteenth century, the people in
their varied household formations—civil society—erupted from
their everyday lives into the public sphere in one small corner of the
world on the Atlantic Rim and laid a claim to this sphere as the sole
source of legitimate political power. They set about to construct a
new form of state—a civil state—and launched a new kind of economy, based on steam power, the factory system, and the unregulated market. With these actions, they initiated a period of unprecedented economic and territorial expansion.

SLAVERY ??

In time, two new domains of power emerged: the bourgeois state
and the corporate economy. Between them, they shared whatever
power they had, gradually strengthening their base of power
through the resources they controlled. Meanwhile, the people, who
for the most part were but poorly organized, returned to their main
business, which was to provide the bulk of low-cost labor to the new
industries and to spend such income as they earned (often mortgag-
ing their future income as well) on consumption for themselves. Except for periodic and mostly symbolic interventions, they withdrew
from the political domain, returning to it as active protagonists only
exceptionally. This was a workable arrangement until the present
crisis re-injected civil society into the political scene as an autonomous force. The evident failures of power, along the axis of state
and corporation, to meet, even minimally, people's needs and aspi-

reason for its politics. Politics involves power, and power involves coercion, deception, negotiation, domination, struggle. But this game of power is constrained by the
will to maintain a common life within fixed territorial boundaries. And so there is a
constitution, there are courts of law, there are habitual practices, and there are un-
spoken rules of conduct—the very stuff of which political communities are made.

rations has meant that today, just as in the eighteenth century, people are once more beginning to take the conduct of public affairs into their own hands (Boyte 1980; Castells 1983).

So, we have been here before. But the second time around, the conditions for people's intervention are very different from what they were two centuries ago. The arena now extends from the immediate locality to the entire globe. Forces of production have everywhere developed unevenly, and the gap between the "haves" and "have nots" is ever widening. World population is many times what it was in the eighteenth century and is continuing to expand by more than 2 percent each year. Machine-interposed communication is instantaneous between people anywhere on the surface of the earth and even into the far reaches of outer space. The resources and destructive potential of what we will soon be justified—what in a certain sense we are *already* justified—in calling the *ancien régime* are still immense and have the capacity to do great harm. The threat of spiritual and physical obliteration hangs in the air.

It is against this somber background that a new social project is taking form. Its objectives are several: individual and collective survival; acts of civil resistance to continued domination by forces that are alien to human life; and dedication to a living harmony with the natural world, so that life can be sustained with dignity for the ten to fifteen billion people who will inhabit the earth a century from now.

We do not yet have a name for the social project that is beginning to take shape. But we do know its general aim, which is to take possession of the terrain of political community, and to transform both state and corporate economy in ways that will place them at the service of human needs at all the relevant levels of public life.

And so, once again, it is the people who move to the center of the stage. Only this time there are no Bastilles to be stormed. In the industrialized countries, the work that needs doing must begin in small ways within local communities, neighborhoods, and the household itself—especially in the last, which is both an economy and a political community, the smallest social entity, and the protoplasm of the social order. It is within the household economy that the new relations of power are being forged, and it is from there that they will weave new patterns of social relation into the encompassing domains of public action.

In the wider struggles for a new society, the concerns of people's life space, which is the intimate sphere of everyday life, will be brought into sharper focus and relation with the economic space defined by work place and the still functioning markets for labor.[18] As Raymond Williams has so forcefully argued, to remake society more is needed than merely to change the dominant "mode of production" and to replace the market with central planning allocations. "The old orientation of raw material for production is rejected," writes Williams. "In its place there is the new orientation of livelihood: of practical, self-managing, self-renewing societies, in which people care first for each other, in a living world" (Williams 1983, 263–267).

The aim, then, of this revolution-in-the-making is not to "capture" the state or even to "smash" capitalism—those hollow phrases of another century—but to remake everyday life. Raymond Williams again finds the true words.

> If our central attention is on whole ways of life, there can be no reasonable contrast between emotions and rational intelligence. . . . This response can develop in several different directions, but where it is rooted in new concepts, now being steadily shaped, and in many kinds of relationship—forms of genuine bonding which are now being steadily renewed and explored—it is already creating the energies and the practical means of an alternative social order. (Ibid. 266–267)

The problem we face is, therefore, in the first instance, a political problem. At issue is the question of personal transformation in the course of changing human relationships. There are, of course, technical components of the political question, and the technical elements tend to increase as we extend ourselves into larger social domains. But the technical problems arise in the context of the political and the personal, which therefore must be addressed as a matter of first priority.

The next two chapters take up this challenge. The political and the personal dimensions of the new project are explored at different levels in Chapter 9. This is followed by an account of the role of the radical planner in furthering, with his or her technical ability and knowledge, the new order that is beginning to be formed.

18. This is particularly true for the politics of urban households in industrialized countries. For peasant populations, the situation is somewhat different and is best described by a concept of "agropolitan" development. On various occasions, I have proposed such a concept as a model for rural development in peripheral economies. (See Friedmann 1985.)

9   The Recovery of Political Community

A Central Guiding Vision

In the closing pages of his classic work, *Ideology and Utopia*, Karl Mannheim made a telling comment about the uses of the future in the present. As many planners do when faced with the sheer impenetrability of the future-as-knowledge, he opted for a future-as-moral-imperative.

> The only form in which the future presents itself to us is that of possibility, while the imperative, the "should," tells us which of these possibilities we should choose. As regards knowledge, the future—insofar as we are not concerned with the purely organized and rationalized part of it—presents itself as an impenetrable medium, an unyielding wall. And when our attempts to see through it are repulsed, we first become aware of the necessity of wilfully choosing our course and, in close connection with it, the need for an imperative (a utopia) to drive us onward. Only when we know what are the interests and the imperatives involved are we in a position to inquire into the possibilities of the present situation, and thus to gain our first insight into history. (Mannheim 1949a, 234; orig. 1929)

For Mannheim, utopia was an image of a transcendent future, a goal, a vision. Its purpose was to spur us on to action and give meaning to what, individually and collectively, we chose to do.

Mannheim's utopian imagery can be misleading. Unlike Fourier, he was not interested in painting agreeable phantasies but in picturing the "possibilities we choose." Centrally preoccupied with a future that is linked to the present, he was concerned with *realistic* utopias.

In this chapter, which sketches some dimensions of the world-historical project that is beginning to emerge, the central guiding vision is what I shall call the recovery of political community. The basic project was explained, somewhat abstractly, in the preceding

343

chapter. It is to shift the axis of power accumulation in society from the vertical, which connects the domain of the corporate economy to the state, to the horizontal, which relates civil society to political community. As its public face, political community is civil society organized for a life in common.[1] And at the core of this conception is the household economy as the first and smallest political community in history.[2]

Above the level of the household, political community takes the specific form of free political associations which, when gathered in assembly, can claim to speak the sovereign will of the people over their common affairs. This universal desire for an autonomous political life arises from within a group of people who, inhabiting the same physical space, empower themselves as the sole source of legitimate action within it.[3]

The justification of this claim to political sovereignty, which, it might be noted parenthetically, is not always successfully asserted, is the interweaving of individual destinies to which joint spatial occupancy contributes. Politics is destiny, and the claims to establish a just political order on the part of any people permanently inhabit-

1. My view of the political derives from Hannah Arendt (1958) and Sheldon Wolin (1960, 1982), and ultimately, of course, from Aristotle's *Politics* (1943). It has nothing to do with the vulgar use of the concept among behaviorists, for whom it signifies merely a struggle among contending interest groups for political power, material advantage, and domination (Lasswell 1936). According to Wolin, "A democratic conception of citizenship . . . means that the citizen is supposed to advance or protect the kind of polity that depends on his being involved in its common concerns" (Wolin 1982, 18). And the problem of a *revolutionary* politics is "to reinvent the forms and practices that will express a democratic conception of collective life" (Ibid. 25). It is in this double spirit that the present chapter is written.

2. The role of the household economy is crucial to the fortunes of the wider political community. I will deal with this in the next section. For now it will be sufficient to note that even though the household economy must be treated as a proto-political community, it cannot be reduced to this, just as it cannot be reduced, as an economy, to a set of social relations in production. Importantly, the household is characterized by strong bonds of affection and continuing mutual obligations of members toward each other—bonds and obligations that both infuse and transcend the household's political and economic dimensions.

3. This is a Rousseauian formulation. I do not wish to insist, however, on the totalitarian implications of Rousseau's *general will* or, of course, on the particularities of a "people's assembly." Nevertheless, the reference to an assembly is not without substance. It is meant to suggest a political system that is rooted in a gathering of the whole people at some level of governance, be it a neighborhood, village, or town. Following Rousseau, we would further posit a political system that is based on the delegation of power. Representative forms of government lead inevitably to a tyranny of minorities. (See Rousseau 1973, Pitkin 1967, and Colletti 1976.)

ing a given territory are difficult, on rational grounds, to deny. As
Michael Walzer has put it,

> [T]he principle of political justice is this: that the processes of
> self-determination through which a democratic state shapes its
> internal life, must be open, and equally open, to all those men
> and women who live within its territory, work in the local
> economy, and are subject to local law. (Walzer 1983, 60)

Although we may, as individuals, escape the common lot by emigra-
tion or death, the community survives the individual loss and, so
long as it survives, its future as a collectivity is a shared future. In
Walzer's words, it becomes a "community of character" a "historically stable, ongoing association of men and women with some special commitment to one another, some special sense of their common life" (ibid. 62).

This does not mean that all its members will be equally affected
by events. Much of the political game is simply an attempt by certain
individuals and groups to shift the distribution of the costs and benefits of any action in ways that will benefit themselves. What constrains self-interested actions, however, and prevents a Hobbesian
"war of all against all," is the recognition that human fates are intertwined, and that by driving one's (temporary) advantage to an extreme, one may, in the long run, place oneself and those for whom
one cares in serious jeopardy. As Fred Hirsch has pointed out, even
as an ideal form of laissez faire, capitalism requires a tacit recognition of shared interests as a condition of its survival (Hirsch 1976).

Characteristically, a given political community will extend its domain over a life space that is, in every case, a physically bounded
area.[4] Having shared their lives, collectively, over a period of time,
often for generations, the members of the community recall a com-

---

4. The boundaries of an area varies with the criterion that is applied. Political authority, for example, is sharply defined in the law but may extend de facto to a much
smaller or larger area, depending on the actual powers of the state to assert an effective presence. Also, political authority will be bounded differently for different purposes. Human rights, for example, tend to be bounded transnationally, while the
right to vote is limited by national constitutions. In addition, national boundaries
tend to inhibit the movement of people and commodities across them (though not
the movement of certain kinds of information), and although internal movement of
people, commodities, and information may be nominally unrestricted, invisible
boundaries of language and religion may, in practice, severely constrain it. Boundedness is thus an extremely complex subject. Nevertheless, politics and boundedness
coincide chiefly because of the crucial question of membership and formal political
authority (Walzer 1983).

mon history (though this history may be told from different vantage points), practice a common cultural discourse, and respect certain political traditions. Despite these basic commonalities, the community is not, within itself, a homogeneous body, but will be fractured into social classes and divisions based on gender, ethnicity, religion, and other associations. Additionally, it will be structured as a hierarchy based on an ascending scale of social integration. The nature of these vertical relations is defined in both custom and law. But expressing relations of dominance and oppression, they will themselves be fiercely contested.

Ranged between the household economy, which is the smallest political conception and the world economy, which is the largest, different levels of spatial integration can be identified. At the present time, the most generally acknowledged community is the national. For global relations, it offers the maximum of protection. But within the nation itself, there may be political communities at regional and urban levels that claim greater autonomy than they actually enjoy, and even urban neighborhoods and rural villages may be mobilized for a political life.

Independent of any spatial hierarchy is an internally differentiated structure of power that is determined by (1) the relative access of individuals and groups to the several forums of collective decision-making and (2) their ability, in these forums, to influence contested outcomes.

With respect to these fundamental divisions of power, a principle of equality is often asserted. Ideally, both access to decision-making and the capacity to influence decisions should be evenly distributed in the relevant population. Historical grounds for inequality are numerous, though differences of gender, ethnicity, class, and income are discovered at the base of virtually all systems of inequality. If people nevertheless insist on the value of equality in political life, the struggle against the bases of inequality, which is a struggle against oppression, must be seen as a permanent struggle.

The institutional conditions for this struggle are fundamental to the vitality of a political community. To function politically, people must have appropriate meeting places for discussing their common affairs. They must also have a guarantee of basic freedom or political rights that, in turn, must be protected by an independent judiciary and press. At a minimum, these rights include those of speech and assembly and, equally important though less widely recognized, freedom from poverty and from fear. None of these freedoms can be taken for granted. They are not gifts to be enjoyed, but high ground that must be won and defended against those who would deny or restrict them. Whenever freedoms are constrained and relative, a political community can be said to exist, if at all, only in forms that are repressed. The struggle for political community, therefore, must include the struggle for its basic grounding in liberty.

Beyond establishing these general conditions for a democratic life, what is meant by the call to reclaiming political community? Why should we make an inclusive democratic polity the central guiding vision for social reconstruction? The most general answer is that the existing imbalances of power in the public domain can be reduced, if at all, only through a reactivated political life that will draw the masses of those who now are relatively powerless into the processes of civil governance.

Forced to become political spectators and consumers, we spend much of our increased "leisure" time absorbed by television, video, and other forms of capital-intensive consumption.[5] We have been seduced into becoming secret accomplices in our own evisceration as active citizens. Two centuries after the battle cries of Liberty, Fraternity, and Justice, we remain as obedient as ever to a corporate state that is largely deaf to the genuine needs of people. And we have forfeited our identity as "producers" who are collectively responsible for our lives.

This situation is morally unacceptable; it is threatening to destroy the foundations of a vibrant civic life. The arrogant assumption of power by a state that has gained control over the principal media of manipulation, and that can harass citizens, divorce them from their livelihood, and threaten them with terror, and an economy that is increasingly controlled by a handful of global corporations whose interest in public benefits is zero, and whose very leadership remains, for the most part, anonymous and unaccountable to the political order, have led us to the growing disorder and unpredictability that we described in the preceding chapter.

The usual countervailing measures no longer suffice. The medicine that allowed an ailing system to limp along for a few decades—Keynesian policies at home, military interventions on the periph-

---

5. Fred Block cites statistics showing that the total number of hours worked in the American economy dropped from 1,045 per capita in 1910 to only 814 in 1979, which is a reduction of more than one fifth (Block 1984, 25). Along with other analysts, he believes that this secular trend, despite occasional reversals, will continue. For the household intent on producing its own life, the choice between paid work and other work will present itself as a genuine choice, since many and perhaps most jobs will be paid at levels much below the market cost of simple reproduction (that is, the so-called poverty line income).

ery—has failed us. Now miracle doctors of every sort promise quick cures: supply-side economics, deregulation, protectionism, religious crusades, immigration controls, constitutional limits on the national debt. With a desperate wish to believe, we try their counsel for a while, but as the sickness continues to spread, disenchantment inevitably sets in. The unthinkable is happening. The political strategies of peasant leaders defeat the war machines of imperialist aggressors. The countries of the semi-periphery, unable or unwilling to pay off massive external debts, are forcing American and European banks to lend them the interest that should be paid to themselves, thereby forestalling a global panic. The random holocaust has become routinely expected or, as Perrow (1984) calls it, a "normal accident." As negotiations on nuclear disarmament have been suspended, atomic scientists have advanced their doomsday clock to within two minutes of midnight.

In the final analysis, it is our instinct for collective survival that leads us to assert as our central guiding vision the recovery of political community from domination by the state and capital. As present contradictions mount, and as the crisis grows more severe, unprecedented opportunities present themselves for a broadly based social movement with inclusive aims.

○ To equalize, through continuing struggle, people's access, both individually and collectively, to the bases of effective social power, among them, the time and space, knowledge and skills, social and political organization, instruments and tools of production, information, social networks, and financial resources that are needed for the collective self-production of life.

○ To enhance people's capacity for independent critical thinking and acting.

○ To assert people's sovereign will at all levels of territorial life, subordinating both state and economy to the political community as the ultimate source of legitimate power in the public domain.

○ Selectively to de-link from the dominant system of market relations, substituting a rich mix of development objectives—social, environmental, economic, cultural, and political—that stresses quality over quantity and points the way to an achievement of a just world order.

○ To generate the main energy for such a development through self-reliant action from within each territorially based community.

The Collective Self-Production of Life

Capitalism introduced an unnatural division into human life. Under its dispensation, production was separated from consumption, work from leisure. Both were organized to serve the interests of capital: the first through labor markets, the second through markets for commodities.

Production was associated with pain for which labor would be compensated, theorists argued, according to the market value of the last unit of whatever they produced, while consumption was portrayed as unalloyed and carefree pleasure—"life"—which one presumably desired madly. In accord with Benthamite principles, the object of the game was for workers to maximize their pleasure and to minimize their pain.

For the most part, production took place in factories, shops, and offices under the immediate surveillance of managers and bosses. Capitalist production required a steely discipline in the organization of the work process, which the owners of capital had skillfully designed to extract the greatest value from the work of labor. Consumption, on the other hand, was regarded as an inherently private activity, carried out in the seclusion of one's home, where personal fancies might be licentiously indulged. Occasionally, paid work might filter into this sacrosanct place, which, during the daytime, belonged chiefly to women and their children, the men in the household being engaged in outside work. On the whole, however, and for reasons of labor discipline and the efficient functioning of labor markets, capital preferred to reinforce its functional division with a spatial separation of work place and home.[6]

This curious arrangement led to a conceptual separation of what people called "work" from "life," with the latter set equal not to what households produced for themselves, but to what they could afford to buy. In the glass-sheathed palaces of supermarket and department store, "life" was put on sale. But as one carried the shopping bags home, one waited in vain for the promised sense of fulfillment. In a perpetual chase of happiness, one would be spurred on to even greater efforts at consumption (Hirsch 1976). Freedom, we were told, meant choosing from among commodities offered for sale: more choice, more freedom.

Almost lost, as one sat down to dinner, was an acknowledgment that there was life activity in the home over which one had substantial control, without which the dinner one ate would never have

6. Capitalists claim their own rewards, it is said, as compensation for their stern self-denial. By postponing smaller pleasures now, they expect to reap greater rewards in the future. This self-denial is sometimes called the cost of capital, or interest.

been produced at all; without which one's children would die of neglect; without which one's home would be a dreary, dirty, lifeless place, unfit for human beings. Most of this productive activity fell on the shoulders of women, though their labors went generally unheralded. It was "just housework," people said; the exciting careers were in the public world, outside. This systematic devaluation of women's labor in the home—the true life activity in which, despite a gender division of labor, other household members would join from time to time, though the role of women was always the more important—was made plausible by the close identification of the household with consumption. Consumption, clearly, was not work. Women's identification with it subtly provided the essential erotic touch.[7]

The logic of this arrangement was vicious. If one were looking for an appropriate symbol to illustrate it, none better could be found

---

7. The gender split between the public and the private spheres, as well as the question of housework, is discussed in a number of feminist studies, among them Zaretsky (1976), Eisenstein (1979), Amsden (1980), Elshtain (1981), and Hayden (1981). The literature continues to flourish. A good part of the more recent work is reviewed from a socialist feminist perspective in Jagger (1983).

The discovery of the household economy as a fit subject for academic discussion is in large measure due to feminist writings. (But see Burns 1977 and Pahl 1984 for non-feminist approaches to the household economy.) It is feminists who first pointed to the household as a productive sphere, dramatizing their insights by demanding "wages for housework," a movement that, for a while, was especially popular in Mediterranean Europe and Canada (Jagger 1983, 329).

In an interesting shift of rhetoric with far more serious implications, Jagger stresses what she calls *procreative* work as opposed to merely *housework*. This new emphasis is especially popular with socialist feminists who have radical feminist (that is, lesbian) leanings. Their argument is that so long as procreation remains primarily women's work, true emancipation is impossible. "We have argued," write Brenner and Ramas, "that historically developed class relations of production, in combination with the biological facts of reproduction, set up a powerful dynamic toward the family-household system, assuring women's continued subordination to men and their exaggerated vulnerability to capitalist exploitation" (Brenner and Ramas 1984, 71). This is all very brave, but it is not clear what alternative the authors have in mind. Abolish children? Abandon them to the state? Abolish the household? But for what? It is curious that only negative solutions come to mind. On the side of affirmation, there is nothing except some vague allusion to the importance of "collective responsibility." (For a descriptive account of the family householding system within a socialist economy, that is, Hungary's, see Barta et al. 1984.)

I should like to emphasize that I am completely unsympathetic to this harsh and to my mind thoughtless rhetoric, which comes very close to saying that women's social emancipation will come about only when women cease to be women and men cease to be men, and both find meaning in loosely structured, androgynous relations within cooperative collective settings. I regard this prospect with a certain dread. It may all come to pass, but I would hope for something different.

than the television screen. Day in, day out, individually or as a group, household members sit huddled in front of the screen that glows into the semi-darkness, gazing at the commercial entertainment, the news, and the sports along with millions of other spectators equally mesmerized, not talking with one another except for laconic exchanges during the numerous commercial breaks, each person silently absorbed into the images dancing on his retina. Television is essentially a solo experience. It has the power to set the public agenda. The average American, it is said, watches more than thirty hours of television a week (World Almanac 1986, 366).

The logic of commodity consumption is for each consumer to feel the tactile sensations of pleasure on his or her skin. Each person with money to spend or capable of exerting pressure on those who have it is a potential consumer. Since there is nothing of any value "produced" at home, there is little need for contact and communication. All one has to do is hunker down by the tube; the rest—fast-food dinners, pizzas—can be ordered from the store.

So long as labor was in short supply, and social reproduction required women's presence in the home, the multi-person household was functional for capital. It allowed owners to pay wages that were below the costs of social reproduction. But with rising productivity and the arrival in the city of a continuing stream of migrants, the labor problem was essentially solved. And consumer conveniences, though not abolishing housework, did succeed in making things easier, so that even a single-person household could mange fairly well by itself.

The new logic was this: each multi-person household might split into separate household amoebas, each containing at least one live adult. The lot together would consume more than they might have done as a combined unit. Women would become independent of men, men independent of women, and children, barely adults, would be off by themselves somewhere, preferably independent of their parents. The singles life was huckstered like any other commodity, with images of fast cars, sexy bodies, hot tubs, and condominiums. As a single person, one was no longer responsible to anyone but oneself. I lead my life and you lead yours: human encounters are between an I and an I of limited commitment. By far the largest number of household formations in America during the present decade are of single persons (Masnick and Bane 1980).

But alone you do not "produce your own life." You work at a job (if you are lucky) and are paid well (if you are doubly lucky), but the job is "owned" by someone else, you do not control this work, and you either fall into line or get out. And when the work is done, and you collect your paycheck, you go home by yourself, you eat, you watch television, you meet a friend, you sleep. And you work out in the gym, and you drive your new car, and you make a down payment on a condominium, and your paid work becomes your life, because that is all you have left, and you need the money to meet the bills that keep mounting, and after a few years, you discover that life has slipped into the cracks; you feel cheated but do not know where to put the blame.

This report is on the charmed life in a southern California metropolis, but it is not unique. The ultimate alienation is simply more visible there than elsewhere. And for reasons too obscure to identify, it suggests an image so captivating and alluring that, if they could, half the world would move to southern California to buy into the glamorous life, where bodies stay forever young and one can live a carefree life in the eternal sunshine armed only with a credit card.[8]

What is wrong with this picture?

Nearly a century and a half ago, the young Karl Marx, working at fever pitch to develop what was to become the philosophical grounding of his later work, used the "production of life" to refer to all purposeful human activity. He meant it to become the central metaphor for his conception of what it means to be a human being. It was also the starting point for his historical and critical analysis of industrial capitalism.[9]

Two major themes flowed together in these early essays. The first we might call the *fundamental democratization* of history. With the American and French revolutions, common people had for the first time entered history as actors, pushing aside the princes and generals who heretofore had occupied the center of the stage. Both the

8. I am aware that I have not described the whole of reality with this sketch. For the 20 percent of the population who live in poverty, the picture I have drawn is irrelevant. It is irrelevant, too, for many of the new immigrant groups in this country seek to gain a foothold in the promised land, and for many other groups, but it holds out the standard to which all would aspire. And in some sense, the glamorous life of Malibu and Beverly Hills *is* attainable in a small way. If you are lucky and strike it rich, if you work hard, if you know the right people, you can make it like a "star." And if you don't, you can always dream about it or shoot your veins with heroin. We all dance around the golden calf.

9. The principal sources I have used include the *Economic and Philosophic Manuscripts of 1844* (Marx 1978d) and Part I of *The German Ideology* (1978b), which was written during the following year in collaboration with Frederick Engels. These essays are also important for the way Marx introduces the categories of alienation and estrangement, which form the basis for his theory of labor exploitation (Ollman 1980). In the present context, however, I do not propose to deal with this aspect of his work.

historical record and actually lived history, argued Marx, were concerned with the everyday social events of people, as they followed their normal pursuits in the material production of their lives. Civil society, which "has as its premise and basis the simple family and the multiple, so-called tribe . . . is the true source and theater of all history. . . . [It] embraces the whole material intercourse of individuals within a definite stage of the development of productive forces" (Marx 1978a, 163). With Marx was born not only the materialist conception of history, but also economic and social history, including the history of everyday life.

The second major, and closely related, theme is that of *radical humanism*. Human beings, says Marx, are the subjects of their own history. Ruled by neither destiny nor alien forces, their achievements and defeats arise out of constant creative activity and struggle. Of course, "circumstances make men, just as much as men make circumstances"; history is not a clean slate (ibid. 165). The world we live in is nevertheless a world we ourselves have made, and because we are its makers, it lies within our collective powers to transform it.

Marx's conception of an active and productive life had nothing in common with supermarkets or hunkering down by the television. To this basic position about human life, he added several additional themes.

1. All work requires the cooperation of others. And because the production of life appears inevitably as a social relation (as well as a relation to nature), humans must be regarded as fundamentally social beings (ibid. 175). Without cooperation among ourselves, we could not survive; genuine history would cease.

2. Conscious life activity is aimed, in the first instance, at the need to maintain one's physical existence. But it is not wholly absorbed by this need. Animals produce exclusively under the dominion of immediate physical need. But "man produces even where he is free from physical need *and only truly produces in freedom therefrom.* . . . Man . . . forms things in accordance with the laws of beauty" (Marx 1978d, 76; italics added).

It is characteristic of human beings, says Marx, that we develop always higher needs, once the needs at an earlier historical stage, including those of physical survival, have been met (Heller 1976). This comes about because, in producing our lives (and the environment enclosing them), we critically confront what we produce as part of an objective world. Man "contemplates himself in a world he has created" (Marx 1978d, 76). This objectification of his life leads to new existential needs.

History moves from need to need in spiral movements, as the product of free, conscious activity. It is the ultimate expression of freedom.

3. At this stage in the formulation of his ideas, Marx did not break down productive work into paid and nonpaid work. And he refused to draw a distinction between work as a means and as an end of life. Life activity, he asserted, stands in the service of existential needs. It is the ends and means of life at the same time. It is "life-engendering life . . . free, conscious activity. . . . Life itself appears only as a means of life" (ibid.).

Let us draw, then, the balance. Capitalism's unnatural arrangement was the separation of production from consumption, in which production was placed under the absolute authority of capital, while workers were left with the dubious freedom of consuming their wages at home. For most men, "life-engendering life" boiled down to working in shop or factory; for most women, it meant working at home, trying to make ends meet with paychecks that were always too little, and that would force them increasingly into the exchange economy, where they would offer their labor at cut-rate, complementary prices. Men regarded their home as a kind of refuge from the battle fronts of capitalism. For women, it was a soft prison. In the end, this prison-refuge was invaded by capital with its secret weapon of television, its endless stream of tawdry entertainment, ideological propaganda, and commercial messages capturing such consciousness as had not yet been absorbed in consumption and survival.

If we are going to recover political community for ourselves, it must be done from within restructured households that have shed their passivity and embraced the "production of life" as their central concern. To do this, we must learn to overcome the opposition between production and consumption, with its adjunct spatial and gender division of labor, overcome as well the opposition between pain and pleasure, and recover a sense of the wholeness of life. As a first step in this direction, we must recover the vision of the multi-person household as a unit of production—a household economy—and as a political community making decisions about its common life.

Arenas for Radical Practice

In outlining some aspects of an alternative to industrial (and post-industrial) capitalism, I am profoundly aware of my temerity in call-

ing it an emerging world-historical project. Mine is not merely a
personal view, however; I have culled from my readings, personal
contacts, and many involvements those elements that seem to be
leading the present search for another society and an alternative
practice. There are a great many people who, to a greater or lesser
extent, already share these visions, and who are working to bring
about relevant change.

Neither am I engaged in writing a political agenda. What is written here is simply a distillation of what a growing number of people
see as a *possible* alternative. The project remains radically open to actually lived history; experience alone will tell us the new directions
it must take. But for now, the past through which we have already
lived is the only source of knowledge we have.

Finally, a word needs to be said about the relation of the present
chapter to planning. In the next chapter, I will identify some tasks
for planners who have committed themselves to work for the alternative. Here, I wish to suggest the substance of what they will be
working on. For radical planners, it is not a matter of indifference
to the tasks, the people, and the ends they propose to work for.
They must themselves become a part of the alternative, not as "consultants for hire" but as committed partisans. As I suggested at the
end of Chapter 6, in radical planning, substance and process have
to be merged.

Four arenas for radical practice will be discussed. They are the
household economy, the regional nexus of work place and home,
the peasant periphery, and the global community. The central object in each arena is the recovery of political community.

The Household Economy

The first and foremost step in this great task is the restructuring of
bourgeois households for the self-production of life. The active life
must be grounded in the circle of intimacy which, in one of its aspects, the household appears to be. Individuals have difficulty
standing alone; by nature, women and men are social beings. And
the self-production of life requires not only a mutually cooperative
effort, involving sustained relations of reciprocity, but also biological reproduction and the nurturing of infants and small children.[10]
For both, the household economy still is and will continue to be the
optimal setting. Neither the state nor the market can provide fully
acceptable substitutes.

10. On the crucial question of reciprocity relations, see S. Price (1978).

In their specific forms and appearance, household formations are a historical construct that is continuously in flux, more so at present, perhaps, than at any other time in history. I propose to write about the household from the perspective of the collective self-production of life. Accordingly, I shall designate by household any social arrangement, sustained over an extended period, that involves a small number of persons—such as lovers, spouses, children, relatives, and friends—who regard their lives as being closely linked to each other, and who customarily make joint decisions concerning the use of their pooled resources of time, energy, and skill. This definition has three principal aspects.

The first is the *circle of intimacy*, or primary closeness. Households tend to come into being when two or more persons decide to share their lives in close proximity to one another, to live, as it were, "under one roof." People may, of course, come together for other reasons as well, but a sense of intimacy, even when it is not sexual, is always present in households. Without a sense of primary closeness, no "life-engendering life" in Marx's sense is possible. In its absence, living together becomes a purely functional arrangement in which individual self-interest is advanced at the expense of the group.

The second principal aspect of householding is *economic*. Above a certain minimum age, each household member commands certain resources, including his or her time, energy, knowledge, and skills.[11] For the well-being of the household as a whole, these resources are, as it were, pooled before they are reallocated to the five different spheres (discussed below) in the collective self-production of life.[12]

A necessarily substantial part of all household resources is invested, first, in the *sphere of the household* itself, where it is used for the care and rearing of children, routine housework, the preparation and eating of meals, home repair work, gardening, caring for the sick and frail, entertaining friends, pursuing personal interests, and so on.

The second sphere that absorbs household resources is the *market*, involving both the sale of labor in appropriate markets and the purchase of commodities for household use. (Since travel is often required, the time, cost, and mode of travel must also be counted in

11. The minimum age may be quite low. Even a three-year-old may perform small household tasks, and at five, most American children are already in school. It could be argued that age is irrelevant. Interpersonal relations bring their own satisfactions, and the small child may contribute more to the household's sense of well-being than a truculent twelve-year-old helping out in the kitchen.

12. This reallocation implies a political process that is not without bitter conflict. As everyone knows, the circle of intimacy is not always harmonious.

this sphere. Another critical variable is the choice of work place, especially in terms of commuting distance.)

The third sphere of household resource allocation is *civil society*, which may include neighborhood projects such as car pooling and urban agriculture, participating in a housing cooperative, informal education, and a wide range of unpaid voluntary activities in church and community.

The fourth sphere in which the household can invest its energies is the wider *political community* of which it is a part, involving activism on behalf of specific causes such as a nuclear freeze, solar energy, neighborhood government, the thirty-five-hour workweek, equal rights, and so forth.

Finally, there is the sphere of the *state*, which demands it share of taxes, a fraction of the householder's time for jury duty, obligatory school attendence on the part of the young, and, during wartime, military service.

The situation facing the household economy is similar to that of any economic unit that is trying to balance its budget. The claims against it are numerous, and they cannot all be satisfied. Thus, only some claims will be selected for an investment of the household's central resources, with the result that the tasks of individual members may be reassigned; savings in one sphere, such as the market, may be used to augment resources in another; claims may be shifted between spheres, as from household to civil society; flexible time arrangements may be sought; travel time may become an important variable. It is clear, then, that complex decisions have to be made. And as a unit which the members must make joint decisions about the use of the household's combined resources for the common good, it reveals its third major aspect, which is that of a *political community*.

Traditionally, households have not been viewed as political, though feminists have pressed the contrary assertion (Hartmann 1981). It is nevertheless evident that, aside from the need to budget its resources, the household meets a number of the formal criteria that define a polity: in its home it has a territorial base; it has a history; and its members may speak a language of gestures, expressions, words, and even dialect among themselves as a token of their feelings of primary closeness. Householding is also a voluntary arrangement (though not for small children), and it may at any time be dissolved, though often at the cost of considerable pain for those involved. More significantly, households, like any other political community, have an internal structure of power: their members have different degrees of access to the bases of social power, especially in their knowledge of the outside world, and a different say-so in household decisions. Although the traditional structure of American households is still male-dominated, the pattern appears to be changing.[13]

This division of the household into circles of intimacy, economy, and political community is useful for purposes of exposition. They are aspects of households which, in practice, function as single, indivisible units. Occasionally, one or the other aspect may dominate, as when the political rises to preeminence in the struggle for the democratization of a household's internal decision processes. Even then, however, the facts of primary closeness and those of economics cannot be ignored. Indeed, the struggle for democratization necessarily touches on all household characteristics and is likely to demand a restructuring of expectations, resource allocations, and social roles that is so far-reaching, it may strain household cohesion to the breaking point.

So far, we have confined discussion to definitional issues from a perspective that sees the household as primarily engaged in the "self-production of life." But what must be done to bring the actually existing household in line with this new understanding?[14] The agenda of action for the recovery of political community begins at this point. It includes the decolonization of the household, its democratization, its self-empowerment, and its reaching out.

Decolonization. To gain their autonomy and to transform themselves into politically active, producing units, households must selectively de-link from the system that keeps them in servitude. Their allocation of time to the exchange economy must be reduced so that resources can be gained for other activities. Households must learn to be more self-reliant in the production of life and do for themselves what they used to obtain from the market.

One of the easiest and most straightforward paths to this end is to cut off television and video as pre-programmed, attention-focusing

13. The extent of male domination in multi-person households probably varies a good deal according to social class, ethnicity, regional folkways, and religion. It is, in any event, not an absolute dominance. In many spheres, such as household management, the children's education, and relations to civil society, the dominant force is likely to be the woman. Whatever the case, the changing political structure of American households is not very well understood and suggests the need for a great deal more research.

14. Since no single form of bourgeois household exists, this is obviously an abstract and schematic way of speaking. What I wish to emphasize is the household's role within industrial capitalism as an entity devoted to passive consumption—an entity which, in its ultimate form, is reduced to the so-called single-person household.

technologies that absorb inordinate amounts of household time even as they colonize one's consciousness and impede critical thinking. The time so saved can be immediately reallocated to self-generated activity in any of the remaining spheres of household production: in the household itself, for example, or with groups of neighbors in cooperative projects (Hayden 1984).

Selective de-linking is portrayed here as a voluntary act. But for many workers it may present itself as a choice that is forced, for instance, when their jobs are suddenly declared redundant. German workers have recently carried out a fierce struggle for the thirty-five-hour week as a means to redistribute work and reduce the amount of open unemployment (Vilmar 1976). In this, they have been partially successful. Similar demands are beginning to be voiced in the United States (Bergman 1984; Block 1984). Over the next twenty years, it is almost certain that the average workweek will be reduced on the side of production. This reduction, too, represents a partial de-linking from the market economy, at least in the labor aspect.

In any event, with the prospect of further industrial decline, social polarization, economic stress, and hyper-inflation, it is not unreasonable to suppose that households will become increasingly self-reliant, using from the economy what they need for the self-production of their lives, and little more. The trend is already underway (Gershuny 1978, 1983; Pahl 1984).

Democratization. It is a basic principle of household economics that there are no unused, redundant resources: every member of a household is a valuable contributor to the well-being of all the other members.[15] Attractive though it is, this formulation implies a fundamental democratization of decision processes that goes considerably beyond the actual practices of bourgeois families. Any hierarchy of decision-making among household members constitutes, in itself, a violation of the circle of intimacy which, ideally, is based on openness, dialogue, and trust. It sets up a class basis for relationships inside the household, where traditionally women and children have belonged to a socially inferior class: "Children are to be seen, not heard." Such hierarchies are divisive.

In the division of tasks among household members, differences in

15. It must be stressed that, in abstract terms, the time of every household member should be valued equally. Thus, the mother's time will be on a par with that of her infant child; the son's time, spent studying, is equal in worth to the father's; and so forth. The *strategic importance* attached to the use of this time will vary, but there is no a priori hierarchy of value-in-use.

technical ability, knowledge, and experience must, of course, be respected. On the other hand, women are not naturally endowed with
less ability than men, and in some capabilities, the younger members of the household often exceed their parents. In modern industrialized society, there is no a priori justification for a gender- or
age-based division of labor.

The democratization of decision-making also assumes a leveling
of differences, to the extent that it is possible, in access to the bases
of social power. One focus for this leveling process involves the
space inside the home, and the need for each member to have his or
her own territorial domain. Another is knowledge, particularly the
knowledge that is gained by engaging in outside activities. The condition of democratization demands an equal sharing of inside and
outside tasks, so that no one person gains an undue advantage from
being exposed to challenging and unfamiliar environments.

In the bourgeois household, public and private spheres are
sharply separated in space and by gender: the first is the man's
world, the second the woman's. In a restructured household, this
line of demarcation between public and private would change from
threshold to zone. Their meanings would change as well. The private would remain the sphere of intimacy for both men and women.
As an exclusive sharing of life with a small number of others, this
sphere must be protected against unwelcome intrusions from the
outside.[16] The public sphere encompasses all the rest and would be
accessible to both as the household economy invests its combined resources in the domains of civil society, economy, political community, and the state.

Self-Empowerment. Social power is the power one needs to produce
one's own life in reciprocal exchange with others. Seven bases of social power can be identified, and households that wish to move toward the collective self-production of life must seek to improve
their access to these bases of power and build their strength in those
areas where they are weak. Some examples will help to illustrate this
point.

    ○ Time. Time for the self-production of life can be gained by
       reducing the consumption of commodities, and by reducing

16. Even this sphere, however, cannot remain wholly private, but must be protected against possible abuses of human rights, exploitation, and violence. Within the
sphere of intimate relations, therefore, individuals also enjoy certain public rights.
By the same token, they must learn to respect public duties, such as civility toward
neighbors, an ecological ethic, and so forth. The sphere of intimacy is surrounded by
and interpenetrates a public sphere in which all participate.

the household's participation in the labor market through various time-sharing arrangements already under active consideration in Western Europe, such as one job for two, flexitime, paternity leaves, sabbaticals, and others (ILO, 1979).

○ Space. Each household needs a space that is adequate for the self-production of life. This requirement underlies the fierce struggle for housing that continues unabated throughout the world (Turner 1977). Especially for poor people, gaining control over adequate housing space requires some form of cooperation with other households. The design of household space must take into consideration the variable needs of each household, including space for larger household units; cooperative arrangements for cooking, eating, and child care; and common access to tools (Hayden 1984).

○ Knowledge and skills. Skills can be learned through formal teaching and through practice, and because people often have quite different skills of which they are proud, the possibilities of teaching each other without the exchange of money are nearly endless (Illich 1971). Knowledge in the sense of an ability to draw information from the environment, to make sense of it, and to think critically about it is more difficult and requires as a first step a de-linking from the main sources of disinformation (popular magazines, television). The best way of learning, however, is by direct engagement in the world and, in open discussion with others, by reflecting on the meanings of what one has seen and experienced. Learning and study centers for regenerative practice can be organized in every neighborhood, linked by computer.

○ Organization. The amount of self-organization within civil society is already at an impressively high level in the United States. One gets a sense of this by looking at umbrella programs such as the Catholic Church's Campaign for Human Development or the Youth Project.[17] The organizations they help to finance in very modest ways are citizen-based: they bring households together in small organizational formats that remain under the direct control of the membership. It is

17. The addresses of these organizations are: The Campaign for Human Development, United States Catholic Conference, 1312 Massachusetts Avenue, N.W., Washington, D.C., 20005, and The Youth Project, 1555 Connecticut Avenue, Washington, D.C., 20026.

through organizations of this sort that people can reclaim control over their life space.

These and other paths to self-empowerment will lead to greater citizen involvement with organizations in the political community, as activists join the long struggle to restructure the state, to make it more responsive to the community, and to achieve the wider goals of social justice in the distribution of societal resources and the treatment of persons. Out of local efforts to gain control over the life space of individual households come social movements with the potential to make a difference in the larger society (Castells 1983).

Reaching Out. The process of self-empowerment implies a reaching outward to successively wider networks of people, as households link up in common struggle to resume control over their lives and their environment. Collective self-empowerment implies connecting with others; there is strength in combined action. Not all potential linkages will be of a territorial nature; some will be functionally organized. But in either case, the inwardness of households will be strengthened through collective involvements, which themselves will become major projects for the investment of household resources.

It is for this reason that a restructuring of the household as both an economy and a political community is the first step toward the recovery of political community at the level of the whole society. Without decolonizing the household domain, without its democratization as a political community, without its self-empowerment as a collective actor in the public domain, without its reaching out to other households in cooperative action to achieve an alternative vision of the future, nothing can be done. So long as people allow themselves to be brainwashed by the media, they will make their peace with a system that holds out to them false promises of happiness. So long as there is patriarchy in the home, women will not achieve equal rights. So long as there is hierarchy in the home, households will accommodate to hierarchy outside and assume that it is natural. So long as people remain locked up in privacy, they remain powerless to affect the world for either good or bad. They remain as objects in the world.

But people are not sitting still. The self-production of life is not a chimera, but increasingly and everywhere a palpable reality. People are beginning to divest themselves of the attitudes and roles they were taught in an earlier era. Despite mistakes and occasional defeats, the political terrain of the household economy is the first to be liberated.

The Regional Nexus of Work Place and Home

Even though the household is regarded as "producing" its own life, a large part of its resources will continue to be invested in paid work in metropolitan labor markets. Participation in these markets raises a new set of political issues and a corresponding agenda for action which, under the impact of industrial capitalism, arises from the separation of political and economic space.

In the preceding section, the household was described as a proto-political community with its own territorial base in the home. The classical political community, however, is not the household but the urban commune.[18] Extending as far back as the Greek city-state, or polis, its traditions are beautifully evoked in the passage quoted earlier from Werner Jaeger's paradigmatic study, *Paideia*. Although its basis was religious, it already contained the major elements that were to form the classical idea of a political community: it was urban, small in scale, bounded against the outside world, governed by laws that were made and enforced by its own citizens, and self-reliant in all things.

This is not the place to recall the history of the commune as an autonomous, self-governing social formation.[19] Its period of great flowering was during the Middle Ages in northern Italy (Martines 1979) and northern Germany (Rorig 1967). As a covenant, it formed the basis of early North American settlement. And Jean Jacques Rousseau, though condemned to a nomadic life, longed to be readmitted as a citizen of Geneva and in all his political writings celebrated the commune.[20]

---

18. The use of the term *commune* in the political sense has become all but extinct in the United States. It will therefore be helpful to recall the dictionary definition.

commune *n.* **1.** The smallest administrative division in France, Italy, Switzerland, etc. governed by a mayor assisted by a city council. **2.** any community organized for local interests, and subordinate to the state. **3.** the government or citizens of a commune. **4.** a close-knit community of people seeking radical personal changes. **5.** see *people's commune*. **6.** *The Commune. Also called* Commune of Paris. *a*) A revolutionary committee that took control of the government of Paris, 1789–1794. *b*) a socialist government of Paris from March 18 to May 27, 1871. (*The Random House College Dictionary*, 1975)

Note the emphasis on self-governance; on the identity of commune as people, government, and territory; on the commonality of interests; on the historicity of the commune; and on its popular, radical tradition.

19. This history is reviewed in Friedmann (1982).

20. Rousseau's political philosophy only makes sense if we interpret it not in the context of the nation-state which was about to emerge, but in the context of the urban communal tradition in which he himself had been raised. One of the best essays dealing with Rousseau's political thought is by Manuel and Manuel (1979, ch. 17).

From this history and the theories to which it gave rise emerge the principal elements of the communal tradition.

○ Political community. The commune is conceived as a corporate entity that has come into being as the result of a "sacred covenant" among its founding members to further and protect their common interests in perpetuity.

○ Sovereign will. The commune is a politically bounded social formation whose sovereign institutions of governance extend over a finite territory or homeland.

○ Continuity in time. As a territorially (and therefore politically) integrated society, the commune acquires a history that extends forward from its original foundation and, intersecting with the present, points toward a common destiny or future.

○ Size. The commune is typically small. Historically, the vast majority of communes have had populations of fewer than 50,000 people. However, they have generally been large enough to provide for a sufficient life.

○ Accountability. All power exercised in the name of the commune is ultimately accountable to the body of its citizens meeting in assembly.

○ Reciprocal claims. The relation of the individual citizen to the commune (that is, to the territorial expression of the political community) is one of reciprocal claims. The citizen has a right to the satisfaction of fundamental human needs that are recognized by the commune. In return for ensuring the citizen's livelihood and safety, the commune can demand appropriate contributions in money or in kind from its adult members.

○ Linkage. The commune is an "open" community joined to other communes through trade and political alliances. However, like all alliances, trade agreements are subject to review and control by the political institutions of the commune.

The communal tradition, then, is one of a political autonomy. Whatever its institutional form, it refers to the body of all citizens gathered in political assembly. (Over the centuries, the definition of who was a citizen became more and more inclusive.) The commune thus stands apart from the local state, which is meant to be merely the executive instrument of its will (Barber 1984).

With the coming of industrial capitalism, three things happened that fundamentally altered this relationship between citizen and state. First, the local state was subsumed as an administrative unit under the national state, which became the political formation that for the next two-hundred years would facilitate and promote the rise of industrial capital. Second, reversing roles with the political community, the national state demanded and, for the most part, obtained the loyalty and allegiance of each citizen, who was thus weaned from his or her identification with the local commune. And third, the state became thoroughly bureaucratized; it became "the administration."

One result of these changes, which for the most part took place during the nineteenth century, was the gradual depoliticization of urban space. Political community grew increasingly weak and its behavior ritualistic. As an economically structured space rose to dominate it, the classical city, as the original embodiment of political community, became, in George Sternlieb's brutal but revealing phrase, a "sandbox."

The structure of space produced by industrial capital to serve its needs can be studied at two levels: (1) the *metropolitan*, reflecting closure of local labor markets as well as localized inter-industry relations, and (2) the *inter-regional* or global.

What can be said about economic space in relation to the existing political spaces over which it extends its dominion?

1. In its physical dimension, economic space exceeds political space at the levels of both commune and nation.

2. Economic space is relatively open to resource flows; it has no boundaries. Political space, on the other hand, is by definition bounded, proclaiming the sovereignty of a people over a given territorial domain. Political boundaries tend to impede economic flows. At the national level, they have much the same effect as would increasing the "friction of distance" between two places.

3. Economic space is efficiently organized for capital accumulation.[21] It is also, and for this very reason, only minimally controlled by political authority, particularly at the level of the classical city. In Manuel Castells's expressive phrase, economic space is a "wild city" (Castells 1976).

4. Economic space generates a primary distribution of income for local communities; that is, it generates a pattern of income

21. This has been elegantly demonstrated for Japan by Koichi Mera (1975).

inequalities that can ultimately be "corrected" in the direction of greater equality only through a political process.[22]

5. Economic space has allowed capital to shift the social costs of production to the political community in two principal ways.

a. Through direct and indirect subsidies that may take form of tax exemptions, gifts of land, low-interest loans, public infrastructure investments, artificially low utility rates, and the costs of the social reproduction of labor.

b. Through direct social costs, such as unemployment, poverty, deteriorated housing, homelessness, pollution, traffic congestion, and the long litany of other well-known evils, imposed on the political community in the form of budgeted expenditures by capital.

These costs appear to be rising quite rapidly. To escape their spiraling impact, many middle- and upper-income people have moved into suburban enclaves and rural towns, pulling along the businesses that cater to their needs and whims. This migration has imposed a double burden on central cities, which now have to cope not only with the normal impacts of capital restructuring but also with the costs generated by the massive abandonment of central cities by those most able to pay for urban services. Reinforced by a sharp decline in the volume of federal transfers to local governments, this polarization of metropolitan space has generated a fiscal crisis without precedent (O'Connor 1973). The social costs of production have become literally unmanageable.[23]

Economic space, then, obeying a very different dynamic, has outgrown the urban commune on its limited domain. This dramatic event has forced the latter's energies into largely residentiary matters or, as Castells has called them, issues of "collective consumption" (Castells 1983).[24] This disjunction of what had once been an organically integrated space centered on the household economy was made possible not only by the increasing scale of economic activities and the metropolitan-wide and even global coordination of production, but by the fact that people with social ties and commit-

22. This principle lies at the root of welfare economics, which traditionally has been more concerned with the question of income distribution than with the "objective" question of the generation of income and the allocation of resources (Little 1957).

23. There are serious fiscal crises also at the level of the national state, especially in the countries of the peasant periphery, but these have a different origin.

24. Castells's whole approach to the city is unfortunately limited by his persistent neglect of urban production.

ments are far less mobile than money. They hesitate moving to where they are strangers (if indeed they are allowed to settle there at all) and tend to value the close-knit relations that we signify with words such as family and community (Marris 1975). Of course, they do move for various reasons, though more reluctantly as the potential distance increases, as frontiers must be crossed, or as new cultural experiences are demanded. But at whatever distance, they move less easily than capital, which, driven by competition, is constantly in search of high profit horizons, and for which infinite geographical mobility is of the essence.

Earlier, in characterizing the communal tradition, I observed that as a political space it is typically quite small. A look at data for the United States are revealing in this regard. In cities of 10,000 or more population in 1978, 81 percent turn out to have had fewer than 50,000 inhabitants, 92 percent fewer than 100,000, and fully 97 percent fewer than a quarter million (*Statistical Abstract of the U.S.* 1978, Table 23). In addition, virtually all townships, constituting nearly 17,000 units, had fewer than 100,000 inhabitants.

Given our national fixation on economic space—the metropolitan giants—the corresponding proportion of total urban population are equally significant. In 1978, fully half the urban people of the United States lived in cities of between 10,000 and 100,000 inhabitants and nearly two thirds lived in cities of fewer than 250,000 people. Moreover, these ratios were significantly higher than they had been in 1960, when they stood at 43 and 56 percent, respectively. The popular view of the United States as a nation of urban giants is one-sided and misleading. It is a view colored by an economic lens. If we take *city* to mean a political unit, we can as readily conclude that Americans, even as they work within a metropolis, are a predominantly small-town folk!

In contrast to the structures of capital, which from the beginning tended toward the limitless spaces of the globe, the urban commune has always been small (Dahl and Tufte 1973). What surprises us, then, is not that urban life in the United States (and indeed elsewhere) is scaled to a small population size, *but that it has survived at that scale*. The relatively small size of most urban communes suggests that quite possibly a size in excess of a quarter million or even 100,000 may be less than optimal for the workings of a political community, that is, for self-governance.[25]

For most households, the physical space of the urban commune

25. There is a good deal of evidence that, from a management standpoint as well, small cities make sense. (See Zimmerman 1972.)

also constitutes their life space, in the sense that it is here, in close proximity to their homes, that households customarily invest most of their resources in the production of life. The size of this space will vary, but for the sake of this argument, let it be an area with a travel radius of 1 mile (3.14 square miles) and a population of between 10 and 20 thousand. According to recent surveys, 10 percent of U.S. household heads work either at home or within 1 mile from home. In addition, most small children attend neighborhood schools, most convenience shopping is done within this area, much neighboring and visiting takes place there, and a good deal of daily and weekend recreation occurs within it. The point I wish to stress is that much of one's life is lived at an extremely local scale.

If we now extend the travel radius to 4 miles, an even larger proportion of a household's effective life space is included. The work places of nearly 40 percent of all household heads are found within this area, together with most of the household's educational activities, social visiting, shopping, and recreation. No longer a neighborhood, it has grown to 50 square miles, larger than the area of many medium-sized American cities.[26] And the corresponding population may run up to a quarter million.

Four miles from home is not, in American terms, a great distance. By car one can traverse it in about 15 minutes. Within a quarter of an hour, then, households can satisfy most of their everyday needs.[27] And this is probably the key to why the small commune has persisted throughout history. Because households' life space and political community are virtually identical, political interaction has a different meaning here than if it were suddenly blown up to, say, metropolitan scale, where high-level abstractions, bureaucratic apparatus, and scientific managers prevail. People, it seems, like their politics on an intimate scale.

Beyond the life space of households, of course, there remains the "wild city" of economic space, created by capital, where people look for work that is paid. For the 60 percent or so who are not in local employment, labor markets extend out from the home for upwards

26. Pasadena, California, for example, has an area of 23 square miles; Lansing, Michigan, 33 square miles; and Allentown, Pennsylvania, 18 square miles.

27. The only study that has attempted to map human activity patterns in urban America was done by Stuart Chapin, Jr. in 1968 (Chapin 1974). Chapin's city is Washington, D.C., and he shows travel distances that, in some cases, are greater than those we have assumed. Thus, in 1968, the locus of shopping activities was, on average, 6 miles from home, reflecting trips to suburban shopping centers. Socializing, recreation, and other out-of-home activities, however, were all contained within an average radius of 3.5 miles.

of 30 miles—1 hour's driving distance. If we were to draw for an aggregate of all households in a metropolitan area a frequency distribution of the time spent by household members in different locations, we would obtain a bimodal distribution of space use over any 24-hour period on weekdays. The bulk would be centered on the home, but the second major concentration would cluster around the distant work place. These two "bulges" in the distribution of space/time would be connected by "ridges" along the most frequently traveled corridors.

From a perspective of political action, two problems emerge from this analysis of the juxtaposition—symbiotic yet contradictory—of economic and political space (the latter identical with the urban commune and roughly consistent with the life space of households).

1. The imposition by capital of the social costs of production on the political community may be viewed as a form of taxation without representation. It is as if a foreign prince were to exact tribute from the city. The "wild city" of economic space must therefore be "tamed," and mobile capital must come, in at least some of its aspects, under the direct control of the relevant political community. The social cost of enterprise must be internalized within the enterprise itself. Although it is likely to slow down the rate of capital accumulation, this practice would help to reverse the entropic course on which we are embarked and, at the same time, enlarge the scope of the household economy.

2. The urban commune, which by constrast with economic space is the city of political order, has to become more self-reliant. In line with the new household economy, it must change from a predominant orientation with collective consumption to one more consistent with the collective self-production of life (Morris 1982, 1984; Ross and Usher 1986).[28]

What specifically can be done to promote these broad purposes? As with the household economy, I do not wish to prescribe a detailed agenda; I would rather suggest the general direction that political action might take.

To tame the wild city, the first step would be to extend an effective political space to the approximate limits of economic space at the metropolitan scales. This strategy would diminish capital's ability to use its built-in mobility as a threat when negotiating for advantages

28. A third problem, which I will not address, is the possible down scaling of political communities that exceed the "optimal" size theshold of 250,000 (100,000?). The problem has been discussed by Kotler (1969).

with local communities, and it would enable the community to impose a tax on enterprise commensurate with the social costs that, in the past, had to be absorbed.

To suggest the expansion of political space to the limits of the metropolis is not, however, intended to weaken existing urban communes, most of which are at the appropriate size for political interaction and self-governance. Rather, it is intended to strengthen them by giving them a legislative voice in a *federated* metropolitan assembly with the power to make laws, subject to ratification by local councils for the entire region.

The present structure of Councils of Governments, which came out of the urban crisis of the sixties, has become obsolete. The formation of a regional legislative assembly, with delegates chosen from local city councils, would enable the political community—so enlarged—to deal with economic questions at a level that is also relevant for capital. It would create another level of political community above that of the urban commune through the instrumentality of a Proudhonian federation.[29]

Once an appropriate political structure has been established, a number of practical things become possible that will slow down the processes of economic restructuring, which are among the major immediate generators of social costs (Bluestone and Harrison

29. See Proudhon (1979). According to Stanley Hoffman:

> The function of the areal division of powers which Proudhon proposes in his *Principe Federatif* is, thus, not to provide for the best political ordering of a democratic community but first to create a framework in which producers and consumers will be the masters of their fate. Political federalism and economic federalism are mingled; the territorial units are, in a word, the shells of economic decentralization. Secondly, the areal division has the function of making a thorough dismantling of state power possible, by replacing as much as possible the law, the symbol of coercion, with the contract, the symbol of liberty.
>
> Hence the curious features of Proudhon's federalism: a strictly contractual construction, in which the contract would really be an agreement to give-and-take, and not, as in Rousseau, a unilateral oath; a system, in which the bigger the unit, the fewer powers it would have—the more numerous the participants, the fewer the common powers would be; a scheme in which the relations between the various levels would be relations of *subordination of the higher to the lower*. The central common government would have power of initiative, but not of execution. The public servies, once created by it, would be run by the public, these including education, justice, and the army, in peacetime. (Hoffman 1959, 133)

This essentially anarchistic solution would unquestioningly require constitutional changes at the state level; it would also substantially reduce the power of the federal states. The present proposal is therefore a "utopian" one.

1982). For instance, before a firm above a certain threshold size may be allowed to close its regional operations, it might be required to give adequate public notice of its intention to do so, allowing workers and local communities to make an appropriate response. Should the firm nevertheless persist in its plans, it might have to pay a severance tax whose proceeds could be used to compensate the community for the loss of employment and other, secondary effects. In addition, it might be compelled to give first option on any infrastructure it intends to leave behind to the local community or its workers. Levying a corporate development tax on large firms would tend to make these firms more socially responsible and help with the upgrading of infrastructure throughout the region.[30]

The second objective, to move toward greater local self-reliance, suggests at least three kinds of possible action.

    1. Developing small businesses, including joint ventures, with community capital and worker-owned enterprise (Carnoy and Shearer 1980; Bowles et al. 1983). Numerous benefits would flow from the implementation of this strategy.

        a. It would generate investment within the community itself.
        b. It would generate new employment (small business firms tend to generate more jobs per unit of investment than do larger firms).
        c. It would raise the density of employment within the life space of households from the present 40 percent to perhaps 60 percent within a 4-mile radius, thus reducing commuting time and encouraging a more flexible integration of the household economy with the exchange economy.
        d. It would stabilize the local economy, allowing it, because

30. A difficulty with this proposal is that footloose capital is free to locate anywhere and can use its high mobility to extract concessions from local communities. The only solution to this situation is to pass mandatory national legislation. Although this might drive some industries overseas, the losses so incurred are likely to be more than made up by gains in community welfare.

It seems highly improbable that such legislation will ever be passed, unless the hazards to the community can be made clearly visible. The nuclear energy industry, for instance, has had to comply with very stringent safety regulations and has been forced to internalize these costs. The result has been a significant slowdown in the construction of nuclear power plants, with more serious consideration being given to alternative, less hazardous sources of energy. This victory of the environmental movement is a clear instance of a campaign that was intended to create public awareness leading to a new legislative framework for nuclear power investments (Brown 1984).

of its lesser dependence on outside capital, to bargain more effectively with large firms wishing to settle within its political boundaries. A strategy of local investment in small firms would also mean strengthening the resistance of the local economy to cyclical phenomena. Following the Swiss model of industrialization, where industrial strength is built on serving specialty markets, it would emphasize highly skilled over unskilled work. And it would help to promote community pride. Who knows? The trademark MADE IN WICHITA, KANSAS, might someday become a world-renowned badge of quality.[31]

2. Creating and expanding community-based services that will facilitate the self-production of life by the household economy. If the household economy is to become the backbone of a revitalized political community, it will need to be helped in a variety of ways through the efforts of the local state. Among these facilitating actions are the expansion of services that are provided in partnership with households, cooperatives, churches, and other civic groups. Examples include child care centers, storefront health centers, legal aid centers, services for foreign immigrants, local community and neighborhood newspapers, arts and crafts centers, shelters for battered women, community garages, continuing education, suicide help lines, services to older people and shut-ins, extension services for urban farming, and alternative housing for adolescents.

One way for the local state to help these and similar services get started and sustain themselves might be through a system of "work-in-lieu-of-taxes," which would allow people to substitute work in community-approved services for a certain amount of direct tax payment to the local state. Different methods of implementing such a system could be tried; most of them would involve some form of wage payment in addition to the units of time credit people would accumulate. Incentive bonuses—earned by accumulating credit units—could be worked in; such bonuses might include free tickets to community-sponsored events or a stint in a community-organized summer camp for young people. (See Offe 1985 for European examples.)

The advantages of this approach to service expansion are readily apparent.

---

31. I am indebted to Charles Hampden-Turner (1975) for this idea. An actual example that comes to mind is the association we make between Solingen (a city in West Germany) and high-quality steel in the manufacture of knives.

a. It would begin to address people's genuine needs.

b. It would recognize volunteer activities as being important to the life of the community as a whole.

c. It would greatly increase the number of people involved in rendering these services as a public gesture.

d. It would build on an already existing tradition of community and volunteer services.

e. It would encourage the household economy to reach out into the wider service economy of the community.

f. It would slow down the bureaucratization of services.

3. Recovering the street for people. Streets are becoming obsolete in America. Their place is being taken by private shopping malls, with their carefully controlled environments. Streets have become not only obsolete but also unsafe, especially for women and children and especially at night, and for the most part, they are boring. They have become places to get through and not to gather, meet, or celebrate in. Yet the urban commune is above all a meeting place, and the public street can serve this need, though it will take a special effort to bring the street back to life (Appleyard 1981). In the life space of the average-sized city, this is not an impossible task, because a radius of four miles or less allows people to rely chiefly on bicycles, electric-powered vehicles, public shuttles, and similar conveyances for their transportation. To get people to use these alternative modes of travel, through-traffic at high speeds must be physically separated from a capillary system penetrating all parts of the city. The conversion of alleyways to alternative corridors that can be traversed by bicycles might make the whole community accessible and at the same time convert a major "dead space" to active use.

To get people accustomed to the idea that the street is a public place and belongs to them, not to the automobile, neighborhood street festivals could be sponsored the year round. To make streets more interesting, zoning ordinances could be changed to encourage the development of mixed-use districts (being mindful of the new emphasis on small business development and community services). And the best way to make streets safe for people, following Jane Jacobs' famous advice (1961), is to have people watch people, a reliable practice that costs nothing and can be supplemented at night by a citizen watch, volunteer escort services, emergency call boxes, and so forth (see also Hayden 1984, ch. 8).

The Peasant Periphery: Toward Collective Self-Reliance
In the preceding two sections, I addressed the recovery of political community at the levels of the household economy and the urban commune in the context of a regional assembly of cities. Our starting point for this discussion was the collective self-production of life. I argued that people's life space, which was shown to be roughly coincident with the territory of an urban commune, would have to be extended outward in a political sense to gain control over the surrounding metropolitan economy. The focus for this discussion was the United States.

I want to stop here, because I believe that the arena for a radical, regenerative practice in the United States does not, at present, include the national state. The great strength of American radicals is the self-organizing capacity of the American people on a local level, and the bastion of the national state is too powerful and too remote from the centers of radical practice to become an arena in its own right. This is not to say that the struggle cannot occasionally be carried to Washington, but in this huge country, America, the political life that holds promise is, *for the time being*, better concentrated in the diversity of its many local communities and the fifty states of the Union.

The matter is very different in the peasant periphery, which encompasses two-thirds of the world's population. Here, the national state is the essential instrument for directing development to avoid the collective misery which, for most countries of the Third World, is the most probable outcome of projected trends. Only the state is able successfully to organize resistance to a heteronomous development that benefits no one but a small minority who float, like cream, on people's misery. And it is only the state which can organize people for an alternative development based on the country's own means of production. But to accomplish these gigantic tasks, the state must first be able to express the genuine popular will of the country. It cannot merely echo the voices that manage the international economy and reap its benefits. *It must be a politically progressive state*.

And just as cities are able to reach their full potential as the historical ground for the collective self-production of life only in a regional assembly of cities, so the countries of the peasant periphery, most of them being small, *must join forces in regional assemblies of countries that share a basic commitment to an alternative development*. Liberation from massive poverty implies collective forms of self-reliance (Galtung et al. 1980, ch. 1).

Countries become periphery by virtue of their mode of integration into the world economy, and of the particular roles assigned to them in the international division of labor and in the processes of global capital accumulation. Over long periods of time, they may change position between core, semi-periphery, and periphery. But overall, the spatial system of the international economy reproduces itself from period to period. Peripheral status is not easily overcome. There are contending schools of thought as to how a country might successfully accomplish a transition from, say, peripheral to semi-peripheral status. All these recipes assume, as they must, that industrial capitalism is alive and well, and that it will soon be pulling out from its present crisis, resuming a course of vigorous expansion. The alternative assumption, that the present is, in some sense, a "terminal" crisis, is rarely entertained.

Naturally, we cannot know the course that history will take. Even if we assume that the more optimistic scenarios will in the long run prove correct, there remain the undoubted facts of the present situation and the relatively modes expectations concerning the development perspectives of most peripheral societies, a forecast on which most experts seem to be agreed.

Examined at closer range, the future of the peasant periphery is a depressing one. Throughout much of the world, peasant populations are increasing without any hope of a significant material improvement in their lives: billions can be expected to eat less, have less land, and remain for much of the time unproductive and idle. The urban proportion of the population will undoubtedly increase over the next twenty years, but the prospective economic situation in most peripheral cities is not much better than in the countryside. Under present models of export-based industrialization, urban employment in the periphery will almost certainly deteriorate, putting additional strain on an informal economy that is already under pressure (Sethuraman 1981).

But the peasant periphery is periphery only for as long as it chooses to remain periphery, that is, only for as long as it remains integrated into a system that systematically "underdevelops" its economy. Countries, like households, can opt out and *selectively de-link* from global economic relations, as they set out on a more self-reliant course of development. This is the option I should like to consider.[32]

32. The following pages reflect an emerging counter-consensus among leading specialists in Third World development. It is manifested in the work of the Swedish Dag Hammarskjöld Foundation; the International Foundation for Development Alternatives, in Geneva; the group associated with Johan Galtung (Galtung et al. 1980); David C. Korten's "people-centered development" (Korten and Klauss 1984); Dieter

Dieter Senghaas, perhaps the most prominent economist arguing for a strategy of selective de-linking, calls it the first imperative.

> In the long run, the Third World has a chance of building up self-reliant and viable economies and societies only if it dissociates the metropolitan economies. . . . Historical experience of capitalistic *and* socialistic development processes that resulted in more or less viable structures shows that without a period of self-centredness, the duration of which may vary from case to case, i.e., *without protection motivated by development policy, an intensive* (as opposed to an extensive) *development of productive forces is hardly possible.*
>
> *[T]rade is a consequence of an inward-oriented dynamic accumulation process* in the sense that it is merely expedient and does not determine the dynamic impetus of the entire reproduction process. Trade must be pursued selectively, and only that form of *selective cooperation* should be practiced which benefits the building up of a viable internal structure in the countries of the southern continents.
>
> For the majority of the countries of the Third World, *dissociation* nowadays means in particular: a break with the traditional, export-oriented economy and instead, mobilization of their *own* resources with the goal of making such resources utilizable for their *own* purposes. This would mean particularly: a break with the production of raw materials which are processed mainly in the metropolitan economies; a break with export-oriented industrialization . . . but also a break with misguided industrialization geared to import substitution which, where it was pursued, patently satisfied chiefly the demand of high-income impoverished masses. (Senghaas 1984, 212–213)

Senghaas manages to capture the essence of "dissociation": to pursue a more autonomous development that will be guided by the needs internal to the country, and whose results will directly benefit the broad masses of the people.[33] He is less than fully candid, how-

---

Senghaas's "plea for dissociation" (Senghaas 1977, 1984); Ignacy Sachs's work on "eco-development" centered at the École des Hautes Études in Paris (Sachs 1982); Richard Falk's "world order project" at Princeton (Falk et al. 1982); Md. Anisur Rahman's work on self-reliance in rural development (1981); and other projects.

33. In the present context, autonomy means essentially to have adequate powers to do four things: (a) define what is (and is not) a matter of public concern, (b) order the priorities for public action, (c) choose an appropriate set of implementing devices, and (d) marshal resources necessary for carrying out the proposed action. Fundamentally political, these powers also define the core meaning of sovereignty.

ever, about the meaning of development under the assumed conditions of dissociation. A self-reliant development by a society, the majority of whose population are peasant farmers, is something quite different from an "inward-oriented dynamic accumulation process." Opting out of the world economic system, even selectively, amounts to a declaration that the accumulation logic of capital is, at least for a peripheral economy, counterproductive. Being substituted is a set of very different concerns, centered on a norm that proclaims a *sufficiency of livelihood for everyone* (see below).

In any event, Senghaas's plea for a self-reliant development presupposes the existence of a powerful and popularly based state that is prepared to mobilize the internal resources of the country, especially labor time, with the aim of "step-by-step, opening up . . . the domestic market by which the mass of the population is integrated into productive activites" (ibid. 213).

Finally, Senghaas asserts, such a development "from within" will require

> new forms of division of labour among the economies of the Third World itself. . . . Dissociated from the world market, the peripheries would have the chance of developing their economies in relation to each other, i.e., by mutually complementary processes. In this connection, importance would attach not merely to the *building up of subregional, regional, and continental infrastructures* with provision for common transport and communication systems, means of transport, insurance companies, news agencies, etc. This would contribute towards *dehierarchization* of the present, grossly hierarchized international society and hence to the formation of effective counterweights to the so-called metropolitan economies. (Ibid. 213–214)

A drastic economic restructuring of this sort has in the past always been viewed as a direct threat to the hegemony of the leading core states of the world economy, especially the United States. The latter's repeated acts of aggression against offenders whose major sin appeared to be their attempt to steer a course of development outside the "logic" of capital forced these countries into a war economy even as they tried, desperately, to carry out far-reaching economic reforms (post-1949 China, Cuba, Chile, Nicaragua, Vietnam, Jamaica, Grenada, Angola, Mozambique). In some of these countries, attempts at a self-reliant development were effectively blocked (Chile, Jamaica, Grenada, Mozambique); in others, such attempts were perverted as the war economy raised military-political elites to a position of unexpected dominance and came to overshadow more peaceful and democratic objectives (Vietnam, Nicaragua).

In any event, the selective uncoupling of a peasant society from international capitalism is but the first, albeit necessary, step in what amounts to a fundamental restructuring of the national economy (Harari 1982, 85–86). A self-reliant development requires the refocusing of priorities around the needs of peasant populations who are in the majority (Lipton 1977). Such a refocusing would be aimed at increasing the productivity of agriculture, for which there is often a substantial margin; expanding rural markets; and developing an industrial base that would, over the next cycle of development, serve primarily the rising needs of an increasingly prosperous peasantry.[34] In a spatial sense, rural development would be articulated through a decentralized system of small- to medium-sized cities (urban communes), which stand in close interaction with, but do not dominate, the surrounding countryside.[35]

To advocate rural priorities is to tacitly acknowledge that peasant societies are primarily societies of small producers who have traditionally met most of their household needs from their own production. In one form or another, a self-reliant development, guided by the state, must enlist the energies and inventive capacities of millions of peasant households in an inclusive, participatory process which I have elsewhere called agropolitan development.[36] Practical

34. Contrary to widely held beliefs, both the rate of productivity increase and the efficiency of capital in agricultural production are comparable to, if not greater than that in other sectors, including manufacturing. (See Hayami and Ruttan 1971.)

35. An equal development of countryside and city is one of the perennial themes of Marxist theory and practice. Its most recent and dramatic manifestation is in communist China. (For discussion of China's difficulties in managing rural-urban relations to avoid the exploitation of the countryside by cities, see Whyte 1983.) But as we now see, such exploitation was already the case in classical antiquity (Ste. Croix 1981, 10–19). Its sublation will probably require the virtual elimination of peasant farming as a way of life and the substitution of capitalist or collectivist methods of production. This has already happened in the United States.

36. See Friedmann (1985). The model of agropolitan development can be described in terms of the following three concepts.

a. As a concept of *socioeconomic change*, agropolitan development refers to a self-reliant development that aims at a substantial increase in the productive forces of rural populations and the betterment of rural life. Through the extension of basic services such as electric power, clean water, modern communications, primary education, and health clinics, agropolitan development looks to the "urbanization of the countryside." Along with the provision of these services, the model proposes the social guarantee of the fulfillment of the "basic needs" of rural households. Finally, it proposes a strategy that relies heavily on the peasantry's capacity for social learning.

experience is unequivocal on this point. In a recent review of its policies, UNICEF reports:

> On the basis of experience and observation, UNICEF is convinced that participatory approaches are the only ones that hold out long-term hopes for effective development. . . . While national policy and master plans can make significant contributions to the solution of family and community problems, in the final analysis it is men and women living out their daily lives and working creatively and resourcefully—participating in the process of development and developing solutions with available resources—who will improve the lives of children. (UNICEF 1982, 132)

In an article entitled "Lessons from Grass-Root Development Experience in Latin America and the Caribbean," Peter Hakim of the Inter-American Foundation confirms this conclusion. He writes:

> * Poor people know what they require to satisfy their interests, meet their needs, and solve their problems.
> * Even though many grass-root organizations are fragile and operate under extremely adverse conditions, they have shown time and time again that they can effectively use development assistance and contribute to the economic and social development of their members.
> * Organizations that are best able to serve the needs of poor people and poor communities share four characteristics: first, they provide tangible economic benefits to their members. Secondly, their membership has an active voice in running the

---

b. As a *geographical* concept, agropolitan development refers to a bounded space, a territory, that defines an area for common decision and action. Lying at the intersection of political, economic, and cultural spaces, this territory constitutes the immediate habitat or life space of the rural population. Agropolitan districts may be operationally defined as containing at least one small urban center and a population of between forty and sixty thousand who live no further than a day's return traveling distance—by nonmechanized means of conveyance—from this center.

c. As a *political* concept, agropolitan development refers to the entire district population as a political community to which is ascribed a capacity for self-determination in matters of common concern. The community regulates access to land and water, and it may call on its members to contribute their time and energy to public works. The community, defined by an agropolitan district and operating through its political assemblies, becomes the principal recipient of government assistance and the major agent, above the level of household, of comprehensive rural development. An "agropolis" as described in these terms is meant to be equivalent in every way to an urban commune.

organization. A third characteristic is that benefits are distributed equitably. Finally, the organizations have or can acquire the managerial and technical skills to use development assistance and perform the tasks at hand.

* Dependency on one imposing leader, particularly from outside the community, is a sign of organizational weakness.

* The development efforts of promising organizations can be frustrated by unrealistic expectations that they can become self-sustaining or produce large gains within a short period.

* The success of self-help organizations and projects is sometimes dependent on the ability of organizations to secure services or resources that only governments can provide.

* The most productive projects are not necessarily those that have achieved their initial goals; rather they tend to be projects in which (1) the local organization and its members have acquired the skills, knowledge, and capacity to solve problems and manage problems; and (2) local resources and initiatives have been mobilized for sustained efforts over time. (Hakim 1982, 138–141)[37]

An agropolitan form of development would require (1) far-reaching reforms to secure a stable and equitably distributed land base; (2) collective command over water resources in the hands of local peasant communities; and (3) a substantial measure of self-determination in matters of resource mobilization, production, and collective consumption. This last condition would imply an equal form of development that seeks equality not only in the conditions of women and men, but also in the regional distribution of social investments, in the guarantee of a sufficient livelihood for everyone, and, above all, in households' access to the primary bases of social power.[38] Finally, a rurally centered development would have to consider a "pyramid" of investment priorities that would articulate the following activities.

1. Production in the primary sectors of agriculture, horticulture, forestry, livestock, fisheries, and mining.

2. Intermediate manufacturing producing inputs to primary production, such as fertilizers, tools, irrigation equipment, and fishing nets.

37. For additional examples from Asia, see Korten (1984).

38. Among the relevant bases of social power are knowledge, skills, and tools. An outstanding example of the sort of knowledge that is useful and is designed to help people solve their own problems is *People's Workbook: Working Together to Change Your Community* (Berold and Caine 1981).

3. Processing industries in support of primary production, such as canneries, meatpacking, glue manufacture, and forest products.

4. Manufacturing industries to meet the basic and evolving needs of individual peasant households, including sturdy clothing, shoes, kitchen utensils, materials for housing construction, furnishings, bicycles, soap, contraceptives, transistor radios, and solar energy stores.

5. Manufacturing industries to meet the needs of collective consumption, such as heavy construction materials, transport equipment, educational materials, and pharmaceuticals.[39]

What can be concluded from this discussion? The peasant periphery is clearly an arena for radical practice, but the struggle must be carried on by the peasants themselves. Those of us who live in the "core" countries and who may declare our sympathies with their heroic efforts can demonstrate solidarity with these struggles, but we have our own agenda to accomplish.

Dieter Senghaas attempts to answer those critics who are skeptical about the feasibility of a self-reliant development (Senghaas 1984, 215–216). In fact, for most countries of the peasant periphery, the future is rapidly evolving toward what is virtually a no-choice situation. Their integration into the global economy as "periphery" has pushed them against the wall; it is forcing them to de-link. The majority of countries, having made themselves dependent on outside capital and markets, now find themselves seriously de-capitalizing as they spend a large and growing percentage of their export earnings on debt-servicing, with a diminishing remainder going for essential fuels, food, and capital equipment. Even the World Bank, with its "can do" spirit, is beginning to recognize that a problem exists. In countries where the land base is limited, the projected increase in rural population means a further subdivision of the land into parcels so small that they can no longer supply a peasant household with food throughout the year, while many peasants are being forced off the land altogether. What makes this situation so desperate is that the creation of new, productive employment along the traditional "modernization" route is completely inadequate for meeting the aggregate needs of the population.

Under these circumstances, a self-reliant development of the peasant periphery will come about simply because it is the only course Third World countries can take if they are to survive. In the long run, American opposition to a self-reliant development will

39. See Senghaas (1984, 213) for a similar list.

make very little difference. The emergence of China as a leader of
the world periphery (Gauhar 1983) may enable countries to escape
being forced to choose between the tutelage of the American or the
Soviet system. Although China is as yet too weak to offer more than
symbolic material assitance to other countries, her political backing
of peasant societies embarked on a course of collective self-reliance
may well turn out to be decisive.

The Global Community

Today's radicals, especially in the West, are inclined to praise the
virtues of local action. It is only in the local community, they say,
that "real" changes can be brought about. The time is unpropitious
for a general attack on problems at the level of the state. As modern
radicals, they harbor a deep suspicion of large organizations, pre-
ferring loosely knit social movements. In taking on the state, *on the
state's terms*, they are afraid of falling victim to Robert Michels' "iron
law of oligarchy." For the Left is no less vulnerable to being suduced
by bureaucratic enticements than anyone else. And so the real
struggles, they will argue, must be fought at storefront levels in the
street.

Our own discussion of the recovery of political community in
household, urban commune, and metro-region was more or less
sympathetic to this point of view, though mindful of Sheldon Wolin's words that "the political limitations of such activity be recognized. It is politically incomplete" (Wolin 1982, 27). When we came
to consider the problems of the peasant periphery, however, our
anti-state position had to be modified. In the peasant periphery, it
was the central state—albeit a progressive, revolutionary state—that
alone would be able to mobilize the internal resources of the society
for a self-reliant development. Although households, "agropolitan"
districts (the equivalent of urban communes), and metro-regions
were still the central arenas for radical practice, the state's role in societal guidance was now regarded as essential.

Most specialists concerned with Third World development would
agree. Of course, even a Johan Galtung or Dieter Senghaas does not
know, abstractly, how to make a revolution that would establish the
basic conditions for "dissociation" and an agrarian-based development. But once a formal restructuring of power at the level of the
state has occurred, adoption of a policy of collective self-reliance will
ensure that whatever promises the revolution held are not forfeited
to history.

Few are the radicals, however, who consider the "global community" as an appropriate arena for political practice. One of them is

Richard Falk. Unlike others working on questions of international relations, Falk is not concerned primarily with maintaining the existing balance of power in world affairs, or with strategic gaming, but rather with *restructuring relationships of power* in ways that will bring humanity closer to a political order based on democratic principles and justice (Falk et al. 1982). It is, of course, the case that the world has never been a political community in this sense. But to focus on the local community, or even on the post-revolutionary state, as the exclusive arena of radical practice would be to overlook the global interdependencies that actually exist, and that demand new institutional arrangements in support of the fledgling efforts at a self-reliant and autonomous development.

Global interdependency is not likely to unravel. It is capitalism's chief legacy to future generations. At some point, we will have to acknowledge the connection that inevitably links the smallest political community to the largest, the household to the world. To help to build a world community—a political order that will sustain diverging local paths to happiness—must be seen as an important task for radicals.

Interdependencies have turned this global community still waiting to be born into an arena for political struggle. Indeed, this struggle helps to define its meaning as community. Three dimensions of interdependency are crucially important.

Ecological Interdependency. In some ways, the world in its entirety must be regarded as an ecosystem in which damage at one point produces negative effects at another, ultimately threatening human life that even in a highly technological society still depends in fundamental ways on "nature." The world is best viewed as a "common," and, if the common fails to be managed in the long-term interests of humanity, the destructive potential of present use is capable of liquidating significant portions of the biosphere (Hardin 1984; orig. 1968). The systematic destruction of tropical rain forests for short-term private gain is proceeding apace in Brazil, Thailand, the Philippines, and elsewhere, setting in motion irreversible processes of resource degradation (Hecht, forthcoming). The desertification of large parts of the world's surface, rendering them uninhabitable, has already reached tragic proportions in the West African Sahel, as well as in a number of other regions (Eckholm and Brown 1977). Ocean fishery resources are under relentless pressure from commercial interests which, in the absence of enforceable rules for sustained-yield management, consistently over-exploit this vital source of food, causing its disappearance from regions that were formerly teeming with life. Air currents carry poisonous wastes over long distances, often beyond national frontiers, until they descend on innocent regions as invisible killers of forests and freshwater fish (Brown 1984). The so-called "greenhouse effect" may be changing the world's climates.

These pervasive and essentially destructive processes can be expected to continue and even to intensify under the combined, cumulative pressure of population and economic growth. Immediate effects are often hidden from view until critical theshold values are reached. In some situations, exceeding threshold values may trigger rapid downward cycles of deterioration and decay. With a possible doubling of world population to ten billion by the middle of the next century, less than a human lifetime away, and economic pressures on the environment that are from four to six times greater than at present, there can be no question but that institutional inventions will have to be forthcoming, reflecting humanity's dependence on a viable environment.[40] It may be overstating the case to forecast, as some have done, the sudden environmental collapse of major world regions (Mesarovic and Pestel 1974); it would be equally wrong to take the comfortable view that because Science and Technology have helped to "save" us in the past, this redoubtable team will continue to extend its safety net indefinitely into the future (J. Simon 1981).[41] The environmental harm that already has been inflicted on humanity—especially in the peasant periphery, where the devastation is boundless—requires the most urgent attention as a problem of global proportions.[42]

40. For a comprehensive perspective on the global environmental problem, see Council on Environmental Quality (1980).

41. A typical posture is expressed in the following quotation from a respected economist.

> The advance of science and technology has enabled modern society to achieve a more productive and better balanced relationship to the natural world than in ancient civilizations or in the earlier stages of western industrial civilization. The rhetoric about "finite earth" is clearly misleading. The impact of science and technology has been to expand the size of "spaceship earth" along those dimensions that are most significant for human existence. (Ruttan 1984, 888)

Unfortunately, the beguiling self-evident character of this statement is belied by many contradictory views on the impact of science and technology, ranging from philosophical questioning to the empirical. Science and technology do not come as isolated social practices but are part and parcel of the capitalist mode of production, which helps to finance the work of scientists and engineers from whom it expects and demands certain kinds of result. The problem is not science as such, but science in the context of capitalist society.

42. I have not even mentioned possible threats arising from nuclear poisoning, the

Economic Interdependency. No matter how successful a widespread movement toward a self-reliant development may be, it will not deconstruct the international economy. Over time, it may change the composition and direction of world trade, but collective self-reliance is not a movement that stands for autarky and isolation. And even as regional blocks of developing peasant societies are forming, and as global capital withdraws from spreading zones of endemic violence, the economic interdependency of nations is more likely than not to increase over the next few decades. Twenty years from now, transnational banks and corporations will undoubtedly be more powerful than at present; international migrations, currently as high as or higher than at any previous time in history, will continue and perhaps even increase, as millions of people seek to escape from poverty and persecution at home; and international commodity trade, which has been rising steadily since World War II, will almost certainly continue to grow in volume. The peasant periphery may try to dissociate, but dissociation will of necessity be selective and of limited duration. In the long historical sweep of things, *the general movement of the last six hundred years toward greater global interdependency is not likely to be reversed.*

If one accepts these propositions, then new institutional arrangements must be found that will normalize economic relations on an international basis and assist peasant societies to achieve an autonomous development within a restructured world economy.

In some ways, the world economy, dominated as it is by transnational capital, seems to be one of the least promising arenas for radical practice. The fact remains that a new international economic order is required, if only to facilitate local policies of self-reliance. The specific concern may be with the world food system, international capital movements, trans-boundary flows of information, rationing and price stabilization of critical commodities in international trade, or scientific cooperation. Imaginative and equitable solutions to problems such as these, based on international agreements, form a necessary part of any post-capitalist conception of the world and therefore constitute an important arena for radical practice.

Political Interdependency. Finally, world political struggles for emancipation are linked by bonds of solidarity into a single movement. Ultimately, the issue is people's control over their life space at all the relevant scales of territorial organization. Whatever its local configuration, the struggle is everywhere the same, whether for self-reli-

---

devastation caused by prolonged "conventional" warfare the destruction of up to one fifth of the world's total species of plants and animals, and similar horrors.

ance, women's rights, political self-determination, cultural identity, an environmental ethic, the right of an indigenous community to find its own way in the world, political liberties, or people's access to social power. Localized though they may be, these struggles are not independent of each other. They need the support of international organizations that are sympathetic to their cause, maintain open lines of communication, keep the rest of the world informed and focus its attention on key struggles, and provide financial assistance and political support when needed. Many such organizations already exist. As a rule, they are loosely structured networks of private citizens who have made a personal commitment to some particular effort. Amnesty International, working on behalf of human rights, may serve as illustration. But many more organizations are needed (Lakey 1976).

The global community, then, is something that is already happening. It is based on the acceptance of cultural diversity, the political autonomy of territorially organized societies, and the facts of global interdependency. Like all political communities, it must be built from the ground up, as an expression of active citizen concern and the world-historical project in which we are engaged.

Summing Up

I have attempted in this chapter to sketch the outlines of the project that is gaining strength in the face of a capitalist system increasingly caught in the grindstones of its own contradictions. The project can be variously described. Its primary objective is the recovery of political community and with it, an active, public life. As a territorial concept, political community is found at different levels of spatial integration, beginning with the household economy and ending, at the other end of the spectrum, with the world economy as a whole. We saw how a process of recovery involves both the "self-production of life" and "collective self-reliance" in territorial development, and how implicit in the territorial approach is a process of cultural differentiation.

I further specified the recovery of political community, with its origins in civil society, by stressing its grounding in fundamental values, including equalizing access to the bases of social power for all persons and households; the fundamental democratization of all social institutions; the rightful claims of political communities to sovereignty over their territory; and their reasonable expectation for survival, peaceful co-existence, and historical continuity.

I argued that the struggles for political community in this sense, occurring simultaneously in four distinct arenas of radical practice, are ultimately converging, becoming part of a dialectical movement that involves both social integration at the global level and territorial differentiation at all lower levels.

Being convergent, these struggles are ultimately linked into a great solidarity front in opposition to the established powers of state and corporate economy, which are increasingly failing to satisfy the basic human need for an active, socially useful life; the self-development of human capacities and skills; freedom from hunger and from fear; the bonds of social solidarity; and a voice in political assemblies.

This great oppositional movement seeks to reclaim what capitalism has taken away.

o A genuine political life with widespread citizen involvement.

o Territorial autonomy in production and politics.

o The collective self-production of life.

o The discovery of one's individuality in the context of specific social relations.

Capitalism, I argued, has in effect colonized civil society, incorporating ever larger spheres of the life of households into the money economy and placing much of what remains under the direct tutelage of the national state. It has proposed a false criterion of rationality ("rational is that which most effectively furthers self-interest") in which all desire for cooperation and community are declared to be misguided. The first step in advancing toward the recovery of political community, therefore, is the selective de-linking of territorial communities from the market economy. This applies specifically to households and peasant societies.

The course of this great oppositional movement will increasingly determine the shape of our lives. Precise outcomes cannot, however, be foreseen. In response to an evolving situation, new social forces will appear that will carry the action forward against an opposition that can be expected to grow in ruthlessness, cunning, and repressive power as its legitimacy in the public eye declines. Those engaged in the struggle will want to write their own agendas.

So far as planning is concerned—and after this long detour, we must at last return to planning—this much is clear: along with the gradual disappearance of the old regime, planning must be reconsidered. Such planning in the public domain as we have known in the West has been dominated by the bourgeois state. It was an integral part of the management of civil society, part of its policy of political pacification. Now the time has come for a regenerative form of planning linked to the practices of social transformation. An account of its characteristics and tasks forms the subject of the next chapter.

10 The Mediations of Radical Planning

Theory and Practice in Social Transformation

In any of the four arenas discussed in the previous chapter, radical practice must be informed and guided by appropriate theory. It must be "saturated" with theory. Without a theory of structural transformation, radical practice has no staying power: it becomes visceral, opportunistic, and reactive. When faced with an intransigent resistance that knows very well what it has to defend and has "theory" to spare, short-term tactics are headed for failure.

What do we mean by a *transformative* theory (as I shall henceforth call it)? It is a set of complexly related statements about the world that:

1. Focuses on the structural problems of capitalist society viewed in a global context—problems such as racism, patriarchy, class domination, resource degradation, impoverishment, exploitation, and alienation;

2. Provides a critical interpretation of existing reality, emphasizing those relations that, from period to period, reproduce the dark underside of the system;

3. Charts, in a historical, forward-looking perspective, the probable future course of the problem, assuming the absence of countervailing, transformative struggles;

4. Elaborates images of a preferred outcome based on an emancipatory practice; and

5. Suggests the choice of a "best" strategy for overcoming the resistance of the established powers in the realization of desired outcomes.

Such theory cannot be arbitrarily invented. It must grow out from and be informed by long periods of sustained oppositional practice. Based on experience, it combines an amalgam of analysis, social vision, and hard strategic thinking with the intent to shape

389

ongoing political practice, even as it continuously absorbs new learning.[1]

The starting point is always a concrete problem. A recent example is the work on "deindustrialization" and plant closings. This has become a major political issue in the older industrialized regions of the world, from Britain (Massey and Megan 1982), to the United States (Bluestone and Harrison 1982), to Australia (Sandercock and Melser 1985). The problem has been laid at the door of "capital restructuring," which is seen as a response to declining rates of profit in key industrial sectors, growing international competition, and advances in production technology that have hastened the obsolescence of industrial processes which until only a short while ago were thought to be "state of the art."

No less well-documented is the political practice that has focused on this question (Metzgar 1980; Luria and Russell 1981; Haas 1985; Morales and Wolff 1985). There were struggles at specific sites, such as Youngstown, Ohio, where workers had hoped to buy up the steel plant that was threatening to shut down and finally did; militant video documentaries carried the basic message to large numbers of people who had previously been unaware of what was happening around them; church-related groups worked shoulder to shoulder with labor unions and local communities to save the plants, devise alternatives, and even protect entire neighborhoods, such as Poletown in Detroit, from being razed to the ground to make way for a "restructured" industry while thousands of working-class homes were being sacrificed to the bulldozer.

These and other forms of radical practice did not accomplish their immediate purpose, which was, first, to prevent the calamity from happening; second, to devise alternatives that would provide jobs and income for the displaced working population; and third, to pass legislation that would prevent or at least mitigate similar occurrences in the future. The tactical failure of these struggles does not mean that the effort was wasted. Resistance is never wasted. The "fight back" struggle against plant closings raised people's consciousness; built a sense of human solidarity in the teeth of profit;

1. This account of transformative theory is drawn directly from the social mobilization paradigm of planning. Contemporary examples include certain varieties of feminist theory, particularly socialist feminism; the radical political theory implicit in *democracy: A Journal of Political Renewal and Radical Change*, edited by Sheldon Wolin and now, unfortunately, defunct; and the emerging theory of a "self-reliant" development.

tested certain proposed solutions (such as worker buy-outs); and built new, collaborative networks within civil society, such as the links that have been made between the major churches, organized labor (especially at the local level), and university-based groups of radical students and faculty. The time may not be ripe for such a coalition to score political victories in the United States; in Latin America, they have been the only significant source of resistance to the rapacious military regimes of Argentina, Brazil, Uruguay, and Chile and, in the first three of these countries, were instrumental in overturning existing dictatorships.

The necessary unity of theory and practice is one of the deep insights of the social mobilization tradition of planning. But dialectical unity is not the same as an identity, and transformative theory has its own distinctive character:

1. An expressive language capable of reaching ordinary people.

2. Consistency in the relation of its several parts to each other.

3. Comprehensiveness with respect to the main variables relevant for system transformation.

4. A formulation that enables the ready adaptation of general theory to unique, specific settings.

A theory having these characteristics must not be allowed to harden into doctrine. Because its usefulness is ultimately determined in practice, critical reflection on practice forms the basis of its continued renewal (Ulrich 1983).

These criteria for an appropriate theory of social transformation also provide us with a clue for identifying the central task of radical planning, which is the *mediation of theory and practice in social transformation.*[2]

---

2. This formulation obliges us to reconsider the third of the three formal definitions of planning offered in Chapter 1. In that definition, "social transformation" was substituted for "societal guidance," but in all other respects, the definition of what we now call radical planning was presented as identical with that of planning by the state (definition II). In both cases, we spoke of "scientific and technical knowledge" as being "linked" to "processes" of social change. Now, this is not at all the same as saying that radical planning is centrally concerned with the "mediation of theory and practice in social transformation." The present chapter is intended to elaborate on this basic understanding. Nevertheless, I propose to retain the earlier formulation, since it allowed us to proceed up to this point. Radical practice does not lies on a logical continuum with planning for societal guidance. It implies an "epistemological break" with past ways of thinking and doing.

On Mediation

The meaning of mediation with respect to radical planning is not immediately apparent. As a start, it is easier, perhaps, to say what, in the present context, it is not.

In mediating theory and practice, radical planners are not neutral agents arbitrating between two disputing parties. Nor do they present themselves as experts on theory and, therefore, on the political guidance of radical planning. Radical planners must not become absorbed into the everyday struggles of radical practice. In short, as mediators, they stand neither apart from nor above nor within such a practice.

Instead, mediation suggests a role for radical planners that is Janus-faced: to shape transformative theory to the requirements of an oppositional practice in specific local settings, to create opportunities for the critical appropriation of transformative theory by groups organized for action, and to rework this theory in ways that will reflect firsthand experience gathered in the course of radical practice itself. In terms of social space, radical planners occupy a position tangential to radical practice at precisely the point where practice intersects theory.

The practice to which their work relates is focused on the familiar problems of people's livelihood—jobs, housing, and providing for themselves. It may be concerned with organizing alternative services for specific sectors of the population, such as children, adolescents, old people, shut-ins, immigrants, and the physically and mentally disabled, for whose needs neither the state nor the corporate economy makes adequate provision. It may also work to protect or restore the built environment—the places people call home—and shield it from the voracious mania that seeks only the highest return on investment. Or it may address more general issues such as war and peace, nuclear power, and the preservation of the natural environment for future generations. In one form or another, these are all emancipatory practices that seek to create a space for the collective self-production of life that lies beyond bureaucracy, the profit motive, or the national obsession with military overkill, unlimited growth, corporate gigantism, and the communist menace.[3]

Given the complex nature of transformative theory—its struc-

3. Each of such practices teaches political lessons. In some, the state or corporate power is directly opposed. In others, their financial assistance will be sought, but their tutelage rejected. Some of the practices are purely local in character, such as tenant struggles (Heskin 1983), while others link up from city to city to build a national movement. What is still missing is the political link-up among single-issue social movements and hammering out a genuine alternative. But to imagine the possibilities of such an alternative can no longer be dismissed as a utopian fantasy.

tural character, its critical reading of existing reality and the near future, its imaging of what is desired, and its broad considerations of strategy—with its double burden of responsibility toward practice and theory, the mediations of radical planning are not easily accomplished. And yet, for all of its apparent weightiness, the planner's role in radical practice is severely restricted. For in social transformation, theory and practice become everyone's concern; responsibilities for both are multiple and overlapping. Terms such as *mediation, mediator,* and *role* suggest a technical division of labor. But in radical practice, the set of mediating role is not clearly defined and, in the language of mathematics, remains a "fuzzy" set.

Before we proceed to a more detailed illustration of the principal mediations of radical planning, it is necessary to consider what sorts of knowledge planners bring to their assignment.

On Thinking and Knowing

The tasks of mediation call for the skills of analysis, synthesis, communication, and managing group processes. Yet mediation is more than a craft.[4] In addition to possessing skills which, when found in combination, are exceedingly rare, radical planners must be able to draw on substantive knowledge. No less than other planners, they must command a ready fund of data, information, and theoretical insight pertaining to a given problem such as the environment, housing, or community economic development. Some of this knowledge will have been acquired from systematic reading, some from personal experience and observation. But all of it remains passive knowledge until the moment it is used in the process of thinking.

Most thinking is discursive and involves what Jürgen Habermas calls "communicative acts," which is everyday speech in the context of action.[5] It is only when we proceed to talk or write about a given problem that knowledge is actualized. In talking and writing, we address an audience, sometimes visible and sometimes not, from whom, sooner or later, we expect a response that will either refute or validate what we say, or else expand on it, refine it, and ultimately

4. This formulation is borrowed from Ravetz (1971, ch. 3), who refers to science, in its inquiring aspects, as "craftsman work": "[W]ithout an appreciation of the craft character of scientific work there is no possibility of resolving the paradox of radical difference between the subjective, intensely personal activity of creative science, and the objective, impersonal knowledge which results from it" (Ravetz 1971, 75). We may recall that the craftsman view of science, not coincidentally, also informs the work of policy analysts, who have gone on record to reject subject matter as a relevant concern. (Cf. Chapter 4; also Wildavsky 1979.)

5. For a splendid critical review of Habermas's ideas on discursive thinking, see Ulrich (1983, ch. 2).

redirect the conversation to produce a new perception of the problem and new modes of practice.

This conversation, intermingled with practice based on theory and close observation of the results, is continuous and does not come to a halt even with a shift in problem focus. As both the oral and written records of this conversation accumulate, a "body of knowledge" is produced which aspiring planners acquire in the course of their studies. But sometimes this record of past conversations is thin, and major disputes remain unresolved. As Jerome Ravetz points out, this situation is common of emerging technical fields in which established facts are few, the problems addressed are urgent, and passions run high (Ravetz 1971, ch. 14). He warns us that there are dangers inherent in the use of such knowledge, particularly in its premature application and the unwarranted expectations it arouses. But on reflection, it would seem wiser to bring even fragile and disputed knowledge to bear on practice (in full awareness of its limitations), and thus to enlarge and deepen the record, than to refrain from speaking out.

It is through communicative acts that knowledge for radical practice comes to be provisionally established. I say provisionally because the knowledge used in planning is inherently ephemeral, and nowhere more so than in the process of social transformation. Therefore, it is preferable to substitute the more dynamic concept of social learning, which is the way we critically appropriate experience for action, for the more solid "knowledge" that suggests a fixed stock of accumulated learning.

This switch to an epistemology of social learning is also indicated, because knowledge in radical planning appears as something distinct from what it is in the sciences, especially the natural sciences. Ravetz speaks of scientific knowledge as "objective and impersonal" (compare note 4, above). But in radical planning, the relevant knowledge, embedded as it is in a transformative theory, is always and necessarily contextual: it points to action, considers strategy, endeavors to reach a critical understanding of the present and near future, and is informed by specific social values. This contextualizing of knowledge is a profoundly social process in which those who stand in the front line of the action—households, local communities, social movements—make a decisive contribution. It is these users of knowledge-in-practice who are the final arbiters of knowledge-in-theory. It is they who must critically appropriate theory and adapt it to their needs. It is activists engaged in daily social struggle who must take part in dialogue with planners and so become immersed in mediated processes of social learning.

The provisional nature of knowledge in planning tells us that the theory of social transformation must never be allowed to harden into dogma but must remain open to even fundamental questioning and reconceptualization. The organizational counterpart to this epistemological commitment is a structure for radical practice that consists of a large number of autonomous (or quasi-autonomous) centers of decision and action whose coordination remains loose and informal. Such a structure encourages a better fit with local environments, a great deal of local experimentation, a maximum of social mobilization, a self-reliant practice, and a nondogmatic view of the problem. It is the very opposite of planning by the state, with its single-track vision, its remoteness from people's everyday concerns, its tendency to gloss over differences in local conditions, and its hierarchical ladders. The essential openness of transformative planning not only imposes on planners certain responsibilities in mediation, not the least of which is careful listening (Forester 1980), but also obliges them to give serious attention to polemical critiques from the front lines of practice, which in this way become integrated with the process of theory formation.[6]

What Radical Planners Do

We are now ready to return to more practical matters. I have argued that the central role of radical planning consists in mediating transformative theory with radical practice, and that in so doing, planners must draw on the tradition of social learning. Mediation was seen to involve specific skills used to confront formal knowledge with knowledge drawn from struggle and experience. As a result, the distribution of roles in radical planning is not clearly defined.

I should now like to illustrate the meaning of this "mediation" by giving some examples that will show how radical planning may contribute to the emergence of a more self-reliant, politically active community. The following discussion will be organized according to the vocabulary used by those who are engaged in struggle for the recovery of such a community. It is intended to complement the earlier discussion of radical planning found at the conclusion of Chapter 6.

Before proceeding, however, I should like to reiterate a point that has been made repeatedly and that we must continue to keep in view. The relevant actors in this struggle for a new society are individual households that have opted for the alternative; organized social groups based in the local community; and larger, more inclusive

6. For the epistemological grounding of this statement, see Ulrich (1983, 305–310).

movements, not bounded by territorial limits. Even transformative social movements, however, whose contact networks may circle the entire globe, have their true strength in the practice of local action groups—the base, as they are sometimes called—where ordinary people are directly involved in struggles close to their everyday lives. Although these struggles must eventually be carried beyond the confines of local communities into the world, the strength and vitality of the movement as a whole are drawn from its myriad struggles at the base. Given this context, what are the concrete tasks facing the radical planner?

Selective De-Linking, Collective Self-Empowerment, and Self-Reliance
These three terms are complementary facets of a single strategy. If you de-link and do nothing else, the gesture remains meaningless. It is equally meaningless to talk about self-reliant development without, at the same time, considering the need for collective self-empowerment, by which I mean a continuing and permanent struggle for the equalization of access to the bases of social power. The relative access of a single-household economy may be visualized as shown in Figure 19.

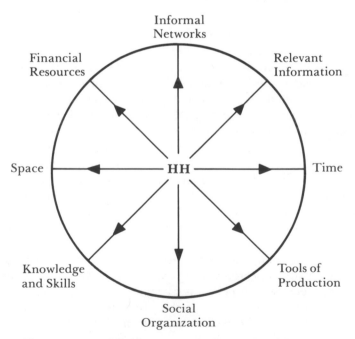

Figure 19. Household access to the bases of social power.

In practical terms and for the household shown in the center of the diagram, self-empowerment means a decision to invest its resources of *time, energy,* and *skill* along one or more of the axes shown in the diagram, for instance, to secure more space, or a more adequately serviced space, under the cooperative control of households. In this instance, space that would facilitate the functioning of the household economy translates into land and housing, and the effort would involve advancing along *all* of the axes of self-empowerment (Hartman et al. 1981).

As this example suggests, getting more adequate housing involves, for poor people at least, a collaborative effort.[7] Attempted self-empowerment by households, acting on their own behalf, would lead to suboptimal results for all. Indeed the bases of social power displayed in Figure 19 presume the existence of other households with whom one links up in a bootstrapping operation. This is plainly evident in terms such as "social organization" and "informal networks"; it is least obvious in the case of "space" and "time." But even here, the terms imply what, in the language of game theorists, is called a positive-sum game. Space must be shared with others, and rescheduling one's own activities involves their priorities as well, all of which must be harmonized.

From our discussion of the process of collective self-empowerment as a whole, the following conclusions may be drawn.

1. Self-empowerment is a mediated process.

2. It necessarily takes place around points of struggle, such as housing.

3. Its effects are synergistic, so that, by linking up with other households in struggle, more power is generated for the full re-

---

7. One of the best studies of "survival strategies" in poor societies was sponsored by the Organization for Economic Cooperation and Development (OECD). The authors write:

> It is our thesis that the only political efforts which have some possibility of success are those in which: i) an appropriate degree of *awareness* of the social, political, and economic situation coincides with ii) the necessary *capacity to organise* protracted actions, with iii) a *realistic appraisal* of the reformist or revolutionary possibilities of the overall situation and with iv) the ability to hammer together the *indispensible alliances with other social groups and actors.* (Harari and García-Bouza 1982, 43)

Radical planners can play significant parts in all these aspects of the struggle. Perhaps the best-documented, most profound study of radical planning is by Max-Neef (1982). The experiences of this self-styled "barefoot economist" come from Latin America but their lessons have validity for all of us.

alization of the objective than would be the case if each household had to "go it alone."

Radical planners mediate theory and practice at each of the relevant bases of social power. Through workshops and other means, they impart relevant knowledge and skills in collective housing struggles; they assist households in organizing themselves as a cooperative or tenant union; they assist them as well with the establishment of community orchards and gardens, workshops for the self-production of home furnishings, or community-operated nurseries, kitchens, and laundries; they help to channel appropriate information, such as impending legislative struggles, to the emerging political community; they help to network local housing struggles to related efforts elsewhere; they offer their grantsmanship skills to obtain outside funding; and they assist households in better organizing their available time for tasks that need attention (for example, through computerized skill banks).

Throughout this effort, radical planners must work to expand people's *horizon of possibilities* by relating pertinent experiences from other parts of the world and discovering ways to broaden collective efforts once the basic objectives of the group have been achieved. In this way, the momentum of radical practice is maintained, as social space is progressively liberated from control by the state and corporate capital.

Thinking without Frontiers

Radical practice, we insisted, must be guided by appropriate theory, but theory itself must come from practice. Divorced from practice, it ceases to be meaningful. The mediations involved here are accomplished through communicative acts in which takes place an exchange of ideas about the proper direction of practice and its wider meaning. In this exchange, radical planners, whose job is partly to shape theory to the requirements of practice, can play a major role.

The kind of thinking involved in this mediation must not acquiesce in artificial boundaries that might constrain the free flow of ideas. What are these boundaries? Four boundaries are frequently encountered.

1. Hierarchy. Social rank, such as university degrees or institutional affiliations, may be used to draw a boundary between "valid" and "invalid" knowledge: only high social rank (it is claimed) possesses "valid" knowledge.

2. Academic disciplines. Knowledge is bounded by self-gov-

erning academic disciplines that claim to be the keepers of the most reliable knowledge in their respective subject areas.

3. Parochialism. What is accepted as true in one set of circumstances is held to be universally true: the local sets the boundaries of "valid" knowledge.

4. Theory/Practice. Formal knowledge embodied in theoretical statements is bounded from practice and is declared to be superior to practice, that is, more perfect than the "real" world. Conversely, informal knowledge drawn from practice is bounded from theory and is declared to be superior to theory.

These and other constraints on thinking can be transcended in dialogue. One of the obligations of radical planners is to ensure that thinking about transformative practice breaks through the traditional boundaries of hierarchy, academic discipline, parochial viewpoint, and the theory/practice dichotomy, as they weave together a single cloth of theory *and* practice that is continuously tested for its fitness and durability in use.

Meaning, Purpose, Practical Vision (Recovery of Wholeness)

As passive consumers, our lives are badly fragmented. We lack a reliable criterion that would enable us to pull together the many fragments of our daily experience into a coherent whole. The more fragmented experience appears to us, the less it holds the promise of meaning, the more alienated we become. Yet human life is based on the assumption that meaning is possible, that life can make sense even under adverse conditions, that striving for particular goals and objectives is more than an exercise in self-deception. People do, indeed, seek meaning, though all too often they seek it in otherworldly contexts that merely reinforce their inclination to quiescence.

It is different for those who, for whatever reason, have decided to shed their passive and compliant attitudes and to become actors on the stage of historical events. For when you set out purposes and try to achieve them, you suddenly discover a firm criterion that helps you to interpret the world: the definition of a problem, the search for an appropriate strategy, and a clear grasp of the values to be realized in practice. Action simplifies by excising irrelevant information. At the same time, it unifies thought by bringing disparate information and experience into relation.

Applying these general considerations to the tasks of radical planning, we can say that households, community-based groups, and social movements can be helped in formulating realistic understandings for their practice in the context of the larger framework of transformative theory. This involves a series of mediations, including the need to bring potential actors to a critical understanding of their own situation and to identify correctly efficient levers for change in terms of which a realistic vision can be stated.

I hesitate to call this participatory planning, though it has a certain affinity to this well-known practice from societal guidance (Oakley and Marsden 1984). The main difference is that, in radical practice, the elaboration of a realistic vision concerns a future for which the people are themselves responsible. Their vision, then, is more than a wish list; *it is a commitment to its realization through practice.* And so the role of the planner changes as well. The traditional advocate planner mediates between the state and the people of a given community, shuttling information back and forth. Whatever people may contribute to the process of decision-making, the final word is spoken by the state. The radical planner, by contrast, must draw from a potential actor, such as a community-based action group, a commitment to engage in a transformative practice of its own. The essential planning mediation is between theory and practice, where both, ultimately, belong to the people.

Cross-Linking, Networking, Building Coalitions
The discussion so far will have made clear my own belief that the small action group plays a decisive role in social transformation. This conviction was the major thesis of an earlier book, *The Good Society* (Friedmann 1979b). What needs to be stressed in the present context is the importance of linking these groups to each other in informal networks and political coalitions. For the problem is not merely to make room for an alternative practice within the interstices of the state and corporate economy—those leftover, marginal areas where social practice is inconsequential, because it poses no threat to the basic configurations of power. At issue is the creation of an alternative social order, which necessarily involves a restructuring of basic relations of power. Social barriers that constrain a self-reliant practice at other than very local and even private levels of experience must be removed. This requires political action and a concerting of wills across a wide spectrum of alternative actions. Groups of often disparate backgrounds and experience, with different "realistic visions" of what is attainable, must be brought together for specific struggles in order to hasten the arrival of the new order.

The first and most immediate level at which coalitions can help to establish politically responsive institutions that will facilitate a self-reliant development is the metropolis. Tentative steps toward creating oppositional movements of this sort have already been taken. Examples include California's Campaign for Economic Democracy (chiefly active in Los Angeles); the Coalition Against Plant Shut-Downs (which is statewide in California but operates primarily in the metropolitan labor markets of Los Angeles and the Bay Area); Barry Commoner's Citizen Party (now active primarily at state and local levels); the National Organization of Women (again with a strong metropolitan accent); the anti-nuclear Alliance for Survival (California); and the grass-roots coalition Jobs and Justice (Los Angeles). What is characteristic of these coalitions is their largely informal character, their foundation in quasi-autonomous local action groups, and the absence of a top-heavy bureaucracy.

In their role as mediators, radical planners are in an excellent position to connect community groups with politically effective social movements. However pragmatic they might be in some respects, coalitions no less than small action groups require the mediations of theory to be effective.

Strategic Action (Focusing)
Action must be focused so as not to dissipate its energies, and this means not merely having objectives in view but also possessing a sense of sequence and timing—what is usually called strategy. Strategies are necessary, because any innovative practice is bound to meet with resistance, and this resistance must be overcome.

For actors to devise a successful strategy, they must (1) be well grounded in *the relevant technical information*; (2) be aware of *the major constraints* on their choices, and what it would take to break them; (3) have a clear sense of the *political options* and of the costs and benefits attached to them; and (4), as the action itself unfolds, be *continuously informed*, as close to real time as possible, about the consequences of their actions and any changes in the objective conditions they confront.

These tasks are among the assignments for mainstream planners who apprise their clients of information that will improve the quality of their decisions. Radical planners are no different in this regard, though their role as information providers may not be formally defined. Since timing is of the essence, and since, in any event, there is no clear-cut division of labor between planning and practice, much of this gathering and evaluating of intelligence takes place informally, by word of mouth, and involves the members of the group in an ongoing dialogue. Appropriate strategies must be devised in the very eye of the storm.

Dialogue, Mutual Learning (Transactive Planning)

Radical practice is self-organized and depends for its effectiveness on interpersonal relations based on trust. It is this requirement, above all others, that determines the small size of action groups and their preferred dialogic mode of communication. In the course of transformative practice, more formal organizations, such as coalitions, may come into existence. But even they decompose into smaller groups whose members stand in a close personal relation to each other.[8]

The process of social learning, moreover, is premised on dialogue, which allows mutual learning between actor and planner to take place. I have called this process, which generally leads to a new synthesis of knowledge relevant for action and incorporates both experiential and formal codes, *transactive planning* (Friedmann 1981). When the theory of transactive planning was first published in 1973, few planners knew what to make of dialogue in planning.[9] Critics failed to appreciate how much planning actually gets done by word of mouth, and they could not conceive of a radical practice except by invoking huge Althusserian abstractions, such as a revolutionary class, in which no one has a need to talk at all.

Yet the evidence pertaining to the efficacy of small groups in which dialogue is practiced is conclusive. Writing from the feminist front, where group dynamics have been used extensively, Cook and Kirk report:

> [F]orming small groups allows women to get to know one another well; provides a basis of trust and mutual support for the action; makes decisions easier to reach; and avoids the need for leaders. It also makes it easier to absorb individuals into the action at the last minute, forming the basis for a future network and future action. (Cook and Kirk 1983, 73)

In Sweden, small-group organization has been introduced on an extensive scale into industrial production. Johnstadt concludes his evaluation of this technique with the following observation:

8. The emphasis on "trust" in transactive planning has been ridiculed by certain critics. One wonders whether they would prefer to put their trust instead in government statisticians, the public pronouncements of the president, the contrived images of television reporting, and the daily press. Trust is a necessary facet of all human relations. With so much conscious and unconscious deception in the management of public affairs, the personal trust among a small number of people who know each other, work with each other, and rely on each other would seem to be essential for moving the world's business.

9. For critiques, see Roweis and Scott (1977) and Camhis (1979).

In the beginning, group dynamics methods are purchased for
the purpose of increasing productivity and profits; under the
surface and in the long run, however, they will lead to a sharp-
ening of political questions about the meaning of and justice
in the way we live and work together. (Johnstadt 1980, 140)

In revolutionary China, the small group, or *hsao-tsu*, was made the
basis for transforming and unifying the Chinese people in a largely
successful attempt at mass mobilization (Whyte 1974).

Many other examples could be cited, from guerilla warfare to literacy training. In a review of the pertinent literature, Gil Court concludes that the small-group tactics of the social learning/social mobilization paradigm of planning are effective compared to other
organizational strategies. "Rather than destroying the current system, it gradually questions and undermines the reality on which it is
built. This may prove a far more effective strategy in the long run"
(Court 1984).

If her conclusion is correct, radical planners will have to get used
to the idea that their business is not primarily to write reports for
their hierarchical superiors but continuously to inform their comrades during the course of the action itself. It is primarily through
interpersonal transactions, grounded in dialogue, that the mediations of radical practice occur.

Transactive planning is not, of course, without problems of its
own. Personalities may clash; personal trust may be unwarranted;
the very nature of radical practice may lead to a cliquishness that
fundamentally negates the style. But more often than not, the conditions for mutual learning are right, and planners, though not centrally engaged in the action itself, will be able to foster an environment conducive to interpersonal transactions at the level of
planning.[10]

Dilemmas of Radical Planning

Although radical planners will not always be professionals—indeed,
a traditional education may be more of a hindrance than a help—
there is no question but that their practice requires certain skills and
knowledge for their mediations. In carrying out their assignment,
radical planners face extraordinary difficulties. It is the purpose of
this section to elucidate some of these dilemmas and to hint at ways

10. Two recent doctoral dissertations provide positive proof that transactive planning based on dialogic relations can be made to work even in public settings, such as
the management of wilderness areas. See McLaughlin (1977) and Stokes (1982).

of overcoming them. I shall discuss them under three headings: critical distance, open inquiry, and the unity of opposites.

Critical Distance

I refer here to the planners' social involvement with the group that is the "carrier" of radical practice. We suggested that, as radicals, planners must be committed to the group's practice and to the global project of emancipation. At the same time, however, they should neither stand apart from the group's practice nor be absorbed by it. As mediators, they must maintain a *critical distance* from the group's practice.

We may visualize planners' social distance along a continuum: beyond a certain point, the closer they come to the action, the less useful are their mediations likely to be. The same holds in the other direction: the further away they move from the immediacies of the group's actions, the less they will be able to accomplish. We posit, then, an optimum critical distance between planners and the front line of action. Planners must be part of the action, but not entirely a part.

It is quite easy, then, for planners to lose the correct location vis-à-vis the group's practice. A basis for their effectiveness is the trust they inspire as people. The position implied by "critical distance," however, suggests that if planners remain too distant and aloof, trust may be dissipated. Alternatively, though trust may be gained by closer involvements with the action, the ability to mediate theory effectively in the thick of the action may plunge to zero.

Open Inquiry

The result of this requirement for effective mediation is the same as that of trying to find the proper social distance from engagement in practice. Planners are expected to bring the "whole world" to bear on local action. Inevitably, this involves a questioning mind. Are you doing things right? Is the theory according to which you are proceeding correct? Planners as mediators are inquirers who place the group's action in perspective through a fundamental questioning of its premises. They are the critical consciousness of radical practice.

This role can lead to situations that will render the planner's task well-nigh impossible. On the one hand, any group committed to action will want to protect itself against fundamental doubt. It does not need to have its hard-won practice undermined by marginally situated intellectuals. The questioning can go on indefinitely and may lose sight of its original purpose. An inquiry that does not respect boundaries and thus has very lax criteria of what constitutes warranted knowledge is obliged to consider even outrageous hypotheses: there is no stopping rule. As thinking goes on and on, from question to question, over an immense expanse, it can paralyze the will to act. But at what point does one say enough is enough, and bring the inquiry to a close?

The Unity of Opposites

One of the most difficult requirements for radical planners is the ability to live with contradictions. Yet one is tempted to say that contradictions define the very essence of radical planning practice.

To live with contradictions is to say that planners must hold in tension two opposing categories, *affirming both*, even where traditional logic tells us that only one of the terms can be asserted without running into unsolvable dilemmas. Some examples of contradictions follow:

○ Theory *and* practice.

○ Empirical analysis *and* normative vision.

○ Critique *and* affirmation.

○ Explanation *and* action.

○ Future vision *and* present reality.

Our natural inclination is to substitute the conjunction *or* for every *and* in the list above. Alternatively, it is to wish the opposite term away and to coin perhaps some new words, indicative of a mixed reality—ugly terms such as "theo-practica." Neither of these escape routes is, in fact, open to planners. The problem has to be faced in all of its complexity and without giving way.

As an example of what I have in mind, let us look at the contradiction between critique and affirmation. In strictly logical terms, critique is something altogether different from affirmation. If standards are made explicit, it is relatively easy to get agreement on what, in given instances, is missing. To formulate these standards and apply them to observable reality is the essence of a good critique. Thus, given an unambiguous concept of open unemployment, it is relatively easy to measure actual unemployment in the economy. And given a concept of gender inequality, the measurement of inequalities in the treatment of women workers is fairly straightforward. People may interpret these measurements in various ways; the numbers themselves commit no one to action. It is quite another matter, however, to build a consensus on what ought to be done. Whereas critique is always about an existing or past event, affirmation concerns a future that is still open to choice. You must assert certain values, alert people to the seriousness of the situation, invent solutions, gauge their probable impact, test them for their feasibility, and consider strategies to overcome resistance. You are now in a different mode of thinking: *you affirm.* For this reason, good critics rarely make good poets and painters. Or even planners, for that matter.

And yet, radical practice and planning must begin with a critique of what, in the present, is so wrong and offensive that it justifies actions to restructure the system. What is the planner to do? Critique can be carried to the point where it virtually eliminates all options. Everything must go, cries the radical critic, and go at once, in one climactic upheaval. All merely partial actions are pronounced useless; worse still, they may be enlisted in the "enemy's" cause.[11] A bland critique, on the other hand, may be inadequate for motivating and sustaining radical practice.

In short, critique and affirmation must be linked in practice, but linked dialectically, in reciprocal action upon each other. That is the core meaning of a "unity of opposites."

A similar analysis can be carried out for each of the pairs of contradictory terms. Carried to an extreme, each term negates the possibility of the other. A theoretical extreme negates the possibility of practice (and vice versa); an extreme of empirical analysis negates the possibility of vision; too much explanation loses sight of the requirements of action; future vision without a link to the present becomes addicted to utopian speculations. But how much is too much?

The dilemmas of radical planning are, in the end, all of the same kind. How much is too much? What is the optimal social distance? When should a halt be called to critical inquiry? None of these questions allows of a formal reply. Yet neither can we say, with Wittgenstein, that if an answer does not exist, the question itself has no meaning. In fact, in the practice of radical planning, it is the absolutely central question. And because it is about practice, the answer to it must come from practice itself and not from pure thought. It is a question about practical reason (Ulrich 1983).

A tentative answer might be as follows (the very terms of the answer remain imprecise: we are now with Michael Polanyi [1966], in the arena of tacit knowing). With an epistemology of social learning, which is the theory of knowledge underlying radical practice, *action*

11. The whole of the Frankfurt School of Critical Sociology might be accused of carrying its critique beyond the critical threshold. The mind, as Gramsci said, is inclined to pessimism. What is needed is to join its pessimism to the optimism of the will.

is always primary. Questions are thus put to theorists from the side of practice and not the other way around. The imperative of action always has priority over the equal imperative of knowing.

So long as the planner keeps this order of priorities in mind, the dilemmas of radical planning practice can be resolved, though only in practice. As planner, you always work within a context that has its own limits of time and place, and you address specific actors with known characteristics. These are the practical conditions that help the planner to find the critical distance, to guide his or her inquiry, and to hold dialectical opposites in reciprocal relation.

Radical Planning and the State

Radical planning, always based on people's self-organized actions, stands in necessary opposition to the established powers and, more particularly, the state. For the state to engage in radical planning poses a contradiction in terms. Still, it would be wrong to ignore the state's existence or to treat it as an adversary only. Its presence is pervasive, and social advances achieved through a radical planning that bypasses the state will quickly reach material limits. To go beyond these limits, appropriate actions by the state are essential. Such actions must be fought over in political struggle for the legitimate claims of the disempowered (Piven and Cloward 1979; Peattie and Rein 1983). The ultimate aim of these struggles—the reassertion of political community in civil governance—will undoubtedly require a permanent restructuring of the state. But this can only be achieved through a step-by-step process of radical reforms and social learning in all of the domains of public action.

Three kinds of politics are relevant. The *politics of empowerment* takes place over claims staked out around the major bases of social power (see Figure 19). One of these bases, time, involves a claim to greater access to a surplus of time over and above what is required for social reproduction. In Western, industrialized countries, this struggle is currently focused on such issues as time sharing, the thirty-five-hour week, flexitime, child care provision near the place of work, and extended maternity and paternity leaves. In Third World cities, struggles over time tend to be merged with those over access to space and the complementary investments that render that space socially useful. By correct planning for space use, settlement, and land in metropolitan areas, time, currently used up in subsistence activities, could become available as "surplus." Land for new urban settlements should be situated near the major sources of employment and enjoy good access to public transportation. The amount of land should be sufficient to allow, in addition to shelter, the development of urban gardens for self-provisioning (Sanyal 1986). The land should be adequately served with water, electricity, and sanitary facilities at a cost affordable to people with very low incomes. Schools and other collective facilities should be planned as an integral part of low-income housing estates.

As this abbreviated catalogue makes clear, the state, whether national or local, must be involved in projects that directly address people's survival needs and liberate their energies for self-development. It is true that struggle over time and space, or indeed over greater access to any of the other bases of social power, will not, in itself, lead to empowerment. Genuine power comes only from successfully engaging in political struggles, and from using the gains in social power to engage in yet further struggles to enhance people's capacity for a development from within.

In view of the massive material needs of the disempowered, the potential costs imposed on the state are very large indeed. To divert the resources required from other, economically more lucrative uses will require a *politics of redistribution* at the national level. Such a politics is likely to favor the disempowered only when advocates for progressive redistribution can count on mobilized grass-roots support. Linked to each other, the politics of empowerment and of redistribution illustrate the intimate association that exists between successful micro-actions on the one hand and a national politics on the other.

Finally, we must consider the *politics of place*, which sets out to defend people's life spaces against the rapaciousness of capital and bureaucratic fiat. Life space comprises the homes and neighborhoods and districts that sustain and support the self-production of life by individual households and communities. People have an inborn desire to preserve and improve its character. They will want to extract from the state assurance of continuity in local production against the rise and fall of business and technological cycles. They will want to control outside investments that, while they will benefit few within the community, are likely to be harmful to many. They will want to provide safeguards against speculative building.

The politics of place is typically conducted at the level of the local state, because the relevant policy instruments, such as zoning, rest in the hands of the state. And yet, these instruments are not likely to be used in the protection of people's life spaces unless the people themselves become engaged in defending them. The state may thus be visualized as a "terrain of struggle" in which different class interests contend over the direction of development and the distribution of the related costs and benefits. This is not to argue the state's neutrality. The state has interests of its own at stake, and it asserts these interests from time to time even as it strikes an alliance with this or that class fraction. But whatever the outcome, the state-as-actor can never become a radical state. For better or for worse, it always acts as a hegemonic force.

Surviving in a Heartless World

To be an outsider, or "radical," is a difficult role to sustain. It means to swim against the stream, to mobilize for action, and always to struggle against resistance. Of course, most so-called radicals do not perceive their actions to be radical at all. They are merely doing what comes naturally to them, fighting for what they believe to be right, for their own survival, for a better and happier existence.

Tenants going on strike tend to see their action as a last resort; they are not radicals. People protesting a nuclear power plant, or organizing a peace march, see themselves as exercising their legitimate right as citizens under the Constitution. Women setting up a shelter for battered women are doing something to help their sisters; they may be angry, but they are not radicals. Energy activists fighting the private utilities for permission to tie alternative power-generating sources, such as wind, into the larger territorial grid, are using a legal means to achieve their purpose. Neighbors planting a community garden to grow fresh produce for themselves are doing a neighborly thing in the time-honored tradition of barn raising. Bicycle enthusiasts lobbying the city council for grade-separated bike paths act like any other pressure group. Workers buying out an abandoned manufacturing plant, perhaps with local community assistance, are not challenging the system; they are battling to save their livelihood. Labor unions negotiating with employers for the thirty-five-hour week, flexible time arrangements, and child care provisions are doing what they have always done: engaging in collective bargaining. Black women forming a local development corporation that will help them get adequate housing for themselves and their children and common services specifically tailored to their needs as single-parent heads of households, all at a cost they can afford, are doing something that is of vital importance to themselves through an institutional mechanism that is already sanctioned.

Yet taken together and blown up to the proportions of society as a whole, these instances of a radical practice constitute a major challenge to the prevailing system. They will make people less dependent on global capital, increase their social power, and expose them to the lessons of political practice. A sense of commonality in the simultaneous pursuit of their separate interests is diffused through network publications such as *TRANET* (Transnational Network for Appropriate/Alternative Technologies) and journals such as *Coevolution Quarterly* (now discontinued). The time for an encompassing, integrative political ideology for the loosely textured radical practice of today may not be here as yet, but the potential exists, and once the movement acquires political potency, it will be quickly perceived as the real threat that it is.[12]

Let tenant activists elect a city council, as they did a few years ago in Santa Monica, California, and real estate and local business elites

12. For a very different and much less sanguine evaluation of what he calls the "new populism," see Carl Boggs (1983). He writes:

> It would be illusory to view the new populism as a fundamentally new strategy that, because of its uniquely indigenous and pragmatic character, could be the basis of a revitalized oppositional movement of the 1980s. On the contrary, the new populism has a deep affinity not only for *traditional* American populism but for the very European social democracy it considers obsolete. . . . Hence, whatever is distinctive "American" language and priorities, the new populism seems destined to repeat earlier failures. The probability is that, where such movements succeed in their own terms, they will end up *stabilizing* the very corporate power structure they ostensibly set out to oppose . . .
>
> The decisive theoretical and strategic limits of the new populism are not a function of its emphasis on "community" over "workplace" organizing or even of the predominant role it assigns to "alliance" politics; it is difficult to imagine any social movement in the U.S. establishing a public presence without *some* kind of community-based, alliance-oriented radicalism—and, moreover, none of the new populist theories have abandoned a commitment to workplace struggles . . .
>
> The basic underlying problem is deeper and more complex. On the one hand, new populist theory contains no critical or transformative approach to power relations, or to domination. The vision of democratic structural reforms is not shaped by any radical conception of the state—that is, it anticipates no overturning of the old social and political hierarchies, no sustained attack on the authoritarian state apparatus, no development of qualitatively new forms of self-management. Lacking such a dialectic, the principles of "economic democracy" ultimately have to be fitted into the design of the corporate power structure. (Boggs 1983, 358–359)

Boggs is not opposed, per se, to the new populism. His call is for a transformative theory that would convert the existing partial movements, with their partial theories, into a radical political force to overturn the state. Although I would agree with the need for such a theory and corresponding political organization, it is simply not realistic to believe that a theory can be produced at will. Either it will come at the appropriate moment or it will not. While the future remains open, present practice, with its more limited ambition, is still worthwhile, creating beachheads for the more extensive struggles to come.

will see the pillars of capital toppling and raise millions of dollars to defeat the incumbents. Not surprisingly, the money is always with those who uphold the status quo. People have only themselves. Their real strength lies in the transactive relations of their dialogue.

Still, groups engaged in radical practice also need money. How shall they finance themselves? Even more to the point, how shall radical planners survive when neither the state nor private foundations pay for their work?

Radical practice does not come dear in terms of money. It is more demanding of time: time for countless meetings that may last long into the night, or for the "sweat equity" that many jobs demand. But time, which is almost always in scarce supply, can be "saved" for radical practice from other activities so long as people are prepared to help each other out. Mutual help, which has its own intrinsic satisfactions, must be organized and requires forethought. To rely on merely spontaneous enthusiasm is not enough.

As for money, if you want it badly enough it will often materialize. Small individual amounts can be pooled. Fund raising helps. Institutions, such as parish churches, can make meeting space available. Foundations can be persuaded to underwrite certain kinds of activity. Even the government may be ready to fund some "radical" projects, perhaps unaware of their connection to the larger agenda. Militant political action may succeed in putting conditions on the use of public pension funds that will channel a larger proportion in the direction of radical projects. Often, there is a tipping point, with the public purse strings suddenly untied after a series of successful struggles which have created a certain aura of respectability for the project.

As for radical planners themselves, their circumstances may be as varied as the sources of financing I have described. Very often, radical planning is not a full-time occupation. In this event, planners come to earn their livelihood in the usual way, not unlike actors, painters, dancers, writers, and poets who work at relatively undemanding jobs while their real work lies elsewhere. In the relatively rare instances when radical planning constitutes the only source of income, the employer may be a radical "think tank," such as the Washington-based Institute of Policy Studies; a progressive labor union, such as the United Electrical Workers; or a church group such as the Maryknollers. Occasionally, radical planners may even work inside the bureaucracy as a kind of "fifth column" in support of radical practice outside. The material situation of radical planning is thus far from hopeless. But it is no way to get rich.

Concluding Comments

Throughout this book, "planning" has been used in a heuristic sense. As such, it has served us well, as we explored the several modes of technical reason in the public domain. But when we came to radical planning, we discovered that we had to step outside the traditions of societal guidance and change the terms of our discourse. We had to substitute the dialectical relation of transformative theory and radical practice for the "linkage" of knowledge to action." Because of this difference, what we have described as radical planning has little in common with the traditions of policy analysis or social reform. And yet, in the attempt to guide the course of human destiny through reason, to place the goal of history in *this* world and not in some transcendental heaven, there is a common root. Both transformative planning and societal guidance are born of the Enlightenment.

In closing my story with a discussion of radical planning, I have no wish to suggest that the other planning traditions have now been superseded. In the case of the peasant periphery, we observed that radical practice will require actions by a revolutionary state without which social mobilization for a self-reliant development cannot take place at all. And the planning by even a revolutionary state tends to have more in common with Saint-Simonian technocracy than with anarchist-inspired forms of radical planning, which are, by nature, oppositional.

Nor is the state in the so-called First World of industrial capitalism about to go away. To speak of its declining powers is not to argue the case for its imminent dissolution. And so, with the state continuing in the hands of technocrats, Saint-Simon lives on, along with a lingering belief in the technical mastery of unlimited progress.

But societal guidance from the top is not, as some liberal theorists would have it, the dialectical other of radical planning (Stöhr 1981). For the latter is not about participation in projects by the state. Its aim is the structural transformation of industrial capitalism toward the self-production of life, the recovery of political community, and the achievement of collective self-reliance in the context of common global concerns. In this context, our task is to wrest from the political terrain still held by state and corporate capital expanding zones of liberation in which the new and self-reliant ways of production and democratic governance can flourish. And for this project, the mediations of radical planning are essential.

Epilogue

Two hundred years of post-Enlightenment reason have brought us to this: the globe has shrunk to a few hours' travel distance and to the mini-seconds of intercontinental communications that shuttle billions of messages each day and transfer billions of dollars in the profitable management of global business—a staggering achievement. It has also led us to the present condition, which we believe to be a structural crisis of long duration and which threatens our livelihood and survival on a scale that is global as well. The countries of the First World, with the United States in the lead, have so far been able to stave off the worst of this, on the economic side by massive expenditures on military and space weaponry and politically by engaging in a global game of power that more often than not has enabled them to enforce their political will (Vietnam is the major exception).

It would be wrong, of course, to blame our present predicament on any single "cause," on a cause even so general and abstract as objective, technical reason. It would be equally wrong, however, to dismiss the connection and to continue with solutions that derive from the traditional responses of rational planning.

The philosophers of the Enlightenment argued that the highest forms of reason would be realized in the service of science and its methods, which were crudely modeled on Newtonian physics. For their part, engineers, who by the end of the eighteenth century were beginning to form their own professional academies for world improvement, would argue that the application of scientific knowledge to the natural world would ensure man's domination over nature. Some of them, such as Auguste Comte, went further, claiming that equal mastery could be achieved over the social world through knowledge of scientific laws and "human engineering."

Planning is to a large extent still practiced in the Comtean manner; as Rexford Tugwell (1975b) put it nearly forty years ago, it is a "scientific endeavor." And in that tradition, the specific agent of mastery and control is, first, last, and always, the state. Planning was to be the finely honed instrument that would enable the state to direct the social forces that operated within its boundaries in accord with principles that, knowable in themselves, could be used to "predict" the future. To predict was to control, Comte had taught, and in the twentieth century, the branch of knowledge concerned with scientific predictions, or forecasting, became an important part of the technology of planning.

Comtean scientism pushed aside the more delicate and philosophical *Geisteswissenschaften*, or disciplines of the spirit which today we call the human sciences. It promised an epistemology without a knowing subject—the phrase is Karl Popper's (1972). Since the only valid knowledge was said to be theoretical, and theory was to be independent of the personal quirks and preferences of scientists, it constituted a refined world of its own. The language in which theory was expressed was often arcane, delighting in mathematical symbols, long words with Greek roots, and an involved grammar. Science was for the specialist. It was an esoteric knowledge.

During the 1920s, the German physicist Werner Heisenberg discovered that subatomic investigations of matter led to indeterminate results and could therefore be apprenhended only as statistical probabilities. The instrument of observation was itself a disturbing element, and what could not be observed "as it really was" could only be interpreted according to the laws of chance. This finding quickly made its way into the social sciences as the uncertainty principle. Typically, it came to be applied to research at the micro-scale, where the presence of the investigator came to be seen as a possible "cause" of the observed behavior. A famous instance of this was the Hawthorne experiment at the Western Electric plant described in Chapter 5. To draw the full implications of the Heisenberg principle would have meant putting the subject back into scientific observation at all levels of social-scientific discourse. Until quite recently, the vast majority of social scientists were unprepared to accept what they sensed would be the probable consequences of this move: the de-objectification of knowledge by making it subject-related, or "intersubjective," and the re-integration of the human with the social sciences and perhaps ultimately with the physical sciences as well. Sporadic efforts along these lines have tended to be viewed with a certain indifference if not outright hostility and have been pushed to languish in the far periphery of the social-scientific establishment.

But of late—given the growing conviction that Popper's world of theoretical objects is taking us nowhere—the far periphery is staging a comeback, laying siege to the Establishment under the fluttering, multicolored banners of hermeneutics, structuration theory, phenomenology, ethno-methodology, universal pragmatics, and similar movements. These shock troops of a social-scientific revolution are at least in agreement on one point: that the world is real, and that it can only be known—to the extent it can be known— through a form of empathic inquiry, which is a way of interrogating a social reality that has the capacity to answer back. Along with this is a gradual rapprochement with the human sciences, as such cognitive fields as mythology, folklore, history, and linguistics are seen to provide important pointers for the proper understanding of observed phenomena.

The implications for planning of this new, holistic, dialogical science are not yet fully understood.[1] We can nevertheless risk three preliminary conclusions. First, the new epistemology renders old-fashioned technocratic planning illegitimate. All knowledge is perspectivist, provisional. Second, on the positive side, the new epistemology turns both scientific and planning inquiries into a dialogic process between the researcher/planner and the subject/actor, who typically proceeds on the basis of unarticulated, tacit knowing. Third, the language of scientific/planning discourse is changed into one capable of expressing subjective realities, a search for meaningful action, and the integration of the human with the social and behavioral sciences.

But a change in the epistemological paradigm is not the only change affecting contemporary planning. A second disturbance in the classical model of rational planning came with the realization that more than one macro-actor was engaged in societal guidance. Under rational planning, the state was seen as the dominant actor in socioeconomic processes. However, radical critiques soon established monopoly capital as a second major actor in the public domain. Since capital is neither elected nor in any way accountable to the people, however, and its interventions are thus lacking in legitimacy, a third macro-actor had to be identified: the people organized for political action on their own behalf—the political community.

Mainstream planners typically worked for the state, articulating the state's interests, while capital employed its own advisors. It is only within recent years that planners have been found in substantial numbers also within civil society, where they work not only with

1. The best theoretical statement is by Ulrich (1983); the best account from practice is by Max-Neef (1982). The two levels of understanding—theoretical and experiential—have not yet been brought successfully together.

the politically mobilized sectors of the population, but also with the legislative assemblies that intersect with the domain of the state.

The traditional model of rational planning has thus been canceled by the very evolution of human consciousness. Because it is roughly divided among the domains of state, capital, and political community, planning had to become politicized, with the planners themselves battling in the front lines of the struggle.

To this general picture, we must now add the perception we have of being engulfed by the consequences of a worldwide structural crisis that presents us with challenges of unprecedented magnitude. Our environments—political, economic, social, and physical—have suddenly become unglued. Most of what we thought we knew has lost its validity; it no longer leads to a satisfactory understanding of reality. The older sciences had assumed fixed parametric relations, and so long as these held, scientific findings had some validity. But now it is precisely the relations that have given way. And so, just at the point when our need for knowledge is greatest, we stand ignorant before events whose long-term implications we can scarcely grasp. Under these conditions, only an epistemology of social learning based on the unity of practice and transformative theory within the context of a continuing process of action and inquiry can give us grounds for hope.

The contemporary situation of planners, then, is much like that which faced the *ancien régime* in France when a king died, and the shout went up from the streets, *Le Roi est mort, Vive le Roi!* We are inclined, with planning in mind, to repeat this phrase. The old planning has died, but we cannot do without planning. We cannot wish to separate knowing from acting. Yet our paradigms are rapidly changing—paradigms of how knowledge is gained, of who the relevant actors are, and of how knowing and acting can be successfully linked to each other. In response to multiple crises, planning is undergoing its own transformations.

In this book, I have advocated a return to radical practice and thus to a form of planning whose intellectual roots are in the tradition of social mobilization. I have done so because I am convinced that we face the most profound crisis since the world was overturned by the triple revolution of the eighteenth and nineteenth centuries: the political revolutions in America and France, the revolution in science, and the industrial revolution. That magnificent era bequeathed to us the several forms of rational planning we have discussed in this volume. The changes through which we are now passing—as revolutionary as any of those that had their origins in the Enlightenment, and which may take several generations to fully work themselves out—will also surely transform the nature of the basic relation of knowledge to action. In the present transition, however, we stand especially in need of planners who will assist with the recovery of an active political community, which alone can engage in an emancipatory practice. We cannot know where this path will lead us. But with Italo Calvino we can say at least this:

The inferno of the living is not something that will be; if there is one, it is what is already here, the inferno where we live every day, that we form by being together. There are two ways to escape suffering it. The first is easy for many: accept the inferno and become such a part of it that you can no longer see it. The second is risky and demands constant vigilance and apprehension: seek and learn to recognize who and what, in the midst of the inferno, are not inferno, then make them endure, give them space. (Calvino 1972, 165)

Appendixes

Appendix A
Planning as a Form
of Scientific Management

Planning*

I. On the Nature of Planning

If it should be decided to "put to work," as the phrase goes in industry, some comprehensive program of better utilization and control of water resources, it becomes of interest to know something of the kind of planning that would be involved in carrying through such a far-flung social undertaking.

1. *Generic Meaning of the Term:* In its common sense "planning" is as old as man. Peasant, husbandman, merchant, industrialist, ruler, have always made plans. Such planning, however, pivots on the individual and carries the limitations of his particular interests, abilities, and facilities, varies as these change, and terminates when his interest ceases.

2. *Technical Meaning of the Term:* Used by those who advocate planning of public affairs the term has come to have the technical meaning given to it by engineering and industry. Engineers in large-scale construction operations and managers of large-scale business enterprises have learned that the condition of success is that this condition can be met only by the creation of an institutional mind which has its power of perception (investigation, research), of memory (records), of reasoning (analysis), and of design (planning). Such an institutional mind is a composite of, and yet is distinct from, the minds of the individuals of which it is composed, who, as individuals, may come and go; has a continuing life coincident with the life of the enterprise; and can think and arrange affairs with that large perspective made possible only by such characteristics. When a Goethals has assumed responsibility for the construction of a Panama Canal, or a Rockefeller has undertaken the creation of an industrial

---

* Chapter contributed by Harlow S. Person to the *Report of the Mississippi Valley Committee of the Public Works Administration* (1934, 221–228).

enterprise, he has invariably set about the development of such an institutional mind as the only reasonable assurance of consistency of component operations and the success of the undertaking.

This capacity to think in terms of experience larger than that which comes to any individual, to define distant goals, to arrange highly efficient ways and means of attaining them, and to pursue these distant ends consistently, yet with a flexibility which permits adjustment to changing conditions, is the dominant characteristic of institutional planning.

3. *Planning and Control:* The attainment of a complicated objective requires, first, the design of an arrangement of ways and means by this institutional mind; second, an actual manipulation of the ways and means—usually by another than the planning agency—in accordance with the predetermined arrangements. Therefore responsibility, authority, and control are inherent in planning. Yet these can be—have been in certain instances—provided for in a manner and with a quality which is valued in a political democracy.

To make responsibility, authority, and control both democratic and effective the planning and the execution must be in accordance with "laws of the situation," the situation including both the objective and its environment. The planner must know as much as science makes possible about all natural and human forces involved in the achievement of the objective, must evaluate their degrees of flexibility and must arrange for either manipulation or conformity in accordance with their natures. This is an inexorable condition of planning, whether individual or institutional. Water cannot be made to flow uphill and ships cannot be made to sail up shallow rapids, but, by an arrangement of materials which takes the form of locks, navigation uphill may be made possible. Navigation may be thus provided, but shippers cannot be compelled to make use of it if it is not to their interest so to do. Therefore in planning, the design must be such that, in execution, the control and authority reflect—now obey and now manipulate—the forces inherent in the situation, and are not the expression of arbitrary desires and unintelligent assumptions.

Planning offers itself as the salvation of essential democracy. As a democratic society develops a more complicated social-economic life, it becomes less capable of surviving uncertainty and drift; of surviving as democracy without continuing purpose, control, and authority. It must therefore develop its institutional planning. Recognition of inflexibilities as well as flexibilities in situations is of especial importance to planning in a democratic society. Over a period flexible and inflexible factors may undergo change with respect to these characteristics, but in making plans at any particular time they must be recognized as they then are. A democracy must make its planning the expression of a genuinely collective interest, purpose, and will; must have regard for inflexible human as well as inflexible physical factors; and must confine its manipulations to the plastic factors inherent in the situations being planned. In this way individual and group relations in adjustment to environment may be organized and brought under control and yet remain democratic.

II. Organization for Planning

1. *Planes of Planning:* Because of the complicated organization and operations of multiple-plant enterprises, these offer the most valuable suggestions for social planning; in fact, theirs is the only pertinent experience on which we may draw. In their experience it has been discovered that the planning least subject to confusion and self-defeat and most effective in coordination is organized on three planes:

a. Directive Planning is concerned with the general direction of a far-flung enterprise, calculates in terms of plants as units, formulates plant programs, schedules, and budgets as directive instruments, and leaves to each plant the more detailed planning in terms of its units. These plant schedules and budgets are the standards by which plant operations are coordinated and their efficiency judged. The comparison of periodic plant-progress reports with these schedules and budgets effects directive control. Control through specifications of major purposes, ways, and means—environmental control—is the characteristic of this plane of planning.

b. General Administrative Planning is the planning by the general management of the individual plant. In conformity with directive specifications it calculates in terms of major departments as units, and formulates programs, schedules, and budgets as controls for these departments. It leaves to the departments more detailed planning for their operating units. General administrative control is effected through comparison of departmental-process reports with the general administrative schedules and budgets. Here again environmental control is more characteristic than specification in detail.

c. Operative Planning is the responsibility of a departmental management. It calculates in terms of orders received, and of the processes and machines of the department. Within the major controls established by directive and the secondary controls established by general administrative planning, it designs the related functional activities of detailed operations. Here specification in detail enters.

With respect to specification in detail—by some called regimentation—two characteristics should be noted:

a. The farther the plane of planning from the plane of actual operations the less detailed is the planning and the larger the units in terms of which plans are made. Detailed planning can be done only by those who are at the scene of operations and know intimately the unit acts to be performed and the processes, machines, and skills involved.

b. Detail in specification is a function of the technological methods necessary for achievement of the objective, not a function of planning itself. Planning does not seek detail in arrangement for its own sake. It seeks rather to discover the least prearranging which the technology of achievement of the particular objective requires.

2. *Steps in Planning:* In directive, general administrative, and operative planning, considered individually or as an integrated whole, there are five inherent major steps:

a. Definition of Purpose: The designing of ways and means for achievement of an objective cannot be begun until the objective is accurately defined. The desired end governs every step of planning. Many failures in planning may be attributed to disregard for this condition precedent. It is a folk saying that a problem well stated is half solved. A precise and complete definition of objective is a long step toward planning for its achievement.

b. Formulation of Policies: Not only does decision to achieve an objective reflect a major policy, but achievement is governed by collateral policies. An entrepeneur may for instance decide to construct and operate a textile mill. The necessary planning will be conditioned by such policies as those respecting the market to be served, the variety of items to be fabricated, and the apportionment of capital between physical equipment and working funds.

c. Formulation of Program: To bring ways and means under organized consideration and evaluation there must be a working formulation of their possible arrangement in the form of a tentative program of action. This program is to planning what an hypothesis is to scientific research—a guide to orderly procedure in discovery, evaluation and application of data.

d. Design of Plan: Revision followed by still more revision of the tentative program, as data are acquired and evaluated, results in a refined final form of the program in which ways and means of accomplishing the objective are brought into precise qualitative, quantitative, and functional relationships. This constitutes the plan.

e. Differentiation of Projects: A plan is usually composed of groups of operations, each group having an integrity which permits it to be carried through as a thing in itself. Such an integral group of operations may be identified as a project. For instance, in building construction the foundation work, the erection of superstructure, or the installation of a lighting or heating system, is each a distinct project. Each can be carried out as a separate sub-objective because coordination has been effected by the general plan of which each is a part.

Anyone of such related projects, if it be large and complicated enough to call for such a division—for instance, the projects involved in the construction of a Panama Canal—may have its particular planes of directive, general administrative, and operative planning.

3. *Process of Planning:* Three major processes are characteristic of planning, whether it be directive, general administrative or operative.

a. Research and Investigation accumulate the data by which the ways and means of achievement that are to enter the final design may be evaluated. Such research and investigation eliminate guess, hunch, and prejudice, discover the degree of flexibility and inflexibility of factors, and increase the probability of the success of the resultant plan. Research and investigation are of two kinds: the continuous research and investigation which arc constantly engaged in accumulating basic data for general subsequent use; and the research and investigation which focus on problems of a particular objective.

b. Standardization translates scientific information into terms pertaining to materials and apparatus to be used and to ways of doing things familiar to those concerned with execution. The specification of a particular type of machine on which to fabricate a particular product, or of a specified grade of materials for a particular piece of construction, is a standard. It is in terms of such basic standards that a detailed operative plan is composed. Such standards are never considered final and are subject to continuous rational revision.

c. Design is the final element of the planning process in which ways and means of achieving the purpose, based on research-determined standards, are formulated into a logical and effective scheme of coordinated, synchronized acts utilizing specified facilities.

Although these elements of the planning process are common to all planes of planning, each uses its appropriate types of research, standards, and design. As has been observed, the farther the plane of planning is from the plan of action and from the planning of constituent projects, the less detailed the specifications. However, the standards and resultant specifications of all planes of planning must be consistent, as they may be if based on the same fundamental researches and checked one against another. Planning, in this technical meaning of the term as understood by large-scale engineering and industry, has not yet been adapted to the social purposes of government in the United States. In the common meaning of the term, individual leaders and individual administrators have had their individual plans, but these pivoted on individuals and have been transitory. A continuing institutional mind, especially charged with the responsibility of formulating some comprehensive long-run social plan, has never been established. However, the complications and confusions of our cultural and economic life are becoming such that the planning of a better adjustment of national life to natural environment appears essential. The technique of such planning cannot make a better beginning than to adapt the technique developed by engineering and industry.

III. Directive Planning of the Utilization and Control of Water Resources

1. *Federal Responsibility:* Comprehensive regional planning of the utilization of water resources is unquestionably a responsibility of the Federal Government. Federal responsibility rests on these

among other facts: (a) the problems transcend state areas and the physical factors cut across state lines; (b) the Federal Government has for years been particularly concerned with navigation and more recently with flood control; (c) water problems have in other respects become increasingly a problem of the Federal Government; (d) it has numerous agencies already experienced in the particular kinds of research and investigation involved, and in formulating appropriate basic standards; (e) national relations and influences play a progressively larger part in cultural and economic life; and (f) many believe the Federal Government should discharge the moral obligation of rectifying the results of unwise early Federal land policies (including water factors) which have permitted in some cases the misguided efforts of individual settlers, with the ultimate consequence of jeopardy to their present welfare and security.

2. *The Evolutionary Point of View:* The application to public affairs of the principles and technique of planning offered by the rich experience of engineering and industry must first of all be conditioned upon the social nature of the proposed planning.

In regional planning the objective must be defined in terms of the desires of an existing society; the standards must take into account its traditions, habits, and prejudices; the planning and executing instruments employed must be insofar as is technically desirable, existing institutions. One of the first problems of regional planning research is to inform itself with respect to such matters and to ascertain how harmony may be brought between existing institutions, mental attitudes, and habits on the one hand, and the developed technique of planning on the other hand. Beginning in this manner social experience in planning will influence traditions, habits, prejudices, desires, and institutions, and also the planning technique itself; and by circular reactions will bring progressively more perfect harmony between principles, technique, and conditions.

3. *Utilizing Available Institutions:* Organizations are constitutionally and legally available to serve as agencies of regional planning and of the execution of plans. These are agencies which may easily be expanded or created by Federal, state and local governments, respectively. From among these should not be omitted interstate and interlocal-government "authorities" which may be created under statutes authorizing compacts. Provided there is a will to plan and a willingness to come into cooperative relations, a great variety of institutions is available for the purpose.

4. *General Resources Planning:* Although here concerned chiefly with directive planning of the control and use of water resources, we should not fail to perceive that water is but one of several related classes of resources and that promotion of the public welfare by wiser use of one particular resource cannot effectively be accomplished without its being incorporated into a master plan of utilization of all resources. Therefore, from the point of view of an agency concerned with directive planning of the use of water resources, its planning should be conditioned by a comprehensive plan for the coordinated control and utilization of all resources. It should begin its planning subject to environmental controls thus established.

5. *Organization for Regional Planning:* In private industry it has come to be realized that the once common assumption that "my business is entirely different from yours" is true only in respect to such matters as materials, technology, and markets, and that all businesses are essentially alike in respect to fundamentals of management, among them planning. The framework of planes, steps and processes of planning, which have been described, is common to all. The differences between a public and a private business do not affect fundamentals or organization for achievement of objectives, provided there is the will to achieve them precisely and economically. Therefore, one may accept the framework of planning developed by private industry as adaptable to public purposes.

Consideration of available public institutions, to which reference has been made, suggests an orderly and logical allocation of planes of planning responsibility among them. Federal agencies would be concerned primarily with directive planning and think in terms of regional objectives and constituent projects. State and interstate agencies would be concerned primarily with general administrative planning of constituent projects; and lesser agencies, public and private, generally with operative planning and execution. This suggestion will be developed more fully below. Likewise the planning would involve steps and processes similar to those characteristic of planning in private industry.

6. *Definition of Objective:* For reasons which have been indicated the Federal directive planning agency would be best equipped to define the purpose and scope of any particular regional undertaking for control and utilization of water resources. It would of course consult with state and interstate agencies in working out the statement of scope and purpose, but on it should rest initiative and ultimate responsibility because its perspective, free from the particularism of

more restricted points of view, is the only perspective adequate for such responsibility.

7. *Research:* It also would be the agency best equipped through association with specialized agencies of the Federal and state governments to organize coordinated researches (conducted by both Federal and local agencies) essential to an adequate knowledge of the waters involved, and their behavior and relations. In this connection attention should be called to the urgent necessity that it should promptly organize the procurement of continuous records of the behavior of water, and accompanying researches, with a scope which has never yet been undertaken. This would involve that at all strategic points in a region provision be made for the accumulation and analysis of continuous records of rainfall, runoff, infiltration, water tables, subsurface deposits, stream flow, low water, floods and erosion; and the relations of swamps, reservoirs, lakes and rivers to other physical and cultural factors. While planning begun tomorrow would have to be content with such meager records of this kind as are now available, the concept of the planning agency as a perpetual institutional mind should inspire it to provide promptly for adequate continuing records and analyses for use twenty-five, fifty, and a hundred years hence. Paralleling such studies of a more strictly hydraulic nature should be studies of the social utilization of water for navigation, power, irrigation, sanitation, recreation, and so on; all designed to afford a more substantial foundation for future planning of the use and control of water in a program of better adjustment of man's life to his environment.

8. *Data and Standards:* Accompanying and consequent on these researches such a Federal directive planning agency should be continuously engaged in the consolidation of basic data and the formulation of basic standards pertaining to materials and methods used in the control and utilization of water, of the nature indicated in an earlier section, and should have them available for use in connection with the succession of programs and projects with which it would come to be concerned. As in industry and engineering, such standards should never be considered final; but at any time the latest revisions should be immediately available for each planning problem that presents itself.

9. *Education:* This Federal agency of directive planning should assume the responsibility of a continuous program of general public education respecting better utilization of water resources and better

control of the destructive conduct of water, especially where, as in the case of erosion, its first destructive forms are insidious, do not attract local attention, and the destructive characteristics are seen only in large perspective. For illustration it might undoubtedly be well worth while to inspire the enlistment of the rural school children of the country—rural Boy Scouts and Girl Scouts—under the guidance of educational and agricultural authorities, in a campaign to combat erosion in its initial, insidious forms of sheet and finger erosion. Similar maneuvers have been organized and carried through in suburban communities with respect to pests like the tent caterpillar. This suggestion indicates how planning may be made a means of enabling all citizens of a democracy to join the ranks of those seeking to thwart destructive [*sic*] and to release beneficial energies.

10. *Specific Programs and Projects:* In the fact of concrete situations calling for better utilization and control of water resources, and with the data and standards being continuously acquired against such times of need, this Federal directive planning agency would be in a position to exercise the more definite planning function. In respect to this, its function would be: to design the over-all regional layout of a program, including any special investigations necessary to the development of a first hypothetical design into a final refined design; to indicate the nature of and relations of constituent projects; to indicate the general character of the layout of each particular project; to indicate the organization of states, localities and authorities for further planning and the execution of plans; to formulate the schedules of action and the budget of costs and their allocations; and not least, by interchange of ideas concerning objective, plans, methods and division of labor, to effect the arrangements whereby the several cooperating agencies would be brought into legal and technical relations for consumption of the plans. All this accomplished, the several parts of the over-all plan would be passed along to the various cooperating general administrative and operative agencies.

11. *Directive Contacts and Controls:* To assure coordination in carrying through the program of any regional development, even though general administrative and operative responsibilities would be passed along to other agencies, this Federal directive planning agency would possess facilities for observing and appraising the progress on all parts of the program, because detailed operative and general administrative plans would be components of and dovetail

into the directive comprehensive plan. It would be in a position to assure the enforcement of all specifications, or correction of deviations therefrom, because of the authority accompanying Federal contributions to projects which are elements of a regional plan.

12. *Exclusively Federal Projects:* Undoubtedly in respect to some parts of an over-all plan or even in respect to an occasional over-all plan in its entirety, it would be found expedient for this Federal directive planning agency to assume the additional functions of general administrative planning, operative planning and execution—as is now the fact respecting major navigation projects. In such a case it should extend its organization to enable it to perform the additional functions. The extension of its organization would be by addition of a unit for the particular general administrative and operating planning, while the execution would usually be left by contract to some private agency or to the Corps of Engineers.

13. *Practicality of Planning:* Because government in the United States has not yet instituted planning with the comprehensive technique which has been here explained, discussion of what might be undertaken cannot avoid a theoretical flavor. However, it should be borne in mind that the technique has been validated by industrial experience and is one of the most practical and vital instruments of private business. Although first developed for control of fabricating operations, it has been applied progressively to merchandising, the general administration of plants, and directive administration of far-flung multiple-plant enterprises. It permits management of large-scale operations with an efficiency seldom realized in the small enterprises of half a century ago. Without it modern large-scale enterprises would be unmanageable, because the larger the scale of operations the more dependent an enterprise on planning. For this reason social enterprise appears to be even more dependent than private enterprise on such a technique of planning.

Appendix B
The Professionalization of
Policy Analysis

Since the late 1960s, policy analysis has moved toward an independent professional status. This direction is illustrated by the proliferation of new professional journals, graduate study programs, professional sub-specializations, and a growing critical self-consciousness. These developments are briefly commented on below, with the appropriate bibliographical references.

New Professional Journals
Since 1967, at least fifteen journals that focus on policy analysis have been started. This does not include journals focusing on particular policy questions (what Majone calls action programs), such as environmental policy, transportation policy, and so forth. The journals listed below are exclusively method-oriented. The date accompanying each is the first year of publication.

The Futurist 1967
Socio-Economic Planning Sciences 1968
Futures 1968
Policy Sciences 1970
Decision Sciences 1970
International Journal of Systems Science 1970
Journal of Applied Systems Analysis 1971
Policy Studies Journal 1972
Policy Analysis 1975
Journal of Policy Analysis and Management 1979
International Journal of Policy Analysis and Information
    Systems 1980
Policy Studies 1980
Performance Evaluation 1981
Policy Studies Review 1981
Forecasting 1982

433

Graduate Study Programs

A number of graduate programs in policy analysis have been established since 1970 when the first of these, The Rand Graduate Institute, opened its doors. Today there are at least seven such programs in the country at major universities, including Berkeley, Carnegie-Mellon, Duke, Harvard, Michigan, Stanford, and Texas. In 1979, the Association for Policy and Management was established as the common meeting ground for academics, students, and practitioners.

Because Rand played a decisive role in the emergence of the field and was the first to offer a curriculum leading to the Ph.D. in policy analysis, its statement of educational objectives may well be taken as definitive. Referring to the aims and objectives of the Rand Graduate Institute, which is the academic arm of Rand, a recent announcement of its program explains:

> The Institute's curriculum trains students to apply and adapt academic theories (e.g., in economics, organization and political analysis, and technological change) and tools (e.g., statistical techniques, survey methods, and operations research), in order to solve real-world policy problems within the often severe constraints of budgets, time, organizational outlook, and politics. The program is intended to cultivate both a taste and a capacity for interdisciplinary analysis—for timely thinking, speaking, and writing across the familiar boundaries of technology, economics, and politics. And through the research activities in which faculty and students are engaged, the Institute contributes to the development of the field of policy analysis. (Rand Graduate Institute 1982–1983, 2)

Areas of Specialization

Overall, the field of policy analysis has been characterized by a focus on method as opposed to more substantive foci (Wildavsky 1979, 414). A good example of this reluctance to be submerged in sectoral specializations and to embrace a methodological position instead is provided by the series of *Policy Studies Review Annuals* published by Sage Publications in Beverly Hills, California. Appearing since 1977, these enormous collections of essays, totaling more than eight hundred pages and over forty chapters each, cover every conceivable aspect of public policy. One is left with the impression that but for practical limitations of time, space, and resources imposed by the publisher on the series, the number of topics could have been indefinitely expanded. Given this bias toward a generic, methodological approach, a number of specializations have nevertheless begun to acquire rough contours of identity.

- ○ Futures research: de Jouvenal (1964), Helmer (1966), Kahn and Wiener (1967), Allen (1978), Ascher (1978), Hughes (1985)
- ○ Technology assessment: Ayres (1969), Jantsch (1972)
- ○ Program evaluation research: Caro (1971), Weiss (1972), Riecken and Boruch (1974), Rossi et al. (1979)

Critical Self-Consciousness
Policy analysis has always been a very self-critical field, so the literature here is extensive. Much of it is reviewed in Chapter 4. Following are some of the key texts: Hoos (1972), Berlinski (1976), Nelson (1977), Lilienfeld (1978), Lindblom and Cohen (1979), Wildavsky (1979), Carley (1980), Majone and Quade (1980).

Appendix C
Marxism and Planning Theory

Essay written by Marco Cenzatti expressly for this volume

The evolution of planning theory and practice on the left has a complex history. Beginning in the 1960s with advocacy planning and linked to the social conflicts of those years, radical planning theory took a major turn about ten years later with the entrance of Marxism into the debate. Whereas advocacy planning had its birth place in the United States and later expanded to Great Britain (Hall 1983), the genesis of the Marxist critique is more complex. Although part of the growth and radicalization of advocacy itself, it also originated from across the Atlantic and had its origin in the lively philosophical debates of post-war Europe (Anderson 1976). Compounded by the social events of the 1960s (the student revolt, the workers movements, and the growth of the welfare state), neo-Marxist studies opened up new areas of inquiry, such as urban sociology and the role of the state, that had previously been either ignored or dismissed as unworthy of serious attention.

Planning theory, however, did not enter as a central object of study in this expansion of the debate; rather, it was added on to other subjects. This resulted in a tension between the more radical fraction of advocacy planning, which was seeking in Marxism some guidelines for an effective planning practice, and the new Marxist studies which dealt with reconceptualizations of the urban terrain, the state, capital, classes, and class fractions. When planning entered the picture at all, it entered as a real activity, that is, as something to be analyzed for its present functions within the capitalist system. It was, therefore, subjected to a negative critique—for what it *was*—rather than advanced as an instrument for change—for what it *could be*.

A glance at the planning literature of the second half of the 1970s clearly reveals this tension. On the one hand, the literature shows the uneasiness with formal definitions of planning. On the other hand, when it embraces a Marxist perspective, it either denies the

437

possibility of planning theory altogether, or proposes compromises based on the relative autonomy of the planner within the state structure. In any event, it is unable to present a convincing alternative vision of the role of planning in the process of social transformation.

If a resolution of this tension was expected in the 1980s, this expectation has been disappointed. Discussions on planning theory have retreated into the background. Rather than asking what kind of planning should be furthered, more people appear to be asking whether planning is necessary at all (as in the present discussion on the necessity for a national industrial policy). As Harvey (1978) insightfully predicted, a new—but not altogether new—"gospel of efficiency" has largely erased the social concerns of the 1970s from the public agenda.

Obviously this involution did not happen without cause. To use Marxist terminology, it took place on the basis of the defeat of the working class that followed upon the crisis of the mid-1970s. The present drive to de-unionization, the decrease in blue collar wages, the increasing use of part-time, minimum-wage labor, the cuts in social security and social programs—all are aspects and signs of the inability of the working class effectively to counter the recovery of profitability that capital is achieving via increased exploitation. In most industrialized countries, labor has been unable to propose alternative forms of restructuring. Given the present political weakness of the left which is also reflected at ideological and theoretical levels, a positive theory of Marxist planning is not emerging. Planning by the left, guided by appropriate theory, would require an ability by labor to impose alternatives to the "austerity of capital." And this ability clearly does not exist at the present time (Campos Venuti 1978, Castells 1980).

This essay proposes to summarize the main differences between the Marxist view of planning and mainstream planning theory. It will point out the "two souls" of the Marxist tradition (action-oriented and analytical) and suggest that the unsuccessful resolution of the tension between them is a symptom of the left's inability to propose viable political alternatives in the present period of capitalist evolution.

Planning Theory

It is always difficult to establish the precise boundaries of Marxist theory. Internally, there are the accusations which different fractions on the left hurl at each other of having either misunderstood or distorted the "real" meaning of Marx. Externally, there is the broad spectrum of positions that incorporates a number of Marxist elements of analysis into frameworks of different intellectual origin (for example, Weberian, Neo-Ricardian). For the purpose of this essay, it is sufficient to point out that the Marxist conception of capitalist society is based on the primary and irreconcilable contradiction between the capitalist and working classes as well as on secondary contradictions between fractions within these classes. The dynamics of society are, therefore, not a linear development toward a single objective, but the continuous redefinition of the contradictions in the dialectical relationships between classes.

Mainstream Planning
From this starting point, a fundamental critique has been developed not only of the current definitions and theories of planning but also of planning practice. Its central point is the conception of the "common good" so fundamental to mainstream planning theory. Mainstream theories that start from definitions of planning such as "laying out . . . a course of action that we can follow and that will take us to our desired goals" (Churchman 1979a) are attacked on two grounds. In the first place, their very generality renders them immune against being disproved. It so separates them from reality as to make it virtually impossible to understand the dynamic processes that create both the problems to be solved and the goals to be achieved. More important, mainstream theories do not tell us what, precisely, these obstacles or goals might be: "Mainstream planning theory engages in a form of generalization that we might designate as *indeterminate abstraction*; and given this proclivity, mainstream theory appears not so much as incorrect as it is simply trivially true" (Roweis and Scott 1977, 1113).

A second point of departure for a radical critique is that in order for planning theory to maintain validity without specifying what "our desired goals" are and without questioning the rationality on which "courses of action" are based, it must be assumed that there is no need for a critical analysis of either the goals or the courses of action themselves. Society is seen as "naturally" proceeding towards objectives that are, or should be, universally accepted in the "public interest." If problems or contradictions appear on this route, they are simply obstacles to be overcome and the planner posits him/herself as an expert technically qualified to restore public rationality and the smooth workings of efficiency (Burton and Murphy 1980).

This function is even more evident in variations of the theory such as Lindblom's incrementalism, which Angotti compares to the theory of the invisible hand in economics: "[Incrementalism] gives the impression that no one group or class rules the state, placing the individual planner in a relatively passive role before the inevitability of the decision-making market" (Angotti 1978, 211).

Advocacy Planning

In what Roweis and Scott (1977) call "the imperfect negation," advocacy planning breaks with the formal definitions of previous planning paradigms. It is nevertheless unable to escape from the same theoretical horizon. In contrast to the system maintenance of mainstream theory, the "negation" consists in the explicit role of advocacy planning as facilitator of social change through the support by the planner of social groups whose interests had previously been excluded from the planning process. The other aspect of the negation is the refusal to "technicize" the issues and to acknowledge the fundamentally political character of planning. Yet, the "imperfection" of advocacy planning remains in its unwillingness to theorize the dynamics of capitalist society. Advocacy planning therefore risks offering a view of a socially balkanized society in which different groups are perpetually fighting one another. Lisa Peattie (1978, 88–89), for example, identifies three forms of advocacy planning.

1. In the classical version, "desirable processes of change are arrived at by a more inclusively pluralistic political process which incorporates into decision-making and intervention the ideas and interests of the broadest social spectrum of people concerned." Citizen participation in public programs is the legacy of this strand of advocacy.

2. In the activist perspective, "whatever desirable modifications of the system may emerge from the activities of the 'advocate planner,' these are not the real output of his work; the real output is the growth of radical consciousness and organizational competence in his constituency, and these will have their payoff when they go into making the revolution."

3. In the most radical view, advocacy "sees radical political change in the base of power in society as necessary, but not sufficient; the revolution, in this view, does not obviate the need for the long march through the institutions. . . . Advocate planners in this stream of thinking find themselves in food coops and communes, the women's health centers, the centers for the study of policy alternatives."

In all three of these positions, even the most radical, the question remains why and how the different groups that advocate planners choose as clients should coalesce around shared interests, rather than fight among themselves, in a sort of radical incrementalism.

"The imperfection of the negation" pivots around this question. Either advocacy moves into a Marxist interpretation, by recognizing in the dynamics between classes the lines of demarcation between the interests of different groups, in which case it is no longer "advocacy planning," or it subscribes to an understanding of the public interest that, although no longer a "given," but constructed through political debate and even conflict, nevertheless is the motor of social processes and the final goal of planning in the public domain.

Planning Practice

The Marxist critique of the public interest is substantiated in the analyses of specific planning practices. These critiques tend to follow a more or less fixed pattern. There is, to begin with, a general critique of mainstream planning theory on the ground of ideology, indefiniteness, and depoliticization. Second, planning activity is linked to the state apparatus. Even planners who try to act outside the state will keep it as a major point of reference, since sooner or later they will have to confront it and are therefore, de facto, acting within it (Fainstein and Fainstein 1978; Peattie 1978). The state is seen as a set of institutions whose task is to guarantee the reproduction of the existing social relations of production and to facilitate a smooth accumulation process by mediating the conflict between labor and capital and by regulating the secondary contradictions within the capitalist class.

The third step is the choice of a particular subject of analysis in which state intervention, and state planning, take a specific form. The choice and the treatment of the specific subject is where the two roots of the Marxist approach reveal their differences. "Academic" Marxism focuses on a specific form of planning as an example of the contradictions managed by the state (urban planning is a favorite subject). The interest of the analysis lies in understanding the workings of the process; the main dynamics are recognized in the hand of capital, and working-class action is seen as reactive to them. By contrast, action-oriented Marxist studies linked to advocacy focus on the collective actor, that is, social movements and community action. Although existing planning practice is recognized as serving the status quo, new forms of social action are actively sought in order to establish different planning practices.

Urban Planning

Castells's study of urban planning in the development of the growth pole of Dunkirk (1978) is a good example of the first approach. His starting point is the apparent paradox between the inability of urban planning to reach its stated goals and its continuous popularity and expansion. After rejecting explanations that see the growth of urban planning as a consequence of the worsening of the urban crisis or a result of the self-interest of the planning profession and its agencies, he identifies three functions of planning: as an instrument of rationalization and legitimation, as an instrument of negotiation and mediation of the differing demands of the fractions of capital, and as a regulator of the pressures and protest of the dominated classes. In the case of Dunkirk, all of these functions were brought to bear on controversies over the priorities of urban and regional development between the old bourgeoisie (linked to the port economy of the city), the old working class (dockers, casual laborers, textile workers), the new industrial interests (the new steel mill, shipyards, petroleum-processing complex), and the new, unionized, industrial working class.

In a more general case, Roweis and Scott (1977) point to the contradiction between the decisions of individual firms and households which have a substantial control over the purchase, sale, and development of land and the aggregate outcome of this conflictive process, or the production of urban land, over which no one has control. The inability to privately produce and consume urban land tends to lead these outcomes away from the efficiency and rationality sought by individual actors. The function of urban planning springs from the continuous attempt to render the chaos of individual decisions more orderly by means of zoning and by supplying urban goods and services, such as low-income housing, public transportation, streets, and so forth. At the same time, urban planning is simply another element of change added to the process and is consequently doomed to chase after a chaos which is always one step ahead.

Harvey (1978) focuses on the conflict between fractions of capital, rather than on individual actors. The interest of landowners and the construction industry, for example, tends to generate clashes not only with tenants (who, if well organized, can push rents downward, so that potential investors turn somewhere else), but also with the interests of industrialists, since a rent increase is likely to trigger demands for higher wages. Although this kind of dynamics is typical for the general working of the capitalist system, the contradictions are amplified in the urban system by the long life and immobility of the artifacts, by the "externality effects" that each element has on the others, and, above all, by the collective character of many urban services. These characteristics make the urban system particularly vulnerable to market failures. Insufficient urban investment creates bottlenecks in production, circulation, and consumption, and can generate social strife and diminish the supply of labor. Over-investment, on the other hand, leads to a devaluation of capital contrary to the interests of capitalists. Some form of coordination among private investments in the built environment has therefore to be reached in order to ensure that aggregate needs of individual producers are met. Through a mixture of repression, co-optation, and integration, urban planning tries to bring about some balance by decreasing the risks of long-term investments and externality effects, by supplying collective goods, and by avoiding the emergence of monopolies in space (such as privately owned mass transit systems) that would have disruptive effects on the social aggregated needs.

These examples offer analyses that lead in different directions. Castells denies the effectiveness of urban planning in the built environment and sees its principal task as that of achieving *social* cohesiveness. Roweis and Scott, on the other hand, not only deny that urban planning will ever succeed in bringing about the efficiency it seeks, but see its role as continuously searching for that efficiency *in the built environment*. Harvey shares with Roweis and Scott the focus on the built environment, but he concentrates on the mediations of planning among the fractions of capital, rather than on the individual actors. What these writers have in common, however, is their silence on the role that the working class has in the urban process. Harvey is explicit in pointing out that "[l]abor is not passive, of course, but its actions are defensive" (Harvey 1978, 217). The consequence of this view is that their analysis focuses primarily on the "active" actor, that is, on capital and "its" planning. It fails to see planning as a possible terrain for class struggle, where the working class plays a more active role, and thus as an instrument for significant change.

Social Movements and Community Action
Marxist studies linked to the advocacy planning tradition share with the previous group the critique of normative planning theory and the role of the state. However, their central interest is the question, What is planning? only insofar as it helps to understand what planning can be. Inherited from advocacy, their focus is on social groups who do not have a voice in the planning process, or, if they do, on how their interests are shaped to fit the present form of planning.

To be sure, the dominant force of the whole planning process is still capital, but understanding how it works is a means to increase the strength of the working class.

In Piven and Cloward's work (1978, 1979), the crux of the matter is the distinction between the organization and the mobilization of the working class. According to these authors, entrusting the possibility of social change to the organization of social protest has two negative results. In the first place the organization itself is, most of the time, structured around channels supplied by the state, so that the social protest is stripped of its innovative potential. A chief example of this is the welfare system, which historically has been used as a safety valve to contain social unrest. In the second place, dangers of "organizing" are also present in the attempts to fit new types of protest into a rigid Marxist schematization of the division between bourgeoisie and proletariat. Marx's analysis was based on nineteenth-century society. Nowadays, capitalist development has created new divisions (between races, between workers of different industries, between workers of "centers" and "peripheries"). If these divisions are dictated by capitalist logic, they also open up new ground for challenge. It is useless and counterproductive for left-wing intellectuals to try to fit this reality into the older and now obsolete categories. By so doing, the new possibilities arising from current contradictions are lost. Even if, in the short run, the mobilization of individual groups may be seen as negative, since it creates conflicts internal to the working class itself, mobilization should be judged for what is possible in a given situation and what is actually obtained. It is not mass organization that should be sought, but mass mobilization.[1]

A different position is presented by Cockburn (1977). Although aware of the pitfalls implicit in the use of state channels, Cockburn sees community participation in the local state in more dialectical terms than Piven and Cloward. Facing the social challenges of the 1960s and early 1970s, the state found it advantageous to allow the participation of the community in local councils. At the same time, the entrance into state channels was advantageous to the working class: "[T]he state's offers of participation and community development are [not] gains *in themselves* for the working class. Rather, they are what the working class *can make them*. They lead class struggle one step onward and bring new dangers and new opportunities"

1. For the debate of this position within the left, see the introduction to Piven and Cloward (1979), Roach and Roach's critique (1978a, b), and Piven and Cloward's reply (1978).

(Cockburn 1977, 103). The first danger to be avoided is the very concept of community action, which is the form in which the state tries to force the entrance of the movement into its structure. The starting point should be that, like struggles at the point of production, conflicts at the point of reproduction are not primarily political, but a part of the social wage and therefore fundamentally economic. In a reversal of Piven and Cloward's position, the task is to coordinate and integrate the two.

Back to Theory

Running through the various positions exemplified in the previous pages, there is a constant critique of mainstream planning theory as ideologically subservient to the needs of production and reproduction of the capitalist system. As the examples show, the alternative proposed in the Marxist framework offers a different starting point. The subject of Marxist analyses is never planning per se, but the state, the urban terrain, and social movements. As real activity, planning is inserted into the study a posteriori, as an instrument that fulfills a specific task after the limits and the possibilities of the subject have been established. There is thus a reversal from mainstream theory which proceeds by inserting the specific area of intervention into an abstract formulation of planning. And, although the possibility of a general theory of planning is denied, it is unnecessary to limit the aim of Marxist analysis to specific instances of planning. Where Marxist analysis can be most effective is in identifying an intermediate level where planning theory, or rather theories, are deemed possible so long as the field of intervention can be independently conceptualized. The state, the urban terrain, and social movements are independent objects of analysis, since the dynamics between classes are present in specific forms; "the plan" is not. To put it differently, the question, What can Marxist planners do? can only find generic and half-hearted answers such as, "The planner can also become the revealer of contradictions, and by this an agent of social innovation" (Castells 1978, 88). Formal definitions of the role of the planner remain undetermined in a Marxist framework because planning does not have its own dynamics but changes according to both the substantive subject of the planning activity and the shifts in power relationships and in the levels of social conflict in different instances.

Yet, if a Marxist general theory of planning cannot exist in the normative sense established by the mainstream approach, there is a different ground on which a general, but not generic, set of principles can be laid out toward a Marxist theory of planning. In order to do so it is necessary, first to clarify what a theory is about.

In mainstream planning, theory is understood as *guidelines for practice*. If, as already stated, a Marxist theory of planning cannot exist in this sense, mainstream planning theory exists only because of its peculiar logic which is circular: the starting point is the various practices of planning; from them, common characteristics are extracted by empirical observation; given the diversity of the fields of planning, the generalizations based on these characteristics render them void of content; via systems analysis, the characteristics are then rearranged and presented as a guide for the practice from which they were extracted in the first place. Thus, even if mainstream planning were to propose structural changes, it would be unable to do so, since it is a fundamentally tautological process. Furthermore, this theory is "free-standing," that is, it is not required to make explicit its underlying assumptions, nor is it linked to a comprehensive and explicated world view.

The Marxist approach presents a different concept of theory which is articulated on two levels. In the analysis of the different fields of planning, theory is understood as a *substantive hypothesis to explain observed phenomena*. In this sense, Marxist theories are typically *post-facto*, in that they explain phenomena already in progress. Although they may help us take a stand on these events, they are also inadequate to deal with emergent situations for which they lack specific counsel. However, these theories are explicitly informed by the Marxist world view. The link between world view and specific theory is the crucial second level of analysis. The continuous changes observable in reality, such as restructuring of capital, the growing importance of the state, changing class fragmentations, the emergence of new forms of protest, should be integrated with the existing framework. At the same time, they should lead to a more or less extensive reexamination of the underlying world view. The tension mentioned in the previous pages, between the work of Piven and Cloward, for example, who emphasize action, and Roweis and Scott and Harvey, who give more attention to analysis, follows from the polarity and interaction between world view and specific instances. The latter authors give more importance to further elaboration of the general framework and insert the specific cases into it, while the former tend to modify the world view, starting from the particular.

The question of linking the two positions is not simply a scholastic debate concerning methodology, but a political question of how class struggle should adjust to social changes and extend into new areas. It is, however, a question that cannot be answered in a discourse exclusive to the planning profession, that is, re-proposing a conception of the planner as an expert and technician. Nor does the answer lie in the spontaneous appearance of new forms of protest that, as the last few years have shown, are ineffective in times of social restructuring. The answer must appear from a conception of planning as a terrain of debate, confrontations, and elaborations of alternatives within the organizations of the working class. Only on the basis of this clarification can Cockburn's "dangers of the state's offers of participation" be avoided and the new opportunities created and seized.

Bibliography

Entries marked with an asterisk constitute a core library in planning theory.

Abbott, Leonard Dalton, ed. (1947). *Masterworks of Government*. New York: Doubleday.

Aborn, Murray (1984). "The Short and Happy Life of Social Indicators at the National Science Foundation." *Items* (SSRC) 38, no. 2/3 (September): 32–40.

*Ackoff, Russell L. (1962). *Scientific Method: Optimizing Applied Research Decisions*. New York: John Wiley & Sons.

*Ackoff, Russell L., and Fred E. Emery (1972). *On Purposeful Systems*. Chicago: Aldine-Atherton.

Adorno, Theodor W. (1978). *Minima Moralia: Reflections from Damaged Life*. London: Verso. (Orig. 1951)

Akerman, Nordal (1979). *Can Sweden Be Shrunk?* Reprint from *Development Dialogue* 2 (1979): 72–114, published by the Dag Hammarskjöld Foundation, Uppsala, Sweden.

Albert, Michael, and Robin Hahnel (1978). *Un-orthodox Marxism: An Essay on Capitalism, Socialism, and Revolution*. Boston: South End Press.

Alexander, Christopher (1975). *The Oregon Experiment*. New York: Oxford University Press.

Alexander, Christopher (1977). *A Pattern Language: Towns, Buildings, Construction*. New York: Oxford University Press.

Alford, Roger R., and Roger Friedland (1985). *Powers of Theory: Capitalism, the State, and Democracy*. New York: Cambridge University Press.

*Alinsky, Saul D. (1969). *Reveille for Radicals*. New York: Vintage Books. (Orig. 1946)

Allee, C. W. (1932). *Animal Life and Social Growth*. Baltimore: Johns Hopkins University Press.

Allee, C. W. (1958). *The Social Life of Animals*. Boston: Beacon Press. (Orig. 1951)

449

Allen, T. Harrell (1978). *New Methods in Social Science Research: Policy Sciences and Futures Research*. New York: Praeger.

*Allison, Graham T. (1971). *Essence of Decision: Explaining the Cuban Missile Crisis*. Boston: Little, Brown.

Althusser, Louis (1972). *Politics and History. Montesquieu, Rousseau, Hegel, and Marx*. London: NLB. (Orig. 1959–70)

*Altshuler, Alan (1965). *The City Planning Process: A Political Analysis*. Ithaca, N.Y.: Cornell University Press.

Amsden, Alice H., ed. (1980). *The Economics of Women and Work*. New York: St. Martin's Press.

Anderson, Perry (1976). *Considerations on Western Marxism*. London: NLB.

Angotti, Thomas (1978). "Planning and the Class Struggle: Radical Planning Theory and Practice in the Post-Banfield Period." In Harvey A. Goldstein and Sara A. Rosenberry, eds., 209–254.

Ansart, Pierre (1969). *Marx et l'Anarchisme. Essai sur les sociologies de Saint-Simon, Proudhon, et Marx*. Paris: Presses Universitaires de France.

Appleby, Joyce Oldham (1978). *Economic Thought and Ideology in Seventeenth Century England*. Princeton: Princeton University Press.

Appleby, Paul H. (1962). *Citizens as Sovereigns*. Syracuse: Syracuse University Press.

Appleyard, Donald (1981). *Livable Streets*. Berkeley: University of California Press.

Apter, David E., and Nagayo Sawa (1984). *Against the State: Politics and Social Protest in Japan*. Cambridge, Mass.: Harvard University Press.

Archibald, Kathleen A. (1980). "The Pitfalls of Language, or Analysis Through the Looking-Glass." In Majone and Quade, eds.

*Arendt, Hannah (1958). *The Human Condition*. Chicago: University of Chicago Press.

Argyris, Chris (1982). *Reasoning, Learning, and Action: Individual and Organizational*. San Francisco: Jossey-Bass.

*Argyris, Chris, and Donald Schön (1974). *Theory in Practice: Increasing Professional Effectiveness*. San Francisco: Jossey-Bass.

*Argyris, Chris, and Donald A. Schön (1978). *Organizational Learning: A Theory of Action Perspective*. Reading, Mass.: Addison-Wesley.

*Aristotle (1943). *Politics*. Translated by B. Jowett. New York: The Modern Library. (Orig. 4th century B.C.)

Arrow, Kenneth J. (1963). *Social Choice and Individual Values*. 2d. ed. Cowles Foundation Monograph 12. New York: John Wiley & Sons. (Orig. 1951)

*Ascher, William (1978). *Forecasting: An Appraisal for Policy Makers and Planners*. Baltimore: Johns Hopkins University Press.

Ashby, W. R. (1956). *Introduction to Cybernetics*. New York: John Wiley & Sons.

*Avineri, Shlomo (1968). *The Social and Political Thought of Karl Marx*. Cambridge: Cambridge University Press.

*Ayres, Robert V. (1969). *Technological Forecasting and Long-Range Planning*. New York: McGraw-Hill.

*Bahro, Rudolf (1979). *The Alternative in Eastern Europe*. London: NLB.

Baldwin, Roger N., ed. (1970). *Kropotkin's Revolutionary Pamphlets*. New York: Dover Publications. (Orig. 1927)

Banfield, Edward C. (1951). *Government Project*. Glencoe, Ill.: Free Press.

Banfield, Edward C. (1968). *The Unheavenly City*. Boston: Little, Brown.

Banfield, Edward C. (1974). *The Unheavenly City Revisited*. A Revision of *The Unheavenly City*. Boston: Little, Brown. (Orig. 1968)

*Banfield, Edward C., and James Q. Wilson (1963). *City Politics*. Cambridge, Mass.: Harvard University Press and MIT Press.

Barber, Benjamin R. (1984). *Strong Democracy: Participatory Politics for a New Age*. Berkeley: University of California Press.

*Bardach, Eugene (1977). *The Implementation Game*. Cambridge, Mass.: MIT Press.

*Barrett, Michele (1980). *Women's Oppression Today: Problems in Marxist Feminist Analysis*. London: Verso.

*Barry, Brian, and Russel Hardin, eds. (1982). *Rational Man and Irrational Society? And Introduction and Source Book*. Beverly Hills: Sage Publications.

Barta, Barnabas, et al. (1984). *Fertility, Female Employment and Policy Measures in Hungary*. Geneva: International Labour Organization.

Bateson, Gregory (1979). *Mind and Nature: A Necessary Unity*. New York: Dutton.

Bauer, Raymond, ed. (1966). *Social Indicators*. Cambridge, Mass.: MIT Press.

*Bauer, Raymond, and Kenneth Gergen, eds. (1968). *The Study of Policy Formation*. New York: Free Press (Div. of Macmillan).

Baumol, William J. (1952). *Welfare and the Theory of the State*. London: G. Bell & Sons.

Beauregard, Robert A. (1978a). "Planning in an Advanced Capitalist State." In Robert W. Burchell and George Sternlieb, eds., 235–254.

Beauregard, Robert A. (1978b). "Resolving Tensions: Planning Theory About and for Local Planners." In Harvey A. Goldstein and Sara A. Rosenberry, eds., 84–98.

*Beer, Stafford (1966). *Decision and Control: The Meaning of Operational Research and Management Cybernetics.* New York: John Wiley & Sons.

Beer, Stafford (1975). *Platform for Change.* New York: John Wiley & Sons.

*Bendix, Reinhard (1962). *Max Weber: An Intellectual Portrait.* New York: Doubleday.

Benne, Kenneth D. (1976). "The Process of Re-Education: An Assessment of Kurt Lewis's Views." In Bennis et al., eds. (1976), ch. 8.1.

Benne, Kenneth D., Leland P. Bradford, Jack R. Gibb, and Ronald O. Lippitt, eds. (1975). *The Laboratory Method of Changing and Learning: Theory and Action.* Palo Alto, Calif.: Science and Behavior Books.

Bennett, Douglass C., and Kenneth E. Sharpe (1984). "Is there a Democracy 'Overload'?" *Dissent* (Summer): 319–326.

Bennis, Warren G., Kenneth D. Benne, and Robert Chin, eds. (1961). *The Planning of Change.* New York: Holt, Rinehart and Winston.

*Bennis, Warren G., Kenneth D. Benne, Robert Chin, and Kenneth E. Corey, eds. (1976). *The Planning of Change.* 3d ed. New York: Holt, Rinehart and Winston.

*Bentham, Jeremy (1948). *An Introduction to the Principles of Morals and Legislation.* New York: Hafner Press. (Orig. 1789)

Bentley, Arthur (1908). *The Process of Government.* Chicago: University of Chicago Press.

*Benveniste, Guy (1977). *The Politics of Expertise.* 2d ed. San Francisco: Boyd & Fraser. (Orig. 1972)

Berglar, Peter (1970). *Walther Rathenau: Seine Zeit, Sein Werk, Seine Persoenlichkeit.* Bremen: Schuenemann Universitaetsverlag.

Bergman, Barbara R. (1984). "A Shortened Work Week is Long on Good Sense." *Los Angeles Times,* July 5, 1984, Part 2, 5.

Berle, A. A., Jr., and Gardiner C. Means (1932). *The Modern Corporation and Private Property.* New York: Macmillan.

Berlin, Isaiah (1969). *Four Essays on Liberty.* New York: Oxford University Press.

Berlinski, David (1976). *On Systems Analysis: An Essay Concerning the Limitations of Some Mathematical Methods in the Social, Political, and Biological Sciences.* Cambridge, Mass.: MIT Press.

Bernstein, Samuel (1955). *Essays in Political and Intellectual History.* New York: Paine-Whitman Publishers.

Berold, Robert, and Collette Caine, eds. (1981). *People's Workbook: Working Together to Change Your Community.* Johannesburg, South Africa: Environmental and Development Agency.

Bester, Arthur E. (1950). *Backwoods Utopias: The Sectarian and Owenite Phases of Communitarian Socialism in America: 1663–1829.* Philadelphia: University of Pennsylvania Press.

Bews, J. W. (1935). *Human Ecology.* Oxford: Oxford University Press.

Biersteker, Thomas J. (1981). "The Limits of State Power in the Contemporary World Economy." In Peter G. Brown and Henry Shue, eds., *Boundaries: National Autonomy and Its Limits.* Totowa, N.J.: Rowman and Littlefield.

Block, Fred (1984). "The Political Perils of Full Employment." *Socialist Review* nos. 75–76:24–29.

*Bluestone, Barry, and Bennett Harrison (1982). *The Deindustrialization of America: Plant Closings, Community Abandonment, and the Dismantling of Basic Industry.* New York: Basic Books.

Boggs, Carl (1976). *Gramsci's Marxism.* London: Pluto Press.

Boggs, Carl (1982). *The Impasse of European Communism.* Boulder, Colo.: Westview Press.

Boggs, Carl (1983). "The New Populism and the Limits of Structural Reforms." *Theory and Society* 12:343–363.

Boggs, Carl, and David Plotke, eds. (1980). *The Politics of Eurocommunism: Socialism in Transition.* Boston: South End Press.

Bookchin, Murray (1971). *Post-Scarcity Anarchism.* San Francisco: Ramparts Press.

Bookchin, Murray (1977). *The Spanish Anarchists: The Heroic Years 1868–1936.* New York: Harper Colophon Books.

Bowles, Samuel, David M. Gordon, and Thomas Weiskopf (1983). *Beyond the Wasteland: A Democratic Alternative to Economic Decline.* New York: Anchor Press/Doubleday.

Boyte, Harry C. (1980). *The Backyard Revolution: Understanding the New Citizen Movement.* Philadelphia: Temple University Press.

*Braverman, Harry (1974). *Labor and Monopoly Capital.* New York: Monthly Review Press.

*Braybrooke, David, and Charles E. Lindblom (1963). *A Strategy of Decision. Policy Evaluation as a Social Process.* New York: Free Press (Div. of Macmillan).

Brenner, Johanna, and Maria Ramas (1984). "Rethinking Women's Oppression." *New Left Review* 144 (March-April): 33–71.

Brown, Lester R. (1984). *State of the World*. New York: W. W. Norton.

Brown, Stuart Gerry, ed. (1941). *We Hold These Truths: Documents of American Democracy*. New York: Harper & Bros.

*Buber, Martin (1949). *Paths in Utopia*. New York: Macmillan.

*Buchanan, James M., and Gordon Tullock, eds. (1962). *The Calculus of Consent*. Ann Arbor: University of Michigan Press.

Bulmer, Martin (1982). "Applied Social Research. The Use and Non-Use of Empirical Social Inquiry by British and American Governmental Commissions." In Rist, ed., 55–82.

Burchell, Robert W., and George Sternlieb, eds. (1980). *Planning Theory in the 1980's*. New Brunswick, N.J.: The Center for Urban Policy Research.

Burnham, James (1941). *The Managerial Revolution*. New York: John Day.

Burns, Scott (1977). *The Household Economy*. Boston: Boston University Press.

Burns, Tom, and G. M. Stalker (1961). *The Management of Innovation*. London: Tavistock Publications.

Burton, Dudley, and M. Brian Murphy (1980). "Planning, Austerity, and the Democratic Prospect." *Kapitalistate* 8:67–97.

Bury, J. B. (1932). *The Idea of Progress: An Inquiry into Its Origin and Growth*. New York: Macmillan.

*Caiden, Naomi and Aaron Wildavsky (1974). *Planning and Budgeting in Poor Countries*. New York: John Wiley & Sons.

Calvino, Italo (1972). *Invisible Cities*. New York: Harcourt Brace Jovanovich.

*Camhis, Marios (1979). *Planning Theory and Philosophy*. London: Tavistock Publications.

Campanella, Tommaso (1981). *La citta del sole: Dialogo poetico* (The city of the sun: A poetical dialogue). Berkeley: University of California Press. (Orig. 1623)

Campbell, Donald T. (1971). "Reforms as Experiments." In Francis G. Caro, ed., 233–261. (Orig. 1969)

Campos Venuti, Giuseppe (1978). *Urbanistica e austerita*. Milan: Feltrinelli.

Capra, Fritjof (1975). *The Tao of Physics: An Exploration of the Parallels between Modern Physics and Eastern Mysticism*. Berkeley: Shambhala.

Capra, Fritjof (1982). *The Turning Point: Science, Society, and the Rising Culture*. New York: Simon & Schuster.

Carillo, Santiago (1977). *Euro-Communism and the State*. London: Lawrence and Wishart.

*Carley, Michael (1980). *Rational Techniques in Policy Analysis*. London: Heineman.

Carneiro, Robert (1970). "A Theory of the Origin of the State." *Science* 169:733–738.

Carnoy, Martin, and Derek Shearer (1980). *Economic Democracy: The Challenge of the 1980s*. White Plains, N.Y.: M. E. Sharpe.

Caro, Francis G., ed. (1971). *Readings in Evaluation; Research*. New York: Russell Sage Foundation.

*Caro, Robert (1975). *The Power Broker: Robert Moses and the Fall of New York*. New York: Vintage Books.

Cassirer, Ernst (1951). *The Philosophy of the Enlightenment*. Princeton: Princeton University Press. (Orig. 1932)

Castells, Manuel (1976). "The Wild City." *Kapitalistate* 4–5 (Summer): 2–30.

Castells, Manuel (1977). *Ciudad, Democracia y socialismo: La experiencia de las asociaciones de vecinos en madrid*. Mexico: Siglo Veintiuno.

Castells, Manuel (1978). "The Social Function of Urban Planning: State Action in the Urban-Industrial Development of the French Northern Coastline." In Manuel Castells (1978), *City, Class and Power*, 62–92. London: Macmillan.

Castells, Manuel (1980). "Cities and Regions Beyond the Crisis: Invitation to a Debate." *International Journal of Urban and Regional Research* 4, no. 1:127–129.

*Castells, Manauel (1983). *The City and the Grass Roots: A Cross-Cultural Theory of Urban Movements*. London: Edward Arnold.

Cavanagh, John, and Frederick Clairmonte (1982). The Transnational Economy: Transnational Corporations and Global Markets. Washington, D.C.: Institute for Policy Studies.

Cerni, D. M. (1982). *The CCITT: Organization, U.S. Participation, and Studies toward the ISDN*. Boulder, Colo.: U.S. Department of Commerce, National Telecommunications and Information Administration, Institute for Telecommunication Sciences.

Chapin, Stuart F., Jr. (1974). *Human Activity Patterns in the City*. New York: John Wiley & Sons.

Chardin, Pierre Teilhard de (1959). *The Phenomenon of Man*. New York: Harper & Row. (Orig. 1955)

Chase, Stuart (1932). *A New Deal*. New York: Macmillan.

Childe, V. Gordon (1956). *Man Makes Himself*. 3d ed. London: Watts. (Orig. 1951)

Child-Hill, Richard (1983). "The Auto Industry in Global Transition." Paper presented at the annual meeting of the American Sociological Association, Detroit, Mich., September 3, 1983.

Chin, Robert, and Kenneth D. Benne (1976). "General Strategies for Effecting Changes in Human Systems." In Bennis et al., eds. (1976), ch. 1.2.

Chonchol de Ferreira, Edy (1982). "Planificación del desarrollo local: Un efoque de pedagogía social." *Revista interamericana de planificación* 16, no. 62 (June): 74–99.

Churchman, C. West (1971). *The Design of Inquiring Systems: Basic Concepts of Systems and Organization*. New York: Basic Books.

*Churchman, C. West (1979a). *The Systems Approach*. 2d ed. New York: Dell. (Orig. 1968)

*Churchman, C. West (1979b). *The Systems Approach and Its Enemies*. New York: Basic Books.

*Churchman, C. West, et al. (1957). *An Introduction to Operations Research*. New York: John Wiley & Sons.

Churchman, C. West, and M. Verhulst (1960). *Management Sciences*. New York: Pergamon Press.

Clawson, A. W. (1984). *Address to the Board of Governors*. Washington, D.C.: The World Bank.

Cleveland, F. A. (1913). *Organized Democracy*. New York: Longmans, Green & Co.

Cloward, Richard A., and Frances Fox Piven (1983). "Toward a Class-Based Realignment of American Politics: A Movement Strategy." *Social Policy* 13, no. 3 (Winter): 3–14.

Cockburn, Cynthia (1977). *The Local State*. London: Pluto Press.

*Cockburn, Cynthia (1983). Brothers: *Male Dominance and Technological Change*. London: Pluto Press.

*Cohen, Stephen (1969). *Modern Capitalist Planning: The French Model*. Cambridge, Mass.: Harvard University Press.

Colletti, Lucio (1976). *From Rousseau to Lenin: Studies in Ideology and Society*. London: NLB. (Orig. 1969)

Connerton, Paul (1980). *The Tragedy of Enlightenment: An Essay on the Frankfurt School*. Cambridge: Cambridge University Press.

Cook, Alice, and Gwyn Kirk (1983). *Greenham Women Everywhere*. Boston: South End Press.

*Coover, Virginia, et al. (1977). *Resource Manual for a Living Revolution*. Philadelphia: Movement for a New Society (New Society Press).

*Council on Environmental Quality and the U.S. Department of State (1980). *The Global 2000 Report to the President: Entering the Twenty-first Century*. Vol. 2, *Technical Report*. Washington, D.C.: U.S. Government Printing Office.

Court, Gil (1984). "Social Learning." Unpublished paper, Graduate School of Architecture and Urban Planning, UCLA.

Crozier, Michel (1964). *The Bureaucratic Phenomenon*. Chicago: University of Chicago Press.

Crozier, Michel, Samuel P. Huntington, and Joji Wanatabe (1975). *The Crisis of Democracy: Report on the Governability of Democracies to the Trilateral Commission*. New York: New York University Press.

*Cyert, Richard, and James B. March (1963). *A Behavioral Theory of the Firm*. Englewood Cliffs, N.J.: Prentice-Hall.

*Dahl, Robert A., and Charles E. Lindblom (1957). *Politics, Economics, and Welfare*. New York: Harper & Bros.

*Dahl, Robert A., and E. R. Tufte (1973). *Size and Democracy*. Stanford: Stanford University Press.

*Daly, Herman E., ed. (1980). *Economics, Ecology, and Ethics: Essays toward a Steady-State Economy*. San Francisco: W. H. Freeman.

Dantzig, George B. (1963). *Linear Programming and Extensions*. Princeton: Princeton University Press.

de Bary, William Theodore, et al., eds. (1960). *Sources of Chinese Tradition*. Vol. 1. New York: Columbia University Press.

*de Jouvenal, Bertrand (1964). *L'Art de la conjecture*. Monaco: Ed. de Rocher. (English translation [1967], New York: Basic Books.)

della Volpe, Galvano (1978). *Rousseau and Marx*. London: Lawrence and Wishart. (Orig. 1964)

de Neufville, Judith I. (1975). *Social Indicators and Public Policy*. New York: American Elsevier.

Derthick, Martha (1972). *New Towns In-Town*. Washington, D.C.: Urban Institute.

Dewey, John (1938). *Logic: The Theory of Inquiry*. New York: Holt.

*Dewey, John (1946). *The Public and Its Problems: An Essay in Political Inquiry*. Chicago: Gateway Books. (Orig. 1927)

*Dewey, John (1950). *Reconstruction in Philosophy*. New York: The New American Library. (Orig. 1920)

Dewey, John (1958). *Experience and Nature*. New York: Dover Publications. (Orig. 1929)

Dewey, John (1963a). *Experience and Education*. London: Colleri Books. (Orig. 1938)

*Dewey, John (1963b). *Liberalism and Social Action*. New York: Capricorn Books. (Orig. 1935)

Dewey, John (1980). *The Quest for Certainty: A Study of the Relation of Knowledge to Action*. New York: Perigee Books. (Orig. 1929)

*Diesing, Paul (1982). *Science and Ideology in the Policy Sciences*. Chicago: Aldine.

Dobzhansky, Theodosius (1962). *Mankind Evolving: The Evolution of the Human Species*. New Haven: Yale University Press.

*Downs, Anthony (1967). *Inside Bureaucracy*. Boston: Little, Brown.

*Dror, Yehezkel (1968). *Policy Making Re-examined*. San Francisco: Chandler.

*Dror, Yehezkel (1971). *Design for Policy Sciences*. New York: American Elsevier.

*Dumont, Louis (1977). *From Mandeville to Marx: The Genesis and Triumph of Economic Ideology*. Chicago: The University of Chicago Press.

Duncan, Otis Dudley (1969). *Toward Social Reporting: Next Steps*. New York: Russell Sage Foundation.

*Dunn, Edgar S., Jr. (1971). *Economic and Social Development: A Process of Social Learning*. Baltimore: Johns Hopkins University Press.

Durkheim, Emile (1958). *Socialism and Saint-Simon*. Yellow Springs, Ohio: The Antioch Press. (Orig. 1895–96)

Eckholm, Erik, and Lester R. Brown (1977). *Spreading Deserts: The Hand of Man*. Washington, D.C.: World Watch Institute.

Eisenstein, Zillah R., ed. (1979). *Capitalist Patriarchy and the Case for Socialist Feminism*. New York: Monthly Review Press.

*Ellman, Michael (1979). *Socialist Planning*. Cambridge: Cambridge University Press.

*Elshtain, Jean Bethke (1981). *Public Man, Private Woman: Women in Social and Political Thought*. Princeton, N.J.: Princeton University Press.

Emerson, A. E. (1946). "The Biological Basis of Social Cooperation." *Transactions of the Illinois Academy of Sciences* 39:9–18.

*Emery, F. E., ed. (1969). *Systems Thinking*. Harmondsworth, England: Penguin Books.

Emery, F. E., and E. L. Trist (1960). "Socio-Technical Systems." In Emery, ed. (1969), ch. 14.

Emery, F. E., and E. L. Trist (1965). "The Causal Texture of Organizational Environments." In Emery, ed. (1969), ch. 12.

*Engels, Frederick (1975). *Socialism: Utopian and Scientific*. Peking: Foreign Languages Press. (Orig. 1880)

*Etzioni, Amitai (1968). *The Active Society: A Theory of Societal and Political Processes*. New York: Free Press (Div. of Macmillan).

Evers, Adalbert (1981). "Social Movements and Political Power: A Survey of a Theoretical and Political Controversy." *Comparative Urban Research* 8, no. 2:29–47.

Fainstein, Norman I., and Susan S. Fainstein (1978). "New Debates in Urban Planning: The Impact on Marxist Theory." In Harvey A. Goldstein and Sara A. Rosenberry, eds., 5–22.

Falk, Richard (1981). *Human Rights and State Sovereignty*. New York: Holmes & Meier.

*Falk, Richard, Samuel S. Kim, and Saul H. Mendlovitz, eds. (1982).

Studies on a Just World Order. Vol. 1, *Toward a Just World Order.* Boulder, Colo.: Westview Press.

Fallows, James (1981). *National Defense.* New York: Random House.

*Faludi, Andreas (1973). *Planning Theory.* Oxford: Pergamon Press.

Faludi, Andreas (1983). "Critical Rationalism and Planning Methodology." *Urban Studies* 20, no. 3 (August): 265–278.

*Feyerabend, Paul (1975). *Against Method: Outline of an Anarchistic Theory of Knowledge.* London: NLB.

Feyerabend, Paul K. (1978). *Science in a Free Society.* London: NLB.

Fogarty, Robert S., ed (1972). *American Utopianism.* Primary Sources in American History. Itasca, Ill.: F. E. Peacock Publishers.

Follett, Mary Parker (1920). *The New State: Group Organization and the Solution to Popular Government.* New York: Longmans, Green & Co.

Follett, Mary Parker (1924). *Creative Experience.* New York: Longmans, Green & Co.

Foner, Philip (1965). *The Industrial Workers of the World, 1905–1917.* New York: International Publishers.

*Foreman, Ann (1977). *Femininity as Alienation: Women and the Family in Marxism and Psychoanalysis.* London: Pluto Press.

Forester, John (1980). "Listening: The Social Policy of Everyday Life (Critical Theory and Hermeneutics in Practice)." *Social Praxis* 7, no. 3/4:219–232.

*Fourier, Charles (1976). *Design for Utopia: Selected Writings of Charles Fourier.* With an introduction by Charles Gide and a new foreword by Frank E. Manuel. New York: Schocken. (Orig. 1901)

Frank, André Gunder (1972). "The Development of Underdevelopment." In James D. Cockroft, André Gunder Frank, and Dale L. Johnson, eds., *Dependence and Underdevelopment: Latin America's Political Economy.* Garden City, N.Y.: Anchor Books. (Orig. 1969)

*Freire, Paulo (1970). *Pedagogy of the Oppressed.* New York: Herder and Herder.

*Freud, Sigmund (1962). *Civilization and Its Discontents.* New York: W. W. Norton. (Orig. 1930)

*Friedmann, John (1965). *Venezuela: From Doctrine to Dialogue.* National Planning Series, no. 1. Syracuse: Syracuse University Press.

Friedmann, John (1966). *Regional Development Policy: A Case Study of Venezuela.* Cambridge, Mass.: MIT Press.

Friedmann, John (1973). "The Public Interest and Community Participation: Toward a Reconstruction of Public Philosophy." With comments by Robert Nisbet and Herbert J. Gans. *Journal of the American Institute of Planners* 39, no. 1 (January): 2–12.

Friedmann, John (1978). "The Epistemology of Social Practice: A

Critique of Objective Knowledge." *Theory and Society* 6, no. 1 (July): 75–92.

Friedmann, John (1979a). "The Crisis of Transition: A Critique of Strategies of Crisis Management." With comments by Martin Bronfenbrenner, Gustav Ranis, and Hans Singer, and a rejoinder by the author. *Development and Change* 10, no. 1 (January): 125–176.

*Friedmann, John (1979b). *The Good Society*. Cambridge, Mass.: MIT Press.

*Friedmann, John (1981). *Retracking America*. Emmaus, Pa.: Rodale Press. (Orig. 1973)

Friedmann, John (1982). "Urban Communes, Self-Management, and the Reconstruction of the Local State." *Journal of Planning Education and Research* 2, no. 1 (Summer): 37–53.

Friedmann, John (1985). "Political and Technical Moments in Development: Agropolitan Development Revisited." *Society and Space* 3:155–167.

Friedmann, John (1986). "The World City Hypothesis." *Development and Change* 17, no. 1 (January): 69–84.

Friedmann, John, and George Abonyi (1976). "Social Learning: A New Model for Policy Research." *Environment and Planning A* 8 (December): 927–940. Reprinted in Howard E. Freeman, ed. (1978). *Policy Studies Review Annual* 2. Beverly Hills, Calif.: Sage Publications.

Friedmann, John, and Clyde Weaver (1979). *Territory and Function: The Evolution of Regional Planning*. Berkeley and Los Angeles: University of California Press.

Friedmann, John, and Goetz Wolff (1982). "World City Formation: An Agenda for Research and Action." *International Journal of Urban and Regional Research* 6, no. 3 (Sept.): 309–344.

*Friedrich, Carl J., ed (1962). *The Public Interest*. Nomos 5: Yearbook of the American Society for Political and Legal Philosophy. New York: Atherton Press.

Froebel, Folker, Juergen Heinrichs, and Otto Kreye (1980). *The New International Division of Labor: Structural Unemployment in Industrialized Countries and Industrialization In Developing Countries*. New York: Cambridge University Press. (Orig. 1977)

Galtung, Johan, Peter O'Brien, and Roy Preiswerk (1980). *Self-Reliance: A Strategy for Development*. London: Bogle-L'Ouverture Publications, Ltd.

Garraty, John F., and Peter Gay, eds. (1983). *The Columbia History of the World*. New York: Harper & Row. Dorset Press edition. (Orig. 1972)

*Gauhar, Altar, ed. (1983). *The Rich and the Poor: Development, Negotiation, Cooperation: An Assessment*. London: Third World Foundation for Social and Economic Studies.

Gaus, John, Leonard White, and Marshall Dimock (1936). *The Frontiers of Public Administration*. Chicago: University of Chicago Press.

*Gay, Peter (1969). *The Enlightenment: An Interpretation*. Vol. 2, *The Science of Freedom*. New York: W. W. Norton.

*Georgescu-Roegen, Nicholas (1971). *The Entropy Law and the Economic Process*. Cambridge, Mass.: Harvard University Press.

Gershuny, Jonathan I. (1978). *After Industrial Society: The Emerging Self-Serving Economy*. London: Macmillan.

Gershuny, Jonathan I. (1983). *Social Innovation and the Division of Labor*. New York: Oxford University Press.

Giddens, Anthony (1982). *Profiles and Critiques in Social Theory*, ch. 1. Berkeley: University of California Press.

Gillespie, Charles C. (1960). *The Edge of Objectivity: An Essay in the History of Scientific Ideas*. Princeton: Princeton University Press.

Glatz, Hans, and Gunter Scheer (1981). "Autonome Regionalentwicklung-eine neue Dimension des Regionalismus?" *Oesterreichische Zeitschrift für Politikwissenschaft* no. 3:333–346.

*Goldhammer, Herbert (1978). *The Advisor*. New York: American Elsevier.

Goldstein, Harvey A., and Sara A. Rosenberry, eds. (1978). *The Structural Crisis and Beyond: The Need for a New Planning Theory*. Blacksburg, Va.: Virginia Polytechnic Institute, Division of Environmental and Urban Systems.

*Goodman, Paul, and Percival Goodman (1960). Communitas: *Means of Livelihood and Ways of Life*. New York: Vintage Books. (Orig. 1947)

*Goodman, Robert (1971). *After the Planners*. New York: Touchstone Books.

Goodsell, Charles T. (1965). *Administration of a Revolution: Executive Reform in Puerto Rico under Governor Tugwell, 1941–46*. Cambridge, Mass.: Harvard University Press.

Gorz, André (1980). *Ecology as Politics*. Boston: South End Press.

*Gorz, André (1982). *Farewell to the Working Class: An Essay on Post-Industrial Socialism*. London: Pluto Press.

Gorz, André (1983). *Paths to Paradise: On the Liberation from Work*. Boston: South End Press.

Gouldner, Alvin (1958). "Introduction" to Emile Durkheim, *Socialism and Saint-Simon*. Yellow Springs, Ohio: The Antioch Press.

*Gouldner, Alvin (1979). *The Future of Intellectuals and the Rise of the New Class*. New York: Seabury Press.

Gourevitch, P. (1979). "The Re-emergence of 'Peripheral Nationalisms': Some Comparative Speculations on the Spatial Distribution of Political Leadership and Economic Growth." *Comparative Studies in Society and History* 21, no. 3:303–322.

*Grabow, Stephen, and Allen Heskin (1973). "Foundations for a Radical Concept of Planning." *Journal of the American Institute of Planners* 39, no. 2 (March): 106–114. For comments, see *Journal of the American Institute of Planners* 39, no. 4 (July 1973) and 40, no. 2 (March 1974).

*Gramsci, Antonio (1971). *Selections from the Prison Notebooks*. Edited by Quinton Hoare and Geoffrey Noel Smith. New York: International Publishers.

Grindle, Merilee S., ed. (1980). *Politics and Policy Implementation in the Third World*. Princeton: Princeton University Press.

Gross, Bertram M. (1966). *The State of the Nation: Social Systems Accounting*. London: Tavistock Publications.

*Gross, Bertram M., ed. (1969). *Social Intelligence for America's Future*. Boston: Allyn and Bacon.

Gulick, Luther Halsey, and Lyndall F. Urwick, eds. (1937). *Papers on the Science of Administration*. New York: Institute of Public Administration.

*Guttman, Daniel, and Barry Willner (1976). *The Shadow Government: The Government's Multi-Billion Dollar Giveaway of Its Decision-Making Powers to Private Management Consultants, "Experts," and Think Tanks*. New York: Pantheon.

Haas, Gilda (1985). *Plant Closures: Myths, Realities, and Responses*. Boston: South End Press.

*Habermas, Jürgen (1971). *Toward a Rational Society: Student Protest, Science, and Politics*. London: Heineman. (Orig. 1968)

Habermas, Jürgen (1973). *Legitimation Crisis*. Boston: Beacon Press.

*Habermas, Jürgen (1979). *Communication and the Evolution of Society*. Boston: Beacon Press. (Orig. 1976)

Hakim, Peter (1982). "Lessons from Grass-Root Development Experience in Latin America and the Caribbean." In UNICEF, 137–141.

*Hall, Peter (1975). *Urban and Regional Planning*. London: Penguin Books.

Hall, Peter (1982). *Great Planning Disasters*. Berkeley and Los Angeles: University of California Press. (Orig. 1980)

Hall, Peter (1983). "The Anglo-American Connection: Rival Rationalities in Planning Theory and Practice, 1955–1980." *Environment and Planning B: Planning and Design* 10:41–46.

Hampden-Turner, Charles (1975). *From Poverty to Dignity.* New York: Anchor Books. (Orig. 1974)

Hansen, Bent, and Samir Radwan (1982). "Employment Planning in Egypt: An Insurance Policy for the Future." *International Labour Review* 121, no. 5 (Sept.–Oct.), 535–552.

Hansen, Niles M., ed. (1972). *Growth Centers in Regional Economic Development.* New York: Free Press (Div. of Macmillan).

Harari, Denyse, and Jorge García-Bouza (1982). *Social Conflict and Development: Basic Needs and Survival Strategies in Four National Settings.* Paris: OECD.

Hardin, Garrett (1984). "The Tragedy of the Commons." In David C. Korten and Rudi Klauss, eds. (Orig. 1968)

*Harrison, J.F.C. (1969). *Quest for the Moral World: Robert Owen and the Owenites in Britain and America.* New York: Charles Scribner's Sons.

Hartman, Chester, et al. (1981). *Displacement: How to Fight It.* Berkeley: National Housing Law Project.

Hartmann, Heidi (1981). "The Family as the Locus of Gender, Class, and Political Struggle: The Example of Housework." *Signs: Journal of Women in Culture and Society* 6, no. 31 (Spring): 366–394.

Harvey, David (1978). "On Planning the Ideology of Planning." In Robert W. Burchell and George Sternlieb, eds., 213–234.

Hawley, Ellis W. (1974). "Herbert Hoover, the Commerce Secretariat, and the Vision of an 'Associative State,' 1921–1928." *The Journal of American History* 61, no. 1 (June): 116–140.

Hawley, Ellis W., ed. (1981). *Herbert Hoover as Secretary of Commerce: Studies in New Era Thought and Practice.* Iowa City: University of Iowa Press.

Hayami, Yujiro, and Vernon W. Ruttan (1971). *Agricultural Development: An International Perspective.* Baltimore: Johns Hopkins University Press.

*Hayden, Dolores (1981). *The Grand Domestic Revolution: A History of Feminist Designs for American Homes, Neighborhoods, and Cities.* Cambridge, Mass.: MIT Press.

*Hayden, Dolores (1984). *Redesigning the American Dream: The Future of Housing, Work, and Family Life.* New York: W. W. Norton.

Hayek, F. A. (1944). *The Road to Serfdom.* London: George Routledge and Sons.

*Hayek, F. A. (1955). *The Counterrevolution of Science: Studies on the Abuse of Reason.* New York: Free Press (Div. of Macmillan). (Orig. 1941–44)

Hecht, Susanna B. (forthcoming). *Deforestation in Tropical South America.* Association of American Geographers Research Series.

Hegedus, Andreas, et al. (1976). *The Humanisation of Socialism: Writings of the Budapest School*. London: Allison & Busby.

*Heller, Agnes (1976). *The Theory of Need in Marx*. London: Allison & Busby. (Orig. 1974)

Helmer, Olaf (1966). *Social Techology*. New York: Basic Books.

Helmhold, Lois Rita, and Amber Hollibaugh (1983). "The Family: What Holds Us, What Hurts Us. The Family in Socialist America." In Steve Rosskamm Shalom, ed.

Herman, Edward S. (1981). *Corporate Control, Corporate Power*. A Twentieth Century Fund Study. New York: Cambridge University Press.

Heskin, Allan (1980). "Crisis and Response: An Historical Perspective on Advocacy Planning." *Journal of the American Planning Association* 46, no. 1 (January): 50–63.

Heskin, Allan (1983). *Tenants and the American Dream: Ideology and the Tenant Movement*. New York: Praeger.

Himmelfarb, Gertrud (1983). "Engels in Manchester: Inventing the Proletariat." *The American Scholar* (Autumn): 479–496.

*Hirsch, Fred (1976). *Social Limits to Growth*. Cambridge, Mass.: Harvard University Press.

*Hirschman, Albert O. (1958). *The Strategy of Economic Development*. New Haven: Yale University Press.

Hirschman, Albert O. (1963). "Models of Reformmongering." *The Quarterly Journal of Economics* 77 (May): 236–257.

Hirschman, Albert O. (1967a). "The Principle of the Hiding Hand." *Public Interest* no. 6 (Winter): 10–23.

*Hirschman, Albert O. (1967b). *Development Projects Observed*. Washington, D.C.: The Brookings Institution.

Hirschman, Albert O. (1977). *The Passions and the Interests: Political Arguments for Capitalism before Its Triumph*. Princeton: Princeton University Press.

Hirschman, Albert O., and Charles E. Lindblom (1962). "Economic Development, Research and Development, Policy Making: Some Converging Views." *Behavioral Science* 7, no. 2 (April): 211–222.

Hitch, Charles J., and Ronald N. McKean (1960). *The Economics of Defense in the Nuclear Age*. Cambridge, Mass.: Harvard University Press.

*Hoare, Quintin, and Geoffrey Nowell Smith, eds. (1971). *Selections from the Prison Notebooks of Antonio Gramsci*. London: Lawrence and Wishart.

*Hobbes, Thomas (1958). *Leviathan, Parts I and II*. Edited by Herbert W. Schneider. Indianapolis: The Bobbs-Merrill Co. (Orig. 1651)

Hobsbawm, E. J. (1979). *The Age of Capital: 1848–1875*. New York: New American Library. (Orig. 1975)

Hoffman, Stanley (1959). "The Areal Division of Powers in the Writings of French Political Thinkers." In Arthur Maass, ed., *Area and Power: A Theory of Local Government*, ch. 6. Glencoe, Ill.: The Free Press.

Hofstadter, Douglas R. (1979). *Goedel, Escher, Bach: An Eternal Golden Braid*. New York: Vintage Books.

*Hoos, Ida R. (1972). *Systems Analysis in Public Policy: A Critique*. Berkeley: University of California Press.

*Horkheimer, Max, and Theodor W. Adorno (1982). *Dialectic of Enlightenment*. New York: Continuum. (Orig. 1944)

*Horowitz, Irving Louis (1961). *Radicalism and the Revolt against Reason: The Social Theories of Georges Sorel*. London: Routledge & Kegan Paul.

*Horowitz, Irving Louis, and James Everett Katz (1975). *Social Science and Public Policy in the United States*. New York: Praeger.

Horvat, Branko, et al. (1975). *Self-Governing Socialism*. 2 vols. White Plains, N.Y.: International Arts and Sciences Press.

Houghton-Evans, W. (1980). "Schemata in British New Town Planning." In Gordon Cherry, ed., *Shaping an Urban World*, 101–128. New York: St. Martin's Press.

*House, Peter W. (1982). *The Art of Public Policy Analysis: The Arena of Regulation and Resources*. Beverly Hills: Sage Publications.

*Hueting, Roefie (1980). *New Scarcity and Economic Growth: More Welfare through Less Production*. Amsterdam: North Holland Publishing Co. (Orig. 1974)

Hughes, Barry B. (1985). *World Futures: A Critical Analysis of Alternatives*. Baltimore: Johns Hopkins University Press.

Hughes, H. Stuart (1975). *The Sea Change: The Migration of Social Thought, 1930–1965*. New York: McGraw-Hill.

*Hughes, H. Stuart (1977). *Consciousness and Society: The Reorientation of European Social Thought, 1890–1930*. New York: Vintage Books. (Orig. 1958)

Huntington, Samuel P. (1981). *American Politics: The Promise of Disharmony*. Cambridge, Mass.: Harvard University Press.

*Hyams, Edward (1979). *Pierre-Joseph Proudhon: His Revolutionary Life, Mind and Works*. New York: Taplinger Publishing Co.

Hyden, Goran (1983). *No Shortcuts to Progress: African Development Management in Perspective*. Berkeley: University of California Press.

International Institute for Applied Systems Analysis (1981). *Energy in a Finite World*. Executive Summary. Report by the Energy Systems Program Group of the International Institute for Applied Systems Analysis, Wolf Hafele, Program Leader. Laxenburg, Austria: IIASA.

*Illich, Ivan D. (1971). *Deschooling Society*. New York: Harper & Row.

*Illich, Ivan (1973). *Tools for Conviviality*. London: Fontana/Collins.

ILO (1979). *Growth, Structural Change, and Manpower Policy: The Challenge of the 1980's*. Report of the Director-General. Geneva: ILO.

*Ionescu, Ghita (1976). *The Political Thought of Saint-Simon*. New York: Oxford University Press.

Isard, Walter, et al. (1960). *Methods of Regional Analysis*. New York: John Wiley & Sons.

Jacobs, Jane (1961). *The Death and Life of Great American Cities*. New York: Random House.

Jacoby, Henry (1973). *The Bureaucratization of the World*. Berkeley: University of California Press.

Jaeger, Werner (1976). *Paideia: The Ideals of Greek Culture*. Vol. 1, *Archaic Greece; the Mind of Athens*. 2d ed. Translated by Gilbert Highet. New York: Oxford University Press. (Orig. 1935)

*Jagger, Alison M. (1983). *Feminist Politics and Human Nature*. Totowa, N.J.: Rowman and Allanheld.

Jaggi, Max, Roger Muller, and Sil Schmid (1977). *Red Bologna*. London: Writers and Readers Publishing Cooperative. (Orig. 1976)

James, William (1974). *Pragmatism and Four Essays from* The Meaning of Truth. New York: New American Library. (Orig. 1907, 1909)

Janowitz, Morris (1970). "Sociological Models and Social Policy." In *Political Conflict Essays in Political Sociology*, 243–259. Chicago: Quadrangle Books,

Jantsch, Erich (1972). *Technological Planning and Social Futures*. London: Associated Business Programmes.

*Jay, Martin (1973). *The Dialectical Imagination: A History of the Frankfurt School and the Institute of Social Research, 1923–1950*. Boston: Little, Brown.

Jenkins, Brian M. (1983). *New Models of Conflict*. R-3009-DNA. Santa Monta, Calif.: The Rand Corporation.

Johnstadt, Trygve (1980). *Group Dynamics and Society: A Multi-National Approach*. Cambridge, Mass.: Oelschlager, Gunn & Hain.

Johnston, William M. (1972). *The Austrian Mind: An Intellectual and Social History, 1848–1938*. Berkeley and Los Angeles: University of California Press.

Jöhr, W. A., and H. A. Singer (1955). *The Role of the Economist as Official Adviser*. London: Allen & Unwin.

Juster, F. Thomas, and Kenneth C. Land, eds. (1981). *Social Accounting Systems: Essays on the State of the Art*. New York: Academic Press.

Kahn, Herman, and I. Mann (1957). *Ten Common Pitfalls*. RM-1937. Santa Monica, Calif.: The Rand Corporation.

Kahn, Herman, and Anthony J. Wiener (1967). *The Year 2000: A Framework of Speculation on the Next Thirty-Three Years*. New York: Macmillan.

Kannappan, S. (1983). *Employment Problems and the Urban Labor Market in Developing Nations*. Ann Arbor: University of Michigan, Graduate School of Business Administration.

*Kanter, Rosabeth Moss (1972). *Commitment and Community: Communes and Utopias in Sociological Perspective*. Cambridge, Mass.: Harvard University Press.

*Katznelson, Ira (1981). *City Trenches: Urban Politics and the Patterning of Class in the United States*. New York: Pantheon Books.

Kautsky, Karl (1914). *Der Politische Massenstreik*. Berlin: Buchhandlung Vorwaerts Paul Singer G.m.b.H.

Kay, Adah, and Mike Thompson (1977). "The Class Basis of Planning." In John Cowley, Adah Kay, Marjorie Mayo, and Mike Thompson (eds.), *Community or Class Struggle?* 101–107. London: Stage 1.

*Keynes, John Maynard (1964). *The General Theory of Employment, Interest, and Money*. New York: Harcourt Brace Jovanovich. (Orig. 1936)

Kidron, Michael, and Ronald Segal (1981). *The State of the World Atlas*. New York: Simon & Schuster.

Kolakowski, Leszek (1978). *Main Currents of Marxism: Its Rise, Growth, and Dissolution*. Vol. 2, *The Golden Age*. Oxford: Clarendon Press.

Koopman, B. O. (1956). "Fallacies in Operations Research." *Operations Research* 4, no. 4:422–426.

Korten, David C. (1980). "Community Organization and Rural Development: A Learning Process Approach." *Public Administration Review* 40, no. 5 (Sept./Oct.): 480–512.

Korten, David C. (1984). "Rural Development Programming: The Learning Process Approach." In David C. Korten and Rudi Klauss, eds., ch. 18.

Korten, David C., and Felipe B. Alfonso, eds. (1981). *Bureaucracy and the Poor: Closing the Gap*. Singapore: McGraw-Hill.

*Korten, David C., and Rudi Klauss, eds. (1984). *People-Centered De-

velopment: Contributions Toward Theory and Planning Frameworks. Hartford, Conn.: Kumarian Press.

Kotler, Milton (1969). *Neighborhood Government: The Local Foundations of Political Life.* Indianpolis: Bobbs-Merrill Co.

Kowarick, Lucio and Milton Campanario (1986). "São Paulo: The Price of the World City Status." *Development and Change* 17, no. 1 (January): 159–174.

Kropotkin, P. A. (1902). *Mutual Aid.* London: Heineman.

*Kropotkin, P. A. (1970). *Selected Writings on Anarchism and Revolution.* Edited by Martin A. Miller. Cambridge, Mass.: MIT Press.

*Kropotkin, Peter (1975). *Fields, Factories, and Workshops Tomorrow.* Edited by Colin Ward. New York: Harper & Row. (Orig. 1888–1890)

*Krueckeberg, Donald A., ed. (1983). *Introducution to Planning History in the United States.* New Brunswick, N.J.: The Center for Urban Policy Research, Rutgers University.

Krygier, Martin (1979). "Saint-Simon, Marx and the Non-Governed Society." In Eugene Kamenka and Martin Krygier, eds., *Bureaucracy: The Career of a Concept.* New York: St. Martin's Press.

*Kuhn, Thomas S. (1970). *The Structure of Scientific Revolutions.* 2d ed., enlarged. Chicago: University of Chicago Press. (Orig. 1962)

Kuznets, Simon S. (1937). *National Income and Capital Formation, 1919–1935. A Preliminary Report.* New York: National Bureau of Economic Research.

Lakatos, Imre (1971). "History of Science and Its Rational Reconstruction." In R. Buck and R. Cohen, eds. (1971), *Boston Studies in the Philosophy of Science.* Vol. 8. Dordrecht, Holland: Reidel.

Lakey, George (1976). *A Manifesto for Nonviolent Revolution.* Philadelphia: Movement for a New Society.

Langer, Susanne K. (1953). *Feeling and Form: A Theory of Art.* New York: Charles Scribner's Sons.

Lasswell, Harold D. (1936). *Politics: Who Gets What, When, and How.* New York: McGraw-Hill.

Lasswell, Harold D. (1971). *A Preview of Policy Sciences.* New York: American Elsevier.

*Lawrence, Paul R., and Jay W. Lorsch (1967). *Organization and Environment: Managing Differentiation and Integration.* Boston: Graduate School of Business Administration, Harvard University.

*Lawrence, Paul R., and Jay W. Lorsch (1969). *Developing Organizations: Diagnosis and Action.* Reading, Mass.: Addison-Wesley.

Lee, D. B. (1973). "Requiem for Large Scale Models." *Journal of the American Institute of Planners* 39, no. 3 (May): 163–178.

*Lenin, V. I. (1973). *The State and Revolution: The Marxist Teaching on* *the State and the Tasks of the Proletariat in the Revolution.* Peking: Foreign Languages Press. (Orig. 1917)

*Lenin, V. I. (1975). *What Is To Be Done? Burning Questions of Our Movement.* Peking: Foreign Languages Press. (Orig. 1902)

*Lenzer, Gertrud, ed. (1975). *Auguste Comte and Positivism: The Essential Writings.* New York: Harper Torchbooks.

Leontief, Wassily (1937). *The Structure of the American Economy, 1919–1929: An Application of Equilibrium Analysis.* Cambridge, Mass.: Harvard University Press.

Leontief, Wassily (1966). *Input-Output Economics.* New York: Oxford University Press.

*Lerner, Daniel, and Harold D. Lasswell, eds. (1951). *The Policy Sciences: Recent Developments in Scope and Methods.* Stanford: Stanford University Press.

*Lewin, Kurt (1948). *Resolving Social Conflicts: Selected Papers on Group Dynamics.* Edited by Gertrud Weiss Lewin. New York: Harper & Bros. (Orig. 1940)

Lewin, Kurt (1951). *Field Theory in Social Science: Selected Theoretical Papers.* Edited by Dorwin Cartwright. A publication of the Research Center for Group Dynamics, University of Michigan. New York: Harper & Bros. (Orig. 1943–1944)

Likert, Rensis (1967). *The Human Organization: Its Management and Value.* New York: McGraw-Hill.

*Lilienfeld, Robert (1978). *The Rise of Systems Theory: An Ideological Analysis.* New York: John Wiley & Sons.

Lin Piao, ed. (1966). *Quotations from Chairman Mao Tse-Tung.* Peking: Foreign Languages Press.

Lindblom, Charles (1959). "The Science of Muddling Through." *Public Administration Review* 19, no. 2 (Spring): 79–99.

*Lindblom, Charles E. (1965). *The Intelligence of Democracy.* New York: Free Press (Div. of Macmillan).

*Lindblom, Charles E. (1977). *Politics and Markets: The World's Political-Economic Systems.* New York: Basic Books.

Lindblom, Charles E. (1979). "Still Muddling, Not Yet Through." *Public Administration Review* 39, no. 6 (Nov./Dec.): 517–526.

*Lindblom, Charles E., and David K. Cohen (1979). *Usable Knowledge: Social Science and Social Problem Solving.* New Haven: Yale University.

Lindholm, Stig (1981). *Paradigms, Science, and Reality: On Dialectics, Hermeneutics and Positivism in the Social Sciences.* Research Bulletin Vol. 9: 1. Institute of Education, University of Stockholm.

Linn, Johannes F. (1983). *Cities in the Developing World: Policies for the*

Equitable and Efficient Growth. Published for the World Bank. New York: Oxford University Press.

Lipietz, Alain (1982). "Towards Global Fordism." *New Left Review* 132 (March-April): 33–47.

Lippitt, Ronald, Jeanne Watson, and Bruce Westley (1958). *The Dynamics of Planned Change: A Comparative Study of Principles and Techniques*. New York: Harcourt, Brace and Co.

Lipton, Michael (1977). *Why Poor People Stay Poor: Urban Bias in World Development*. Cambridge, Mass.: Harvard University Press.

Little, I.M.D. (1957). *A Critique of Welfare Economics*. 2d ed. Oxford: Oxford University Press.

*Locke, John (1948). *An Essay Concerning the True Origin, Extent and End of Civil Government*. In Sir Ernest Barker, ed., *Social Contract: Essays by Locke, Hume, and Rousseau*. New York: Oxford University Press. (Orig. 1690)

Lorwin, Lewis L. (1932). "The Origins of Economic Planning." *Survey* 67, no. 9 (February): 472–475.

*Luce, R. D., and Howard Raiffa (1957). *Games and Decisions*. New York: John Wiley & Sons.

Luria, Dan, and Jack Russell (1981). *Rational Reindustrialization: An Economic Development Agenda for Detroit*. Detroit, Mich.: Widetripped Press.

*Luxemburg, Rosa (1937). *Reform or Revolution*. New York: Three Arrows Press. (Orig. 1899)

*Luxemburg, Rosa (1971). *The Mass Strike*. New York: Harper Torchbooks. (Orig. 1906)

Lynch, Kevin (1960). *The Image of the City*. Cambridge, Mass.: MIT Press.

Lynch, Kevin (1976). *Managing the Sense of a Region*. Cambridge, Mass.: MIT Press.

*Lynch, Kevin (1981). *A Theory of Good City Form*. Cambridge, Mass.: MIT Press.

Lynd, Robert Stoughton (1939). *Knowledge for What? The Place of Social Sciences in American Culture*. Princeton: Princeton University Press.

McCluskey, John E. (1976). "Beyond the Carport and the Stick: Liberation and Power without Control." In Bennis et al., eds. (1976), ch. 9.3.

McHarg, Ian L. (1969). *Design with Nature*. New York: American Museum of Natural History.

MacKenzie, Findlay (1937). *Planned Society: Yesterday, Today, and Tomorrow*. A Symposium by Thirty-Five Economists, Sociologists, and Statesmen. New York: Prentice-Hall.

McLaughlin, William James (1977). *The Indian Hills Experiment: A Case Study of Transactive Planning Theory.* Ph.D. diss., Colorado State University. (Available from University Microfilms International, Ann Arbor, Mich.)

McLellan, David (1979). *Marxism after Marx: An Introduction.* Boston: Houghton Mifflin.

McLennan, Gregor (1981). *Marxism anad the Methodologies of History.* London: NLB.

*Macpherson, C. B. (1962). *The Political Theory of Possessive Individualism: Hobbes to Locke.* Oxford: Oxford University Press.

McWilliams, Wilson Carey (1973). *The Idea of Fraternity in America.* Berkeley: University of California Press.

Maeda, N. (1983). "A Fact-Finding Study of the Impacts of Microcomputers on Employment." In OECD (1981), 155–180.

Majone, Giandomenico (1980). "Policies as Theories." *Omega: The Journal of Management Science* 8, no. 2 (April): 151–162.

*Majone, Giandomenico, and Edward S. Quade (1980). *Pitfalls of Analysis.* New York: John Wiley & Sons.

Majone, Giandomenico, and Aaron Wildavsky (1979). "Implementation as Evolution." In Pressman and Wildavsky, ch. 9.

*Mandel, Ernest (1975). *Late Capitalism.* London: NLB.

Mannheim, Karl (1937). "On the Diagnosis of Our Time." In Kurt H. Wolff, ed. (1971), *From Karl Mannheim.* New York: Oxford University Press.

*Mannheim, Karl (1949a). *Ideology and Utopia.* New York: Harcourt-Brace. (Orig. 1929)

*Mannheim, Karl (1949b). *Man and Society in an Age of Reconstruction.* New York: Harcourt-Brace. (Orig. 1940)

*Mannheim, Karl (1951). *Freedom, Power, and Democratic Planning.* London: Routledge & Kegan Paul. (Orig. 1950)

*Manuel, Frank E., and Fritzie P. Manuel (1979). *Utopian Thought in the Western World.* Cambridge, Mass.: The Belknap Press of Harvard University Press.

Mao Tse-tung (1965). "Analysis of the Classes in Chinese Society." In *Selected Works of Mao Tse-tung.* Vol. 1. Peking: Foreign Languages Press. (Orig. 1926)

*Mao Tse-tung (1968a). "On Practice." In *Four Essays on Philosophy.* Peking: Foreign Languages Press. (Orig. 1937)

Mao Tse-tung (1968b). "Where Do Correct Ideas Come From?" In *Four Essays on Philosophy.* Peking: Foreign Languages Press. (Orig. 1963)

*March, James G., and Herbert A. Simon (1958). *Organizations.* New York: John Wiley & Sons.

*Marcuse, Herbert (1964). *One-Dimensional Man: Studies in the Ideology of Advanced Industrial Society*. Boston: Beacon Press.

Markham, F.M.H., ed. (1952). *Henri Comte de Saint-Simon (1760–1825): Selected Writings*. Oxford: Basil Blackwell.

*Marris, Peter (1975). *Loss and Change*. Garden City, N.Y.: Anchor Press. (Orig. 1974)

Marris, Peter (1983). "The Future of Social Policy in America." Unpublished manuscript, Graduate School of Architecture and Urban Planning, UCLA.

*Marris, Peter (1982). *Community Planning and Conceptions of Change*. London and Boston: Routledge & Kegan Paul.

*Marris, Peter, and Martin Rein (1982). *Dilemmas of Social Reform: Poverty and Community Action in the United States*. 2d ed. Chicago: University of Chicago Press. (Orig. 1967)

Martines, Lauro (1979). *Power and Imagination: City-States in Renaissance Italy*. New York: Alfred A. Knopf.

Marx, Karl (1965). *Capital*. Vol. 1. Moscow: Progress Publishers. (Orig. 1867)

*Marx, Karl (1978a). *Critique of the Gotha Program*. In Robert C. Tucker, ed., *The Marx-Engels Reader*. 2d ed. New York: W. W. Norton. (Orig. 1875)

*Marx, Karl (1978b). *The German Ideology, Part I*. In Robert C. Tucker, ed., *The Marx-Engels Reader*. 2d ed. New York: W. W. Norton. (Orig. 1845–46)

Marx, Karl (1978c). "Theses on Feuerbach." In Robert C. Tucker, ed., *The Marx-Engels Reader*. 2d ed. New York: W. W. Norton. (Orig. 1844)

*Marx, Karl (1978d). *Economic and Philosophic Manuscripts of 1844*. In Robert C. Turker, ed., *The Marx-Engels Reader*. 2d ed. W. W. Norton. (Orig. 1844)

*Marx, Karl, and Friedrich Engels (1978). *The Communist Manifesto*. In Robert C. Turker, ed., *The Marx-Engels Reader*. 2d ed. New York: W. W. Norton. (Orig. 1848)

*Maslow, Abraham (1968). *Toward a Psychology of Being*. 2d ed. New York: Van Norstrand.

Masnick, George, and Mary Jo Bane (1980). *The Nation's Families: 1960–1990*. Cambridge, Mass.: Joint Center for Urban Studies of MIT and Harvard University.

Massey, Doreen, and Richard Meegan (1982). *The Anatomy of Job Loss*. London: Methuen.

Max-Neef, Manfred (1982). *From the Outside Looking in: Experiences in "Barefoot Economics."* Uppsala, Sweden: Dag Hammarskjöld Foundation.

Mayo, Elton (1933). *The Human Problems of an Industrial Civilization.* New York: Macmillan.

Meadows, Donella, John Richardson, and Gerhart Bruckman (1982). *Groping in the Dark: The First Decade of Global Modelling.* Chichester, England: John Wiley & Sons.

Meisner, Maurice (1974). "Utopian Socialist Themes in Maoism." In John Wilson Lewis, ed., *Peasant Rebellion and Communist Revolution in Asia.* Stanford, Calif.: Stanford University Press.

*Meltsner, Arnold J. (1976). *Policy Analysis in the Bureaucracy.* Berkeley: University of California Press.

Mera, Koichi (1975). *Income Distribution and Regional Development.* Tokyo: Tokyo University Press.

Mesarovic, Mihajlo, and Eduard Pestel (1974). *Mankind at the Turning Point.* New York: Dutton.

Metzgar, Jack (1980). "Plant Shut-down and Worker Response: The Case of Johnstown, Pennsylvania." *Socialist Review* 10, no. 5 (Sept.-Oct.): 9–50.

Meyerson, Martin, and Edward C. Banfield (1955). *Politics, Planning, and the Public Interest: The Case of Public Housing in Chicago.* New York: Free Press (Div. of Macmillan).

Michels, Robert (1915). *Political Parties: A Sociological Study of the Oligarchical Tendencies of Modern Democracy.* New York: Heart International Library.

Miles, Ian, and John Irvine (1979). "Social Forecasting: Predicting the Future or Making History?" In John Irvine and Jeff Evans (1979), *Demystifying Social Statistics.* London: Pluto Press.

Miliband, Ralph (1969). *The State in Capitalist Society.* New York: Basic Books.

*Mill, John Stuart (1974a). *On Liberty.* Harmondsworth, England: Penguin Books. (Orig. 1859)

*Mill, John Stuart (1974b). *Utilitarianism.* Edited by Mary Warnock. New York: New American Library. (Orig. 1863)

Mintz, Jerome R. (1982). *The Anarchists of Casas Viejas.* Chicago: Chicago University Press.

*Mishan, Edward J. (1976). *Cost-Benefit Analysis: An Introduction.* New York: Praeger. (Orig. 1971)

Mishan, Edward J. (1981a). *Economic Efficiency and Social Welfare: Selected Essays.* London: Allen & Unwin.

Mishan, Edward J. (1981b). *Introduction to Normative Economics.* New York: Oxford University Press.

*Mississippi Valley Committee (1934). *Report of the Mississippi Valley Committee of the Public Works Administration.* Washington, D.C.: U.S. Government Printing Office.

Mitchell, Wesley C. (1937). *The Backward Art of Spending Money and Other Essays*. New York: McGraw-Hill.

Monod, Jacques (1971). *Chance and Necessity: An Essay on the Natural Philosophy of Modern Biology*. New York: Alfred A. Knopf.

Monroe, D. H. (1967). "Jeremy Bentham." In *The Encyclopedia of Philosophy*. Vol. 1. New York: Macmillan.

Montagu, Ashley (1956). *The Biosocial Nature of Man*. New York: Grove Press.

Moore, Wilbert E., and Melvin M. Tumin (1964). "Some Social Functions of Ignorance." In Bernard Rosenberg et al., eds. (1964), *Mass Society in Crisis*. New York: Macmillan.

Morales, Rebecca, and Goetz Wolff (1985). *Los Angeles Labor Union Responses To Plant Closings and Growth in the Immigrant Labor Force*. Los Angeles: UCLA Institute of Industrial Relations.

Morgenstern, Oscar (1963). *On the Accuracy of Economic Observations*. 2d ed. Princeton: Princeton University Press. (Orig. 1950)

*Morris, David (1982). *Self-Reliant Cities*. Washington, D.C.: Institute for Local Self-Reliance.

*Morris, David (1984). *The New City States*. Washington, D.C.: Institute for Local Self-Reliance.

Morris, David, and Karl Hess (1975). *Neighborhood Power: The New Localism*. Boston: Beacon Press.

*Mumford, Lewis (1938). *The Culture of Cities*. New York: Harcourt, Brace and Co.

Mumford, Lewis (1961). *The City in History: Its Origins, Its Transformations, and Its Prospects*. New York: Harcourt, Brace and World.

Murray, Robert K. (1981). "Herbert Hoover and the Harding Cabinet." In Hawley, ed. (1981).

Myint, Hla (1948). *Theories of Welfare Economics*. Cambridge, Mass.: Harvard University Press.

*National Planning Board (1934). *Final Report, 1933–34*. Washington, D.C.: U.S. Government Printing Office.

*Nelson, Richard R. (1977). *The Moon and the Ghetto*. New York: W. W. Norton.

*Noble, David F. (1977). *America by Design: Science, Technology, And the Rise of Corporate Capitalism*. New York: Alfred A. Knopf.

Nora, Simon, and Alain Minc (1981). *The Computerization of Society*. Cambridge, Mass.: MIT Press. (Orig. 1978)

Nordhaus, William, and James Tobin (1972). "Is Growth Obsolete?" National Bureau of Economic Research, Fiftieth Anniversary Colloquium V. *Economic Growth*. New York: Columbia University Press.

*Novack, David, ed. (1965). *Program Budgeting: Program Analysis and the Federal Budget*. Cambridge: Harvard University Press.

*Novack, George (1975). *Pragmatism versus Marxism: An Appraisal of John Dewey's Philosophy*. New York: Pathfinder Press.

Oakley, Peter, and David Marsden (1984). *Approaches to Participation in Rural Development*. Geneva: International Labour Office.

*O'Connor, James (1973). *The Fiscal Crisis of the State*. New York: St. Martin's Press.

O'Connor, James (1984). *Accumulation Crisis*. New York: Basil Blackwell.

OECD (1981). *Microelectronics, Productivity and Employment*. Information, Computer, Communications Policy. Vol. 5. Paris: OECD.

OECD (1983). *Industrial Robots: Their Role in Manufacturing Industry*. Paris: OECD.

Offe, Claus (1974). "Structural Problems of the Capitalist State." *German Political Studies* 1:31–56.

Offe, Claus (1975). "The Theory of the Capitalist State and the Problems of Policy in Formation." In L. Lindberg et al., eds., *Stress and Contradiction in Modern Capitalism*. Lexington, Mass.: Lexington Books.

Offe, Claus (1985). *Disorganized Capitalism: Contemporary Transformations of Work and Politics*. Edited by John Kean. Cambridge, Mass.: MIT Press.

Ollman, Bertell (1972). "Toward Class Consciousness Next Time: Marax and the Working Class." *Politics and Society* 3 (Fall): 1–24.

*Ollman, Bertell (1980). *Alienation: Marx's Conception of Man in Capitalist Society*. 2d ed. Cambridge, Mass.: Cambridge University Press. (Orig. 1971)

*Olson, Mancur (1965). *The Logic of Collective Action: Public Goods and the Theory of Groups*. Cambridge, Mass.: Harvard University Press.

*Omi, Michael, and Howard Winant (1983). "By the Rivers of Babylon: Race in the United States." *Socialist Review* Part 1 (Sept./Oct.): 31–65; Part 2 (Nov./Dec.): 35–68.

*Owen, Robert (1972). *A New Society and Other Writings*. New York: Dutton.

Paauw, D., and J. Fei (1975). *The Transition in Open Dualistic Economies: Theory and Southeast Asian Experience*. New Haven: Yale University Press.

*Padilla, Salvador M. (1975). *Tugwell's Thoughts on Planning*. San Juan: University of Puerto Rico Press.

*Pahl, Ray E. (1984). *Divisions of Labor*. Oxford: Basil Blackwell.

Parsons, Talcott (1949). *The Structure of Social Action: A Study in Social Theory.* 2d ed. New York: Free Press (Div. of Macmillan).

Parsons, Talcott (1964). "Introduction." In Max Weber (1964).

Peattie, Lisa R. (1978). "Politics, Planning, and Categories—Bridging the Gap." In Robert W. Burchell and George Sternlieb, eds., 83–94.

*Peattie, Lisa, and Martin Rein (1983). *Women's Claims: A Study in Political Economy.* New York: Oxford University Press.

Peccei, Antonio (1969). *The Chasm Ahead.* London: Collier-Macmillan.

Perlman, Janice (1979). "Grassroots Empowerment and Government Response." *Social Policy* 10, no. 2 (Sept./Oct.): 16–21.

Perloff, Harvey S. (1950). *Puerto Rico's Economic Future.* Chicago: The University of Chicago Press.

*Perloff, Harvey S. (1957). *Education for Planning: City, State, and Regional.* Baltimore: Johns Hopkins University Press.

Perloff, Harvey S. (1969). *Alliance for Progress.* Baltimore: Johns Hopkins University Press.

*Perloff, Harvey S. (1980). *Planning the Post-Industrial City.* Washington, D.C.: Planners Press (APA).

Perrow, Charles (1984). *Normal Accidents: Living with High-Risk Technologies.* New York: Basic Books.

Piaget, Jean (1970). *Genetic Epistemology.* New York: Columbia University Press.

*Pigou, A. C. (1932). *The Economics of Welfare.* 4th ed. London: Macmillan. (Orig. 1920)

Pitkin, Hanna Fenichel (1967). *The Concept of Representation.* Berkeley: University of California Press.

Piven, Frances Fox, and Richard A. Cloward (1978). "Social Movements and Social Conditions: A Response to Roach and Roach." *Social Problems* 26, no. 2: 172–178.

*Piven, Frances Fox, and Richard A. Cloward (1979). *Poor People's Movements: Why They Succeed. How They Fail.* New York: Vintage Books. (Orig. 1977)

Piven, Frances Fox, and Richard A. Cloward (1982). *The New Class War: Reagan's Attack on the Welfare State and Its Consequences.* New York: Pantheon.

*Polanyi, Karl (1957). *The Great Transformation.* Boston: Beacon Press. (Orig. 1944)

*Polanyi, Michael (1962). *Personal Knowledge: Towards a Post-Critical Philosophy.* New York: Harper & Row. (Orig. 1958)

*Polanyi, Michael (1966). *The Tacit Dimension.* Gardena, N.Y.: Anchor Books.

Policy Studies Review Annual (1977–). Beverly Hills: Sage Publications.

Popper, Karl (1972). "Epistemology Without a Knowing Subject." In K. R. Popper (1975), ch. 3.

*Popper, K. R. (1974). *The Open Society and Its Enemies.* 2 vols. London: Routledge & Kegan Paul. (Orig. 1945)

*Popper, K. R. (1975). *Objective Knowledge: An Evolutionary Approach.* Oxford: Clarendon Press. (Orig. 1972)

Portmann, Adolf (1956). *Zoologie und das neue Bild des Menschen: Biologische Fragmente zu einer Lehre vom Menschen.* Hamburg: Rowohlt. (Orig. 1951)

*Poulantzas, Nicos (1980). *State, Power, Socialism.* London: Verso. (Orig. 1978)

*Pressman, Jeffrey L., and Aaron Wildavsky (1979). *Implementation.* 2d ed. Berkeley: University of California Press. (Orig. 1973)

*Preteceille, Edmond (1982). "Urban Planning: The Contradictions of Capitalist Urbanization." In Chris Paris, ed., *Critical Readings in Planning Theory.* Oxford and New York: Pergamon Press. (Orig. 1974)

Price, Lorna (1983). *The Plan of St. Gall in Brief.* An overview based on the three-volume work by Walter Horn and Ernest Born. Berkeley: University of California Press.

Price, Sally (1978). "Reciprocity and Social Distance: A Reconsideration." *Ethnology* 17, no. 3 (July): 339–350.

Proudhon, Pierre-Joseph (1846). Système des contradictions economiques, ou philosophie de la misère. Paris: Guillaumin.

*Proudhon, Pierre Joseph (1970). *What is Property? An Inquiry into the Principle of Right and of Government.* New York: Dover Publications. (Orig. 1840)

*Proudhon, Pierre Joseph (1979). *The Principle of Federation.* Toronto: Toronto University Press. (Orig. 1863)

*Pyziur, Eugene (1968). *The Doctrine of Anarchism of Michael A. Bakunin.* Chicago: The Henry Regnery Co. (Orig. 1955)

*Quade, Edward S. (1963). *Military Systems Analysis.* Memorandum RM-3452-PR. Santa Monica, Calif.: The Rand Corporation.

Quade, Edward S., ed. (1966). *Analysis for Military Decisions.* Chicago: Rand McNally.

Quade, Edward S. (1968). "Pitfalls and Limitations." In Quade and Boucher, eds. (1968).

*Quade, Edward S. (1975). *Analysis for Public Decisions.* New York: American Elsevier.

*Quade, Edward S., and W. I. Boucher, eds. (1968). *Systems Analysis* *and Policy Planning: Applications in Defense*. New York: American Elsevier.

Rada, J. (1980). *The Impact of Micro-Electronics: A Tentative Appraisal of Information Technology*. Geneva: International Labour Organization.

Rada, Juan F. (1981). "The Microelectronics Revolution: Implications for the Third World." *Development Dialogue* no. 2:41–67.

Rahman, Md. Anisur, ed. (1981). "Participation of the Rural Poor In Development." *Development: Journal of the Society for International Development* no. 1 (special issue).

RAIN Staff (1981). *Knowing Home: Studies for a Possible Portland*. Portland, Oreg.: Rain Umbrella Inc.

Rand Graduate Institute (1982). *Bulletin 1982–1983*. Santa Monica, Calif.: The Rand Corporation.

Rathenau, Walther (1921). *In Days to Come*. London: George Allen & Unwin.

Ravetz, Jerome R. (1971). *Scientific Knowledge and Its Social Problems*. New York: Oxford University Press.

Reder, Melvin W. (1947). *Studies in the Theory of Welfare Economics*. New York: Columbia University Press.

Rexroth, Kenneth (1974). *Communalism: From Its Origins to the Twentieth Century*. New York: The Seabury Press.

Ridley, Clarence E. and Herbert A. Simon (1943). *Measuring Municipal Activities*. Chicago: International City Managers Association.

*Riecken, Henry W., and Robert F. Boruch (1974). *Social Experimentation: A Method for Planning and Evaluating Social Intervention*. New York: Academic Press.

Rist, Ray C., ed. (1982). *Policy Studies Review Annual*. Vol. 6. Beverly Hills: Sage Publications.

*Rittel, Horst W. J., and Melvin M. Webber (1973). "Dilemmas in a General Theory of Planning." *Policy Sciences* 4:155–169.

Roach, Jack L., and Janet K. Roach (1978a). "Organizing the Poor: Road to a Dead End." *Social Problems* 26, no. 2:160–171.

Roach, Jack L., and Janet K. Roach (1978b). "Disunity and Unity of the Working Class: Reply to Piven and Cloward." *Social Problems* 26, no. 3:267–270.

*Robinson, Ira, ed. (1972). *Decision-Making in Urban Planning*. Beverly Hills, Calif.: Sage Publication.

Robinson, James Harvey (1921). *The Mind in the Making: The Relation of Intelligence to Social Reform*. New York: Harper & Row.

Roethlisberger, F. J., and William J. Dickson (1939). *Management and the Worker: An Account of a Research Program Conducted by the*

Western Electric Company, Hawthorne Works, Chicago. Cambridge, Mass.: Harvard University Press.

*Rogers, Carl R. (1980). *A Way of Being.* Boston: Houghton Mifflin Co.

Rorig, F. (1967). *The Medieval Town.* Berkeley: University of California Press.

*Ross, David P., and Peter J. Usher (1986). *From the Roots Up: Economic Development as if Community Mattered.* New York: The Bootstrap Press.

Ross, Edward Alsworth (1901). *Social Control: A Survey of the Foundations of Order.* New York: Macmillan.

Ross, Robert (1982). "Regional Illusion, Capitalist Reality." *democracy* 2, no. 2 (April): 93–99.

Rossanda, Rossana, et al. (1979). *Power and Opposition in Post-Revolutionary Societies.* London: Ink Links. (Orig. 1978)

*Rossi, Peter, Sonia Wright, and Howard Freeman (1979). *Evaluation: A Systematic Approach.* Beverly Hills: Sage Publications.

Rostow, W. W. (1961). *The Stages of Economic Growth: A Non-Communist Manifesto.* Cambridge: Cambridge University Press.

Rostow, W. W. (1978). *The World Economy: History and Prospect.* Austin: University of Texas Press.

*Rousseau, Jean-Jacques (1973). *The Social Contract and Discourses.* Translated and introduced by G.D.H. Cole. New York: E. P. Dutton. (Orig. 1750–1762)

*Roweis, Shoukry T., and Alan J. Scott (1977). "Urban Planning in Theory and Practice: A Reappraisal." *Environment and Planning A* 9:1097–1119.

Ruttan, Vernon W. (1984). Review of Julian Simon (1981), *Economic Development and Cultural Change* 32, no. 4 (July): 886–889. Quotation is from an article which appeared in the *American Journal of Agricultural Economics* (December 1971).

Sachs, Ignacy (1982). *Ecodesarrollo: Desarrollo sin Destrucción.* Mexico, D.F.: El Colegio de Mexico.

Ste. Croix, G.E.M. de (1981). *The Class Struggle in the Ancient Greek World.* Ithaca, N.Y.: Cornell University Press.

Sandercock, Leonie, and John Friedmann (forthcoming). "Planners and Employment Policy: The Next Stage of the Debate." *Journal of the American Planning Association.*

Sandercock, Leonie, and Peter Melser (1985). " 'Like a Building Condemned': Planning in an Old Industrial Region." *Built Environment* 11, no. 2 (Spring): 120–131.

Sanyal, Biswapriya (1986). "Urban Cultivation: People's Response to Urban Poverty in East Africa." Cambridge, Mass.: Manuscript, MIT Department of Urban Studies and Planning.

Sarbib, Jean-Louis (n.d.). "The University of Chicago Program in Education and Research Planning." Unpublished manuscript. A shortened version of this paper appeared in *Journal of Planning Education and Research* 2, no. 2 (Winter 1983): 77–81.

Sassen-Koob, Saskia (1986). "New York City: Economic Restructuring and Immigration." *Development and Change* 17, no. 1 (January): 85–120.

Savage, L. J. (1954). *The Foundations of Statistics*. New York: John Wiley & Sons.

Schafers, Bernhard (1969). "Voraussetzungen und Prinzipien der Gesellschaftsplanung bei Saint-Simon und Karl Mannheim." In *Zur Theorie der Allgemeinen und der Regionalen Planung*. Edited by Zentralinstitut für Raumplanung an der Universität Münster. Bienefeld: Bertelsmann

*Schaff, Adam (1970). *Marxism and the Human Individual*. New York: McGraw-Hill. (Orig. 1965)

*Schein, Edgar H. (1969). *Process Consultation: Its Role in Organization Development*. Reading, Mass.: Addison-Wesley.

Schiller, Herbert I. (1981). *Who Knows: Information in the Age of the Fortune 500*. Norwood, N.J.: Ablex.

Schmitter, Philippe C. (1983). "Experimenting with Scale: Changes in the Units of Production, Culture, and the Governance in Western Europe." *Items* 37, no. 1 (March): 1–7.

*Schön, Donald A. (1971). *Beyond the Stable State*. New York: W. W. Norton.

Schroedinger, Erwin (1956a). *Die Natur und die Griechen: Kosmos und Physik*. Hamburg: Rowholt.

*Schroedinger, Erwin (1956b). *What Is Life and Other Scientific Essays*. Garden City, N.Y.: Doubleday Anchor.

Schultz, Theodore W. (1949). *Production and Welfare of Agriculture*. New York: Macmillan.

Schumacher, E. F. (1973). *Small Is Beautiful: Economics as if People Mattered*. New York: Harper & Row.

*Schumpeter, Joseph (1954). *Economic Doctrine and Method: An Historical Sketch*. London: Allen & Unwin. (Orig. 1912)

Scitovsky, Tibor (1976). *The Joyless Economy: An Inquiry into Human Satisfaction and Consumer Dissatisfaction*. New York: Oxford University Press.

*Scott, Mel (1969). *American City Planning Since 1890*. Berkeley: University of California Press.

Seers, Dudley (1976). "The Political Economy of National Accounting." In Alec Cairncross and Mohinder Puri, eds., *Employment, Income Distribution and Development Strategy: Problems of the Developing Countries*. Essays in honour of H. W. Singer. London: Macmillan.

Sen, Amartya (1983). "Economic Development: Some Strategic Issues." In Altaf Gauhar, ed.

Senghaas, Dieter (1977). *Weltwirtschaftsfordnung und Entwicklungspolitik: Pladoyer fur Dissoziation*. Frankfurt: Suhrkamp.

Senghaas, Dieter (1984). "The Case for Autarchy." In Charles K. Wilber, ed., ch. 13. (Orig. November 1980)

Sethuraman, S. V., ed. (1981). *The Urban Informal Sector in Developing Countries: Employment, Poverty, and Environment*. Geneva: ILO.

*Shalom, Steve Rosskamm, ed. (1983). *Socialist Visions*. Boston: South End Press.

Shannon, C. E., and W. Weaver (1949). *The Mathematical Theory of Communication*. Urbana: University of Illinois.

*Simon, Herbert A. (1957). *Models of Man: Social and Rational*. New York: John Wiley & Sons.

*Simon, Herbert A. (1976). *Administrative Behavior*. 3d ed. New York: Free Press (Div. of Macmillan). (Orig. 1945)

*Simon, Herbert A. (1982). *The Sciences of the Artificial*. 2d ed. Cambridge, Mass.: MIT Press. (Orig. 1969)

Simon, Herbert, Don Smithburg, and Victor Thompson (1950). *Public Administration*. New York: Alfred A. Knopf.

Simon, Julian (1981). *The Ultimate Resource*. Princeton, N.J.: Princeton University Press.

*Skinner, B. F. (1969). *Walden Two*. London: Macmillan. (Orig. 1948)

Skinner, B. F. (1971). *Beyond Freedom and Dignity*. New York: Alfred A. Knopf.

Sklar, Holly, ed. (1980). *Trilateralism: The Trilateral Commission and Elite Planning for World Management*. Boston: South End Press.

*Skocpol, Theda (1979). *States and Social Revolutions: Comparative Analysis of France, Russia, and China*. New York: Cambridge University Press.

Social Science Research Council (1983). "The Council's Program in Social Indicators." *Items* 37, no. 4 (December).

*Soja, Edward W. (1980). "The Socio-Spatial Dialectic." *Annals of the Association of American Geographers* 70: 207–225.

Somavia, Juan (1981). "The Transnational Power Structure and International Information." *Development Dialogue* 2:125–152.

*Sorel, Georges (1950). *Reflections on Violence*. Foreword by E. A. Shils. London: Collier. (Orig. 1906)

Spretnak, Charlene (1984). "A Green Party: It CAN Happen Here." *The Nation* (April 21): 472–478.

Starr, John Bryan (1979). *Continuing the Revolution: The Political Thought Of Mao*. Princeton: Princeton University Press.

Starr, John Bryan (1983). "On the Possibility of a Pragmatic Ideology: Pragmatic Elements in Maoist Thought and Praxis." Unpublished manuscript.

Statistical Abstract of the United States, 1978. Washington, D.C.: U.S. Department of Commerce.

Stavenhagen, Rodolfo (1984). "The Ethnic Question and the Social Sciences." Unpublished paper.

Steward, Julian H. (1955). *Theory of Culture Change*. Urbana: University of Illinois Press.

Stöhr, Walter B. (1981). "Development from Below: The Bottom-Up and Periphery-Inward Development Paradigm." In Stöhr and Taylor, eds., *Development from Above or Below? The Dialectics of Regional Planning in Developing Countries*. New York: John Wiley & Sons.

Stokes, Gerald L. (1982). *Conservation of the Blackfoot River Corridor: An Application of Transactive Planning Theory*. Ph.D. diss., Colorado State University. (Available from University Microfilms International, Ann Arbor, Mich.)

Stouffer, Samuel Andrew, et al. (1949). *The American Soldier*. 2 vols. Princeton: Princeton University Press.

*Sussman, Carl, ed. (1976). *Planning the Fourth Migration: The Neglected Vision of the Regional Planning Association of America*. Cambridge, Mass.: MIT Press.

Szanton, Peter (1981). *Not Well Advised*. New York: Russell Sage Foundation.

*Taylor, Frederick Winslow (1919). *The Principles of Scientific Management*. New York: Harper & Bros. (Orig. 1911)

Theil, Henri (1964). *Optimal Decision Rules for Government and Industry*. Amsterdam: North Holland Publishing.

Theil, Henri (1966). *Applied Economic Forecasting*. Amsterdam: North Holland Publishing.

Thomas, Carol G. (1981). "The Greek Polis." In Robert Griffeth and Carol G. Thomas, eds., *The City and State in Five Cultures*. Santa Barbara, Calif.: ABC-Clio.

*Thomas, Paul (1980). *Karl Marx and the Anarchists*. London: Routledge & Kegan Paul.

Thompson, John B., and David Held (1982). *Habermas: Critical Debates*. Cambridge, Mass.: MIT Press.

Thurow, Lester C. (1981). *The Zero-Sum Society: Distribution and the*

Politics of Economic Change. Harmondsworth, England: Penguin. (Orig. 1980)

Tinbergen, Jan (1951). *Econometrics*. Philadelphia: Blakiston.

*Tinbergen, Jan (1952). *On the Theory of Economic Policy*. Amsterdam: North Holland Publishing.

*Tinbergen, Jan (1964a). *Central Planning*. New Haven: Yale University.

Tinbergen, Jan (1964b). *Economic Policy: Principles and Design*. 4th ed. Amsterdam: North Holland Publishing. (Orig. 1956)

Toffler, Alvin (1970). *Future Shock*. New York: Random House.

*Toffler, Alvin (1980). *The Third Wave*. New York: Morrow.

"Towards a New Information and Communication Order." (1981). *Development Dialogue* (special issue).

Truman, David B. (1951). *The Governmental Process*. New York: Alfred A. Knopf.

Tugwell, Rexford G. (1932). "The Principle of Planning and the Institution of Laissez Faire." *American Economic Review* 22, no. 1 (March): 75–103.

*Tugwell, Rexford G. (1935). *The Battle for Democracy*. New York: Columbia University Press.

Tugwell, Rexford G. (1940). "The Superpolitical." *Journal of Social Philosophy* 5, no. 2 (January): 97–114.

Tugwell, Rexford G. (1970). *A Model Constitution for a United Republics of America*. Santa Barbara, Calif.: Center for the Study of Democratic Institutions.

Tugwell, Rexford G. (1974). *The Emerging Constitution*. New York: Harper's Magazine Press.

Tugwell, Rexford G. (1975a). "Implementing the General Interest." In Salvador M. Padilla. (Orig. 1940)

Tugwell, Rexford G. (1975b). "The Study of Planning as a Scientific Endeavor." In Salvador M. Padilla. (Orig. 1949)

Tugwell, Rexford G. (1975c). "The Fourth Power." In Salvador M. Padilla. (Orig. 1939).

Tugwell, Rexford G., and Edward C. Banfield (1951). "Governmental Planning at Mid-Century." *The Journal of Politics* 13:133–163.

*Turner, John F. C. (1977). *Housing by People: Toward Autonomy in Building Environment*. New York: Pantheon.

*Ulrich, Werner (1983). *Critical Heuristics of Social Planning: A New Approach to Practical Philosophy*. Bern: Verlag Paul Haupt.

UNICEF (1982). *Assignment Children*, nos. 59–60.

Union of Concerned Scientists (1984). "Reagan's Star Wars." *The New York Review of Books*, April 26, 1984, 47–52.

United Nations Centre of Transnational Corporations (1982). *Transnational Corporations and Transborder Data Flows: A Technical Paper*. New York: United Nations. ST/CTC/23.

Urwick, Lyndall F. (1938). *Scientific Principles and Organization*. Institute of Management Series, no. 18. New York: American Management Association.

Urwick Lyndall F. (1956). *The Pattern of Management*. Minneapolis: University of Minneapolis Press.

*Veblen, Thorstein (1983). *The Engineers and the Price System*. With an introduction by Daniel Bell. New Brunswick, N.J.: Transaction Books. (Orig. 1921)

Vickers, Sir Geoffrey (1965). *The Art of Judgement. A Study of Policy Making*. New York: Basic Books.

Vidal, E. (1959). *Saint-Simone e la Scienza Politica*. Milano.

Vilmar, Fritz (1976). "Notwendig: Systematische Arbeitszeitverkürzung." In Michael Bolle, ed., *Arbeitsmarkttheorie und Arbeitsmarktpolitik*. Opladen: Leske Verlag.

von Bertalanffy, Ludwig (1960). *Problems of Life: An Evaluation of Modern Biological and Scientific Thought*. New York: Harper & Row. (Orig. 1952)

von Bertalanffy, Ludwig (1962). "General System Theory: A Critical Review." In *General Systems*. Yearbooks of the Society for General Systems Research 7:1–20.

*von Bertalanffy, Ludwig (1968). *General System Theory: Foundations, Development, Applications*. New York George Braziller.

von Neumann, John, and Oskar Morgenstern (1953). *Theory of Games and Economic Behavior*. 3d ed. Princeton: Princeton University Press. (Orig. 1944)

Wachs, Martin (1985). "Ethical Dilemmas in Forecasting for Public Policy." In Martin Wachs, ed., *Ethics in Planning*, ch. 13. New Brunswick, N.J.: The Center for Public Policy Research, Rutgers University.

Waldo, Dwight (1948). *The Administrative State: A Study of the Political Theory of American Public Administration*. New York: Ronald Press.

*Walker, Pat, ed. (1979). *Between Labor and Capital: the Professional-Managerial Class*. Boston: South End Press.

*Walker, Robert A., (1950). *The Planning Function in Urban Government*. 2d ed. Chicago: University of Chicago Press. (Orig. 1941)

Wallerstein, Immanuel (1974). *The Modern World-System: Capitalist Agriculture and the Origins of the European World-Economy in the Sixteenth Century*. New York: Academic Press.

*Walzer, Michael (1983). *Spheres of Justice: A Defense of Pluralism and Equality*. New York: Basic Books.

Watson, James D. (1969). *The Double Helix*. New York: The New American Library. (Orig. 1968)

*Weaver, Clyde (1984). *Anarchy, Planning, and Regional Development*. London: John Wiley & Sons.

Weber, Max (1956). *Soziologie, Weltgeschichtliche Analysen, Politik*. Edited by Johannes Winckelmann. 2d ed. Stuttgart: Alfred Kroner.

*Weber, Max (1964). *The Theory of Social and Economic Organization*. Edited by Talcott Parsons. New York: Free Press. (Orig. 1947)

*Weiss, Carol H. (1972). *Evaluation Research Methods for Assessing Program Effectiveness*. Englewood Cliffs: N.J.: Prentice-Hall.

Weiss, Carol H. (1977). "Research for Policy's Sake: The Enlightenment Function of Social Research." *Policy Analysis* 3, no. 4 (Fall): 531–545.

Weiss, Carol H. (1982). "Policy Research in the Context of Diffuse Decision Making." In Ray C. Rist, ed. (Orig. 1981)

Wells, H. G. (1964). *Mind at the End of Its Tether*. In *The Last Books of H. G. Wells*. London: The H. G. Wells Society. (Orig. 1945)

Wheatley, Paul (1971). *The Pivot of the Four Quarters: Preliminary Enquiry into the Origins and Character of the Ancient Chinese City*. Chicago: Aldine.

White, Leonard (1926). *Introduction to the Study of Public Administration*. New York: Macmillan.

Whyte, Martin King (1974). *Small Groups and Political Rituals in China*. Berkeley: University of California Press.

Whyte, Martin King (1983). "Town and Country in Contemporary China." *Comparative Urban Research* 10, no. 1:9–20.

Wiener, Norbert (1950). *The Human Use of Human Beings*: Cybernetics and Society. Boston: Houghton Mifflin.

*Wiener, Norbert (1959). *Cybernetics: Or, Control and Communication in the Animal and the Machine*. New York: John Wiley & Sons. (Orig. 1948)

*Wilber, Charles K., ed. (1984). *The Political Economy of Development and Underdevelopment*. 3d ed. New York: Random House.

Wildavsky, Aaron (1973). "If Planning is Everything, Maybe It's Nothing." *Policy Sciences* 4, no. 2 (June): 127–153.

*Wildavsky, Aaron (1975). *Budgeting: A Comparative Theory of Budgetary Processes*. Boston: Little, Brown.

*Wildavsky, Aaron (1978). *The Politics of the Budgetary Process*. 3d ed. Boston: Little, Brown. (Orig. 1963)

*Wildavsky, Aaron (1979). *Speaking Truth to Power: The Art and Craft of Policy Analysis*. Boston: Little, Brown.

Wildavsky, Aaron (1980). *How to Limit Government Spending*, or How a Constitutional amendment tying public spending to economic growth will decrease taxes and lessen inflation. Berkeley: University of California Press.

Williams, Raymond (1983). *Year 2000.* New York: Pantheon.

Williams, William Appleman (1981). "Radicals and Regionalism." *Democracy* 1, no. 4 (October): 87–98.

Williams, William Appleman (1982). "Procedure Becomes Substance." *democracy* 2, no. 2 (April): 100–102.

Williamson, Jeffrey G. (1965). "Regional Inequality and the Process of National Development: A Description of the Pattern." *Economic Development and Cultural Change* 13, no. 4, Pt. 2 (July): 3–45.

Wilson, Edward O. (1975). *Sociobiology: The New Synthesis.* Cambridge, Mass.: The Belknap Press of Harvard University Press.

Wilson, Edward O. (1978). *On Human Nature.* Cambridge, Mass.: Harvard University Press.

Wilson, William H. (1983). "Moles and Skylarks." In Donald A. Krueckeberg, ed.

Wilson, Woodrow (1887). "The Study of Administration." *Political Science Quarterly* 2 (June): 197–222.

Winner, Langdon (1977). *Autonomous Technology: Technics-Out-of-Control as a Theme in Political Thought.* Cambridge, Mass.: MIT Press.

Wittfogel, Karl August (1959). *Oriental Despotism: A Comparative Study of Total Power.* New Haven: Yale University Press. (Orig. 1951)

Wolfe, Alan (1983). "Why Is There No Green Party in the United States?" *World Policy Journal* 1, no. 1 (Fall): 159–180.

Wolfe, Marshall (1981). *Elusive Development.* Geneva: United Nations Research Institute for Social Development.

*Wolin, Sheldon S. (1960). *Politics and Vision: Continuity and Innovation in Western Political Thought.* Boston: Little, Brown.

Wolin, Sheldon S. (1982). "What Revolutionary Action Means Today." *democracy* 2, no. 4 (Fall): 17–28.

Wollstonecraft, Mary (1975). *Vindication of the Rights of Women.* Harmondsworth, England: Penguin Books. (Orig. 1792)

Wood, Gordon S. (1972). *The Creation of the American Republic, 1776–1787.* New York: W. W. Norton. (Orig. 1969)

*Woodcock, George (1962). *Anarchism: A History of Libertarian Ideas and Movements.* New York: New American Library.

World Almanac, 1986. New York: NEA.

World Bank (1983). *World Development Report, 1983.* New York: Oxford University Press.

Wright, Arthur F. (1978). *The Sui Dynasty: The Unification of China, A.D. 581–617*. New York: Alfred A. Knopf.

*Zaretsky, Eli (1976). *Capitalism, the Family and Personal Life*. London: Pluto Press.

*Zimmerman, J. F. (1972). *The Federated City: Community Control in Large Cities*. New York: St. Martin's Press.

Index

action, 39, 45, 48, 135, 151, 158n, 173n, 174, 179, 181, 183, 202, 210, 217, 399, 406; and non-action (Habermas), 267; communicative (Habermas), 267; community, 122, 441; defined, 44; for societal guidance or social transformation, 298; from below, 200, 297; group, task-oriented, 186; in social anarchism, 241; in social learning, 183; innovative, 122; linked to knowledge, 74; local, 382; political, 291; programs, 175, 176; public domains of, 339; radical, types of linkage, 302; rational, 19; strategic, 401; top-down, 202

Active Society, The (Etzioni, Amitai), 8, 59, 134, 137

actors, 183, 186, 201; as outside change agents, 206; in the public domain, 44–46

administration, 33; public, 149n

Administrative Behavior (Simon, Herbert), 49, 55, 78, 150n

administrative man, 150

Adorno, Theodor W., 265, 266n

Adviser, The (Goldhammer, Herbert), 179

advocacy in policy analysis, 173n

advocacy planning. *See* planning

Agricultural Adjustment Act, 106

agropolitan development, 342n, 378n, 380–81

Albert, Michael, and Robert Hahnel, cited, 283

Alinsky, Saul, 286; cited, 284–85

Alliance for Progress, 112

Allison, Graham, 159; cited, 158

allocative planning. *See* planning

Althusser, Louis, 327

American Soldier, The (Stouffer, Samuel A.), 147

Analysis for Military Decisions (Quade, Edward S.), 152

anarchists, 55, 83, 100, 281, 283

Anderson, Perry, 247n

Angotti, Thomas, cited, 440

Appalachian Regional Commission, 34

Apter, David E., and Nagayo Sawa, cited, 35n

Archibald, Kathleen, cited, 171

Arendt, Hannah, 261n, 344n

Argyris, Chris, 13, 57, 202, 215

artificial intelligence, 140, 150

Ashby, W. R., 11n

autonomous policy space, 175

Ayres, Robert, 168

Bakunin, Michael, 239, 279, 281n, 288, 292, 298

Banfield, Edward C., 37, 120, 126, 132n, 135, 331; cited, 121; and James Q. Wilson, cited, 120

Battle for Democracy, The (Tugwell, Rexford G.), 106

Beer, Stafford, cited, 141–42

Benne, Kenneth D., 210; cited, 207

Bennis, Warren G., 13, 202

Bentham, Jeremy, 51, 61, 99, 101, 105, 129, 134–35, 168, 230, 234, 328, 349; cited, 329

Bentley, Arthur, 331n

Benveniste, Guy, cited, 163

Berle, A. A., Jr., and Gardiner C. Means, 91n

Library of Congress Cataloging-in-Publication Data

Friedmann, John.
  Planning in the public domain.

  Bibliography: p.
  Includes index.
    1. Planning—History. 2. Political planning—
History. I. Title.
HD87.5.F745 1987   361.6   87–3194
ISBN 0–691–07743–6 (alk. paper)
ISBN 0–691–02268–2 (pbk.)